THE
PILGRIMAGE OF BUDDHISM
AND
A BUDDHIST PILGRIMAGE

THE PILGRIMAGE OF BUDDHISM

AND

A BUDDHIST PILGRIMAGE

BY

JAMES BISSETT PRATT, PH.D.

GYAN

Published by

GYAN

Gyan Publishing House
5, Ansari Road
Daryaganj, New Delhi-110002
Phone: 011-47034999, 9811692060
E-mail: books@gyanbooks.com

Distribution Network
gyanbooks.com
India, USA, Canada, UK, Australia

ISBN: 978-93-6208-482-8 (HB)
First Published, 1928

2nd Impression 2024

Printed at: Gyan Press, Delhi.

THE PILGRIMAGE OF BUDDHISM AND A BUDDHIST PILGRIMAGE

Author: JAMES BISSETT PRATT

THE PILGRIMAGE OF BUDDHISM

THE PILGRIMAGE OF BUDDHISM

AND

A BUDDHIST PILGRIMAGE

BY

JAMES BISSETT PRATT, PH.D.
PROFESSOR OF PHILOSOPHY IN WILLIAMS COLLEGE

New York
THE MACMILLAN COMPANY
1928

TO

MY BELOVED FELLOW PILGRIM
THROUGH THE WORLD AND DOWN THE YEARS
MY COMFORT AND SUPPORT
IN ALL THE HARDSHIPS AND PERILS OF THE ROAD
AND MY GUIDE TO ALL THE SACRED PLACES

PREFACE

THERE are so many books on Buddhism already that I shall not apologize for writing another. But the reader, if there be such an one, who cares enough for Buddhism to embark upon so large a volume as this may be interested in knowing how I happened to undertake the years of investigation that made it possible. The answer is quickly told: I wanted to get a synthetic view of Buddhism, to grasp it as a whole, and also to discover the actual conditions of the religion as it is believed and lived to-day. To do these things the reading of many books was helpful, but most important of all were the two pilgrimages that my Fellow Pilgrim and I made, in two Sabbaticals, to Buddhist lands. And now that I have gained some of the understanding I sought, it seems only right I should hand it on to others who may be as interested as I was.

I hope, in other words, that my book will give the reader two things which he may not find in more learned volumes. First I want him to get, with me, a sense for Buddhism as a whole, for the organic unity of its life and growth, for the organic identity of the Buddhism of contemporary Japan with that which originated nearly twenty-five hundred years ago in India. I want him to share with me the tremendous impression of the advance of this religion from land to land, gathering further enrichment in every stage of its progress, growing like an immense snowball as it goes, yet assimilating its increments as an organism its food, moving irresistibly onward till it reaches "the sea that ends not till the world's end." I hope that at least faintly this way of conceiving Buddhism may be suggested to the reader by the title I have chosen. For this great Traveler is also an exile and a pilgrim —perhaps the figure of a missionary would have been more appropriate—driven from his native land and carrying the blessings of insight and love to the long and colorful succession of peoples and countries that fringe the Indian Ocean, the Bay of Bengal, the Gulf of Siam, the China Sea, and the Western Pacific. For pictorial simplicity I have written as if the "Buddhist Pilgrimage" which my Fellow Pilgrim and I pursued had followed in the exact footsteps of the Great Pilgrim. As a fact, our pilgrimage had to be spread over two Sabbaticals with an interval of nine years between them. But at one time or another, and in one order or another, all the lands whose religion is described in this volume have been studied by us with greater or less care and detail; so that what I have ventured to say about them is at any rate based in large part upon personal observation.

And that brings me to the second thing I hope the reader will be able to find in these pages: namely, a fairly intimate understanding of Buddhism as it is actually *lived* to-day. If this is to be done some knowledge of its origin and its history is essential; hence the historical chapters of this volume. But the history of Buddhism one can find much more learnedly presented elsewhere. The thing I have sought chiefly to do is to make Buddhism *plausible*. It would be possible with sufficient study to write a learned book on Buddhism which should recite the various facts with scholarly exactness yet leave the reader at the end wondering how intelligent and spiritual men and women of our day could really be Buddhists. I have sought to avoid this effect and have tried in addition to enable the reader, when he has turned the last page, to understand a little *how it feels to be a Buddhist.* To give the feeling of an alien religion it is necessary to do more than expound its concepts and describe its history. One must catch its emotional undertone, enter sympathetically into its sentiments, feel one's way into its symbols, its cult, its art, and then seek to impart these things not merely by scientific exposition but in all sorts of indirect ways.

There is one notable omission which will at once strike the reader of this book. I have said nothing whatever of the Buddhism of Tibet, Nepal, and Mongolia. This has not been due to lack of space but to deliberate intention. The form of religion which prevails in these lands is so mixed with non-Buddhist elements that I hesitate to call it Buddhism at all. At any rate, if I was to give a unified notion of Buddhism, it seemed to me necessary to confine myself to the Hinayana and the Mahayana.

It will be a privilege before closing this preface to mention a few of the many friends and acquaintances in Buddhist lands who by their assistance and their information helped to make my book possible. First of all in order of time would naturally come those kindly Indians, Ceylonese, and Burmans who gave me so much assistance in my first visit to the Far East; but as several of these were named in "India and Its Faiths" I shall omit them here. But of the many who helped me on my more recent visit I must surely mention the following: Mr. Nai Leck of Bangkok; Rev. J. D. Olsen of Saigon; Rev. F. R. Millican of Ningpo; Mr. Ouyang and Dr. Reichelt of Nanking; Bishop Roots, formerly of Hankow; Bishop Gilman, Professor Francis Wei, and the monk Tai Hsü of Wuchang; Rev. Mr. Warren of Changsha; Rev. C. F. Howe of Ichang; Rev. W. S. Dudley of Chungking; Mr. Mei and Mr. Yü of Tsinan Fu; Rev. and Mrs. A. W. Hummell, formerly of Fen Chow (Shansi); Mr. T. C. Yen, Dr. Hu Shih, Mr. Kwai, Mr. Teng, Mr. Carrington Goodrich, Mr. R. F. Johnston, and Baron Stael Holstein of Peking; Dr. Deming of Seoul; Rev. Mr. Blair of Taikyu (Korea); Dr. Anesaki, Dr. Kato, Dr. Mochitzuki, Rev. D. Shimaji, and Dr. Armstrong of Tokyo; Prof. D. T. Suzuki, Rev. E. S. Cobb and Rev. J. A. Welbourn of Kyoto; Prof. Akizuki of Koyosan; and Mr. Y. Suzuki of Kobi.

To all these and to many more I owe much. But no one who reads this book through will need to be told that my chief indebtedness is to the eyes and memory, the quick apprehension, the sympathetic understanding, and the unfailing encouragement of my Fellow Pilgrim.

CONTENTS

CONTENTS

THE PILGRIMAGE OF BUDDHISM

THE PILGRIMAGE OF BUDDHISM

CHAPTER I

THE FOUNDER

I HOPE I shall not forget the impression that we both received as we drove in a tika-gari through the early hours of that January morning from Gaya to Buddh Gaya. Possibly in my own case the strength of the impression could be attributed in part to other causes, for I had been a student of Buddhism—in a desultory way—many years. But I am sure it was not wholly the sentiment I brought with me that produced the intimate sense of great calm that clothed the landscape. For my Fellow Pilgrim, whose knowledge of the "Blessed One" and of his teaching was but slight, felt the same compelling charm of the quiet hills and of the listening country, as if the footfalls of him who was to be the Light of Asia had only then died away.

Nor was the goal of our journey unworthy of the expectant preparation. An ancient garden surrounds the place, cared for with reverence but not too minutely, where Nature and Art are not at war, where ancient statues are half concealed by climbing vines and fresh spring flowers, and where picturesque decay gives the last touch of reverence and suggestiveness to never-ceasing piety and love. In the center stands the great pagoda, product of combined Buddhist and Hindu adoration for a lofty soul, marking the spot where, according to a well authenticated tradition, Gotama spent that night of illumination when he became the Buddha. Close to it grows a vigorous specimen of the *ficus religiosa*, said to be descended from the "Bodhi Tree," under whose sheltering branches he sat during those hours so fateful for all Eastern Asia.

Nearly twenty-five centuries ago, that famous night. And we who, peering back through the ages, long to know what manner of man it was who sat under the tree find our sight dimmed by the distance and interrupted by the loving mythology that has sprung up, like tropical vegetation, between ourselves and him. The oldest books that tell of his life and teaching were not put completely into writing till about the year 30 B.C.[1] Doubtless they go back in the oral memory of the Buddhist community very much farther than this; and some of the materials from which they were formed may have been derived from the immediate disciples of the Founder, some may have come from his very lips. But how much of the canon goes back to his time, and how trustworthy in detail it is, we shall never know with certainty. All we can do is to use what critical methods our Pali scholars can devise in selecting the most credible of the texts, and then exert what judgment we possess in forming our own tentative opinions.

Based upon such uncertain and disputed foundations, modern opinions of the Founder and of what he taught naturally differ. Was he a rationalistic moralist? A Yogin? A supernaturalist who thought himself a god? Or did he, perhaps, never really live at all; is he merely a sun myth? Pretty certainly, I think, we may say he was not the latter.[2] But in each of the three other answers just noted there may well be an element of truth. Fortunately in making up our own opinions we are not dependent entirely upon the expositions of the disagreeing doctors. A few Pali scholars, to whom our gratitude can never be fully expressed, have worked out the most trustworthy texts of much of the sacred literature of Buddhism, and have translated into either English or German the four principal Nikayas—the oldest records of his dia-

[1] Some put the date at 80 B.C.

[2] This hypothesis has been put forward more than once. The most recent presentation of it with which I am acquainted is that given by H. Kern, in Vol. I of his *Histoire du Bouddhism dans l'Inde* (Paris, Leroux, 1901). This is not the place to discuss the question, and I can only say that Kern's arguments leave me quite cold. The question is briefly discussed in the Introduction and on pp. 216-26 of Dr. E. J. Thomas' *Life of Buddha* (London, Trübner, 1927).

logues—and the more important parts of the fifth.[3] Whoso would form for himself an opinion as to the character and the teachings of the Founder of Buddhism may, therefore, if he be willing to consecrate the time to it, go with the Pali

[3] The Canon of Pali Buddhism, known as the Tripitaka, consists of three grand subdivisions, each known as a Pitaka or basket. The first of these is the Vinaya Pitaka, or the rules of the monastic Order; the second is the Sutta Pitaka, or teachings of the Buddha; the third is the Abhidhamma Pitaka, which is later than most of the others are and is devoted to the metaphysical and psychological refinements of the later scholastic systematizers. The five Nikayas, of course, make up the second of these divisions, the Sutta Pitaka. These five, though containing much identical material, are of varying degrees of value. By far the most important of them are the Digha and the Majjhima. Although marred like the others with much repetition, they both contain a large number of dialogues of rather striking insight and beauty. Though much alike, their emphasis is not quite the same. The Digha is emphatically the rationalistic Nikaya. Its interest is almost exclusively upon questions of the moral life, earnestness, and self-control. The Majjhima is also more interested in these things than in anything else, but it puts greater stress than does the Digha upon Yoga methods, the gods and their heavens, and the Buddha's supernatural knowledge. The Samyutta Nikaya is pretty evidently later than the Digha and Majjhima. It bears the marks of scholastic organization without the freshness of the earlier dialogues. In content it is characterized by two rather diverse tendencies: a great delight in stories about the gods, and an extreme rationalistic, positivistic, ethical tendency, often more pronounced than that of the Digha. It emphasizes the causal chain of the Twelve Nidanas, the ubiquity of sorrow, and hence the importance of the Four Noble Truths. The Anguttara Nikaya is inferior to the three others except for a few passages. It is characterized chiefly by form rather than by content. The teachings of the other Nikayas are here rearranged in numerical groups, the *numbers* of virtues, of vices, of obstacles, of methods, etc., etc., are set out with scholastic detail. This, of course, points conclusively to its later date. There are a few passages of the Anguttara, however, which are of real value and which contain material not found in the other Nikayas.

When one refers to the Nikayas, it is usually these four books that are intended. There is, however, a fifth Nikaya, called Khuddaka, made up of a strange variety of material. It is, in fact, a collective name for some fifteen independent books of varying value and varying date. In their present form they are thought to be later than the first four Nikayas, but some of them, notably the Sutta Nipata, the Udana, the Jatakas, and the Dhammapada, contain ancient material, some of it drawn from the older Nikayas and put in new form. The most important of these books that make up the fifth Nikaya are the four just named, the Iti-vuttaka, the Thera Gatha and the Theri Gatha (or Psalms of the Brethren and Psalms of the Sisters), and the Khuddaka-patha. All of these, as well as the first four Nikayas, have been translated into either English or German. As I have no Pali my knowledge of these books is based on these translations. To save needless repetition I shall, as a rule, in referring to the sources, give only the names of the books, and shall here once for all indicate the translators to whom I am indebted, together with the titles of their translations and their publishers. The reader may, therefore, refer back to this list, if he cares to do so, when reference to the Pali books is given.

Digha Nikaya, trans. by T. W. Rhys Davids, under the title *Dialogues of the Buddha*, three vols. (Oxford Univ. Press, 1899, 1910, 1921).

Majjhima Nikaya, trans. by Karl Neumann under the title *Die Reden Gotamo Buddhos*, three vols. (München, Piper, 1922). About half of the Majjhima has also been translated into English by Lord Chalmers and entitled, *Further Dialogues of the Buddha* (Vol. I, Oxford Univ. Press, 1926).

The Samyutta Nikaya, trans. into German by Wilhelm Geiger, but not yet completed. Vol. II has been published by Schloss (München) in 1925. The content of what is to be Vol. I is appearing at present (1927) in the *Zeitschrift für Buddhismus*. The Samyutta has also been translated into English by Mrs. Rhys Davids and F. L.

doctors to the sources themselves and drink from waters as near the original spring as is now possible for anyone.

Even so, of course, the opinions of different readers will vary. The best one can do is to start one's study with as few prejudices as possible, to read with both critical and sympathetic eyes, and to report one's impressions as honestly as one may. With these principles in mind I, who, alas, am no Pali scholar, have gone through all the Nikayas [4] in English or German, as well as the Vinaya, and shall try to set down in this and the following chapters what seems to me the most probable truth concerning the character and the teachings of the Buddha.

I may say at once that the general impression I bring away from this reading is of a very great personality—a personality whom to know, even at this distance and in this unsatisfactory manner, is a benediction. In spite of the wearisome repetitions of the Nikayas it is a precious experience to spend a little time each day reading the accounts they give of his discourses, and enjoying the passing glimpses they furnish into his daily life.

> So as I enter here from day to day
> The tumult of the time disconsolate
> To inarticulate murmurs dies away
> While the eternal ages watch and wait.

Before going further I should say a few words about the commonest of the many names used by Buddhists to desig-

Woodward, under the title *Kindred Sayings*, three vols. (Oxford Univ. Press, 1917, 1922, 1925).

The first part of the Anguttara Nikaya was translated by E. R. J. Gooneratne (Galle, Ceylon, 1913), and continued by A. D. Jayasundere (Adyar, Vasanta Press, 1925). A third volume is promised.

The Jatakamala has been translated, under the title *The Jataka*, by Cowell and others in six volumes (Cambridge Univ. Press, 1895-1907). A Sanskrit version of the first thirty-four stories has been translated by J. S. Speyer (Oxford Univ. Press, 1895).

The Dhammapada, trans. by Max Müller, and the Sutta Nipata, trans. by V. Fausboll, are published in one volume in the *S. B. E.* series (Oxford, Clarendon Press, 1881).

The Thera Gatha and the Theri Gatha have been translated by Mrs. Rhys Davids under the titles *Psalms of the Brethren* and *Psalms of the Sisters* (London, Frowde, 1909, 1913).

The Iti-vuttaka, trans. by J. H. Moore (New York, Columbia Univ. Press, 1908).

Udana, trans. into German by Seidenstücker, 1920.

Khuddaka-patha, trans. by Childers, *Jour. Royal Asiatic Soc.*, 1870.

I should add to this list of translations from the Sutta Pitaka, the translation by Rhys Davids and Oldenberg of the Vinaya Texts, in the *Sacred Books of the East*.

[4] I mean all the four principal Nikayas, as well as the eight books of the Fifth Nikaya that are available in English or German.

nate the Founder of their religion. The term Buddha is, of course, not a proper name but a title, as is the word Christ. As Christ means the Anointed One, so Buddha means the Enlightened One, or the One Fully Awake. According to Buddhist theory there has been a long line of Buddhas. The family name of the one we know was Gotama (in Sanskrit Gautama), and his personal name Siddhatha (Sanskrit Siddhartha). He came from the Clan of the Sakyas, and hence came to be known in later years as Sakyamuni, or the Sage of the Sakyas—the name most commonly given him in the Far East. His disciples, both those who knew him and those who have been his followers through all the years, frequently speak of him as the Blessed One. Perhaps the commonest title found in the Pali books is Tathagata, which has no exact English equivalent but which means approximately the Perfectly Enlightened One.

Possibly I should add here, for the benefit of those readers, if such there be, who are not familiar with the story of the Buddha, a few dates and a few biographical facts. Gotama was born at Kapilavastu in northern India, on the borders of Nepal, about the year 560 B.C.,[5] the son of a wealthy and powerful prince. He received the usual education of an Indian noble, married, and had a son (Rahula, by name). Oppressed by the unsatisfying nature of worldly pleasures and by all that is changeful, he renounced the world at the age of twenty-nine and left his home in search of truth and deliverance. He became a mendicant and studied with two distinguished teachers, but finding that their teachings did not solve the problem of human sorrow, he left them and tried the ancient Indian method of asceticism in its extremest forms. This proving even more futile than the teachings of his former masters he gave it up also, and apparently through the double process of hard thinking and semi-mystical practices of mind control, he gained the insight he had sought. This "enlightenment" seems to have been sudden, and took place during one night, as he sat under the Bodhi Tree at Buddh Gaya. Immediately thereafter he began "turning the wheel of the Dhamma" (or Law)—i.e., he

[5] To be exact, it was most likely in 563 B.C. See the discussion of the point in Geiger's Introduction to his translation of the Mahavamsa (London, Frowde, 1912).

preached his first sermon—in a deer park (now Sarnath) in the suburbs of Benares. This was at the age of thirty-five. The remainder of his eighty years he spent in spreading his doctrine, and founding and administering an order of monks which was to carry his teaching eventually over all the East. He died about the year 480 B.C.[6] surrounded by his devoted followers, between the twin Sala trees at Kusinara.

But to return to the character of this man of many names and many deeds. As I read the Nikayas, perhaps the most striking thing about him is his almost unique combination of a cool scientific head with the devoted sympathy of a warm and loving heart. The way in which he kept that perfect balance during the forty-five years of teaching and in the varied situations recorded in the Buddhist books is indeed very extraordinary. His pity for every sort of suffering sentient life and his devotion to its needs seem to have been boundless. Yet apparently he never lost his head, and never was misled or blinded by sentiment.

I think the Rhys Davids and Oldenberg and Neumann are in part right in picturing the Buddha as a rationalistic moralist; but Keith and Franke and La Vallée Poussin are also right in pointing out that there were other sides to his character and teaching. He made repeated use, as we shall see, of methods of meditation borrowed from the Yogins of his time and taught them to his disciples; and he took for granted (often in somewhat amused fashion, to be sure) the gods of Indian tradition. He considered them of less account than a good Buddhist, and felt himself to be immeasurably superior to them all;[7] but we have no reason to suppose that he denied their existence, since in fact he repeatedly referred to them as beings taken for granted with whom in previous births he had been well acquainted.[8]

[6] Presumably 483 B.C.

[7] In a passage in Chap. IV of the Anguttara Nikaya, which may be late, the Buddha is depicted as asserting that he is neither a god nor a man. His surprised questioner asks what, then, he can be. To which he responds that before his enlightenment he had been both, many times, but now he is an Enlightened One, a Buddha. Jayasundere's trans. of Part II, p. 54.

[8] In § 22 of the Iti-vuttaka (which belongs to the fifth Nikaya) the Buddha is represented as saying that he himself once occupied the position of the great Brahmā, and that he had been Sakka, ruler of the gods, thirty-six times. It was and is the Indian conception (or *an* Indian conception) that different individuals occupy the position of Brahma and of each of the gods. The name of a god thus is really a title, the name of an office, rather than the appellation of an individual.

For all that, both the gods and the heavens and hells which he described and the Yoga methods which he practiced and taught are all kept in unquestionable and explicit subordination to the supreme question of the wise way to live.

The great mass of the dialogues left us are concerned with moral and humanistic matters. The Buddha was primarily a moral teacher. It was on the questions of right living that he placed supreme emphasis, and upon the psychological analyses and the spiritual training which he considered helpful or necessary for attaining the ideals of human life. And yet the impression one gets from the dialogues is very different from that given by the Confucian Analects. Confucius, in spite of his great reverence for the cult of his national religion, was essentially a sage. The Buddha, in spite of his ridicule for cult and his refusal to discuss the ultimate problems of philosophy, was a saint, or even a mystic and a prophet. Confucius was a humanist; the Buddha was the founder of a religion.[9] This feeling that one inevitably gets on reading the dialogues is doubtless due in part to the repeated references they make, as already noted, to gods, places of reward and punishment, transmigration and the exact justice of the Cosmos, the practice of mystic methods of meditation and the rest. Yet this is but part of the explanation. More important still in producing the impression one gets of the Buddha is the evident veneration felt for him by nearly everyone who meets him, and the sense that the reader comes to share with his followers that here we see something very like Omniscience incarnate before us. The Buddha does not, indeed, claim omniscience for himself.[10] Yet it is plain that his disciples, clerical and lay, seem to have attributed it to him; and he himself plainly felt that he was in possession of knowledge far deeper than that of any other man or god. Like other great men of the first order, such as Christ and Confucius, he was conscious of his own superiority. Though devoid of the littleness of conceit and of the hardness of pride, and though never despising others,

[9] Cf. the excellent comparison of the two men in Irving Babbitt's *Democracy and Leadership*.

[10] Cf. Majjhima Nikaya LXXI.

he had immense self-confidence.[11] The humility of a Saint Francis belonged to him no more than it did to Jesus.

Indeed such humility would hardly have been compatible, in either Jesus or Gotama, with the deep-seated sense of a supreme mission that each of them seems to have entertained. Immediately after his enlightenment, so we are several times assured in the Nikayas (and one can well believe the source of this oft-repeated story was the Founder himself), the Exalted One looked out in thought and imagination over the world and "saw souls whose eyes were scarcely dimmed by dust and souls whose eyes were sorely dimmed by dust, souls sharp of sense and souls blunted of sense, souls of good and souls of evil disposition, souls docile and souls indocile, some of them living with a perception of the danger of other worlds and of wrong doing." [12] It had been one of the temptations of Mara, the Evil One, so the accounts repeatedly tell us, to suggest to the Tathagata that his newly discovered truth was too deep for this world to understand and that he should therefore withdraw into Parinirvana and leave it unrevealed. But in answer to this temptation came the thought of needy beings, seen now clearly with the Buddha eye, and out of pity for them he put behind him the thought of his own ease and the glory of Parinirvana, and for forty-five years, till his head was white and his steps infirm, he toiled up and down the dusty roads of India to save from sorrow all who had ears to hear. So strongly did the call of pity for the world rush into his heart, as he sat there under the Bo Tree, with such almost external imperiousness did it come to him, that he seems to have felt it was suggested by the great god Brahma. Whether or not we take the story as literally as did his disciples who edited the Nikayas, the power of his pity and of his determination to save the world can hardly be doubted. This consciousness of an almost cosmic mission is one of the things most certain

[11] His self-confidence was not such as to make him slow in taking suggestions from others or in acting on their advice when it seemed good. The institution of the fortnightly confession among the monks, the fortnightly preaching, and the custom of remaining in the monastery during the rainy season, according to the Vinaya, were all decreed by the Buddha as a result of suggestions from his disciples.

[12] I have taken this version of the oft-repeated phrase from Mrs. Rhys Davids' translation of the Samyutta I, 174. I might quite as well have chosen her husband's version in the Digha, II, 32, or Neumann's rendering of the Majjhima, I, 396.

about the Buddha, for it dominated his whole life, and has become crystallized in one of those formulas, found in several of the Nikayas, which are presumably among the very oldest phrases of Buddhist literature, and which may well go back in something like their present form to the Founder himself. Repeatedly he is described, or describes himself, as one "born into the world for the good of the many, for the happiness of the many, for the advantage, the good, the happiness of gods and men, out of compassion for the world." [13]

To the carrying out of this mission the Buddha devoted all his days after the achievement of enlightenment. His time was divided betwen feeding the lamp of his own spiritual life by solitary meditation—just as Jesus spent long hours in lonely prayer—and active preaching to large audiences of his monks, instructing the more advanced in the subtle points of inner development, directing the affairs of the Order, rebuking breaches of discipline, confirming the faithful in their virtue, receiving deputations, carrying on discussions with learned opponents, comforting the sorrowful, visiting kings and peasants, Brahmins and outcasts, rich and poor. He was a friend of publicans and sinners, and many a public harlot, finding herself understood and pitied, gave up her evil ways to take her refuge in the "Blessed One." Such a life demanded a variety of moral qualities and social gifts, and among others a combination of democratic sentiments with an aristocratic *savoir faire* which is seldom met with. In reading the dialogues one can never forget that Gotama had the birth and up-bringing of an aristocrat. He converses not only with Brahmins and pundits but with princes and ministers and kings on easy and equal terms. He is a good diner-out, with a fund of anecdote and apparently a real sense of humor,[14] and is a welcome guest at every house. A distinguished Brahmin is pictured as describing him thus:

> The venerable Gotama is well born on both sides, of pure descent . . . is handsome, pleasant to look upon, inspiring trust, gifted with great

[13] Cf. Digha Nikaya XIX 5; Iti-vuttaka, § 84.

[14] Cf. the story of "Darky" in Majjhima Nikaya XXI, and his oft-quoted fable of the blind men giving their diverse accounts of the elephant (Udana VI 4). Possibly here should be classed also his remarks to Cunda the Smith concerning the food at his banquet (Seidenstücker's *Udana*, p. 95).

beauty of complexion, fair in color, fine in presence, stately to behold,[15] virtuous with the virtue of the Arahats, gifted with goodness and virtue and with a pleasant voice and polite address, with no passion of lust left in him nor any fickleness of mind. He bids all men welcome, is congenial, conciliatory, not supercilious, accessible to all, not backward in conversation.[16]

But what appealed most to the India of his time, and has appealed most to India through the ages, is expressed by the Brahmin in these words:

> The monk Gotama has gone forth into the religious life, giving up the great clan of his relatives, giving up much money and gold, treasure both buried and above ground. Truly while he was still a young man, without a gray hair on his head, in the beauty of his early manhood he went forth from the household life into the homeless state.[17]

Such a life as his demanded not only pleasant manners, sympathy, and kindness, but firmness and courage. When the occasion required it,[18] he could be calmly severe with those who worked evil for the Order. Physical pain he bore not only with equanimity but with no diminution of his inner joy.[19] Courage also was needed, and was found; as, for example, in the Buddha's calm attitude during Devadatta's various attempts to assassinate him,[20] in facing threats of murder,[21] and in the conversion of the famous bandit in the Kingdom of Kosala, whom all the countryside feared, and whom the Buddha visited, alone and unarmed,

[15] He seems to have been extremely handsome. The impression he made upon all sorts of people at first sight, and the charm of his personality which was never-failing through years of intimacy are among the notable things that strike one's mind in reading the canonical books. The Psalms of the Brethren contain several instances of this. For example the learned Brahmin Vakkali: "When he had grown wise and had learnt the three Vedas, and was proficient in Brahmin accomplishments, he saw the Master. Never sated by looking at the perfection of the Master's visible body, he went about with him. And when in his house he thought, 'I shall not here get a chance of seeing him constantly'; so he entered the Order and spent all his time doing nothing else but contemplating the Exalted One." So strong was this fascination that the Buddha, for the man's own spiritual good, had to rebuke him and finally to send him away (*Psalms of the Brethren* No. 205).

[16] Digha IV. Cf. also *Mahavagga of the Vinaya* V. 13, 4.

[17] Digha IV.

[18] Cf. Majjhima XXI, XXII, XXXVIII, LXVII. Also his dealings with schism in the Order, Vinaya Mahavaga X; with discipline, Kullavagga I.

[19] Mrs. Rhys Davids' trans. of the Samyutta I, 138-39.

[20] Kullavagga of the Vinaya VII. 3.

[21] Cf. Fausböll's Sutta Nipata, pp. 30, 45, and Mrs. Rhys Davids' Samyutta, pp. 275-76.

in his lair, changing him from a scourge of the kingdom to a peaceful member of the Order.[22] Neither pain, danger, nor insults marred his spiritual peace. When he was reviled he reviled not again.[23] Nor was he lacking in tender thoughtfulness for those who needed his comfort and support. The twenty-second chapter of the Samyutta describes how Tissa, one of his disciples, became bewildered and discouraged in his efforts at following the Way, how the Buddha heard of it and sent for him and by a parable presenting a Buddhist Pilgrim's Progress he instilled in him the hope and courage so much needed. "Be of good cheer, Tissa," he added. "Be of good cheer, Tissa. I to counsel you, I to uphold you, I to teach you." [24] The Master's tender words to Ananda, the beloved disciple, just before his own death,[25] are often cited in popular lives of the Buddha. Less tender but more thoughtful was the message which he sent at about the same time to Cunda the smith, at whose house he had eaten the food which was the immediate cause of his death. In the midst of his suffering he thought of the possibility that poor Cunda might be blamed for having been, unintentionally, responsible for the Tathagata's passing away; so he laid a last command upon Ananda to tell the smith that of all the meals of his life two stood out in his memory as especially fruitful and full of blessing. One was that in the strength of which he had attained insight under the Bo Tree; the other was that given him by Cunda, through which he was entering into the complete liberation of Nibbana.[26]

Like many other men of spiritual discernment he had a power of reading character which to his followers seemed

[22] Majjhima LXXXVI.

[23] A Brahmin in the neighborhood of Rajagaha "sought the presence of the Tathagata and there reviled and abused the Tathagata in rude and harsh speeches. When he had spoken thus the Tathagata said:

" 'When thou receivest visits from friends and colleagues, dost thou make ready for them food?'

" 'Yet, Master Gotama, sometimes I do.'

" 'But if they do not accept thy hospitality, whose do those things become?'

" 'If they do not accept them, those things are for us.'

" 'Even so, Brahmin. That wherewith thou revilest us who revile not, wherewith thou scoldest us who scold not, abusest us who abuse not, *that* we accept not at thy hands. 'Tis for thee only, Brahmin, 'tis only for thee!' " (Mrs. Rhys Davids' trans. of the Samyutta I. 202.)

[24] Woodward's Samyutta III. 90-92.

[25] Digha XVI. 14.

[26] Udana VIII. 5.

nothing short of miraculous. Many a time, according to the Psalms of the Brethren (which presents at least the impression of him entertained by the Early Church), he saw in some new seeker or even distant aspirant or needy soul "the conditions of Arahantship (sainthood) shining within his heart like a lamp in a jar,"[27]—as in the story of Sunita, a poor outcast, a scavenger of withered flowers in the city streets, not making enough even by this despised labor to still his hunger.

> Now in the first watch of the night the Exalted One, attaining that mood of great pity so largely practiced by the Buddhas, surveyed the world. And he marked the conditions of Arahantship in the heart of Sunita, shining like a lamp within a jar. And when the night paled into dawn he rose and dressed, and with bowl and robe, followed by his train of monks, he walked to the city for alms, and sought the street where Sunita was cleaning. Now Sunita was collecting scraps, rubbish, and so on, into heaps, and filling therewith the baskets he carried on a yoke. And when he saw the Master and his train approaching, his heart was filled with joy and awe. Finding no place to hide in on the road, he placed his yoke in the bend of the wall, and stood as if stuck to the wall, saluting with clasped hands. Then the Master, when he had come near, spoke to him in a voice divinely sweet, saying, "Sunita, what to you is this wretched mode of living? Can you endure to leave the world?" And Sunita, experiencing the rapture of one who has been sprinkled with ambrosia, said, "O Exalted One, if such as I may in this life become a monk of yours, why should I not? May the Exalted One suffer me to come forth!"

So the Blessed One, knowing the conditions of sainthood in the heart of the flower scavenger, made him at once a member of the Order.[28]

As I have already indicated, the Buddha's moral qualities, as he is depicted in the Nikayas (and I should add in the Vinaya also), were balanced with equally striking intellectual gifts. He had a way of seeing to the heart of a question, brushing aside incidentals, and arguing matters out on purely rational grounds. He never appeals to authority, but desires to stand only as the representative of reason. If in reading the Dialogues one can abstract from the wearisome

[27] *Psalms of the Brethren*, Nos. 220, 227, 242.

[28] *Ibid.*, Mrs. Rhys Davids' trans., pp. 271-72. For other cases of rapid character reading that seemed to the beholders almost magical see Psalms Nos. 205, 218, 220, 227.

repetitions (doubtless introduced in part because of the demands of oral reproduction), one feels oneself in the presence of an extremely alert and agile intellect. Always ready for his intellectual opponents and willing to discuss with them at any time any point of his doctrines, he is represented as invariably and overwhelmingly successful. Not only is he a clear expounder, but he has also a good deal of the Socratic ability of putting questions, and, like Socrates, can lead on his unsuspecting critic to admissions which undermine the whole position.[29]

An oft-repeated formula, that probably goes back to very early Buddhist days, sums up several of the qualities I have here sought to present, and gives a succinct account of the attitude toward the Buddha maintained by his successors, and probably by his contemporaries.

> The Blessed One is an Arahat, a fully awakened one, abounding in wisdom and goodness, happy, with knowledge of the worlds, unsurpassed as a guide to mortals willing to be led, a teacher for gods and men, a Blessed one, a Buddha. He by himself thoroughly knows and sees, as it were, face to face this universe—including the worlds above of the gods, the Brahmas, and the Maras, and the world below with its recluses and Brahmins, its princes and peoples—and having known it he makes his knowledge known to others. The truth, lovely in its origin, lovely in its progress, lovely in its consummation, doth he proclaim both in the spirit and in the letter; the higher life doth he make known, in all its fullness and in all its purity.[30]

Yet neither this nor any other description of the Tathagata, the Perfectly Enlightened One, ever fully satisfied his disciples. After words had done their uttermost there was ever, as they viewed him, a residue of mystery in the nature of their Master, ever unplumbed depths which their language could not express nor their thought fathom. So much was he as they saw and knew, revered and loved; but more was there than they could ever hope to exhaust. "Deep is the Tathagata, unmeasurable, difficult to understand, even like the ocean." [31]

[29] E.g., Majjhima LVI.

[30] Digha IV. The same formula recurs frequently in various parts of the Digha and also in the other Nikayas, as well as in the Vinaya Mahavagga VI. 34, 13; 35, 1.

[31] Majjhima LXXII. This formula is found in several other passages and, I expect, is very ancient.

The Tathagata has suffered, from the western reader's point of view, in being too well reported. Like every wise teacher, he knew the necessity of repetition if his disciples were to grasp thoroughly and remember and hand down the main points of his doctrine. He taught for forty-five years, and nearly every year saw an influx of hundreds of novitiates into the Order. These had to be taught the simpler elements, while the more advanced disciples needed deeper instruction, and the rank and file who had been several years with him needed constantly to hear afresh the essentials of the doctrine in fresh words. The call for both repetition year after year, and also for variety of expression, was much greater than is demanded of a college professor, who for forty years gives courses in some large subject. The Buddha's situation and the demands upon him were thus very different from those of Jesus who taught only two years and had only twelve regular disciples, all of whom were, so to speak, in the same class. Thus it was natural that various presentations of a given subject, differing but slightly in expression, should have been treasured up by various disciples and added, after the Master's death, to the precious spiritual possessions of the Order. The Buddhist Suttas would probably be pleasanter reading had the Buddha taught only a few years and trained only one small group of pupils.

But a more unfortunate effect has flowed from the many repetitions of the Nikayas than tedium for the reader. The repetitions being in part fortuitous, it is impossible to determine with certainty the relative emphasis that the Buddha intended to be placed upon his various teachings. Most of the disagreement among western interpreters of his doctrine has arisen from this fact.

Some light can be thrown on the proper reading of his sayings if we keep in mind the intellectual situation of the times in which he lived. He was highly educated in the learning and philosophy of his day, and this must mean that he was thoroughly versed in the Vedas, possibly in the thought of the Upanishads, and certainly in the many new metaphysical theories which were springing up on all sides in that intellectually stimulating and fertile century. The Samkhya philosophy and probably its off-shoot, the Yoga, had been developed in their more ancient forms, and there is good reason to suppose that one or both of Gotama's most famous teachers, during the years just prior to his enlightenment, were at least well versed in the doctrines and methods of these schools.[32] In addition to these philosophies, and to the ancient and orthodox Vedic doctrine and cult, there was a wild growth of new schools of thought—the Buddha mentions some sixty-two philosophical views, each with its ardent expounders and followers. Prominent among these were the Jainas, whose founder was an older contemporary of Gotama. Some of these schools were materialistic, insisting that man is merely a combination of physical elements, with no soul, no rebirth, no reward or punishment. Other schools that did not go so far as this and still acknowledged a soul, maintained that deeds have no fruits, that all man's fate is determined for him, regardless of his acts, and that the will is never free. Still others denied all possibility of knowledge.[33] A large number of schools agreed on the value and importance of asceticism and practiced various extreme and fantastic forms of self-torture.

All of these views the Buddha had to meet and against all of them he protested. It is hardly correct to picture him as an Indian Martin Luther; but if not a "Protestant" he was at least a protestor against the various forms of conservative superstition and radical nonsense with which his times were seething. Against all of of these he armed himself with the sword of the intellect. Nothing, he insisted, should be taken on authority. "Do not accept what you hear by report, do not accept tradition, do not accept a statement because it is found in our books, nor because it is in accord with your belief, nor because it is the saying of your teacher." [34] The test of every doctrine is to be found in one's own experience and in reason. Nor is the traditional cult of India any more worthy of respect than belief on authority.

[32] Cf. Oldenberg, *Die Lehre der Upanishaden und die Anfange des Buddhismus* (Göttingen, Vandenhoeck, 1915), 317ff.

[33] Numerous references to these views are to be found in both the Digha and the Majjhima. A helpful account of them is given by Keith in his *Buddhist Philosophy in India and Ceylon* (Oxford, 1923), Chap. VII.

[34] Anguttara III. 65. I have slightly abbreviated the passage from Gooneratne's translation. The admonition is repeated several times in the Anguttara and also in the Majjhima.

Repeatedly the Tathagata ridicules the ancient meticulous observances of Brahmanic ritual and prayer to the helpless gods.[35] Asceticism comes in for even severer rebuke in many striking passages.[36] But the sharpest words are reserved for the folly of self-indulgence. In contrast to both these latter the Buddha calls his doctrine the Middle Way [37]—the Golden Mean as we should say—between indulgence and self-torture. Moreover the will is free, effort is worth while, man makes his own fate, deeds have consequences, knowledge is possible, the body is not the real self, and its death is not the end.

So much for the Buddha's point of view. A detailed study of his ethical and philosophical teachings must be reserved for the following chapters.

[35] Cf. Majjhima VII; Digha XIII.
[36] E.g., Digha VIII, XXV; Majjhima XL, XLV; Anguttara III. 92, 151, IV. 198.
[37] Cf. the Mahavagga of the Vinaya I; and Majjhima CXXXIX.

CHAPTER II

THE MORAL TEACHINGS OF THE FOUNDER ON THEIR NEGATIVE SIDE

THE central theme of the Buddha's teachings is the moral life. Morality, however, is itself a large theme. Is there any central principle in Gotama's moral teachings from which all the others may be deduced, or around which, at any rate, they should all be grouped? I expect almost every reader whose knowledge of Buddhism is derived from books *about* Buddhism will respond at once: There is such a central principle, and that is the pessimistic view of this world, the universality of sorrow, the derivation of sorrow from desire, and the consequent exhortations to root out desire in every form —in short, the Four Noble Truths. For my own part, this was certainly the view of Buddhism I held, as a matter of course, for many years—in fact, until my first visit to Southern Buddhist lands. On talking with Buddhist monks and laymen in Burma and Ceylon I was surprised to find that the Four Noble Truths and the conception of desire as always evil and the source of all our woe, though of course familiar, occupied no such central position in modern Buddhism as they hold in Western books about Buddhism. It was only after my return from this first visit to Buddhist lands that I turned seriously to the ancient sources. Here once more, particularly in the Majjhima Nikaya, I had somewhat the same experience as in talking with my Burmese and Ceylonese acquaintances. The Four Noble Truths do indeed hold a prominent position in the Nikayas, and it would not be difficult even to show by chapter and verse that they form the one basal doctrine of the system.[1] But one could prove the same thing, again by chapter and verse, of several other

[1] E.g., "He preached what is the principal doctrine of the Buddhas, namely suffering, the cause of suffering, the cessation of suffering, the path," Vinaya, Mahavagga I. 6, II. 4. "It is just sorrow and the ceasing of sorrow that I proclaim," Samyutta XXII. 86. See also Udana V. 3.

Buddhist principles.[2] And if one takes the teachings of the Buddha as a whole and in the large, noting the actual emphasis of the Nikayas, it becomes very difficult to give the Four Noble Truths the all-dominating position that our Western convention assigns them. The Buddha indeed recognizes sorrow in the world, but he also recognizes joy. And there is certainly no such emphasis in his teaching upon pessimism as we in the West commonly suppose. The explanation of our interpretation is, I believe, in part due to the historical accident that interest in Buddhism was introduced into Europe largely through the influence of Schopenhauer, who naturally emphasized those concepts in the Eastern religion most in accord with his own philosophy.[3] Another reason for the emphasis upon sorrow and desire is perhaps to be found in the fact that the first of the canonical books to be translated (in 1855, by Fausböll) was the Dhammapada. This beautiful anthology of Buddhist sayings, selected and arranged some time after the Master's death, gives much more decided emphasis to sorrow and desire and fleeing from the world than do the Nikayas as a whole. Not only was it the first book of the Buddhist canon that we of the West possessed. It is to this day probably the most commonly read. I expect, too, that Edwin Arnold's *Light of Asia*, with its poetic picture of the pathos of this world, has had its share of influence in forming the common view.[4]

[2] Cf., for example, the notable Seventy-seventh Dialogue of the Majjhima, which discusses the question in what respects the Tathagata is superior to other teachers. His superiority, we are told, consists in the following points: his virtue, his truthfulness, his wisdom, his teaching of the way to avoid sorrow, his emphasis upon constant self-control, effort of the will, insight, the "Eight Deliverances," the raptures, supernatural knowledge, conquest of illusion. In this list the Four Noble Truths play a part but a very subordinate part, and the concept of desire as the cause of all evil is not mentioned. In the "Book of the Great Decease" (Digha, No. 16) an account is given of the Buddha's last address to his disciples. At the close of it he is presented as giving a list of his most important teachings. The list is as follows: "The four earnest meditations, the fourfold great struggle against evil (to prevent and put away evil, to produce and increase goodness), the four roads to saintship, the five moral powers, the five organs of spiritual sense, the seven kinds of wisdom and the Aryan Eight-fold Path." It is noticeable that in this list only the last of the Four Noble Truths is mentioned. Nothing is said of the universality of sorrow nor of desire as its cause.

[3] The influence of Schopenhauer upon several German Buddhist scholars is particularly notable: e.g., Dahlke, whose *Buddhist Essays* was published in the seventies (Eng. trans., Hodder and Stoughton, 1875), and Grimm, whose *Doctrine of the Buddha* appeared in 1926.

[4] Further confirmation of the view that the West has exaggerated the importance of the Four Noble Truths is to be found in the fact that in Asoka's elaborate expositions of Buddhist morality (as found in his inscriptions) they are not mentioned.

I would not be understood as denying to the Four Noble Truths, especially to the evil of desire, a very important place in the Buddha's teaching, as found in the Nikayas. I am merely urging that we are hardly justified in setting them down as constituting the one central principle of Buddhism from which all else flows. Almost or quite equal emphasis is given in the Nikayas to ignorance, to energy of will, to the law of causation, to Yoga training, to the psychological analysis of man. The Buddha's moral teaching, as I view it, is thus more inclusive, more human, more persuasive, than is commonly thought, and consequently less striking and less original.

If we are to find a fundamental principle in the Buddha's ethical system, we must discover something more directly related to all his moral teachings than are the Four Noble Truths, and something also more truly basal than they. This principle is not difficult to discover. If we examine his directions for the moral life, his praise of the virtues and his denunciations of vice, we shall find that in every case in which he justifies his position (and to do so is a common practice with him) his argument is by appeal to reason and to recognized human values. There are good things in life and bad things; this is taken for granted. And moral conduct is based upon wise discrimination of values, separating true goods from spurious ones, and consists in an earnest cultivation of those tendencies and acts which produce or preserve the true values of life, and destroy life's evils. This principle cuts deeper than the Four Noble Truths. They may be justified by it and are derivable from it; but the reverse would be impossible.

This rationalistic view of morality at once determines the Buddha's position toward mere conventions or approved tradition, and thus sets his ethic at variance with that of Confucius. It also makes impossible any such conception of sin as the Hebrew or Christian. Sin is not for the Buddhist, as it is for the Jew and the Christian, "a transgression of or want of conformity to the Law of God." For the Buddha there is no God in the Jewish or Christian sense; and even if there were, the dominant position of the inner or subjective view in his thought would have prevented his attributing any ethical importance to the objective transgression of a God's decree. The Buddha would have accepted—in a sense he almost anticipated—Kant's doctrine of the Autonomy of the Will. Kant's formalism, however, would have made no appeal to the Buddha; the actual and foreseeable consequences of acts were to him of primary importance. Sin in his opinion is essentially irrational conduct, conduct that tends to destroy more values than it creates, either for the actor or for other sentient beings whom it affects. An act is characterized by its probable consequences. A good act is one that may be counted on to produce good results, in this life or the next, to the actor or to others.[5] His system may be classed as a form of altruistic hedonism in which the higher spiritual pleasures are rated much more important than those of the body. Pleasure of the senses, according to the Buddha, is seldom really desirable, in the long run; those who seek and find it discover that it does not permanently satisfy. Nor is desire as a psychological state truly desirable. Peace, freedom, equanimity—these are the things that are worth while, both for the actor and for all. It is in the inner life, insists the Buddha, that the true goods and ills are to be found. His rationalistic ethics must be interpreted in the light of his constant emphasis upon inwardness.

An ethical point of view based upon rationality and value will naturally have both a negative and a positive aspect. The negative side of such a doctrine would, of course, deal with negative values and point out whence they came and how they may be avoided. This in effect is what the Buddha presents in his famous doctrine of the Four Noble Truths.

The first and most famous formulation of the Four Noble Truths is that found in the Tathagata's first sermon, delivered in the Deer Park near Benares (now Sarnath) to the five ascetics who had been his companions, had become his scornful critics, and were now destined to be his first disciples. As given in Rhys Davids and Oldenberg's translation of the Vinaya it runs thus:

[5] Illustrations of the Buddha's insistence that all moral matters are questions of val[ue] will be found in the following passages: Rhys Davids' trans. of the Digha III. 175-7 Neumann's Ger. trans. of the Majjhima II. 622-23, 625, III. Nos. 114, 129, 13[0] Vinaya Mahavagga I. 22, 5.

This, O Bhikkhus,[6] is the Noble Truth of Suffering: Birth is suffering; decay is suffering; illness is suffering; death is suffering. Presence of objects we hate, is suffering; separation from objects we love, is suffering; not to obtain what we desire, is suffering. Briefly, the fivefold clinging to existence is suffering.

This, O Bhikkhus, is the Noble Truth of the Cause of Suffering: Thirst, that leads to re-birth, accompanied by pleasure and lust, finding its delight here and there. [This thirst is threefold] namely, thirst for pleasure, thirst for existence, thirst for prosperity.

This, O Bhikkhus, is the Noble Truth of the Cessation of Suffering: [it ceases with] the complete cessation of this thirst,—a cessation which consists in the absence of every passion,—with the abandoning of this thirst, with the doing away with it, with the deliverance from it, with the destruction of desire.

This, O Bhikkhus, is the Noble Truth of the Path which leads to the cessation of suffering: that holy eightfold Path, that is to say, Right Belief, Right Aspiration, Right Speech, Right Conduct, Right Means of Livelihood, Right Endeavor, Right Mindfulness, Right Meditation.[7]

It will add to our understanding of the Buddha's position if we read this careful presentation of the Four Noble Truths carefully and consider it to have been intended as we find it. If we read merely what is said and add nothing of our own we shall get from the First Noble Truth a list of sorrowful things which all will acknowledge to be such and which we should, doubtless, all like to get rid of. Certainly the Buddha does not here assert that everything is sorrow, nor can any such conclusion be deduced from these words. The pessimistic picture of the world commonly associated in the West [8] with the First Noble Truth is not to be derived from this presentation of the matter. And the presentation here given is typical not only of the Vinaya but of all the careful expositions of the First Noble Truth found in the Digha, Majjhima, and Anguttara Nikayas. In many passages, moreover, in which the Four Noble Truths are presented, especially in the Anguttara,[9] the First Truth reads: "*This* is sorrow." In Digha XXII. 17 the First Truth is expressed thus: "Herein a brother at the thought 'This is ill!' is aware of it as it really is." This way of putting the matter rather plainly shows that the intention is to emphasize discrimination be-

[6] Monks or hermits who get their food by begging.
[7] *Sacred Books of the East*, Am. Ed., IV. 95-96.
[8] Cf., for example, Dahlke's and Grimm's treatment of the subject.
[9] See Eng. trans. I. 145, 189, 265, II. 229, 238.

tween good and bad. It is ability to recognize evil things and things that under the surface are full of sorrow and of sorrowful consequences that is particularly stressed. Attention should be drawn also to the fact that in several expositions of the Four Noble Truths *illusion* is substituted for sorrow,[10] and in at least one case *body* is substituted.[11]

We are indeed told [12] that all the parts of the body and of the mind are transient and that all things are without permanent being. Is this assertion surprising or peculiar to Buddhism? Have not our Western philosophy and science and religion usually taught as much? And is there anything in this assertion from which it follows that this is a thoroughly evil world? As we shall see in another connection, the Buddha recognizes many of the solid (though of course transient) values of life as real values. There are transitory forms of happiness which he expressly approves and recommends. In fact the whole sting of transiency is to be found in the very fact that these passing things *are* good. That is why it is sad to lose them.

It will, I think, be difficult to find in the Vinaya, the Digha, Majjhima, or Anguttara any solid justification for the view that this is wholly a bad world. It is a sad world, of course, for the beautiful is certainly fleeting, and we should, therefore, not set our hearts upon it, but lay up our treasure where moth and rust do not corrupt. Buddhism realizes the sadness and uncertainty of this world quite as much as Christianity; probably it is even more emphatic in pointing out these characteristics. But if we confine ourselves to the four great scriptures named above we cannot justly class it with such a philosophy as Schopenhauer's or describe it as thoroughly pessimistic.[13] The Nikayas have little that could be called *Weltschmerz,* little of that gentle

[10] See Neumann's Majjhima II. 458, III. 26, 160, 338.

[11] Mrs. Rhys Davids' Samyutta III. 133.

[12] E.g., Neumann's Majjhima I. 530; Gooneratne's Anguttara, p. 300.

[13] When we turn to the Samyutta Nikaya we find a somewhat different situation. The other Nikayas point out that all worldly things are transitory; the Samyutta goes on and asserts, "Whatever is transient is full of sorrow." (Cf. Geiger's version II. 78, 173; and Mrs. Rhys Davids' version II. 165, III. 21, 39, 43, 59, 80). One passage in the Samyutta adds that consciousness is suffering. (III. 23. See also p. 19.) The tone of the Samyutta is on this matter (and we shall see it is on other matters also) very like that of the later canonical books, the Psalms of the Brethren and the Sisters, the Dhammapoda and the Sutta Nipata.

melancholy one finds in Japanese Buddhist poetry. They are hardly more melancholy than the Gospels.

I hasten to add that it is of course true that the Indian belief in transmigration, which the Buddha accepted and taught, adds greatly to the impression which the sorrowful side of life presents.[14] Behind each of us stretches an infinity of lives, each of which repeats the sad old round of birth, old age, death; birth, old age, death, till the thought grows unbearable and one longs for release from the sorrowful, weary wheel.

> Less are the waters of the oceans four
> Than all the waste of waters shed in tears
> By heart of man who mourneth touched by Ill.[15]

The Truth of Sorrow is certainly not the supremely important thing in Buddhism that it is sometimes pictured. But it is as certainly *one* of the important things; and a comprehension of the Buddha's position and of his ideal is not possible without grasping it. One must realize the real sadness of this world if one is to be filled with zeal for the ending of it.

To end sorrow one must know its cause. That the causal law is universal is one of the things most stressed by the Buddha and one which his disciples, at any rate, considered original with him. The Buddha gave years to the search of this cause. He is depicted as having found it on the night under the Bo Tree, but this was of course merely the consummation of long pondering. This persistent attempt to destroy sorrow for the world by discovering its cause is a marked illustration of what, in the preceding chapter, I called his rationalistic, objective, scientific attitude. The First Noble Truth in a sense sets his problem, provides him with the symptoms of the disease. He now goes at his task like a physician. He throws myth and cult and faith to the winds and asks himself: Sorrow being present, what is always present with it, what is absent when sorrow is absent? The cause of sorrow is plainly not any lack of things, and sorrow

[14] Cf. Geiger's version of the Samyutta, pp. 234-51.

[15] From Mrs. Rhys Davids' version of the *Psalms of the Sisters*, pp. 71, 173. Cf. also Samyutta XV. 3, XXII. 99.

can never be rooted up by the production of pleasure. To do that is but to heap fresh fuel on the fire. We must go deeper for the cause. And so he comes to his solution which is expressed in the Second Noble Truth, which, it will be recalled, reads thus: "This is the Noble Truth of the Cause of Suffering: Thirst that leads to rebirth, accompanied by pleasure and lust, finding its delight here and there. This thirst is three-fold, namely, thirst for pleasure, thirst for existence, thirst for prosperity."

The word that Rhys Davids here translates *thirst* is more commonly rendered *desire,* though *thirst* or *craving* probably gives the truer connotation. We are sad because we long for things and are therefore the slaves of things. And desire is *essentially* insatiable. The natural man, like Carlyle's bootblack, would still be miserable if you gave him half the planet; even if he had the whole planet, in fact, he would, like Alexander, sigh for more worlds to conquer. It is desire that leads us to give pledges to Fortune, and so to put ourselves at Fortune's mercy. No assured happiness is possible until we have freed ourselves from such serfdom to Chance.

It is possible but not easy to overemphasize the importance in Buddhist thought of the Second Noble Truth. Perhaps no other single thing, with the one exception of the evil of illusion or ignorance, is so stressed in the Nikayas. It is, I have said, possible to exaggerate it; for in a considerable number of passages other causes of sorrow are cited. Hatred is sometimes set down as the cause, and more often self-centeredness. Most commonly of all, illusion or ignorance is given as even more fundamental than desire, for desire comes from it.[16] This is particularly noticeable in the famous causal chain, or "Twelve Nidanas," which figures so prominently in the Buddha's teaching. In this account of the origin and development of human ill, desire is merely one of the links (the eighth) in the chain, while the first link, or better perhaps the hook from which it all hangs, is ignorance. In this sense ignorance is more fundamental than desire, and it receives correspondingly larger emphasis

[16] Cf. Neumann's Majjhima III. 622-24; Geiger's Samyutta, pp. 35, 60, 87, 90, 101, 114, 116-17; Mrs. Rhys Davids' Samyutta II. 175, III. 17, 114; Gooneratne's Anguttara I. 223; Seidenstücker's Udana, p. 34; *Psalms of the Brethren,* No. 250.

throughout the Nikayas. Yet if one ask what is meant by ignorance, the answer must be that it is, in part, ignorance of the Four Noble Truths, of which the central one is doubtless the Truth that sorrow is the result of desire.

That sorrow springs from desire was a real discovery and a piece of genuine insight. How far it was original with the Buddha I cannot say. That it was not entirely so is plain from the references to desire in the Upanishads.[17] Yet it was probably the Buddha who first realized the universality of its application and who first expressed it in explicit form. It is an insight that goes very deep into the general theory of value, and I expect few thinkers would deny its profound truth. To strike at desire is to strike at the very root of sorrow. No wonder that this truth colored a large part of the teachings of primitive Buddhism.

The amplification and application of this insight fill many of the discourses of the Buddha. Desire is "empty, false, and vain."[18] It is unsatisfying, full of pain, and essentially insatiable.[19] It is like flaming straw which a man holds before him and which burns him up.[20] One who yields to it is like a thirsty man who drinks from a beautiful cup a sparkling liquor which in reality is deadly poison.[21] Desire is the cause of envy and selfishness,[22] of contention, lamentation, arrogance, and slander;[23] it stands in the way of knowledge, insight, and true wakefulness.[24] It is the strongest of fetters.[25] Only by its total destruction can spiritual freedom be won.[26]

Does this mean that *all* desire is evil? A positive answer is sometimes given to this question: rarely by Buddhist monks, not uncommonly by Western writers on Buddhism. It would not be difficult to produce some evidence from the Nikayas for this interpretation. Yet I am entirely convinced that such a conclusion would be mistaken. If we take the Founder's teaching and life as a whole we shall find a balance of evidence for a less extreme position. I think it is obvious that the meaning which the Buddha himself put into his

[17] Cf. the Brihadaranyaka IV. 4, 6, 7.
[18] Neumann's Majjhima III. 84.
[19] *Ibid.*, I. 207, II. 514ff.
[20] *Ibid.*, II. 54.
[21] Geiger's Samyutta II. 152-53.
[22] Rhys Davids' Digha II. 310-11.
[23] Fausböll's Sutta Nipatta, pp. 164-65.
[24] Neumann's Majjhima I. 563.
[25] Dhammapada XXIV.
[26] Rhys Davids' Digha II. 316.

words and the sense in which he wished them to be taken should be interpreted in the light of his own conduct. When a man pursues one steady and consistent course, without deviation, during a period of forty-five busy years, that course and that aim are surely most relevant commentaries upon the meaning of his words. It is perfectly plain that the Buddha desired a number of things—perhaps not in such a way that his inner peace would have been destroyed had he failed in their achievement,[27] yet in some very real sense. He was filled with pity for suffering humanity and for even the beasts and insects; he dedicated his life to the dissemination of a truth which should free all who accepted it from endless woe; he labored unceasingly for the upbuilding and enlargement of the Order, for the education of its members, and also for the instruction of laymen and of all that came his way. To say that he labored so persistently for these ends yet never desired their realization could hardly mean anything else than that one wished to establish some new and limited definition of the word desire.

As a fact, moreover, if we are to accept the statements of the Nikayas, the Buddha repeatedly taught his disciples that there are two kinds of desire, good and bad, and that good desires were to be inculcated and cultivated. The attainment of the "raptures" [28] is often referred to as something which one may and should wish for, as is also the acquisition of supernormal powers and knowledge.[29] More worldly things also are sometimes mentioned as at least not improper objects of desire, such as a favorable rebirth,[30] the good will of one's fellows and the necessities of the monastic life.[31] Occasionally the disciples are encouraged to wish that those who help them may acquire merit.[32] The objects of desire more commonly mentioned with approval are, naturally, spiritual gifts,[33] the overcoming of lust, ill will and ignorance,[34] insight into the truth,[35] the various virtues,[36] the

[27] We have at least one instance in which the Buddha's peace seems to have been temporarily disturbed; this was brought about by dissension in the Order. See Vinaya, Mahavagga X. 4.

[28] E.g., Neumann's Majjhima I. 70, 574-75, 671.

[29] E.g., Ibid., pp. 71-75.

[30] E.g., *Ibid.*, pp. 244-45.

[31] E.g., *Ibid.*, p. 68.

[32] E.g., *Ibid.*, p. 69.

[33] E.g., *Ibid.*, II. 624.

[34] E.g., *Ibid.*, I. 71.

[35] E.g., *Ibid.*, II. 27.

[36] E.g., Iti-vuttaka § 22.

destruction of evil desires,[37] and (most common of all) complete liberation or Nibbana.[38] I recall but one passage in which it is said that one must give up even "the desire for the holy life"; [39] and shortly after this the Buddha is made to assert, "With the aid of craving does one eliminate craving." [40]

The same rational and by no means ascetic or merely negative position on the part of the Buddha comes out plainly from a study of various passages in the Nikayas which deal with happiness. Repeatedly is the explicit statement made that there are good as well as evil forms of happiness. In one passage the Buddha recounts his own experience, how after trying in vain the extremes of the ascetic method he recalled the joy of rapture which he had once known. Questioning whether joy of this or any sort were not a danger to be feared, he answered himself, "No, I will not fear this joy!" [41] From that time on the Buddha seems, like Socrates, to have considered himself the happiest of men.[42] The joy of rapture and the other spiritual delights of the enlightened are good things which one should seek. They are far removed from evil desire.[43] Joy in heavenly things [44] is a unity of the spirit, an inner blameless peace like the calm of the sea.[45] It is indeed so inward and so deep that no change in the environment can destroy it; [46] yet the monk may well take delight in the solemn and purifying beauties of nature, and especially in the dark silence of a solitary forest. The *Psalms of the Early Buddhists,* notably those of the Brethren, are full of poetical expressions of keen delight in these woodland solitudes,[47] and to the Tathagata is attributed this same joy of the nature-lover.

> 'Tis the high hour of noon; the birds rest silently.
> Boometh the mighty forest; enchanting that sound to me.[48]

[37] E.g., Neumann III. 85. Cf. also *Psalms of the Brethren,* No. 262.

[38] E.g., Samyutta I. 1, 3; I. 6, 9.

[39] Jayasundere's Anguttara II. 58.

[40] *Ibid.,* p. 189.

[41] Neumann's Majjhima, II. 569.

[42] Jayasundere's Anguttara II. 118.

[43] Neumann II. 813; Digha XXVI. 28.

[44] Neumann, II. 346-47.

[45] *Ibid.,* I. 204: "*die innere Meeresstille.*" See also pp. 623, 656, 700-01.

[46] Cf. Sutta Nipata I. 2. *Psalms of the Brethren,* Nos. 51-54, 192.

[47] Mrs. Rhys Davids' *Psalms of the Brethren,* pp. xxxvii-xxxix, and Nos. 18, 19, 119, 167, 186-7, 246-47, 249-50, 252, 267, 363-64, 379, 386. See also Dhammapada VII.

[48] Mrs. Rhys Davids' Samyutta I. 11.

The principle on which the good and the evil forms of happiness are to be distinguished is explicitly stated. It is the principle of utilitarianism.

> Happiness [said the Buddha], I declare to be twofold, according as it is to be followed after or avoided. And the distinction I have affirmed in happiness is drawn on these grounds: When in following after happiness I have perceived that bad qualities developed and good qualities were diminished, then that kind of happiness is to be avoided. And when following after happiness I have perceived that bad qualities were diminished and good qualities developed, then such happiness is to be followed.[49]

It is plain, then, that there are both bad pleasures and good, both evil desires and good desires. A careful reading of many of the passages in which the evil of desire is most emphasized seems to indicate that it was chiefly (though not exclusively) those of a sensuous nature that the Buddha disapproved.[50] This, however, is not always the case; and in fact it would not be difficult to cite passages in which the Buddha denounces as evil a desire for some of the things mentioned in the preceding paragraph as truly desirable. To live a good life in order thereby to go to heaven is, he tells us, really impossible;[51] for the desire for heavenly delights vitiates the efforts at virtue. Possibly some of the seemingly contradictory statements in the Nikayas are due to an actual uncertainty in the Buddha's thought, or to failure on the part of his reporters to grasp and hand on his true meaning; but much of the apparent contradiction can be explained in other and quite natural ways. We must distinguish, for one thing, between the life of the layman and the life of the monk. Normal human pleasures will not defeat your purposes if all you want is happiness and a good rebirth. If, however, you are aiming (as a monk should) at Nirvana, the matter may be different. Furthermore, the Buddha seems to have distinguished between desires not chiefly by their content or objects, but by the form and nature of the desires themselves as psychical states. This is quite characteristic of him and falls in with the whole trend of Buddhism to emphasize in-

[49] Digha XXI. 3. See also XXIX. 23, 24. A much more elaborate but less philosophical dichotomy of happiness is given in Anguttara II. 7.

[50] Cf. Rhys Davids' Digha II. 340-44; Neumann's Majjhima I. 240, 406, 516, III. 69. Geiger's Samyutta II. 151.

[51] Neumann's Majjhima I. 244-45.

wardness. That this is the basis of his distinction, a fact plain enough from a careful reading of the English and German translations of the Nikayas, comes out more strikingly, according to Mrs. Rhys Davids, in the Pali original. In some of our translations, she tells us, "the word *desire* is made to do duty for no less than seventeen Pali words." [52] In its choice of terms the Pali canon distinguishes between *desire* in its merely psychological sense and the kind of desire that deserves moral disapproval. If moral value is intended special words or special qualifications are used.[53]

But while it is true that the Buddha did not condemn all desire as such, and whatever his principal distinction between good desires and bad may have been, certain it is that he placed on the evil side of the line many desires which most other ethical teachers have considered either entirely proper or even praiseworthy. In a typical passage of the Digha [54] we are told craving takes its rise from material things that are pleasant and dear to us, and not only from sensations and feelings related to them but from intentions concerned with sensuous objects and deliberations about them. Craving, or the evil kind of desire, is not justified or transformed by the goodness of the object longed for. Attachments to any ephemeral object of affection lays one open to the slings and arrows of outrageous Fortune and therefore, seemingly, should be avoided. In the Eighty-seventh Dialogue of the Majjhima, a discussion is described concerning the Tathagata's assertion that attachment to parents, wife and children brings sorrow. Some of his hearers insist that instead of sorrow these human ties bring joy. The Buddha does not deny that they bring joy, but shows by many examples of the loss of dear ones the conditions of dependence upon chance and of constant liability to overwhelming grief which is the lot of everyone who has not broken the ties of personal affection. He does not say such affections are wicked; he states the fact that they are pledges to Fortune, and that he who breaks the ties and exchanges family life for that of

[52] "On the Will in Buddhism," *J. R. A. S.*, 1898, p. 54.

[53] "Want or wish becomes *craving* or *thirst*; for desire we get *lust, lusts of the flesh, sensual delight*, etc." *Op. cit.*, p. 49.

[54] XXII. 19.

the monk has an assured peace which the "householder" can never possess.

A similar situation is reported in the Udana VIII. 8. A woman who has just lost a very dear grandchild comes to the Buddha for comfort. He asks her would she like to have as many children and grandchildren as there are people in the city of Savatthi. On her reply in the affirmative, he points out that if it were so, she would probably lose several every day, so all her life would be filled with grief. "Those who have a hundred dear ones have a hundred woes; those who have ninety dear ones have ninety woes . . . those who have one dear one have one woe; those who hold nothing dear have no woe." [55]

In the Samyutta (which, it will be recalled, is probably later than the Digha and the Majjhima) the sorrow that arises from all worldly attachments comes more often to the fore and is made more central to the moral life. "The well-taught disciple asks himself: 'Is there, I wonder, aught in all the world which I can cling to without sin?' Then he knows for certain: 'No! There is naught in all the world that I can cling to without sin.' " [56] An interesting instance of the struggle that must have been felt in the heart of many an ancient disciple between this rather austere doctrine and the natural outpourings of human affection in the finest of personal relations is given in the twenty-first chapter of the Samyutta, in which the greatest of the Buddha's disciples, Sariputta, is faced with it.

> The venerable Sariputta said this: "As I was meditating in seclusion there arose this consideration: Is there now anything in the whole world wherein a change would give rise in me to grief, lamenting, despair? And methought, No, there is no such thing." Then the venerable Ananda said to the venerable Sariputta: "But the Master—would not the loss of him give rise in you to grief, lamenting, despair?" "Not even the loss of him, Friend Ananda. Nevertheless, I should feel thus: O may not the mighty one, O may not the Master so gifted, so wonderful, be taken from us!" [57]

[55] Similar instances of the Buddha's rationalistic type of comfort to the bereaved will be found in the *Psalms of the Sisters*, Nos. 33, 47, 50, 63.

[56] XXII. 80. See also I. 2, 9, XXII. 3. A similar view is presented in the *Psalms of the Sisters*, Nos. 28, 68.

[57] I have used Mrs. Rhys Davids' translation. Cf. also the laments of Ananda and Moggallana over the death of Sariputta, *Psalms of the Brethren*, Nos. 260, 263. Note

What has been said of the danger of attachments should not be taken to mean that friendship is taboo. The Buddha was on terms of warm friendship with many of his disciples and with some of his lay followers. A good friend is commended as a great treasure.[58] Leading members of the Order lived together on terms of mutual regard and service.[59] When the venerable Udayi reproved the venerable Ananda (the "beloved disciple") for expressing delight at the glory of his Master, the Tathagata defended Ananda, saying that his gladness of heart would redound greatly to his heavenly reward.[60] It seems to have been the general opinion, however, that Ananda's tardiness in attaining Arahantship (or complete liberation) was largely due to the personal and emotional nature of his attachment to his Master. And while friendship of a calm and mutually helpful sort was commended, it is plain that the ideal monk must be on his guard lest he make his inner peace dependent on his friend.

In the later parts of the canon—notably in the Sutta Nipata,[61] the Dhammapada,[62] and the Theragatha, or Psalms of the Early Buddhists, fear of human attachments and the exhortation to break all the ties is carried much further than in the Nikayas, both in extreme form of statement and in the emphasis of repetition—from which I think we are justified in supposing that the Founder himself laid less stress upon it than did his followers who developed his thought. None the less he himself plainly spoke in some such wise at times, and there is no gainsaying the fact that the fear of all human ties was a logical consequence of the Second Noble Truth.

The similarity between the Buddha's attitude toward desire and that of the Stoics has often been pointed out; and the distinction he draws betwen good and evil desires seems related to their distinction of those things that are in our

also the contrast in the attitude of the different monks when the death of the Buddha was announced. Those "not yet free from their passions stretched out their arms and wept: some rocked to and fro in anguish; but those free from passion bore their grief collected and composed." Cullavagga XI. 1.

[58] Digha XXXI. 21, 5.

[59] Cf. Majjhima XXXI. Vinaya Mahavagga X. 4.

[60] Anguttara III. 80, 5.

[61] Cf. Fausböll's version, pp. 3, 6ff, 77, 90, 154-55, 165.

[62] Cf. Müller's version, p. 57: "Let no man love anything; loss of the beloved is evil. Those who love nothing and hate nothing have no fetters."

power and those that are not in our power.[63] With Saint Paul the Buddha at times urges his disciples to covet earnestly the best gifts: and these it will be noted are chiefly or entirely conditions of the inner life the achievement and preservation of which lies entirely with us, and which, as Spinoza would say, beget in us a "love toward that which is immutable and eternal and which we really have within our power.[64]

The Buddha's ethic might, then, well be called Stoic, but the principle underlying and justifying his Stoicism, to which he makes appeal when argument is needed, is his fundamental utilitarianism or (altruistic) hedonism. On the general principle involved the Buddha would find a large amount of agreement, in the West as well as in the East. It is not good to desire things that in the long run will bring more pain than pleasure to all concerned, nor is it good to desire at all if the very psychological state of desiring will bring a balance of disappointment, sorrow, and defeat. Not here is the line to be drawn between the Buddhist point of view and, let us say, the Christian, or the Western in general. The difference between the two points of view lies in their contrasted evaluations of good and evil things, which in its turn seems based upon a rather fundamental difference in temperament. Like Epicurus and his followers, the Buddha is suspicious of the more violent pleasures. The calm, impersonal satisfactions of intelligence and virtue, since they are the "purest"

[63] Cf. Epictetus, Encheiridion, Chap. V.

[64] The whole passage from Spinoza is worth quoting, so Buddhistic is it in tone: "One should note that griefs and misfortunes have their chief source in an excessive love of that which is subject to many variations, and of which we can never have control. No one is solicitous or anxious about anything unless he love it; nor do injustices, suspicions, enmities, etc., arise, except from the love of things of which no one can really have control. Thus we easily conceive what power clear and distinct knowledge, and especially that third kind of knowledge, the foundation of which is the knowledge of God and nothing else, has over the emotions; if it does not, in so far as they are passions, absolutely remove them, at all events it brings it about that they constitute the least part of the mind. Furthermore, it begets love toward that which is immutable and eternal, and which we really have within our power; a love which, consequently, is not stained with any of the defects inherent in common love, but can always become greater and greater and take possession of the greatest part of the mind, and affect it everywhere" (*Ethics*, V, 20). Cf. also the following from the *Imitation of Christ:* "If thou seek this or that, and wouldst be in such or such a place, the better to enjoy thine own profit and pleasure, thou shalt never be at quiet or free from anxiety: for in every instance something will be found wanting. Man's welfare, then, lieth not in obtaining or multiplying any external thing, but rather in despising it and utterly rooting it out from the heart" (Chap. XXVII).

(i.e., the least mingled with pain) are the best. So great are the dangers of strong desire which result from intense pleasure that the wise man, according to both the Buddha and Epicurus, will often express his goal in negative terms—"the freedom of the body from pain and of the soul from confusion." [65] To all pleasures and pains of a sensuous sort and of a personal sort, the good Buddhist should feel complete indifference. For the Buddhist the choice of what seems to us negative values is often a choice of a positive good. "Whatsoever may be the delights of sense in this world or even in heaven, these are not worth the sixteenth part of the delight that lies in the disappearance of thirst." [66] Nor is Buddhism any more afraid of bodily pain than the West, and it is surely even less afraid of bodily discomfort than we. But turmoil of mind, inner disturbance, disappointment, the weariness of weakness and of old age, the grief that comes from the loss of dear ones and the defeat of ambition: these to it seem very dreadful indeed, so dreadful, in fact, as far to outweigh the joy that comes from health, successful effort, and human love. Buddhism at times seems to us almost pathologically afraid of sorrow. It is perhaps no more pessimistic than is Christianity; but sorrow seems to the Buddhist a more dreadful thing than it does to the Christian or to Westerners in general. The typical Westerner is willing to take the risk that the desired object will bring more joy than its loss will bring pain, or he is sanguine enough to hope that in his own time the desired object may not be lost. From such a risk Buddhism shrinks back. Better be on the safe side, it counsels; better give no pledges to Fortune; better take no chance of the loss of inner peace, even if your security be purchased by the sacrifice of all the uncertain and ephemeral joys. Buddhism seems femininely sensitive to sorrow, while the West seems relatively masculine, thick-skinned, imprudent, and willing to take a chance. Buddhism takes the attitude of wise and somewhat timid old age: the West (except when really old) takes that of inexperienced and possibly rash youth. A philosophical friend of mine well past middle life recently made the remark: "I am making no new friends now; I do not dare to." The attitude thus ex-

[65] Epicurus, as expounded by Diogenes Laertius.

[66] Udana II. 2.

pressed is not uncommon with many of us Westerners as we grow older. It is typically Buddhist in its fear of possible sorrow.

The Second Noble Truth is the central element in the negative side of Buddhism, and I have therefore dwelt upon it at length. The Third Noble Truth need not detain us long. It is the "Noble Truth of the Cessation of Suffering"—the truth that by killing out evil desire we may become free from sorrow. This in a sense merely makes more explicit the Second Truth; yet it is not merely that. For it involves the fundamental confidence and insistence of the Founder that not only are we slaves to sorrow when slaves to desire, but that *something may be done about it.* We may break our bonds and end our slavery when we will, for our acts are neither determined for us by Fate nor devoid of real consequences, but free and efficacious. The Fourth Truth, which consists of the Noble Eightfold Path that leads to the cessation of suffering is, in effect, a course of habit training and character training through which the peace of perfect freedom may be obtained, and with which we shall deal later on.

The Four Noble Truths are concerned chiefly with the cessation and avoidance of suffering, and thus represent, as I have pointed out, the negative side of the Buddha's utilitarianism. Because of the exceptionally intense fear of sorrow which characterizes Buddhism, and because of its extreme prudence and unwillingness to take risks, the negative side of the moral life inevitably receives greater stress than it does in more virile systems, such as Zoroastrianism and Christianity. A large part of the moral exhortations of the Nikayas are taken up with warnings *not* to kill, *not* to steal, *not* to desire, *not* to be unkind, *not* to make trouble, etc. It would be a mistake, however, to suppose that the Buddha confined his teaching to negations or failed to see that positive good must be cultivated if positive evil were really to be avoided. He was too wise a psychologist to be ignorant that human nature as well as inorganic nature "abhors a vacuum." If the seeker after release merely realizes that the desires bring no satisfaction, he cannot free himself from them; but when he adds to this knowledge the realization of a Better outside of the desires, then he is their slave no longer.[67] In the Seventh Dialogue of the Majjhima a long list of vices is given, covering many pages, and in each case the method of overcoming the vice, which is through the cultivation of the corresponding virtue. The moral rule not to kill must, the Tathagata insists, be interpreted to mean not merely abstention from taking life but also positive sympathy, good will, and love for everything that breathes; [68] and the same principle is to be applied to the other seemingly negative commands. One of the Buddha's lay followers once reported to him the teaching of a non-Buddhist ascetic, to the effect that the highest ideal consisted in the absence of evil deeds, evil words, evil thoughts, and evil life. The Buddha's comment upon this is significant. If, said he, this were true, then every sucking child would have attained the ideal of life. Much more than this negative condition of mere innocence is needful. The first requisite of the virtuous life is knowledge of good and evil; and after that the exchange of evil deeds, words, thoughts, and life, for good ones. This is to be brought about only by a long and determined effort of the will.[69] In the Anguttara Nikaya the Buddha is quoted as distinguishing between a good man and a very good man by saying that one who abstains from killing, stealing, unchastity, lying, and drunkenness may be called good; but only he deserves to be called very good who abstains from these evil things himself and also instigates others to do the like.[70]

The Buddhist ethic, then, is not merely negative. And while its emphasis is more decidedly upon the negative aspects of morality than is that of Christianity, it is a misrepresentation to depict it (as Western books not infrequently do) as primarily and chiefly negative. Its positive and constructive teachings are really more fundamental than are its negations and prohibitions. To these more interesting themes we shall turn in the following chapter.

[67] Neumann's Majjhima I. 208.
[68] *Ibid.*, I. 668.
[69] *Ibid.*, II. 432-36.
[70] Jayasundere's version, II. 279-80.

CHAPTER III

THE POSITIVE SIDE OF THE BUDDHIST ETHIC

THE two cardinal virtues of Buddhism are wisdom and love. The moral life begins with knowledge and ends in wisdom. The Buddha came to save the world, and his method for the accomplishment of this end is the destruction of ignorance and the dissemination of knowledge as to the true values of life and the wise way to live. The Buddha, indeed, cannot save us: we must do that for ourselves. But the way to save ourselves is, in large part, through the attainment and application of his knowledge or insight. Insight, to be sure, is not the whole of the Buddhist method of salvation, but it is the alpha and omega of it. The central part of the method is training and love, but the first step is knowledge of true values and of the causes of evil, while the last stage is a deep and almost mystical apprehension of the highest potentialities of the mind. Ignorance, as I have pointed out in another connection, is held up as the source of evil perhaps even more commonly than desire. A passage in the Anguttara says, "Lust [or desire] is slightly sinful and its removal is slow; hatred is highly sinful and its removal is rapid; ignorance is highly sinful and its removal is slow." [1] Ignorance is the first of the twelve "Nidanas" or links in the Causal Chain, which end in old age, sickness, and death. It is the source not only of sorrow here and now, but of the perpetual repetition of birth which keeps us endlessly upon the weary round of passionate and painful life. In fact, passion itself is but a form of ignorance [2]—a doctrine which recalls forcibly the position of Spinoza in Part IV of the *Ethics*.

It is particularly ignorance of the true nature of self, or rather the delusion that one's self is to be identified with one's

[1] Gooneratne, I. 223.

[2] See Sutta Nipata, Mahavagga 12, vss. 4, 5.

body, one's consciousness, or one's phenomenal personality in general that works most of our woe.[3] The Buddha's treatment of the self in its theoretical aspect will concern us in a later connection; here it is necessary simply to point out that ignorance about the self leads to self-centeredness, and self-centeredness has as much to do in causing sorrow as has even desire; it seems at times, in fact, to be almost a synonym for desire. A very large part of human unhappiness is produced by our constant and unnecessary preoccupation with the thought of ourselves. The animals who are not yet self-conscious know nothing of this artificial woe, and the saints who have transcended separate self-consciousness know nothing of it. The great bulk of our woe, thinks the Buddha, most of us bring upon ourselves quite needlessly by viewing everything from its bearing upon our little selves. "'Tis self whereby we suffer." Once rid of this self-centered habit, we should taste the new joy of spiritual freedom.

The importance of insight into the true nature of the self, of human weal and woe and their causes, immediate and remote, calls for a large amount of detailed advice concerning the conduct of life, often in the form of moral directions, maxims, exhortations, some of them enunciating large and general principles, some going into the minutiæ of daily living. Moral discussions of this sort fill a large part of the dialogues of the Buddha as reported to us in the Nikayas. It was on these subjects that he most frequently talked to laymen and beginners in the Path. "To them he discoursed in due order," says the Digha, depicting a typical conversation of the Tathagata; "that is to say, he gave them illustrative talk on generosity, on right conduct, on heaven, on the danger, the vanity and the defilement of lusts, on the advantages of renunciation."[4] The detail of these moral exhortations would fill a volume. From the mass of them certain special virtues and special sins or sources of danger and evil stand out with particular and repeated emphasis. Self-control, of course, looms very large—a peculiarly Buddhist virtue, which, in a sense, is the precondition of nearly

[3] *Diese von Gluten erfüllte, gänzlich in den Berührungen befangene Welt erklärt die Krankheit für das Ich* (Seidenstücker's Udana, p. 33).

[4] Rhys Davids' version, I. 34. See also Vinaya Mahavagga V. 1, 9, VI. 26, 8, VI. 36, 5.

all the rest. "If one man conquer in battle a thousand times a thousand men, and if another conquer himself, he is the greatest of conquerors." [5] Humility is often praised; the ideal Buddhist must be "poor in spirit," and pride is one of the most dangerous of stumbling blocks. Both these virtues —self-control and humility—are of course notably matters of the inner life, which thus receives the characteristic stress of Buddhism. In a lively discussion with a distinguished Jaina sophist the Buddha is presented as upholding the thesis that evil thoughts are much worse than evil deeds or evil words; and in quite Socratic manner he forces his opponent into admitting the truth of the doctrine. Out of the heart are the issues of life. But from this inner source rise many of the splendid virtues of action. There are few qualities more highly praised by the Buddha than generosity—a peculiarly Buddhist virtue which has characterized the followers of the Blessed One in every land to which his teaching has been carried. And generosity does not mean merely giving. It is, as usual, intended in the inner even more than in the outer sense. It means the generosity of spirit that understands and forgives. "These two are wicked: he who does not see and admit the wrong he has committed, and he who does not forgive when the wrong has been confessed and forgiveness is implored." [6] Closely related to generosity are the qualities of mercy, sympathy, fellow-feeling, which lie so deep in Buddhism that even in the most degenerate Buddhist monasteries of today the scent of this choice rose still hangs around the broken vase. From generosity and good will flow naturally good manners: and it is in keeping with the Founder's heart and head and aristocratic birth that he should have regarded good manners and the kind of politeness that comes from the good breeding of a noble nature as a part of morality.[7]

Greatest among the vices, dangers, and sources of evil stand lust, ill will, and ignorance, and the slavery that comes from too much care for the objects of sense. Indolence, laziness, and lack of energy in the spiritual struggle also come in

[5] Dhammapada VIII. See also XXIII.
[6] Gooneratne's Anguttara I. 79.
[7] Jayasundere's Anguttara II. 55. Cf. also the Patimokkha rules of the Vinaya.

for repeated denunciation.[8] The Buddha was careful that the silent meditation which he taught—the strenuous mental activity of the true "Aryan" or man of noble nature—should not be confused with the mere *dolce far niente* which doubtless in the case of many a "holy man" goes under some more pious name. That self-excused laziness was a temptation even to the greatest members of the Order in their novitiate days is seen by a story concerning Moggallana the Great—counted by the Master the second in importance of all his followers. "After Moggallana had been ordained a week, torpor and sleepiness assailed him, so that the Master aroused him with the words: 'Moggallana, idleness is not the same as Aryan silence.' "[9]

In addition to the Buddha's careful teaching about special virtues and vices such as those mentioned in the preceding paragraph, one finds in the Nikayas—notably in the later ones—elaborate analyses and systematizations of ethical and psychological matters. How much of this came from the Founder and how much from his scholastic followers who faced the difficult task of handing on his teaching through the centuries without the aid of written records, is a question no one can answer. A good deal of it, at any rate, probably originated with the scholastic transmitters. Thus we have the Five Bonds of the Senses, the Five Factors of Grasping, the Five Hindrances (desire, malice, torpor, worry, doubt), the Four Intoxicants (sensuality, becoming, delusion, ignorance), the Four Attachments (to sensual pleasure, continued existence, erroneous views, illusion), and the interminable and wearisome numerical lists of virtues and vices in the Anguttara Nikaya and in the last two dialogues of the Digha.[10] But whatever the source of these scholastic analyses, there can be little doubt that the Five Precepts came from the Founder. These are as follows: Not to kill, not to steal, not to be unchaste, not to lie, not to drink intoxicants.[11] These, as we have seen, were intended by the Tathagata to be taken in a liberal and positive manner; the first includes

[8] Cf. *Psalms of the Brethren* No. 225.

[9] *Psalms of the Brethren* No. 263.

[10] See also Udana V. 5 (7, 8).

[11] The first four of these precepts are shared by both Hindu and Jaina monks. For the fifth Hinduism substitutes a vow of liberality, and Jainism one against covetousness.

sympathy and good will to all, the second generosity, the fourth precludes slander, back-biting, idle talk, and trouble-making. Against lying the Buddha is at times particularly bitter. The liar and the man who speaks ill of the good and tries to soil a good name is in danger of hell fire.[12] "He who does not shrink from conscious lying is in a condition to do every evil thing. Therefore, Rahula, resolve: Not once even in jest will I speak a lie." [13] Thus did the Buddha counsel his own son.

The central position of the moral values in the Buddha's view of life, the magnitude and number of the dangers that constantly threaten one's peace, and the detail of psychological analysis set forth in the teaching as an almost indispensable tool for the achievement and retention of virtue necessitate a constant watchfulness and self-consciousness in him who is really in earnest in his aim to reach the goal. The teaching of the Tathagata, and the training which he outlines, point out the way; but the way must be trod by one's own strength. In the last analysis the victory must be won by sheer force of will. I know not whether Pali Buddhism has a word which corresponds exactly with our word *will*, but the thing is there, described as the fundamental necessity of moral victory in no uncertain terms. "Those who follow the Way might well follow the example of an ox that marches through the deep mire carrying a heavy load. He is tired, but his steady gaze, looking forward, will never relax until he come out of the mire, and it is only then he takes a respite. O monks, remember that passions and sins are more than the filthy mire, and that you can escape misery only by earnestly and steadily thinking of the Way." [14] Like the ox one must take no respite, no "moral holiday." Even the slightest evil tendency may be but the entering of the wedge, which, unless stopped at once, may end by cleaving and destroying the entire character. "Let no one think lightly of evil, saying 'It will not come nigh me.' Even by the falling

[12] Sutta Nipata, Mahavagga 10.

[13] Majjhima LXI.

[14] From the Sutra of the Forty-two Chapters. This in its present form is a late anthology—one of the first Buddhist books carried by missionary monks into China. The spirit of it, however, is thoroughly Buddhist. It has been translated into English by Prof. D. T. Suzuki in the vol. entitled *Sermons of a Buddhist Abbot* (Chicago, *Open Court*, 1906).

of water drops a water pot is filled. The fool becomes full of evil even if he gather it little by little." [15]

Until complete victory is won, the moral life, to be successful, must be a constant struggle. One must be ever on one's guard, ever fighting off the temptations of evil, night and day.[16] Constant effort,[17] eternal vigilance, is the price of liberty. Diligence is pointed out as the one quality by which the monk may acquire and retain well-being both in this life and in that which is to come.[18] In preparation for the battle with evil one should put on the whole armor of righteousness.[19] The true monk repeatedly "arouses his will" that new evil shall not arise within him, that so much as has arisen shall be driven out, that the good already within him shall grow, and that new forms of goodness shall come into being.[20] Even the most unfavorable of circumstances must not be allowed to diminish one's persistence or the strength of one's resolve.[21] A sick old man once came to the Buddha for comfort and advice, complaining of his many physical ills. The Buddha made no attempt at working a miraculous cure and held out no deceiving hopes for bodily health. "True it is," he said, "that your body is weak and encumbered. For one carrying this body about to claim but a moment's health would be sheer foolishness; Wherefore thus should you train yourself: 'Though my body is sick my mind shall not be sick.' Thus must you train yourself." [22]

Neither longing for the past nor hoping for the future will aid one: [23] nothing will aid but determined and unremitting effort in the living present. Every expedient and every method should be tried till the victory is won, the last resource being the sheer heft of the will.

When evil and unworthy thoughts arise in the mind, images of lust, hatred, and infatuation, the monk must win from these thoughts other

[15] Dhammapada IX. 121.

[16] Majjhima CLI; Dhammapada II, XXII, XXIII.

[17] Samyutta I. 2, 6.

[18] Samyutta III. 2, 7.

[19] Majjhima LXXXV. This armor consists of five pieces: confidence, strength, honesty, courage, wisdom.

[20] Neumann's Majjhima II. 410-11, III. 550; Jayasundere's Anguttara II. 19, 124-25, 319-20; Geiger's Samyutta, p. 207.

[21] Majjhima CXXII.

[22] Woodward's Samyutta III. 2.

[23] Majjhima CXXXI.

and worthy images. When he thus induces other and worthy images in his mind, the unworthy thoughts, the images of lust, hatred, and infatuation cease; and because he has overcome them his inner heart is made firm, tranquil, unified, and strong. If in spite of these efforts unworthy thoughts still arise, with images of lust, hatred, and infatuation, the monk should go over in his mind the misery that comes from such thoughts and images. . . . He should pay no attention to these evil thoughts and images. . . . If in spite of these efforts evil thoughts and images still rise in his mind, he should let them go to pieces, one by one. . . . If this method does not succeed, then with teeth pressed against each other, with his tongue pressed against his gums, he should by the exertion of his will overthrow, press down, destroy these evil thoughts.[24] . . . You may attain the goal of a stainless life if you are strenuous in your continuous and indefatigable efforts with the firm resolve: "We will not discontinue our strenuous effort without gaining that spiritual perfection which can be secured by manly vigor, manly ability, manly exertion, so long as our skin, nerves and bones remain, even if our flesh and blood were to dry up.[25]

This constant watchfulness against every form of temptation or evil, this unremitting preoccupation with one's spiritual progress, results in a certain self-consciousness, which robs Buddhist morality of some of the charm it might otherwise possess. The monk who has not yet attained perfect self-mastery must keep a perpetual watch on each object of each of the senses and see to it, with clear and explicit awareness, that it rouses no desire in his mind.[26] Rahula, the Buddha's son, is urged by his father to watch himself constantly as in a mirror: to reflect before each deed, while performing it, and after it is done whether it was spiritually helpful or harmful to himself and to others; to go through the same process with each word and each thought. "Thus by thinking over and over will we purify our deeds, words, and thoughts."[27] A form of exhortation given more than once to the monks is the following:

How does a brother become self-possessed? He acts in full presence of mind whatever he may do, in going out or coming in, in looking forward or in looking around, in bending his arm or stretching it forth,

[24] Neumann's Majjhima I. 288-92.

[25] Gooneratne's Anguttara I. 70. Cf. also the Samyutta XII. 22, XXI. 3. For examples of the way in which some even of the women followers carried out the strenuous efforts commended, see *Psalms of the Sisters*, Nos. 40, 45.

[26] Neumann's Majjhima I. 632.

[27] Majjhima LXI.

in wearing his robes or in carrying his bowl, in eating or drinking, in masticating or smelling, in obeying the calls of nature, in walking or standing or sitting, in sleeping or waking, in talking or being silent.[28]

It can hardly be supposed that the Buddha seriously meant such preoccupation with one's own moral character to be carried on through all the waking hours of the day. Much of what he said on the subject must be taken as directions for the training of the character by frequent but not continuous meditations, or as exhortations that the thought of watchfulness should be kept ever in the background of one's mind. Since for him morality was equivalent to rationality, he would have agreed with Professor Fite that to be moral is to be self-conscious—to know what one is about. It must be remembered, too, that those who, like the Buddha and his more spiritual and proficient followers, had attained complete enlightenment are no longer troubled by the constant temptations that assail the rest of us and so, having perfected this training, need it no longer.[29] It may be true that we who are not Arahants, if we are to win to the heights of the Buddhist ideal, need to be constantly on the watch and clearly aware of the moral and immoral nature of all that we do, and just how much we may gain or lose thereby. Yet most of us, I think, after reading the long exhortations in the Nikayas upon "mindfulness" in all its sophisticated details, turn with a certain wistfulness toward those spontaneous yet beautiful souls who act with no struggle and with little reflection, who "do by knowledge what the stones do by structure," as Emerson puts it, and "whose acts are all regal, graceful, and pleasant as roses."

However we may think about this, it is the Buddha's opinion that for beings such as most of us, the moral ideal is attainable only through long processes of self-conscious and Puritanical self-training. So difficult is the task that it is hardly to be expected anyone can achieve it, in this world at any rate, without going at it professionally, that is, by joining the *Sangha,* the monastic order. It is to these professionals, who are devoting their entire lives to moral train-

[28] Digha XVI. 13. See also Digha XXII; Majjhima X.

[29] For the monk who has fully overcome illusion there is no backsliding, Majjhima LXXVI.

ing, that the great bulk of the discourses in the Nikayas is addressed. This is important to remember, for it explains the monastic flavor of much of Buddhist moral teaching. The ideal monk is described repeatedly and in great detail. Such an one realizes the dangers and temptations in the life of the householder and wearies of it, renounces the world, cuts his hair and beard, clothes himself in the orange-colored robes, and goes forth from the household life into the homeless state. He becomes a recluse, uprightness is his delight, he trains himself in the precepts, in self-control, and in all the minutiae of the minor moralities, he becomes an adept in meditation, enters into the mystic absorptions of contemplation, and at length attains to complete insight, is born again, becomes a new creature.[30] Of course this goal is not attained by all in this life, but the good monk who has not achieved it in its perfection is ever seeking it with unfailing alertness. He is never lazy. All his time beyond the minimum needed for sleeping, begging his food, and eating his one daily meal, he devotes to meditation (a large part of the night as well as of the day is spent at this), to getting and giving instruction, and to pious conversation. To outward appearance he is a rather sober fellow and his life seems possibly somewhat drab. He must not dance nor listen to music. He may laugh a little, but only with moderation, and not so heartily as to show his teeth.[31] Loud talk and discussion of worldly themes are for him unseemly; he should choose between edifying conversation and holy silence.[32] He may enjoy a little simple food if he be without greed or longing and be watchful of danger; though it is doubtless better to be quite indifferent to all tastes, whether good or bad.[33] In spite of his rather dull and unexciting life, when the occasion calls for it, he can command any amount of manliness and fortitude. Brother Adhimutta, attacked by highwaymen and about to be slaughtered as an offering to their cruel deity, "stood undaunted and without blenching." The robber-chief was so astonished that he gave him his liberty, and asked for the explanation for courage greater than he and his fol-

[30] See Digha II, XIII; Majjhima XXVII, XXXVIII, CXII, CXXV; Anguttara XX. 198.
[31] Anguttara III. 103.
[32] Udana III. 8.
[33] Samyutta XX. 9.

lowers had ever before witnessed. The monk had no difficulty in replying. His courage was the direct and necessary outgrowth of the Buddha's teaching. "There is no fear for him who hath no wants." [34]

The ideal monk is not only self-possessed and courageous. He seeks constantly for greater enlightenment from those wiser than himself, and he does what he can to instruct those less advanced in the Way than he is, whether they be fellow monks or laymen.[35] He seeks to promote harmony in the Order; [36] nor does he limit his good will to it, but often sends out thoughts of love in all directions [37] and does what he can for others in active fashion when the opportunity offers. Once a year during the Buddha's lifetime a large number of monks were sent out on missionary expeditions, and some of the more advanced members of the Order were put in charge of separate monasteries or even large regions. A part of the work of the monks on these expeditions and in these separate divisions consisted in spreading the doctrine.

Self-discipline and the perfection of their own character, however, was the first aim of all. The Buddha held the view, almost universal in India, that one's first duty is self-development; [38] that this is the condition of one's being able to do anything of importance for anyone else; and that in the measure in which one does become spiritually perfect one's influence will spread to others without great effort on one's own part.[39] The ideal monk seeks first the perfection of his own inner life, insight, self-control, spiritual freedom; he is at last master of himself, "has his heart in his own power and is not in the power of his heart." [40] It may be that this Buddhist ideal overstresses the individualistic side of morality and says too little of the social side. But at any rate there is something attractive in the spiritual independence of the Buddhist ascetic who breaks all the ties and "wanders alone like a rhinoceros."

[34] See the noble "psalm" of this brother in Mrs. Rhys Davids' trans., pp. 292-94.
[35] Neumann's Majjhima I. 517.
[36] Ibid., I. 621-22.
[37] Ibid., I. 656, and many other passages.
[38] Jayasundere's Anguttara II. 128.
[39] Cf. Ramakrishna's view, as presented in the little book of his sayings, *The Gospel of Ramakrishna* (N. Y., Vedanta Society, 1907).
[40] Neumann's Majjhima I. 503.

Without covetousness, without deceit, without craving, without detraction, having got rid of passion and folly, being free from desire in all the world, let one wander alone like a rhinoceros.

Having left son and wife, father and mother, wealth and corn and relatives, the different objects of desire, let one wander alone like a rhinoceros.

Wishing for the destruction of desire, being careful, no fool, learned, strenuous, considerate, restrained, energetic, let one wander alone like a rhinoceros.

Like a lion not trembling at noises, like the wind not caught in a net, like the lotus not stained by water, let one wander alone like a rhinoceros.[41]

The Buddha seems to have felt that his mission consisted primarily in founding an order of men and women who should devote their time exclusively to the spiritual culture of themselves and their fellows, in an environment where real spiritual perfection might be achieved. The life of the layman or householder was too full of temptations and of purely worldly activities to admit of the achievement of this goal; hence he and his monks sought to win as many as they could out of this dangerous condition and bring them into the Order. It would be a mistake, however, to suppose that the Buddha had no place in his scheme of life for the world of the layman. Like St. Francis, he not only founded an Order of Monks and an Order of Nuns, but also worked among laymen and urged his monks to do the same, gave careful directions and earnest exhortations for the best conduct of the household life, laid down certain rules for those laymen who would be his followers—in short, instituted what might well be called a Tertiary Order. The lay follower, like the monk, takes the "three refuges," namely, in the Buddha, in the Dhamma or doctrine, and in the Sangha or Order. This does not mean, as it does with the monk, that he joins the monastic order, but that he takes it as a part of his Trinity of Guides.

In his exhortations to laymen the Buddha urges the usual virtues and warns against the common temptations and vices that conventional morality at its best in all civilized lands and in all the historical religions has so repeatedly dealt with. One might almost imagine, at times, it was not Gotama

[41] Fausböll's Sutta Nipata, pp. 6-11. Cf. also *Psalms of the Brethren,* Nos. 137, 138.

speaking but Confucius or Solomon or Ptah Hotep.[42] Particularly is the duty of filial piety emphasized.[43] The Buddha also points out duties to teachers, to wives and husbands, to friends, to one's servants, and to recluses. The Five Precepts, cited on a previous page—not to take life, steal, be unchaste, lie, drink intoxicants—are intended for the layman quite as much as for the monk.[44] The lay follower, moreover, or, as he might be called, the member of the Third Order, should cultivate firm faith, and learn what he can of sound doctrine. Faith, virtue, liberality and wisdom should be his characteristics, and he should get rid of greed, avarice, ill will, sloth, distraction, worry, lust, and doubt.[45] He cannot, to be sure, hope to become in this life fully enlightened [46]—only the professional, as I have called the monk, can do that; but he may become a "never returner"—i.e., be reborn in one of the heavens and there gain at length supreme enlightenment.[47] The Buddha has great respect and admiration for a really good layman.

> There are three sweet odors that travel with the wind and not against it [but there is only one sweet odor that travels both with the wind and against it, and that is] the fame or sweet odor of a man or woman living in a village or town who has taken the Buddha, the Dhamma, the Sangha as his guides, who refrains from killing, stealing, adultery, lying, and strong drink, who is religious and virtuous, who lives the life of the householder with thoughts devoid of avarice, and is liberal in giving. . . . The odor of flowers travels not against the wind, nor that of sandal, nor the fragrant powder of frankincense or jasmine; but the sweet odor of good men travels with the wind and against it.[48]

The innocent values of the layman's life, so far as they do not rouse undue longing and lead into temptation, are recognized by the Buddha as good in their way, though of course some of them may be hindrances to the monk. Occasionally (though rarely) they are even held out to the lay-

[42] Cf. Digha XXXI; Anguttara VIII. 1; Sutta Nipata I. 7, II. 4 and 14.

[43] E.g., Digha XXXI; Anguttara II. 4, III. 31 and 45, VII. 3; Samyutta VII. 2, 9.

[44] The third of these is, of course, interpreted less extremely for the married layman than for the monk.

[45] Anguttara VII. 1.

[46] Neumann's Majjhima II. 305-06; but see Keith, p. 131.

[47] Ibid., p. 320.

[48] Anguttara III. 79.

man as rewards for virtue—much after the manner of the Book of Proverbs.

> There are five advantages to the moral man through his success in virtuous conduct. In the first place he acquires through industry great wealth. Secondly, good reports of him spread abroad. Thirdly, whatever assembly he attends, whether of nobles, Brahmins, householders, or members of a religious order, he enters confident and undisturbed. Fourthly, he dies with lucid and assured mind. Fifthly, he is reborn to a happy destiny in a bright world.[49]

The layman, it is recognized, naturally desires wealth honestly won, a good name for himself, his family, and friends, long life, and a blessed rebirth.

> These are the four things which in the world are welcome and pleasant but hard to gain. For the attainment of them there are also four conditions. These are the blessings of faith, of virtuous conduct, of liberality, and of wisdom.[50]

I trust that what I have said concerning the Buddha's praises of the virtues and his detailed advice for the cultivation of the moral life, his repeated emphasis on the need of

[49] Rhys Davids' Digha III. 226. See also Seidenstücker's Udana, p. 100; Vinaya Mahavagga VI. 28, 5.

[50] Jayasundere's Anguttara II. 87-88. Cf. also Woodward's Samyutta III. 10. The Khuddaka Patha (one of the books belonging to the Fifth Nikaya) has a passage on the sources of happiness and the nature of true blessedness which I here transcribe from Childers' translation.

"To serve wise men and not to serve fools, to give honour to whom honour is due, this is the greatest blessing.

"To dwell in a pleasant land, to have done good deeds in a former existence, to have a soul filled with right desires, this is the greatest blessing.

"Much knowledge and much science, the discipline of a well trained mind, and a word well spoken, this is the greatest blessing.

"To succour father and mother, to cherish wife and child, to follow a peaceful calling, this is the greatest blessing.

"To give alms, to live religiously, to give help to relatives, to do blameless deeds, this is the greatest blessing.

"To cease and abstain from sin, to eschew strong drink, to be diligent in good deeds, this is the greatest blessing.

"Reverence and lowliness, contentment and gratitude, to receive religious teaching at due seasons, this is the greatest blessing.

"To be long-suffering and meek, to associate with the monks of the Buddha, to hold religious discourse at due seasons, this is the greatest blessing.

"Temperance and chastity, discernment of the four great truths, the prospect of Nirvana, this is the greatest blessing.

"The soul of one unshaken by the changes of this life, a soul inaccessible to sorrow, passionless, secure, this is the greatest blessing.

"They that do these things are invincible on every side, on every side they walk in safety, yea, theirs is the greatest blessing."

(*J. R. A. S.*, IV, 313-14.)

strenuous willing and the cultivation of the moral will, the ideals he held out for the monk and for the layman have made it abundantly plain that his moral teaching is not merely negative. The center of the more positive part of his teaching is to be found in his emphasis upon love. Outside of Christianity, at any rate, there is no other religion which has put so much stress upon love as has Buddhism. Universal pity, sympathy for all suffering beings, good will to every form of sentient life, these things characterized the Tathagata as they have few others of the sons of men; and he succeeded in a most surprising degree in handing on his point of view to his followers. The Jataka Stories, which reflect the feelings of the Buddhist community concerning their Master in the centuries immediately following his death, pick out as his most memorable characteristic his unselfish love, clothing it in many forms of beautiful and at times (from our point of view) even fantastic devotion. Nor is it without significance that the frescoes and carvings with which early Buddhist piety decked the topes and cave temples of the faith drew their subjects most largely from these tales of the Founder's unselfishness. The form these Jatakas took was often exaggerated but the spirit behind them was the very spirit of the Founder. The true monk, he taught, must "cultivate a heart of love that knows no anger, that knows no ill will." [51] "As a mother at the risk of her life watches over her own child, her only child, so also let everyone cultivate a boundless (loving) mind toward all beings. And let him cultivate good will toward all the world, a boundless (loving) mind above and below and across, unobstructed, without hatred, without enmity. This way of living is the best in the world." [52]

He who would follow in the footsteps and obey the injunctions of the Tathagata should spend many hours cultivating good will for all beings. Such an one "lets his mind pervade one quarter of the world with thoughts of love, and so the second, and so the third, and so the fourth. And thus the whole wide world, above, below, around, and everywhere, does he continue to pervade with heart of love, far-reaching,

[51] Digha VIII. 16. Cf. *Psalms of the Brethren*, No. 244.

[52] Fausböll's Sutta Nipata, p. 25.

grown great, and beyond measure."[53] This meditation was a common practice of the Founder and in many passages in the Nikayas he enjoins it upon his more promising disciples. Possibly some of us practical-minded Westerners may be tempted to say that the time thus spent in meditation should have been devoted to helping the poor, or in some more efficient and outward fashion. Your Buddhist—and, in fact, any typical Oriental—will reply that without this spiritual preparation no activity of an external sort for the welfare of others can be really efficient. It is the inner life that counts, he will assure us, and unless the proper state of mind be cultivated all our mere money gifts and mere physical activity will bring but slight blessing. It is manifestly impossible to be actually giving manual help to the needy at every moment; and to keep up the central fire of good will much more time must be spent in cultivating the spirit of love than the West sometimes realizes. Hence, perhaps (the Buddhist may suggest), the somewhat slight spiritual harvest from the sowing of our elaborate and expensive, but mechanical and impersonal, charities. In this matter I am sure the Christ, who was also an Oriental, would side with the Buddha. The East believes that to give with the hand brings little blessing unless we give with the heart as well.

This cultivation of inner good will is twice blest: it blesses him who gives as well as him who takes. The "liberation of the will through love" is one of the most helpful means of attaining spiritual freedom.[54]

> All the means that can be used as bases for doing right are not worth the sixteenth part of the emancipation of the heart through love. That takes all those up into itself, outshining them in radiance and glory. Just as whatsoever stars there be, their radiance avails not the sixteenth part of the radiance of the moon; that takes all those up into itself, outshining them in radiance and glory. . . . Just as in the night when the dawn is breaking, the morning star shines out in radiance and glory, just so all the other means that can be used as helps towards doing right avail not the sixteenth part of the emancipation of the heart through love.[55]

[53] Rhys Davids' Digha I. 317-18. See also III. 44-45; Neumann's Majjhima I. 656, 687, II. 785, 818; Gooneratne and Jayasundere's Anguttara I. 207-08, II. 163, 237.

[54] Samyutta XX. 3 and 4.

[55] Iti-vuttaka § 27. I have used the translation of this passage given by Rhys Davids in his article on Buddhism in the *Encyclopædia Britannica*, as the wording seems better than that of Moore.

For aims more immediate than ultimate emancipation the practice of loving thought is also helpful. The Venerable Vangissa, finding himself tempted by the sight of beautiful women, discovers that he can drive out of his heart thoughts of lust by concentrating his mind on thoughts of the nobler love—the "loyal" love for all.[56] The Tathagata instructs Ananda that when divisions and jealousies have broken out within the Order, or are on the verge of breaking out, the true monk should serve his fellows with loving deeds, with loving words, with loving heart, and pleading with them should offer to take upon himself their guilt and share with them his blessing.[57]

It goes without saying, I expect, that the love which the Buddha urged upon his followers is of the universal and relatively impersonal sort. His expressions in praise of love should be read in connection with passages of another type, such as this verse from the Dhammapada: "Let no man love anything: loss of the beloved is evil. Those who love nothing and hate nothing have no fetters."[58] The Buddha distinguishes clearly three attitudes of the mind which, in spite of their obvious difference, get themselves expressed in English by the one word *love*. The first of these is sexual lust. The second is tender personal affection for an individual of a sort so strong and uncontrollable that it tends to occupy one's thoughts and make one's peace dependent on the loved one's presence, or at least on his life and welfare. The third meaning of *love* is earnest and even tender good will for all, of a universal and impersonal sort. As is indicated in the words *good will,* this attitude belongs quite as much to the voluntary and conative as to the emotional side of human nature. Now of these three kinds of love the Buddha sternly condemns the first, he regards the second as an unnecessary and avoidable opening to the attacks of sorrow, and he approves thoroughly only the third, the impersonal love which seeks the welfare of all.

The distinction between the second and third of these kinds of love is in essence the distinction that Professor Palmer draws between *love* and *justice*.

[56] Samyutta VIII. 1. [57] Majjhima CIV. [58] XVI. 211.

> Love is ever selective. It chooses one and leaves another. It is exercised only toward definite persons, a little group, preferably two. The smaller the number the warmer the love. . . .
>
> Justice seeks to benefit all but all alike. It knows no persons, or rather it knows everyone as a person and insures each his share in the common good. All the altruism of love is here but without love's arbitrary selective and limited interest. . . . Justice is therefore thoroughgoing love, its mutuality guarded, rationalized, stripped of personal bias, and brought near us through the avenues of our special work.[59]

I am not sure that the Buddhist doctrine of love is (except for its fear of sorrow) very different from the Christian. Christian discussions of love as a rule are, to be sure, not so explicit in their distinction between personal tender emotion and universal good will as is the Buddha's treatment of the matter; yet when one examines a really typical exposition of love from some authoritative source, the distinction seems implicit, and the love commended is usually of the type the Buddha also would have praised. Take for example the oft-quoted thirteenth chapter of First Corinthians. The Greek ἀγάπη, translated in the King James version *charity* and in the Revised *love,* seems to mean something midway between the two; a universal and impersonal yet tender good will. This surely is not far from the meaning the Buddha put into the word our translators render *love* (or *friendship*), in those cases where he praised it and urged its cultivation upon his followers. Nor is there any evidence, as I interpret the Gospels, to show that Jesus advocated the more personal type of emotion.[60]

The impersonal love and good will which the Buddha urged upon his followers by no means ended in subjective contemplation. It was carried out in the world of action and guided almost the entire life of the Founder himself, and much of the conduct of his more faithful disciples. Mutual love within the Order and within the little groups of friendly monks got itself expressed in mutual helpfulness and the giving up by each of his own will for the sake of the others.[61] Charity and generosity as the fruits of good will are repeatedly urged. Protection should be given to those who are

[59] *Altruism, Its Nature and Varieties* (N. Y., Scribner's, 1919), pp. 115, 123-24.

[60] Cf., for example, Matthew XII. 46-50. The love advocated by à Kempis in the *Imitation* is, of course, notably impersonal.

[61] Cf. Majjhima XXXI and CIII.

afraid.[62] The Brethren must care for each other and wait upon each other and minister to each other's needs: "Whosoever waits upon the sick waits upon me." [63] But most important of all one should carry the good tidings of the Buddha's truth to all who can be reached and who have ears to hear. The formula of reproof repeatedly used by the Tathagata in case a monk had performed some unworthy act consisted in pointing out that such conduct "will not do for converting the unconverted." [64] The conversion of as many as possible to the truth was one of the chief functions of the Buddhist Brotherhood. The world was filled with souls "whose eyes were scarcely dimmed by dust and souls whose eyes were sorely dimmed by dust, souls sharp of sense and souls blunted of sense, souls of good and souls of evil disposition, souls docile and souls indocile"—all of whom were in danger of suffering endless and needless woe, in this life and many others, on the "sorrowful weary wheel" of rebirth, unless they gained the insight and followed the Path which the Buddha could teach them. Hence soon after the founding of the Order the Buddha sent out his monks in little groups, and every succeeding year he sent them out, on missionary journeys with this commission:

> Fare ye forth, brethren, on the mission that is for the good of the many, for the happiness of the many, to take compassion on the world, to work profit and good and happiness to gods and men. Go not singly: go in pairs. Teach ye the Truth, lovely in its origin, lovely in its progress, lovely in its consummation. Both in the spirit and in the letter proclaim ye the higher life in all its fullness, in all its purity. Beings there are whose eyes are hardly dimmed with dust perishing because they hear not the Truth.[65]

How well the spirit of this command was carried out, even in the details of daily helpfulness toward lay followers, is seen in the accounts left us of the early years of the Order; and how widely the missionary campaign spread we shall see in later chapters.

[62] Iti-vuttaka, § 30.
[63] Mahavagga of the Vinaya VIII. 26, 3.
[64] The formula occurs many times in the Vinaya, e.g., Mahavagga III. 14, 3.
[65] I have quoted Rhys Davids' version (Digha XIV. 22) of this oft-repeated passage, though it occurs in many other places. It is repeated in the Buddha's last talk with his monks (Digha XVI). It occurs also in the Mahavagga of the Vinaya I. 12, 1.

The good will which the Buddha taught was not to be confined to those who returned it. When reviled one must not revile again.[66] If one's efforts for the welfare of others resulted in angry rebuffs, the follower of the Buddha must not respond in anger.

> Hatred does not cease by hatred at any time; hatred ceases by love. This is an old rule.[67]. . . If some one curses you, you must repress all resentment, and make the firm determination, "My mind shall not be disturbed, no angry word shall escape my lips, I will remain kind and friendly, with loving thoughts and no secret spite." If then you are attacked with fists, with stones, with sticks, with swords, you must still repress all resentment and preserve a loving mind with no secret spite.

Your good will should be as inexhaustible as the waters of the Ganges.[68]

How well some, at any rate, of the Buddha's disciples learned the lesson he had to give and caught his own spirit of universal love is shown in the account of the mission of the Venerable Purna. He wished to preach the Doctrine among the Western Suner, a wild and dangerous folk. To test him the Buddha said,

> "But, Purna, these are violent, cruel, and furious men. When they get angry and curse you what will you think?" "I will think (answered Purna) that they certainly are kind and good men, they who address me in insulting words, they who are angry and curse me, but who do not beat me with their hands nor with stones." "But," said the Buddha, "if they do beat you with their hands and stones, what will you think?" "I will think that they are kind and good men, since they do not attack me with clubs and swords." "And if they do attack you with clubs and swords?" "I will think they are kind and good since they do not kill me." "And if they do kill you?" "I will then certainly think that they are kind and good, since they deliver me with so little pain from this vile body." "Very well, very well, Purna," replied the Buddha; "with such perfect patience you are allowed to fix your abode in the country of these violent men. Go, Purna, yourself delivered, deliver others; yourself arrived at the other shore, bring others there; yourself having attained Nirvana, conduct others to it." [69]

[66] Cf. *Psalms of the Brethren*, No. 221.

[67] Dhammapada I. 5. See also Vinaya Mahavagga X. 2.

[68] Majjhima XXI. Cf. also CIII. A boyish member of the Order was given by the Master an exercise of meditation on fraternal love. As a consequence of this he attained insight and bade the other monks "make no difference between those who were to them friendly, indifferent, or hostile. For all alike their love should be one and the same in its nature and should include all realms, all beings, and all ages" (*Psalms of the Brethren*, No. 33).

[69] Majjhima CXLV. I have used chiefly the French trans. of La Vallée Poussin.

Such, then, in outline is the moral teaching of the Buddha. Such is the ideal that he held up. Such is the nature of his salvation. But to attain this ideal, to participate in this salvation is no child's play; the Noble Eightfold Path is no royal road. To follow it to the end and attain the prize requires persistence and long training. What this training is, and whither it leads, we shall in part see in the next chapter.

CHAPTER IV

THE ROAD TO SPIRITUAL FREEDOM

THE true Way of Life, the Dhamma—so the Buddha tells us—is in many respects like the great ocean. One of these points of similarity is the following: "Just as the great ocean has only one taste, the taste of salt, just so has this doctrine and discipline only one flavor, the flavor of deliverance."[1] The deliverance of the individual from evil, the achievement of spiritual freedom, this is the Buddha's single aim. The comprehension of theory, the acceptance of creed may be necessary for the achievement of the practical aim of deliverance, but only as a means to this has it value. The Buddha spent his life teaching the truth not for the sake of the theoretical and intellectual enlightenment of his hearers, but that they through it might be saved. And salvation is never a matter of intellectual adhesion to a creed. It is a new manner of life. Hence the importance of long and steady training and self-discipline if the lessons of the Teacher are to be of real value; for they can become of real value only in the measure in which they are assimilated to the very life of the individual, only as they work themselves down into the mind and dominate all its parts, volitional and emotional as well as intellectual, subconscious as well as conscious.

The achievement of this end is a long process and not to be accomplished in a day or a year; for many hardly in a lifetime. For some it may, in fact, take many lives to achieve complete deliverance, but for the Indian with his faith in numberless rebirths this does not greatly matter, for he has all the time that is needed for the moral task. One must have patience and pursue the shining goal through stage after stage of persistent character training. "Just as the great ocean

[1] Cullavagga of the Vinaya IX. 1, 4; Udana V. 6.

gets gradually deeper, slope following on slope, hollow succeeding hollow, and the fall is not precipitately abrupt, just so in this doctrine and discipline is the training a gradual one, work following on work and step succeeding step, with no sudden attainment of complete insight."[2] "One cannot attain insight at the beginning. One achieves it gradually by earnest effort, by fighting, by pushing one's way forward step by step."[3] Hence the importance of training in the moral life of the Buddhist, and the repeated and minute instruction recorded in the Nikayas concerning the details of this training.

I shall not attempt to give anything like a complete account of the various methods of self-culture inculcated by the Buddha. All or nearly all of them may be included—explicitly or by implication—within the Noble Eightfold Path. Of this I must say something. The Noble Eightfold Path, it will be recalled, constitutes the Fourth Noble Truth. When read over hastily it appears a somewhat heterogeneous collection of ideals; but in reality it has a very real unity, the unity of a single aim. This aim is the transformation of character, and the Path as a whole is really a course in systematic habit formation. To follow the Path means constant concentration of mind. It means unremitting suppression of impulse, of self-assertion, of craving. It means forming the habit of turning away from the delights of the flesh and accustoming oneself to the thought that the usual objects of ambition and the world's values are really worthless. It means a constant guard on one's acts, on one's words, on one's thoughts and emotions; in short, the psychical making over of the whole man. The Buddha was probably the greatest psychologist of his age; at any rate, he had a keen insight into human nature; and knowing what he did, he realized that the transformation of character at which he aimed could not be achieved by any mere change of creed however revolutionary, by any emotional experience however intense, by any single act of will however strenuous and determined.

[2] Cullavagga IX. 1, 4; Udana V. 1.

[3] Majjhima LXX. Cf. also CXXV, CLI; Anguttara I. 3-8, 16, 17; Samyutta XXII. 101.

The eight steps of the Noble Eightfold Path, let me remind the reader, are these:

Right views
Right aspiration
Right speech
Right behavior
Right livelihood
Right effort
Right mindfulness
Right concentration

Both religion and morality are more than mere creed or belief, yet every religion and every form of morality involve a belief, and true religion and true morality involve knowledge. Right views are by no means the whole of the ideal life, but they are an essential part, and from the point of view of the teacher they constitute the first part, for it is only with them that the teacher can begin the training of the pupil. In the previous chapters we have seen the evil effects of ignorance. The right view, or knowledge, is thus the cornerstone of right life and character.[4] With most learners knowledge begins as faith. "By faith," writes Mr. Narasu, "is meant the conviction that truth can be found. . . . While reason rejoices in the truths it has already found, faith gives confidence and helps it to further conquests."[5] Confidence in the Tathagata is mentioned, in a famous discourse between the Buddha and a prince, as the first of five qualities needed for spiritual victory.[6] For exceptional persons, to be sure, this initial confidence in a teacher is not necessary; but for the ordinary man saving knowledge begins as faith in an inspiring personality. Of course it must not end here. Faith must become knowledge; one must see for oneself, and one's own experience, reason, and insight must take the place of trust in the authority of another. And

[4] Cf. Anguttara I. 17, II. 22.

[5] *The Essence of Buddhism* (Madras, Varadachari, 1907), p. 38.

[6] Majjhima LXXXV. In Dialogue No. 70 the Buddha raises the question: How does one gradually attain illumination? and answers it thus: "An arouser of faith appears in the world. One associates oneself with him. One gives ear to his teaching. One remembers it and ponders over it. The teaching gives one insight. One delights in it and adopts it. One acts upon it and thus realizes in lively fashion the highest truth."

this saving insight, of course, means insight in the truth which the Buddha taught—however insight be gained.

The five steps in the Noble Path following right views are fairly obvious in their meaning and call for little comment. The second step means, on the negative side, right aspiration toward renunciation of the false values, desires and ambitions of the world; on the positive, right aspiration for benevolence, kindness, and universal love. Right speech means abstaining from slander, lying, abuse, and idle talk. Right behavior means the observance of the Five Precepts,[7] and of the moral life in general, as described in the previous chapters; for morality, as a matter of course, is the most important thing of all in character formation. In a sense, of course, the whole Noble Path is just morality, and the means of its attainment. Right livelihood means, negatively, abstaining from any of the callings which are forbidden because of the harm they do to sentient life,[8] and for him who is in earnest with the search for deliverance it means, on the positive side, joining the Order and participating in the monastic discipline. Right effort means the inhibition of incipient evil mind states, the eradication of those that have arisen, stimulation of good mind states and the perfecting of them; in other words, the control of the passions, avoidance of evil thoughts, emotions, and volitions, and concentration on good ones.

The seventh stage of the Path, right mindfulness, needs more comment than its predecessors, as several of the specific methods of mental training which the Buddha inculcated upon his professional followers naturally fall under this heading. As it is largely the senses that rouse man's evil desires, the Buddha gave special attention to them and by training his followers how to use them, sought to keep these servants of the mind in their proper place. The principle involved in this training of the senses is exactly right mindfulness. It is the attempt to behold every object of sense "as it really is," to destroy the hypnotic power which many sensuous things have upon us because of their appeal to irrational passion.

[7] Not to kill, steal, be impure, lie, or drink intoxicants.

[8] Notably the occupations of the caravan-trader, slave-dealer, butcher, publican, and poison-seller.

The same principle of objective, coolly scientific apprehension is applied also to the higher activities of the mind; each is to be regarded "as it really is." When a monk is affected by a feeling of pleasure he is to recognize the fact and objectify the state as he would a stone or a mathematical truth. It is no part of him, as we shall see—one of the most fundamental teachings of Buddhism—and therefore must be taken merely intellectually, not emotionally.

> So too does he control his consciousness when affected by a painful feeling or by a neutral feeling. So does he, as to the feelings, continue to consider feeling both internally and externally. He keeps on considering how the feelings are something that comes to be and something that passes away. . . . Thereby mindfulness becomes established far enough for the purposes of knowledge and of self-collectedness. And he abides independent, grasping after nothing in the world.[9]

In a previous chapter I pointed out that the Buddha's aim is intense and constant self-consciousness. One must be wide awake, steadily aware of what one is about. One should set aside an hour or so every now and then—possibly every day—for more intense training in this practice of wakefulness. Going alone into the solitude and silence of the forest, one should repeat to oneself exactly what is happening in one's mind and body, and attend carefully and self-consciously to all that one is doing.[10] The Buddha of course did not mean that one should do this all the time: it was an exercise. As an exercise he and his followers found it helpful in producing singleness of mind and power of self-mastery. This very method is used today by some of the most successful psychiatrists in restoring normal mental balance to their patients.[11]

[9] Digha XXII. 11. See also Majjhima X, LXII.

[10] Minute directions for this are given in several of the Dialogues, e.g., those mentioned in the preceding note.

[11] Notably by Dr. Roger Vittoz. The method will be understood from the following extracts from his book, *The Treatment of Neurasthenia* (London, Longmans, 1921): "Let us first take a simple movement, for example, bending the arm, which we will ask the patient to do. To be well under control the movement must be sufficiently conscious, concentrated and voluntary, that is to say, the patient must know what he is doing, he must exert enough strength to do it and he must keep his mind on the movement until accomplished. . . . Tell the patient to take four or five steps, and while doing so, to have the definite sensation (in his brain) that he is putting his right and left foot forward alternately. Then ask him to realize clearly the movement of his leg and then of his whole body, teaching him at the same time to know whether the movement is sufficiently supple and easy. He will soon see that he

These exercises for producing right mindfulness lead without break into the eighth step of the Path, right concentration. It seems to have been the custom of the Buddha to provide each of his followers, at least in the early stage of his monastic life, with a type of meditation adapted to his peculiar needs. Several of these meditations aim at obvious moral results. Notable among them are the meditations on the body and on death. One should seat oneself at the foot of a great tree in the forest, or go into a charnel field where dead bodies and skeletons are lying, and contemplate the body "as it really is," both in life and in death.[12] The purpose of this contemplation is twofold. For the beginner who is still in love with the flesh and a prey to sensuality this picturing of the body "as it really is"[13] produces disgust and the destruction of desire. It was greatly valued by those who were earnestly seeking to follow the Way and free themselves from the flesh, and resulted in much spiritual profit.[14] For those more advanced, who had already overcome the more passionate appeals of the flesh, the meditation on the body was still of value in breaking the false though instinctive notion that one's body is a part of one's self. Full enlightenment is impossible until the native tendency of the mind to accept this fallacy has been overcome to such an extent that we shall be able to contemplate our own death or the death of our friends with perfect equanimity. To this coldly rational position we can attain only as we are able to objectify the body and view it, not as a part of self, but "as it really is"—an object like every other object, in many

will be very much less tired if he controls his walking from time to time. . . . The patient should take some object in his hand and determine mentally the exact sensation of its form, weight, temperature, consistency, etc. . . . As we have already said, the person lacking control often looks without seeing; in order to correct this the brain must be taught to pay attention to everything that strikes the eye, and to see all things clearly and distinctly. As an exercise pass some object, say an engraving, quickly before the patient's eyes, and then ask him to describe what he has seen. . . . By this continual attention he can acquire a habit which will be very useful to him. If all he does is really well done he will feel calmer, better balanced and more master of himself. When his brain is always concentrated on something definite, it will become less and less troubled. He will regain confidence in himself and his mind will always be under control" (pp. 45-47, 49).

[12] Directions for this meditation are frequently repeated and in detail: e.g., Digha XXII; Majjhima X, CXIX; Samyutta XXII. 95; Sutta Nipata I. 11.

[13] "Impure, ill-smelling, filled with various kinds of stench, and trickling here and there" (Sutta Nipata I. 11, 13).

[14] Cf. *Psalms of the Sisters*, Nos. 19, 26, 27, 41, 52, 66, 71.

ways a rather repulsive one, and destined to speedy decay.[15] In this unterrified determination to face the facts as they are, resolutely to see and stare out of face the worst that Nature and Fate can produce, Buddhist and Christian monasticism are at one.[16]

Meditation on disgusting and fearful things is a part but only a part of the moral discipline. A large portion of the themes on which the Buddha taught his followers to meditate were of a more positive and a more joyful nature. One of the best ways of overcoming vices and temptations, so the Tathagata taught his monks, is to concentrate one's mind on the virtues, to picture vividly the desired ideal.[17] Specially great emphasis was given by the Buddha to the exercise of loving thought for all creatures. Love, to be sure, cannot be forced, but it may be fed, and loving contemplation of the needy, vividly imaged, has great power over the human mind. The Buddha understood his followers. There is much in common, as to both moral aim and psychological method, between the Buddha's systematic meditations and the Spiritual Exercises of Ignatius.[18]

For the adept, the eighth stage of the Noble Path leads up to a series of mental concentrations which were greatly prized by the more advanced members of the Order, and which, though the Buddha by no means considered them essential to the achievement of complete insight,[19] were in his opinion frequently helpful means for attaining it. These are the eight *Jhanas* or absorptions.[20] Whether we accept or not La Vallée Poussin's view that Buddhism as a whole grew out of Yoga,[21] there can be no doubt that these psychi-

[15] Cf. Ernst L. Hoffmann, "*Die Bedeutung des Körpers in der Meditation,*" *Zeitschrift für Buddhismus*, VII (1926), 67-74.

[16] Cf. the skeleton-filled crypts of the Cappuccini. The practice, psychologically considered, is not unlike that sometimes utilized by psychiatrists in having their patients face in meditation various unpleasant subjects, thus getting those disturbing complexes out of the subconscious region of the mind.

[17] Cf. Majjhima XIX, XX.

[18] Cf. Van Dyke, *Ignatius Loyola* (New York, Scribner's, 1926), Chap. XVIII.

[19] Cf. Majjhima LXIV, CXIII; Samyutta XII. 69.

[20] I use the word *absorption* rather than the common translation *rapture* or *ecstasy*, because, as Grimm so well says, "Such conceptions [as rapture] mean states wherein man abandons himself without restraint to the feelings that well up in him, so that clarity of understanding is obscured and the freedom of the will circumscribed" (*The Doctrine of the Buddha*, Leipzig, Drugulin, 1926, p. 457, note).

[21] See his little book *Nirvana* (Paris, Beauchesne, 1925).

cal and semi-hypnotic methods of Buddhism came from Yoga as a part of that large Indian heritage which Gotama took over into his Dhamma. The reader of the Nikayas who has formed his conception of Buddhism antecedently from a perusal of the rationalizing accounts given by many Western (and some recent Eastern) books will be surprised to note how large a part of many of the Dialogues is devoted to detailed accounts of these Yoga-like exercises, including even methods of breath control [22] and resulting supernormal powers.[23] The aim of these psychic practices as utilized by the Buddha seems to have been chiefly concentration of mind and immediate apprehension of the nothingness of this passing and deceitful world. For the moment the adept was caught up into a new sphere of being,[24] and he returned to the light of common day with a sense of the *Umwerthung aller Werthe.*[25]

These mystic experiences of the early Buddhists, though derived from the ancient Yoga practices that go back at least as far as the Rig Veda, do not seem to have ended in unconscious trance or to have aimed at a somnolent condition. Sir Charles Eliot is in the main justified when he writes:

> It is clear that the Buddha did not contemplate any mental condition in which the mind ceases to be active or master of itself. When at the beginning the monk sits down to meditate, it is "with intelligence alert

[22] Cf. Majjhima X, LXII, LXXXIII, CXVIII.

[23] Cf. Digha II, XI, XXV, XXVIII, XXXIV; Majjhima LXXIII, LXXVI, LXXVII, LXXIX, LXXXV, CVIII; Anguttara I. 14, III. 100; Samyutta XVI. 9. These powers are not a part of salvation (Samyutta XII. 70). There are three mystic wonders; but of these the wonder of education is by far the best and greatest (Digha XI, Anguttara III. 6, 60). In Digha XI the Buddha even says he loathes and abhors all the wonders except that of education. This rationalistic view is not found in the Majjhima passages.

[24] In a sense these meditations are creative. Says Hoffmann, "*Die Meditation ist der schöpferische Akt einer Neueinstellung, einer Welterneuerung, ja mehr noch: einer Weltschöpfung, nämlich der Schöpfung einer inneren, wirklicheren Welt*" (*op. cit.*, p. 69).

[25] I shall not go into the detail of the eight absorptions—a vast subject of considerable interest psychologically but not necessary for the purposes of this book. The reader who cares to study it for himself will find descriptions of the various Jhanas in the following passages: Rhys Davids' Digha I. 248-51, III. 75-76, 97-111, 123-24, 203, 216, 256; Neumann's Majjhima I. 376-79, 408-09, 426-27, 487-91, II. 121-22, 240-41, 418-20, 455-56, 569-70, III. 24-27, 97-98, 109, 114-16, 140-42, 159-60, 252-55, 288-89, 337, 516f., 551; Gooneratne's Anguttara I. 41, 73-74, 103-04, 187-88, 207; Jayasundere's Anguttara II. 62-63, 160-62, 236. For two rather opposed Western interpretations of the Jhanas (both of them useful) see Keith's *Buddhist Philosophy* Chap. VI, § 2, and Grimm's *The Doctrine of the Buddha*, IV, 4. B. Jasink has two chapters on the subject in his *Die Mystik des Buddhismus* (Leipzig, Altmann, 1922).

and intent"; in the last stage he has the sense of freedom, of duty done, of knowledge immediate and unbounded, which sees the whole world spread below like a clear pool in which every fish and pebble is visible.[26]

From the ecstasies of the Christian mystic the Buddhist absorptions are also to be distinguished. Both, to be sure, are mystical or semi-mystical experiences, but the Buddhist Jhanas seem to be rather more intellectual and less emotional in content than the Christian ecstasy. In fact, according to Buddhist theory, all emotional quality disappears in the Fourth Absorption and only pure cognition is left. The word "absorption," I should say in passing, must not be taken as implying the absorption of the soul in some Over-soul or Absolute, but merely the complete absorption of the individual in thought, which becomes less discursive and more intuitional as one advances. This intuition of the higher Jhanas, although all emotion is explicitly denied them, is far from being merely intellectual in the ordinary sense of the word. It is a kind of immediate insight, a revelation of being which cannot be put into words and which only those who have experienced it can comprehend. And while these Yoga-like experiences are not essential to salvation and final illumination, the illumination, when it comes and by whatever path, has always, like the Jhanas, a touch of the mystical. It does not consist in a merely intellectual acceptance of the truths of Buddhism, nor can it be attained by any process of simple learning by rote or even of accurate ratiocination.

The Buddha's own experience we may consider typical, in this matter, since he plainly considered it so himself. In the Eighty-fifth Dialogue of the Majjhima he tells us that his first feeling for the way of deliverance came to him while still a youth, before leaving his home, when, seated in the cool shadow of an apple tree and deep in thought, he suddenly experienced the first of the absorptions. It seems to have been to him a faint foretaste of deliverance and he said to himself: This is the way to enlightenment.[27] The memory

[26] *Hinduism and Buddhism* (London, Arnold, 1921), I. 222.

[27] Dahlke deals with this passage, and with the Buddha's treatment of the Jhanas in general, in such a way as to imply that the Buddha's attitude toward conceptual knowledge was much the same as Bergson's. Although he does not refer to Bergson by name he seems to interpret the Buddhist absorptions as a case of Bergsonian intuition. See Chapters III and IV of his *Buddhism and Its Place in the Mental Life of Mankind* (London, Macmillan, 1927), esp. p. 62.

of this experience remained with him all his life, and at a critical moment in his career redirected his search. Soon after this slightly mystical experience further meditation upon the sorrow of the world and the wearisome repetition of birth, old age, and death, together with growing disgust for the vanities of a worldly life, sent him out upon the great renunciation. He studied with two teachers who trained him in the first four of the absorptions. This, however, gave no complete solution of the problem of human woe and its cure; so he tried extreme asceticism. The physical torture he vainly inflicted upon himself very likely contributed nothing to his final illumination save a knowledge of its uselessness; but his long and dreadful hours of meditation in the terrible loneliness of the charnel field through the black hours of the night may well have left an influence upon his mind that played its part in the final solution. Much serious and purely rational thought was mingled with all this training during the six years of his search and contributed, possibly, more than anything else to the outcome. But the outcome was not merely the attainment of a scientific theory. It was that, but it was also a definite and new form of experience; a revelation of what life might be. It is necessary to understand this or we shall fail utterly in comprehending the power that Buddhism had over the souls of men in the triumphant centuries of its early progress. Something happened under the Bodhi Tree, and something has happened in every Buddhist's attainment of enlightenment, which cannot be set down wholly in terms of the intellect. In Western and Christian parlance it was a kind of conversion experience. In Gotama's case all the influences I have mentioned in his early career were factors in the final result; and much the same thing is noticeable in all the cases of illumination among his followers, which are told us in any detail. There seems to have been regularly a process of what Western books on the psychology of religion call subconscious ripening.[28] When the conscious and subconscious factors are ready, the longed-

[28] See, e.g., Starbuck, *Psychology of Religion* (N. Y., Scribner's, 1903), Chap. VIII; James, *Varieties of Religious Experience* (London, Longmans, 1903), Lectures IX, X; Pratt, *The Religious Consciousness* (New York, Macmillan, 1920), Chap. VIII. For examples of the ripening process in Buddhism see Anguttara III. 100; *Psalms of the Sisters*, Nos. 53, 54, *et passim.*

for illumination comes. Sometimes, doubtless, it is a gradual process, but in many cases like that of the Buddha during the epoch-making night under the Bodhi Tree, it manifests itself in the form of a perfectly definite and datable experience comparable in the specificness of its recognizable character with the receiving of the Holy Ghost in the early Christian Church.[29] At times the experience comes with great suddenness, reminding one of the cases of sudden conversion presented in James' *Varieties,* and of the attainment of *satori* by members of the Zen sect in medieval and modern Chinese and Japanese Buddhism.[30]

When this state of insight has been reached, the searcher "becomes conscious that birth is at an end, that the higher life has been fulfilled, that all that should be done has been done, and that after this present life there will be no more becoming." [31] Thus he becomes an *Arahant,* a perfectly enlightened one, and enters at once, while still in this life, into Nibbana—or as we Westerners usually call it (using the Sanskrit rather than the Pali term), Nirvana. Primarily Nirvana means extinction: that is, extinction of the evil elements of the human mind, notably of lust, ill will, and ignorance. It is the extinction of the process of becoming, the end of the acquisition of new *Karma,* or merit and demerit which have to be worked out in future lives. Life, to be sure, continues for a little while even after the attainment of illumination, because the Karma of former lives is still not fully exhausted, just as the potter's wheel continues to revolve a few moments after the vase is finished, and the fire continues to burn after the last of the fuel has been heaped upon it. So, for a while, the saint or Arahant lives on in the enjoyment of Nirvana even in this world.

This state of the soul, freed from desire, from temptation, from ignorance, anger, and fear, with the unfailing consciousness that the great task has been accomplished and that one is no longer a slave to things nor to Fate nor to one's own little self, is not the *way* to salvation: it *is* salvation.

[29] This is very notable in the accounts of illumination among the early Brothers and Sisters, e.g., *Psalms of the Brethren,* Nos. 43, 44.

[30] Cf. *Psalms of the Brethren,* Nos. 1, 115, 119, 129, 147, 239, 240, 260. *Psalms of the Sisters,* Nos. 17, 21, 28, 29, 47, 64. See also the Mahavamsa V, XIV, XVI.

[31] The oft-repeated formula of triumph.

For the Buddhist, salvation does not mean going to heaven when you die. The Founder taught, to be sure, that good but unenlightened Buddhists do go to heaven when they die; but going to heaven is only a relative and passing good. The only good that is absolute and permanent is the state of the soul achieved by the Arahant.

Frequent reference to this permanent consciousness of deliverance, this supreme goal, is made in the Nikayas, but little positive description. For more positive accounts we must look to some of the later books, notably to the Psalms of the Early Buddhists. Many of these hymns are shouts of exultation at having achieved the goal. In reading them one seems to be listening to what evangelical Christians used to call an "experience meeting." One rather surprising thing in these expressions of delight at the achievement of Nirvana (surprising at least to the Western reader) is that almost no reference is made to any future state, to any continuance of Nirvana after the death of the body. As Mrs. Rhys Davids has put it, the *Theri* or Buddhist *Santa* [32]

> is never led to look forward to bliss in terms of *time*, positive or negative. If Death be conquered, it is not through winning, in Arahantship, of eternal living, but because, when Death comes, his eternally recurring visitation ceases. It may be that in harping in highest exultation how they had won to and touched the Path Ambrosial, Nibbana, they implied some state inconceivable to thought, inexpressible by language. . . . Nevertheless, their verses do not seem to betray anything that can be construed as a consciousness that hidden glories, more wonderful than the brief span of "cool" and calm they now know as Arahants, are awaiting them.[33]

Mrs. Rhys Davids has sought to analyze the descriptions of Nirvana given by these ancient Sisters, and finds the following qualities often enumerated. On the negative side, extinction of evil, freedom, the end of discomfort and of becoming, the end of craving, rest. Of positive qualities she finds the following: mental illumination, happiness and calm content, self-mastery.[34] An analysis of the *Psalms of the Brethren*

[32] We have no English word for *Theri* (such as *saintess*), and I cannot bring myself to write *female saint*.

[33] *Psalms of the Sisters*, p. xxxi. The same is true of the Brethren. See *Psalms of the Brethren*, pp. xlvi, xlviii.

[34] *Op. cit.*, p. xxxvii.

would not differ very greatly in the qualities of Nirvana discovered, except perhaps for the fact that the monks seem more introspective than the nuns, and less occupied with external matters,[35] and also that they stress more than the nuns the delights of solitude.

To give a less elaborate analysis of the mind state of the Arahant, as it finds expression not only in the *Psalms* but in the whole canon, I should say that the four qualities which stand out most prominently seem to be peace, freedom, joy and insight. The first of these is the most commonly and the most specifically emphasized. Nirvana in this life means primarily the attainment of the great peace. It means deliverance from the fear of death and every other fear, a large equanimity, a carelessness of all happenings, an inner calm, often compared to the stillness of the sea. Peace is closely connected with spiritual freedom; in a sense it comes from it. But the sense of spiritual freedom belongs, perhaps, somewhat more to the active and energetic side of one's nature. The Arahant knows himself to be a spiritual athlete, he is conscious of his powers of self-mastery, he delights in the thought that he is free from temptation, free from craving, free from praise and blame, free from Fate: that he is independent and can when he likes "wander alone like a rhinoceros." Joy, of course, is linked with both peace and freedom, and possibly it should not be mentioned as a third quality, for it is obviously dependent on the others. Yet some of the exultant cries of the emancipated Buddhists say more of joy, and some speak more of peace or freedom. The joy, so far as I can judge from the *Psalms*, is frequently a contrast effect, and consists largely in comparing the Arahant's present state of freedom and peace with the self-made ills he suffered in the past or that the unenlightened are now suffering.[36] There are, I should say, fewer expressions of pure

[35] *Psalms of the Brethren*, pp. xxxi, xxxii.

[36] Cf. the story of Bhaddiya who had abdicated a throne in order to join the Order. "Now at that time the venerable Bhaddiya, who had retired into the forest to the foot of a tree, into solitude, gave utterance over and over again to this ecstatic exclamation: 'O happiness! O happiness!' And a number of Bhikkhus went up to the place where the Blessed One was, and bowed down before him, and took their seats on one side. And so seated, they [told the Blessed One of this and] added, 'For a certainty, Lord, the venerable Bhaddiya is not contented as he lives the life of purity; but rather it is when calling to mind the happiness of his former sovereignty that he gives vent to

and intense joy among these Buddhist saints than one would find in an anthology drawn from an equal number of Christian saints. Buddhist joy is inevitably of a rather restrained and "unemotional" sort; violent joy is hardly compatible with "indifference." Yet a mild serenity certainly does shine through many of these Buddhist testimonies of the spiritual life, and no one can read Buddhist literature without feeling that the Buddhist saint is no long-faced killer of delight, but outwardly gracious and inwardly filled with his own kind of calm and quiet joy. A fourth quality of the state of sainthood on its inner side is, I have suggested, of a more intellectual nature. It consist in a satisfying grasp of the truth, a clear insight into the really important matters. We cannot too often remind ourselves that this is one of the things which, to human nature as actually constituted, is worth while on its own account. "All men by nature desire knowledge," said Aristotle, and to see the truth eye to eye is one of the supreme satisfactions of life. The Buddhist insight in its highest form, moreover, is, as we have seen, not merely intellectual apprehension; it is an insight and an intuition with something of the mystical about it—a kind of immediate experience of reality. It would seem to be not unrelated to what Spinoza called the intellectual love of God.

Perhaps the quality of Nirvana most often praised in Buddhist books and hailed by the Arahant with greatest delight consists in its marking the end of becoming.[37] This world of *Samsara*, of recurring *happenings*, of endless rebirth, this overwhelming vista of endless, monotonous, repe-

this saying.' So the Blessed One summoned brother Bhaddiya and asked him what he meant by his exclamation. To this Bhaddiya replied, 'Formerly, Lord, when I was a king, I had a guard completely provided both within and without my private apartments, both within and without the town, and within the (borders of my) country. Yet though, Lord, I was thus guarded and protected, I was fearful, anxious, distrustful, and alarmed. But now, Lord, even when in the forest, at the foot of a tree, in solitude, I am without fear or anxiety, trustful and not alarmed; I dwell at ease, subdued, secure, with mind as peaceful as an antelope's. It was when calling this fact to mind, Lord, that I gave utterance over and over again to that cry, "O happiness! O happiness!" ' " (See Cullavagga VII. 1 and also *Psalms of the Brethren*, No. 254).

[37] "*Aufheben des Werdens ist das Nirvana*" (Geiger's Samyutta II. 163). "*Aus dem Wissen erfolgt die Erlösung.*" "*Und was erfolgt aus der Erlösung?*" "*Aus der Erlösung erfolgt die Erlöschung* (Nirvana)." "*Und was erfolgt aus der Erlöschung?*" "*Überschritten hast du das Fragen, man kann den Begriff der Frage nicht fassen. Denn um in die Erlöschung zu münden wird das Asketenleben geführt, in die Erlöschung geht es ein, in der Erlöschung geht es auf*" (Neumann's Majjhima I. 702).

titious years which lead nowhere, this to the Buddhist is the greatest pain of all. Hence the joy in the thought that with the achievement of insight one is emancipated forever from this slavery.

> Looking for the maker of this tabernacle [the recurrent body] I shall have to run through a course of many births so long as I do not find it; and painful is birth again and again. But now, maker of this tabernacle, thou hast been seen; thou shalt not make up this tabernacle again. All thy rafters are broken, thy ridge-pole is sundered; the mind approaching Nirvana has attained to the extinction of all desires.[38]

In the *Psalms of the Brethren* no thought is commoner than this. One of the expressions of it is repeated again and again by successive Arahants. It may have originated with Ananda, the beloved disciple: at any rate, tradition has it that he said it over "as he lay a-dying his last death." It reads thus:

> The Master hath my fealty and love,
> And all the Buddha's ordinance is done.
> Low have I laid the heavy load I bore,
> Cause of rebirth is found in me no more.[39]

[38] Dhammapada XI. 153-54.

[39] Mrs. Rhys Davids' version of the *Psalms of the Brethren*, p. 358. See also pp. 268, 306, 325, 330, 349.

CHAPTER V

MAN AND HIS DESTINY

THE matters discussed toward the close of the last chapter may well have raised in the reader's mind the question: What becomes of the saint after death? Is Nirvana for this life only? The questions are natural and the second permits of a perfectly definite answer. The word Nirvana, or the extinction of evil, is not confined in its use to the condition of the saint in this life. The Buddhist canon recognizes a double application of the word: in reference to what is this side of death and to what is beyond.[1] In cases where the distinction needs to be made specific the word Parinibbana (Sanskrit Parinirvana) is used for the complete "extinction" of all becoming that the Arahant enters into on the death of the body.

The reader, however, will doubtless remain unsatisfied by the mere recognition of this distinction. What, he will demand, is Parinirvana? What is the condition of the Arahant after he has died his last death? The question is almost inevitable, and was, in fact, asked of the Buddha by some of his disciples. More specifically, the question was phrased: Does the Arahant exist after death? The Buddha refused to answer this question, further than to insist that it was so badly put that any yes or no reply to it must necessarily be wrong. It would be equally false to assert that the saint exists after death or that he does not. To our Western minds, with our black and white distinctions and our exact dichotomies, this reply will at first seem absurd. To understand the significance of it and piece together the implications of the Buddha's indirect assertions and his silences we had best make a long detour and consider first the Buddhist conception of the nature of man and of some other things that may throw light upon this almost baffling problem.

[1] Cf. Iti-vuttaka § 44.

I shall not attempt to go into the details of Buddhist psychology further than to outline the conception of human nature and the empirical self involved in it. The human personality as an object for psychological study is analyzed in the Nikayas into five *Khandas* or aggregates.[2] The first of these is the body, the remaining four constitute what we should call the mind. The second of the Khandas is feeling; the third sense-perception; the fourth is known as the *Samkharas* or mental processes that produce latent tendencies; the fifth is cognition.[3] From another point of view the empirical self is sometimes analyzed into the five senses, with their physical organs and resulting sensations, plus the mind which is referred to as a sixth sense and which, like the common sense of Aristotle's psychology, unifies the products and the workings of the five. Cognition awakens when one of the sense organs makes contact with its object, and with cognition all four of the mental Khandas arise—for indeed they constitute consciousness and are really inseparable from each other except in theoretical analysis. Neither of these psychological expositions of the empirical self is above reproach; and both probably suffer from the common Buddhist tendency to depict psychology in terms of morals[4] (for the moral aim of self-conquest and the destruction of craving is often quite obvious), a weakness by no means peculiar to Buddhism.[5]

Two other concepts of Buddhism must be mentioned even in this hasty sketch (which omits so much) of human personality. These are *Tanha* and *Karma*. *Tanha* means craving, and particularly craving for life, or (to use Schopenhauer's term) the will to live. *Karma*, which originally means work, is used most commonly for the individual's

[2] These are sometimes referred to collectively as *Namarupa*, a term borrowed from Hinduism which means literally "name and form," but really denotes mind and body.

[3] The Khandas are referred to many times in the Nikayas, a typical passage being Digha XXII. 14. Later scholastic analysis elaborated the concept. For contemporary Western presentations of the subject see Mrs. Rhys Davids' *Buddhist Psychology* (London, Bell, 1914), Chaps. II-VI; Grimm's *Doctrine of the Buddha*, I. 2; and Keith's *Buddhist Philosophy*, Chap. IV. Mrs. Rhys Davids and Herr Grimm in their attempts to present the matter sympathetically perhaps read into Buddhist psychology more than they should; while Dr. Keith seems bent on showing that Buddhist psychology is very stupid.

[4] A defect pointed out by both Keith and Mrs. Rhys Davids.

[5] McDougall has shown how repeatedly European psychology has been vitiated by the same moral purpose. See *The Group Mind* (Putnam, 1920), Introd.

store of merit and demerit laid up in the past, and which one carries with one till it is worked out in reward and punishment, or till an end is put to all becoming by enlightenment. It is Tanha, craving, that keeps one on the weary wheel of rebirth and brings one back after the death of the body to birth in a new one. That one's Karma was the cause of rebirth was a Brahmin and Jaina concept; hence the ideal of worklessness as a means of salvation, referred to so repeatedly in the Bhagaved Gita, and the attempt of the Jainas to extinguish acquired Karma through ascetic practices and avoid the acquisition of new Karma. Against these conceptions the Buddha set up his new psychological theory (if so we may style it) that rebirth was due not to Karma but to craving; and that by rooting out evil desire and the will to live one could escape from rebirth, regardless of the Karma one had brought with one to this life. This, of course, was a much more hopeful and moral doctrine, and one for which a certain amount of empirical evidence based on analogy could be produced. The influence of Karma, according to the Buddha's teaching, was to be found not in the fact of rebirth but in the kind of rebirth.[6]

When a man dies, the first of his Khandas, the body, obviously is dispersed and goes no farther. Like all other things it is impermanent and in a few years at most after death it completely dissolves. In one sense (as the Buddha several times insists) the mind of man is even less permanent than the body.[7] The four mental Khandas change every moment. They form together a constantly changing "stream of consciousness," to use James' term, and possess no more substantiality or unity than does the succession of "present moments" which constitute the self in James' psychology.[8] Yet each momentary wave or ripple in the stream gives birth to the next. Thus there is between any two sections of the stream a causal connection; and there is also as a rule a certain amount of similarity between them. They form a relatively continuous, though constantly changing, bundle. Now when

[6] This contrast between the Buddhist and the Jaina points of view is brought out clearly by Thomas in his recent *Life of Buddha*, pp. 204-06.

[7] Cf. Digha IX. 21f. and Samyutta XII. 61.

[8] See the *Principles of Psychology* (New York, Holt, 1896), Vol. I, Chaps. IX, X.

a man transmigrates (to use a common phrase which should be made much more exact than it is) from one body to another, the old body does not go with him, but there is a sense in which it may be said that his consciousness or cognition (the fifth Khanda) does. That is, there is the same sort of connection, through continuous causation and similarity, between the first pulse of consciousness in the new life and the last one of the old life that obtained between two given pulses of consciousness in any one lifetime. And as the four mental Khandas are inseparable, there is a sense in which one may say that the whole bundle of them transmigrates. It has been kept together and continued in existence by the power of craving, which is one of its elements. Thus the same kind of unsubstantial pseudo-identity is retained between births that existed within the successive epochs of a given life. To use an illustration from the Milindapanha, personality passes over from life to life in much the same way as a flame passes from candle to candle.[9] And of course one's accumulated Karma goes with one's personality.

The doctrines of transmigration and Karma were by no means original with the Buddha. He simply accepted them, as he did many other conceptions, from the common Indian heritage of his age. Not, indeed, that they were universally accepted. There were several sects that denied both, particularly the latter, and against these schools of thought the Buddha protested. The thought of retribution involved in the Karma doctrine was especially important in his eyes. It was fundamental to his system, and was bound up both with his moral postulate that what we sow we shall reap, and with his doctrine of universal causation.[10] Possibly I overstate his position in using the word *universal;* for though he seems to have believed that the law of cause holds in every realm, he consistently refused to make statements about purely theoretical or external matters. In this respect his emphasis upon cause is different from that of the modern scientist. He confined himself to the field of human nature, and here he found the causal law supreme. He was con-

[9] *The Questions of King Milinda,* Rhys Davids' trans., *S. B. E.,* XXXV. 64.

[10] Cf., for example, Digha XIV, Majjhima XXXVIII, LXXIX, CXV, Samyutta XII. 20-29.

vinced that everything within a human stream of consciousness except its will-acts had its cause, and he seems to have held that this cause was to be found (in whole or in part) in some event that occurred earlier in the stream. One of the teachings which he considered most important was his analysis of this causal chain by which the evils of old age and death might be followed back to their original source. For lack of space I shall say nothing more of this famous chain of the "Twelve Nidanas,"[11] further than to remind the reader that they begin with ignorance, and may therefore be destroyed by insight, and that they emphasize and illustrate the way in which we make our own fate not only for the rest of this life but for our initial position and our initial character in the next. Not for all the details and deeds of our next life, however. The Buddha, with all his belief in causation, never doubts that man's will is free. The free act of the enlightened will is able to put an end to the consequences of past action. If, however, one does not take advantage of this great human opportunity, he will be reborn, and will be reborn in just the set of circumstances and just the kind of world that he deserves.[12] The great law of Karma is eternally just. The moral laws are more fundamental, at any rate, in that part of the Cosmos that has to do with human fate than are the laws of physics and chemistry. Of course the Buddha did not put it, and did not think it, in these terms; but after all this is what his teaching necessarily means.

It is a common Western misunderstanding to suppose that Buddhism taught and teaches transmigration *in contrast* to

[11] The Causal Chain runs as follows:

From ignorance come the dispositions which lead to rebirth (Samkharas).
From the dispositions comes consciousness or cognition.
From consciousness come name and form (i.e., the personality).
From name and form come the five senses and the mind.
From the five senses and the mind comes contact.
From contact comes feeling.
From feeling comes craving.
From craving comes grasping, or attachment to existence.
From grasping comes becoming.
From becoming becomes birth.
From birth come old age, sickness, death.

The Causal Chain is frequently repeated, especially in the Samyutta. The most striking presentation of it is in the Digha XIV, XV.

[12] Cf. Majjhima XLI, LVII, LX.

the Christian and Mohammedan doctrine of heaven and hell. As a fact Buddhism, both primitive and present, makes almost as much use of heaven and hell as do Islam and Christianity. The doctrine of transmigration, in fact, includes them; for it teaches that most bad men are reborn in hell and most good men in heaven. After a period of punishment in hell the bad individual may be born on this earth in animal form and eventually once more as a man. A good man who has been rewarded by a long life in heaven will also be reborn as a man unless, in his heavenly life, he has attained to deliverance. Some men may be reborn in human form at once after their death. An interval in heaven or hell, however, seems to be the rule.[13] The Buddha accepted the Indian universe of his day ready-made. As a teacher he was not interested in non-human matters, and the constitution and geography of the material universe did not seem to him worth discussing. Presumably he believed in the common view.

Whatever may have been the Buddha's personal opinion, the Buddhism of the Nikayas at any rate believes that there are innumerable worlds, each constructed on the same general plan. In each of them, in ours certainly, there are three great divisions. The lowest of these (the one in which we live) is called the Kamaloka, or the realm of desire. In this there are six subdivisions—the "six regions" or "six paths" frequently referred to in Buddhist literature. One of these six regions consists in eight or more hells, the second is the realm of animals, the third the realm of ghosts, the fourth the abode of the Asuras or demons, the fifth the realm of men, and finally, as sixth, the abodes of the lower gods. The second great division of our world is Rupaloka (the world of material form), with sixteen divisions or "Brahmalokas" in which dwell the gods who are free from desire. The third and highest division is Arupaloka, the formless world, in which dwell those lofty souls who are superior in spiritual attainment to the highest of the gods. But he who through self-conquest and insight has attained to the "incomparable security of Nibbana" is superior to the greatest of these.

[13] For the fate of good but unenlightened and of the bad see Digha XVI, XXVII; Majjhima XII, XIX, XLI, LXXI, LXXXVI, XCVII, CXX, CXXIX, CXXX; Anguttara III. 35, VI. 5; Samyutta I. 5, 9, XIX. 1.

The highest of the gods holds his lofty position but for a time and must at last die and be reborn, unless he attains to supreme enlightenment. A mortal who acquires sufficient merit may hope to be born not only in one of the heavens but even as one of the gods.[14] Thus the good Buddhist may look forward to a future life with confidence and great hope. The Buddhists who die in the Nikayas face their fate with a certain brave and delightful buoyancy. "What matters it how far we go?" they seem to say.

> There is another shore, you know, upon the other side.
> The further off from England the nearer is to France.[15]

This confidence in a blessed hereafter for the good is very notable in the Nikayas, and constituted later on one of the chief attractions of Buddhism when as a missionary religion it invaded foreign lands. One of four alluring lots is secure to him who diligently follows the path.

> Four kinds of fruit [says the Buddha] are to be expected [from such a life]. Firstly, the case of a brother who by complete destruction of the three fetters [false belief in the substantiality of the phenomenal self, doubt, and belief in ceremonial] becomes a stream-winner, saved from disaster hereafter, certain to attain enlightenment. Secondly, the case of a brother who by destruction of the three fetters has so diminished lust, ill will, and ignorance, that he has become a once-returner, and returning but once to this world will make an end of ill. Thirdly, the case of a brother who by the complete destruction of the five last fetters [those mentioned above plus attachment to sensuous things and antipathy] will be reborn in another world [presumably one of the Brahmalokas], thence never to return, there to pass away. Fourthly, the case of a brother who, by destruction of the mental intoxicants,[16] has come to know and realize for himself, even in this life, emancipation of intellect and emancipation of insight and therein abides.[17]

For such an one there is no rebirth anywhere.

What becomes of him? This is the problem with which

[14] The gods of the Vedic and Brahmanic times had in the sixth century B.C. come to be regarded as offices rather than as individuals, and these divine positions were held in turn by individuals who had acquired sufficient quantities of good Karma. The Iti-vuttaka represents the Buddha as saying that he himself had once been Brahma (the highest of the gods in Rupaloka) and had been Sakka, ruler of the lower gods, thirty-six times (§ 22).

[15] As the whiting said to the snail.

[16] Sensuality, becoming, delusion, ignorance.

[17] Digha XXIX. 25. See also XVI. 7, XXVIII. 13.

the present chapter began, but we must still ask one more preliminary question before facing this. We have learned, in outline, what was the Buddha's theory of the empirical self—the personality or the bundle of the five Khandas. Is there, in addition to this, a noumenal, ultimate, or transcendental self? Plainly this question will be of the utmost importance to us in making up our minds how we should answer the earlier question concerning the fate of the Arahant after death. For the Arahant has succeeded in destroying craving and has put an end, thereby, to all rebirth for the Khandas or empirical self. Hence if there be no ultimate or noumenal self, no self that is more than appearance behind all appearances, there will be nothing to survive, and our question concerning the fate of the Arahant will be answered.

The scholastic systematizers of the centuries following the death of the Founder developed a doctrine, in conscious opposition to the growing Vedanta, that there is no *Atta* or ultimate self. This view came to be known as the *Anatta* doctrine, or doctrine of no-self.[18] It seems to be the accepted view in the *Katha-vatthu* and *The Questions of King Milinda*, and it has been handed on as the orthodox view in both the Hinayana and Mahayana forms of Buddhism—though there was much early opposition to it. Most Western writers on Buddhism [19] have adopted this view of the self and emphasized it in their expositions of the teachings of the Buddha. The serious though amateur student of Buddhism, however, would be ill-advised to limit his study to books about the Buddha's teachings, and should go direct to the Nikayas for those teachings themselves. If, now, we search the pages of these ancient books we shall find the Buddha repeatedly discussing the question of the self. The great majority of the passages in which he deals with this subject read essentially as follows:

> "Is the body perishable or permanent?"
> "Perishable, O Gotama."
> "Is that which is perishable full of pain or of joy?"

[18] From what students of Greek would call α-privitive, and *Atta*, the word for self, the Pali equivalent of the Sanskrit *Atman*.

[19] Notably Oldenberg in Germany, Rhys Davids in England, and Stcherbatsky in Russia.

"Full of pain."

"That which is perishable, painful, changeable—can one assert, 'This belongs to me, this am I, this is my Self'?"

"Certainly not, O Gotama."

The same questions are then asked, and with the same conclusions, concerning feeling, sense perception, the mental processes, and cognition—in short, concerning all the five Khandas; and the conclusion is that the self is none of these things.[20] And the argument repeatedly used, as in the passage quoted, to prove that these phenomenal characters are not the true self is precisely because they are impermanent and painful. Consciousness, in particular, the Buddha points out, must not be identified with the self; because consciousness is even more impermanent than the body and is always passing away.[21]

This represents the most typical treatment given by the Tathagata to the question of the self. There are other discussions of the matter and they lead almost without exception to the same sort of conclusion. Thus the parts of the body and the activities of the mind are taken up in turn: the eye, the ear, the nose, the tongue, self-consciousness, perceiving, etc. Each is shown to be incapable of identification with the self for the same two reasons as those noted above: namely, because each of these organs and activities is perishable and painful.[22] Similarly none of the many perishable forms to be found in the world, past, present, or to come, can be really ours or can be our true selves;[23] nothing composed of any of the five elements is the true self or can really belong to us;[24] the universe is not our true self.[25]

The view of the self thus presented, if it does not answer all our questions, is at any rate self-consistent and luminous. So far as I have been able to discover there are only two pas-

[20] The passage quoted is from the thirty-fifth Dialogue of the Majjhima, but exactly the same argument and conclusion are to be found in the first, forty-fourth, one hundred and ninth, and one hundred and thirty-first Dialogues of the Majjhima; Digha XV; Anguttara XIX. 1, XX. 6; Samyutta XII. 70, XXII. 1, 33, 46, 59, 83; Mahavagga I. 6.

[21] Digha IX. 21f.; Samyutta XII. 61.

[22] Majjhima CXLVII, CXLVIII.

[23] Anguttara XX. 6.

[24] Majjhima CXL, Anguttara XVIII. 6.

[25] Majjhima XXII. Does the Buddha here refer to the Upanishadic view?

sages in the Nikayas that present a view inconsistent with this, and both of these are in the Samyutta which, as we have seen, was a later compilation than either the Digha or the Majjhima, and was obviously put together under the influence of the rising scholasticism to which reference has been made.[26] If we leave these out of account and base our opinion of the Founder's self-doctrine on the passages I have cited, certain conclusions seem to me perfectly obvious and altogether different from the conclusions found in most Western books on Buddhism. If a man says to me, This material which I see on the ground cannot be snow because it is neither white nor cold, I should hardly conclude that he was trying to assert that there is no such thing anywhere as snow. Similarly, to start with the argument that the body and the conscious states cannot be the self since they are ephemeral and painful, and to draw from it the conclusion that there is no self at all, seems to indicate an extraordinary method of deduction. I submit that the obvious conclusions from the Buddha's argument are the following: First, the real self is not the phenomenal personality. It is neither the body nor the content of consciousness, nor the functions of the mind, nor the peculiarities of the character. Second, it is not an animistic double, nor identical with the "soul" of several other religions. Third, there is a real self which is none of these things. One cannot say, however, that the self exists; for existence is a term that means having a position in Samsara, the stream of becoming.[27] This is, perhaps, only another way of denying the identity of self with the stream of consciousness or with any of its parts, and is directly re-

[26] These passages are in V. 10, XII. 12. The first of them puts into the mouth of the nun Vajira a view of the self identical with that of the great scholastic Nagasena, as expressed in *The Questions of King Milinda.* Oldenberg thinks this conclusive evidence that the Nagasena denial of any kind of self was a continuation of the original doctrine. See his *Buddha* (Stuttgart, 1906), pp. 302-03. In the other passage the Buddha is represented as refusing to answer the question *Who* takes nourishment? *Who* is born? *Who* dies? etc., on the ground that the questions are not rightly put. They imply, that is, a self, no matter how answered; hence any answer would be false. As I have indicated, the apparent view of these two passages is so out of keeping with the many expressions of the Buddha upon the self, particularly in the Majjhima, that they seem to me the expressions of the age of scholasticism rather than of the Founder.

[27] It is thus that I interpret Digha XV. 31 which argues against the view that the self has the property of sentience, since according to that view if sentience had ceased one could not say, *I myself am.*

lated to my next conclusion from the Buddha's way of presenting the matter: namely, Fourth, the self is enduring, not subject to change, and as such, when by itself, not painful.

That the Buddha believed in some sort of ultimate and noumenal self is made more plain by a consideration of his teaching as a whole. His Dialogues are filled with references to his own previous existences and those of his followers and with predictions as to their future lives. The entire point of many of these references of his lies in the thought that the same man who lived in the past in another body lives now in this, or will live in still a different one. Particularly biting is this consideration from the point of view of responsibility and reward and punishment.[28] These things lose all their significance if there be no more identity in a series of lives than the identity found in successive bundles of Khandas—the identity discoverable in a flame passed from candle to candle. The moral earnestness of the Buddha and his insistence on responsibility would seem to demand some kind of real, identical, and abiding self.[29]

The real significance of the Anatta doctrine as found in the Nikayas would therefore seem to be the assertion that of the many visible, namable, experiencable things in this world of becoming not one is the self. The self is real, the Buddha seems to teach, but its nature is not such as many personalists both in and out of India consider it. It is not a part of

[28] I am glad to note that several scholars who know a great deal more about the subject than I do hold much the same view as that expressed above. Thus I gather that neither La Vallée Poussin nor Keith would seriously disagree with me, while Radhakrishnan, Grimm, Schrader, and Professor W. E. Clark have said much the same thing. See Radhakrishnan in *Mind,* XXXV, 168, and his *Indian Philosophy* (Macmillan), I. 386f.; Grimm's *Doctrine of the Buddha,* I. 4; Schrader, *On the Problem of Nirvana* (*Jour. of the Pali Text Society,* 1904-05); and Clark's article "Buddhism" in the *Dictionary of Religion and Ethics* (N. Y., Macmillan, 1921), p. 60. Oldenberg in his *Lehre der Upanishaden und die Anfänge der Buddhismus* (Göttingen, 1915) still clung to his original insistence that the Buddha denied a real self. But he comes perilously near the opposite view, and the general view he adopts in Chap. III would be more consistent if he had explicitly recognized the implication of a real self in the Buddha's teaching. Much the same might be said of the lip-service (I can hardly call it more serious than that) which Sir Charles Eliot does to the traditional Anatta doctrine. See Vol. I, Chap. X of his *Hinduism and Buddhism.*

[29] Stcherbatsky himself recognizes the force of this consideration and admits that the position of a philosopher trying at once to deny the self and to insist on moral responsibility "was not an easy one." (*The Conception of Nirvana,* Leningrad, 1927), p. 3.

the pantheistic Brahma; it is not a "soul" of the animistic sort; it is not consciousness nor character nor a substance that performs the various mental functions. Of the many things that exist—that is, that change and become in this ephemeral world of Samsara—the self is not one; in other words, the self does not exist. Hume was right in saying you could never find it. The Buddhist soul would seem to be like the Upanishadic in this, that it is always subject and never object.

Most of these things I have said about the self are negative. What positive views did the Buddha hold concerning the self, further than those involved in the matters discussed? The Nikayas do not tell us; for the good reason that the Buddha never told his followers. Some [30] think the Buddha made no further statements concerning the nature of self because he had no further opinions; others [31] believe that the Buddha knew very well what he thought as to the positive nature of selfhood but refrained from telling because further discussion of the matter would be purely theoretical and not helpful toward the one great aim of spiritual deliverance.[32] Still others think that the nature of self is a matter which is essentially incapable of being expressed in words, and that the way to know it is the way the Buddha taught—namely, by reaching the intuitive insight of the Arahant. Certain it is that whenever the Buddha discusses the self—and this is rather frequently—it is with a distinct moral purpose. The common notion which would find in the body or in some conscious state the true self, or would identify the self with some imaginary animistic double or homunculus dwelling inside the body, is (in the Buddha's opinion) the source of endless sin and endless woe.[33] In this sense

'Tis self whereby we suffer

and (as we have seen) the destruction of this particular form of ignorance the Buddha considers perhaps the most important step in the new life. Self-centeredness is the source of

[30] E.g., Prof. Jacobi.

[31] E.g., Schrader and Radhakrishnan.

[32] He often refers to the uselessness of such purely theoretical discussion concerning the self. E.g., Majjhima II, CXL.

[33] Cf. Chap. II of this book. See especially Majjhima XXII, Anguttara XX. 9.

most sin and sorrow and of most divisions among men. The clear recognition that nothing in the whole world of becoming and existence is our true self—that all such things as wealth, body, mental processes, and feelings belong to us and are to be identified with us no more than so much dried wood which a peasant burns up [43]—this is almost the alpha and omega of the spiritual life. If only we could fully realize this truth, we should be freed from all personal fear and anger and grief, and should come to love each other as ourselves.

The bearing of all this on the question of Parinirvana is plain enough. If one holds, with so many Western writers, that there is no self but the phenomenal and ephemeral personality—the five Khandas—it is plain that when these are destroyed at the last death of the Arahant nothing will be left, and that therefore Parinirvana will mean simply nonbeing in the absolute sense of that word. It will not mean annihilation for there is nothing real to annihilate, but it will mean that absolutely nothing is left of the saint and that the death of his body is the end of all. If, on the other hand, there be a real self, a self to be sharply distinguished from the phenomenal personality, a self that has never been really a part of Samsara and one which is essentially permanent, then the whole conception of Parinirvana appears in a new light.[35]

But it will not do to argue too far on this matter in purely *a priori* fashion. Let us consult the Buddha himself. Unfortunately the Buddha has disappointingly little to say. The question whether the saint exists after death is one of the things which he regarded as purely theoretical and there-

[34] Cf. Majjhima XXII, Samyutta XXII. 33.

[35] The proper interpretation of Nirvana has long been a matter of disagreement and discussion among Buddhist scholars, East and West. The most recent contribution to the subject consists in a controversy between La Vallée Poussin and Stcherbatsky, each of whom has written a book upon the theme. The French scholar, who considers Buddhism an outgrowth of Yoga, insists that by Nirvana the Buddha meant "*la beatitude par excellence*" (*Nirvana*, pp. 60-61). The Russian, whose book (*The Conception of Buddhist Nirvana*), published in Leningrad in 1927, is intended expressly as a reply to La Vallée Poussin's, upholds the common view that Nirvana is absolute nothingness. (See also his review of La Vallée Poussin's *Nirvana* in the *Bulletin of the School of Oriental Studies*, Vol. IV, Part II, pp. 357-60.) Stcherbatsky's treatment of the question is to me much less persuasive than his opponent's because of his almost complete dependence upon relatively late and Abhiddharma writings, notably Vasubhandhu's Adhiddharmakoca.

fore not a suitable subject for discussion,[36] and when asked the question point blank he either avoids the issue or flatly refuses to answer. This much he will say, that Parinirvana is not a continuation of this life. It is the antithesis of Samsara. It is not what the Christian commonly means by "personal immortality." The saint at death is freed not only from sorrow but from change,[37] and that means that he is freed from perception, feeling, and cognition; for consciousness *as we know it* is dependent on perfectly definite physiological and psychological conditions and is unthinkable apart from change and causal relations.[38] The departed saint ceases to be a part of this phenomenal world; neither gods nor men behold him more.[39] He has passed away with "that utter passing away which leaves nothing whatever to remain behind." [40]

The Buddha realizes that this assertion will bring deep disappointment to those who still cling to the notion of an animistic soul, or to any of the other doctrines of a particular soul-substance held by the various schools of personalists. Such disappointment, however, is due to the false notion of selfhood with which they start. Presupposing that the self is what they erroneously imagine, they take his doctrine to mean the destruction of the self.[41] The truth is they have put their question wrongly. Those who hold to the personal immortality of a conscious soul-substance and those who assert that the saint after death has ceased to be are equally mistaken.[42] Of the venerable Vakkali, an Arahant

[36] Cf. Majjhima LXIII, LXXII; also Samyutta XVI. 12; Sutta Nipata II. 12.

[37] With this dislike of the Buddha for change and Samsara, compare the following from Baron von Hügel: "I still think that a downright observation on the part of those Buddhists as to the sickening character of all mere change, with their longing for Nirvana, for the complete cessation of all consciousness such as theirs, thus penetrated with a sense of mere change and hence of pure desolation, I think that this is quite magnificent as a prolegomenon to all religion. I take it to my mind quite simply as one of the most striking effects of the Real Presence of God also in those men's minds. It is because they have the dim, inarticulate sense of what the Abiding means that the mere slush of change is so sickening—a change not of growth, not of full establishment in Faith and Light, but a sheer racket: something fairly like what the evening newspapers of our most enlightened times tend to produce in the minds of their unhappy devotees" (from a letter of Baron von Hügel, of Nov. 29, 1922, taken from a little volume, privately printed, entitled *Some Letters of Baron von Hügel*, 1925).

[38] Majjhima XXXVIII; Udana IX.

[39] Digha I. 73-74.

[40] Digha XVI. 8.

[41] Cf. Majjhima XXII.

[42] Digha XV. 32.

who has just died, the Buddha says, "He has no consciousness anywhere and is utterly well." [43]

We must not allow ourselves to be deceived by the fact that the Buddhists use the words *consciousness* and *being* or *existence* in ways different from ours. In Nirvana the saint gets beyond the realm of being and beyond definite and changing consciousness; but he does both these things, we are told, in the seventh and eighth absorptions. He experiences non-being, both in this life and in the next; and he who experiences non-being surely must be.[44] Consciousness ceases in Nirvana; but also in this life "for him who both inwardly and outwardly does not delight in sensation, for him who thus wanders thoughtful, consciousness ceases." [45] In Nirvana the saint does not exist; but as Sariputta reminds the doubting brother Yamaka, it would be false to say that the true self of the Arahant exists even in this life.[46] In Nirvana the saint becomes extinct; but in later Sutras [47] we find the expression "utterly extinct" used of Buddhas who are, in the same breath, described as still very real and certainly by no means dead. In other words, Buddhist thought insists that the concepts existence and non-existence do not exhaust the possibilities; there is a *tertium quid*. An interesting illustration of this is to be found in the cases of two skull-tappers, related in the *Psalms of the Brethren*. A skull-tapper was a man who made his living by the skull-spell: the skull of some dead man would be given him and "when he had muttered the spell and tapped with his nail on the skull, he would declare, 'This person is born in such a sphere.' " Now the skull-tapper Migasira once came to the Buddha and offered to display his art. So

> the Exalted One had the skull of a monk brought who had attained Parinibbana, and said, "Tell the destiny of him to whom this skull belonged." Migasira muttered and tapped, but saw neither the beginning nor the end. Then the Master said: "Art not able, Wanderer?" He replied, "I must first make sure," and turning the skull round never so much—for how could he know the goings of an Arahant?—stood ashamed, perspiring, dumb.[48]

[43] Samyutta XXII. 87.

[44] Cf. Descartes' *"Cogito ergo sum."*

[45] Sutta Nipata V. 14.

[46] Samyutta XXII. 85, 86.

[47] E.g., the Saddharma Pundarika.

[48] *Psalms of the Brethren*, No. 151. A similar story is told of one Vangissa in No. 264.

The Arahant belonged neither to the realm of existence nor to that of non-existence. He was completely beyond all Migasira's categories.

An even more illuminating story is the conversation between Vaccha, a wandering ascetic of some non-Buddhist sect, with the Tathagata. Vaccha insisted on an answer to the question, "Where is an Arahant reborn after death?" The Buddha replied,

"The word *reborn* does not apply to him."

"Then he is not reborn."

"The term *not-reborn* does not apply to him."

"To each and all of my questions, Gotama, you have replied in the negative. I am at a loss and bewildered."

"You ought to be at a loss and bewildered, Vaccha. For this Dhamma is profound, recondite, hard to comprehend, rare, excellent, beyond dialectic, subtle, only to be understood by the wise. To you it is difficult—who hold other views and belong to another faith. So I in turn will question you for such answer as you see fit to give. What think you, Vaccha, if there were a fire blazing in front of you, would you know it?"

"Yes, Gotama."

"If you were asked what made that fire blaze, could you give an answer?"

"I should answer that what made it blaze was the fuel consisting of bracken and sticks."

"If the fire went out, would you know it had gone out?"

"Yes."

"If now you were asked in what direction the fire had gone, whether to east, west, north, or south, could you give an answer?"

"The question is not rightly put, Gotama. Since the fire was kept alight by bracken and sticks and since it had consumed its supply of fuel and had received no fresh supplies, it is said to have gone out for lack of fuel to sustain it."

"Just in the same way, Vaccha, all things material—feelings, perceptions, forces, consciousness—everything by which the Arahant might be denoted, has passed away for him. Profound, measureless, unfathomable, is the Arahant even as the mighty ocean; *reborn* does not apply to him nor *not-reborn,* nor any combination of such terms." [49]

To understand this simile of the fire (which in slightly different words is used again in the Sutta Nipata [50] and the Udana) [51] we must forget our modern and Western ideas of that element and take in its place the Indian view. Accord-

[49] Majjhima LXXII. I have here used Chalmers' trans. I. 343-44.
[50] V. 7. [51] IX.

ing to Schrader "the common Indian view is, since the oldest time, that an expiring flame does not really go out but returns into the primitive, pure, invisible state of fire it had before its appearance as visible fire." [52] The fire figure thus seems to suggest a conception at least remotely related to the thought of the Upanishads that at the death of the enlightened, the self returns to Brahma, its divine and impersonal source. We must not, of course, press the fire simile too far, or forget that the pantheistic side of the Upanishadic tradition the Buddha definitely rejected. But certainly the fire figure seems plainly to show that the Arahant at death does not cease to be. And we may, perhaps, go a little farther in the direction of the Upanishads than this—at any rate if we take the Udana as representing the Buddha's thoughts; for it quotes him as saying:

> Just as all rivers lose themselves in the great ocean and all the waters of the air pour into it, yet the great ocean thereby knows neither increase nor diminution; so when many Arahants become extinguished in the pure realm of Nirvana, the Nirvana realm knows neither increase nor diminution.[53] There water, earth, fire, air are not. There no candle gives light, no sun beams, no moon shines, no darkness is. And when the enlightened has attained in stillness to insight, then is he free from form and formlessness, from pleasure and from pain.[54]

If we may for a moment consider the matter quite apart from the direct expression of the Nikayas, let us ask ourselves: What must naturally and logically be conceived as the goal to which the life of the Arahant points, the completion of its nature? We must remember that the universe of the Buddha is one in which the causal law holds sway, flowers grow into fruit, seeds develop according to their kind, and natures fulfil themselves. On the one hand, the life of the Arahant is increasingly one of independence from particular events, of growing freedom from cares, passions, processes. It has less and less to do with the detail of life, with things that happen to the body, and in fact with things that *happen* at all; more and more its inwardness increases and unflickering

[52] "On the Problem of Nirvana," *Jour. of the Pali Text Society*, 1904-05, p. 167. Keith takes exactly the same view (*Buddhist Philosophy*, pp. 65-66). Eliot very nearly agrees (*Hinduism and Buddhism*, I. 232, note.)

[53] Udana V. 5.

[54] Udana I. 10.

peaces takes the place of the change that characterizes other lives. But it is just these changes in consciousness, these events that have locus in time and space, that characterize *existence* in the technical meaning given that term by many contemporary philosophers. Of course so long as the spirit remains organic to a body this tendency away from the particular, the temporal, the changing, must be constantly thwarted. But now do away with this bodily connection and allow the tendency of the enlightened nature to be carried on without let or hindrance, as we may suppose, on Buddhist principles, to be actually the case at the last death of the Arahant. We cannot describe the state to which this would lead, but we can see the direction.

On the other hand we must remember another aspect of the saintly life. Deliverance and enlightenment do not result in a reduction but in an enhancement of being. In the Buddha as his disciples knew him there was immeasurably more of reality (a most inadequate and clumsy expression, but I know of none better) than in any other mortal. And if we may trust the implications of their testimony, each of them, as they advanced on the Buddhist path toward deliverance, felt an increase of inner, spiritual being. Their development was not a process of shriveling but of expansion and realization. They became more and more real as they grew in grace. Of course while connected with a material body full of imperious demands and humiliating limitations, this growth had bounds beyond which it could not pass. But now suppose this connection with the body severed once for all and no new bodily tie substituted. Let all bonds be broken and suffer the spirit to develop indefinitely in the course it has begun toward increase of being. Again we cannot describe, we cannot imagine the resulting state, but we know the direction.

Now put this thought with the one in the previous paragraph—the increase of being with the freedom from particulars that make up existence—and note the point at which the two converging lines meet. Can this be better described than in the words of the Buddha—a state that is "neither existence nor non-existence"? "There is, O monks, an unborn, non-existent, not-made, not-compounded. Were there not, there would be no deliverance from the born, the existent, the made, the compounded."[55]

It may be these considerations and these passages from the canon will throw a little light on the nature of the ultimate Nirvana as the Tathagata conceived it. We should, of course, like to know much more than this. We should like to ask him many questions. Is Parinirvana a state of unchanging and desireless joy? Is it so different from everything we call consciousness that no terms of ours apply to it? Is it absorption in some Absolute? . . . The Buddha refuses to answer.

Why is he silent? As Professor Radhakrishnan has pointed out,[56] there are three possible ways of accounting for his silence. One is that he held a purely naturalistic view of things, considering the self to be nought, and Nirvana to be complete nothingness, but refrained from telling what he thought for fear of hurting sensitive feelings. This view of the Buddha's position is so plainly out of harmony with most of the things he said that it needs no discussion here. The second hypothesis is that the Buddha was himself agnostic on all the ultimate problems; that he refused to answer the questions asked him because he did not know the answer himself. This is a perfectly possible hypothesis. It is the hypothesis of Professor Keith; and in the absence of more definite statements in the Nikayas it will probably always remain one of the possibilities. Personally I do not accept it. With Professor Radhakrishnan and (I gather) with Sir Charles Eliot, I prefer the third interpretation of the Buddha's silence. I prefer it chiefly because it is the interpretation of the Buddha himself. In a famous passage of the Majjhima [57] one of the Buddha's disciples asks the Buddha a number of these ultimate questions and insists on an answer. The Buddha not only refuses to give a reply but tells his disciple explicitly why he does so. The reason is a moral one: namely, because these matters "profit not, have not to do with the fundamentals of religion, tend not to absence of passion, quiescence, supreme wisdom, and Nirvana." The Buddha knew the

[55] Iti-vuttaka § 43; Udana VIII. 3.
[56] "Indian Philosophy, Some Problems," in *Mind,* XXXV.
[57] LXIII. See also LXXII; Digha VI, IX, XXIX; Anguttara VIII. 7.

danger—especially among a people such as the Indians—of the attention's being turned away from the great problem of right living into various purely speculative channels. He was determined that if he could help it his teaching and way of life, his Dhamma, should not become a matter of creed or of hair-splitting, and he would give no opening to the danger he feared by answering questions on these matters or permitting discussion of them in the Order. As the sea's taste is only salt, so the one taste of his Dhamma is deliverance. That he had no opinion on these matters himself seems unlikely when we remember that he was an Indian thinker, and when we recall the agility of his mind in the many discussions of other matters that are recorded. It was plainly the opinion of his followers that he knew the answers to these questions. He himself asserts in more than one passage that he knows much more than he has ever revealed.

Another reason for the Buddha's refusal to deal with cosmic problems not directly connected with human life may very likely have been the impossibility of putting the ultimate truth in words. Human language was forged for human needs and there may well be cosmic themes that can hardly be communicated by so rough and purely practical a tool. Most of the great religions have known this, and hence have tried to express the ineffable in poetry and symbol. The Buddha might have done the same, but he did not. Apparently he feared that the symbols, should he use them, would come in time to be taken as literal expressions, and thus once more creed and myth would take the place of earnest living.

The Buddha did not tell his ultimate philosophy of the universe. Can we guess it? At once the monistic absolutism of the Upanishads suggests itself as a position he may have adopted. But on the whole question of the influence of the Upanishads upon his thought we have too little definite information to justify our forming any opinion.[58] Nor can we with security on *a priori* grounds argue that if he viewed the

[58] Prof. Radhakrishnan is convinced the influence was great. La Vallée Poussin, on the other hand, thinks it was *nil*. (See his *Nirvana*, pp. 52, 56-57.) "Not in close contact with Upanishadic thought," says Thomas (*op. cit.*, p. 199). Oldenberg thinks the Buddha adopted his antithesis of the Changing and the Changeless from the Upanishads. Both he and Neumann think many passages in the Buddhist canon show direct Upanishadic influence. Eliot and several others insist that on some points the Buddha was directly antithetical to the Upanishads.

self and Nirvana in the way suggested in this chapter he must therefore have believed in an Absolute Reality.

One thing about his universe we do know: namely, that it was fundamentally moral. The law of Karma, of strict retribution, is the most fundamental law in it; and all other laws, chemical or physical, are bound to conform. From the Western point of view concerning nature, we must say that the Buddha's universe is supernaturally just.

May we from this argue further and conclude that the universe must therefore be conscious, or must be guided by a supreme and moral intelligence? We may so argue; but the Buddha does not. On all these matters he is silent. Doubtless he has his reasons.

> Others abide our questions. Thou art free.
> We ask and ask; Thou smilest and art still.

Deep is the Tathagata, measureless, unfathomable, like the great ocean.

CHAPTER VI

THE STORY OF INDIAN BUDDHISM

No new religion is ever entirely new. Were it so it would make no appeal and get no following. Buddhism appears to have possessed as many original elements as any of the great religions; in fact, I am inclined to think, rather more than any other. Yet necessarily a large part of what the Buddha believed and taught he derived from the common inheritance of Indian thought which he shared with his generation. To this he added the results of his own pondering over the problems of human life and death, the new ways of viewing things, the new analyses and conclusions to which his thought and his personal experiences led him. Finally he faced humanity and its problems with an attitude of loving devotion, which, while it contributed nothing of a conceptual nature, gave the religion which he founded a character that early distinguished it from all other faiths and sects of central or eastern Asia. It will be useful to keep in mind these three sources of early Buddhism.[1]

The first of the three, the traditional Indian element, including such things as belief in transmigration, the general geography of the universe with its heavens, hells, and gods, was of course brought into the religion not only by the Buddha but by all its early converts. This factor of Buddhism was, as Alessandro Costa has pointed out, "the spontaneous product of the popular mind, fixed in certain general lines by the powerful personality of Gotama; but one which retained the elasticity which characterizes the things thought out and felt by many." [2]

[1] For further comment on this triple aspect of Buddhism see *India and Its Faiths* (Boston, Houghton, Mifflin, 1915), pp. 410-16.

[2] *Il Budda e la Sua Dottrina* (2d ed., Torino, Bocca, 1921), pp. 54-55. Mrs. Rhys Davids suggests that the early disciples, especially the five ascetics who were the first converts, may have contributed some of the ideas which are commonly attributed to the Founder, see "The Unknown Co-founders of Buddhism," *J.R.A.S.*, April, 1927.

This traditional element seldom finds itself in conflect with the intellectual element of the Buddha's teaching; for they deal, as a rule, with such different themes that there is little room for conflict. The same cannot be said of the relation between the second and the third factors. That part of the Buddha's intellectual teachings which has to do with the evils of desire and the importance of cultivating indifference can only with difficulty be kept from conflicting with what might be called the heart element of Buddhism, the love and sympathy which the Founder felt and taught for all needy sentient life. It is, to be sure, only craving and desire for harmful things that the Buddha disapproves, but, as we have seen, many of the natural affections of the heart weaken the defenses of one's peace; wives and children are pledges to Fortune. The logic of the situation, if pressed to its extreme, might drive one even farther than this. Pity for the suffering may be a source of sorrow; and to fix one's heart on the success of a cause may lead to great distress if the cause fail. This almost irrepressible conflict between heart and head was noticeable within Buddhism from very early times. The first Jataka story tells us that Gotama as a Bodhisattva (one destined to be a Buddha and on the way to Buddhahood) in a previous birth, on seeing a starving tiger, "though composed in mind was shaken with compassion by the sufferings of his fellow-creature as Mount Meru is by an earthquake. It is a wonder," the writer comments, "how the compassionate, be their constancy ever so evident in the greatest sufferings of their own, are touched by the grief, however small, of another."[3] This is not history but it points to a situation which must have arisen not once but many times. To be "composed in mind" yet at the same moment to be "shaken with compassion" is a difficult performance. A more historical example of this conflict is to be found in Mahavagga X. 4, which shows how the dissensions among his monks—the temporary defeat of one of his life purposes—for a short time troubled the Tathagata and prevented him from living at ease.

So far as I am aware this inner conflict is never faced by Buddhist books as a matter of theory; and the result is that

[3] Speyer's trans., p. 4.

each Buddhist is left to fight it out for himself. To the heartless and self-centered, the logical inference from the Second Noble Truth—desire is the cause of sorrow, therefore desire nothing and love no one—has resulted in a certain hard selfishness. The solution which the Buddha and his greater disciples acted upon, though so far as I know they did not express it, seems to have been that of living their lives on two levels. One may be distressed and disappointed, and one's efforts may be frustrated; yet if one takes a larger view he need not allow these things to determine the whole tone of the inner life. Pleasure is not compatible with sorrow, but joy and the Great Peace may be. When the ideal Buddhist suffers with the pain of the wounded animal or feels the woe of the whole sentient world, he is with Saint Paul "as one sorrowful, yet always rejoicing."

When the Buddha died he left his disciples the Dhamma to be his representative. According to the Samyutta he had already in life said, "He who seeth the Dhamma, seeth me; he who seeth me, seeth the Dhamma." [4] This Teaching and Way of Life, combined with one's own reason, was to be the individual's guide. The Buddha departed into Nirvana, which, whatever else may be said of it, is out of all conscious and active relation with the affairs of this world.

Yet the Brethren who were left behind could not break the spell or forget the charm of their radiant Master. Even before he died the thought of him, though far distant, formed one of the strongest psychological helps in the spiritual struggle. Aged and infirm Pingiya sings the praises of Gotama, and Bavari asks how he can stay away from one so luminous and dear. Pingiya replies: "I do not stay away from him even for a moment, from Gotama of great wisdom who taught me the Dhamma. I see him in my mind and with my eye, vigilant night and day; worshiping I spend the night. Therefore I do not stay away from him. As I am worn out and feeble my body does not go there, but in my thoughts I always go there, for my mind is joined to him." [5]

Those who had revered and loved the Master in this way could not at the death of his body drop out of their lives all

[4] XXII. 87.
[5] Sutta Nipata V. 17. Cf. also Samyutta XI. 3; Majjhima LXXXV.

that he personally had meant to them. And this personal attachment that they felt was passed on by a kind of inevitable spiritual contagion to those who came by their words to believe on him. Though long since in Parinirvana, he was still the first of the Three Refuges named in the formula of "joining the Church" as we should say:

I take my refuge in the Buddha,
I take my refuge in the Dhamma,
I take my refuge in the Sangha.

The characteristic stanza already quoted in another connection from the Psalms of so many of the Brethren, shows how this feeling of personal loyalty as a part of the religion was handed on through the generations:

The Master hath my fealty and love
And all the Buddha's ordinance is done.
Low have I laid the heavy load I bore;
Cause of rebirth is found in me no more.

In church theory the Buddhist truth is accepted because revealed by the Buddha. Faith, which means trust in the Buddha and right belief (the first step of the Noble Path) is of great importance.[6] Meditation is for the purpose of making faith more vivid by means of deeper experiences, not for the sake of discovering new truths.[7] But, as we have seen, the Buddha himself constantly made appeal to reason. His discourses were more like those of Socrates than like those of Mohammed. He insists that his disciples shall really understand and not simply take his word.[8] Each man must work out his own salvation with diligence. "Therefore be ye lamps unto yourselves. Be ye a refuge unto yourselves. Betake yourselves to no external refuge. Hold fast the Truth as a lamp. Look not for refuge to anyone besides yourselves." [9]

The authority of the Buddha in his church is midway between that of Christ in Christianity and that of a great scientist or scholar in the intellectual world. The Buddha *knew;*

[6] Cf. Digha XVI. 9.
[7] Cf. La Vallée Poussin, *Bouddhisme* (Paris, 1909), pp. 129-78.
[8] Cf. Majjhima XXXVIII.
[9] From the Buddha's last address to his disciples, Digha XVI. 26.

hence by listening to his word we shall learn the truth. If we could have got at the truth in some other way it would have done as well. And since the Buddha's teaching is true, one way to get at his real meaning is by the use of our reason. Thus great liberty of discussion and very divergent views have almost always been possible within Buddhism. So far as authority is exercised within the church it is for the sake of unity. Heresy becomes a sin only when it leads to schism.

That primitive Buddhism and the Buddhism of the early centuries deserves to be called a religion rather than a moral philosophical society has often been questioned. It believes, to be sure, in many "gods," but these are merely heavenly rajahs and not at all equivalent to God in the Christian sense. It has then no "personal God," nor does it teach a pantheistic God nor an idealistic Absolute. For my own part I think it should be called a religion because it decidedly takes an "attitude toward the Determiner of Destiny" [10]—in this case the moral universe and Karma. Yet it must be confessed it lacks two things which are almost invariably found in religion: namely, a cosmic philosophy expressed in more or less symbolic fashion, and a cult. The Buddha feared the effect of both of these things; he had seen the evil effects of a perversion or exaggeration of both, and he determined to have his followers make the experiment of getting on without either.[11] In one sense the experiment worked; so long as the Founder lived and for a few years after his death, the Buddhist community followed his injunctions with a fair degree of strictness and success. In another sense the experiment failed; for very soon after his death a simple form of cult was introduced, and as the years went by a few cosmic symbols crept into the thought of his followers. In this latter respect, however, the Southern form of Buddhism has kept fairly close to the Buddha's injunctions: the cosmic questions are still in theory taboo and not even in symbolic form are they answered. There is a certain negative gain in this, since much nonsense and superstition is thereby avoided. On the other

[10] The definition of religion suggested in my book on *The Religious Consciousness.*

[11] As to cult see Digha XIII; Majjhima VII; concerning cosmic beliefs see preceding chapter.

hand, the Buddhism of the masses in the lands of Southern Buddhism is incrusted with much animistic mythology that has crept in from lower and non-Buddhist forms of belief; and the pure Buddhism of the more learned has a certain hard-headedness, this-worldliness, and lack of mystical lure and cosmic largeness which certainly are not marks of strength or inspiration. The cosmic vistas which the other great religions give their followers through the symbolic expression of metaphysical ideas are possessions of great value, and Southern Buddhism is the poorer for their lack.

It was more difficult for human nature to resist the demand for some kind of cult than for philosophy; and, as I have indicated, not long after the death of the Founder certain simple forms of it began to creep in. Both the Udana and the Mahavagga (of the Vinaya) repeat a story that a certain young monk named Sona was directed by the Buddha to intone before the assembly of the monks "all the verses in the Atthakavaggikani" [12] (which is thought to be Book IV of the Sutta Nipata). This would indicate that, if not actually during the life of the Buddha, at any rate shortly after his death, the repetition of portions of the Dhamma was becoming a sort of ritual. We can easily see how this would be. The Master's words were not at first recorded in writing but were treasured in the memory of those who had heard them from his lips or (later on) from the lips of those who had learned them at second or third hand. It was desirable that as many members of the Order as possible should participate in this communal memory—both for the sake of the Order as a whole and for the individual advantage that each member would thereby gain. To make more sure of this a large number of passages from his teachings would be recited in unison at frequent meetings of each of the chapters. This solemn chanting of sacred words inevitably became a liturgy, which was regarded as having value in itself.

Another form of cult began, very naturally, immediately upon the death of the Founder. His body was ceremoniously burned, and his ashes and bones were distributed as precious possessions among the faithful. Over each of these sacred relics a cairn was piled, which later on was replaced

[12] Udana VI; Mahavagga V. 13, 9.

by a massive structure of masonry called stupa or dagoba. The Digha justifies this practice (which in India was probably common enough) by putting into the mouth of the Buddha himself directions for the doing of what was actually done, together with a rationalization for the practice: "At the four cross roads a cairn should be erected to the Tathagata. And whosoever shall there place garlands or perfumes or paint, or make salutation there, or become in its presence calm in heart—that shall long be to them for a profit and a joy." [13]

Reverence to the relics of the Buddha—including, probably, not only his bones and ashes but some of the articles most associated with him in life, notably his begging bowl—was probably the first step in the direction of worship, if indeed we may speak of "worship" in early Buddhism at all. The reverence for the relics was practiced originally in order "to become calm in heart." It had desirable subjective effects which were empirically verifiable. It is chiefly in this subjective sense that we are justified in speaking of worship among the intelligent early Buddhists. That "subjective worship" [14] should have begun thus early in Buddhism and that it should have had the sanction of the Nikayas is interesting and significant, for, as we shall see, it tends to characterize the religion throughout its history.

There was also, however, a belief that the reverential attitude toward sacred relics was in itself a good act and that as such it (like all other good acts) must result in good Karma. Not only reverence for relics produced this perfectly objective result, in the opinion of early Buddhism; the same result might be attained by pious pilgrimage to the four places at which the four great events of the Tathagata's life occurred: his birth at Kapilavatthu, his enlightenment under the Bodhi Tree (at Buddh Gaya), his first sermon or "turning of the wheel of the Dhamma" at the deer park at Sarnath near Benares, and his Parinirvana at Kusinara.[15]

[13] Digha XVI. 11. It is of course perfectly possible that the Buddha himself may have given these directions, but it seems more probable that the passage was composed after his death to justify the practice.

[14] By this I mean worship the purpose of which is the subjective effect it produces on the worshiper. See *The Religious Consciousness*, Chap. XIV.

[15] A prophecy of the veneration of these places is put into the mouth of the Buddha in Digha XVI, and the practice is thereby stamped with his approval.

Pilgrimage to these sacred places must be set down as one of the earliest forms of Buddhist cult. Out of them, according to Foucher's hypothesis, came the first religious symbols of Buddhist art—the tree, the wheel, the stupa, found so frequently in bas-relief upon early Buddhist monuments.[16] Figures of the Buddha were for a long time avoided; in fact they were introduced into Buddhist art only through the influence of Greek artists in the northwest, during the reign of Kanishka, in the first or second century of our era.[17]

The type of Buddha image thus created has been carried over all the East. Slight variations have been introduced here and there but in fundamental characters the image of the Buddha is everywhere the same.[18] The product of Indian tradition and symbolism and of Greek art, it is worthy of its double ancestry, and to one who understands it today with its two thousand years of history it is rich with significance and beauty. Foucher has pointed out that it is composite in other ways than origin. The body is robed as a monk but the head, instead of being shaven as every monk's must be, retains an elaborate arangement of long and beautiful hair. The model chosen for the head .by the Hellenic or Hellenized sculptors was not the Indian monk but the Greek god. The Buddha image thus presents us with a being half human, half divine—the monk and the god, who is neither god nor man but a wholly unique being.

Once introduced into Buddhist monasteries, the Buddha image inevitably became the center of the simple ritual that was developing, and the room in which the monks assembled to chant together pasages from the Dhamma became a shrine or temple. The influence of this development on the attitude of the less learned toward the Buddha must have

[16] Foucher believes that pilgrims to each of the four places brought home with them an appropriate memento. Thus the tree was used to indicate Buddha Gaya, the wheel Sarnath, and the stupa Kusinara, see *Beginnings of Buddhist Art* (Paris, Guethner, 1917), Chap. I.

[17] *Ibid.*, Chap. IV.

[18] Thus Stein says that in the frescoes of the Tun-Huang caves "the Chinese artists seem to have given free expression to their love for ·ornate landscape backgrounds, graceful curves and bold movement. But no local taste had presumed to transform the dignified serenity of the features, the simple yet impressive gestures, the graceful richness of folds with which classical art, as transplanted to the Indus, had endowed the bodily presence of the Tathagata and his many epiphanies," *Ruins of Desert Cathay* (London, Macmillan, 1912), II. 25.

been very considerable; and we can see how naturally the later worship of the Buddha before his image developed from these simple and rather Puritanical beginnings.

Hand in hand with this development of the cult there went a corresponding transformation in the conception of the Founder. During his later years he seems to have been regarded by his faithful disciples as the source of all authority and as possessing unfathomable and all-inclusive knowledge, yet subject still to the limitations of a human body. So he was remembered by those who had known him in the flesh. But when the last of these had followed him into Parinirvana, his form took on larger and more supernatural proportions. No longer joined to a body, he came to have a place in a cosmic scheme which it is hard to suppose he himself would have accepted. At great intervals, so the theory ran, when the World's need called for it, a Buddha regularly appeared and taught the eternal Dhamma. Gotama Buddha was thus only the latest of several omniscient teachers. The eternal Dhamma, too, which all the Buddhas taught, took on a new and awful glamour. And the Order or Sangha which the Buddha founded—not just this collection of fallible men and women, but the ideal Sangha, the institution, eternal too, or at least refounded by each recurring Buddha—this also demanded and received the reverence of worship. Thus "Buddha, Dhamma, Sangha," the three refuges, became the "Three Jewels" or the "Triple Gem" and were hymned as the supreme object of adoration.[19]

Buddha and Dhamma have been treated at length in these pages. Something further must now be said of the last member of the three jewels, the Sangha. As we have seen, the Buddha at the very beginning of his career formed a society of followers who took him as their master, lived a monastic life, and sought to follow the Dhamma. The idea of a group of men who had renounced the household life and chosen a teacher was not original with Gotama. For many centuries it had been the custom in India for men who were in earnest with their personal salvation or who desired to attain supernatural powers, to leave the household life and live as homeless wanderers. Many of these "Paribrajakas" lived as lonely

[19] See the hymn in the Khuddaka Patha VI.

hermits, many grouped themselves around some leader whose teachings they sought to learn. The Buddhist Sangha was one of these groups of earnest seekers. It differed from the others in its rapid growth but chiefly in the nature of the Dhamma which its teacher imparted, and the consequent aim which it sought. Here indeed was an original contribution to the monastic and religious life of India, a contribution which came not so much from the Buddha's head as from his heart. His devotion to the service of all needy creatures he was able, to a considerable extent, to infuse among his followers, and the Sangha recognized the spreading of the truth among those who knew it not, as one of its chief ideals. This was something relatively new in India. It is to the Sangha and its missionary ideal more than to anything else that Buddhism owes its long life, its wide spread, the comparative purity of its doctrines, and the continuity of its tradition and its teaching. It has been one of the most influential institutions in history.

The Order of Nuns was initiated by the Buddha with much misgiving and (if we are to accept the account in the canon) only at the urgent request of Ananda, the cousin and personal attendant of the Founder. Once started, however, it seems for years to have been a thriving institution, and it is quite probable that the story of the Tathagata's reluctance to admit nuns to the Sangha and his prediction that as a consequence of his doing so the religion would come to a temporary end in five hundred years, originated at some time subsequent to Asoka, when the Women's Order was in a state of serious decline. During the Buddha's lifetime and for long after, the nuns received systematic instruction from the more learned monks, who seem to have taken turns in preaching at the convents. The elderly nuns also instructed the novices and made many converts among lay women.[20] In fact, as Mrs. Rhys Davids puts it, "the Order, refuge though it proved, was primarily an organization for the propaganda of the Dhamma, and its members were all more or less, wholly or at times, saviours and good shepherds of stray sheep." [21]

[20] Cf. *Psalms of the Sisters,* Nos. 48, 49, 50.
[21] Introduction to the *Psalms of the Sisters,* p. xxxv.

The Sangha is an interesting example of collective life organized for the sake of individual religion. In guiding its development during its early years the Buddha showed constantly that elasticity of mind, that ability ever to distinguish the end from the means, which characterized him in every field of thought. He never lost from sight the one great aim—or double aim—of the Order: the stimulation of the spiritual life in its individual members and the missionary effort to spread the truth throughout all the world. But in the prosecution of this aim he tried all sorts of expedients, never allowed himself to be bound by tradition or precedent, accepted and acted upon all manner of suggestions, used different methods with different individuals, and in general adapted the means to the end and treated every new situation on its merits. So long as he lived he was the source of authority, and after he died his method was followed by the Sangha itself, so that it developed in much the same empirical fashion as the British Constitution. As Mr. Dutt has pointed out, most of the rules of the Vinaya, as we have it today, though attributed to the Buddha, are probably of later origin and were made, as the occasions for them arose, by the Sangha.[22] This process continued for many years.

For these many rules, whatever their origin, there is here no space. Mention should perhaps be made in passing of the custom called Uposatha, a gathering of all the monks of each chapter at new moon and full moon.[23] Its original aim was that each chapter of monks might recite together the many rules of the Order, the list of which was known as the Patimokkha, and that opportunity for public confession might thus be given to any brother who had broken some of the rules. This recitation of the Patimokkha later "became a mere ceremonial observance, serving the same purpose among the Buddhist Bhikkus as the Holy Communion amongst the Christians, being nothing but the formal embodiment of the corporate life of a cenobitical society."[24] The rules thus read over by the group seem to have varied at different times. There are ten rules, however, which stand out with special

[22] *Early Buddhist Monachism* (London, Trübner, 1924).

[23] Reference is made to this custom in so early a passage as Majjhima LXXVII.

[24] Dutt, *op. cit.*, p. 100. I am not sure that Mr. Dutt fully understands the purpose of the Christian sacrament.

prominence and have been recognized from the Buddha's time to our own, namely, the "Five Precepts" already alluded to more than once,[25] which all Buddhists, lay as well as cleric, must observe, and five additional precepts for the monks as follows: (6) not to eat at forbidden times, (7) not to dance, sing, or attend theatrical or other spectacles, (8) to abstain from the use of garlands, scents, and ornaments, (9) to abstain from the use of high or broad beds, (10) never to receive money.[26]

The Buddha's two chief disciples during his lifetime were Sariputta and Moggallana. Both of these died before their Master, and at the time of his death the most important members of the Sangha seem to have been Kassapa, Ananda, Anuruddha, and Upali. The tradition preserved in the Cullavagga and the Mahavamsa describes how, under the leadership of Kassapa,[27] five hundred leading Arahants assembled during the following rainy season at Rajagaha in order to discover how far they agreed as to the teachings of their departed Master on the various points of doctrine and discipline. This meeting is known in Buddhist history as the First Council.[28] Its existence has been called in question, but the thing itself is so very likely that it seems more reasonable to accept the fact, if not the details, of the Rajagaha Council.

A hundred years later, according to tradition, a large group of monks living in or near the city of Vesali became so dissatisfied with the stringency of the rules that they decided to disregard—or reinterpret—some of them.[29] The attention of the stricter monks being called to this fact, a meeting of representatives of the Order was held at Vesali. Here the question of the rules was decided in favor of the conservative party; so little to the satisfaction of the minor-

[25] Not to kill, steal, lie, be unchaste, or drink intoxicants.

[26] Found in several passages, e.g., Mahavagga I. 56.

[27] The northern tradition speaks of Kassapa as the First Patriarch or head of the Order after the death of the Tathagata, and makes Ananda his (almost immediate) successor. The Southern tradition recognizes Kassapa as the presiding officer of the First Council, but makes Upali the first patriarch.

[28] It is described in the Cullavagga XI and Mahavamsa III. Upali is said to have recited the Vinaya and Ananda the Sutta. A later account adds that Kassapa recited the Abhidhamma.

[29] Notably the rule which forbade the acceptance of money.

ity, however, that they seceded from the Order (though by no means from Buddhism) and formed a new order or school of their own. This Vesali meeting is known in Buddhist history as the Second Council.[30] It is notable as marking the end of complete union in the Order and the beginning of the many schismatic schools or sects or denominations into which later Buddhism was divided.

This Second Council (whose existence, like that of the First is seriously questioned by several Western students), if it convened as tradition says a century after the Founder's death, must be dated about 380 B.C We have little knowledge of the history of Buddhism during the next century. But in 270 B.C. there came to the throne of the Indian Empire a man who was to do more for Buddhism than anyone before or after him, saving only the Founder. This man was Asoka. I referred to his domain as the "Indian empire" because his grandfather, Chandragupta, King of Magadha, had conquered all of northern India, his father Bindusara (Chandragupta's son) had added much of southern India, and he himself, during the early years of his reign, rounded out his realm by the conquest of Kalinga, on the southeastern coast, thus uniting under his sway all of India from Kabul and the Himalayas to an east-and-west line a little north of Madras. According to his own confession, the sufferings which he had produced by his bloody conquest of Kalinga caused him "remorse, profound sorrow, and regret"; and it was possibly in part as a result of these feelings that he became, shortly after, a Buddhist; and two years later actually joined the Order and became (while still emperor) a monk.

This in effect made him head of the church as well as head of the state. But Buddhism did not thereby become the state church, at least not in the ordinary sense of the word. For the emperor was a man of great liberality toward all sincere faith, and the teachings of the Buddha only encouraged this tolerant attitude. All religions were state religions, in that they all received aid from the emperor. Buddhism, however, being in his opinion the truest and best of all, naturally received the greatest aid. It is interesting to note what

[30] Our knowledge of it is based on Cullavagga XII, Mahavamsa IV, and the Dipavamsa.

Buddhism meant in the third century B.C.—at least what it meant to the emperor. We are enabled to see this because he has told us in letters engraved on enduring stone, in a series of remarkable inscriptions set up by him in all the corners of his immense empire. Buddhism meant to him chiefly one thing: morality. Many of his inscriptions are moral sermons, based on the Dhamma and set up for the sake of spreading the Dhamma. In some of the inscriptions he shows how he himself has practiced it: for example, by digging wells, planting trees, providing remedies (hospitals also may be intended) for both men and animals, and looking out for the comfort of travelers. In another very Buddhist way he also followed the Dhamma and obeyed the injunctions of the Founder: he sent out missionaries to spread the knowledge of the true religion both in his own dominions, in Ceylon, and to the Greek Kingdoms of Asia, Europe, and Egypt. According to the Mahavamsa he also sent missionaries to Pegu in Burma, but as this is not supported by the inscriptions it is not generally accepted. What was the result of his missions to Africa, Europe, and Asia outside of his own realm, is quite unknown; but Ceylon, to which he sent his son (or younger brother?), Mahinda, was rapidly converted; and his efforts to spread Buddhism in his own broad empire were so successful that, as Vincent Smith has expressed it, "he succeeded in transforming the local doctrine of a local Indian sect into one of the great religions of the world." [31]

The missionary zeal which Asoka inherited from the great Founder has characterized Buddhism throughout its history and marked it off from all the other religions of southern and eastern Asia. Hinduism, to be sure, had a certain limited spread outside of India, but this extension was not of the missionary sort. As Sir Charles Eliot has put it:

> Wherever we find records of Hinduism outside of India the presence of Hindu conquerors or colonists is recorded. Hinduism accompanied Hindus and sometimes spread round their settlements, but it never attempted to convert distant and alien lands. But the Buddhists had

[31] *The Early History of India*, 4th ed. (Oxford, 1924), p. 197. An epitome of the inscriptions referring to the Dhamma will be found in Rhys Davids' *Buddhist India* (N. Y., Putnam, 1903), pp. 294-97.

> from the beginning the true evangelistic temper: they preached to all the world and in singleness of purpose; they had no political support from India.[32]

And as to the native religions of China the contrast is perhaps even greater. To quote again from Eliot:

> Whereas Indian missionaries preached Buddhism in China, the idea of making Confucianism known in India seems never to have entered the head of any Chinese.[33]

According to the Ceylonese tradition Asoka not only did his best to spread Buddhism over all the world; he also sought to purify the Buddhist Order at home by calling a Third Council, held at his capital, Pataliputra. The historicity of this Council, like that of the others, has been seriously questioned by Western scholars: all the more so because it is not mentioned in any of Asoka's inscriptions, and rests on the authority of the two Ceylonese chronicles and Buddhaghosa.[34] Vincent Smith,[35] Eliot,[36] and Havell [37] accept the Council as probably historical. According to the tradition, the occasion for calling the Council was the fact that many heretical or utterly irreligious persons, for the sake of enjoying the advantageous lot held by Buddhist monks under Asoka, had joined the Order, and by their loose lives and impure faith were bringing the Sangha into disrepute. The Council, presided over by the very venerable Tissa Moggaliputta, is said to have purified the Order by driving out these unworthy members, established the true doctrine, and fixed the canon. That it fixed the Pali canon as we have it today is certainly not the case, but it may well have recognized definitively the canonicity of the older books.

Tissa, the presiding officer, is said to have written the Katha-vatthu, as a kind of compendium of the theoretical conclusions established by the Council and a refutation of

[32] *Hinduism and Buddhism*, III. 5.

[33] *Ibid.*, p. 3.

[34] Mahavamsa V. Buddhaghosa's account will be found in Aung and Mrs. Rhys Davids' translation of the Katha-vatthu (*Points of Controversy*, London, Milford, 1915), pp. 1-7. There is no translation of the older Ceylonese chronicle, the Dipavamsa.

[35] *Op. cit.*, p. 169.

[36] *Op. cit.*, I. 271.

[37] *The History of Aryan Rule in India* (London, Harrap, 1918), p. 96.

the false positions held by the heretical sects. At this time—and for a thousand years thereafter—some eighteen sects were recognized, to which, from time to time, still others were added. The points of disagreement were seldom of a philosophical sort and even then were not often fundamental. On matters of theory the sects of Buddhism kept pretty closely together, or where they diverged it was most often on what seem to us hair-splitting distinctions. Much subtle thinking and discussion went on during Asoka's reign and during the centuries that followed it, and this resulted in the writings known as the Abhidhamma, the third part of the canon, in which the scholastic mind had full sway. The tendency of most of the schools was toward the refinements of analysis, and the majority of the schools (though by no means all) developed the Anatta doctrine not only into an absolute denial of a real self but into a "radical pluralism" which analyzed all things into elements known as "dharmas."

> The conception of *dharma* [according to Stcherbatsky] is the central point of the Buddhist doctrine. In the light of this conception Buddhism discloses itself as a metaphysical theory developed out of one fundamental principle, viz., the idea that existence is an interplay of a plurality of subtle, ultimate, not further analyzable elements of Matter, Mind, and Force. These elements are technically called *dharmas*, a meaning which this word has in this system alone. Buddhism, accordingly, can be characterized as a system of Radical Pluralism: the elements alone are realities, every combination of them is a mere name covering a plurality of separate elements. The moral teaching of a path toward Final Deliverance is not something additional or extraneous to this ontological doctrine, it is most intimately connected with it, and, in fact, identical with it.[38]

While the conceptual side of the religion was undergoing this development, the cultus and the more popular forms of belief did not remain unchanged. The reliefs on the stone railings of the Bharut and Sanchi topes, though they have no representation of the Buddha, present us with a rich variety of demigods and demigoddesses, fairies and genii, borrowed largely from Hinduism, or rather the common possession of all Indians. These great topes were erected by pious Buddhists during the second century B.C. and show how

[38] *The Central Conception of Buddhism and the Meaning of the Word Dharma* (London, Royal Asiatic Society, 1923).

large a part mythology played in the religion of the Buddhist masses at that period. In the commentary to the *Psalms of the Sisters*, which, though written in the fifth century A.D., consists almost entirely of much more ancient stories, reference is several times made to forms of worship which surely would have won the disapproval of the Founder —such as making a golden *tee* or umbrella as an offering to the shrine where some of his relics were buried, or offering flowers to a former Buddha and gaining merit thereby.[39] For by this time the many Buddhas who had preceded Gotama had begun to occupy a large place in the thought of the faithful and to enjoy a growing cult.

But to return to the outer history of Buddhism at the point where we dropped it. The great Asoka died about 230 B.C. and his dynasty was overthrown about 182 by the commander-in-chief of the army, Pushyamitra by name, an ardent partisan of the Brahmanic religion and an equally ardent foe of Buddhism. Under the dynasty which he founded Buddhism was at a disadvantage. It is possible that the tales of persecution recorded by late Buddhist writers were unfounded, but it is plain that a religion so largely monastic as Buddhism was at that time must have suffered considerably when a hostile ruler took the place of an ardent devotee.[40]

It was fortunate for Buddhism that only a few years after the overthrow of Asoka's dynasty a new defender of the faith appeared in the northwest. This was the Greek King Menander, whose difficult name the Indians approximated as nearly as they could by calling him Milinda. Several of the Greek rulers of Bactria (by this time largely colonized by Greeks) had, before Milinda's time, invaded northwestern India; and if we may trust Hindu tradition he pushed his conquests to the gates of Pataliputra, the ancient capital of Magadha, and was stopped only by Pushyamitra.[41] Milinda is of interest to us not because of his conquests but because of his devotion to Buddhism, and also because of the famous

[39] See Mrs. Rhys Davids' version of the Psalms, pp. 22-27.

[40] See Kern's discussion of the subject in his *Histoire du Bouddhisme dans l'Inde*, II. 380-83.

[41] See Vincent Smith's *Oxford History of India*, p. 118; and "The Indian Empire" section of the *Imperial Indian Gazetteer* (Oxford, 1909), II. 287.

and illuminating conversations he carried on with one of the ablest of Buddhist scholars and thinkers, the great Nagasena.[42] During his reign Buddhism spread rapidly in the northwestern regions, Kashmir, Kabul, Bactria—where, in fact, it already had gained a considerable foothold in Asoka's time. In the Deccan (i.e., southern India) also Buddhism had some success from, roughly, the year 200 B.C. onward, as is shown by the Buddhist monuments and Chaitya halls at Karli, Nasik, Ajanta, and elsewhere.[43] In fact, right on till the end of the first century of our era Buddhism seems to have been the popular religion with the upper classes in most parts of central and southern India,[44] in spite of the overthrow of Asoka's dynasty. The influence of Pushyamitra's Hindu dynasty in Magadha, however, steadily told against Buddhism in that region and in the first centuries of our era the center of the religion seems to have been shifted to the extreme northwest. The Græco-Bactrian kingdom of western India was indeed overthrown soon after the death of Milinda, but its place was taken by a new foreign invader, which like its predecessor was easily won over to the young missionary religion of the Blessed One. These invaders were the Kushans, a sub-division of the Yueh-Chi nomads. The greatest of their kings was Kanishka, whose exact date is still a puzzle, but whose reign seems to have fallen somewhere in the first or second century A.D.[45]

Whatever his date, King Kanishka was a liberal patron of Buddhism, whether from religious or political motives is not plain. Though not sharing the great Asoka's undivided

[42] Reported in the Milindapanha, trans. by Rhys Davids (*The Questions of King Milinda*) in *S.B.E.*, XXV, XXXVI.

[43] See Fergusson's *History of Indian and Eastern Architecture* (London, Murray, 1876), Book I, Chap. V, Kern *Histoire du Buddhisme dans l'Inde*, 388-89. A description of the present condition of some of these cave temples will be found in Dey's *My Pilgrimages to Ajanta and Bagh* (London, Butterworth, 1925).

[44] This is indicated by the numerous Buddhist monuments and inscriptions of this period as compared with the Brahmanic monuments of the same centuries. Cf. Eliot, *op. cit.*, II. 69.

[45] Vincent Smith dates Kanishka's accession at approximately 120 A.D. (*Oxford History of India*, p. 130; *Early History of India*, 4th ed., pp. 271-74). Eliot says, "At present the majority of scholars place his accession at about 78 A.D.," and he seems inclined to accept this date. Stael Holstein puts it later than Vincent Smith, while some put it as early as 58 B.C. See Eliot's *Hinduism and Buddhism*, II. 64. His dominion included Kabul, Kashmir, Gandhara, and a large part of western India, and toward the close of his reign he seems to have conquered Khotan, Yarkand, and Kashgar, taking them from China.

loyalty to Buddhism,[46] he was exceedingly generous toward the official representatives of the faith, and he followed Asoka's example by holding a Council, the Fourth General Council if we accept Asoka's and its two predecessors as historical. By this time the new kind of Buddhism known as Mahayana, or "Greater Vehicle" was gradually forming, and the contrast between it and the more conservative Hinayana, or "Lesser Vehicle" was beginning to be felt. Kanishka's Council was called to straighten out, if possible, some of the difficulties thus produced and some of the disputes between the eighteen older sects, and to settle certain questions about the canon. The Sarvastivadins, a Hinayanist sect, seem to have dominated the Council; but it is recognized by the Mahayanists of Tibet and China, and quite disregarded by the Hinayanists of Ceylon, Burma, Siam, and Cambodia.[47]

The technical questions to which this Council of Kanishka's gives rise are many and difficult, but fortunately we need not enter upon them. It is sufficient for our purposes to note that the Council was a fairly successful attempt to harmonize various schools of Buddhist thought and practice, and that apparently both Hinayanists and Mahayanists were represented in it.

The two schools continued to develop side by side in many parts of the land for several centuries. Particularly in the mountainous regions of the northwest were they successful in making new converts. When about 400 A.D. the Chinese pilgrim Fa-Hien made his way through the Gobi desert and across the Palmirs to northwestern India, he very early came upon regions that honored the Dharma. The first of these he met with, which he calls the country of Shen-shen, supported some four thousand Buddhist monks "all of the Little Vehicle," and much the same situation he found in the next stage of his journey. In Khotan, where "all without exception honor the Dharma," the monks (who "number even several myriads") principally belonged to the

[46] Many of Kanishka's coins have been found, and though the Buddha is honored on some of them, many of the others bear the images of Greek, Persian and Indian deities. See Vincent Smith, *Oxford History of India*, pp. 131-32.

[47] The principal source of our knowledge of Kanishka's Council is Hiuen-Tsiang—in Beal's trans. (*Buddhist Records of the Western World*, London, Trübner), I. 151-56. For further discussion of the questions involved see Kern, *Histoire du Bouddhisme dans l'Inde*, II. 391-97, and Eliot, *op. cit.*, II. 78-82.

Great Vehicle.[48] Further south, in Udyana, he found five hundred monasteries, all belonging to the Little Vehicle without exception.[49] And so his account continues, throughout his description of the various Buddhist communities in India proper, though in some places he finds monks belonging to both systems dwelling promiscuously together.[50] On the whole the picture of Indian Buddhism which one gets from Fa-Hien shows the Hinayana still enjoying a larger following than the Mahayana but the Mahayana rapidly overtaking the older form of the faith.[51] In the sacred region where Buddhism was born, from Sravasti, through Kapilavastu (= Kapilavatthu) to Kusinara, along the base of the mountains in the north of Oudh and of western Bengal, there were many deserted Viharas. Especially round Kapilavastu the country was a great desert where few people were met with on the roads "for fear of lions and white elephants." [52] But except for this region Buddhism on the whole was in a most flourishing condition in all the parts of India that Fa-Hien visited. The Guptas, to be sure, who ruled most of northern and central India from 320 to 480, were Hindus, and during their dominance there was a decided revival of Hinduism,[53] but the kings of this dynasty, especially the earlier ones, were tolerant, and Buddhism seems to have reached the height of its popularity during their rule. Like most things Indian it suffered somewhat from the invasion of the Huns, who dominated many parts of the northwest from 480 to 530; but the immediate effect of their depredations does not seem to have been very striking. At any rate, the Chinese pilgrim Sung-Yun, who traveled through this region in 518-21, gives us a picture in which Buddhism is quite as thriving as it was in Fa-Hien's time.[54]

[48] See Chaps. II and III of his Fo-Kwo-Ki. In Legge's trans. (*Fa-Hien's Record of Buddhist Kingdoms*, Oxford, Clarendon Press, 1886), pp. 12-16; Beal's trans. in the Introd. to his *Buddhist Records of the Western World*, pp. xxiii-xxv.

[49] Legge, Chap. VII.

[50] *Idem*, Chap. XVII. Cf. also Chap. XXXVI.

[51] Cf. also Kern, *op. cit.*, II. 439.

[52] Chap. XXII.

[53] See Havell's *History of Aryan Rule in India*, Chaps. X, XI.

[54] See his account of his travels, trans. by Beal in the Introd. to his *Buddhist Records of the Western World*, pp. lxxxv-cviii. Apparently the anti-Buddhist propensities of the invading Huns had little influence on the mass of the population. The ceremonious Chinaman seems to have been more struck with the bad manners of the

The next picture we get of Indian Buddhism, however, namely, that given us by the great pilgrim Hiuen-Tsiang (629-45) shows us plainly that the religion had reached its acme either during Fa-Hien's time or shortly after, and was rather rapidly starting down the decline. In Magadha, to be sure, it was still prosperous [55]—possibly even more prosperous than during Fa-Hien's visit. This is probably to be accounted for in part by the natural strength of the religion on its native soil and also by the encouragement given it by the Emperor Harsha (606-47), who became a Hinayana Buddhist during his reign and was converted to the Mahayana by Hiuen-Tsiang himself.[56] But a comparison of the accounts of outlying regions given by Fa-Hien and Hiuen-Tsiang shows unmistakable and rather striking signs of rapid decay.[57] The northwest, once the stronghold of Buddhism,

Huns and especially of their king than with their paganism. "Their rules of politeness are very defective," he tells us; and on one occasion he undertook to read a lecture on the subject to the King himself.

[55] Asoka's capital, Pataliputtra, however, had sadly decayed, and Hiuen-Tsiang found only two or three monasteries where there had been several hundred. See *The Life of Hiuen-Tsiang* by his disciple Hwui-li, trans. by Beal (London, Kegan Paul, Trübner, 1911), p. 101.

[56] Hiuen-Tsiang not only converted King Harsha (who is always referred to in the Life of Hiuen-Tsiang by his title Siladitya-raja); at a grand *mela* held by the King, the Chinese scholar displayed a series of theses in support of the Mahayana which he was willing to defend against all comers. As no one dared to debate with him or dispute his position, he converted large numbers of learned Hinayanists. See the *Life,* pp. 175-81.

[57] Notably in Gandhara, Takshasila, and Kashmir. Cf., e.g., the following passages descriptive of Udyana (the region north of Peshawar on the Swat river): (1) "The religion of Buddha is very flourishing. In all they have five hundred Sangharamas [monasteries]. They belong to the Little Vehicle without exception" (Fa-Hien, Chap. VIII). (2) "The King of the country religiously observes a vegetable diet; on great fast days he pays adoration to the Buddha both morning and evening. . . . In the evening the sound of the convent bells may be heard on every side, filling the world. The earth is covered with flowers of different hues which succeed each other winter and summer, and are gathered by the clergy and laity alike as offerings for the Buddha" (Sung-Yun, Beal's trans., p. xciv.) (3) "They practise the art of using charms. They greatly reverence the Dhamma of the Buddha and are believers in the Great Vehicle. On both sides of the river there are some 1400 old sangharamas. They are now generally waste and desolate: formerly there were some 18,000 monks in them, but gradually they have become less, till now there are very few. They study the Great Vehicle; they practise the duty of quiet meditation and have pleasure in reciting texts relating to this subject, but have no great understanding as to them" (Hiuen-Tsiang III. 120 of Beal's trans.). Concerning Gandhara Fa-Hien says merely, "The people of this country mostly study the Little Vehicle" (Chap. X). One hundred and twenty years later Sung-Yun found it in possession of the conquering Huns whose King "did not believe in the Law of the Buddha but loved to worship demons. The people of the country had a great respect for the Law of the Buddha and loved to read the sacred books when suddenly this king came into power who was strongly opposed to anything of the sort" (Beal's trans., *op. cit.,* p. c.). About one hundred and fifteen years still later Hiuen-Tsiang says of this region and its people: "The disposition of the people is timid and soft. Most of them belong to heretical schools; a few believe in the true

was rapidly forgetting the Tathagata. All over the north Hinduism was coming back into its own, and the rather precarious foothold which Buddhism had been able to gain in the south was being lost to Jainism. It is interesting to note that the two great divisions of Buddhism seem to have suffered about equally in the general decline. In fact, if we may trust Hiuen-Tsiang's rather incidental figures, there were still many more Hinayanist monks than Mahayanist.[58] It should be said in this connection, however, that judging from the pictures given us by the Chinese pilgrims, the Hinayana of these centuries in India was less pure than of old, and was being largely colored by Mahayana practices, if not by Mahayana philosophy,[59] and furthermore that the Mahayana had probably greater strength with the laity than had the Hinayana, and this strength of course is not shown in Hiuen-Tsiang's figures.

The last of the Chinese pilgrims who have left us descriptions of Indian Buddhism is I-tsing, who was in India and Sumatra from 671 to 695. In the interval between Hiuen-Tsiang's visit and his own, things seem to have gone from bad to worse. The pilgrim himself is conscious of the fact and bemoans the decaying state of the religion that he loves.[60] At the close of his narrative the curtain falls on India, or at least a veil falls between our eyes and it, through which we can see only the general tendencies, with now and then some

Dharma. There are about 1000 monasteries which are deserted and in ruins. They are filled with wild shrubs and solitary to the last degree. The stupas are mostly decayed. The heretical temples to the number of about one hundred are occupied pell-mell by heretics" (p. 98).

[58] Eliot has tabulated Hiuen-Tsiang's figures as to Buddhist monks in India, with the following results: Hinayanist, 96,000; Mahayanist, 32,000; students of both systems or residents of monasteries where both were permitted, 54,500. On this Eliot significantly comments: "Some writers speak as if after one era Mahayanism was predominant in India and the Hinayana banished to its extreme confines such as Ceylon and Kashmir. Yet about 640 this zealous Mahayanist states that half the monks of India were definitely Hinayanist, while less than a fifth had equally definite Mahayanist convictions," *op. cit.*, II. 101.

[59] In the Mathura region, for example, where in Fa-Hien's time there were many monks and nuns of both the Hinayana and the Mahayana, "the Bhikshunis principally honor the tower of Ananda; the Sramaneras mostly offer to Rahula; the masters of the Abhidharma offer to Abhidharma; the masters of the Vinaya offer to the Vinaya. Men attached to the Mahayana offer to the Prajnaparamita, Manjusri, and Avalokitesvara." Fa-Hien, Chap. XVI. For a summary of the conditions of Indian Buddhism in Hiuen-Tsiang's time see Watters, *On Yuan Chwang* (London, *J.R.A.S.*, 1904), I. 161-68.

[60] See his *Record of the Buddhist Religion as Practised in India and the Malay Archipelago*, trans. by J. Takakusa (Oxford, Clarendon Press, 1896).

striking fact. Harsha, the Buddhist emperor, had died a quarter of a century before I-tsing's visit, and for many centuries thereafter India was in a process of political disruption, during which Buddhism continued steadily to decline. In its home land, Magadha, to be sure, much was done for it by a new and loyal Buddhist dynasty, the Palas, which ruled from 730 for four or five centuries, and the inscriptions indicate a revival in the religion from the eighth to the tenth century.[61] But outside of Magadha the decay of Buddhism proceeded with notable rapidity. Most of the Indian rulers were Hindu, and Hinduism seems gradually to have absorbed Buddhism. In the Deccan, Buddhism had nearly ceased to exist by the year 1000.[62] It was approximately in this year 1000 that the last attack upon Buddhism began, which was to give it its *coup de grâce.* This was the invasion of India by the Moslems. The first serious incursion in the northwest was begun in the year 1001 by the zealous and able soldier Mahmud of Ghazni, and he kept up his work of conquest and plunder for a quarter of a century. What Buddhist monasteries were left in the northwest were probably destroyed by his hosts of iconoclasts, who felt themselves commissioned by Allah to enforce the first and second of the Mosaic Commandments. In all the western region conquered by Mahmud, however, there seems to have been but little living Buddhism to destroy. It was during his reign that the distinguished Moslem scholar, Alberuni, visited the Punjab and made a careful study of Indian philosophy and science. He was a man of great intellectual curiosity and liberality of thought, and has left us a book descriptive of India and its peoples. He has much to say of Vaishnavism, which he found very strong in the regions he visited, but he hardly so much as mentions Buddhism.[63]

Mahmud's example was followed by other Mohammedan warriors from the northwest; and in the year 1193 Magadha, the last stronghold of Buddhism, fell before their swords. After this Buddhism lingered on in various isolated commu-

[61] See Neumann's notes in II. 830-31 of his *Die Reden Gotamo Buddhos,* based upon Bühler's investigation.

[62] According to Eliot there are no traces of the existence of Buddhism in the Deccan after 1150, *op. cit.,* II. 108.

[63] *Alberuni's India,* trans. by E. C. Sachau (London, Trübner, 1910).

nities, especially in Bengal and Orissa. In fact there are still remnants or traces of it in the degenerate worship of a few villages here and there. But the fall of Magadha was really the death-knell of Indian Buddhism; and today there is hardly a vihara or temple worthy of the name Buddhist in all the land of the Tathagata.[64]

But long before the fall of Magadha Buddhism had been carried to all the neighboring countries and to peoples far away by devoted followers of the Blessed One, who had caught something of his missionary spirit and had not forgotten the great command that he gave his disciples:

> Fare ye forth, brethren, for the good of the many, for the welfare of the many, out of compassion for the world, for the good, for the gain, for the welfare of gods and men. Preach the doctrine which is glorious in the beginning, glorious in the middle, glorious in the end, in the spirit and in the letter. Proclaim a life of holiness, consummate and pure.

Thus Buddhism became an exile from the land of its birth, and began that long pilgrimage which we are to trace in the remaining pages of this volume.

[64] I should add that Ceylonese and Burmese Buddhists have recently built a temple in Calcutta and are constructing a vihara at Sarnath.

CHAPTER VII

CEYLON AND BURMA

Asoka's son,[1] the Prince Mahinda, made a happy choice when he determined upon Ceylon as the scene of his missionary labors. A fairer island it is hard to find. Surrounded by the blue expanse of the Indian Ocean, covered and crowded with luxurious tropical vegetation, its central mountains descending in graceful ridges to the foothills and the sea, this emerald in a setting of lapis lazuli shines with almost uniquely radiant beauty. Jungle of magnificent strength and fierceness covers much of the central section, paddy fields stretch up from the coast, spice-trees, rubber and tea and the giant bamboo cover many of the hills, and the white waves wash the shore. Coconut palms, betel palms, Palmyra palms, royal palms, and many another kind whose names have long escaped my poor memory, wave their feathery branches in the spice-laden air, and among them grow the cinnamon, the nut-meg, the breadfruit tree, with the coffee plant and the pepper vine, the bright red hibiscus, the crimson cassia, and the wild acacia whose flower loves every hue from palest lavender to the deepest pink.

At the time of the Emperor Asoka most of Ceylon had been united under the sway of a dynasty which traced its origin to India and whose capital, Anuradhapura, was already a city of some magnificence. Thither the young monk-prince made his way. There are today two routes to Ceylon, one by sea, the other across "Adam's Bridge"—the line of islets which, except for one break of twenty-two miles, connects the main island with southern India. But if we are to believe the Mahavamsa, the Buddhist missionaries made use of neither of these routes but came, in quite modern fashion, through the air. They alighted, so tradition says, on a hill near the capital named Mahintale. Now King

[1] According to the Mahavamsa; Hiuen-Tsiang calls him Asoka's younger brother.

Tissa [2] had started that day on a royal hunt at the foot of the hill. An elk-stag (which was really the deva of the mountain) led him up the hillside and into the presence of the prince-missionary. Mahinda told the king that he and his monks were disciples of the King of Truth, that out of compassion for the Ceylonese they had come from India, and when he had tested the king's intelligence with a few bits of Indian logic, he preached to him and to his courtiers the message of the Blessed One. The king and his company took the Three Refuges, and on the following day Mahinda and his monks were conducted with great ceremony to the capital. Here they instructed the king and his court still farther in the Dhamma and in a short time converted most of the city and a considerable part of the kingdom. His Majesty built for the monks a large monastery known as the Mahavihara [3] to the south of the city, and there many of the new converts who had taken Orders received their training, and there they handed down the orthodox tradition for many centuries. Soon after this vihara was completed, the great Asoka sent as a priceless gift to the new Buddhist land a scion of the sacred Bodhi tree which was still living in his day and which was honored and even "worshiped" (i.e., reverenced) by the emperor and his court. Asoka had a branch of it cut off and sent it, according to a tradition which there is little reason to doubt, in the care of his daughter Samghamitta, who had taken the vows, and who not only conducted the sacred branch to Anuradhapura but there joined in the missionary labors of her brother Mahinda and instituted in Ceylon the order of Buddhist nuns. The sacred branch was planted in the grounds of the Mahavihara and, from the frequent mention of it in Ceylonese history, it seems to have lived to our day and to be the very tree still venerated by the monks of the ancient monastery and by all Buddhist Ceylon. Many relics were also brought from India and for these King Tissa built suitable shrines. For the collar bone of the Buddha the king built the great Thuparama Thupa or Dagoba, which still stands guarding its precious

[2] His full name was Devanampiyatissa, but since the Mahavamsa itself takes liberties with his name we may do as much.

[3] Great Monastery.

relic, probably the oldest dagoba in Ceylon, perhaps the oldest in all the world. So the king filled his capital with stately dagobas for the remembrance of the Blessed One and with wide-spreading viharas for the increasing numbers of the Order. But Prince Mahinda loved best to live in his cell on Mahintale, and there in his sixtieth year he passed into Nirvana, and there a thupa was built over his ashes.

The thupa still stands on Mahintale hill, where a few monks dwell and guard it, surrounded by a wild tangle of trees and vines through which a broad stairway of a thousand steps conducts the pilgrim to the sacred shrine, from the ruins of the ancient capital. From the summit of the hill a broad expanse of forest greets the eye, broken only by the immense dagobas of the city which, after being for a thousand years the capital of the island, and adorned with Buddhist monuments in massiveness second only to the pyramids of Egypt, was at last deserted by men and swiftly overrun by the hungry jungle, until its ruins were rescued, during the last century, by the ax of the excavator.

Buddhism seems to have spread rapidly during King Tissa's reign and for some time thereafter, and has been the national religion of the Ceylonese ever since. It has had its battles to fight, at first against the animism which preceded it, and later against the Hinduism of the invading Tamils who came from southern India and ultimately occupied much of the northern portions of the island. But Hinduism, while it slightly infected Ceylonese Buddhism with some of its external forms, made but few converts and the Ceylonese as a people, though often politically subject to Hindus and Europeans, have been throughout their history very faithful to the religion which their great Saint Mahinda brought them in the third century before Christ.

The form of Buddhism which was brought them and which they have scrupulously maintained is the Buddhism of the Nikayas which we studied in the first five chapters of this volume. The various heretical sects condemned by the Second and Third Councils seem to have secured but little following in the island. Not that the Ceylonese Church has always been of one mind on all points. The Mahavihara, which the writers of the Mahavamsa consider the bearer of the orthodox tradition, had rivals, especially in the Abhayagiri vihara, built and embellished by one of the kings shortly before the beginning of the Christian era. But the differences between these two great centers of Buddhism appear to have been very slight indeed. There are a few traces of Mahayana influence in Ceylon, such as images of one of the Mahayana Bodhisattvas,[4] and references in the Mahavamsa indicate that at certain periods other forms of Buddhism hardly consistent with the pure Hinayana of the *Theras* (the ancient saints) had some following. But these influences were largely superficial and they came to a final end with the synod of 1165, held under the auspices of one of the most powerful of the kings; and since then the Pali Canon has been the one authority in the island.

This does not mean, however, that the Buddhism of Ceylon has always, or even usually, been of the sort that would have won the complete approval of the Tathagata. The Buddhism of Magadha under the great Asoka would hardly have done that; for in the third century B.C. much relic worship and other forms of cult had crept in which the Founder would surely have viewed with sorrow. Asoka himself, if we may trust the Mahavamsa, in his adoration of the Bodhi tree, went to the extent of abdicating his throne in its favor.[5] It was this form of Buddhism with its cult, its beliefs about the supernatural power of relics, its recognition of many Hindu deities as well as with its admirable moral teachings, that came to Ceylon; and the Ceylonese certainly did not reduce the relative importance of its external aspects. King Tissa, following Asoka's example, "worshiped the Bodhi tree by bestowing upon it the great kingship." [6] His example of importing relics and worshiping them was followed by his more pious successors, and in the early part of the fifth century of our era the most famous relic of all, the left canine tooth of the Tathagata, was procured from southern India and came to be, as Eliot calls it, the "talisman of the king and nation." [7] Fa-Hien, the Chinese traveler who visited Ceylon a few years after its arrival, describes an an-

[4] Coomaraswamy in *J.R.A.S.*, 1909, pp. 283-97.
[5] Mahavamsa, Chap. XVIII.
[6] Mahavamsa, Chap. XIX.
[7] *Op. cit.*, III. 26.

nual religious procession in honor of the tooth, from its home chapel to one of the great viharas in the city. The route was lined with "representations of the five hundred bodily forms which the Bodhisattva [Gotama before his enlightenment] had assumed in previous births." As the tooth proceeds on its way, "religious offerings are made to it," and when it reaches the vihara "the clergy and laity all assemble in vast crowds and burn incense and light lamps and perform every kind of religious ceremony both night and day without ceasing." [8] The tooth has continued to hold a place of great reverence in the eyes of Ceylonese Buddhists to this day although the Portuguese claim to have destroyed it in 1560 (and probably did so) and although it was twice presented a few months later to the King of Burma.[9] Plainly at least two "fake" teeth were produced at that time, but whether both impostures were performed by the two rival Buddhist kings, or one by a Buddhist and one by a Portuguese Christian will probably be an eternal mystery.

It must not be supposed, however, that Ceylonese Buddhism was at any time mere externalism. The strict moral rules of the Founder seem to have been pretty faithfully followed, at any rate by the monks, and the work of preaching to the laymen was not forgotten. In Fa-Hien's day a public preaching service was held three or four times a month in the capital; and the virtues of pity and generosity were impressed upon the people through the memorable stories of the Jataka, which have always been very popular in Ceylon. The writer of the Mahavamsa, to be sure, seems interested in recalling only the shining deeds of external munificence of the monarchs, yet at times we can see that the spirit of the Founder still shone on in the hearts of his followers; and in the midst of the recital of the founding of thupas and the bestowal of rank upon the Bo Tree and the Dhamma, we find modest mention of food given to the poor, remedies to the sick, and the earnest preaching of the truth to all classes.[10]

It was shortly after Fa-Hien's visit to Ceylon that the Tamils of southern India began their series of invasions which

[8] Beal's trans. in his Introd. of *Buddhist Records of the Western World*, lxxv-lxxvi.

[9] For an account of the tooth see Tennent's *Ceylon* (London, Longmans, 1860), II. 197-202.

[10] Cf. Mahavamsa, Chap. XXXII.

finally resulted in driving the native dynasty, and to a considerable extent Buddhism, out of the northern part of the island. In the eighth century the capital was moved from Anuradhapura to Pollannaruwa. A short interlude to the steady decay of the old kingdom was the reign (during the eleventh century) of Vijaya Bahu, an ardent Buddhist who not only defended his people from the invaders but purified the Order, and discovering that the apostolic succession, as we should call it, had been broken, sent to Burma to validate the monastic ordination. His successor was even more forceful than he, and at his command a synod was called which put an end to heresy and schism. But after his death the Tamils regained their ascendancy. The Portuguese arrived in 1505 and conquered all the coasts of the island, the native dynasty retaining only the highlands with Kandy as capital. The Dutch succeeded the Portuguese but never conquered Kandy. During the eighteenth century the Order very nearly died out for a second time. The king sent to Siam for a new validation, and ten Siamese monks were despatched from Ayuthia (the Siamese capital) and founded what is now known as the Siamese school. A second and more democratic school of monks was initiated at the beginning of the nineteenth century (known as the Amarapura school) and this got its ordination from Burma. It was just before this that the British ousted the Dutch, and finally in 1815 they put an end to the native kingdom and brought all the island under their sway.[11]

But the national religion survived the monarchy, and though Tamil Hindus are to be found in every part of the island, all the southern section, where the native Ceylonese are in the majority, is still predominantly and intensely Buddhist.[12] Wherever one goes in this really Ceylonese region one finds tiny *pansalas* or monasteries, dagobas, sacred pipal

[11] In writing this account of the history of Ceylonese Buddhism I have depended chiefly on the Mahavamsa, Tennent, and Eliot.

[12] The census of Ceylon for 1921 gives the following analysis of the population:

Buddhists	2,769,000
Hindus	982,000
Christians	443,000
Moslems	302,000
Total	4,496,000

trees, and the lemon-colored robe of the bonze. Beautiful Kandy, with its great temple where the sacred tooth is still kept, with many a spacious monastery in its environs, Matale with its ancient vihara in the cleft of a rock where the great scholar Buddhaghosa is said to have translated the Singhalese commentaries into Pali, Adam's Peak, the highest mountain on the island, crowned with a Buddhist shrine, city temples and remote hermitages, all testify to the hold the ancient religion still possesses. And so Buddhism follows the traveler as he journeys to the very tip of the island, along the coast south of Colombo where for seventy-five miles an almost unbroken palm forest meets the sea, to the town of Galle, with its sleepy old Dutch fort, its little harbor, dreaming of long-vanished sailing ships, its spacious viharas, hidden in the gloom of palm groves, till at last one can go no further and where even Asoka's missionaries had to stop, because there is nothing beyond but the deep blue waters of the Indian Ocean, stretching away to the endless distance, and luring one's thoughts, like the half-suggested hints of the Dhamma, into unmapped spaces and regions unexplored.

Here begins the sea that ends not till the world's end.

But the ships that, sailing from Colombo, round the southern point of the island and turn into the northeast, plow through the shining waves of the Bay of Bengal and reach at last another land to which the missionaries of ancient Buddhism made their way not long after Mahinda and his monks alighted on Ceylon. How and when these first missionaries reached Burma will probably never be known with certainty. The Mahavamsa says that Asoka sent missionaries to "Suvannabhumi," [13] which has usually been taken to mean Burma. A Burmese tradition supports this view. In the opinion of most Western scholars today the Mahavamsa is mistaken, or else Suvannabhumi does not mean Burma. There is much dispute not only as to the date of the arrival of Buddhism in Burma but also on the question whether the Hinayana or the Mahayana was the first to ar-

[13] Chap. XII.

rive.[14] According to Mr. G. E. Harvey, whose *History of Burma* contains the latest, and to me the most persuasive, contribution on the subject, Indians had been drifting into Burma for centuries before Asoka's time, both by sea to Thaton and the coast region of the south, and over the mountains of Assam to the north. They settled among both the Telaings of the coastal region and the Burmese of the central Irrawaddy, and brought with them their civilization which was rapidly taken over by these less cultured peoples. Their religion of course was among the cultural elements which were thus disseminated. This at first meant Hinduism (in the broad sense), but after Asoka's conquest of Kalinga (on the eastern coast of India) and its partial conversion to Buddhism, Buddhist elements began to mix with the Hinduism thus introduced and before long dominated it. Thus the introduction of Buddhism was at first gradual and its extension was slow until the fifth century A.D., when the rise of the great Hinayana center at Conjeveram (near modern Madras) led to a more rapid propaganda. But the Mahayana also drifted in, partly by sea and partly through Assam.

Burma was inhabited in these centuries by four [15] related but distinct peoples: the Burmese in the center, the Shans to the north, the Telaings along the southern coast, and the Arakanese on the west coast. Racially the Burmese and Shans and possibly the Telaings are Mongolian,[16] but culturally they are much more Indian than Chinese. The first unification of Burma as a whole (except for Arakan) was brought about by the conquests of the Burmese king, Anawrahta (1044-77) who made his capital at Pagan, which is on the Irrawaddy about four hundred miles from the coast. The religion of the capital was at this time in the hands of Buddhist priests known as Aris, who seem to have belonged to a degenerate (and probably Tantric and Tibetan) form of the Mahayana.[17] The king, learning that

[14] Geiger in a note on Chap. XII of the Mahavamsa says, "It is a fact that Buddhism reached Burma from China in the Mahayana form and not before the fourth century A.D." Temple in his article "Burma" in *H.E.R.E.* says the same, and so does Taw Sein Ko (quoted in Harvey's *History of Burma*, p. 337). Eliot is much more sympathetic with the view that the first missionaries were sent by Asoka (*op. cit.*, III. 50-51).

[15] Five if we include the Pyus, whose capital was near modern Prome, but who early disappeared as a separate people and were absorbed by the others.

[16] Harvey, *History of Burma* (London, Longmans, 1925), p. 6.

[17] *Ibid.*, pp. 17, 313.

there was a purer form of Buddhism (and one with slighter ambitions for political meddling) at the Telaing city of Thaton on the coast, made war on the Telaings, captured their capital, and brought to Pagan many of the Thaton (Hinayana) clergy and their Pali scriptures. Thus the Hinayana superseded the Mahayana at Pagan and ultimately throughout Burma.

Pagan remained the capital of the country for over two centuries (1044-1287) and all its kings were zealous Buddhists. Too zealous, in fact, for the wealth of the land was spent in the lavish foundation of hundreds of pagodas, at the capital and elsewhere. It was an era of temple building, comparable to that which was going on at the very same time in Europe, and in it both king and people enthusiastically joined. Pagan in particular became one of the great religious centers of the world, and one which for its architectural splendor had few rivals. It has long since been deserted, but the ruins of its nine thousand temples extend for eight miles along the Irrawaddy and for two miles back from it, and present to the traveler a bewildering sky line of upward-pointing pinnacles and immense cathedral-like structures.

The fall of Pagan may have been hastened by the waste of wealth on these costly religious foundations. Harvey writes, "for two centuries Pagan had witnessed the spectacle of a whole population filled with a passion for covering the earth's surface with pagodas, and now she was perishing to the drone of prayer." [18] But two hundred and forty years is a long period for a Burma dynasty, and one may question whether without the enthusiasm for religion which built the pagodas Pagan would have been able to hold her own for more than half that time. The *coup de grâce* was given her by an army of Kubla Khan's soldiers, who having conquered all of China made a foray over the border from Yunan and took the Burmese capital. For centuries after the fall of Pagan Burma was much of the time divided among warring kingdoms, the Shan peoples usually having the better of it against both Burmese and Telaings. All of these peoples, however, were Hinayana Buddhists, and so were the able Burmese Kings of the Toungoo dynasty who reunited Burma

[18] *Ibid.*, p. 63.

(once more with the exception of Arakan) in the sixteenth century, and the equally able kings of the Alaungpaya dynasty who ruled from 1752 to the end of Burmese independence. In 1852 Great Britain annexed lower Burma, and upper Burma in 1886. As the religious history of the country knew but few changes during these centuries, I shall not trouble the reader with the bloody campaigns which these kings carried on, both throughout Burma and against their neighbors, Arakan and Siam, the six terrible sieges of Siam's capital, Ayuthia, and its final destruction at the hands of the Burmese, the murders and torturings of individuals, the turning of the richest lands of Burma into a wilderness and the partial extirpation of the Telaing people, which make Burmese history such painful reading and form such a commentary on the effects of absolute power. One must add also that they form a commentary on the influence of Buddhism, for these cruel kings were ardent Buddhists. To be just, however, we must also remember that the Christian kings of Europe throughout the major portion of the Christian era frequently showed but slight influence of the New Testament. The monks seem to have disapproved of the bloody acts of their pious sovereigns and did not directly share their guilt. In speaking of the cruelty of the kings to shipwrecked mariners, Harvey writes:

> But here as in so much else the harshness of the rulers was mitigated by the humanity of the monks: if the distressed mariner wandered into a monastery he was safe, for the monks would bind up his wounds, feed him, clothe him, and send him as if in sanctuary with letters of commendation from monastery to monastery till he reached Syriam [where the French had a factory], there to await the chance of some passing ship.[19]

There is no evidence that the Burmese as a people were cruel. The cruelty of their kings was the result of arbitrary power. None the less, it is significant that but seldom was any protest made or any public opinion aroused against the monarch's actions on the score of humanity. Buddhism from its beginning has been interested in the salvation of the individual, not in the reform of society; and it is characteristically significant that the Burmese monks should themselves

[19] P. 206.

have refrained from unkindness, should have helped the unfortunate who came their way, but should have done nothing to attack the root of the evil or to rouse a sentiment among the people at large against such abuses of arbitrary power. Shall we lay this lack to the score of Buddhism, or is it primarily and chiefly oriental? If the Burmese had been Christian instead of Buddhist in those days, would they have acted differently? The Christian nations of the West have usually shown more feeling for society, more energy in politics, and more initiative in reform than the Buddhist nations of the East. Is it because they are Christian or because they are Western? I wish I knew!

The actual nature and conditions of Hinayana or Southern Buddhism as practiced today is of much more interest to me personally than its history, and I imagine that most readers will feel as I do. In spite of that, however, I shall treat of present conditions in Ceylon and Burma briefly because on this matter I have already published about all I have to say,[20] and because I mean to say a good deal about the less-known Hinayana lands, Siam and Cambodia, and fear to wear out my readers' patience with repetition. In general, Buddhism may properly be described as in a fairly flourishing condition in both Ceylon and Burma, and more particularly in the latter. One gets the impression that it fills a much larger place in the life of the Burmese layman than in that of the Ceylonese. The monasteries of Ceylon are frequently in very remote regions, appropriate for the solitary meditation of the three or four monks who dwell in them, but difficult of access from the town or village; whereas in Burma they are much more likely to be found near the centers of population, and are in fact located there purposely so that the laymen may come thither for their devotions and the little boys for their studies. Hence it is common to find the Buddhist shrines in Burma frequented much of the time by lay worshipers, while in Ceylon it is usually only on *poya* or preaching days (two or four times a month) that one comes upon laymen in the temples. In Ceylon, in fact, the temples are closed much of the time and the image is often hidden, while the shrine of the Burmese

[20] In Chaps. XVI-XIX of *India and Its Faiths*.

pagoda is open all the day and the image is invariably visible. In Burma, moreover, Buddhism has no real rival; eighty-five per cent of the entire population are Buddhist, and the non-Buddhist elements are chiefly concentrated in Rangoon and on the extreme frontiers. In Ceylon, on the other hand, only sixty-one per cent of the inhabitants are Buddhist.

The form of Buddhism found is about equally pure in the two countries, for while Burma has its *nats*, Ceylon has its *devatas*. These devatas Buddhism took over from the devas of Hinduism. In theory there are said to be thirty thousand of them, but the only ones of much importance are Sakara (the Vedic Indra), Brahma, Vishnu, Ishvara, Siva, and the deva of the Bo Tree. Images of these—particularly of the first three—are frequently found in the viharas, guarding it from evil spirits and attending on Sakyamuni. For it should be said at once that though their aid is frequently sought in prayer, they retain always their subordinate position very modestly and are no more rivals to the Buddha than the saints of Roman Catholicism are to Christ and the Madonna. Corresponding to these are the *nats* of Burma. The nats come not from Hinduism [21] but from the native animism of the land.[22] They were the gods of Burma before the Buddha arrived. But as soon as he came they learned their place as merely subordinate spirits, and they have kept their place very well ever since. The number of nats is uncertain, but there are a great many of them, thirty-seven of whom are of special importance. Like the devatas they hear and answer prayer. The good ones keep away evil spirits (for there are bad nats as well as good) and they are represented in (and on) all the larger monasteries.[23]

The Buddhism of the two countries differs more in ecclesiastical architecture than in creed or custom. The ancient dagobas or thupas of Ceylon are more massive than any Burmese masonry of equal age. But when we come to modern times or relatively recent centuries, the advantage is all

[21] The thirty-seven chief nats, however, are supposed to have some connection with the thirty-three gods of Hinduism.

[22] Some are evidently nature spirits and some are ghosts.

[23] There is an excellent chapter on the thirty-seven nats, with delightful illustrations in color, in J. G. Scott's discussion of "Indo-Chinese Mythology," Vol. XII of the *Mythology of All Races* (Boston, Jones, 1918).

on the Burmese side. A Ceylonese monastery is a pleasant place but has nothing memorable to show from an architectural point of view. A white dagoba built, presumably, over a relic, a semi-sphere of solid masonry, surmounted by a "tee" and usually white-washed, is the central and most sacred of the structures within the compound. Then there are one or two low dormitories, open at the sides—hardly more than a roof supported on columns—and a low tower, reminding one a little of a Lombard campanile. There will be also a small shrine, usually closed, with a Buddha image. A pipal tree, usually of handsome dimensions, completes the equipment of the monastery. The roofs are straight, and most of the architecture is simple, obvious, and in many respects quite western in appearance, so that one carries away from it no distinct or striking impression. A Burmese vihara or pagoda, on the other hand, one can never forget. At the very entrance, or near it, one is greeted by a pair of those monstrous mythological beasts known as lions in lands where lions have never been seen, and which remind one that India now lies behind and that one has entered that series of countries so well called *Indo-China.* Many of the temples or monasteries of Burma (the two functions of shrine and dormitory are usually performed by one large building) give the appearance from the exterior of having many stories, though as a fact they have but one, and this affords the architect opportunity for an elaborate arrangement of roofs and gables in which he delights. Frequently there is a five-story or seven-story tower. The ends of the gables turn upward and end in finials, frequently crowned with gilt tees and from them are suspended little metal bells—the "tinkly temple bells" of Kipling—which in every little breeze sing joyously the praises of the Blessed One. Most monasteries are of teakwood, though a few are built of brick, and like nearly all dwellings in Indo-China, they are usually elevated several feet above the ground, on stilts, with a vacant place beneath, and approached by an ornate flight of steps or (in the case of the simpler *kyoungs* of the jungle) by a step-ladder. On the interior there is one large room with a lofty ceiling, which serves as meeting-place, dining room, temple, and usually as dormitory also, though in the larger kyoungs there may be separate sleeping rooms. The eastern end of the great hall is reserved for the Buddha and his altar, surrounded with offerings of flowers, flags, and candles. The Buddha almost invariably sits there alone: or if there be other images they also are images of the one Buddha, Gotama. The Buddhists believe there have been other Buddhas and that there will be at least one more (Maitreya), but these are seldom represented. Neither does one find the Buddha accompanied, as in Siam, with some of his chief disciples—except, of course, in those cases where his death or entrance into Parinirvana is presented. Most frequently he is seated, though sometimes he stands or reclines.

Both interior and exterior of the monastic building are decorated in high color, with much red and mosaic; large surfaces are covered with minute mirrors which give the effect of shining silver; and there is a surprising and extravagant expenditure of gold-leaf. There is also much carving—especially of friendly nats—and perhaps frescoes, especially of the curiosities of hell.[24]

Beside the monastery there is frequently a small pagoda in the temple compound, or an immense Buddha image in the open air.[25] Sometimes one comes upon a small and simple shrine, in addition to the one in the central monastic hall, with its solitary Buddha image and altar always decked with flowers. Most memorable of all these ecclesiastical structures are the great pagodas, such as those at Prome and Pegu. In particular the great Shway Dagon pagoda at Rangoon must remain in the mind of every one who visits it as one of the two or three most memorable structures in the world. Higher than Saint Paul's Cathedral, its four long stairways bright with flowers and pretty Burmese youths and maids, its bewildering platform halfway up that runs around the gilded dome which is surrounded on both sides with shrines of every shape and size and color and form of decoration, a platform like a street or rather a kind of religious "Midway Plaisance," crowded with orange-robed monks and brilliantly clad, happy, yet reverent, worshipers—well,

[24] The reader will find interesting descriptions of the Burmese monastery in J. G. Scott's *The Burman* (London, Macmillan, 1882), Vol. I, Chap. XIII.

[25] In Pegu there is a reclining Buddha one hundred and eighty-one feet long.

there is no use trying to describe it. Let the reader go to Rangoon for himself; otherwise he will never know what can be done with teak and lacquer and color and gold and bells and carved nats and mysterious Buddhas and joy and reverence.

To build a pagoda is one of the chief means, in Burma, of acquiring merit. Hence many a rich man builds one at his sole expense and "owns" it. Poorer men, or those less devout, may club together to build one, or take up a collection throughout the village, or even board trains and pass the hat among the passengers. Unfortunately no great amount of merit accrues from repairing an old pagoda unless it be one of special sanctity. The result is that Burma is covered with pagodas new and old and in all stages of decay. This gives the stranger the mistaken impression that the present generation is quite inferior in religious zeal to its predecessors. Fortunately for the artistic impression of the land a dilapidated pagoda is often more beautiful than a new one. As Eliot puts it, "A pogoda understands the art of growing old."

In Ceylon there are three orders of monks—or three divisions or schools of the Order—the Siamese, Amarapura, and Ramanya. The first of these, as its name implies, got its ordination from Siam, the second and third got theirs from Burma. The Siamese Order will accept members from only the highest caste [26] (for caste exists in Ceylon as well as in India), while the two other Orders admit any of the three upper castes. The Ramanya is the smallest of the three schools and the most strict, insisting on absolute poverty and refusing to admit Hindu deities. The Burmese monks are of two schools,[27] the Mahagandi, or easy-going, and the Sulagandi, or Puritanical. Both go back to Ceylon for their ordination, thus tracing their succession through Mahinda. The heads or abbots of the three schools in Ceylon are on an equal footing, with no primate, while in Burma a superior for the whole Order is elected by the monks. In both coun-

[26] A schism is threatened at present within the Siamese Order on the question of ecclesiastical government, one section being unrepresented in the governing body and threatening to secede.

[27] There is a small anti-clerical sect of Burmese Buddhists who refuse to recognize the Sangha at all.

tries the higher offices of the Order are elective.[28] There are a few Buddhist nuns in Burma; but in Ceylon they have quite disappeared.

The monks of the two lands differ not much more than do their costumes. In Ceylon their robes are yellow, in Burma orange. In both countries they live a life of simplicity and leisure. In Burma they go the rounds of the village every morning with their alms bowls, even in those monasteries where food is provided by some rich layman. In this case the rice brought back from the begging expedition is given to the poor. In many parts of Ceylon this ancient custom of begging one's food has fallen into abeyance. In both countries the number of monks in a single monastery is usually small, though in Burma, particularly in Mandalay, a large number of Kyoungs may be united in one compound and under the control of one abbot. The larger monasteries in both countries, and some of the smaller ones in Ceylon, are endowed, and receive revenues from lands which they own. In both countries before British times many of the monasteries or "pagodas" owned slaves. The life of the monks in the two countries does not greatly differ, though one sees much less of them in Ceylon than in Burma, and their influence is, I suspect, correspondingly smaller than is that of the Burmese clergy. In both countries the chief attraction of the Order seems to be the desire to assure one's own salvation and perhaps the life of security and leisure which it offers. There is little of the ardent wish to help the world. The reform movement in both lands is primarily a layman's movement. Nor can it be said that any considerable proportion of the monks use their leisure in the pursuit of Buddhist learning. There are learned monks in both lands, but the great majority are decidedly ignorant. In both countries some of the monks read from the Dhamma at public meetings of the laity on full and new moon, in some cases at two other times in the month as well. In both countries they also meet twice a month and recite the Patimokkha or list of rules, as in ancient times. Twice a day,

[28] An interesting account of the election and induction of the new abbot of the Siamese sect in Ceylon—the official announcement to the government, the elaborate procession through Kandy, the speeches, etc.—will be found in *The Maha Bodhi* (of Calcutta) for June, 1925, p. 329f.

at dawn and at bedtime, they assemble before the Buddha and chant some verses in his praise from the Dhamma. In Burma also they have the task of educating the small boys of the near-by village. If they like, they may study or meditate. The life is not strenuous. Still the influence of the monks is said to be considerable—in Burma much more so than in Ceylon.[29] And in both countries they have the respect and the affection of the people at large.

The worship that one sees at the shrines in Burma, whether by monks or by laymen, impresses one—at least it impressed my Fellow Pilgrim and me—as a very real, reverential, and religious act. It is purely individual worship. No priest is there to mediate between the worshiper and the object of his thought, there is no congregational singing or responsive reading, and (fortunate Buddhists!) no "long prayer." A family may come in together, or two or three friends, their happy voices hushed in reverence as they take off their straw sandals and enter the little shrine. Each bears in his hand a flower or a candle. Before the altar, where sits the Buddha on his lotus, they bow, touching the floor with their heads; then seated before him, hands pressed together in the attitude of prayer and holding thus the flower or candle, they recite, half aloud or silently, some Pali verses they have learned from the monk or it may be some petition of their own. Then they may sit a few moments in silence, gazing at the Buddha. The prayer and meditation finished, they place the candle or flower on the altar before the Blessed One, and go back to their work or their play, and, I expect, with a calmness of spirit they did not feel before.

In Ceylon this sort of thing is not so common as in

[29] According to both Nisbet and Fielding Hall the influence of the monks in Burma is a very fine thing. Hall's enthusiasm over them is pretty well known, and the reader who wishes a pleasing picture of the Burmese monkhood would do well to read Chapters X and XI of his *The Soul of a People* (London, Macmillan, 1911). Nisbet is almost as enthusiastic. He writes: "The strong hold which the Pongy (a monk who has belonged to the Order for ten years or more) undoubtedly possesses over his coreligionists in Burma arises mainly from the two facts that his life is, save only in most exceptional cases, one of purity, and that for century after century the monastery has, until comparatively recently, been the only seminary in which the arts of reading, writing, and elementary arithmetic have been taught. Residence in a monastery is no life of mere mock modesty cloaking debauchery and sensuality. It is, even allowing for the relaxation that now exists from the primitive austerities, still a life of self-denial and continence," *Burma Under British Rule* (Westminster, Constable, 1901), p. 147.

Burma, for there the shrines are usually closed except on *poya* days (the four religious days of each lunar month); on those days the shrines are often crowded. But in principle the form of worship is the same in both lands. Both Ceylonese and Burmese, moreover, have home shrines, with a small image of the Buddha and perhaps a picture or two of some event in his life; and before these shrines daily offerings and daily prayers are made.

There is, of course, much that is external in the worship of the Buddhist masses.[30] The most ignorant may perhaps view the Buddha image as a veritable idol and I have been told that some of them pray not only to the image but to the pagoda. They also "worship" the sacred pipal trees found in nearly every monastic inclosure in both lands; only we must remember that "worship" for the Buddhist, and for the Oriental in general, has a different meaning from that which it suggests in our ears. To the Buddhist it means chiefly "pay reverence to"; they would say that we "worship" the flag; and all but the most ignorant know that in "worshiping" the pipal tree they are merely holding it in affectionate regard for having sheltered the Blessed One on that famous night of his illumination. The Pali prayers universally recited before the Buddha are in one sense a matter of form, and sometimes, no doubt, the meaning is unknown to the worshiper who pronounces them. This at one time would have seemed to me a gross case of superstition and externalism. I have since learned that such externalism very often hides from the onlooker a genuine spiritual experience. I remember hearing the voice of a woman in a lonely shrine in Mandalay, shrill and clear and impassioned, with the heart's longing in every syllable, appealing to the Lord Buddha, repeating her prayer over and over, intensely, wildly, filling all the courtyard of the deserted vihara. The prayer was in Pali and very likely she understood not a word of what she said. Not a word perhaps; but she understood the prayer. The seemingly meaningless words, sacred to her since childhood's days, she took and filled with a meaning of her own.

[30] And for that matter of many of the clergy. To most Westerners the veneration of the Tooth seems particularly superstitious. It is, of course, about on a par with the various sacred objects that Greek and Roman Catholicism still venerates in and around Jerusalem. Western admirers of Buddhism can only regret that so many intelligent Buddhists still make so much of it, and of relics in general.

That meaning, perhaps, like the meaning of music, could not have been put into words. But the prayer had a very real meaning for her; it had a meaning even for me; and I am sure if the Lord Buddha was for the moment roused from the mysterious realm of Nirvana—as well he might have been—that he, too, heard and understood that woman's prayer.

Of course many of the laymen make petitions of their own to the Buddha. This, however, is not logically consistent with the orthodox theory of the Buddha's present condition—for he is in Nirvana beyond all touch of change and Samsara. Many of the laymen know this, yet in religious and non-theoretical moments pray to him just the same. If they are careful to retain their consistency, yet wish to make petitional prayers, they will place their requests (as even the monks do) not before the Buddha but before the nats or the devatas. This, however, a monk in Galle told me, has nothing to do with religion. It is a matter of business—one contracts with the devata for his assistance, agreeing that when the requested aid is actually given, one will make an offering to the Buddha and transfer the merit thus acquired to the devata. It is, said he, no more religion than is dealing with the government. Religion has to do with the Teacher.

Some Buddhists pray, that is repeat sacred verses, because, as they believe, the Buddha has commanded that his followers should do so; and if they do so with a pure heart they will receive a blessing in return. In strict theory, however, the intelligent Buddhist prays because of the good subjective effects which the act of prayer produces in his own mind and character. This is, of course, a perfect example of what I referred to in a previous chapter [31] as "subjective worship." A monk in Rangoon said to me, "Prayer and offering are not received by the Buddha in the sense that they have any effect upon him, nor in the sense of being means of procuring anything from him. Their value is subjective purely. A prayer for peace or purity is likely to bring about its own fulfillment, especially if accompanied by the thought of the Buddha as our ideal. The Buddha, indeed, is for practical purposes quite dead, but he is the ideal of what human-

[31] Page 98. For a detailed discussion of the matter see *The Religious Consciousness*, Chap. XIV.

ity might be and of what each of us ought to be. Thus prayer for the enlightened Buddhist is not supplication but mental discipline."

It is said that when, in 1877, Bishop Titcomb, the first British bishop of Burma, went out to take up his duties in that land, he visited a Buddhist temple soon after his arrival and seeing a monk at his devotions asked him, with typically British abruptness, "To whom are you praying and for what?" To which the monk replied with equal promptness, "I am praying to nobody and for nothing."[32]

But there is a third theory of prayer, which, since it is something of a compromise between the subjective and objective views, is perhaps the commonest of all. This universe is governed primarily by the moral law of justice or Karma. Merit can never fail to produce good results. Now though the Buddha cannot—or at any rate does not—hear and answer prayer, it is still true that the repetition of the Buddha's words with reverence and a pure heart are infallible means of acquiring merit and cannot lose their reward. The thing works automatically. Thus your father is ill. You do not make a petitional prayer to the Buddha for his recovery. But you chant sacred Pali verses, or get the holy monks to do so for you, with the mental intention that the merit thus acquired shall be applied to your father's account. It will not infallibly restore his health any more than in Christian theory a prayer to God would do so. But it will infallibly *tend* to do so; and even if his (or your) evil Karma be so great that he dies just the same, your prayer cannot be of no effect, for it will have counterbalanced some of the evil Karma which he or you have acquired.

I need not here go into the various questions of Buddhist belief which have been already dealt with as they appear in the Nikayas and which we must again consider in connection with Siamese and Cambodian Buddhism. Suffice it to say that both Ceylonese and Burmese Buddhists in theory accept the Anatta doctrine in the scholastic sense, as denying all reality to a self.[33] One would expect as a consequence of

[32] Reported by Nisbet, *op. cit.*, p. 89.

[33] Cf. two articles in the *Buddhist Annual of Ceylon* on this subject; one by Ariya Dhamma in the number for 1922, pp. 55-57, the other by C. A. Pereira, in the 1923 number, p. 34ff.

this that they would identify Nirvana with complete death. Many of the more learned monks do this. Such a view carries with it, of course, the conclusion that the Buddha is quite dead; as several monks expressed the thought in their somewhat broken English, "Buddha finish." Not all will agree with this conclusion, however. One learned Abbot told me that Nirvana was like a distant house of which we can see only the outside. What it is like within we cannot even guess; yet we know that it is real. One very well informed layman told me that Nirvana is "eternal comfort," sheer and inexpressible but very conscious bliss.

All are agreed, however, that it is something which no one even approximates in this life; for there are no more Arahants. Not only was I unable to learn of any one who had even heard of the attainment of complete enlightenment within modern times; it is held as a definite theory that there are no more Arahants and that there will be none till the coming of Maitreya, the next Buddha—he who is now awaiting in the Tusita heaven to descend to earth and restore the Dhamma. This, however, will not happen till Buddhism has so degenerated that the Teachings of the Buddhas have been all forgotten. Some of the monks with whom I talked, particularly in Burma, felt that we were already witnessing the decline which the Buddha had prophesied and which is to precede Maitreya's descent to this earth.

Of the Four Noble Truths I heard, as I have already said, less in all the Hinayana countries than I had been led to expect. I heard more of them in Ceylon and Burma than in Siam and Cambodia. The influence of the First Truth is seen occasionally in a certain melancholy among the happy Burmese. This comes out notably in Fielding Hall's books, and I have found traces of it in both clergy and laity. Most of the monks especially with whom I talked assured me that life was dreary and the nothingness of Nirvana far preferable—though one of them added, rather naïvely, that it was difficult for him to remember this fact at meal time. The evil of desire and the necessity of cutting all the ties is of course one of the beliefs that lead men to join the Sangha. The logical and egoistic deduction from this Second Noble Truth is sometimes clearly faced and accepted. During a visit we were making at a vihara near Kandy, while I was examining the Buddha image, my Fellow Pilgrim asked the leading monk some questions about the monastic life and its service to others. He said in reply: "I have mother and father and sisters but leave them all to themselves and think of myself only and my salvation. I have to think of my own salvation only and not somebody else's. You have mother and father and sisters? Leave all to themselves and think only of yourself, pay no attention to them. If you get rid of lust, anger, and ignorance you will have happy life. To love your husband or your father very dangerous. If you live pure life without attachments you will be young and good-looking when you will attain eighty or hundred years. If I live good life I will be young and well with no infirmities when I get old."

Since I have brought in this representative of the more selfish side of Buddhism, I ought to say a few words about one who stood for its more generous aspect, even at the risk of repeating what one or two of my readers may possibly have read in *India and Its Faiths*. This man was a upasaka—a layman who on poya days keeps three of the five additional Precepts of the monk, and who every day seeks to keep the first five Precepts in generous fashion. Thus the first Precept, not to kill, he takes in the positive sense of earnestly wishing well to every one, of never thinking of any one without good will, and of lending what aid he can to all who need him. The second Precept means to him not merely abstaining from theft, but giving to the needy. It means making offerings at the vihara daily to the Buddha and his monks. Rather unexpectedly it also means non-resistance—if struck the upasaka must not strike back nor retaliate in any way. So at least my upasaka informed me. And the other Precepts are interpreted in an equally large way. It is usually women rather than men that take on them these upasaka vows, but some men do so, and we were certainly fortunate in finding one of them.

It was in fact he who found us. Overhearing a question of mine, in a crowded temple, he offered his services and for three days in succession gave up the major part of his time in assisting us to see the Kandy and Matale monasteries, acting as guide, interpreter, and instructor in Buddhism. He was a teacher, I learned, and his few days of vacation he was spending "as upasaka." For the love of the Buddha as well as the Buddha's peace shone through his face and echoed in his words. Though he made no effort at proselytism, it was evident he longed to bring us both to take our refuge in the Blessed One, so that we too might at the last go with him to Nirvana. Nirvana occupied much of his thought and of his conversation; and to him it meant emphatically a conscious state of endless joy. Much as he longed for it, however, he once said, quite incidentally, "Of course if I could bring my brother to Nirvana by going to hell myself, I should want to do so." He tried to give me his most precious possession, a small sheet of brass on which was etched a seated Buddha. This was a talisman over which two thousand Pali verses had been said by the monks; and he carried it always with him and was convinced it kept him safe. When, before saying good-by, I urged him to let me give him something for the three days' service he had rendered me, he said there was just one thing he would accept: he wished I would write and give to him a note of introduction to strangers in Kandy notifying them that he would like the opportunity of showing them about the town and its environs without any remuneration. When the train was about to carry us away from him he put his hands together in the attitude of prayer and said quite simply, "May Lord Buddha keep you! May devata keep you!" Before we sailed a telegram came from him reading, "May self and lady travel healthily"; and after our return to America we had several letters from him, one of which said: "I will not forget you, gentleman and lady, and that affection will I hope not efface until the last moment, and I pray Sakyamuni [34] and meditate to take the same affection till I, we, attain Nirvana, with my soul. I hope according to Buddha's teachings that we might meet at the same place and attain Nirvana—the everlasting comfort." It is this man's religion more than anything else that most often comes to my mind when I think of

> . . . Ceylon's isle,
> Where every prospect pleases
> And only man is vile.

[34] A common name for the Buddha.

We must not leave Ceylon and Burma without a word or two concerning religious education and the attempts that are being made at reform and propaganda. The influence of subjection to foreign governments long ago broke down the ancient Ceylonese custom of sending all the boys of the community to the viharas for their education. The result of this has been disastrous to the religious training of the young. In the eighties and nineties a movement was begun by the Theosophical Society, under the guidance of Colonel Olcott, to found Buddhist schools, and later on the Maha Bodhi Society took up the work. There are now over 560 of these schools [35] in the southern part of the island, in which boys and girls are given a fair general education and are taught some of the principles of Buddhism—with, of course, more or less of the usual nonsense thrown in which theosophists in the East so often mix with the good things they teach. These schools, of course, are private and the poor who cannot afford to pay tuition send their children to government schools, where they get no religion at all, or to missionary schools where they learn to substitute Christianity for Buddhism. Some poor families send their boys to the monks occasionally for a little religious instruction outside of school hours. Besides the Buddhist schools (which are naturally for the lower grades) there are five Buddhist institutions called colleges [36] in which Buddhism and Pali are taught, and at least one college for the education of monks; and land has just been purchased in Kandy, through the generosity of an American Buddhist lady (Mrs. Mary F. Foster of Honolulu) for an "International Buddhist Seminary," to train youths for the clergy.[37] A movement to open Buddhist Sunday schools, I should add, has also been initiated, and (according to the *Buddhist Annual* for 1925 and 1926) is steadily spreading.

In Burma the ancient custom of using the monasteries as schools has never been abandoned; and though some of the

[35] There are about 1500 Christian schools. I take both these figures from *The Young East* for March, 1927.

[36] Ananda College, Mahinda College, Maha Bodhi College, the Buddhist Girls' College of Colombo, and the Dharmaraja College which "has formulated an ambitious building scheme and has already purchased an excellent site," *Buddhist Annual of Ceylon* for 1923.

[37] *The Maha Bodhi* (of Calcutta) for Feb. 1925.

more progressive families and those who wish their sons to study English and science make use of the government schools, a large part of the population still gets its education from the monks. Here they learn reading, writing, and arithmetic, the fundamentals of Buddhism, and good manners. By the fundamentals of Buddhism I mean at least the Three Refuges and the Ten Precepts. These are contained in the first and second chapters of the Khuddaka Patha, which is the common textbook, and which contains, besides, a list of the thirty-two parts of the body,[38] the sources of happiness (or the Buddhist Beatitudes) to be found on page 48 of this volume, and a few other fundamental Buddhist teachings. Many of the boys learn these (at least in Pala), as well as the Refuges and Precepts. The words are said to be remembered better than the meaning, but this may be slander. At any rate, all the Burmese know the Five Precepts, the girls as well as the boys, the old folks as well as the young. Girls, of course, cannot go to the monastic boarding schools, but they get a little religious instruction from the monks at the pagodas. To counteract the alluring influence of the government and mission schools an effort is being made by the Association for the Propagation of Buddhism to found schools which shall teach English and the practical branches as well as the government schools do, and also teach the Buddhist religion. The movement has been slightly successful. The higher education also has received some attention, and a bright boy can now find a place to study Buddhist philosophy and the Pali scriptures without first becoming a monk. Moreover, whether they have studied at government schools or with the monks, almost all Burmese boys go to the monastery at the age of fifteen to spend at least a week, and many stay during the four months of the rainy season. They wear the yellow robe of the novice and in theory take the first steps toward entering the Sangha.

The adult Buddhist gets his religious instruction (if he gets any) by going to the viharas twice a month (a few go four times a month) where the monks read the Dhamma and

[38] This list is used by monks and pious laymen as a basis for meditation, to draw them from the world of sense.

expound it during a large part of the night. They also read the Jataka stories in their homes and go occasionally to a religious drama which performs much the same office of instruction as did the medieval miracle plays. Sometimes a zealous monk announces a special sermon. The preaching consists in reading from the scriptures and exhorting to the Buddhist virtues, with little philosophy and little reference to the Four Noble Truths or to the more abstruse principles of Buddhism.

A new but not very active movement toward religious revival has been under way since the late nineties, in both Ceylon and Burma. The two most important institutions in this revival are the Young Men's Buddhist Association (the Y.M.B.A.) founded in Ceylon in 1898, and the Maha Bodhi Society founded there in 1891. The aim of the former is, of course, to do for young Buddhists what the Y.M.C.A. does for Christians. The objects of the latter are of a more missionary nature. The primary purpose was to rescue the site of the Buddha's enlightenment at Buddh Gaya from non-Buddhist hands; to establish a Buddhist college in India; to revive Buddhism in India; to disseminate Buddhist literature and a knowledge of Buddhism all over the world; and to help in the cause of Buddhist religious education in Ceylon. It has established several educational institutions in the island, has a press in Colombo where it publishes a religious journal in the vernacular, holds an All-Ceylon examination for students in the Buddhist Sunday schools, with prizes for the best students, and in Calcutta it publishes a monthly in English, *The Maha Bodhi.* A branch of the Society has been started in Germany and another in England.[39]

[39] Another society which has at least an elaborate program is the Burma Buddhist Mission. It lists some thirty-seven aims, one of the most important of which is religious education. To this end it has devised a rather original method. It offers the degrees of B.D. (Bachelor of Dharma) and D.D. (Doctor of Dharma) to those who will pass examinations set by the Mission. Its International Field Secretary writes me thus: "There is an Esoteric Department of the Mission to get deserving individuals initiated into the Occult practice of Yogacharya Buddhism corresponding to the self-concentration at the Maggaphalanayana. The Evangelistic Department of the Mission is doing very successful work. The President-Founder of the Mission, a veteran Buddhist preacher of nearly seventeen years' standing, a great scholar of Sanskrit, and an untiring spiritual researcher for the last thirty years, is addressing thousands of people as often as he can. The Evangelistic activities of Sreemati Jeevamba Devi, the first Lady-Member of the Mission, are simply wonderful. Many of her disciples have made large strides on the path of Yogacharya Buddhism. Everyone of them have seen the self-light. Fellows

There are several other societies for the revival and propagation of Buddhism in both Ceylon and Burma.[40] The Ceylonese societies unite every December in an annual "Congress of Buddhist Associations in Ceylon." (The eighth meeting took place in December, 1926.) Several Buddhist periodicals are published in both countries devoted to the interests of reform and propaganda.[41]

It must be said that considering the number of these societies not as much has been accomplished as might be wished. With all the talk of the great need of sending missionaries to India and with the many societies which have been formed for the spread of Buddhism all over the world, not one missionary so far as I have been able to discover has been sent.[42] With a few great and outstanding exceptions, such as the late evangelist and writer, Ledi Sadaw [43] and Mr. Dharmapala, founder and head of the Maha Bodhi Society, most Burmese and Ceylonese Buddhists seem to expend their missionary zeal in founding societies, starting periodicals, and holding meetings. A Ceylonese Buddhist writing recently of the foundation of a new religious periodical in Colombo by some enthusiastic young Buddhists adds the comment: "One only hopes that their enthusiasm is not

of the Mission who are increasing in number day by day, are doing a little bit of evangelistic work in their own way. There is the Dept. of Education of the Mission, which promotes the study of comparative religion by holding examinations for degrees in Dharma. There is the Department of Publicity carrying out the publicity work of the Mission in a vigilant manner. Much propagation work is done by this department. The enrolment of Fellows of the Mission, Trustees of the Mission Fund, Members of the Mission, sermons to masses and groups of individuals, prayer-meetings (rather Bodha-meetings), the establishment of Bodhasalas, the opening of branches of the Mission, the advancement of the knowledge of Dharma, the Dept. of Conversions, and the pushing up of Publicity work in various ways, etc., etc., are the means by which the ends of the Mission are being achieved from day to day."

[40] E.g., in Ceylon the International Buddhist Brotherhood, the *Banddharakshaka Sabha,* the *Dharmadutha Sabha,* the Servants of Buddha, the *Kulangana Samitiya* (an association of Buddhist women for the purpose of looking to the religious education of Buddhist girls) and (very remarkable) a Young Bikkhus Association, which it is hoped may do something to wake up the clergy. In Burma there is, or was, an Association for the Propagation of Buddhism, a Mandalay Society for Promoting Buddhism, a Rangoon College Association, the Burma Buddhist Mission, an Asian Buddhist Mission, and I know not how many others.

[41] The most important of these periodicals in Ceylon are the *Sinhala Baudhaya* and the *Buddhist Annual* (of Colombo)—perhaps the best known in Burma are the *Ledi Religious Instructor* and the *Pivot of Buddhism* (both published in Rangoon).

[42] Ceylonese and Burmese monks, making pilgrimage to Buddh Gaya or Sarnath, sometimes preach on their way through the country. But I know of no permanent and regular missionaries, such as Japanese Buddhism sends out.

[43] He died June 27, 1923.

of the variety that usually soon pegs out."[44] The presiding officer of the Congress of Buddhist Associations in Ceylon recently remarked in his presidential address, "The Congress of Buddhist Associations has become a social gathering of Buddhist workers, the opportunity being made use of for passing several resolutions expressing many pious hopes."[45]

Every one who has the cause of religion and of moral living and human kindness and good will at heart should wish well to the Buddhist reformers in their efforts at deepening the religious life of their countries. The Buddhism of Ceylon and Burma is, indeed, not all that one could desire, and is far from what the Founder would have desired. But taken in the large and as a whole, the blessing it has brought to these fair lands is quite immeasurable. So at least my Fellow Pilgrim and I felt as we sailed away from Ceylon with its mountains and its palm groves and its quiet viharas hidden deep in the forest. So we felt as we sailed down Burma's great river, the Irrawaddy, for a thousand miles between flowering forests and banks crowned with golden pagodas, from Bahmo to the sea.

[44] *Young East* for May, 1926, p. 399.
[45] *Maha Bodhi* for March, 1924, p. 122.

CHAPTER VIII

THE EXTERNAL ASPECTS OF SIAMESE BUDDHISM

THE Gulf of Siam forms an appropriate and beautiful gateway between the lands of Southern Buddhism. Adjacent to the seas that border Burma and Ceylon, and washing the coasts of both the other Hinayana countries, it seems to have absorbed something of the calm, something of the spirit of the great Indian Teacher; and I wonder if there be not, in some hidden page of Buddhist literature unknown to me, a story of his laying his command of peace upon this sea, so that its waves and winds have ever since obeyed him. At any rate, the typhoons, which visit the adjacent China seas in every month of the year with deadly effect, have seldom been known to venture into the Gulf of Siam, and the great mass of Indo-China, interposing its miles and its mountains, has completely cut off from these waters the north-eastern monsoon, which for so large a portion of the year blows a steady gale on the coasts of Annam. One day of golden light and of blue sky and water follows another, as the merchant or the tourist—or the coolie or the pilgrim—sails over its mirror-like waters, without a wave for miles and miles "except the jiggle from the screw."

The sunsets on the Gulf of Siam are justly famous. I remember one—which I think I shall hardly forget—of turquoise sea stretching north and south to the illimitable horizon, while directly to the west, between ship and sun there was a bank of cloud that seemed surely not more than three or four miles away. It was like an island, there, so close by that I could have sworn one could row out in no time in a little boat and land upon its gravelly shore. Only it was no ordinary isle, this; rather one of the Islands of the Blest, lying there in the Western Paradise, all effulgent with lavenders and golds, until the sun, setting beyond it, shot some of its last rays through the island's solid base and poured rose leaves and then red blood over all its coasts. And when scarlet and purple, gold and blue, had faded, through all the scale of opalescent hues to dull grays, there came suddenly a sign of tremendous conflagration at the opposite pole, just beyond the eastern horizon, as if all Cambodia were in a blaze. It grew redder and brighter; and then we saw the ancient moon, lopped off into a fantastic oblate, rise dripping from the sea.

There is nothing sudden or dramatic about one's first sight of Siam. Long before land is seen one is prepared for it by the change in the sea's color, from blue to the tawny brown of the muddy Menam. Small floating islands of greenery sail past the ship, following an invisible current, and the narrow green line of the land comes into view so gradually that one hardly distinguishes it at first from the familiar sharp horizon of the sea. Then one sees it clearly, the green line of the low-lying coast and the low-growing forest. Small sailing ships are seen in increasing numbers, many modern-looking Siamese boats, and a few ancient junks from southern China, much more picturesque with their strange broad and rounded sails, patched with incredible care, and as one nears the shore, small sampans, propelled by nearly naked oarsmen, the big one standing in the stern, silhouetted against sea and sky, looking like the king of the Cannibal Islands. The Gulf of Siam now rapidly narrows, the pilot is taken aboard, and we are in the broad mouth of the Menam, which winds through flat country some forty miles between Bangkok and the sea. The thicket comes down to the water's edge—a forest of palms and bamboos and creepers, eagerly bathing their feet in the brimming river. Now and then one passes the mouth of a canal or a salt creek flowing into the stream and giving one a momentary and tantalizing vista into the heart of the tropical jungle. The river narrows, and one gets a more intimate view of its banks. Natives rush down on the approach of the ship to haul in their large fish nets, naked children play in sampans and on the shore, Siamese huts of the ancient and national model stand on stilts, with canals on three sides of them and the river on the fourth, being thus surrounded by water on all possible sides but one. A palm tree peeps out at us over the roof of the house, a bamboo thicket stretches beyond it, and a grove of banana trees lines the water's edge. Farther on the sharp point of a pagoda attracts the eye, and standing near it the typical double roof of the Siamese wat, where the monks in their bright yellow robes chant to the Buddha every night and morning. Then more palms, more houses, more Siamese half asleep in their sampans or basking in the warm shade of their open porches.

The Siamese like to bask. They are an intelligent race who know what they want, and who have not as yet been persuaded by either Europeans or Chinese that they want something quite different. "Better is a dinner of herbs where love is, than a stalled ox and hatred therewith," says King Solomon; and the Siamese agree with him. Better a coconut and a few bananas and a long nap than all the "comforts" of "civilization" with no leisure to enjoy them. We are doing our best to convert them from their heathen point of view and to bring them to a realizing sense of a thousand artificial needs, but as yet with relatively slight success. A fair amount of work in his own paddy field the Siamese is willing to do; but he does not care to hire out as a laborer in other people's vineyards nor on other people's railroads, nor to bother his brains with shopkeeping and commercial enterprises; and since no end of Chinese coolies and Chinese merchants can be imported to do all these difficult and uninteresting things, he is very content to let them come. Unnecessarily hard work is well enough for those who like it; for his own part, he prefers to be, in the country a small but independent proprietor, or in the city either an official or one of the nobility. He and the king are of one mind about the desirability of officials. The nation of Siam is very carefully run. There are officials to do everything you can think of, and supervisors to see that they have done it, and secretaries to make a note that it was done. The best job of all is, naturally, that of being a prince; and Siam—the only absolute monarchy left in these uninteresting days save Abyssinia —has no dearth of princes. The Kings of Siam have not been negligent in their duty in this respect. One of the late sovereigns increased the number of princes and princesses of the blood by upward of a hundred. He is remembered with affectionate gratitude. I think he is called the Father of his country.

But I do not wish to ridicule these likable and very sensible people. Which of us would not be a prince of the blood if he only could? And Siam is notable for many things besides its princes. In the words of a recent American Consul-General at Bangkok:

> Siam is the one officially Buddhist state, the one remaining absolute monarchy, the one nation with an inconvertible paper currency with more than its nominal gold value, the one nation whose national debt is less than five dollars per capita, one of the few nations without strikes, lockouts, unemployment, or Bolshevism and with a large excess of exports over imports, a paying state-owned and state-operated railway system, and a gilt-edged credit in the world's money market. Here is a country with all the charm of the Orient, undisturbed as yet by commercialism or tourist catching: its capital a fascinating city where you cannot find a professional guide or a souvenir shop; a city of wide shaded boulevards and picturesque canals: of red, blue, and gold temple roofs: of swarming native quarters and delightful shops and streets eight feet wide where one may buy all the myriad things that delight the oriental eye and palate and tickle the occidental fancy.[1]

In all probability Buddhism did not come to Bangkok by the route I have been describing. And if I am to say anything of the way it reached Siam and of its history after it got there, it will be necessary for us first of all to get before our minds as clear a picture as we can of the principal peoples of Indo-China. This peninsula, as the reader may know, is divided by Nature into four or five rather sharply distinguishable regions. To the west lies Burma, centering round the valley of the Irrawaddy. Next to it is the valley of the Menam, now belonging to Siam. Parallel to the Menam and still farther east runs the great Mekong, along whose shores dwell the Laos or Laotians in the north, the Cambodians in the middle, and the Chams in the south. The Mekong, like the Irrawaddy and the Menam, follows in general a southerly course, flowing through the whole length of the peninsula, and is cut off from the eastern coast by a long range of mountains. Between these mountains and the China Sea, and reaching all the way from the

[1] James Porter Davis, in the *China Weekly Review.*

mouth of the Mekong to the borders of China dwell the Annamese.[2]

That is the present situation. In the first centuries of our era the Cambodians or Khmers and the Chams occupied or dominated nearly all the territory now comprised in Siam, Cambodia, Cochin-China, and Annam: just as the Telaings (whose capitals were at Thaton and Pegu) occupied and controlled all of southern Burma. The Cambodians and Telaings are thought to have been closely related, and probably had drifted down the river valleys from the northern mountains. The Chams seem to have been of Malay origin. At any rate, these three peoples, in the early centuries of our era, received and adopted the culture and religions of India. Indian merchants and Indian colonists traded and settled on all these shores, bringing with them Hinduism and Buddhism, which were quickly absorbed by all three of these intelligent peoples.

We have seen how the Burmese seized the Telaing capital in 1057 and from that time on steadily gained in power over the civilized southerners. Much the same thing happened in the central and eastern parts of the great peninsula. The unification of the Chinese Empire under the Han and T'ang dynasties had gradually driven out of Yunan and other southern and western provinces of China a people known as the Thai. These people filtered into the mountainous region in the northern part of Indo-China, now known as Laos, and thence spread westward and southward. Those who went west into Burma (and those who remained in Yunan) came to be known as the Shans, and it was these who dominated Burma during the thirteenth, fourteenth and fifteenth centuries. Those who remained in the mountain districts of the north and along the upper reaches of the Mekong are known today as the Laos or Laotians. Finally the third branch of the Thai who drifted down the Mekong and thence over into the valley of the Menam came to be known as the Siamese. The Siamese are thus a Mongolian people, related to the Chinese, and when they came into Indo-China the culture they possessed was presumably derived from China. As yet

[2] For the facts in this and the following paragraphs I am largely indebted to René Grousset, *Histoire de l'Asie* (Paris, Crès, 1921), Vol. I, Chap. III.

they had experienced no direct Indian influence. Yet it is thought they brought a certain kind of Buddhism with them. This Buddhism must have been derived from China; hence must have been either of the Mahayana or of the Tibetan type.

When the Siamese arrived in the region of the Mekong and the upper Menam, the empire of the Khmers or Cambodians was at its height. It had driven the Chams from most of the Mekong valley, and the incoming Siamese were for some centuries subject to them. They were subject to them not only in political but in cultural fashion, for the Khmers were highly civilized. The Khmer religion at this time was Brahmanism and Mahayana Buddhism, and the Siamese must have been considerably influenced by both of these through imitation of the dominant race. In the early twelve hundreds, however, the Siamese won their independence and in a hundred years more had occupied nearly all of the Menam valley. During most of these prosperous years the seat of the most powerful branch of the Siamese was at Sukhothai, on the middle course of the Menam, and this is frequently spoken of as the first capital of Siam. About 1350 the city of Ayuthia was built—or rebuilt—and it gradually supplanted Sukhothai in importance and in the next century became the capital.

In the thirteenth and fourteenth centuries Burma was in a condition of chronic civil war and its power was in eclipse. Hence the Siamese were able to push their influence and sometimes their control as far as Pegu. Even before this they must have come into close contact with the (Hinayanist) Telaings of southern Burma. It is probably in this manner that they first became acquainted with Hinayana Buddhism,[3] which from that time on gradually spread among the Siamese and at length completely supplanted both the Mahayana and Brahmanism. According to A. W. Graham:

> In the ruined temples and timeworn relics with which the whole country is strewn, the ancient coexistence of Brahmanism with Buddhism, and also the gradual supplanting of the former by the latter can without much difficulty be traced. Upon the sites of the oldest cities, bronze statues of various Brahman gods are continually found mingled

[3] Eliot, *Hinduism and Buddhism*, III. 80.

with images of the Buddha. In the less ancient ruins such relics of Brahmanism are almost entirely absent, whilst Buddhist remains are exceedingly numerous. Finally in the modern cities, with the exception of one small section where Brahmanism still holds its own as a distinct religion and in one temple in Bangkok which is the headquarters of the court Brahmans, representations of the Brahman gods are rarely seen, or, if present, are relegated to quite subordinate positions as attendants on, or adorers of, the Buddha.[4]

That not only Brahmanism but Mahayana Buddhism rapidly declined before the Hinayana and that the latter was soon looked upon as the national religion seems to be indicated by the fact that about 1360 the king sent to Ceylon for an abbot or Sangharaja.[5] This prelate brought with him, of course, the validation of the ordination for future Siamese monks, who thus, like the Burmese monks, were thereafter able to trace back their apostolic succession through the Mahavihara of Anuradhapura to Prince Mahinda. Not long after this a branch of the Bodhi Tree and various sacred relics were imported from Ceylon and India.

During this period of prosperity, in the fourteenth and fifteenth centuries, the power of Siam extended not only to the west but still more to the east. Its former mistress, Cambodia, was humbled and seriously weakened; Angkor, the Cambodian capital, was captured and pillaged four times[6] by Siamese armies, and at length abandoned with all the region of the middle Mekong. The fame of Siam as a great Buddhist power was spread abroad, and as we have seen, the king of Ceylon in 1750 sent for Siamese monks to reintroduce valid ordination into the island.

If we may judge by its jungle-covered ruins, Ayuthia must have been a large, magnificent, and intensely Buddhist city. It had four centuries of brilliant life, and was filled by its devout kings and devout population with immense religious edifices and great Buddhas, now overgrown and hidden by the almost irresistible forest. It underwent six different sieges by the Burmese, in three of which it defied their utmost power. In 1564 and again in 1569 it was taken, but

[4] *Siam* (London, Moring, 1912), p. 488.

[5] Eliot, III. 83. Eliot points out that though the King whose inscription related the importation of the Ceylonese prelate was plainly Hinayanist, his religion retained a few Brahman and Mahayana elements.

[6] In 1357, 1394, 1420, and 1460.

in neither case was it seriously damaged. In 1767 it was again captured by the Burmese (all of them good Buddhists, one must recall) and completely destroyed.[7] The Siamese people, however, soon recovered their spirits and most of their power. A new dynasty, the present one,[8] came to the throne in 1782, which has ruled ever since, characterized equally by its genuine patriotism and its zealous yet liberal devotion to the Buddhist religion, in the new capital of the land.

Thus we are brought back again, after a considerable detour, to Bangkok and Buddhism. Even to the passing tourist with no special interest in religion, the one outstanding thing about Bangkok is its magnificent *wats* or temples. The Siamese wat is hard to describe. It is, roughly speaking, a religious enclosure—one can hardly word it more exactly—surrounded by a wall and containing a large number of buildings, small and great, and several other things besides. Its principal axis runs east and west, with the entrance on the east. There is no regular plan, such as is found in Chinese temples, but all sorts of things are clustered together in delightful irregularity, as the exigencies of space, the munificence of donors, or the chances of history have dictated. Thus it comes that no two wats are alike, and the visitor never knows exactly what to expect, but may usually count on finding something unexpected. The simplest form of wat, such as one comes upon in the rural districts, contains one hall for worship and at least one, usually several, pagodas. Almost all wats contain at least two worship halls and a considerable number of pagodas. In the larger wats the buildings and pagodas are multiplied into a bewildering maze, through which the pilgrim wanders in a daze of wonder, and from which plan and system and even the points of the compass at first seem to have been banished. The central hall of worship, which is never lacking in even the smallest wat, is known as the *bot*. It is usually very much of a building and much more like a Christian church than anything you will find in the Burmese or Ceylonese vihara. Here the morning and evening services are held, here the laity come

[7] For the six sieges see Harvey's *History of Burma*, pp. 159, 167, 169, 181, 241, 251f.
[8] The eighth monarch of this dynasty is now (1928) on the throne.

on preaching days to listen to the reading of the scriptures, and here (in most wats) the consecration of young monks takes place. If there are two or more halls in the wat, the bot is distinguished externally from the others by being surrounded, at the four corners and on the four sides, by eight stones carved into the shape of a conventionalized cobra's head, reminiscent of the ancient myth of the cobra protecting the Founder [9] and really significant of the early connection of Buddhist worship with the Naga cult.

The roof of the bot is a very unique construction, one roof apparently having been superimposed upon another, and sometimes a third upon the second, the angularity of the gables being accentuated by long and narrow horns which extend out from the corners skyward. The coloring of the roofs moreover is characteristic. Instead of the brilliant tones of Burmese temples we find here all manner of subdued tints—olives, maroons, tans, and various browns. The gable ends, on the other hand, and sometimes much of the walls are brilliant with colored tiles and gold mosaic. The interior of the wat is frequently very ornate. The lofty ceiling is usually supported by eight or more square columns, which, in common with the walls, are decorated with scenes from the life of the Buddha. Near the middle of the hall is a kind of throne for the preacher, its back toward the altar, and facing a double row of mats which cover all the floor between it and the central doorway. Upon these the lay congregation sit at preaching services. More mats cover the floor between the preacher's throne and the altar, and on these the monks sit (or kneel) at the daily and weekly offices. Beyond them, at the farther end of the hall, is the altar, and rising high above it, the glorious throne of the Buddha, who is thus seated in a position from which he can survey all his worshipers. Around him, on the lower steps of the throne, are sometimes other Buddha images, standing or sitting, all of them images of one and the same historical Gotama, and not, as in China and Japan, images of other

[9] According to the Udana (Chap. II), directly after attaining insight Gotama sat for seven days and nights, with crossed legs, rejoicing in the new-found blessedness. A great storm, with rain and cold wind, raged all through these days, but the Naga King, in order to protect the Tathagata, wound his coils about him seven times and held his hood over the Buddha's head.

Buddhas. There may also be images of two monks, usually worshiping toward the central figure. These represent Moggallana and Sariputta—known in Siam as Mokhala and Saribut—the two most proficient of the Buddha's disciples during his lifetime, and whose names are missing in the list of patriarchs presumably only because they both preceded the Founder into Parinirvana.

The altar, a long table in front of the throne, is piled with offerings of various sorts. Candles in elaborate candlesticks, flowers in most ornate vases, incense and incense burners, gold or gilded images, French clocks, are among the commonest of these votives. The fondness of the oriental for occidental clocks is one of the things which the pilgrim from the west first notices, especially in Siamese and Chinese temples. Being so precious in the eyes of the eastern Buddhists, it is but natural that they should be offered to the Buddha. One finds them on the large public altar, one finds them in the secluded holy of holies. Sometimes they are wound up and going, occasionally they are on time, as a rule they have long since stopped. It does not greatly matter. Presumably the Buddha knows the time without their help. Moreover in Nirvana—and in the true Reality, as the Northern Buddhists would say—there is no time; so perhaps the clock with hands stationary is a more appropriate offering for a Buddhist temple than one kept always wound and always correct to the second.

Besides the bot there is usually a second large hall in the wat compound, much like the bot in structure and contents, but not used for preaching and consecrations and not marked off by the eight cobra-like stones. This is called the *wihan*—the familiar word vihara in its Siamese form. It usually contains some special image of the Buddha, or a considerable collection of images. Besides these buildings there may be a special preaching hall and a number of small image houses or covered corridors, with long lines of seated Buddhas, ranged along the walls facing outward into the court. The pagodas are of any size, from those a few feet high to hill-like structures such as that in the wat Chang, looking down upon the adjacent river from the height of 250 feet, or the even higher wat Sa Ket, crowning an artificial hill in the center of the city. The pagodas are of two types, the commoner called Phra-Chedi, in the shape of a bell and terminating in a sharp point, almost identical in form with those in Burma: the other type borrowed, not from Burma, but from Angkor in Cambodia—Phra-Prang it is called—thicker, less pointed, less Siamese in appearance and ending always with a finial of three crescents set one above another on an upright point and borrowed, I suppose, from the worship of Siva. Less Siamese in appearance, I have called them, for Siamese architecture and sculpture is characterized by its love of exaggerated elongations and sharp points. The favorite Siamese type of pagoda ends in a long needle-like pinnacle: the gable ends of the bots are extended into long and narrow gilded horns: and the head of the Buddha is regularly crowned by a pointed flame, which takes the place of the halo in Indian, Chinese, and Japanese religious art.

This may be as good a place as any to say a few words about the Siamese form of Buddhist images. There are only two, instead of three, common attitudes for the Buddha in Siam, the seated and the standing. Except for a few very large and very special images in some of the temples, the Nirvana of the Buddha is seldom met with. There is one in the wat Po in Bangkok, one hundred and sixty feet long, which therefore ranks well for size with the great Buddhas of Pegu, Rangoon, Nara, and Kamakura. But the regular cult images of the temples and the images for votive offerings and for domestic shrines are all either of the sitting or the standing variety. Between Burmese and Siamese Buddhas there is little difference. The latter have not quite as long ears as have their Burmese cousins, the lobes not touching the shoulders as they so often do in Burma; nor are the fingers regularly of the same length; they vary as do the ordinary human fingers. The hair, as I have said, usually ends in a sharply pointed flame; or if in a knot as in Burma, the knot is usually pointed instead of round. The waists of both Burmese and Siamese Buddhas are much narrower than those of Chinese Buddhas, though not so pinched as those found in Nepalese images. The general effect of the Siamese Buddha when reasonably well done is excellent—at least to one who has any feeling for Buddhas at all. It invariably possesses dignity and frequently impressiveness and the sense of calm for which it supremely stands.

In some respects, one of the most impressive Buddhas I have ever seen is in the ruin of an ancient wat at Ayuthia—though no doubt it owes much of its memorable quality to its setting. The destruction of the ancient capital was very thorough, and what ruins were left were so quickly and completely reclaimed by the jungle that only a few walls and a few pagoda pinnacles still lift their tops over the luxuriance of tropical growth, which, with almost conscious and savage delight, has wound its hundred mighty arms around the little area of which, for a brief period, it was once deprived. The place reminds one somewhat of Anuradhapura; but there has been but slight attempt at any reclamation of the ruins. The most impressive portion of the ancient city centers at one of the large wats. To reach it you must drive or walk through a mile or more of forest to the end of the road, then leaving your gari, follow a footpath for perhaps fifteen minutes that crosses a clearing and plunges into the thicket. Over the mass of greenery you get a glimpse of a pagoda top, then of another, at last of a line of them, and at one point you can count thirteen of these white slender pinnacles still towering above the trees. The vast brick base of some ancient building you pass, and beyond it a turn of the path leads you into a small clearing, from which you view a high brick wall with an enormous breach from base to summit. Through this, as you look inward, you see upon a lofty throne of ancient brickwork, which was once his lotus seat, adorned now not with porcelain tiles and gilt mosaic but with the fresh greenery of the forest, a colossal Buddha. In contrast to the destruction of all about him, the image is in perfect repair. City wall, temple wall, buildings, and the other images all fell before the pillaging Burmese. The protecting devatas with their terrifying faces and enormous arms failed to frighten or deter them. But the great Buddha was untouched. In the front wall of the temple there is a breach as large as that at the side, and through this the Buddha gazes out into the jungle. One cannot help wondering what he sees out there, and what he thinks. That calm face so plainly indicates contemplation and peace. And he has seen so many things these four hundred years that he has sat there: groups of worshipers, following each other as the generations passed; the bristling bands of the Burmese as they destroyed all about him on that tragic day; and since then the quiet desolation of the jungle, the works of man destroyed by man, their ruins going over into the kindly keeping of Nature and disintegrating with slow certainty before her greater force. . . . "Is there anything put together which shall not dissolve? You know what I have told you; sooner or later we must part with all we hold most dear. This body of ours contains within itself the power which renews its strength for a time; but also the causes which lead to its destruction. But you too shall be free from this delusion, this world of sense, this law of change."

What the Ayuthia wats were like in the days of their pride we can imagine by walking through the great wats of Bangkok to-day. Perhaps the most interesting and certainly the largest is the wat Po—a wilderness of buildings large and small, of Phra-Chedis and Phra-Prangs, of outer and inner walls with gateways protected by guardian spirits—at one notable gate the place of the conventional devatas having been taken by gigantic stone Europeans with silk hats. Then there are pipal trees, as in Burma and Ceylon, shrines to the spirits with offerings before them, small bell towers, the schoolrooms, open at the side, for the boys who study at the wat, and just outside the outer wall several long lines of small one-room houses, built of cement, the dormitories of the many monks. The newest of the great wats, the Benchamabopit, is simple in plan, with only one large building besides the school buildings; but it is perhaps the handsomest of all, constructed as it is entirely of white marble, with decorations of gold mosaic on all the eaves and roofs. The great wat Chang across the river is the highest and in some ways most striking, a mass of Chinese porcelain two hundred and fifty feet high, its walls literally covered with plates and saucers, and pieces of broken cups, set there at a time when Chinese porcelain was still beautiful. Most startling of all the wats in the extreme and bizarre shapes of its structures and the brilliant gilding and coloring of its pagodas, is the wat Phra-Keo, adjoining the palace. A wat that I liked as much as any, though unmentioned in the guide books, is the wat Rajabopit. Its central structure is a great pagoda, containing some ancient stone Buddhas, clustered in unconscious impressiveness. Around the pagoda is another building, following its circular shape, with four great gabled gateways which are really halls. The walls of all the buildings are covered with porcelain tiles from the apex to the base, and the doors are inlaid with mother-of-pearl, carved and incised with minute and loving care. Then there are schoolrooms open at three sides, dormitories for monks, and, what I liked best of all, a garden marked off from the rest by a wall, though within the same general enclosure—a garden of palms and pagodas. It has flowering trees of many sorts, cannas and crotons, lace-like bamboos, the Bougainville, tombs of ancient abbots, great bronze vessels holding miniature lotus ponds, and a strange little building with three towers of the Cambodian type, three stairways whose balustrades are threatening snakes or Naga images with uplifted heads, and above the stairways high reliefs of un-Buddhist-looking gentlemen of martial air and triple crown, and still more un-Buddhist-looking ladies with bare and ample breasts. Other pagodas there are, of various shapes and sizes, some in fresh repair, some of gray old stone, stained and blotched and covered with lichen, and all mingled together with tropical trees like an immense and variegated bouquet before the altar of the Blessed One.

The excellent repair of most Siamese wats forms a pleasant contrast to the many decaying pagodas of Burma and the many uncared-for and even filthy Buddhist temples in large parts of China. The good condition of the wats in Siam is due in part to the fact that the repairing of an ancient temple is almost as meritorious as the building of a new one. As compared with the Chinese, moreover, the Siamese are exceedingly devout Buddhists, and, like the Burmese, are lavish in their gifts to the sanctuary. But the government also must be given considerable credit for the excellent appearance of at least the larger temples. For in Siam Buddhism is emphatically the state religion. The present king is an enthusiastic Buddhist. So was his brother who preceded him (he died in 1925). During the first years of his reign, especially, he seemed to be emulating Asoka and Kanishka. It is, in fact, due largely to him that the wats are kept in the excellent repair one finds today. Before his advent to the throne the wats of Siam were in much the same condition as those in Burma—a few important ones kept up, the rest allowed to fall into decay. From his exhortations and his example the Siamese learned to repair temples as well as to build them. The king, moreover, was—and is—exceedingly generous toward many of the monasteries. A large portion of the monks receive from him their robes, in an annual ceremony of some magnificence. Several of the state ceremonies, moreover, have religious elements and require the cooperation of the Buddhist church. Finally the king appoints the patriarch; state confirmation is required for the election of the various abbots; and if a new monastery is to be formed the consent of the government must first be obtained.

The monastic orders are, however, in most respects self-governed. On the death of an abbot, the monks of the chapter elect his successor, and only formal confirmation from the state is required. While the great majority of the monks belong to one order, there are two other orders each of which has a considerable following. One of the three, known as the Ramanya, was brought many years ago from Pegu. The two native orders are sprung from one stock, which divided during the reign of the fourth king of the present dynasty. This sovereign (Mongkut by name) was abbot of the wat Bavaranies (where the present prince patriarch now presides). He felt that the monastic life was in need of reform and founded the Dhammayut or Reformed Order to which the great majority of Siamese monks today belong. Not all the monks, however, followed the king out of the old unreformed order and it has been continued down to this day under the name Maha Nikaya. The differences between these three orders are not doctrinal but disciplinary.

The monks of Siam have, on the whole, a good reputation. They hold the respect and even the affection of the Buddhist laity. Even the Christian missionaries, many of whom I fear would like to think rather ill of their clerical rivals, while dwelling at length on their ignorance, their laziness, and their lack of religious devotion, will tell you that as a body they lead a pure and somewhat ascetic life, are pretty faithful in the observance of their vows, and are undoubtedly a real influence for moral good in the community. I got the impression that they are about on a par with the monks of Burma, a little less learned and a little more devoted than the monks of Ceylon. Certainly their life is not a strenuous one and it gives ample opportunity for laziness—an opportunity which in many cases is gratefully embraced. Many of the monks are ignorant of the nice points of their own religion: and in the country districts some of them cannot even read or write. In Bangkok, on the other hand, the average level of intelligence and education among the monks is fairly high. The abbot of the wat Po (a very authoritative dignitary) told me that while not more than one monk out of a hundred knew any Sanskrit, perhaps ninety-nine out of a hundred knew some Pali. By this he undoubtedly meant that ninety-nine out of one hundred knew by heart the Pali verses which form part of the prescribed chants. Still, many of the monks have really studied Pali, and while the great majority can read the sacred Books only in translation, they have at least an elementary knowledge of the principles of Buddhist thought. A persistent effort is being made, moreover, in most of the city wats to increase this knowledge. A certain amount of information is required before admission to the order. After this admission, the young monk is encouraged to continue his studies and take examinations of higher and higher grade in successive years. There are, altogether, nine of these grades of learning, and while only a few reach the ninth, many go beyond the first. In fact a considerable stimulus has been given to even the most unscholarly and unambitious monk in the rough path of learning by the recent law requiring military service of all young laymen. The first effect of this law was to give a great new impetus to the religious life. Young men piled into the priesthood in such numbers that the church threatened to swamp the laity and destroy the army. Something had to be done about it: so an additional law was passed making it impossible for a monk to escape military service unless he had passed the first of the nine examinations to which I referred above—that is one additional examination beside that required to admit him to the order. This examination is no simple thing, but a really formidable barrier for the ignorant and lazy. It consists, in fact, of four written examinations, taken on four successive days. On the first day the student writes a composition outlining the doctrines of Buddhism. On the three following days he is given examination papers with specific questions which must be answered in writing—dealing on the second day with the rules of proper living, on the third with the life of the Buddha, and on the last day with the Sangha and its monastic discipline, the Vinaya.

The examination for all Bangkok novitiates is given in the wat Moha-Tetu—which is regarded as the center of Buddhist learning in the capital. I visited it on the second day of the annual examination just after the applicants had finished their papers. The court of the wat was overflowing with yellow-robed young hopefuls—or doubtfuls—who were discussing with each other the various questions that had been asked, much as American students do after an important examination, and swarming up the two broad staircases that lead to the examination hall, where older monks sat at tables, pencil in hand, betel box at side, and often cigar in mouth, reading and marking the papers. Here are some of the questions that were asked: What are the chief points concerning conduct which must be inculcated upon novitiates? Can humility beautify people? Can passion do so? What is the duty of the monk in relation to food? to touching, tasting, and smelling? to the commandments? What should be the monk's state of mind on receiving (a) the yellow robe, (b) food, (c) shelter, (d) medicine? The answer to this last question, by the way, is that he should not think of beautifying himself or enjoying himself, but should consider only the necessity of these objects. I happen to know because I was shown not only the examination paper but the long list of answers, made out in duplicate by the chief examiner for the use of the subordinate examiners who were to mark the papers. The examination was planned and carried out, the reader will observe, with quite Western efficiency. This system of thorough examination, throwing out of the church and into the army all those who do not pass, can hardly fail in a very few years to raise materially the standard of intelligence and scholarship of the Siamese monkhood.

The total number of monks in Siam, in February, 1924, was 114,349; to which should be added some 60,141 novices.[10] All but 110 of the monks are native Siamese; 54 being Annamese, 38 Chinese, and 18 Burmese. All of the larger wats are in Bangkok, the largest of all (the Mahadhatu) having 250 resident monks.

The life of the monk is regulated with care, and follows, as it does in Burma and Cambodia, pretty closely upon the ideal set up in the ancient Vinaya. The monks rise at about five, pray (that is, repeat the proper verses) individually, and then go their daily rounds, bowl in hand, to receive from the lay community their daily food.[11] This is, of course, entirely vegetarian, and consists chiefly of rice and fruit. About six in the morning the streets of the upper part of Bangkok are yellow with monks, over forty being sometimes found at once on one block. After returning from their begging expedition and depositing their food in one place they assemble in some shrine of the wat or in their private oratory about nine for a service of chanting. At the conclusion of this service they read, meditate,[12] or rest till their one daily meal, which comes at eleven. As it is necessary for them to eat enough to last them till the next morning, this meal is usually one of considerable size, and it is not surprising that after

[10] These figures were supplied by the Ecclesiastical Department of the Siamese Government, and came to me through the kindness of my friend and former colleague, Dr. F. B. Sayre, Foreign Advisor to the king in 1923-24.

[11] In Northern Siam the monks do not beg their meals. The food is brought to the monasteries by the women of the lay households. Siamese monks when on their begging rounds do not sound a gong as the Burmese monks do.

[12] Several kinds of meditation are followed. *Kammathan* is analytic meditation. "He who exercises it fixes his mind on any one element and reflects on it in all its conditions and changes, until, so far as that element is concerned, he sees that it is only unstable, grievous, and illusory. To aid this kind of meditation there are formulas. A list of elements is repeated, and the ordinary exercise of Kammathan is probably a mere mumbling of these formulas. One of these is the list of the thirty-two elements of the body." *Phawana* is a second form of meditation. It means concentration of thought, either upon charity, pity, joy, sorrow, or indifference. To practice the first of these five forms of Phawana "it is necessary, as a preliminary, to abstain from doing evil and then, seeking a solitary place, to reflect on Charity or universal love, repeating a number of texts appropriate to the occasion and calculated to remove from the heart every feeling opposed to universal charity." A third form of meditation is Chian (Sanskrit Dhyana), a series of states of abstraction or trance, the attainment of which is the highest accomplishment of a Buddhist saint. By them one secures rebirth in the heavens of form and formlessness." I take these descriptions from Alabaster, *The Wheel of the Law* (London, Trübner, 1871).

it most monks feel the need of a nap. After the nap they do as they like till the afternoon or evening chanting service, which comes in some wats at four, in some at eight. By nine P.M. their day is ended and they go to bed.

The life of the monk is therefore far from strenuous. He has plenty of leisure which he may use for study, meditation, or plain loafing, as he likes. Some of them, I should hasten to add, teach religion in the wat schools. For all Siamese children have to go to one of the schools provided by the government, and in these schools religion is a required course and is taught by a monk. "Religion" here of course means Buddhism, and it is the moral side of Buddhism, the Five Precepts, their interpretation and application, etc., that is stressed. I should add that most young men, when they reach their twentieth year, live in the monasteries for at least a short time, as do the young men of Burma and Cambodia.

Besides teaching the boys, a few of the monks read or expound the Dhamma to the laity on preaching days. Naturally it is only the learned and energetic ones who do this, and there is wide play within the calling for any taste. The abbots in particular have an opportunity for luxurious and scholarly ease which to many a Siamese must be very inviting. I remember having an opportunity one morning to get a glimpse into an abbot's study (if so I may call it) in one of the wats, while he had his back turned, and to observe both his room and him. It was, in fact, much more than a glimpse, for he was absorbed in his reading and I could note down everything in the room. Against the wall stood a bookcase with fifty-two volumes (I counted them) handsomely bound in European style, most of them being in Siamese. The lower shelves of the case were filled with personal photographs. More photographs, most of them framed, hung on the walls—pictures of Buddhist processions, groups of monks, famous Buddhist buildings, etc. On the two sides of the bookcase hung very large clocks, both of them going and both of them on time. Why two clocks were needed within five feet of each other would not be plain to most Americans, but the question would seem absurd to most Siamese. There were two tables in the room and a dozen chairs, most of them easy chairs. In one of these—a very easy chair indeed—sat the abbot, reading his pamphlet, his feet resting on a large table in front of him. In addition to his feet the table contained two teapots, six teacups, two fruit dishes, a large and handsomely bound volume, a betel box, two bowls, and four spittoons. Other abbots that I visited, however, were far less luxurious in their surroundings. The elderly abbot of the great wat Po I found sitting on the floor with his back against a pillar, evidently meditating on the transiency of life or on the sermon he had to preach the following day at the cremation of the princess of Sri Ratana Kosindra. His room was spacious but contained neither bookcases, photographs, nor spittoons. At any rate all I remember in it was a rather beautiful shrine at one end with some meditative Buddhas, and the old man in his yellow robe, leaning against a pillar and struggling between a desire to be courteous and a natural feeling of annoyance at the intrusion of an American interviewer when his thoughts should be on higher themes. The reception room of the prince patriarch, the King's uncle, whom I called upon the following day, was even simpler in its furnishings, as well as smaller, and the elderly patriarch, while possessing the gracious manners of a prince, had also all the appearance of the true Buddhist ascetic.

For though the monk's life is far from strenuous and gives ample opportunity for laziness, there is an ascetic element in it, and the heads of the order make earnest efforts to keep up the nobler moral tone of the monkhood. A little pamphlet which is widely distributed and read among both monks and laity is devoted to ten rules of life for the ideal monk—rules, it must be noted, which must not be confused with the Ten Vows or Precepts imposed on entering the order; but in part repetitions, in part additional recommendations. They are, in very brief summary, the following:

(1) The monk must wear only the yellow robe.

(2) He must get each day only enough food for that day's use and save nothing over. He must eat what is given him and not pick and choose.

(3) He must give to the needy, keep the Precepts, and say his prayers.

(4) He must not scold.

(5) He must pay courteous attention to whatever is

said to him, whether he acts on the suggestions given or not.

(6) He must remind himself that all living things are mortal and that nothing is permanent.

(7) He must remind himself that there is punishment and reward, in hell and heaven, after death.

(8) He must be attentive in whatever he does and try constantly to do better.

(9) If he is really in earnest in the desire to become holy, he must go for meditation to a lonely place, such as the forest, the jungle, or a quiet part of the wat.

(10) He must study to become learned, so that he need not be ashamed when questions are asked him.

But these moral precepts have led us quite beyond the external aspects of Siamese Buddhism to which this chapter was to have been devoted. The inner aspect of the religion, with its beliefs and practices, will be considered in the next chapter.

CHAPTER IX

THEORY AND PRACTICE IN SIAM

THE latter part of the previous chapter made it evident that the study of the Dharma and some knowledge of Buddhist theory are considered necessary for the ideal monk. In matters of theory it must be said that Siamese Buddhism, like that of Burma and Ceylon, has kept fairly close to the teachings of the Master. There are, of course, wide differences here, as in other Buddhist lands, between the beliefs of the more learned monks and those of the ignorant monks and laymen, but the leaders, at least, know more or less of their Pali books, and while doubtless they neglect much of ancient Buddhist theory, what theory they have is fairly pure.

The monks whom I consulted with one voice insisted that there is only one Buddha. I do not understand them by this to deny the earlier Buddhas. But their interest in the question is pragmatic, as a good Buddhist's should be; and their meaning I think is that for this period of history and for the purposes of our worship and our guidance there is only one Buddha. I brought to the attention of several of the monks the fact that the Chinese and Japanese believed in a number of Buddhas and worshiped them. They were usually surprised and clung to their monistic position unmoved.

The belief in Maitreya (in Siam called Allenya Metai), the coming Buddha, is in a sense a kind of poly-Buddhism, and it seems to be a living part of the faith for many of the laity. At his arrival the world is to enter into a happy period, and many a layman's prayer is the wish, "Oh, that I might live to see Allenya Metai!" Some of the less learned monks share this position. Not so, I was assured by the prince patriarch, does the ideal monk. The princely head of the church showed that he felt very strongly on this point. I judge he regarded such a belief as the entering wedge of poly-

Buddhism, from which he is resolved to keep the Siamese church pure. Maitreya, he said (or as he called him, Phra Sri An) is a Boddhisattva, but he is not really coming as a Buddha. There is no coming Buddha.

Sakyamuni, therefore, as the one and supreme Buddha has nothing to fear from Maitreya. Neither need he fear anything from Amida, his great rival or supplanter in all Northern lands. Few of the monks and hardly any of the laity had even heard the name Amida. The one monk I found who knew anything about him assured me he was not a Buddha at all, but one of the disciples of the Buddha.

This does not mean that the Buddha has no rivals in Siam. The worship, offerings, and prayers of the Siamese he has to share with the many local spirits who correspond to the nats of Burma. Even in the wats, yes even in the wats of Bangkok, one finds little shrines to these little godlets—doll houses they look like—with a few incense sticks and streamers in front of them. But if they do this in the center of Buddhist learning and purity what shall be expected in the more remote parts of the land? In northern Siam, among the Laos, and in and about Chieng Mai (the second center of Siamese Buddhism), the worship—or at least the buying off—of these animistic spirits forms a large part of the religious, or superstitious, life of the people. As the cult of these ancient fays, tree spirits, local genii, is much the same as it is in many other parts of the world I need say nothing of it here. It is to them that many, perhaps most, of the actual petitions are made. But they are not regarded as in any sense comparable to the Buddha. Upon his absolute supremacy all Siam is agreed.

On the present state of the Buddha there is no such unanimity. The average devout layman believes as a matter of course that the Buddha is a kind of God in heaven, who dwells in eternal bliss, who is conscious and sees our offerings and hears our prayers. The less educated among the monks share the same view. The more learned monks, on the other hand—the abbots and the monks who have passed the higher examinations—know perfectly well that the Buddha is in Nibban and neither sees, hears, nor knows anything. One monk expressed it to me by saying that the Buddha is now like smoke that has been dissipated and has disappeared. So he has disappeared and dissolved. In translating his expressions my interpreter used the exact phrase so often used by the English-speaking monks of Burma and Ceylon: "Buddha finish."

The Buddha, in short, for the orthodox Hinayana, whether in Siam, Burma, Ceylon, or Cambodia, belongs now to the world of the ideal rather than to that of the actual. On this point Buddhism is a kind of Asiatic Platonism. To make use of a distinction common in the philosophical language of our day, the Buddha is subsistent but not existent. He is real—eternally real. So is the perfect circle and the idea of the Good. But by no means all that is real is actual. It is not all to be found within the realms of time and space. The eternal Buddha is in no place. He inhabits the spaceless and timeless worlds. He belongs not with you and me and other finite things that change and pass, but with the eternal Ideas of the Platonic realm. For all that, he is none the less real; rather the more real is he. Nor is he out of all relation to the actual and existent, any more than is the perfect circle, which all our imperfect existent circles seek to—and in some measure do—exemplify. Just because he has passed out of the realm of the actual into that of the ideal with no taint of the existential upon him, is he a supremely fit object for our worship and our aspiration. So, at any rate, thinks the orthodox Hinayanist.

With the nature and present condition of the Buddha is inevitably bound up the nature of prayer and worship. One would expect those who think of the Buddha as a kind of god in heaven to think of prayer, and to practice it, in much the same way as the average Christian. To some extent this is the case. Yet it is surprising to note how relatively rare is this obvious point of view and how seldom it is consistently acted upon. Some of the more ignorant laymen pray to the Buddha in this—shall I say somewhat naïve?—fashion, but their number is surprisingly small. Even the laymen in the country districts rarely make petitions for specific things to the Buddha. They bring offerings to the Buddha in the temples and pray, not to gain particular goods, but that by these means their stock of merit may be increased. In case of illness they pray, as a rule, not to the Buddha but to the spirits. This is of course in part due to the fact that illness, in the country districts of Siam, is always caused by the spirits; in every case there is some hungry spirit that has not been sufficiently fed. In indirect fashion, however, even in the case of illness one may pray to the Buddha. The power of the hungry spirit over the sick man has been made possible because of lack of merit in the latter; hence offerings and praises to the Buddha, by increasing one's stock of merit, may aid in one's recovery. Merit is also at times transferable; and, as in Burma, the merit you acquire through the chanting of Pali verses may be applied toward the recovery of your father.

Another form of prayer more nearly approaching direct petition is the strong expression of a wish. Thus, as I said in another connection, a common prayer of the layman is, "Oh, may I live to see Allenya Metai!" Even this, however, it must be noted, avoids at least the form of direct request. Some laymen, to be sure, make petitions to the Buddha in quite Christian and Moslem fashion; but the great majority seem to have a feeling against doing so.

The less educated monks seem to be in a rather uncertain position on the question of prayer. One young monk in the wat Benchamabopit told me (quite glibly and confidently) that the Buddha is conscious and knows, but that one does not pray to him. One says prayers in his memory but does not make petitions for specific things. If one wants something one must act rightly and not seek help from another. On being pressed, however, as to whether one could not pray to the Buddha in case one's father were ill, he said that one could, and that the Buddha might answer the prayer and heal the sick man. We were sitting in the young monk's room shortly after the morning devotions, in the hour commonly given to study or conversation. One or two other very young men in yellow robes—friends and neighbors of my interlocutor—had come in to listen to and take part in the discussion and had draped themselves around the room in various graceful and youthful attitudes. I was disagreeable enough to point out that the two answers given me were not consistent and could not both be true: in typically impolite Western fashion I insisted that one either could pray to the Buddha or could not. The boy was silent for a while, and so were his friends. Then he said that the question was a very hard one and that he hadn't yet passed his examination, so didn't know the right answer; but that he would take me to a learned one who could answer it. Thereupon, after considerable bowing, we all started out together, the young monk leading the way and the rest of us following, down the stairs, along the little line of white cement two-room dormitories, and up another stair, to a room much like the one we had left, where we were greeted by a somewhat older monk with all the grave courtesy of the East. When we had disposed ourselves around the room I detailed to the Learned One our discussion up to the point where it had broken off and at which we had found ourselves in need of his wisdom. He responded quite readily that the younger monk had been right in what he said at first and wrong in his second answer. One ought not to make any petitions at all. Prayer, he continued, has three purposes: (1) to honor the Buddha; (2) to honor the Dharma by repeating and memorizing it; (3) to honor the Sangha, the present followers of the Buddha, and the work they are now doing in obedience to him. Petitional prayer is useless. We cannot influence health or anything else by that sort of prayer. When the time comes for one's father to die he will die. That time must be determined by his merit, and prayer will have nothing to do with it whatever. I asked him whether prayer might not increase merit and this be transferred, so as to benefit the health of a sick father (as in Burma). He answered with assurance that it could *not* work in this way. Merit, he said, was sometimes transferable, as in building a wat or giving alms, but not always so, and certainly not in the way I had suggested.

The prince patriarch gave me an explanation of the actual practice not altogether confirmatory of the views expressed by the Learned One. The prayer of the monks, he said, consists in the chanting of verses from the Suttas, by means of which merit is acquired. If a family of the laity, for example, is in trouble they send for the monks, and the monks go and chant verses at the house. This may result in acquiring merit for the family, which may, in turn, put an end to their trouble by putting an end to its cause (demerit). If there is a drought word is often sent out to all the wats to have the monks pray for rain. This praying for rain consists in chanting some passage from the Suttas which has to do with rain—any such passage will do. The chanting of such a passage may acquire merit and this may bring rain. Very much depends, however—and this the patriarch emphasized—upon the mental state of the monks while doing the chanting. Merely the mechanical repetition of the sacred words would be useless. The sacred words, coming as they do from the Buddha, have great power, but this only when united with the proper intention on the part of the chanter. If this intention is present, the words will produce merit of a general sort and this may result in various specific benefits. But such chanting, the patriarch insisted, is not petition to the Buddha. The Buddha does not hear prayers. He is unconscious. He is in Nibban.

The question of Nirvana or Nibban is, like the question of prayer, linked up with the question of the present condition of the Buddha. The more naïve of the laity who think of the Buddha as a conscious God in eternal bliss, of course regard Nibban, which is his present state, as a condition of consciousness and joy. Some of the most learned monks on the other hand take the sternly logical view of the situation; as, for example, the abbot of the great wat Po, who told me that Nibban is a state of complete unconsciousness, and the Learned One, to whom I referred a few pages back, who described the Buddha as really quite dead and added that Nibban for us, should we attain it, would mean complete extinction. Most of the monks, with whom I talked, sought to take a mediating view between these two extremes. Even the patriarch who insisted that the Buddha does not hear and does not know would not assert that Nibban means extinction or is by any means equivalent to death. Nibban, he said, is unknowable. It can be described only by negatives. There is in Nibban neither heat nor cold, neither the soft nor the hard, no color, no sound, no material body. It is, he added, somewhat to my surprise, a state of indescribable joy. Joy, he said, is commonly thought to come from sensations and from the possession and use of material things. This is a great mistake. True joy is possible only when all sensations and all material things and with them the body, have been abandoned. Then we find our true selves. That is Nibban.

A somewhat similar view was expressed by the group of monks with whom I was conversing in the examination hall, to whom I referred in the previous chapter. They had been marking examination papers, and when I got one of them into conversation several others gathered around us and joined in. Our talk had followed a sinuous course and ended up, finally and appropriately, with Nirvana. Nibban, they told me, was a condition that cuts off everything. It cuts off love, sorrow, pleasure, old age, death. Does it cut off life? I asked. To this the monks answered No. We are still alive in Nibban. This answer, of course, sounded a bit odd, and apparently they were not quite sure of it after all; so they led me to the chief examiner, who sat in a kind of open office or platform in the middle of the big room. He was a very different type from most of the monks I had met—a man of perhaps thirty-five or forty, on whose face thought had left its marks; very self-confident, very intelligent and mentally alert, an adept at the intellectual game, quick and laconic and sure in his responses. On being asked a question he would remain silent a few moments, then, after a little thinking and a little knitting of the brows, he would give his answer with a quick decisiveness of thought and speech that reminded you of the working of a steel trap. In spite of the obvious keenness of his intellect, however, I felt that he was, without knowing it, something of a slave to his formulas; though he certainly knew how to manipulate his formulas with great skill. He was, in short, the able and typical scholastic.

We gave him some account of our discussion and asked him for light on the nature of Nibban. In response he made the seemingly paradoxical statement that in Nibban there is no consciousness, yet there is ineffable happiness. I pointed out that this was difficult to grasp, for happiness is a form of consciousness, hence happiness without consciousness seemed a contradiction in terms. He thought a moment with bent brows, and then, making use of a formula of Buddhist psychology, replied that happiness is not a form of consciousness, it is, instead, an element like cold and hot. Cold and hot do not know anything, they are not themselves conscious nor are they forms of consciousness. They simply exist. His thought here was much like that of the Neo-realists who would agree with him that the world is constituted of elements—"neutral entities" to use their term—which are in themselves neither physical nor psychical. Cold and hot, they would assert, are not conscious—not conscious themselves nor in need of being made the objects or content of consciousness. Professor Holt would go so far as to maintain that such things as beauty, the sadness of a "pathetic" scene, the joyfulness of a brilliant day, have nothing subjective in them, and are in no more need of consciousness than are stones or atoms.[1] It was apparently a position related to this that the monk was supporting. Hot and cold are not forms of consciousness but elements, and the same is true of happiness. Happiness, he said, is an element and stays by itself and cannot be mixed. So Nibban is unconscious but it is happiness. In answer to a further question he added that it is that part of what we call ourselves which does not desire—it is that which reaches Nibban and is happy. The Buddha is in Nibban. He is not conscious. He cannot see our acts nor hear our prayers. But he is not dead. Between being dead and being in Nibban there is a great difference. When a man is dead the element of desire still remains. Hence death brings birth again. But in Nibban there is no desire and hence from it there is no rebirth. He described Nibban further by enumerating a great number of things which it is not, his words recalling vividly the negations by which Dionysius the Areopagite and other mystics of the Neo-Platonic school have sought to describe the mystic vision of the invisible. I asked whether there is in Nibban anything other than these negations, anything positive. He said there may be something which we have not yet seen nor conceived: such, for example, as America is to him. He has not seen America, cannot think it, knows only that it exists. It has its

[1] *The Concept of Consciousness* (New York, Macmillan, 1914), Chap. VI. Professor Whitehead's views are also somewhat comparable to the monk's.

own qualities, all of them positive; but he can describe it only in negatives.

For all laymen and for most monks the nature of Nibban is a purely academic question. Of much greater practical interest are heaven and hell. If you ask almost any monk or any layman what happens to a man after death, he will tell you that it depends on the man's deeds: that the good go to heaven and the bad go to hell. If you ask him how long one stays in these places he will very often tell you that one stays in heaven till one's merit is used up and then one is reborn in hell, and vice versa. Never once without my having first asked a leading question did any Siamese proffer any information about rebirth in human and animal bodies. If you ask them whether one may be born as an animal or reborn as a man they will usually say, "Oh, yes," but plainly rebirth is a purely theoretical possibility for them. They had not thought of it. Even on the theory of the matter they feel rather muddled. And this is true not only of the ignorant. Some even of the educated monks I have found very uncertain as to the relative desirability of these various forms of future state; apparently you have to pass a good many of the nine examinations before you know much about the next life. The learned abbot of wat Po was very clear on this—as he was on all the things I asked about. There are five possible conditions after death, he said, and they stand in the following order of desirability: (1) Nibban, (2) Heaven, (3) Rebirth as man, (4) Rebirth as an animal, (5) Hell. Of these only Nibban is eternal. All the monks, of course, and most of the laymen know that rebirth is one of the possibilities; but it is quite noticeable that rebirth plays a very slight part in their thoughts, whereas heaven and hell are very vivid to them. Some of the missionaries, in fact, complain of this, criticizing the heathen for their unorthodox and non-Buddhistic views, and feeling, apparently, that these Buddhists have stolen some of their thunder or their brimstone. The truth is, of course, that we of the West have been brought up to give transmigration a more important place in Buddhism than it has ever held and to neglect almost entirely its teachings about hell and heaven. As a fact, from very early times Buddhism has dwelt at length upon the rewards of heaven and the punishments of hell and has often made much more vivid use of them as sanctions of the moral life than of the pains and pleasures of rebirth. Hell is a very Buddhistic conception—as any one familiar with the frescoes on the walls of Buddhist temples ancient and modern, Southern or Northern, will realize. Still it must be acknowledged that the almost exclusive emphasis upon heaven and hell, and the desuetude and neglect into which transmigration seems to have fallen, are relatively recent developments.

If you ask the average monk what it is that is reborn or that goes to heaven or hell, he will probably fail to understand your question. If he does understand it at all he will probably say it is just you yourself that is thus rewarded or punished and will fail to realize that he is treading on very difficult and very famous ground. Those who have passed the nine examinations, however, will probably know well the doctrine. I confess I had little success in finding any one who realized there was a problem of the self at all. But the prince patriarch knew all about it and expounded the true scholastic position. The doctrine, he said, teaches that there is no real substantial self. The seeming self is only a temporary knowing, and a wrong knowing at that. And it is just this wrong knowing—this "knowing the wrong fact"—that is reborn; this and nothing else.

It is a little surprising that a doctrine so fundamental to Buddhist Scholasticism as the non-existence of the self should not be more widely understood in Siam than it is. Still more surprising is the unimportant position in Siamese Buddhism held by the Four Noble Truths. At least I should have been greatly surprised had I not previously found much the same situation in Burma and Ceylon. The monk in wat Benchamabopit whom I referred to some pages back as the Learned One had, apparently, never heard of the Four Noble Truths. At any rate he could not tell me what they were. This was not true of all the monks whom I asked, but few if any seemed to have got hold of the real significance of the Four Truths, the fundamental position of desire in the Buddha's view of suffering, or the logical consequences that follow inevitably from that view. I could not find a single monk who of his own motion defended the orthodox position that since desire and love are the sources of sorrow one should "cut all the ties" and give up even personal love for one's friends and family. One of them told me that monks ought to get rid of personal love but still insisted the laity should cherish it. A rather significant discussion of this subject was one I had with the group of monks in the examination hall; significant because it revealed what seems to me an inherent self-contradiction within Buddhism. One of the monks had rehearsed to me, quite correctly, the Four Noble Truths, and I had brought him back by further questions to the fact that desire is the cause of sorrow and that it is the aim of Buddhism to avoid sorrow. Does this desire, I asked, include love for other people and desire for their welfare? Yes, he replied: love—love quite as much as hate—is one of the causes of sorrow. Then, said I, we ought not to love each other or desire each other's welfare? Oh, yes, he said, Buddhism teaches us to love each other and to desire the welfare of all. When I pointed out the fact that he had contradicted himself he recognized it, but that that what he meant was this: We ought to get rid of love quite as much as hate, but we cannot fully do so till we reach Nibban. It is really wrong to love other people and we should seek to avoid both love and hate. One of the other monks, standing by, was quite dissatisfied by this admission and tried to save the situation by making a distinction. There are two kinds of love, he said, sex love and love for people's welfare, the desire to do them good and help them. Sex love is bad, love for people's welfare is good.[2] But, I asked, does this second kind of love bring sorrow—when, for example, those one loves are ill or die, or when the good we desire for them cannot be attained. He admitted that this kind of love also may and often does bring sorrow; only, he said, this is unavoidable. I pointed out that its unavoidability, if true, is quite irrelevant. So he followed his predecessor in admitting that we really ought to get rid of both kinds of love. At this point a third monk could stand it no longer and protested that this could not be. It was surely our duty to love our parents and to desire good things. Unfortunately the discussion here got shunted off

[2] As we have seen in Chapter III, something like this, though more discriminating, seems to have been the Buddha's position.

onto the nature of Nibban, and we adjourned to discuss the latter question with the chief examiner in the manner already described.

In the sixth chapter of this book I pointed out what seemed to me the essential incompatibility between the Buddhist doctrine that desire is the root of all evil, and the fundamental Buddhist emotion of pity and the sentiment of love for all sentient creatures. If it be true, as the position given the Four Noble Truths by the Founder would indicate, that one great end of religion is to enable men to avoid sorrow, and that this can be done only by rooting out all the desires that lay one open to the slings and arrows of outrageous Fortune, then it is hard to see how religion can consistently teach men earnestly to desire the welfare of others. If the religious ideal is the cultivation of indifference to all that can happen, the cutting of all the ties, the ending of all personal loves which may bring anxiety, break one's peace, and act as perpetual pledges to Fortune, then the religious ideal cannot consistently include the cultivation of a love for others of such a living sort that the death or the misfortune of those loved will bring sorrow or inner disturbance to the mind of the lover. Yet Buddhism has always sought to do both these seemingly incompatible things at once. Most Buddhists, I suspect, have tried—and successfully—to blind themselves to the inner contradiction involved in such a dual ideal, and practically have solved the difficulty by making a compromise which has done scant justice to both sides. The more coldly logical and the constitutionally selfish have stressed the evils of desire and love, and have lived their own lives in monastic establishments with pleasant neighborliness but no strong attachments and with small attempts at social cooperation. They have in short "wandered alone like a rhinoceros." Many of the more learned monks of Ceylon and Burma would seem to have chosen this side of the Buddhist ideal. But the modern tendency all over the Hinayana world, and especially I should say in Siam, is to emphasize the sympathetic, cooperative side of the Master's teachings, or rather to follow less his teachings than his example, to choose as the decisive ideal the life his heart prompted rather than the life his intellect devised. If I am right in this, it is a step in the development of Buddhism which is of the profoundest importance. Buddhism, like Christianity, has always been a religion of growth; one that has felt and responded quickly to the varying needs of the different countries to which it has been carried and the different ages to which it has ministered. It is not strange, therefore, that it feels today the strong tendency to social cooperation which so characterizes the century in which we live. It is more difficult today than it has ever been before to wander alone like a rhinoceros.[3]

But if the quiet shelving of the Four Noble Truths marks a great step in the socialization of Buddhism and enables its deeply altruistic impulses to have a new and unprecedented freedom, it must be recognized that something of real value is in danger of disappearing with them. There is, perhaps, no great gain without some slight loss; at any rate I fear there may be some loss in this case. For while the ideal based upon the Four Noble Truths and the avoidance of sorrow logically led to a kind of spiritual selfishness, there was a great insight involved especially in the Second Truth, which it is a pity to lose out of Buddhism. That desires are weak points in our defenses, that every man should have a central tower into which he may retreat and from which he may defy the whole world, that the value of life should not be *wholly* dependent on anything that can happen, that peace and spiritual independence can be gained only in the measure in which we despise all external chances—these are great truths, and the application of them has produced in all the centuries a characteristically Buddhist or Stoic type of character which has a certain real nobility. There is something rather fine, after all, about the rhinoceros who has it in him to wander alone in the jungle—"not frightened by noises," "not caught in a net," "not stained by water." For my own part, therefore, I should regret to find the Four Noble Truths and the fundamental position of desire altogether neglected by modern Buddhism. They have given Buddhist morality a certain

[3] The difficulty in question is not in principle confined to Buddhism; it presents itself to every religion and every individual that would cultivate both spiritual freedom and social sympathy. In Buddhism the difficulty comes more sharply to the attention than elsewhere merely because of the Buddhist extreme dislike of inner disturbance. In Chapter VI I suggested that Gotama's own practical solution of the matter was much like that of St. Paul.

characteristic note, which, when not allowed the dominant position, has had a real value. I may be wrong, but I fear that this great aspect of the Buddha's teaching is being watered down by many of his followers rather too much, and that there is a tendency in Buddhist morality to become quite commonplace, just a collection of Precepts with no central principle to justify them.

This, however, at most is only a tendency, and we must not forget the other and more important tendency already pointed out, namely that toward universal love, which is becoming increasingly central and dominating within Buddhism—a tendency for which there is the more hope now that the selfish impulse of dodging personal sorrow at all costs is receiving the less emphasis. A much greater evil and danger for Buddhist morality lies in its emphasis upon the acquisition of merit—an emphasis which, after all, involves the same spiritual selfishness as sorrow-dodging, only in a more subtle form. The next hundred years, I should be willing to predict, will witness a struggle between these two ideals within Buddhism—the ideal of sympathy and human helpfulness, on the one hand, and on the other that of the acquisition of a stock of merit for one's own personal benefit in this life and the next. We shall not live to see the outcome of this struggle; but it seems to me that the whole conception of merit is bound to wane, and that of human cooperation and helpfulness must gain steadily upon its rival. The great tendency toward racial adjustment and integration and the steady waning of most supernatural conceptions will both fight in this direction. We shall in short—this is my belief—witness the steady approximation of the Buddhist and the Christian moralities.

The central part of the content of Buddhist morality as taught and practiced today consists of the Five Precepts, with the various interpretations and applications given them by preachers, teachers, and individual consciences. In addition to the Five Precepts, the monks have the five further, monastic precepts, or vows, handed down from antiquity, and also the numerous rules of the Sangha, many of which are on the border line between morals and manners. The laity as well as the monks know the Five Precepts pretty generally, being well grounded in them in the wat schools during boyhood. The more earnest laymen, moreover, seek to carry out some of the five additional precepts meant especially for the monks, and are urged to do so by the preachers. The ten rules of life for the ideal monk quoted at the close of the preceding chapter were taken from a pamphlet distributed among the laity, and are held up to them as counsels of perfection. The excellent influence of these various moral teachings upon the lay community is, I think, admitted by all.

The religious observances of each zealous Buddhist family begin early in the morning and end only at night. They are, indeed, not nearly so meticulous and detailed as those of the Hindu, but they are sufficient to keep one at least in mind of one's religion most of the time. The day must be opened with prayer. Then, while it is still very early, food must be prepared against the visit of the monk. One must keep one's eye peeled, for the monk will not knock at the door, but merely stand outside with averted head and wait. Some member of the family must then go out and empty the dish of rice or other offering into his capacious bowl. Once a day an offering must be made, with suitable verses or prayers, at the domestic shrine. And in the evening there is another "hour of prayer." Besides this regular daily round of religious observance, the more zealous Buddhist goes once a week to the service of prayer and of reading the Dhamma in the wat, at which time he both listens to the reading or preaching, and to the chanting of the monks and himself makes offerings at the altar and recites various sacred prayers or verses before the Buddha. The use of the Buddha image in the wats and in the home must not be taken for idolatry, at least in the usual deprecatory sense of the word. Except with the very ignorant it would be a great misunderstanding to suppose that the Buddhists, whether lay or clerical, worship the images. That some do so is probably the case; but among laymen of average intelligence this, I think, is rare. As one layman expressed it to me, the image of the Buddha is used by his worshipers only to remind them of the Buddha and make their thought and memory more vivid. One does not worship the image; one worships the Buddha. And the educated, be it remembered, know that the Buddha is no longer an existent being. In worshiping him, therefore, they are worshiping an ideal. With the more intelligent, worship thus becomes aspiration; with the more sophisticated it is conscious self-culture.

The domestic shrine is a part of every Buddhist home. In its simple form it consists of an image of the Buddha such as one can buy for a few ticals in the bazar with perhaps a colored print of some episode in the Buddha's life, procured from a center of Buddhist propaganda in Colombo. One rather elaborate domestic shrine which I saw in the house of a very simple layman consisted of two altars, the chief one, on the left, containing some twenty-one images of the Buddha and a reliquary, while the altar on the right held five Buddhas and nineteen figures of other, subordinate, beings—servants of the Buddha, my host called them, and teachers of Buddhism. One of these was of considerable interest to me—an antique bronze, well executed which had been handed down in the family for several generations. It was a four-handed figure, holding symbolic objects—a noose, a trident, etc., which showed it to be Siva—a fact quite unknown to its owner and worshiper. Here, apparently, was an unrecognized remnant of an ancient Siamese Siva cult. My host called the image *Norai* (= Tathagata) and regarded it as the image of some ancient teacher of Buddhism and helper of the Buddha. As such he worships it—and all the rest of the images—every day; bowing before them and at times making offerings of food; I should add that this man's Buddhism was of the very naïve sort which pictures the Buddha as a god in heaven, hearing and answering prayer.

Preaching services, as I have stated, are held in the wats four times a month. As services of this sort seem to me of considerable importance in the life and influence of a religion, I shall describe at some length one which I attended in the wat Benchamabopit, which I have reason to believe is very typical. About a third of the way from the altar to the door was the preacher's throne. In front of it, when I entered, were about twenty monks seated on mats on the floor, while behind the throne or pulpit sat the audience, also on mats. Immediately behind the pulpit was a rack with the candles offered by the audience as they entered, also two large vases with lotus buds, and several fruit dishes containing offerings of pan and betel. The service had not begun when I arrived, and the congregation—about forty-five in number—were having a pleasant social time, chatting, chewing betel, drinking tea, one or two of the men smoking, and some of them quietly praying. Men and women were present (I confess it was hard to tell which was which) as well as a few children. Each newcomer took off his shoes on entering, got down on hands and knees and crawled to his mat, bundle in hand (for all come pretty well armed), and on reaching his place proceeded to unpack and arrange his possessions. First the candles had to be handed up through the audience to the man nearest the candle rack, and by him lighted and put in place. Then the betel box, spittoon, and perhaps teapot and teacup must be conveniently located near the mat. These things being attended to, the newcomer would put his hands together, extend them toward the Buddha, and make a little silent prayer. The service began with chanting by the monks, during which most of the audience was silent and attentive—except for one old woman who was telling the old man next her about an accident that had happened to her arm. The old man listened and chewed but said nothing. Another old man quietly and reverently smoked throughout the chanting. The chanting was in unison on a single low note and the monks kept the note admirably. It was varied with responses between the leader and the body of the monks but always in a low and rather fine monotone. No gong or other instrument was used. The chanting was interspersed with bowing, and at a certain recognized phrase the audience also bowed deeply, touching their heads to the floor, and then followed the chanting with greater attention and reverence than before. Even the woman stopped talking and the old man stopped smoking, and all the members of the audience put their hands together in the attitude of prayer and followed the chanting of the monks with silent but moving lips. Plainly they knew the verses by heart and were very serious and reverent in reciting them. This sacred chant continued some ten or fifteen minutes, and then one of the monks came forward and seated himself, cross-legged in the preacher's throne, facing the audience but, at first, holding before his face a small screen or fan, while he led in a new responsive chant. At the close of the responses the preacher put aside his screen and took up a manuscript case, drawing out of it a long palm-leaf manuscript from which, after intoning a few sentences, he proceeded to read. He read in a monotone, but slowly and distinctly, and, so far as I could see, with no interpretations thrown in. The people were extremely attentive, nearly all holding their hands in the praying position, some with arms and heads touching the floor. The reading lasted some twenty minutes. The preacher then left the pulpit, the monks chanted two or three sentences, everybody bowed with heads touching the floor, the monks arose and filed out, and the audience drank tea. Betel boxes were rearranged, new choice bits prepared for chewing, and conversation began once more, in subdued tones. A man came from the front part of the temple with a pile of Siamese pamphlets and distributed them to the people. The pamphlet was devoted to various moral injunctions. Nearly every one took a copy and a great many dipped into it at once, some reading with evident interest. A few collected their betel boxes, tea baskets, and spittoons and went out one by one, depositing two satangs in the collection box at the door as they passed. Most of them stayed, talked, read, and chewed betel. An old gentleman lighted up his cigarette. As the majority seemed to have camped out for the rest of the morning I deposited my two satangs in the box, and left them to their betel and their talk.

Nearly two hours later the same morning I passed the preaching hall of the wat Saket and found an audience of sixty people, seated on mats, listening, as the other audience had done, to a monk reading from a palm-leaf manuscript. They were just as attentive as the first had been, with hands together in the position of prayer, and in silent, reverent attitude. The monk continued his reading, in slow, clear tones, for almost twenty minutes after I arrived. He then uncurled his legs and got down from the throne, and another monk took his place, opened a new manuscript, and began a new reading. I stayed till lunch time and then left alone. How long the audience had been listening to the

Law before my arrival and how long it continued to do so after my departure, I do not know.

The manuscripts from which the monks read to the people are prepared with a line of the Pali Sutta followed by a line of translation in Siamese. The monk reads straight along, slowly and distinctly, but with no pause or change of tone on passing from one language to the other. The audience, however, are accustomed to this type of reading and follow the Siamese translation without difficulty, in spite of its interruption by the Pali lines. By this method, moreover, many of them in time come to understand a certain amount of Pali.

The interest of the more earnest of the common people in the intellectual side of their religion was brought home to me when my young Siamese friend and interpreter (a former Buddhist, now a Christian) took me to the rooms of the "Sala Sandana Tham," or "Society for the Discussion of Buddhism." The Society is run by two laymen, the leader being an employee of an electrical plant. They have two moderate-sized rooms—really an ordinary shop with a front room and a back one. The front room has a pulpit. Its walls are adorned with lithographs from Colombo, depicting scenes from the life of the Buddha. Before one of these pictures are some incense sticks, candles and flowers. The back room contains only a large platform on which the women sit during the teaching service. The men stand out in the street. The audience varies from fifteen to thirty, the majority being men. The audience is small because the aim of the society is serious. It gives not exhortation but teaching. Two meetings are held every week, each meeting lasting four hours or more—one on Saturday evenings, the other on Sunday afternoons. They open with a short reading from a Pali Sutta by a monk, seated in the pulpit. After the Sutta has been read the monk translates it into old and scholarly Siamese and then expounds it. The rest of the time is occupied by the lay leader who stands and teaches in the popular Siamese of today. His teaching is chiefly concerned with "moral matters and the duties of life and the use of Buddha to the world." I quote here the words of the lay leader as translated to me by my young friend.

And what, I asked, is the use of Buddha to the world? "The use of Buddha to the world," he answered, "is to make people cease to be selfish and jealous. Also Buddha teaches us that death is not the end but that man is immortal, that only the body dies but the soul lives on. We shall have everlasting life in Nibban. We shall have eternal happiness there. It is a happiness that cannot be lost. But Buddha said, If you are to be happy in Nibban you must obey the Teaching and do good. The man who really puts his heart into his prayer will get a blessing from it. The Buddha hears and knows our prayers, and is doing his best to help us."

So I was given a little Buddhist sermon: a sermon by a layman who was apparently ignorant of the nice points of his religion; a sermon which differed considerably, I suspect, from the long one the learned abbot of wat Po was preaching that very afternoon before king and court, at the cremation of the royal princess; and yet a sermon of much earnestness and with much of the real Buddhist spirit of today. And different as it may have been in many respects from such a sermon as the abbot or the patriarch would have preached, it emphasized one point that they too would have emphasized: namely that Buddhism today teaches unselfish living. To several of the monks with whom I conversed I repeated the accusation so commonly made against Buddhism, that it is essentially selfish. They all denied the allegation. Buddhism, they insisted, teaches that we ought to love one another and be mutually helpful. I think, myself, that in their zeal to defend their religion they left out of consideration certain important principles, namely the doctrines of the destruction of sorrow and of the acquisition of merit. But as I have pointed out, one of these is already on the wane and the other is probably destined to decay; while the leaders of the religion, both lay and clerical, by their very faith that Buddhism is unselfish, will probably have much to do in making it so.

The influence of Buddhism on the Siamese people is generally admitted to be, from the moral point of view, excellent. That is the chief reason, many missionaries will tell you, why Christian missions have made such slow and slight progress, especially in those parts of Siam, like Bangkok, where Buddhism is at its best and at its strongest. The Buddhists are so satisfied with their own religion that it is difficult to make them see they need another. So the missionaries tell me. Buddhism is, moreover, probably the greatest force for democracy in Siam. The poorest peasant may become a monk, and once a monk he is spiritually on a level with the King. For the happiness of its adherents Buddhism also does much—as the words of the electrician and lay preacher quoted two pages back will indicate. Not so much, certainly, as Christianity will do, yet something. It teaches its followers that this is an ideal world, that the forces which ultimately control it are moral forces, that what a man sows he inevitably shall reap, and that death is not the end.

In my interview with the patriarch I asked him to tell me what comfort Buddhism had for the dying man. The Christian, I pointed out, faces death with the assurance that his sins are forgiven and that God will take care of his soul. Has Buddhism, I asked, any analogous consolation to offer. The patriarch's answer was in essence as follows: "The doctrine teaches that the body must be destroyed. This the dying Buddhist has long known and hence he is prepared for death. He has learned that he must not think about the body but let it go according to the laws of nature. The people around the dying man will tell him to think of the good deeds he has done [4]—such things as building temples, and helping the poor. If he have no good deeds of his own of which he may think, then he may fix his thought on the Buddha and his work."

Cold comfort many a Christian will call this. Yet it is not so cold for the Buddhist as it would be for one brought up in the Christian creed. For the Christian the sting of death is sin and the strength of sin is the Law. But the Christian conception of sin, as an offense against a personal Deity who will be our Judge, is entirely foreign to the Buddhist. He feels no need of pardon—in fact the notion of pardon for sin would seem to him almost as incongruous as pardon for having cut off one's own hand. Sin, for Buddhism, is an offense against one's self, hence pardon is some-

[4] Almost this identical thing is said by Fielding Hall, in *The Soul of a People*, p. 285.

thing the Buddhist can hardly conceive of, much less desire. There is, moreover, for him, no personal Judge, no living God, into whose hands he is about to fall. There is, instead, an eternal Law that whatever he has sowed that he must surely reap. Brought up with such conceptions as these, his best comfort, facing death is to be found in the philosophical, even stoical, point of view, reinforced with what hope he can muster by fixing his attention on his own good deeds and on the merit which he has through them acquired. The comfort may be cold but it is real. Moreover, the Buddhist would doubtless insist, it is all the comfort which either reason or morality can justify. It would be cheating the dying with false hopes, it would be misleading the living with the promise of an easy way of avoiding the consequences of sin, it would be watering down the great conception of an implacably just Cosmos, to teach that at the last moment one may evade the fate one has built for oneself by calling for help upon some one else. The Siamese Buddhists consider Buddhism the supremely moral religion because of its emphasis on the law of causes, because of its teaching that each man must work out his own salvation with diligence.

How does Buddhism compare with Christianity? I put this question to the two most able Buddhists I met in Siam—the prince patriarch and the monk I have called the chief examiner. The patriarch responded that Christianity teaches the necessity of prayer and the necessity of help from God. If God does not help, the Christian feels helpless. Buddhism, on the other hand, instead of telling its followers to seek help from God, teaches them to study the word of the Buddha and do it, thus helping themselves in accordance with and by the guidance of his precepts. This response was deeply characteristic of Buddhism. But the reply of the chief examiner was no less so. On hearing my question he was silent a moment, with brows knit, and then he responded in that quick decisive way of his, that if he should undertake to answer me he would be forced to dwell upon the superiority of his own religion, and this would involve him in self-satisfaction, pride, and sin; he must therefore refuse absolutely to give any answer to my question.

I do not think either of these monks knew a great deal

about Christianity. I do not think it would be difficult to show that in many real ways, such as the production of happiness and of morality, Christianity is superior to Buddhism. Yet I must confess—as I think this chapter will have indicated—that I bore away from Siam a great respect for the religion of that sunny land. Its marble wats, its golden shrines, and much more the simple, steady faith of the laity, the training given them by the monks in the fundamentals of morality, the impress, still so deep, of the Founder's limitless devotion—these rather than the undoubted defects of his teaching, fill one's thoughts as one embarks once more upon the tawny Menam and sails slowly downstream, past the jungle vistas, past the native huts, past the last little wat on the bank of the widening river, out into the gulf, until Siam has become again merely a thin green line between sky and sea, and the ship turns into its steady course towards Cambodia.

CHAPTER X

CAMBODIA

JUST how Buddhism came to Cambodia and when it came are questions to which we shall probably never have the answer. In fact, it is impossible to say how the Cambodians themselves came and whence and when. It is pretty certain, however, that at any rate by the year 400 A.D. and probably before that date, their reigning house and their nobility and priesthood were Hindus. Indian influence was felt along all the southern coasts of "Farther India" and even in Java and Borneo at a very early period. It was probably brought at first by traders and then by colonists. Presumably it reached Cambodia in this fashion at first; but there is good reason to suppose that some sort of conquest was also involved, and that a migrating group of Indians (probably Kshatriyas with some Brahmins) actually seized the throne of the country and founded a dynasty that ruled over the Khmers or Cambodians for many a century. They brought with them their Indian culture, the Dravidian architectural skill and fondness for immense structures, and also their religions. These religions were Brahmanism and Mahayana Buddhism, as is shown by the early inscriptions. The first inscriptions are in Sanskrit, and begin shortly after 600 A.D. The kings were primarily worshipers of Siva but Mahayana Buddhism was also in high favor with them and with the higher classes; and in fact, as Eliot suggests, "the idea that the two systems were incompatible obviously never occurred to the writers of the inscriptions, and Buddhism was not regarded as more distinct from Sivaism and Vishnuism than these were from one another."[1]

From about the year 800 till the middle of the fourteenth century Cambodia was the greatest power of Indo-China. Much of the time it was at war with the Chams, to the south

[1] *Op. cit.*, III, 120.

and east, but, though the fortunes of war varied, the Khmers usually had the best of it, and finally aided the new invaders of the peninsula, the Annamese, who came down from the north along the eastern coast, in putting an end to Champa as an independent kingdom. It was during these great centuries that the Cambodian kings and nobility erected those immense palaces, fortresses, and temples in and around Angkor which have only within our time been in part brought back to light from the savage jungle which took possession of them at the final overthrow of the Khmer power. These temples were mostly Hindu and were sacred especially to Siva, so they do not concern us here. We should note in passing, however, that some of the lesser temples and monuments were Mahayanist. For while the kings right through this period seem to have been faithful to their Hindu religion—largely through the influence, we may surmise, of the hereditary Brahmin priesthood of the court—many of the nobility seem to have favored the Mahayana.

A greater change was, however, in progress than that from Hinduism to a Brahmanical form of Mahayanism. The Siamese, as we have seen, had made themselves independent of Cambodia in the thirteenth century and in the next century humbled their former rulers in several wars, even capturing Angkor a number of times. We must suppose that while the Siamese borrowed from the more cultured Khmers a good deal of their Indian civilization, the common people of Cambodia began to borrow from the Siamese the Hinayana form of Buddhism, which they themselves were at the same time borrowing from southern Burma. At any rate, when the Chinese traveler Chou Ta-kuan visited Cambodia in 1296 he found that the Hinayana had already largely supplanted the Mahayana.[2] Incidentally he makes one remark which goes far to explain the subsequent course of Cambodian religious history: to the effect, namely, that all the children who went to school at all got their instruction from the Buddhist monks.

As might have been expected, during the course of the following century Hinayana Buddhism not only supplanted

[2] It is also significant that from about 1300 on the Buddhist inscriptions are no longer in Sanskrit (the language of the Mahayana) but in Pali.

the Mahayana but, except at court, supplanted Hinduism as well. The chief reason for this change was very likely the fact just quoted, namely, that all the laymen who got any education at all got it from the monks and in so doing were largely won over to the Hinayana. Doubtless there were other causes. Leclère connects the religious revolution with a change of dynasty that came about in 1320.[3] More important still, the Hinayana appealed to the people and became the democratic creed of the cities.

> Brahmanism was exclusive and tyrannical. It made no appeal to the masses but a severe levy of forced labor must have been necessary to erect and maintain the numerous great shrines which, though in ruins, are still the glory of Camboja. . . . When Siamese Buddhism invaded Camboja it had a double advantage. It was the creed of an aggressive and successful neighbor, but while thus armed with the weapons of this world, it also appealed to the poor and oppressed. If it enjoyed the favor of princes, it had no desire to defend the rights of a privileged caste; it offered salvation and education to the average townsman and villager.[4]

After the fourth capture of their capital by the Siamese (in 1460) the Cambodians abandoned it to their enemies and to the jungle. Much of their territory they lost to Siam and some to the invading Annamese. Champa had already been destroyed by these invaders, and its Buddhism wiped out. The Indian part of Indo-China ends at the border of Annam and Cochin-China. To this rising Annamese power the king of Cambodia for many years paid tribute, at the same time recognizing the suzerainty of Siam. The French intervention in 1862, while it made Cambodia a part of the French empire, at least put it on an equal footing with the other states of eastern Indo-China. It has its own king still, who, like the kings of Annam, Tonkin, and Laos, is subject to France and is guided in his acts by a French agent.[5]

But in spite of the many humiliations of the last five centuries, Cambodia is still itself—very unspoiled, very Buddhist, very Cambodian. The French have treated its people

[3] *Le Buddhisme au Cambodge* (Paris, Leroux, 1899).

[4] Eliot, III, 128.

[5] In this sketch of Cambodian history I have depended chiefly upon Grousset, Leclère, and Eliot.

with sympathy and appreciation, and have returned to it the site of its former glory, so long in the hands of the Siamese, the Angkor region with its magnificent ruins, its swamps and its jungle. From the Grand Lac, near which the ruins are situated, the mighty stream of the Tonlé Sap flows southward and at Pnom Penh unites its waters with those of the Mekong, which from this point to the sea is one of the most majestic rivers of Asia. Except for a slightly elevated watershed along the coast to the west, covered with marshy forests, most of the land is as flat as a billiard table, with an occasional hill or some far-away symmetrical peak, gazing at one from the dim distance. The charm of the land lies not in its geographic features (except, perhaps, for its magnificent river) but in the primitive simplicity of its villages, its little winding streams, hardly wider than the launch which carries you, the roads (wonderful roads of French construction) busy with the life of the country people and yellow with monks and little boys, the modest monasteries, hidden away by the bank of a stream or near the village, spreading among all these simple, happy country folk the gentle calmness of the Buddha, as they have done ever since the Hinayana came to them from Siam.

The Buddhism of Cambodia, being thus an offshoot of the church we studied in the preceding chapter, it will need but a relatively brief treatment here. It might almost be sufficient simply to indicate the differences between the religions of the two lands and for the rest merely refer the reader back to what has been said of Siam. I shall hardly treat it as cavalierly as that; but it may be well to begin what I have to say of Cambodia with a brief indication of the principal ways in which Cambodian Buddhism differs from Siamese. First of all I might mention the *general feeling* one gets on landing in Cambodia, that (except for one particular which will be mentioned later) one is farther away from India and closer to China. "Indo-China" is a most appropriate term for this great peninsula of southeastern Asia; and in all parts of it one feels the ever-present influence of one or the other or both of its two mighty neighbors, the two great sources of almost everything of importance in all the Far East. Thus, to mention only external things, the architecture slowly but noticeably changes its shape as one advances from Burma toward China. There are, of course, sharp lines of cleavage, as one passes some racial and linguistic border, but there has always been some preparation for the change, and it is this gradual transition I have specially in mind—a faintly noticeable transition such as that one experiences on traveling out of the tropics into the temperate zone. The costumes of the people rather notably mark the waning of one influence and the waxing of the other. Burma is almost as blazing with color as India itself. Siam is still brilliant, but its colors are not so varied nor so flaming as the Indian and Burmese. The Siamese *panung* or sarang (the garment wound around the legs and serving as trousers for both sexes) is often gay enough, in tints that astonish the stranger; yet one misses the brilliant beauty of the many-colored sari. In Cambodia, the color has somehow faded from most of the costumes; and among the Annamese, though a long purple coat may occasionally be seen, the prevailing tone is decidedly subdued. So one insensibly passes from the rainbow of India to the solemn blacks, whites, and blues of China.

Cambodia is midway in this passage. It is also midway in other and less pleasant things. The betel chewing becomes gradually less common, the hawking gets louder, the spitting more reckless. The same gradual transition is noticeable in matters of religion. When the lover of Hinayana Buddhism first enters a Cambodian wat his immediate reaction is one of pleasure in finding so much that he had come to prize in Burma and Siam, but his second will probably be a slight sense of protest against what he may call (if he be a Hinayana purist) the taint of China. On the lower step of the golden throne, below the Buddha he may find a fat Milei-Fo, the Chinese representative of Maitreya, the coming Buddha, a contented and friendly grin upon his face, and his arms scarcely reaching around his immense paunch. On the altar there will be endless artificial flowers, and strung along by its side several bunches of paper money. So China and its Mahayana begins, very guardedly and gently, to steal in.

An equally important contrast to Siamese Buddhism is to be found in what might be called the taint of India. It will be recalled that in both Burma and Ceylon various Vedic and post-Vedic devas and devatas held subordinate rôles in Buddhist temples. In Siam one sees very little of this Indian influence, but in Cambodia it reappears. The admixture of Hinduism in Cambodian Buddhism will be easily understood after what has been said in the earlier and historical part of this chapter. Hinduism has not crept into Cambodian Buddhism. It has always been in it. The first form of Buddhism that came to Cambodia, it will be recalled, was the Mahayana; and the Mahayana had in it a large element of Hinduism. If one will look into the opening passages of what is perhaps the most fundamental of the Mahayana books—the Saddharma Pundarika Sutra—he will find Indra, Brahma, and a goodly company of devas, Nagas and Garudas. Long ago, to be sure, Hinayana Buddhism supplanted the Mahayana in Cambodia; but it could not throw off all the inheritance which the Mahayana left it—though plainly some effort was made to do so, as is shown by the iconoclasm of some of the mediaeval monks toward the images of Siva in various small shrines in the neighborhood of Angkor, and also by the Cambodian legend of the victory of the Buddha over Siva and Vishnu. But Hinduism and Buddhism in Cambodia had been on friendly terms too many years, and the commingling of ideas and images had gone too far for the purists to be able to make Cambodian Buddhism as free from Hindu elements as is that of Siam, Burma, or Ceylon. The buildings at Angkor, moreover, with their marvelous decorations, had inevitable effect upon the architectural and sculptural themes of the whole country, and their influence could hardly be escaped even in Buddhist wats and pagodas. Hence the Nagas with their cobra heads and gigantic tails, the Garudas, with their full-breasted spouses, and the four-faced Sivas have found their places in most Buddhist architecture. And not only in Buddhist architecture. Inside the shrine one will occasionally find Siva, Vishnu, Kali, or the elephant-headed Ganesh. I am told also that Nandi and Siva's lingam sometimes appear. These Hindu deities occupy positions subordinate to the Buddha, but they are there; and they get their share of the worship, at least from the more ignorant of the laity. Even on the belief of the bonzes Hinduism has had some influence. Some of them will tell you that at the beginning of each kalpa the race is recreated by the act of Prom, that is, Brahma;[6] while Siva, Vishnu, and Indra keep their place in popular mythology. The Cambodians worship these Hindu gods no longer and make no new images of them; but they cannot forget that it was Siva and his colleagues who built Angkor Wat.

It would be a mistake, however, to emphasize the Hindu element in Cambodian Buddhism and Cambodian temples. At its greatest it is always a subordinate element and in most of the wats or temples it hardly appears at all, except in some incident of the decoration. The usual Cambodian wat is, in fact, except for its greater simplicity, almost identical in form with the wat of Siam. It has the same characteristic double roof, the same horns extending out from the gables, and the same general plan. It is usually smaller than its Siamese sister, its coloring has shared the common fate of most coloring as one gets farther away from India—it is faded and tired looking—and in the arrangement of buildings simplicity has been substituted for complexity. The wats of Pnom Penh, for example, have no such bewildering wilderness of bots, wihans, Phra-Chedis, Phra-Prangs, and I know not what else, as half a dozen of the Bangkok wats present; while the country wats have in most cases nothing but the one hall of worship, without a single pagoda or other extra structure. There are, of course, always the dormitories for the monks, very simple wooden structures as a rule, propped up on stilts like most houses in Cambodia, and with thatched, undecorated roofs, in a little group next to the temple enclosure. The royal wat (the Phra-Keo) is, of course, somewhat of an exception. Its buildings are not numerous—there are within the temple enclosure, beside the central hall, only two pagodas (both mausolea), two small bell towers, and an artificial mound capped with a shrine covering a "footprint" of the Buddha; but in elaborateness and costliness of decoration and of contents it rivals anything in Bangkok except the royal wat, and in some respects it outshines even that. Its white walls are adorned with gold-

[6] J. Moura, *Le Royaume de Cambodge* (Paris, Leroux, 1883), I, 156.

crowned windows, it has a triple roof and a pointed central tower. But it is the interior that is especially famous. All that the kings of Cambodia could do to make this outdo its Siamese prototype and rival has been done, and if one is impressed by gold and diamonds one may prepare for thrills. A solid silver floor one hundred and twenty feet long by thirty feet wide, an emerald Buddha, a standing Buddha six feet high of solid gold, several other gold Buddhas wearing large diamonds on their brows and chests—these and other wonders the visitor will see, and if he is as impressionable as I suppose one should be he will come out feeling as the Queen of Sheba did when King Solomon had shown her all his treasures: "She had no spirit in her." The exterior may perhaps affect him in the same wonderful way, too; it evidently did the editor of the Japanese guidebook. "As visitors stand between these edifices," he tells us, "and look upwards, they will observe that the sky is pierced by the pointed roofs of all these buildings and that the variegated colours of their tiles present a strange harmony of beauty against the azure sky. They will feel that they are in a dream land."

For my own part, while I must confess to a weakness for pointed roofs that pierce the sky, I am unfortunately thick-skinned when it comes to emerald Buddhas and diamond-studded collars, and feel much more impressed by a poor bronze image which people are actually worshiping. Much more typical of Cambodian Buddhism as a living religion than is the palace temple, and therefore to me much more interesting, is a smaller wat near the palace, with neither golden Buddhas nor sky-piercing roofs. It consists of an enclosure surrounded by an iron fence, containing a central hall of worship, a pagoda behind it within which is a shrine with several Buddha images, and, along the sides of the central hall, about twenty small and solid pagodas, which (like most pagodas in Cambodia) mark the graves of departed worthies. These Cambodian pagodas are not so slender and pointed as the Phra-Chedis of Siam, yet they are not like the Phra-Prangs—a form which Siam borrowed from the towers of Angkor and which are seldom seen in the enclosures of Cambodian wats. The central hall of worship (it would be called the bot in Siam) has the usual double roof, but this is not accentuated, and the colors of its tiles are of a rather discouraged tint. The interior is a single room, with a high ceiling supported by columns, and walls covered with frescoes. It was the noon hour when I entered, and half a dozen monks, who had just finished their one daily meal, were lying or sitting on the floor, and more strolled in later on. They were loafing, smoking, chatting, napping. Some had brought with them an armful of palm-leaf manuscript, but none were reading. They were all very courteous and kindly (as I have invariably found Buddhist monks to be) and made no objection to my going anywhere I liked, in their sight or out of it, blindly trusting that I would not pocket any of the little votive Buddhas that sat in tempting attitudes upon the altar. In my wanderings I opened the door of the pagoda at the rear of the hall of worship, and found three Buddha images—the largest one a "sleeping Buddha"—and a monk at full length on the floor imitating the Master's example. I shut the door quickly and quietly, so as not to disturb the slumbers of either Master or faithful follower, and returned to the hall to examine the altar and the Buddha throne. The altar consisted of two low tables with elaborate candles that had never been lighted, artificial flowers, and the usual incense. At other wats I have often noticed oil lamps as a favorite offering—modern-looking, cheap lamps, seldom if ever lighted, but in a sense taking the place of the ubiquitous clocks of Siam. Paper money and paper banners are also common offerings. Near the altar—in this wat and in most—is the pulpit, an elaborate chair on which the preacher or reader sits, his legs curled up under him, on preaching days. At the back of the altar is the Buddha throne, with a large and ugly Buddha seated upon it, while below him are several standing Buddhas and one Chinese Milei-Fo, with hands clasped as usual around his precious belly.

The Buddhas of Cambodia are much like the Siamese, yet with enough difference to make them usually distinguishable. As in Siam the seated and standing ones are by far the commonest. Most of them have a pointed flame issuing from their heads, but the flame is less pointed, its base broader and its upper angle more obtuse than in Siam. Frequently the

Cambodian Buddha wears a kind of band or cap over his forehead, from which the flamelike point issues. His ears are of about the same length as those of his Siamese brothers, but his four fingers are frequently all of the same length, as in Burma. The larger Cambodian Buddhas are usually rather ugly, with sensual, almost African lips, and broad noses. The Cambodians also paint the eyes of their large Buddhas so as to give them a more realistic and human appearance, with a result that is not always pleasing.

A partial exception to what I have said is to be found in the great Buddha at Oudong. Oudong was an ancient capital of Cambodia, now deserted and overgrown and lost in the jungle, save for what was the central part of it—three small hills that rise abruptly from the marshy plain, the only break for miles in the flat paddy and swamp lands that flank both sides of the upper Mekong and the Tonlé Sap. On two of the hillocks of this little triplet are lofty pagodas marking royal tombs, while on the central one is a large wat, and near it a little monastery. The monks, noting your arrival, send up a boy to the top of the hill who opens the door of the great hall. On entering it you are halted almost immediately by an arresting sight. The lofty roof is supported by two rows of enormous round whitish columns, perhaps seven feet in diameter, and at the farther end of the nave, between the columns, you see a gigantic and triumphant golden Buddha, seated on a lofty throne, his knees hidden behind the further columns and his crown touching the very top of the high roof. The building must have been built around him. He is unique among the Buddhas of my acquaintance. His face and posture give little suggestion of Nirvana, nor yet is his face sensual. Rather, as I have indicated, it is triumphant, triumphant and strong. Perhaps without sufficient reason, on viewing it I found myself thinking of the last scene in the Passion Play at Brixleg in the Tyrol, which I have twice witnessed—a tableau of the risen and triumphant Christ sitting in judgment on the world. That Christ had little of pity but was the embodiment of victory and infinite reserve power. So of the Buddha of Oudong. It expresses little of the Buddhist sympathy, little of the other-worldly calm which the Burmese Buddha so well symbolizes. A kind of calm, indeed, it does express, but a calm that comes from conscious power. There is peace in the eyes, while in the mouth there is triumph; and before that gigantic figure, seated between those exaggerated columns, you feel oppressed by your own littleness.

I do not think that the Cambodian bonzes are much affected by the expression of their Buddhas, one way or another. Very likely it was purely imagination on my part, but in Burma and Ceylon I had the feeling that the Great Peace on the face of many of the finer images did have its influence upon the yellow-robed worshipers who spent so much of their time before that striking symbol. In Cambodia I had no such feeling. They impressed me as being on the whole less learned, less intelligent, and less spiritual than the monks of the other Hinayana lands. A certain amount of knowledge of their religion they must, indeed, possess; for they are admitted to the full rank of monks only on passing an examination—usually at about the age of twenty-two. They are numerous enough, certainly—some forty thousand, I was told, out of a total population of two million. As to the nature of their influence there are various opinions. Some of the Frenchmen will tell you their influence is excellent; others that it is a great bar to progress. I heard no accusation against them on the ground of immorality, but much on the ground of laziness and ignorance. They have, at any rate, the profound respect and reverence of the people.[7]

The monk rises at dawn, dresses, repeats his prayers, tidies up his cell, and at seven starts out with the others on his rounds with his begging bowl suspended from his left shoulder. On returning he kneels before some older monk and

[7] I must here transcribe Leclère's opinion of the Cambodian clergy: "*Ce que le Buddha a voulu qu'ils fussent, ils le sont encore: des cadavres vivants, non pour l'action entre les mains de leurs chefs comme nos jesuites, mais pour l'exemple qu'ils doivent au peuple et leur propre salut. Ils n'aspirent ni au gouvernement des hommes, ni au gouvernement des consciences; ils se bornent à prêcher l'exemple et à enseigner la doctrine sans l'imposer. Et ils n'ont aucun pouvoir politique, aucun pouvoir temporel. S'ils ne sont jamais consultés, en matière civile, ils sont resté un clergé respectable et respecté, parce qu'il ne s'est jamais compromis; leur doctrine est admise par tout le monde, indiscutée, parce qu'ils sont demeurés étrangers à toutes les revolutions qui ont tout ruiné autour d'eux, parce qu'ils sont restés des hommes de foi religieuse, et rien d'autre chose*" (*op. cit.*, p. 396).

confesses[8] any fault he may have committed since waking. All the monks then go to the main hall (or Sala) and eat some of their breakfast. They also repeat prayers at this time and throw some grains of rice to the birds before eating. They eat in silence and without choosing their food. The rest of the morning up to 11:30 they spend at various tasks, teaching the lay students, doing some of the necessary work for the monastery or praying and meditating. Their methods of meditation do not differ materially from those of their Siamese brethren: so I need say nothing of them here. At 11:30 they eat again—their last meal of the day—following it by a "rather long grace." After this they disperse, most of them for a nap. In the afternoon they may continue the occupations of the morning or go out and visit their relatives or other laymen, provided they do not go alone. The monk is always chaperoned. They are also always grave and dignified, or at least are taught to be so. But though dignified their gravity is not oppressive; they are welcome visitors and they mix with the villagers quite freely. The country roads, the city streets, and the banks of all the little rivers gleam with the yellows and browns of their robes. They do not confine themselves to any one shade, as do their fellows in Burma and Ceylon and to a considerable extent in Siam, but wear any shade of brown or yellow that suits their fancy, frequently wearing both colors at once. Everywhere they are received with deference; sometimes, I am told, with fear. They have apparently much to do in forming the public opinion of the land.

Their contribution toward the life of the community consists chiefly in education and prayer. Nearly all the boys are sent for at least a brief period to the monastic schools, where they study reading, writing, arithmetic, religion, morals, and manners. The monks also read the Dhamma to the people and expound it four times a month. They conduct funeral services and they represent the community before the throne of the Buddha. It may seem odd to mention this as one of their contributions to the society in which they live, yet there can be no doubt that most of the laity would

[8] The Patimokkha is recited regularly as in Ceylon. There is no public confession; however, guilty monks simply abstaining from attendance (Eliot, III, 131).

regard the proper performance of the proper acts of worship, at regular times and on special occasions, as among the chief functions and duties of the bonzes. Nor would a good Christian of the medieval centuries have seen anything peculiar in such a view. Today, in fact, one of the regular duties of the priest in the Roman Catholic church is to say the daily office, which he does not for the benefit of his own soul but that God may be duly worshiped. An arrangement is made, moreover, by which different sections of the Roman church universal shall devote certain hours to consecutive worship in cooperation with each other in such fashion that prayer and praise shall be constantly ascending from some quarter or other to the throne on high. It is a little difficult for us Protestants to get this purely objective view of the value of prayer, as something intrinsically worth while, yet it is a very simple view and it has been a very common one in many religions. Most of us have become so sophisticated on the question of prayer that we do not realize we are sophisticated at all. The situation in Buddhism is, to be sure, a little different from what one finds in Catholic Christianity; for in the latter the conception lying back of the custom is probably that God is somehow gratified by this stream of unending devotion that rises night and day from earth to heaven. Buddhists of the Southern school, believing as they do (when orthodox) that the Buddha is quite beyond hearing any mortal praises, do not think their chantings please him. Nevertheless, it is a good thing to give thanks unto the Lord and to sing praises unto the name of the Most High. It is a good thing in itself, it is worth while for its own sake, it is one of the things one ought to do, and as such it cannot fail to have its good results. Hence morning and night a little company of faithful bonzes gather together in every monastery of the land and repeat the sacred verses that have become hallowed through two thousand years of pious repetition.

These services are not as a rule public, nor are the laity expected or desired to attend. They are not held (in the larger monasteries at any rate) in the central hall of worship but in a more private and secluded oratory close to or within the dormitories of the monks. In one of these I remember finding not only a shrine with many Buddhas but a life-size statue of a learned monk (they called him "Professor") who had recently died. In a smaller monastery I was present at the regular six o'clock evening service. The oratory was undecorated and in a state of considerable confusion, as a room inhabited and cared for only by bachelors is likely to be. Yellow robes were strewn about the floor, in the middle of things a large pile of palm-leaf manuscript, and there was the usual chorus of spittoons. On the altar, beside the principal image, were ten smaller Buddhas and eight lamps. Three of the lamps were lighted, the others, mostly with broken chimneys, apparently functioned merely as offerings. On the floor in front of the altar were kneeling two old monks and two novices, boys of perhaps sixteen. By no means all the members of a monastery participate in every service, but there are always enough faithful ones to see that the proper worship is offered every morning and every night. The chant was in a monotone, various verses, which all knew by heart, being repeated several times over. At intervals the chant would cease and all would bow their heads to the floor. The oldest of the monks, who led the chanting, would at times intone a few sentences alone, and then the others would join in once more. When they caught sight of me, an uninvited intruder upon their worship, one of the monks brought me a chair. Then the chanting continued, their thoughts being apparently on higher things than strange Americans.

The theology, if so I may call it—rather I should say the *theory*—of Cambodian Buddhists is almost or quite identical with that of the Siamese, and I shall therefore be brief about it. Spite of a little harmless incense to Siva or Ganesh or perhaps to a dead "Professor," Sakyamuni has no serious rival. I specially inquired as to how many Buddhas there were. The word Buddha, I was told, is popularly used at times to mean any sort of supernatural being, but as an object of religious veneration Preasac-mannac-cudom (the Cambodian name for Sakyamuni) stands alone. As I was being conducted about the palace at Pnom Penh by an intelligent and ardent young Buddhist, I pointed out to him the four faces on the central pinnacle—obviously copied from the Siva faces of the Angkor wat towers—and asked him whose faces these were. "*Bouddha à quatre faces,*" was his reply. In one of the palace shrines I found an elephant-headed Ganesh and asked who it might be. "*Bouddha à l'elephant,*" he answered. Another Hindu deity turned up in the next shrine, this one with eight arms. In response to my question, I was informed that this was "*Bouddha à huit bras.*" How many Buddhas are there? I asked. "*Beaucoup,*" he said. But when I asked if he prayed to them all, he told me very decidedly that he did not: that he prayed to only one, namely to "Prea Soumantakodam," [9] whose name he carefully wrote out in my note-book. This, he said, is "*le Bouddha Cambodgien,*" and all Cambodians pray to him and to no one else. And the "*Bouddha à quatre faces*" I discovered on further questioning has another name. He is "Bouddha-Siva."

Not many monks, I think, would have made even the beginning of the confusion between the Buddha and his ancient rivals which this young man did. I asked explicitly from one of them how many Buddhas there were and was told there was but one. I told him that in China and Japan there were several. He was mildly interested, but responded that in Cambodia at any rate there was but one.[10]

The present condition of this one Buddha I took pains, as usual, to inquire about. The laity, as elsewhere, consider him as in conscious bliss, and quite able to hear and answer their prayers. The clergy as usual are divided. I called on one of the principal abbots of the capital to get his opinion on this point. His house—the largest of the houses in the dormitory section of the monastery, and standing like the rest on stilts—was a two-story building, with one large room taking up the entire lower floor. A flight of steps led up from this to the sleeping apartments above. A monk went up to announce my call and I had time to look around before the right reverend old gentleman came down. The ceiling of the room was in process of redecoration and things were in considerable confusion, the tables and the floor being covered with a litter of teapots and spittoons. Few books—I think

[9] Evidently another spelling for Preasac-mannac-cudom.

[10] This belief in but one Buddha does not preclude a lively faith in the coming Buddha Maitreya, whom they call Prea-Mittay, and whose advent is to begin a period of universal happiness. See Moura, *op. cit.*, p. 152.

none—were in sight. Undoubtedly the abbot had the usual supply of palm-leaf manuscripts or books, but kept them in his bed chamber. He came downstairs smoking an immense cigar, his brown robe flung loosely over his shoulders, disclosing much of his very fat paunch, which gave him a striking likeness to Milei-Fo. As he descended, the two laymen in the room fell upon their faces, and he ordered chairs and cigarettes for the guests in a tone that, I think, has seldom been heard in Europe since the days of the late czar. He asked me so many questions about Ceylon, in which he was evidently much interested, that it was with difficulty I brought around the conversation to the Buddha and his present condition. The Buddha, he finally told me, is dead, and has been dead a long time. He no longer hears or knows anything. When one prays to him he does not hear it or know it. When I asked why, then, one prays to the Buddha, he failed to see any incongruity. For him, in fact, there was none. If one's father is ill, he said, one goes to the monks and they say prayers to the Buddha and this may help the sick father. I asked him to give me an example of the prayer the monks might make if asked to pray for a sick man, and he kindly prayed aloud for me. The prayer was in Pali. Such prayers, of course, are not petitions but sacred verses that have indeed little to do with the particular situation or desire but which have a value in themselves so that their repetition produces merit; and merit is useful in many ways. Not that petitional prayer is unknown. The unintelligent laymen frequently make direct requests to the Buddha, and Eliot says he has heard in Cambodia prayers for peace and against war [11]—apparently from monks. Still this is not orthodox. The learned monks "recall the Buddha's deeds, teach his doctrine, revive his memory; they do not call upon him for help because they know that he cannot help them, that he cannot respond, since he is no longer an active personality." [12]

As this quotation shows, and as I have previously pointed out, the theory of prayer follows, of course, directly from the theory of the present condition of the Buddha; and the theory of Nirvana is no less directly related to it. When

[11] III, 130. [12] Leclère, p. 330.

Moura was preparing his great work on *Le Royaume du Cambodge*, over forty years ago, he made a point of asking a number of the clergy as to the nature of Nirvana. As might have been expected, he got varying answers. The head of the ecclesiastical order told him that *Nippean* was eternal salvation in a celestial body, with unending calm joy. On the other hand, the Prea Soccon, which Moura interprets as "viccar general," and who in this case was recognized as the most learned Buddhist in the kingdom, insisted that Nippean was complete annihilation. As to the common people, Moura says three-fourths of them have never heard of Nippean, and those who have consider it a place of delight.

The conception of Nirvana held by the learned monks with whom M. Leclère discussed the matter was in most respects the orthodox view contained in the Nikayas. Nirvana is neither existence nor non-existence, neither pain nor pleasure. It is the end of individuality and of change; yet one could not identify it with annihilation or absolute nothing.[13] But a quite new aspect of the concept is revealed in some pages of M. Leclère's valuable volume, which seems to indicate that the ancient Brahmanism and Mahayanism of six hundred years ago has more influence on the thought of Cambodian Buddhism than one would otherwise suppose. This is connected with the belief in *Preas Prohm.* Preas Prohm is the god Brahma of Hinduism, but he seems also to be mixed up with the impersonal Brahma of the Upanishads and suggests the idealistic Absolute of the Mahayana. As a kind of god he recreates the world of men at the beginning of each new kalpa; [14] some of the monks who talked with M. Leclère said that Preas Prohm is eternal, uncreated, and out of time. All things exist eternally in Him. In their transitory forms they are for our eyes only, not for his. He is changeless peace. It is a common saying among the people (for they know that He exists but little else about him) "Preas Prohm awakes for the Buddha." This is explained by the learned as follows: by his "sleep" is meant the period in which his nature expresses itself in the ordinary course of events; by his awakening at the appearance of a Buddha is meant the expression of his nature in an extraor-

[13] *Ibid.*, Book VIII, Chap. 4.

[14] Moura, *op. cit.*, p. 156.

dinary way, i.e., in a personality of great sanctity who has attained not only to holiness but to a comprehension of Preas Prohm. It is not rare to find a highly educated monk, such as the head of a monastery, who will say "Nippean (Nirvana) and Preas Prohm are one and the same thing." [15]

Preas Prohm has no cult and plays but a small rôle in the thoughts of any but the most learned and philosophical. Nippean, too, is not a matter of much practical importance. Heaven and hell, on the other hand, are much more lively, definite, and interesting conceptions for both laity and clergy. Heaven is a kind of terrestrial paradise situated on Tray-trong (Mt. Meru of Indian mythology). It has three gradations, in an ascending scale: namely, that of the laity, the bonzes, and the ascetics. These heavens play a much more prominent place in the minds of Cambodian Buddhists than either Nirvana or rebirth. Hell is no less real, and is a constant peril to the unwary. The young Buddhist layman who took me through one of the wats I noticed carefully taking off his shoes before entering the building. As this had never been required of me in Siam I had gone in with my shoes on; but noticing his action I asked if I should remove mine. My guide responded that it was not necessary but that it was advisable; for if I did not do so I should go straight down to hell, and the soles of my feet would be cut off. The words were accompanied with such earnest and vivid gestures that I hastened to shake off the offending shoes. I have seen too many pictures of the Buddhist hell to take any unnecessary chances with it.

Most laymen and most monks, too, believe not only in the Buddha but in the Neaca-ta,[16] the spirits of the land which correspond to the nats of Burma, though with none of their picturesqueness. They are simply the ancient animistic godlets who were in Cambodia long before the Buddha came and with whom the Buddha and his disciples have never seriously quarreled. In front of many of the wats there are little shrines to the Neaca-ta, frequently three, distantly suggesting bird-houses or dog-kennels, and containing no images, but usually supplied with a few incense sticks. It is especially to the Neaca-ta that the Cambodians pray when sick,

[15] Leclère, *op. cit.*, Book I, Chap. I. [16] Moura, p. 172.

just as the Laos in Siam do to their tree-spirits. This is largely an homage of fear: it can hardly be called worship. It bears much the same relation to the Cambodian's worship of the Buddha that usury bears to the loyal devotion one owes and gives to one's king.

For the Buddha is worshiped with loyal devotion in both temple and home. Offerings of flowers and incense are brought by the laity to his public temples, and each Cambodian home has its domestic shrine in which there is a little image or picture of the Buddha. The worship given in the public temple varies considerably, the women going often, the men perhaps only once a year. In the domestic shrine worship is paid every day. Four times a month, as in Siam, there is a public service of prayer in the wat, followed by preaching. The monk reads to the people from the Dhamma in Cambodian and expounds its meaning. The subject matter of this preaching, the abbot told me, consists chiefly of moral injunctions.

Almost every boy, as we have seen, spends some time in one of the wats, wearing the yellow robe, and learning manners and morals from the bonzes. How much technical Buddhism the boys learn varies, I presume, considerably with the monastery and the individual. The two very intelligent young men who acted as interpreters for me—loyal and enthusiastic Buddhists—had both spent over a year wearing the yellow robe, and both knew the content of the Five Precepts; but neither knew them *as* the "Five Precepts," nor did they recognize what I meant when I asked what the Five Precepts or Vows were. In Siam this could hardly have happened. As to the proportion of the male population who in boyhood study with the bonzes and take the yellow robe for at least a short time, I have no statistics. Both Leclère and Eliot say that all or nearly all do so. In driving through the country or walking through the towns you get the impression that every boy from thirteen to sixteen is in yellow. Yet I am told that the practice is not universal, even in loyal Buddhist families, and that the proportion of those who take the robe is not so great as it used to be. This is due to the establishment of modern schools by the French authorities. The great educational superiority of these over the schools of the bonzes is evident to many parents, and this is slightly reducing the number of boys that take the yellow robe.[17]

That Buddhism has exerted and still exerts an elevating and ennobling influence upon the people of Cambodia is hardly to be denied. M. Leclère (writing in the nineties) considers the Cambodian Buddhists much more religious than the Christians of Europe. "Nowhere else and in no other religion do I find a greater exaltation of sentiment so well adapted to elevate men, induce kindly customs, and pleasant social relations, and to make man a hero of mildness, charity, and love." [18] Possibly M. Leclère exaggerates: I do not know. But that the Cambodians appear, to a hurried yet greatly interested pilgrim, a deeply and earnestly religious people, of mild manners and pleasing courtesy and helpful human ways, I can attest; and that their religion, which emphasizes just these things, has had much to do with achieving this result seems hard to deny.

Whatever one may think of the value of Buddhism in Cambodia the intensity of its present influence is patent to every eye. The Cambodians today are universally and enthusiastically Buddhist. As my friend the missionary repeatedly puts it, they are very "fanatical." They are so fanatical that it is most difficult to convert them to Christianity. Their fanatical loyalty to Buddhism is the great obstacle to missionary progress. From the Gulf of Siam to the Annamese border, and following up the Mekong, surging past Angkor, the ruined monument of dead Hinduism,

[17] More rapid change, I was told, might be expected after the death of the king, a very old man. He has since died (on August 10, 1927). He was an ardent Buddhist, and the whole weight of his influence had always been back of the bonzes; but the heir apparent, my informants said, was a man of European education and western ideas and he was expected to cooperate with the French Government in its attempt to modernize Cambodia.

[18] He cites many instances of what he means. Thus: "I see every day around me acts of charity and love for others, for all beings, acts which are not known to the Christians. Here, for example, is a boatman who for charity and love's sake, in order to acquire merit, takes gratuitously on his boat all those who present themselves. Here is a devout man who feeds travellers without asking recompense and also lodges them and waits upon them. Here is a poor man who for charity and love's sake has received in his home and feeds one poorer than himself. Here is an old man who spends all he has on the construction or repair of a pagoda, or of a hall for travellers. Here is a dying person who asks his children that after his death his flesh be torn off his bones and given as alms to the birds of the air. . . . Here is an old woman who frees some slaves out of charity; sometimes it is a man who frees them and puts them on some of his fields; these now become the property of the slaves" (pp. 520-21).

on over into Siam, the triumphant Hinayana holds its undivided sway. From the coast to the capital, and from there up and down the great sweep of the great river, or following its little tributaries, the broad flat plain of Cambodia with its marshes and its jungles and its paddy fields presents to your sight ever-recurring reminders that you are in the land of the Buddha. Modest little wats raise their roofs among the trees in all sorts of unexpected places, and every village and every country road and river bank is dotted with the yellow robes of boys and bonzes.

As you travel southeastward, from Pnom Penh towards Saigon—whether by the Mekong or some of its tributaries, or by automobile over the splendid roads of Cambodia—these tokens of the Hinayana follow you. Then at a certain point you begin to feel that something has happened. You miss something. No, there are no more yellow robes in sight, and it is some time since you have seen a wat. You think back and note that they stopped rather suddenly. If you have been watching the mile-stones you may recall that the last sign of robes and wats was at about the stone which bore the inscription "Saigon 65 kilomètres." A new kind of temple, moreover, has begun to appear—Chinese temples with dragons on the roof. Burying grounds of the Chinese style are also appearing for the first time. You have passed the watershed, the boundary line between Hinayana and Mahayana.

It is surprising how sharply this line is drawn. It follows very closely the political line between Cambodia and Cochin-China, the racial and linguistic line between the Khmers and the Annamese. Starting from the Gulf of Siam near the Point of Cambodia, it runs in a northeasterly and then northerly direction some distance east of the Mekong, right up to the borders of China, with the Annamese on the east of it and the Khmers and Laos and Siamese on the west. On reaching Yunan it goes onward in a northwesterly direction, with Burmese and Shans west of it and Chinese to the east, then turns west and southwest, separating the Burmese from the Tibetans. Between the Burmese and Tibetans, however, there is an indeterminate belt of some width, the inhabitants of which are chiefly nat worshipers, though they call themselves Buddhists. Between Burma and Assam the line turns southwestward and ends at the sea. This is the region of the Hinayana, this plus the southern part of the island of Ceylon; and within it Hinayana Buddhism reigns supreme. Outside of it the Hinayana is almost unknown. Saigon is within a few miles of the Cambodian border, but not a bonze nor a wat is to be found in its streets.

As one looks back at the lands of the Hinayana—Ceylon, Burma, Siam, Cambodia—they shine in one's memory with a very grateful light. The artistic wats and pleasant viharas, the pagodas and stupas, the pipal trees, the bonzes, and the great Buddhas, with their suggestion of peace and their message of pity, the unquestionably moral influence of the religion and the earnest attempt to inculcate it in each rising generation—all these memories together produce a really considerable effect, when massed in one general impression within the mind of any unprejudiced and sympathetic observer. With this impression still fresh, on first arriving in Saigon, one goes in search of a Buddhist temple. It is one's first entry, let us suppose, into a Mahayana land, and one is eager to see this northern form of Buddhism. It is not easy to find a Buddhist temple in Saigon. There are a number of Chinese temples, some of which have an image of the Buddha occupying a subordinate position among the many gods before whom incense is burned. But anything like a temple given up only to Buddhism I was unable to find within the city. I found one, however, in the suburbs. It was a simple building, guarded by an Annamese monk who was almost indistinguishable in costume from other Annamese. He unlocked the door and led us in. The central shrine had eleven images. The three upper ones were all Buddhas, so the monk said; though whether they lived before Sakyamuni or after him he did not know—nor even whether they had ever lived as men at all. Below them was an image of Sakyamuni and on each side of him a Chinese god. Other subordinate deities filled out the shrine. In a second shrine, farther back, was a fourteen-handed image which was called a Buddha, and in the extreme rear of the temple a third shrine with four figures, the central one of which represented an Annamese princess of antiquity. This shrine seemed to have attracted more worship than any of the others, judging from the incense sticks and sticks for fortune-telling placed in front of it. The temple as a whole seemed little used, and what use it had consisted evidently of fortune-telling and incense burning. . . . With such an introduction to Northern Buddhism, one's thoughts go back to the Hinayana.

Yet such a contrast is not really fair. For Northern Buddhism is at its worst and weakest in Indo-China; and at its best, the Mahayana is a complicated affair, and appreciation of it is an acquired taste. Let us not judge it, therefore, by this first impression and this unfair contrast. We can understand it rightly and judge it fairly only after studying its rise and its history. Such a study will take us back again to India, and to the India of long ago. It will involve much difficult philosophical analysis. We shall have to trace the course of this new development of Buddhism not only in ancient India but in medieval China, Korea, and Japan. But only after such rather laborious research can we venture to form any intelligent idea whatever of this very complicated system. To this somewhat dull and difficult study we shall now turn in the following chapter.

CHAPTER XI

THE RISE OF THE MAHAYANA

So we come back again to ancient India. For we must now seek the origin and trace something of the development of a new form of Buddhist doctrine and Buddhist aspiration and expression, which was destined to be carried in triumph over the Himilayas and across the vast plains of China, and, leaping the straits of Shiminoseki, to be stopped only by the salt waves of the North Pacific. To ancient India, therefore, we return, and to very ancient India indeed. For if we are to seek the origin of the Mahayana we cannot stop short of the teachings and the life of the Founder himself. Not that the Mahayana doctors are justified in holding that the Tathagata gave two kinds of teaching, an exoteric Hinayana doctrine for simpler minds and an esoteric Mahayana doctrine for the more profound. This is surely the invention of a late school, without any historical justification. But while the Southern school has doubtless clung much more closely to the teachings of the Founder than has the Northern school, the seeds of many of the doctrines and practices and ideals that were to prevail in the North are clearly to be seen in the Pali texts themselves.

In this connection it will be helpful to revert to the suggestion made in the sixth chapter of this book as to a possible triple division within the teachings and practices of early Buddhism. It will be recalled that we found it useful to distinguish, first, beliefs and customs which, by the force of social inertia, were carried over into Buddhism from the common store of Indian life and thought, second, those original (or partly original) teachings of the Buddha which were of a strictly intellectual nature, and third, the influence of his life and example, the influence of his heart rather than of his head. Now each of these elements had its share in the origin and development of the Mahayana, and no account of the Mahayana which leaves out these very early tendencies can give a true picture of the real lineage of the Northern school. There were, of course, other sources for the Mahayana as well. Many of the most important things in Mahayana doctrine and practice were derived from Hindu influence, and some even from foreign influence. These we should note and emphasize; but that there were in primitive Buddhism the seeds of many of the later growths of Mayayana thought and worship we must not forget. It will be impossible to treat separately the lines of development that grew out of these three distinguishable aspects of original Buddhism, for the lines of influence from each are many, and they intertwine in bewildering fashion. But it will be helpful for the reader to keep these sources in mind in at least a general way.

In the Pali Suttas Gotama though obviously a man, with many of the human limitations, is yet not quite a man either. In knowledge, enlightenment, self-control, and moral mastery he is always supernatural, and his supernatural power in other realms is sometimes revealed. From the day of his death, and apparently even during his life, unique veneration was felt for him, and to "take refuge in the Buddha" was one of the essentials of salvation. As we have seen in an earlier chapter, it was not long before this veneration developed into something closely akin to worship.

The Pali texts, moreover, recognize that Gotama was not the only Buddha. Only one Buddha, to be sure, may be active at a time, but there had been several before Gotama, and there will be at least one more in the future.[1] The Bharut tope erected about 200 B.C. bears a relief of seven Bo Trees, and seven thrones inscribed with the names of seven Buddhas, Gotama being the last.[2] These seven Buddhas are recognized by very ancient Pali documents also. Before the close of

[1] In the Maha Parinibbana Suttanta, of the Digha Nikaya, for example, reference is made to the "Able Awakened Ones" of the past and of the future (an expression synonymous with the word *Buddhas*), and the words are used in a way to indicate that the conception of a long line of Buddhas was already common property and taken as a matter of course. It should be noted, however, that in this passage there is no suggestion that a Buddha or Able Awakened One is supernatural in any other sense than that of knowledge and virtue. See Rhys Davids' translation of the Digha Nikaya, *Dialogues of the Buddha*, II, 88-89.

[2] See Foucher, *The Beginnings of Buddhist Art*, p. 72.

the Pali canon the number of Buddhas is raised from seven to twenty-five.[3] The process of increasing the number of Buddhas and at the same time of transforming the veneration paid to them into something more and more like the worship paid to Hindu deities was probably brought about in large part through the influence of the great number of rather ignorant converts from Hinduism. These men and women doubtless meant to be good Buddhists at their conversion, and always considered themselves such, but they could not divest themselves of the unconscious influence of the polytheistic point of view in which they had been brought up, nor of the desire for personal worship and for help from a personal deity. Hence in the first and second centuries of the Christian era the Buddha assumed a more supernatural character in the minds of his followers, and, especially in northern India, an increasing number of Buddhas came to be recognized. In the Larger Sukhavati Vyuha, which must have been written at least as early as Kanishka's time,[4] Sakyamuni is pictured as giving a discourse on the Vulture Peak in which he enumerates some eighty-one Buddhas by name, all of whom lived in the remote past.[5] The first of these eighty-one was Dipankara; but the Saddharma Pundarika Sutra tells us of a Buddha antedating Dipankara by incalculable ages. In a later section of the Sukhavati Vyuha we are told of a sermon preached by the eighty-first Buddha of this list recounting the excellencies of the Buddha fields belonging to some eighty-one hundred thousand *niyutas* of *kotis* of Buddhas.[6] As a *niyuta* is one million and a *koti* ten million, the number of Buddhas here referred to exceeds the power of the English language to express, but it can be represented by mathematics thus: 81,000,000,000,000,000,000.[7] The Laliṭa-vistara and the Saddharma Pundarika Sutra refer to Buddhas in equally overwhelming numbers. Of course no Buddhist takes Buddhist figures very seriously, and the passages just referred to

[3] Cf. La Vallée Poussin, *Bouddhisme*, 264-65.

[4] It is said to have been translated into Chinese between 148 and 170 A.D. Cf. Nariman, *Literary History of Sanskrit Buddhism* (2nd ed., Bombay, Indian Book Depot, 1923), p. 79.

[5] Section 3. In Max Müller's trans., *S. B. E.*, XLIX, Part II, p. 7.

[6] *Op. cit.*, § 5. In Max Müller's trans., p. 10.

[7] It is not surprising that the sermon took "a full koti of years."

are to be interpreted simply as meaning that the number of Buddhas is as infinite as space and time. An infinity of divine beings, moreover, ceases in a sense to be pluralistic. Being necessarily impersonal they merge into each other in the imagination as a kind of *pleroma*, an impersonal cloud of divine rays, so to speak, expressing in their joint capacity the divine nature of the universe. Two or three deities are really much more dangerous for monism than eighty-one hundred thousand *niyutas* of *kotis*.

Yet Mahayana Buddhism—at any rate in its popular form—verges upon something akin to polytheism. For out of the infinitude of Buddhas past, present, and to come, it singles out a few for special adoration, and some of these to the popular mind have become something very like the greater devas of Hinduism.[8] Several different groups of Buddhas have been popular at different times and in different Mahayana lands. The largest of these lists counts twenty-four Buddhas[9] beginning with Dipankara[10] and ending with Sakyamuni. Another list includes simply the last seven of the twenty-four.[11] A third, rather more popular than either of the two just mentioned, is composed of the five Buddhas of the present kalpa.[12]

All of these are known as Manushi Buddhas—that is, Buddhas who at one time historically combined the qualities of Buddhahood and humanity. They have lived on earth as human Buddhas. There are other Buddhas who have never been human, or if so, never lived upon earth in human form after their enlightenment.[13] The five most important of

[8] We must constantly keep in mind the fact that during the centuries when the Mahayana was being formed, Buddhism was making its large numbers of converts from Indians who had been brought up to worship the many Hindu devas.

[9] Twenty-five, if we include Maitreya.

[10] It was during the human appearance of Dipankara that Gotama (then known as Megha) first prayed to become a Buddha. Dipankara granted the request and predicted his future Buddhahood.

[11] See Getty, *The Gods of Northern Buddhism* (Oxford, Clarendon Press, 1914), p. 9.

[12] See Hardy, *Manual of Buddhism* (2nd ed., London, Williams and Norgate, 1880), p. 98. These five Buddhas are important not only as the five Buddhas of the present kalpa but also because they are the Manushi or historical Buddhas corresponding to the Five Dhyani Buddhas, Cf. Getty, p. 9. Their names are Krakucchanda, Kanakamuni, Kasyapa, Sakyamuni, Maitreya.

[13] Amitabha, for example, is said to have gone through many human births while a Bodhisattva; but he is not a Manushi Buddha but a Dhyani Buddha.

these[14] are known as the Dhyani Buddhas, or Buddhas of Contemplation. Each of these is associated with one of the five Manushi Buddhas of the present kalpa referred to at the close of the last paragraph, and each also has an especial Dhyani Boddhisattva. Each of these five groups of three is a kind of trinity: the three are conceived as, in some sense, merely different forms of one identical being.[15] This conception of non-historical Dhyani Buddhas, and the systematic arrangement of the five trinities was late in making its appearance, and has received its greatest development in Nepalese and Tibetan Buddhism, a form of Buddhism with which this volume will not deal. I mention the Dhyani Buddhas here because the conception has had a certain influence in China and Japan, and a cursory acquaintance with it is necessary for an understanding of the mythology of the Mahayana.

The importance of the groups of Buddhas I have mentioned is but slight in the Buddhist world of today outside Tibet and Nepal. There are, however, five Buddhas of very considerable importance in modern Mahayana lands, and to these we must give rather more attention. These five are Sakyamuni, Amitabha, Vairocana, Bhaisajaguru, and Maitreya.

Of Sakyamuni nothing need here be said. In all Buddhist lands he is revered or worshiped as the latest of the Buddhas, the light of the world for the present dispensation. In gratitude and reverence toward him and in conscious recognition of the enlightenment and inspiration and spiritual assistance that comes through him, Hinayana and Mahayana are at one. With the name Amitabha we come upon something quite new. His name means Measureless Light, and

[14] I say the five most important of these to avoid the implication that all Buddhas who are not Manushi Buddhas are Dhyani Buddhas. There is, apparently, an infinitude of Buddhas in the infinite number of Buddha kshetras who are not Dhyani Buddhas and who have never lived upon this earth. Kern speaks of Dhyani Buddhas as those not required to pass through the stage of the Bodhisattva (*Manual of Buddhism*, Strassburg, Trübner, 1896, p. 64). Bhattacharyya follows him in this (*Indian Buddhist Iconography*, Oxford Univ. Press, 1924, Chap. 1). To say this, however, is to forget that Amitabha, the most popular of the Dhyani Buddhas, is generally regarded as having gone through all the usual course of spiritual life, including even the human.

[15] The five Trinities—or the three Pentads—may be indicated thus:

Dhyani Buddhas: Vairocana, Akshobhya, Ratnasambhava, Amitabha, Amoghasiddhi.
Manushi Buddhas: Krakucchanda, Kanakamuni, Kasyapa, Sakyamuni, Maitreya.
Dhyani Bodhisattvas: Samantabhadra, Vajrapani, Ratnapani, Avalokitesvara, Visvapani.

his secondary name, Amitayus, means Measureless Life. According to the Larger Sukhavati Vyuha, he was a Bhikshu in the days of the Buddha Lokesvararaja.[16] His name at that time was Dharmakara (the Japanese give it as Hozo). Being filled with love for all suffering creatures, he sought out the Buddha and kneeling before him made forty-six famous vows. Each of these vows describes some quality of the Buddha-kshetra or divine region which his merit, accumulated through many kalpas, was destined to produce, or names some class of persons aspiring to salvation, and ends always with the solemn wish that if the quality described be not granted to his region, or the class of persons named be not admitted, then may he, Dharmakara, not obtain the highest perfect knowledge, i.e., Buddhahood.

That vow was made many kalpas ago, and during the unimaginable years that followed, Dharmakara through many lives, human and superhuman, acquired so great a mass of merit that his wish became certain of eventual achievement: which means that his longed-for Buddha-kshetra became a reality and that he received assurance that hereafter whosoever directs his thought toward the highest perfect knowledge and meditates upon Him, shall be received into that glorious country. Having obtained this assurance the former Dharmakara consented to become at last a Buddha. But, according to the Sukhavati Vyuha, this does not mean that he has passed away into Nirvana. "Neither has that Tathagata passed away nor has he not yet come, but that Tathagata, the holy, having obtained the highest perfect knowledge, dwells now, remains, supports himself, and teaches the Law in the Western quarter, in the Buddha country, in the world which is called Sukhavati, and he is known as Amitabha. He is surrounded by innumerable Bodhisattvas and worshiped by endless Sravakas, and in possession of the endless perfection of his Buddha country." [17]

The three other Buddhas referred to above can be passed over much more briefly. Vairocana is intimately associated with the sun—both in Sanskrit Buddhism and in modern

[16] The eightieth Buddha after Dipankara.—See the list in § 3 of the work cited, *S. B. E.*, XLIX, Part II, p. 7.

[17] *Op. cit.*, § 11.

Japan. He is apparently a Buddhist adaptation of the sun-worship, which was common in India from the earliest days, and which during the formulation of Mahayana thought was receiving reinforcements from the sun-worship of Persia.[18]

Bhaisajaguru is, as his name indicates, the "Healing Teacher," the King of Medicine. He made twelve vows, somewhat like those of Amitabha, for the benefit of his followers. He is the Buddha of the Eastern quarter.[19] In the Buddhism of India he was never very important, but in China as Yao-shih Fo, and in Japan as Yakushi; he assumes a prominent position.

Maitreya, the last of our list of five popular Buddhas, in one sense does not belong on any list of Buddhas at all, for he is not yet a Buddha, but a Bodhisattva only. He is at present dwelling in the Tusita heaven, and at the expiration of a period whose length is variously reckoned, he is to descend to this earth and be born as the next Buddha. By that time the Dharma will have been nearly or quite forgotten, but he will establish it once more, even as his innumerable predecessors, the blessed Buddhas of old, have done.

Maitreya, I have said, is as yet a Bodhisattva. The conception of the Bodhisattva goes back to the Hinayana, where it is applied to Gotama during his previous births and throughout the earlier years of his historical life up to the time of the enlightenment. A Bodhisattva, then, is, originally, a future Buddha, on his way to enlightenment. Etymologically the term means simply one whose being consists of insight. But the Mahayana seized upon the conception and made it over into a new ideal, which became, perhaps, the central characteristic of the new form of the religion. To understand this ideal it is necessary to go back to what I have referred to as the heart element in the teaching and life of the Founder. His own example, as I have so often pointed out, was quite free from that implication of selfishness or narrowness, which a natural interpretation of the Four Noble Truths and their logical consequences might well suggest. Whatever might be the natural deduction from his teaching

[18] Eliot surmises that Amitabha also may have been of Zoroastrian origin. See *Hinduism and Buddhism*, III, 219-21.

[19] Getty, p. 23.

that each of us should avoid giving pledges to Fortune and should seek the desireless and sorrow-free life, his own heart was so full of love for every form of suffering creature that he long postponed his own Parinirvana for their sake, and fired the imaginations of many of his disciples with the longing to be of service to others at any cost. It was this aspect of the Buddha's teaching and example that the Mahayana thinkers seized upon and it was on this that they based their moral ideal. The typical Arhat (= Arahant), busy about his own salvation, wandering alone as a rhinoceros, they felt to be narrow and unworthy, and they erected in his stead the ideal of the earnest seeker after the welfare of others, who in unselfish devotion to his fellow creatures accumulates great stores of merit and dedicates it not to his own salvation but to that of all suffering beings. For in the faith of the Mahayana, there are many such ardent saviors of others. All the Buddhas had dedicated themselves, for ages before their complete enlightenment, to this unselfish task: and as there will be an endless line of Buddhas in the infinite future, as there has been in the infinite past, so there must now be an incalculable multitude of future Buddhas, i.e., Bodhisattvas, who have dedicated themselves to the same endless task as that for which Gotama went through so many births and deaths. This faith involves not only a new ideal but a new conception of the acquisition of merit and of salvation. Merit is thought of by the Mahayana as being transferable. Suffering and goodness are vicarious. The Bodhisattva is able to present his merit to a needy world, and for its sake he is willing to be himself a meritless sinner. In the words of the New England theology, he is willing to be damned for the glory of God.

This conception of vicarious suffering and the transference of merit is hardly in harmony with what I have called the intellectual aspect of the Founder's teaching and his emphasis upon self-help. On the other hand, it is the natural, perhaps even the necessary, outcome of the heart element of Buddhism, of the Founder's devotion and of the devotion of all loving souls. If the great enlightenment was not merely an intellectual achievement but a new experience of sharing the common life, we may perhaps say with Professor

Suzuki that the possibility of sharing our merit with others is the "logical outcome of enlightenment-consciousness."

> What made Buddhism great as a universal religion [Suzuki adds] was due to the discovery of this principle. . . . The law of Karma may be true and should be made to work in our practical and intellectual plane of life, but it is too rigid, too exclusive, too individualistic, and above all, it goes against our religious yearnings. We want to suffer for others and when this is not practicable we want to send out our thoughts and sympathies to them. If we are at all spiritual beings capable of enlightenment, this thought communication or mystical interpenetration must be possible.[20]

So deeply to heart has the Mahayana taken this ideal of self-forgetting service that it would be difficult to find in the whole round of the world's religious literature more radical and sincere expressions of it. Repeatedly in reading Mahayana devotional books is one reminded of George Eliot's poem, "Oh May I join the Choir Invisible." Listen, for example, to the following from Asanga: "If another does harm to the Bodhisattva he endures with patience the worst injuries, with the idea that it is a benefit he has received. To think that the offender does one a service, this is to conduct oneself in accord with the example of the Perfect Ones."[21] Or this, from Santi-deva's Bodhi-Charyavatara, "*The Path of Light*":

> I would fain become a soother of all sorrows of all creatures. May I be a balm to the sick, a healer and servitor, until sickness come never again; may I become an unfailing store for the poor, and serve them with manifold things for their need. My own being and my pleasures, all my righteousness in the past, present, and future, I surrender indifferently that all creatures may win to their end. The Stillness lies in surrender of all things and my spirit is fain for the Stillness. I yield myself to all living things to deal with me as they list: they may smite or revile me forever, bestrew me with dust, play with my body, laugh and wanton: I have given them my body, why shall I care? Let them make me do whatever works bring them pleasure; but may never mishap befall any of them by reason of me. May all who slander me or do me hurt or jeer at me gain a share in Enlightenment. I would be a protector of the unprotected, a guide of wayfarers, a ship, a dyke, and a bridge for them

[20] "Development of the Pure Land Doctrine in Buddhism," *Eastern Buddhist*, III, 311-12.

[21] From Asanga's Mahayana Sutralamkara, trans. by Sylvain Levi (Paris, Champion, 1911), Chap. VIII.

who seek the further Shore: a lamp for them who need a lamp, a bed for them who need a bed, a slave for them who need a slave.

By constant use the idea of an "I" attaches itself to foreign drops of seed and blood, although the thing exists not. Then why should I not conceive my fellow's body as my own self? That my body is foreign to me is not hard to see. I will cease to live as self and will take as myself my fellow creatures. By constant use man comes to imagine that his body, which has no self-being, is a "self"; why then should he not conceive his self to lie in his fellows also? Then as thou wouldst guard thyself against suffering and sorrow, so exercise the spirit of helpfulness and tenderness towards the world. Be thou jealous of thine own self when thou seest that it is at ease and thy fellow in distress, that it is in high estate and he is brought low, that it is at rest and he is at labour. Make thine own self lose its pleasures and bear the sorrow of thy fellows. Cast upon its head the guilt even of others' works. Darken its glory by telling of the greater glory of others. Make it a carrier in thy fellow creatures' service, like a mean slave. It is made of sin, and because it may have some chance morsel of goodness from without, it is not therefore worthy of praise. Let no man know its goodness. In short, let all the wrong that thou hast done for the sake of thine own self to others fall upon thine own self for the sake of thy fellow creatures.[22]

It is not surprising that lovers of the world who found their aspirations expressed in words like these should have felt that the older ideal of the Arhat was decidedly inferior to their own. It was for this reason that they referred to the older method of salvation as the Lesser Vehicle, and called the new devotion which inspired them the Greater Vehicle. There is no doubt that they exaggerated the contrast between the two ideals—and that some western writers have done the same. The Arhat who really understood the teachings of the Tathagata in their fulness, with its denial of a separate individual self and with the illustration of his own limitless devotion, was a Bodhisattva in spirit. One need only recall Purna and his eagerness to go as a missionary to the Western Suner. But Purnas are always rare, and there can be no doubt that the tendency of the Hinayana was toward self-centeredness, in spite of the Anatta doctrine, and that the new emphasis of the Mahayana marked a real advance in the widening and socializing of the actual interests of Buddhism.

It is seldom possible for a Buddhist thinker to believe in the importance of a being or condition without proceeding

[22] Barnett's trans. of Santi-deva's *The Path of Light* (N. Y., Dutton, 1909), pp. 45, 88-89. Somewhat condensed.

to subject it to minute analysis and systematization. Even in late Hinayana writings the concept of the Bodhisattva began to be developed in scholastic fashion, and the procedure was carried on in great detail by Mahayana writers. The Mahavastu, a late Hinayana work, gives a list of ten stages[23] in the progress of the Bodhisattva, and the same number is retained, with modifications in detail, by the Mahayana authorities. According to the theory thus elaborated, the disciple enters upon the course of the Bodhisattva by taking the vow not to forsake his fellow creatures but to preach the Dharma (Sanskrit form of Dhamma), comfort the afflicted, and accumulate merit through many incarnations for the use of others, and not to enter into Nirvana till all are rescued. He feels now that he is born into the family of the Buddha, that he is "a seed of the Buddha," "a son of the Buddha."[24] During the following six stages he cultivates the six *Paramitas* or characteristic virtues, namely, generosity, morality (both negative and positive), patience, energy, meditation, wisdom or insight. At the eighth stage, the doctrine teaches, he is certain of achieving the final goal: a doctrine comparable to the Presbyterian belief in "the perseverance of the saints." He now could, if he chose, enter at once into Nirvana, but with the encouragement of the Buddhas he denies himself and continues on his course, that he may be the more helpful to the suffering and ignorant world. On reaching the tenth stage he becomes almost equal to the Buddhas. The Buddhas consecrate him and he acquires various supernatural powers. He receives the excellent Rain of the True Law, and having become himself a Cloud of the Law, he sends upon needy creatures the good rain which lays the dust of the passions and causes the growth of the harvest of merits.[25]

It is not surprising that a being at once so powerful, so merciful, and so active as the fully developed Bodhisattva

[23] See La Vallée Poussin's article "Boddhisattva in *H. E. R. E.*

[24] It was important for scholastic theory to determine upon the exact moment at which the individual crossed the line, so to speak, and became a Bodhisattva. Vasubandhu defines this as the moment at which he commences to perform the acts which have for their retribution the thirty-two marks of Bodhisattvahood. See his "Abhidharmakosa," trans. by La Vallée Poussin, III (Paris, Geutner, 1924), 220-21.

[25] La Vallée Poussin, article "Bodhisattva," *H. E. R. E.*, II. See also S. Schayer, *Mahayana Doctrines of Salvation* (London, Probsthain, 1923), Part III.

should be besieged by the prayers of the needy and should become an object of worship with many of the faithful. In fact, to quote La Vallée Poussin, "Chandrakirti says in so many words that, just as the new moon is celebrated and not the full moon, so must the Bodhisattvas be worshiped and not the Buddhas, even though the latter are of greater dignity. The Buddhas have more majesty, the Bodhisattvas more influence." [26]

It will be gathered from what I have said that the term Bodhisattva covers so large a number of volunteer saviors as to be a bit indefinite. According to Mr. R. F. Johnston, "At the present time the vows of a bodhisattva are taken every year by scores of newly ordained monks who thereafter (at least in China) are respectfully addressed by their disciples and novices as *Ta-pusa* (great Bodhisattva)." [27] Several historical scholars and saints are recognized as Bodhisattvas. But the term usually connotes, in the ears of the Mahayanist, a being far excelling, in wisdom and power, anything that can properly be called human. The great Bodhisattvas who are objects of worship may once have been human, just as many of the Buddhas have been human; but the days of their earthly pilgrimage are so many kotis of kalpas ago that they are really quite as exalted above the earth as are the devas of Hinduism. In the eyes of the devout Buddhist they are, of course, immeasurably superior to the devas.

These heavenly Bodhisattvas are, like the Buddhas, innumerable. Yet there are certain members of this heavenly cloud of witnesses who have been singled out for special reverence. As Eliot has shown, the development of these personifications of Buddhist moral ideals into beings which in other religions would have been called gods ran quite parallel with a similar movement within Hinduism. Hindu and Buddhist neighbors all over India were feeling the same need and satisfying it in much the same way.

So far as we can judge, the figures of these Bodhisattvas took shape just about the same time that the personalities of Vishnu and Siva were acquiring consistency. The impulse in both cases is the same, namely, the

[26] Article "Adibuddha," *H. E. R. E.*, I.
[27] *Buddhist China* (London, Murray, 1913), p. 76.

desire to express in a form accessible to human prayer and sympathetic to human emotion the forces which rule the universe. But in this work of portraiture the Buddhists laid more emphasis on moral and spiritual law than did the Brahmans; they isolated in personification qualities not found isolated in nature.[28]

A group of eight of these prominent Bodhisattvas[29] has been singled out by Buddhist art and thus made famous beyond their fellows. And quite aside from all recognized groups, there are five (in addition to Maitreya) who have become in China and Japan especially popular. A word should be said of each of these, in order to introduce to the reader in their ancient form and under their Sanskrit names this circle of venerated beings with whom he will become better acquainted if he ever goes to China and Japan or ever reaches the chapters in this book which deal with those lands.

The most important of all the Bodhisattvas are Avalokitesvara and Manjusri, personifications of the two great Buddhist virtues mercy and wisdom. The origin of each is shrouded in mystery. Some scholars think it probable that Avalokitesvara had an actual human origin—some great saint who lived near Potala, which was either near the mouth of the Indus or in Southern India. No one would maintain that this hypothesis could possibly be verified. The Bodhisattva may equally well have been borrowed from some popular figure of Indian mythology. Beal's guess that he originated from some deity of Southern Arabia has little to support it.[30] The name means "he who looks down"—presumably in pity. He has compassion on every form of suffering, saves from every kind of ill, gives all sorts of good things, notably children, and is closely associated with the merciful Amitabha. He seems to have been popular in India a little before the Christian era[31] and until the seventh cen-

[28] *Buddhism and Hinduism*, II, 12.

[29] These eight are the following: Avalokitesvara, Aksagarbha, Vajrapani, Kshitigarbha, Sarvanirvana-vishkambhin, Maitreya, Samantabhadra, Manjusri. See Getty, pp. 42-99.

[30] See his *Chinese Buddhism* (London, Society for Promoting Christian Literature, 1884), Chap. XI. Beal is typical of a school of writers on Buddhism who seem to think it necessary to derive Buddhist divinities from some foreign source—as if there were not thirty-three million gods in India to choose from.

[31] Getty, p. 54.

tury he was one of the most prominent figures in Indian Mahayana Buddhism. His principal development, however, has been in China and Japan, where we shall meet him again under the names Kwan-Yin and Kwannon, and usually metamorphosed into the opposite sex, as the "goddess of mercy."

Manjusri, as I have said, is the symbol and personification of wisdom, knowledge, meditation.[32] It is he to whom Arhats and even Bodhisattvas appeal for information and instruction. He is thus unusually equipped, in part, presumably because of his innate intellectual powers, in part because of his long experience and perfect memory. He has been a follower of the Buddhas and a listener to their expositions for a longer time than many of the Buddhas themselves. Many kotis of kalpas before the appearance of Dipankara, the first Buddha on the list of twenty-five, Manjusri was already learned in the Law.[33] As the representative of the intellectual side of Buddhism rather than of its emotional aspect, he never holds the power over men's hearts possessed by Avalokitesvara or Amitabha. He commands respect rather than love. But so large is the intellectual element in Buddhism that among the great Bodhisattvas he ranks easily second. In China he is known as Wen-Shu, in Japan as Monju.[34]

The three other Bodhisattvas who deserve mention in this place can be passed over briefly, as their chief development is in China and Japan. The name Kshitigarbha means "receptacle of the earth," or "womb of the earth," and some scholars think that he is a Mahayanist transformation of the Vedic earth goddess Prithivi or of some other ancient goddess of the earth. He seems never to have been very popular in India and his worship was relatively late. The stories told in China of his former births probably originated either toward the close of Indian Buddhism or perhaps in China itself. He is much more popular in China today, as Ti-tsang, than ever he was in the land of his origin; but it is especially

[32] Both Levi and Eliot think it probable Manjusri may have originated in Central Asia.

[33] Cf. the Lotus, Chap. I.

[34] For further details concerning Manjusri as well as concerning the manner of his representation in art, see Bhattacharyya, *Indian Buddhist Iconography*, Chap. II.

in Japan, under the name of Jizo, that he attains the climax of his greatness.

Samantabhadra seems to have held a higher place in the esteem of the Indian Mahayana than did Kshitigarbha. He was the first of the Dhyani Bodhisattvas and represented universal kindness and the highest intelligence—combining thus the characteristics of both Avalokitesvara and Manjusri. He is commonly associated with Manjusri in art, their images being frequently placed side by side, or on the two sides of Amitabha. In China he is known as P'u-hien; in Japan as Fu-gen.

Mahasthanaprapta, as his name declares, is "he who has obtained great strength." He is sometimes spoken of as the deification of Gotama's famous disciple Moggallana.[35] He was of no great importance in India, nor is he often met with in China, but in Japan he is a common figure, as Daiseishi, where he is grouped with Amida and Kwannon.

In connection with the Bodhisattvas should be mentioned two other classes of advanced spiritual beings, all or nearly all of whom are human or once were human. These are the Arhats or Sravakas and the Pratyekabuddhas. A Pratyekabuddha is one who had been a learner and follower of some Buddha in a previous incarnation, yet did not succeed during the life of that Buddha in attaining arhatship, and who in a later birth, while no Buddha exists in the flesh, succeeds by solitary meditation in attaining complete enlightenment and who thereupon enters Nirvana without attempting, as the perfect Buddhas or Buddha saviors do, to pass on the enlightenment to others. The Pratyekabuddha is therefore contrasted with the Bodhisattva in much the same way as is the ordinary Arhat: both are thought of as relatively self-centered. The Pratyekabuddha is a lonely and solitary, meditative figure who emphatically "wanders alone like a rhinoceros." He differs from the Arhat, however, in that he attains to enlightenment not through the direct teaching of a Buddha but by the ripening of much accumulated merit and by his own meditation which develops a seed planted long long ago by some ancient Buddha.[36]

[35] Getty, p. 100.
[36] See La Vallée Poussin's article "Pratyekabuddha" in *H. E. R. E.*, X.

The word Sravaka is sometimes used as synonymous with Arhat, but more often it has the additional connotation of indicating a preacher of the truth. It is sometimes limited in its application to what one might call the Fathers of the Church—the early Arhats who gained enlightenment under Sakyamuni and who carried on the spreading of the new Gospel. Quite as often it is used to refer to the doctors of the Hinayana; in fact, the word Hinayana is synonymous and interchangeable with the vehicle of the Sravakas.

The word Arhat means, in general, the same thing in Mahayana as in Hinayana. Not long after Kanishka's time—possibly earlier—certain traditional Arhats were singled out for special honor. We have seen that in some Hinayana lands images of Sariputta and Moggallana—the two most prominent of Gotama's disciples up to the time of their death—are often placed on the two sides of the Buddha image in the temples. In China this honor is given to the two other great Arhats, Kassapa and Ananda—the two favorite disciples at the time of the Master's death, and the first two patriarchs—for it will be remembered that Sariputta and Moggallana preceded the Tathagata into Parinirvana. An early Mahayana tradition relates that Sakyamuni at his death commissioned four great Sravakas to remain in the world as guardians of the law till the coming of Maitreya.[37] A more popular tradition and one with wider consequences asserts that this commission was given not to four but to sixteen Sravakas and these are sometimes spoken of as the Arhats, *par excellence.* The earliest literary reference to them is in a Sanskrit Sutra of the fourth century [38] or earlier, which speaks of them incidentally thus: "There are the Arhats Pindola, Rahula, and similar men, sixteen in all, all great Sravakas who lived scattered about in all the *dvipas* [regions]." Another Sutra [39] tells us that "When the Buddha was about to enter into Parinirvana he entrusted the Su-

[37] These four are Kasyapa (= Kassapa), Kundopadhaniya, Pindola, and Rahula. Miss Getty identifies the Kasyapa of this tradition, not with the great Sravaka but with the Buddha of the same name. *Op. cit.,* p. 14. But see de Visser, *Ostasiatische Zeitschrift,* IV.

[38] The Mahayanavataraka Sastra, which was translated into Chinese during the Liang dynasty (397-439 A.D.).

[39] *The Record of the Abiding of the Law,* trans. into Chinese by Hiuen-Tsiang in 654.

preme Law to the sixteen great Arhats and their followers, ordering them to protect and maintain it and prevent its being extinguished." Pindola and Rahula again are named among this number. Pindola, I should explain, was one of the personal disciples of the Buddha and had been rebuked by him for a vain display of supernatural powers.[40] Rahula was the Buddha's son. These sixteen Arhats "by means of their transcendental knowledge lengthen their own lives. As long as the Supreme Law shall remain in the world they shall always protect and maintain it." When at length knowledge of the Law shall be extinguished in this world, they shall assemble, shall collect the relics of the Tathagata's ashes, and shall together enter Parinirvana. And after that Maitreya shall come.

There is another and less famous group of Arhats that should be mentioned in passing, namely the Five Hundred Arhats. These are referred to by Hiuen-Tsiang, and in his time were believed to inhabit the caves of the Buddhavanagiri. Not much is known about them, but they seem to have been suggested by and may have been identified with the Five Hundred Arhats of the First Council. It seems probable that they too were to await the extinction of the Law or the coming of Maitreya.[41] Both the Sixteen and the Five Hundred Arhats loom rather large in China and have some importance in Korea and Japan.

As the coming of Maitreya forms the climax of all these Arhat traditions, something further should be said of it here. We have already seen that the hope of Maitreya's coming forms a living part of the Buddhist faith in Hinayana as well as in Mahayana lands. The Mahayana, however, has developed the thought in much greater detail than the Hinayana. Ernst Leumann [42] has analyzed five early accounts of

[40] To show his magic power ("Iddhi") Pindola once rose high in air, circled round, and seized a sandalwood bowl, which a rich layman had elevated on several long bamboo poles. The layman was much impressed and presented the bowl to Pindola. When the Buddha heard of it he rebuked Pindola for using the sacred power of Iddhi merely to show off before laymen and "for the sake of a miserable wooden pot." See Kullavagga of the Vinaya V. 8.

[41] The account I have given of the four, sixteen, and five hundred Arhats is based chiefly on M. W. de Visser's article, "The Arhats in China and Japan," *Ostasiatische Zeitschrift*, I-IV, 1920-23, and Watters, *The Eighteen Lohans of Chinese Buddhist Temples* (Shanghai, Kelly and Walsh, 1899).

[42] *Maitreya-samiti, des Zukunftsideal der Buddhisten* (Strassburg, Trübner, 1919).

the future reign of this Buddhist Messiah, all of which are in substantial agreement, the description being put, as a prophecy, into the mouth of Sakyamuni. When Maitreya arrives prosperity shall fill the earth. There shall be large quantities of fragrant rice and many lotus ponds. Seed time shall come only once a year but harvest ten times. There shall be abundance of rain but it will rain at night only. The earth shall be full of good men, of blessed and believing men who have put off their sins. The length of man's life shall be eighty thousand years, and girls shall be given in marriage at the age of five hundred. Many other details are given, similar in effect. Soon after his coming, Maitreya shall go with a great following to the mountain where the First Patriarch, the great Sravaka Kassapa is now hidden, waiting through the ages. The mountain shall remove itself and all shall see the ancient saint, sitting within the deep opening, wrapt in contemplation. He then shall fall at the feet of Maitreya, and after some conversation shall perform various miracles, and Maitreya shall preach a typically Buddhist sermon, saying that the most important things are not miracles but virtue, wisdom, and mercy.

Kassapa's ability to prolong his contemplation, perfectly oblivious to everything else, through the long ages till Maitreya comes, is one of the marks of his Buddhistic perfection. The use of meditation and contemplation leading even to trance was one of the things which Gotama borrowed from the Hinduism of his day and recommended to his disciples as a useful mode of cultivating the spiritual freedom which he and they so highly prized. Both the Hinayana and the Mahayana have continued these practices which are as ancient and as Indian as the Vedas. This effort to produce by carefully devised methods certain desirable forms of psychosis is typical of every form of Buddhism, with its constant emphasis on the subjective state and the inner life. The Hinayana monks, as we have seen, still have their methods of contemplation; and the Mahayana monks have made even more of the practice than have their southern brethren. There is, thus, a continuous and unbroken tradition from the munis of the Rig Veda, through Gotama and his Sravakas, to the Dhyani sect of the Mahayana, Bodhidharma, the Ch'an of China, and the Zen of Japan.

A distinctly allied phenomenon of Buddhism as a religion is to be found in the development of the emotional side of the religious consciousness within the Mahayana. This has its roots, indeed, within the earliest days of the Buddhist church, when emotional loyalty to the living Master, and later on to his blessed memory, became the first condition of church membership, as we might call it, and of salvation. For the first of the Three Refuges is in the Buddha. As his mighty figure gained in power over men's imaginations through the mists of the receding years, and as reverence for him grew into something like worship, the increasing importance of this emotional loyalty within Buddhism found itself reinforced through the influence of the rise of the Bhakti sects [43] in Hinduism. For it was during the four centuries that immediately surrounded the beginning of the Christian era, i.e., between 200 B.C. and 200 A.D., that the devotional and emotional movement arose which sought salvation through the grace of Siva and of Vishnu and through faith in and love for these great Hindu devas; and it was in just these centuries that the Mahayana was forming. The thing was in the air. Both popular Hinduism and popular Buddhism were longing for a means of salvation less sternly intellectual than the teachings of the Sravakas or the abstractions of the slowly-forming Vedanta. It was perhaps the inevitable association of Sakyamuni with the more intellectual side of Buddhism that, in spite of the unfailing loyalty always felt for him, made him a less suitable figure for this purely emotional type of religion to center round than were the non-historical and more easily molded figures of Amitabha and some of the heavenly Bodhisattvas. It was, at any rate, to them, rather than to the Founder, that this new evangelical type of Buddhism ardently clung. Some of the Mahayana devotional books are full of hymns and prayers of adoration and aspiration which recall the Bhagavad Gita and the hymns of the later Shaivite mystics. For example this, from the Bodhicaryavatara: "I have no health in me. I am poor. I have

[43] Those sects, that is, which worshiped a personal deity with emotional loyalty and trusted for salvation to faith and grace.

nothing in the world with which to express my adoration. But in their great charity toward me may the Protectors themselves accept my offering. I give myself to the Buddhas with all my heart and all I have and also to their sons [the Bodhisattvas]. Take possession of me, Sublime Beings. I adore you and I vow to be your slave." [44]

This new sense of devotion was associated (as it was in the Hindu Bhakti sects) with a new belief as to the method of salvation. Gotama had said, as the final summary of his doctrine, "Work out your own salvation with diligence," and the Hinayana Sravakas had taught that no outside assistance save that of instruction could help one in the struggle. But Amitabha and many of the merciful Bodhisattvas of the Mahayana had been busy these endless kotis of kalpas piling up merit which (by the new discovery of the times) was transferable and therefore available by any poor sinner who earnestly centered his thought upon these masters of mercy. The Larger Sukhavati Vyuha (written before 148 A.D.) holds out the hope of Amitabha's assistance in gaining salvation, but in what was probably its original form (as found in the extant Sanskrit text), it still demands for salvation a considerable amount of the usual Buddhist requisites. A change in the conception of one school of the Mahayana is reflected in what appears to be a slightly later recension [45] of this important scripture in which the famous eighteenth vow of Amitabha is modified so as to bring in the conception that nothing is needed for salvation but faith in him. This conception of salvation by faith is made more explicit by the (somewhat later) Smaller Sukhavati Vyuha which says, in speaking of Amitabha's Paradise, "Beings are not born in that Buddha country as a reward and result of good works performed in this present life. No, all men and women who hear and bear in mind for one, two, three, four, five, six, or seven nights the name of Amitayus [Amitabha] when they come to die, Amitayus will stand before them in

[44] Quoted by La Vallée Poussin in *Bouddhisme, Etudes et Matériaux*, London, Luzac, 1898.

[45] The Sanskrit original of this no longer exists. It was translated into Chinese in 252 A.D. and it is this version of the Sukhavati which forms the basis of the present Pure Land sects of China and Japan. See J. W. Ingles, "The Vows of Amida," *Journal of the No. China Branch of the R. A. S.*, XLVIII, 1-11.

the hour of death, they will depart this life with quiet minds, and after death they will be born in Paradise."[46]

This Paradise of Amitabha is described in glowing colors and with an appeal to desires not indeed evil in themselves according to our western view, but of a sort which the original Buddhism would have regarded as hindrances to spiritual liberation. At first the Western Paradise, the "Pure Land" of Amitabha, seems to have been regarded merely as a stepping stone to Nirvana, a place in which Nirvana might easily be attained. Later on, and in the more popular mind, the thought of Nirvana was often lost from sight and the Western Paradise of Amitabha took its place—just as the personal presence of Vishnu-Krishna in the Gita takes the place of the total absorption of the individual in the Brahman of the Upanishads. This new conception of the ultimate destiny of the soul and of the new and evangelical method by which it is to be attained, though it originated in India, was never so popular there as it has since become in China and Japan.

If one contrasts this new point of view concerning salvation and heaven with the austere teachings of the Buddha and of the Hinayana Sravakas, one sees that it is a component part of the general tendency that invented the Bodhisattvas, multiplied the Buddhas, and substituted worship and prayer for lonely contemplation. The Hinayana was for monks chiefly; the Mahayana is for everyone. As we shall see in the next chapter, it has its abstruse philosophy for the thinker, but it has something also for the simplest and even for the most superstitious. It believes in milk for babes, and meat for only strong men. It practices, sometimes unconsciously, sometimes very consciously and explicitly, an elaborate pedagogical method. Its thinkers were well aware of Hegel's distinction between religion and philosophy at least sixteen hundred years before Hegel was born. The truths of philosophy need not be studied in their abstruse form by the beginner; for him the simpler and symbolic figures that speak to the imagination may well suffice. Hence the Mahayana made a popular appeal that the Hinayana found difficult. This greater appeal to the world was largely brought about by a change

[46] § 10 Max Müller's trans. (slightly abbreviated), *S. B. E.*, XLIX. 98-99.

in the world itself. The India of Kanishka's time was no longer the India of Gotama. The ideal of the passive saint, spurning the world and overcoming his passions in solitude, no longer fascinated as it once had done the Indian imagination. "The Church in vain affirmed its disdain of the world: it lived with the world, reflected it, was inspired by it and accommodated itself to it." [47] In the words of Coomaraswamy, "the development of the Mahayana is the overflowing of Buddhism over the limits of the Order into the life of the world." [48]

Thus Buddhism became a religion for the layman quite as much as for the monk. As the Bodhisattva took the place in men's imaginations of the Arhat, so the householder took the place of the hermit; so the old fear of the world, the fleeing from the world was replaced by the desire to live *in* the world, while yet being not *of* the world. The ancient emphasis upon the inward life was not abandoned, but inwardness was given a new application. One of the ideals for human life cherished by the Mahayana is still indeed the holy monk; but the godly and efficient layman it admires no less: as exemplified, for example, in the figure of Vimalakirti as described in a Sanskrit work that goes by his name.[49] This wealthy householder, it tells us, resided at Vaisali, but

> only for the sake of the necessary means for saving creatures; abundantly rich, ever careful of the poor, pure in self-discipline, obedient to all precepts, removing all anger by the practice of patience, removing all sloth by the practice of diligence, removing all distractions of mind by intent meditation, removing all ignorance by fullness of wisdom; though he was but a simple layman yet observing the pure monastic discipline; though living at home, yet never desirous of anything; though possessing a wife and children, always exercising pure virtues; though surrounded by his family holding aloof from worldly pleasures; though using the jewelled ornaments of the world, yet adorned with spiritual splendour; though eating and drinking yet enjoying the flavour of the rapture of meditation; though frequenting the gambling house, yet leading the gamblers into the right path; though coming in contact with heresy, yet never letting his

[47] Sylvain Levi, in the introduction to his translation of Asanga's Mahayana Sutralamkara, II, 17.

[48] *Buddha and the Gospel of Buddhism* (N. Y., Putnams, 1916), p. 228.

[49] The Vimalakirti-nirdesa, called in English, "Vimalakirti's Discourse on Emancipation." The Sanskrit original is lost, but it was translated into Chinese sometime between 188 and 907 A.D. Professor Idumi, from whose English translation I quote, points out that the original must have antedated Nagarjuna, since he refers to it.

true faith be impaired; though having a profound knowledge of worldly learning yet ever finding pleasure in the things of the spirit as taught by the Buddha; though profiting by all professions, yet far above being absorbed by them; benefiting all beings, going wheresoever he pleases; ever teaching the young and ignorant when entering the hall of learning; manifesting to all the error of passion when in the house of debauchery; persuading all to seek the higher things when at the shop of the wine-dealer; preaching the Law when among wealthy people; teaching the Kshatriyas patience; removing arrogance when among Brahmans; teaching justice to the great ministers; teaching loyalty and filial piety to the princes; teaching honesty to the ladies of the court; persuading the masses to cherish virtue.[50]

The figure of Vimalakirti as thus presented has much in common with that of the Founder; for though Gotama left his family and renounced the world, his life was by no means that of the ascetic or hermit. He mingled much among men, visited all sorts of people in their homes, conversed on easy terms with harlots, was in a sense a friend of publicans and sinners. But too many a Hinayana writer drew from that life only the example of retirement from the world, the cutting of the ties. To the figure of Vimalikirti it is a far cry from the ideal of the ancient anchorite who "wanders alone like a rhinoceros."

[50] Trans. by Professor Hokei Idumi in *The Eastern Buddhist*, III, 138-39.

CHAPTER XII

THE PHILOSOPHY OF THE MAHAYANA

It will be recalled that Gotama had always carefully avoided purely theoretical questions and had earnestly warned his disciples against all metaphysical discussion that did not bear directly on the moral life. It was hardly to be expected, however, that so metaphysically minded a people as the Indians could be permanently restrained by this ancient veto from following out their insatiable urge to speculation. The surprising thing, in fact, is that the veto was respected by so many of them, and that the Hinayana is still so largely obedient to it. But early even within Hinayana history attempts were made to reason out some of the problems which the Blessed One had not elucidated; and as Buddhism made increasing numbers of converts from Brahmin thinkers, it was inevitable that the almost universal Indian insistence upon metaphysical inquiry should more and more make itself felt within the fold. That the conversion of thinkers already saturated with Hindu metaphysics and accustomed to theoretical speculation through half a lifetime of training must have had its effect upon Buddhism is obvious enough. Nor are we left to merely *a priori* probability in this matter. The traditions that cluster round Asvaghosha and Nargarjuna, round Asanga and Vasubandhu may be in their particular application untrustworthy. But it is not without significance that all of these men, the four great founders of the Mahayana, should have been closely associated by tradition with Brahmanism.[1]

When men like these came over into the Buddhist fold they found an intellectual freedom which converts to Christianity or Mohammedanism or Judaism have seldom enjoyed. The Tripitaka (the Buddhist canon), to be sure, was deeply

[1] Both Asvaghosha and Nargarjuna are said to have been converted to Buddhism from Brahmanism; and the father of Asanga and Vasubandhu was a Brahmin.

reverenced, but there was no doctrine of its literal inspiration or final authority. It was unthinkable that all the truth the Omniscient One had to give was contained within these relatively simple books. His revelation, it was felt, must be understood to include not merely the literal teachings found in these books but also all that reason could find implicated by them. By the more daring of these new Buddhist thinkers, the ancient teaching in its literal form was regarded as purely provisional and preparatory. I need hardly add that this new presentation of Buddhist thought associated itself with the new ideal and with the new attitude toward the many Buddhas and Bodhisattvas dealt with in the preceding chapter, and that the three when combined grew into a kind of Buddhism sufficiently distinct from the old to be recognized by a separate name. Together they constituted the Mahayana. The more conservative and less speculative thinkers remained within the narrower limits of the Hinayana.

Yet it must not be supposed that Mahayana thought came out of the blue or descended suddenly from the Tusita heaven, nor that it was imported wholly from Brahmanism. That it was influenced by Brahman philosophy and also by Hindu Bhakti there can be little doubt; but it had its roots in the teachings of the Founder and developed naturally out of the Hinayana. To understand how this came about it will be necessary to dip into some of the developments of Hinayana thought—a tangled skein which I have tried to spare the reader. There were many Hinayana schools. Most of them were realistic in their philosophy and most of them clung to the orthodox Anatta doctrine—the denial of a substantial self. Fortunately we need trouble ourselves with only one of these schools—that of the Sautrantikas. These thinkers accepted, as most other schools did, the ancient doctrine of impermanence, but analyzed it and made it specific. The stream of consciousness, they maintained, was continuous, but was composed of an endless number of momentary pulses, or dharmas. These dharmas, or pulses of being, are consecutive and never overlap: each drops out of existence as its successor arises.[2] Each is charged with the whole past

[2] Each comes to an end spontaneously; its cessation is not caused by the act of its successor. See Vasubanhu's Abhidharmakosa, Chap. IV.

and carries the influence of the past on into the future. The reader will be reminded of Professor James' doctrine of the self as a stream or succession of moments which follow each other not in unbroken and seamless continuity but in cinematographic jumps, each of them being the heir of all its predecessors and each of them a bridge between past and future.[8]

The Sautrantika series of dharmas is infinite backwards and will be infinite forwards unless ended by the destruction of desire and the other Buddhist methods of salvation. The ancient doctrine of causation was also retained, each dharma being regarded as the cause of its successor. The kind of causation here intended was, of course, the purely phenomenal sort, which in the West is associated with the name of David Hume. A dharma does not *act upon* its successor, for it no longer exists when its successor has come into being. Causation holds between the successive dharmas in the Humean sense of invariable sequence. Not the action of a given dharma but its being is causal for the next dharma. That is the way the universe is made, and Buddhist phenomenalism does not ask why.

Since this series of momentary pulses or dharmas is continuous, the conception has some of the advantages of the rejected, non-Buddhist concept of a real self, yet it remains loyal to the Anatta doctrine. The empirical facts of life are capable of being expressed in terms of it. It also makes transmigration without a self fairly intelligible, for the first dharma of the new life is said to be caused by and to be continuous with the last dharma of the preceding life. Some of the Sautrantika thinkers, moreover, applied their formula not only to living and conscious beings but to the non-sentient, material world. Material things they still regarded realistically, as did nearly all Hinayana schools, but each material thing was said to be merely a series of temporary existences. The jug which I now see is not the same jug that I saw a moment ago, any more than I am the same as the one who, a moment ago, saw it. Impermanence characterizes the material world as thoroughly as it does the physical. But

[8] See his *Principles of Psychology*, I, Chap. X.

continuity also characterizes both. The present jug came from the preceding jug.

This Sautrantika view of the nature of being is of more importance to us than most Hinayana doctrines because it was at least one of the sources of a central part of Mahayana thought. Nagarjuna who, with Asvaghosha is commonly considered the founder of Mahayana philosophy and who (tradition says) was won over from Brahmanism about 150 A.D.,[4] seems to have taken his starting point from the Sautrantika doctrine, or at least to have used it as a useful object of criticism from which he might lead on to his own "Madhyamika" philosophy. Like other Mahayana thinkers he could not be satisfied with the phenomenalism, the positivism of the Hinayana. Such a succession of real dharmas as the Sautrantikas maintained necessitated, in his opinion, some real ground for them. Such a real ground for things would be fatal to the Anatta doctrine, and would lead one on to the conception of a real underlying self, comparable to the Atman of the Vedanta. One might suppose that Nagarjuna would therefore have concluded to the existence of a real self. But the Anatta doctrine was too important to be surrendered; so he took the opposite and incredibly daring course of denying the reality of the dharmas altogether, without putting anything in their place. The consequence of this step, once fully understood, is enough to make a Western reader gasp. It means that all things, whether conscious or material, are composed entirely of what is absolutely unreal. The parts being unreal, the wholes which they compose must be. Nothing is—nothing is except the Void.[5] This *Sunyata* doctrine is the fundamental principle of the Madhyamika philosophy.

Astonishing as is this position, it is by no means absolutely unique. There are things in the philosophical teachings of Zeno, Parmenides, Eucleides of Megara, of Plato and Plotinus,[6] and, in our own days, in Mr. Bradley's position, that more or less closely resemble it. Nor did Nagarjuna and his

[4] On Nagarjuna's date see Keith, *op. cit.*, p. 228.

[5] The Void was a conception already popular with earlier schools of Buddhism, but with them it was chiefly an ethical term. See Carpenter, *Buddhism and Christianity* New York, Doran), p. 263.

[6] Cf. Inge's *Plotinus* (London, Longmans, 1918), pp. 107-12.

school base their view merely on the unquestioning acceptance of the Anatta doctrine and its consequences. In closely reasoned works, rather strikingly like Part I of Bradley's *Appearances and Reality,* Nagarjuna and his followers subject an impressive list of the concepts of common-sense and philosophy to critical examination and conclude that they are shot through with contradictions which make them unthinkable.[7] Logic, moreover, for these thinkers is more trustworthy than sight or touch. And they have the courage of their convictions. They are sure the self-contradictory cannot be real—appearances to the contrary notwithstanding. In other words they would say, "If we are going to play the game of philosophy at all, let us play it according to the rules."

Nagarjuna and his followers are willing to draw the consequences. Not only are the objects of common belief demonstrably unreal; the same bitter logic is carried out among the most sacred of Buddhist concepts. In the *Four Odes of Nagarjuna,* the writer sings of the Tathagata: "The permanent cannot transmigrate, nor can the impermanent: Thou sayest that transmigration is but a dream."[8] There is nothing but the Void. "In this emptiness there is no form, no perception, no name, no concepts, no knowledge. There is no eye, ear, body, mind; no taste, touch, objects; no knowledge, no ignorance, no destruction of ignorance, no decay, no death, no Four Noble Truths, no obtaining of Nirvana."[9] In the Vajrakkhedika or *Diamond Cutter,* perhaps the most highly revered of all the Madhyamika scriptures, the Tathagata is made to say: "As many beings as there are in the world of beings must be delivered by me in the perfect world of Nirvana. And yet when I have thus delivered innumerable beings, not one single being has been delivered by me. And why? If a Bodhisattva had any idea or belief in a being he could not be called a Bodhisattva."

[7] Cf. Nagarjuna's Madhyamika-sastra, trans. by Walleser under the title *Die Mittlere Lehre des Nagarjuna* (Heidelberg, Winter, 1911); Santi-deva's Bodhicaryavatara, in La Vallée Poussin's trans. (Paris, Blond, 1907), Chap. IX; Keith's summary of the Madhyamika argument, *op. cit.,* pp. 237-39; and Radhakrishnan's *Indian Philosophy,* I, pp. 647-57.

[8] From La Vallée Poussin's French trans., Museon, XIV (N. S.) 1913.

[9] The Smaller Prajna-Paramita-Sutra. In Max Müller's trans., *S. B. E.,* XLIX, 153-54.

Stars, darkness, a lamp, a phantom, dew, a bubble,
A dream, a flash of lightning and a cloud,
Thus should we look upon the world.[10]

It is difficult to determine just how literally the expressions of the Madhyamika school should be interpreted. Professor Suzuki argues that the term *Sunyata* or the void could not have been meant to express absolute nothingness, and that the Madhyamika system cannot rightly be termed a form of nihilism. In support of his view he refers to the use of terms concerning the highest truth which "convey the sense of affirmation."

What the Cunyata doctrine positively insists on [he tells us] is the denial of sensationalism, and the annihilation of the imagination that means a dualistic world conception. If this could be called a nihilism, every intellectual attempt to reach a unitary view of the universe would be nihilistic, for it declares the untenability of a separate existence of matter and thought, me and not-me, etc.[11]

Professor Radhakrishnan takes much the same view,

The whole show of Nagarjuna's logic [he writes] is a screen for his heart, which believed in an absolute reality. The outer scepticism was in the interests of the inner truth. Nature is an appearance, yet there is the eternal foundation, the infinite, from which everything springs and into which everything retires. Only when talking about it we must drop all categories relative to our empirical life. . . . To attain truth we must cast aside the conditions which are incompatible with truth. . . . To the Madhyamikas reason and language apply only to the finite world. To transfer the finite categories to the infinite would be like attempting to measure the heat of the sun by the ordinary thermometer.[12]

[10] Sections III, XXXII, from Max Müller's trans., *S. B. E.*, XLIX. 113-14, 144.

[11] See Suzuki's trans. of Asvaghosha's *Awakening of Faith* (Chicago, Open Court, 1900), p. 58 note.

[12] *Indian Philosophy*, I, pp. 656, 663. Professor Dasgupta, in his *History of Indian Philosophy* (Cambridge, 1922), does not commit himself on the question how Nagarjuna should be interpreted. McGovern takes much the same view as Suzaki and Radhakrishnan. The doctrine of the Void, he says, "has been frequently totally misunderstood in the West and taken to mean the theory of the non-existence of the Universe, or purely Nihilistic Idealism. In reality Cunya is simply an insistence that all things have no self-essence; that they are compounds, unstable organisms even in their elemental stage. . . . There is nothing that cannot be broken up until we reach the great transcendent reality which is so absolute that it is wrong to say that it is or that it is not. This underlying reality—the principle of eternal relativity, non-infinity—permeates all phenomena, allowing expansion, growth, and evolution which would otherwise be impossible" (*Introd. to Mahayana Buddhism*, London, Trübner, 1922, pp. 21-22).

Dr. Schayer takes a somewhat different point of view from either of those outlined above. For him the *Cunyata* doctrine is related to the Buddha's original dislike of purely theoretical discussion and is to be interpreted neither as a denial of the phenomenal

As opposed to this view both Professor La Vallée Poussin and Professor Keith insist that the expressions of the Madhyamika mean exactly what they say and only by special pleading can be interpreted in any other sense than that of nihilism. And, indeed, it would be hard to contrive modes of expression by which a nihilistic view could be more explicitly and exactly and persistently stated than the way in which the Madhyamika books actually put it. The writers of these books would seem to be bent on making sure that no one should misunderstand them and that no one should water down their courageous assertions. If it be possible to say that only Nothing is, they have said it.

It may, however, be questioned whether it be possible to say that only Nothing is. For a negation loses all meaning without something positive to negate. The reality of any particular fact or event or being may be denied; but when you deny reality to *all* being you have defeated your own purpose and have said nothing. Tell me, for example, that there is no life beyond the grave and you trouble me; add that there is no life on this side the grave either and you comfort me, for now I see that you have made no assertion at all about the thing I mean by life, and its reality. If all reality is "emptiness" then "emptiness" turns out to be just a new name for reality.

It is hard to believe that so obvious a thing as this was not seen by such astute hair-splitters as Nagarjuna and his school. And if this is the case it would be an argument for something like Suzuki's and Radhakrishnan's interpretation. However that may be, the "Void" of the Madhyamika thinkers certainly had a very different emotional connotation for them than for us. The Void was real, and it meant rest from multiplicity, from change and impermanence, from effort and longing. The world of duality and of many things was unreal, the little dharmas of which this world was thought to be composed were unreal, the relations between things and the separateness and contrasts between

world (in any absolute sense) nor as an affirmation of a more fundamental Real below the surface, but rather as a persistent refraining from judgment. It "in no way involves a direct denial of objective existence but merely asserts its unimportance and its emptiness" (*Mahayana Doctrines of Salvation*, p. 41).

finite beings—all these were unreal. This denial of multiplicity was seemingly the important thing for the Madhyamika school, whatever they may have thought of the problem of an ultimate nihilism.

Yet not even Nagarjuna and his most extreme followers cared to deny that the world of multiplicity had a certain relative reality, nor that assertions about it possessed a certain relative truth. They made use, in fact, of a doctrine concerning truth which was popular with all Mahayana thinkers and with the Vedantists as well. According to this ancient Indian view there are different levels of truth and reality—a view almost identical with that held in the West by the Hegelians and Neo-Hegelians of our time. It is, in fact, not different in essentials from that expounded in Greece five hundred years before Christ by the philosopher Parmenides, nor very distant from Plato's view as expressed by the famous illustration of the cave, in the *Republic*. The Madhyamika form of this doctrine maintains that there are three levels of truth or reality. The first is Absolute Truth or the Void. Next to this comes the level of relative truth—this phenomenal world and our practical assertions and beliefs about it. Finally there is the world of dreams and illusions. A famous illustration of the differences between the three is that of the monk with poor eyesight (or perhaps suffering from hallucination) who sees hairs in his begging bowl, when, as a fact, there are no hairs there. A man with normal vision persuades the monk that there are no hairs in his bowl. The monk still continues to suffer from his poor eyesight, he still sees hairs in his bowl, but he now realizes that these visual images are illusory, and that as a fact there are no hairs in the bowl. His condition is now no longer that of complete hallucination but of what western psychologists would call pseudo-hallucination. The two conditions of the monk may be used to illustrate the two lower levels of truth and reality. The progress made by him after having been persuaded of the non-reality of the hairs which he still sees illustrates the advance made by the common man when he learns the truth of the Madhyamika philosophy, but before he has gone far on the road of the Bodhisattva. The philosopher *knows* the truth, but is still under the illusion of the senses. He is under illusion but not in error. He sees the hairs but denies their reality. But the man of normal vision does not see any hairs in the bowl at all, he does not have to deny their existence for it never occurs to him to think of them. For him they are not even an illusion. This man with the normal eye illustrates the Buddha.[13] The true knowledge which the Buddha has is thus of a kind of not-knowing. It is the absence of all idea about the self or the material world or change or motion or phenomena or ignorance. All assertions about these things would be assertions about illusions, and as such would seem to imply their reality and hence from the point of view of absolute truth, they would be false. If the reader, with this illustration in mind, will go back and re-read the passages quoted on page 238 from the Smaller Prajna-Paramita Sutra and the Diamond Cutter, the paradoxes there expressed will, I think, appear in a different light.

The Madhyamika school, therefore, by no means leaves the world of phenomena and multiplicity out of account any more than the wise physician leaves out of account the illusory vision of his patient. After all,

> Dreams are true while they last:
> And do we not live in dreams?

The phenomenal world is ultimately unreal, but it is of enormous practical importance even for the Madhyamika. "It must be practically treated as if it were real." [14] And the Madhyamika school is as much concerned with individual salvation and as devout in its attitude toward the Buddhas and Bodhisattvas as any other.[15]

The Madhyamika has had an immense influence on Mahayana thought. This influence, however, has been largely indirect. Its extreme and complete teaching has seldom been accepted outside of India. A school that has had a much more direct influence on the Mahayana of today was that of the Yogacaras or Vijnanavadins. This school originated

[13] Cf. La Vallée Poussin, *Buddhism*, pp. 192-95.

[14] Keith, *Buddhist Philosophy*, p. 241.

[15] I need only remind the reader that Santa-devi, whose noble words on the aspiration of the Bodhisattva were quoted in the last chapter, was an enthusiastic member of the Madhyamika school.

during the renaissance of Indian thought that took place in the fifth century A.D. under the famous dynasty of the Guptas. The founders of the school, according to tradition, were two brothers, Asanga and Vasubandhu by name—sons of a Brahmin father. Early in life they became Hinayana Buddhists. Asanga was the first of the two to feel dissatisfied with the Lesser Vehicle, and, we are told, used the supernatural powers gained by his study of it to rise into the Tusita heaven, where he had an interview with Maitreya. Maitreya converted him to the Mahayana; and he converted his brother Vasubandhu. In Asanga there seem to have united several diverse influences. His home was Purushapuru, the modern Peshawer, a place where, in the fifth century, many forms of thought, Indian and foreign, confronted each other. Zoroastrianism, Judaism, possibly Christianity, and probably Manichaeism, and various Hellenistic views, all were represented, and probably had some influence on the developing thought of the young philosopher. But the Indian and distinctively Buddhist influences were far more influential with him than the foreign ones. Among these Indian influences should especially be mentioned Yoga, the ancient method for the cultivation of the psychical powers and the ancient confidence in the declarations of the mystic intuition, which loomed so large in Brahmanism and were given so important a place by Gotama himself and in the Hinayana school which followed him. The developing Vedanta philosophy also must have had its influence upon Asanga and his brother. But most directly of all they probably felt the logic of Nagarjuna and his Madhyamika school.[16]

It is, in fact, from the Madhyamika that the Yogacara philosophy starts. To a great extent Asanga and his brother accept the doctrine of the Void. The phenomenal world of duality and multiplicity is an illusion. But to assert the reality of the Void seems necessarily to imply the conception of something which is void. If there is emptiness there must be something which is empty.[17] Hence the Yogacara school

[16] In this description of the influences at work in the formation of Asanga's thought I have followed Levi's introduction to his translation of Asanga's Mahayana Sutralamkara.

[17] "For vacuity to be a justifiable position we must first have the existence of that which is empty, and then the non-existence of that by the absence of which it is empty;

concludes that there is not only a Void but also some kind of a "container." Moreover, if one asserts that the phenomenal world is an illusion one cannot stop there. A *mere* illusion is unthinkable. It cannot stand by itself. There must be some consciousness (not necessarily a personal one) which is under illusion, or the illusion could not be. Illusion implies some form of consciousness. To reinforce these *a priori* considerations, Asanga was not without empirical evidence. He was not only a philosopher, but like most Buddhist philosophers he was a psychologist as well, and his psycho-analysis seemed to provide him with just the concept needed. Buddhist psychology had long recognized six kinds of consciousness or *Vijnana*, namely one connected with each of the senses, and a more general form related to the *Manas* or mind as each of the five others is related to its respective sense organ.[18] Now Asanga insisted that further refinement of analysis was needed. To the six forms of Vijnana or awareness already recognized he added a seventh and an eighth. The seventh is that whose function it is to distinguish between the self and the not-self. But it is the eighth Vijnana that chiefly concerns us, for it may be called almost the cornerstone of the Yogacara philosophy and it was the door to one of the most important subsequent developments of the Mahayana. Asanga called it the *Alaya-vijnana,* which means "repository consciousness," for it includes or is basal to all the other forms of awareness. It is from it that the alternative name of the Yogacara school, the *Vijnanavadin,* is derived. In Levi's opinion, Asanga concluded to this deeper form of awareness because of his experience with Yoga. His analysis "discovers under the incessant flux of phenomena a new sensation, the sensation of the profound *Alaya-vijnana,* the permanent reservoir whence emerge the acquired effects while they wait the hour of their transformation into causes. It is not a person, it is not an ego, it is the affirmation of the being which is involved in all our judgments and all

but if neither exists, how can there be vacuity?" From the Sarvasiddhanta Sarasamgraha, quoted by Radhakrishnan, *op. cit.,* p. 628. See also Keith, p. 244.

[18] For an exposition of this portion of Buddhist psychology see any of the following: McGovern, *Manual of Buddhist Philosophy,* I (Cosmology) (London, Kegan Paul), 1923, pp. 89-96; Keith, *Buddhist Philosophy,* pp. 84-91; Mrs. Rhys-Davids, *Buddhist Psychology,* pp. 52-56.

our sensations." [19] It is distantly comparable to the Subconscious of James and Myers.

It is this Alaya-vijnana, this most basal and impersonal form of awareness, which careful psycho-analysis discovers under or within all our variegated conscious states, it is this that is presupposed by the Void and its illusions. This is the container, this is the Real, and from it flow all the other forms and all the content of our minds. Itself is devoid of all distinctions and all characters and qualities. If we may apply to it a term from Western philosophy, it seems to be pure awareness. Thus the Yogacara school, taking the seeming nihilism of the Madhyamika, turned it into an idealism.

The material world, the world of multiplicity, has thus only relative and derived reality. It is the product of our minds, which in turn are the product of the pure awareness at the basis of our conscious lives. This alone is ultimately real. The particular things and events of the so-called objective world are merely content of consciousness. They are produced by our imagination.[20] Ultimately therefore all

[19] Levi's Introd. of his trans. of Asanga, p. 20.

[20] "Comme un Trompe-l'œil, ainsi s'explique l'Imagination de ce qui n'existe pas; comme l'effet d'un Trompe-l'œil s'explique Perreur de dualité.

"Comme un Trompe-l'œil, comme un Signe d'Erreur, morceau de bois, motte de terre, etc., traité par des formules d'enchantement, telle est l'Imagination inexistante, c'est-à-dire la Nature Imaginaire. Comme l'effet d'un Trompe-l'œil, comme une figure d'elephant, de cheval, d'or, etc., qui dans cette opération apparait comme si elle existait de même, dans cette Imagination inexistante, l'Erreur de dualité apparait en tant que Prenant et Prenable sous l'aspect de Nature Imaginaire. (Asanga, *op. cit.*, Chap. XI, § 15.)

Cf. also the Madhyamakavatara of Chandrakirti, trans. by La Vallée Poussin in the Museon, VIII (1907), esp. pp. 326-27. The arguments used by the Yogacara school in Sankara's time in defense of their form of idealism are expounded and criticized at length in his commentary on the Vedanta Sutras. Some of the Yogacara reasoning has the familiar ring of Bishop Berkeley. For example the following: "We must necessarily admit that the ideas have the same forms as their objects. But if we make this admission, from which it follows that the form of the objects is determined by the ideas, the hypothesis of the existence of external things becomes altogether gratuitous. From the fact, moreover, of our always being conscious of the act of knowledge and the object of knowledge simultaneously, it follows that the two are in reality identical. When we are conscious of the one we are conscious of the other also; and that would not happen if the two were essentially distinct, as in that case there would be nothing to prevent our being conscious of one apart from the other. For this reason also we maintain that there are no outward things. Perception is to be considered as similar to a dream and the like. The ideas present to our minds during a dream, a magical illusion, a mirage and so on, appear in the twofold form of subject and object, although there is all the while no external object; hence we conclude that the ideas of posts and the like which occur in our waking state are likewise independent of external objects; for they also are simply ideas. If we be asked how, in the absence of external things, we account for the actual variety of ideas, we reply that that variety is to be explained from the impressions left by previous ideas. In the beginningless *Samsara* the phenomenal world and all possible appearances have their source in the Alaya-vijnana. In this sense it is sometimes spoken of as the womb of the Tathagata. The universe potentially lies within it, and actually issues from it.

When used in this generic sense the term Alaya-vijnana plainly no longer stands merely for the basal form of the individual's consciousness. The concept doubtless had its source as a term of individual psychology, but even in the hands of Asanga the term tends to take on—and in some passages decidedly does take on—an over-individual significance. If we may use the word *soul* without implying personal selfhood, we may say that the Alaya-vijnana tends to become an over-soul. Better still, perhaps, it may be compared to Bradley's "Reality" which, though decidedly impersonal, is as certainly spiritual. Profesor Radhakrishnan writes of it thus:

> Through meditation and other practices of self-examination, we realize that our waking or superficial consciousness is a fragment of a wider whole. Every individual has in him this vast whole of consciousness, the great tank, of the contents of which the conscious self is not fully aware. Our personal consciousness knows but a small fraction of the sum total of our conscious states, the *alayavijnana.* There are indications that the alayavijnana was sometimes used in the sense of the absolute self. It is said to be without any origination, existence and extinction. It is the permanent background of the endless variety of feelings and ideas, common to all minds. It alone exists; individual, intellectual products are mere phenomena, phases of the *alaya.* It is the sole foundation of the false belief in the existence of the world. All things in the universe are in it. Particular phenomena are manifestations of the *alaya* according to the number and nature of the conditions. . . . *Alayavijnana* is the absolute totality, originality and creativity, unconditioned itself by time and space, which are modes of existence of the concrete and empirical individuality. Things of nature are deposits from the great sea of thought. They can all be taken back into its transparent unity and simplicity, which is the mother sea of consciousness, out of which things arise and into which they again return. It is the living base from which come the members which again withdraw themselves. It is the highest or perfect

ideas and mental impressions succeed each other as causes and effects, just as the plant springs from the seed and seeds are again produced from the plant, and there exists therefore a sufficient reason for the variety of ideas actually experienced. That the variety of ideas is solely due to the impressions left on the mind by past ideas follows, moreover, from the following affirmative and negative judgments: we both (the Vedantins as well as the Bauddhas) admit that in dreams, etc., there presents itself a variety of ideas which arise from mental impressions, without any external object; we (the Bauddhas) do not admit that any variety of ideas can arise from external objects, without mental impressions. Thus we are again led to conclude that no outward things exist" (*S. B. E.*, XXXIV, pp. 419-20).

knowledge in which no thing is known, no difference is felt. It is always the same, and therefore perfect. *Alaya* becomes the universal subject, and not the empirical self.[21]

The tendency to make the Alaya-vijnana a cosmic rather than an individual term, a metaphysical rather than a psychological concept, is carried still farther, and maintained more consistently in the little book called *The Awakening of Faith in the Mahayana.* This book is attributed to Asvaghosha, but as it seems to presuppose both the Madhyamika and the earlier phases of the Yogacara philosophy, it can hardly have been written by him, if (as is generally held) he lived at least as early as Nagarjuna.[22] The term most frequently used by the writer of this work to name the ultimate cosmic principle is *Bhutatathata,* which seems to be almost synonymous with Alaya-vijnana [23]—yet not quite synonymous. The Alaya-vijnana is rather the form in which the Absolute (as we may perhaps call the Bhutatathata) expresses and "affirms" itself.[24] The usual English rendering of Bhutatathata is "suchness." This, is seems to me, is a misleading term; for it plainly indicates quality, and quality is one of the concepts which a thorough-going mystical philosophy like the Yogacara is most concerned to avoid. Western idealism often divides reality into the two aspects of quality and actuality, the "what" and the "that." Following this lead, one might perhaps render Bhutatathata as *thatness.* Care must be taken, however, to avoid including in this conception the connotation of substance (in the Aristotelian sense), for the Yogacara means to get beyond and back of substance as well as quality. Professor Keith [25] suggests for Bhutatathata the

[21] *Op. cit.,* pp. 629, 631. Some of the contemporary interpreters of the Yogacara philosophy in China and Japan maintain that *Alaya-vijnana* was never intended by the founders of the school as a cosmic, but only as an individual and perhaps psychological term. The expressions of Asanga will hardly bear this interpretation, and no writers on the subject with whom I am acquainted—whether European, Japanese, or Indian, agree with this individualistic version. There is, indeed, in the Yogacara use of the word a certain amount of wobbling, but that a cosmic sense is often given to it is hardly to be denied.

[22] Cf. Keith, p. 228; Nariman, *Literary History of Sanskrit Buddhism,* pp. 39-40.

[23] Cf. p. 61 of Suzuki's trans. It will be noted that Suzuki suggests a slight difference between the two, hardly indicated by the text. See also p. 77 ("the *alayavijnana* is practically identical with *bhutatathata*").

[24] Keith, p. 253.

[25] In a personal letter to the writer. For further discussion of the meaning of *bhutatathata* see Suzuki's *Outlines of Mahayana Buddhism* (London, Luzac, 1907), Chap. V.

rendering *thusness*. However we translate the term, the Yogacara intends by it the indefinable background of all being, of which neither existence nor non-existence in the ordinary sense can be predicated. It should be added that Mahayana philosophy more and more tends to make of this indefinable and ultimate reality an idealistic Absolute.

It would be difficult to exaggerate the significance of the change brought about in Buddhist thought by the modifications in the Madhyamika philosophy we have been considering—the introduction of the Alaya-vijnana, the gradual transformation of it from an individual to a generic and inclusive term, and the acceptance of the frankly cosmic and monistic Bhutatathata. It meant the transformation of Buddhism from an individualistic and either pluralistic or nihilistic philosophy into a monistic and spiritualistic view, an absolute idealism in many ways strikingly similar to neo-Hegelianism. Several influences must certainly have been at work in this development, and it will be worth our while to suggest what may have been the more important. First of all there was, of course, the logical working out of the situation as above described once the Madhyamika view was accepted. As we have seen, Asanga's psychological analysis and his possible mystical experiences probably also played their part. Important also, in all likelihood, was the steady influence of the Upanishads and their spiritualistic monism, which has had such an incomparable hold over the Indian mind and which during the time of the formation of the Yogacara was steadily developing into the Vedanta of Badarayana and Sankara. The parallel streams within Hinduism and Buddhism must have given mutual encouragement and stimulus to each other. There was one further influence, moreover, of a logical nature, which, as it seems to me, must have been of very great importance in working out the peculiar form which Mahayana monism finally assumed and which is, so far as I know, quite unique in the history of thought. This was a natural dialectic from the concept of the Buddha when the full significance of this concept was thought out in the light of the presuppositions of idealism. The Buddha, it will be remembered, had from the beginning been characterized in the minds of his followers first of all by his insight, and before the formation of the Mahayana he had come to be regarded as the embodiment and personification of omniscience. Very early in the development of Mahayana thought, the idealistic interpretation of all reality came to be accepted as an unquestionable certitude. The fundamental thesis of idealism is, of course, the identification of being with knowledge. Knowledge and its object are for it indistinguishable and cannot be thought apart. Reality *is* only so far as it is known or experienced; it and the knowledge of it are one. Complete knowledge and the sum total of reality must therefore coincide. But the Buddha *is* complete knowledge. Knowledge, insight, is the very being, the total nature of the Tathagata. Hence the conclusion which to the western mind at first must come with something of a shock, but which logically considered is inescapable, that the Buddha in his true nature *is* the absolute and all-inclusive Real; and that Reality in its ultimate nature is the Buddha. This was exactly the step taken by the Mahayana philosophy. Other religions have made their founders into gods and sons of God; Buddhism makes its founder into the Ultimate and Only Reality, which underlies, produces, and includes all things.

It is plain that such an astounding identification will have its effects not only upon the resulting picture of the world, but on the concept of the Buddha. Of this matter we shall speak in the next chapter. But first of all we must make plain the general outlines of the cosmos in the new world view. The Yogacara accepts the common Indian doctrine of different levels of truth. In the last analysis reality is a pure unity. Bhutatathata, the ultimate spiritual essence, is all in all. From this point of view "all things appear under the forms of individuation only on account of our confused subjectivity. If we could overcome our confused subjectivity the signs of individuation would disappear and there would be no trace of a world of individual and isolated objects." [26] Space itself "is nothing but a mode of particularization and has no real existence of its own. . . . It exists only in relation to our particularizing consciousness." [27] Pure being, if so I may for the moment render Bhutatathata,

[26] The *Awakening,* Suzuki's trans., p. 56. [27] *Ibid.,* p. 107.

is above all predicates. It can best be expressed as the mystics have always expressed it, by negatives: "*Bhutatathata* is neither that which is existence nor that which is non-existence; it is neither that which is unity nor that which is plurality, nor that which is at once unity and plurality, nor that which is not at once unity and plurality." [28]

Yet there is a sense in which the world of multiplicity is real. It has its source in the Absolute essence. To the process by which this is brought about the author of the *Awakening* devotes considerable space and considerable care, though it must be admitted that, when all is done and said, the matter is far from clear. The Bhutatathata produces, or is, the Alaya-vijnana, and through this the process of multiple production is performed: through this and "ignorance," which the author brings in without explanation, and without which this world of the partially illusory *many* could obviously not be explained. *Bhutatathata* and *Alaya-vijnana* are pure spirit or pure awareness without multiplicity or character; but they are infected with multiplicity through the action of ignorance, a process which the author seeks to make plainer by the simile of "perfuming." Just as our clothes when new have no odor but are scented by the perfumes which we put upon them, so the pure, undifferentiated mind is "perfumed" by ignorance.[29] From this perfuming there results the mind of man, and from it the dream or vision of an external world —a world of things which are nothing but the percepts of the various observers.

> The three domains [*triloka*] are nothing but the self-manifestation of the mind [i.e., Alaya vijnana which is practically identical with suchness, Bhutatathata]. Separated from the mind, there would be no such things as the six objects of sense. Why? Since all things, owing the principle of their existence to the mind (*alaya-vijnana*) are produced by subjectivity (*smrti*), all the modes of particularisation are the self-

[28] *Ibid.*, p. 59.

[29] The use of this figure of course really explains nothing, and no conceptual or satisfactory explanation of the derivation of the many from the one is ever given by the Yogacara philosophy. In this respect, however, the Yogacara is surely no worse off than Hegelianism or any other form of monism. As Professor Ward has expressed it, "the way upward to this [the Absolute] by abstraction and idealisation is comparatively easy—though such methods can not pretend to knowledge; but the way back has in fact only been possible by means of myths and metaphors, which are not even logically consistent" (*The Realm of Ends*, Cambridge, 1911, p. 38).

particularization of the mind. The mind in itself being, however, free from all attributes, is not differentiated. Therefore we come to the conclusion that all things and conditions in the phenomenal world, hypostasized and established only through ignorance (*avidya*) and subjectivity (*smrti*) on the part of all beings, have no more reality than the images in a mirror. They evolve simply from the ideality of a particularizing mind. When the mind is disturbed, the multiplicity of things is produced; but when the mind is quieted, the multiplicity of things disappears.[30]

The figure used in the antepenultimate sentence of the section just quoted is a favorite illustration of the reality and non-reality of the many. The things reflected in a mirror, taken, that is, as reflections or images, are in one sense real, in another sense not real. The only genuine reality involved is the mirror. And the mirror as such is not affected by the passing reflections upon it; just as the Bhutatathata is unchanged and uninvolved in the changes of this world of changing illusions which could not be but for it and which exist only in it.[31] Another common illustration of the relation between the Absolute and the phenomena that rise and fall upon its surface is that found in the sea and its waves.

> The water can be said to be identical [in one sense] and not-identical [in another sense] with the waves. The waves are stirred up by the wind, but the water remains the same. When the wind ceases, the motion of the waves subsides; but the water remains the same. Likewise, when the mind of all creatures which in its own nature is pure and clean is stirred up by the wind of ignorance, the waves of mentality make their appearance. Neither the mind nor ignorance has any form and attribute of its own. They condition each other. But the mind itself not being the principle of disturbance, its movability will cease when ignorance is gone, though its essence, wisdom, remains unmolested.[32]

The different matters that we have been considering are discussed in several books of the Yogacara school beside the *Awakening* and the works of Asanga and Vasubhandhu. One of the most helpful treaties I have found is the Surangama Sutra, as translated from its Chinese version by Beal.[33]

[30] *The Awakening*, pp. 77-78. Cf. also pp. 72, 96-97.

[31] Cf. p. 69, *The Awakening*.

[32] *Idem*, pp. 67-68 and note. I have combined the older Chinese translation with the later, as the older seems here the more consistent.

[33] In his *Catena of Buddhist Scriptures from the Chinese* (London, Trübner, 1871). The Chinese name for the Sutra is the Shan-leng-yan-King.

As is so often the case with Mahayana Sutras, a conversation is depicted as taking place in the presence of a large number of disciples and Bodhisattvas in the Jetavana Monastery, and in reply to one of Ananda's questions the Tathagata has been expounding the idealistic view of the world with which we are now familiar.

Every phenomenon that presents itself to our knowledge [he insists] is but the manifestation of Mind. This is the true substratum of them all. . . . All the thousand connections of matter and the various modifications of ideas, all these are but what the Heart originates. [The word which Beal translates as *heart* evidently refers to the inner mind, the eternal subject, which is one with the Absolute Mind.] Your mind and body themselves are but things made manifest in the midst of this mysteriously glorious and true essence called the perfect heart.[34]

Ananda, who throughout the Sutra is treated as the representative of the Hinayana, seeking for the light of the Mahayana, asks in his dear human way for further explanation. The earnestness of his desire for the truth and the honesty of his doubts, which are the doubts of most of his Western readers, make him a decidedly lovable figure, and the vividness of characterization with which he is presented, as well as the logic of his questions and the subtlety of the Buddha's answers, make this Sutra strongly reminiscent of the Platonic Dialogues.

Following the deep, and loving words of the Buddha's argument with tears coursing down his face and his fingers clasped in anxious expression, Ananda spoke thus: "World-honored One, if my sight be the same as the sight-nature of the Tathagata, everywhere diffused, how is it that now, as I sit in this hall, I see but this alone? Is it possible that this power [this Absolute Mind which is said to be identical with my mind] can be changeable, sometimes great and sometimes small? Or can the impediment of a wall confine that which is so vast in its nature? I am unable to explain in what the just solution of this difficulty is to be found. Would that your compassionate love would exercise itself in explaining this matter on my account."

[The Buddha replied] "The description of all worldly things as great or small, within, without, square, round, etc., results from the shifting nature of the phenomenal world and in no way can it be justly attributed to the contraction or expansion of the seeing [or thinking] power."

The relation between the true mind and the various limited perceptions he then compares to the relation between space

[34] P. 313.

and the shape of a hollow square vessel. The shape is square but space is not square. Sight as such and thought as such is no more limited by the walls of this room than space as such is round or square. And "if you become able to understand the real character of all objects, then you become the same as the Tathagata, immovably fixed, enabled to embrace within your mental grasp the infinite worlds."[35] We shall never attain to true understanding if we persist in a realistic interpretation of the material world and found upon so-called material objects our conceptions of the real and the unreal. For "sight and the associations of sight [i.e., all visual and all sensuous phenomena] and all the attributes of [individual and limited] thought are but as an empty flower of space—an aurora. In their real character they are unsubstantial." The illusion of a real material world is a defect of true vision; it is, as it were, the effect of a cataract on the spiritual eye. This world of multiplicity is indeed ultimately attributable to, it flows from, the One Reality—here we find the Mahayana philosophy asserting the same general thesis as Spinoza. Like Spinoza again,[36] the Mayayana does not pretend to be able to follow out the details of the derivation. To ascertain the precise point where the many appear and where they disappear is not possible; for that we must look to the Supreme Nature, and beyond that we can ascertain nothing. But we know that the many are illusory, like the "flower-shaped apparition" which a man would get "who with perfect sight, beheld the pure void of space, but fixed his eyes on one particular spot, beyond which he did not look or move his eyes, staring until his sight was fatigued." To use another illustration, the "false and shadowy appearances around us" are like the space in an empty jar.[37]

The question whence arises in our finite minds the illusion of the many is never completely and satisfactorily answered. The Mahayana struggles with it, as does the Vedanta, but seldom, I fancy, do its attempts at explanation fully satisfy the Western reader. The root ideas of the explanation seem to be the distinction between different levels or degrees of

[35] P. 320. I have slightly modified Beal's wording to bring out the obvious meaning.
[36] Cf. p. 331.
[37] P. 333.

reality, and the thought that an illusion, being itself really a negation of reality, consisting, that is, essentially of non-being, requires no explanation. Since it is, in the last analysis, a non-being, a form of nothing, it is not necessary to attribute to it a cause.

The mysterious effulgence of the Divine is identical with your own originally perfect and intelligent nature. But you have used the word *illusion* as if illusion were Something. What cause can you assign it? If there is any real cause or ground for it, then it is, so far forth, not really an illusion [for an illusion is exactly an unreal appearance that has no ground]. It is an idea that has sprung up entirely from incoherent thoughts; these thoughts have intertwined and intermingled; and increasing deception from age to age, they have resulted in these successive eras of false speculation.

This, then, in general, is the explanation of the world of multiplicity; this expresses the way in which the many evolve from the One through the intervention of ignorance. If it is not wholly clear to the reader, let him blame neither himself nor me. Who indeed has ever been able to answer the question *Cur deus homo?* To the Tathagata of the Surangama Sutra the matter is doubtless clear, as are all things; but I am not sure that Ananda was fully satisfied. And if we turn from Sutras in which the Tathagata himself is presented as speaking to merely human treatises, we find a different situation. Thus the author of the *Awakening* does not claim to have the matter clear nor fully to understand it himself. In fact, he tells us that "the mind which starts from the perfuming influence of ignorance which has no beginning cannot be comprehended by common people nor even by Sravakas and Pratyekabuddhas. It is partly comprehended by some Bodhisattvas; but even those who have reached the highest stage of Bodhisattvahood can not thoroughly comprehend it. The only one who can have a clear and consummate knowledge of it is the Tathagata."[38]

So far as the weak intellect of common people like ourselves will permit, we have sought to trace in outline what might be called the downward road, comparable to the closely similar process in the philosophy of Plotinus from the One outward through the realms of Intellect and Soul to the

[38] *Awakening,* p. 78.

things of the World of the Many. But as with Plotinus, so with the Yogacara, there is an upward pathway, back from the confusing multiplicity of relative illusion to our divine Source, to "God who is our home." The world of the many, coming as it does from the Absolute Essence, cannot be wholly illusory and unreal. The true essence is the inner nature even of it. In it, therefore, we have hold at least of a thread of reality which properly followed will lead us back out of relative illusion to the light. As Professor Radhakrishnan says concerning this aspect of Buddhist thoughts, "the real and the phenomenal are not ultimately different. They are two moments of the same thing, one reality with two aspects. The universe would be utterly unmeaning, absolutely unreal, if it were not in some way the expression of the real. The realm of birth and death is the manifestation of the immortal. It is the appearance in time and space, the actualization of the absolute." [39]

This upward pathway back from the phenomenal to the Real is the path of the Bodhisattva. One enters upon it by cherishing unselfish love and by realizing more deeply the relative falseness of multiplicity. One *acts as if* suffering were real, though knowing that it is not, and thus one steadily practices unselfish kindness. Nor are we alone in this struggle. The Spirit itself beareth witness with our spirits, and helpeth our infirmities. Not only does ignorance "perfume" the Bhutatathata; the Bhutatathata also perfumes ignorance.

In consequence of this perfuming the mind involved in subjectivity is caused to loathe the misery of birth and death and to seek after the blessing of Nirvana. This longing and loathing on the part of the subjective mind in turn perfumes suchness. On account of this perfuming influence we are enabled to believe that we are in possession within ourselves of suchness whose essential nature is pure and immaculate; and we also recognize that all phenomena in the world are nothing but the illusory manifestations of the mind (alayavijnana) and have no reality of their own. Since we thus rightly understand the truth, we can practise the means of liberation, can perform those actions which are in accordance [with the Dharma]. Neither do we particularise, nor cling to. By virtue of this discipline and habituation during the lapse of innumerable *asamkhyeya kalpas*, we have ignorance annihilated. As ignorance is thus

[39] *Indian Philosophy*, I, p. 596.

> annihilated, the mind [i.e., alaya-vijnana] is no more disturbed so as to be subject to individuation. As the mind is no more disturbed, the particularisation of the surrounding world is annihilated. When in this wise the principle and the condition of defilement, their products, and the mental disturbances are all annihilated, it is said that we attain to Nirvana and that various spontaneous displays of activity are accomplished.[41]

It is important to note here once more the great change, pointed out in the preceding chapter, which has come over the Buddhist view since the Founder's last words were spoken, "Work out your own salvation with diligence." The Mahayana accepts this command and (except in the more extreme forms of the Pure Land sect) urges the necessity of individual effort in the pursuit of the goal. But it no longer stops here. With St. Paul it would reword the Buddha's sentence so as to read: "Work out your own salvation with fear and trembling, for it is God who worketh in you, both to will and to do of his good pleasure." It is the divine essence, the Buddha nature within us all, that unites itself with our wills in the struggle against ignorance and desire. Without this more than human aid, this reinforcement which streams into our nature from the exhaustless source of spiritual life, our pigmy efforts against the forces of separation and illusion would probably be fruitless. In the sincere yearning of our hearts after the Ultimate Unity we have the aid, for we are but voicing the longing, of unseen forces.

The turning away from multiplicity toward the One is of course also a turning away from separateness toward a union and a communion of all beings with one another. As we enter into the one Buddha nature we find ourselves uniting with other beings in a unity of the spirit which is both moral and metaphysical. For the identification of self with others, and the loving of others as ourselves, which as we saw in the preceding chapter, is held up before us as the ethical ideal of the Bodhisattva, is now seen to have its foundation in the central principle of metaphysics. I should love my neighbor *as* myself—not merely *as much as* myself but as genuinely identical with myself, for the profound reason that, properly understood, he *is* myself. The two great virtues of Buddhism thus justify each other: knowledge justifies

[40] *Awakening*, pp. 86-87.

love, and love is prophetic of knowledge. The sadness and despair of ultimate and hopeless separation between finite beings natural to many of us occidentals, with our unquestioned belief in the substantial soul, the metaphysically isolated individual, here finds unhoped-for glad tidings. Mathew Arnold's well-known poem *Isolation* gives so much of the feeling for this matter that I cannot forbear quoting some lines from it here:

Yes; in the sea of life enisl'd
With echoing straits between us thrown,
Dotting the shoreless watery wild,
We mortal millions live *alone*.
  The islands feel the enclasping flow,
And then their endless bounds they know.
* * * * * * * *
Oh then a longing like despair
Is to their farthest caverns sent:
  For surely once, they feel, we were
Parts of a single continent.
Now round us spreads the watery plain—
Oh might our marges meet again!

Who ordered that their longing's fire
Should be, as soon as kindled, cooled?
Who renders vain their deep desire?
A God, a God their severance ruled:
And bade betwixt their shores to be
The unplumbed, salt, estranging sea.

To this Mahayana Buddhism replies, Not so. It was not a God who ruled their severance; not a God but a kind of cosmic Ignorance. And since it was the deed of Ignorance it is not irremediable. The estranging sea need not forever flow betwixt us. Surely once we were indeed parts of a single continent; and by the unfailing development of unselfish love and of deep self-knowledge our marges may yet meet again!

Writes Asanga: "The tenderness that the sons of the Conquerors [i.e., the Bodhisattvas] feel for all creatures, their love, their indefatigability—this is the marvel of all the worlds. But no! It is no marvel at all, since other and self are for them identical." [41]

[41] Mahayana Sutralamkara, Levi's trans., p. 170.

And not only does the metaphysical justify the moral; according to the Mahayana it endows it with a new power.

> Rivers in so far as they have separate beds and separate waters and perform their functions separately, have little water and profit only the few creatures that come to drink of them. But once they lose themselves in the ocean, they have thereafter but one bed, they are but one mass of water; they commingle their functions; and they profit the multitude of creatures who seek their waters perpetually. So long as the sages have separate being, separate ideas, and separate functions, they have but finite intelligence and profit only a small number of creatures: for they have not penetrated into Buddhahood. But once entered into Buddhahood they have but one being, but one infinite intelligence, but one united function, and they render service to multitudes of creatures forever.[42]

[42] *Idem.*, p. 92.

CHAPTER XIII

THE ETERNAL BUDDHA

WE must now turn back to the problem of the Buddha which we glimpsed and then postponed in the preceding chapter. The Hinayana had taught that the true nature of the Buddha was his insight, his enlightenment, his Dharma. According to the Mahaparanibbana Sutra, he himself said at his death that the Dharma should take his place.[1] To know the Dharma and all its implications is to know the Buddha. With the change from the realism of the Hinayana to the idealism of the Mahayana, this identification of the Buddha with his infinite knowledge involved, as we have seen, an unexpected dialectic. And the Mahayana did not shrink back from it. Absolute knowledge cannot be other than Absolute Reality; hence the Buddha nature cannot fall short of the inclusive and ultimately Real. Enlightenment, the Dharma, was the one true characteristic of the Tathagata, much more truly representative of him than his material body. As for the early Christians the church was the body of Christ, so for these early Mahayanists the absolute enlightenment, the sum total of the Real, was the true body of the Buddha, or, as they called it, the Body of the Law, the Dharmakaya. It is as the Dharmakaya that the Buddha is the basal and absolute Being. Each school of the Mahayana therefore uses the word Dharmakaya as synonymous with its own Ultimate; the Madhyamika identifying it with the Void (Çunyata), the Yogacara with the Alaya-vijnana, the author of the *Awakening* with the Bhutatathata. It is the inner nature of all that is. It is "undefiled, unchanging, unique in its kind, diffused, transcendant, and to be known by everyone in himself."[2] It is "that which constitutes the Ultimate foundation of existence, the one great

[1] Digha, Sutanta 16; Rhys Davids' trans., II, p. 171.
[2] Keith, p. 268.

whole in which all forms of individuation are obliterated, in a word, the Absolute."[3] It is intuition and true knowledge. It is the womb of the Tathagata, from which all things come. It is to be found in every being that is real to the extent that the being is real at all. The Buddha nature is in all things.[4]

This is what the Buddha is really and in himself. From which it follows plainly that all the Buddhas, infinite though they are in number, once fully understood, are one.[5] Owing to the fact, however, that among finite beings there are all degrees of enlightenment and ignorance, the Buddha not only *is* but *appears*. The finite beings to whom he appears are divisible into two great classes, namely Bodhisattvas and all those who stand below them in enlightenment, including common people, Sravakas, and Pratyekabuddhas. This is a rather subtle thought, that though the Buddha is one, the nature of the Buddha for each soul will be unique and will depend on the nature of the soul. So,

> Life like a dome of many-colored glass
> Stains the white radiance of eternity.

To each of the two classes named above the one Buddha has his characteristic form of appearance or body. The form he takes before the eyes of the blessed Bodhisattvas is known as the Sambhogakaya, or Body of Bliss. As there are countless groups of Bodhisattvas, so there are countless Sambhogakayas. The white ray of the Infinite One is broken into endless prismatic colors by the differentiating consciousness of the blessed but as yet finite Bodhisattvas.[6] The eyes of common people and even of Sravakas could not stand this sight. Or rather, just because their minds are incapable of understanding and conceiving such high things, the vision of the Absolute which they receive is much less glorious. The ap-

[3] Suzuki, *Outlines of Mahayana Buddhism*, p. 62.

[4] For further discussion of the Dharmakaya see Suzuki's *Outlines of Mahayana Buddhism*, Chap. IX.

[5] Cf. Asanga IX. 62 (Levi's trans., p. 87): the *Awakening*, p. 103. Sometimes this necessary conclusion is lost from sight and different Dharmakayas are spoken of. Obviously this will not bear logical examination and those Mahayanists who hold it merely fail to understand their own philosophy.

[6] This vision of himself which the Tathagata grants to the eyes of his sons is closely related, both in description and in fundamental conception, to the vision of himself as Vishnu which Krishna, according to the Bhagavad Gita, vouchsafed to Arjun. Bhagavad Gita, Chap. XI.

pearance of the Tathagata to the unenlightened, the "third body of the Buddha" is called his Nirmanakaya, or Body of Transformation. This is what we should call the earthly or historical appearance of the Buddha.

But:

> Beings of this class [below the rank of Bodhisattvas] do not know that the Body of Transformation is merely the shadow [or reflection] of their own evolving consciousness. They imagine that it comes from some external source, and so they give it a corporeal limitation. . . . Bodhisattvas are able to recognize the finer form of activity [of the Dharmakaya]. Their insight is more penetrating than that of others. As they firmly believe in the Bhutatathata they can have a partial insight into it and understand that the Body of the Tathagata is not departing, is not coming [i.e., that the Tathagata's work is eternal and constant], that everything is but a reflected shadow of the mind. When they reach the height of Bodhisattvahood their insight becomes perfect. As long as they are possessed by the activity consciousness they perceive the Body of Bliss. But when they are liberated from it, all traces of individuation become obliterated. For all Tathagatas come from one and the same Dharmakaya, have no distinction of thisness and thatness, have no corporeal forms that are characterized by reciprocal limitation.[7]

The doctrine of the Body of Transformation has, obviously, a direct bearing on the conception of the historical Buddha. The historical Buddha, like the visions which the Bodhisattvas enjoy in the various Buddha fields, was only an appearance, only a vision. This conclusion of the Mahayana was by no means something entirely new. Quite early in Hinayana history some of the more daring thinkers began to feel that so great a being as the Tathagata could hardly have descended into the womb of Maya and been born a mere baby. Hence a docetic view arose at least as early as the third century B.C., recalling strikingly the docetic doctrines of certain early Christian heresies that were touched with gnosticism. The Katha-vatthu mentions among the heresies which it condemns one which held that men and gods of Sakyamuni's time had known only a phantom Buddha and that the real Sakyamuni had never ceased to reside in the Tusita heaven,[8] but had sent down a phantom form which

[7] *Awakening*, pp. 100-03. I have omitted much and in one place slightly rearranged the sequence.

[8] XVIII, 1, 2. In Aung and Rhys Davids' trans., pp. 323-25. See also Oltramare, *Un Problem de l'Ontologie Bouddhique*, Museon, 3d Series, I (1915), pp. 1-23, and Anesaki's article on "Docetism," *H. E. R. E.*

taught the Dharma to Ananda. Early Mahayana sects maintained that Sakyamuni survives in a prolonged trance and in fact that he has been in it since he entered Buddhahood; and that after he gained enlightenment under the Bo Tree it was only his body that continued to act and speak, he himself not being in the body but in a heavenly state. Probably before the doctrine of the three bodies of the Buddha was devised, many Buddhists believed that all the earthly life of the Founder had been merely a magical substitute for the real Buddha. It is obvious how easily this docetic view led into the three-body doctrine and how naturally it adjusted itself to the larger metaphysical conception.

The result of this combined tendency was to place the historical Buddha in a position of relatively slight importance. India has commonly cared little for historical fact, and the Indian tendency here again made itself felt. He who knows the eternal Buddha, what should he care for the details of a particular occurrence—itself probably illusory—which took place during certain years at Kapilavastu, Gaya, and Kusinara? Thus as we pass from the Hinayana to the developed Mahayana we find a complete change in the center of gravity. The facts of the Founder's life, and even the details of his teaching came to have a steadily decreasing importance. Buddhism comes to be less a continuation of the teachings *of* the Buddha and more a collection of teachings *about* the Buddha—teachings which are no longer historical but purely metaphysical in their nature. The Buddha whom the Mahayana doctors adore is not the Sakyamuni of Kapilavastu, but the eternal Buddha. Paraphrasing the words of St. Paul they might well have said, "Yea, though we had known the Buddha in the flesh, now know we him no more."

The reference to St. Paul suggests a parallelism between the change that took place in Buddhism and a change that took place in Christianity, which is too striking and, in its way, instructive, to be passed by without notice. As the Mahayana substituted for the Buddha of history the eternal Buddha, so St. Paul and the writer of the Fourth Gospel substituted for the Christ of history the eternal Christ. I can make more plain the parallel movements in the two religions by quoting here a passage from Pfleiderer's *Primitive*

Christianity, which, though written with no thought of Buddhism, shows clearly the same metaphysical tendency of the human mind flinging out its declaration of independence from all merely historical or empirical facts.

> The object of the Pauline faith was not Christ after the flesh, not the Jewish Messiah born of David's seed, not the Jew born of a woman and subject to the Mosaic law; of him Paul says expressly, "If we have known Christ after the flesh, yet now we know him no more." And accordingly, "If any man is in Christ he is a new creation; the old has passed away; behold, it has become new." (2 Cor. v. 16f.) . . . The earthly life of Jesus was, according to Paul, only an episodic appearance of the Heavenly Man in our fleshly body; as this body was derived from David's seed the earthly Jesus belonged to the Jewish people and was also, in so far, subjected to the Jewish law. But this existence in earthly flesh was not the true and proper mode of being of the Son of God, but only a form of outward manifestation foreign to His heavenly spiritual existence, which He again laid aside in death in order to become, at His resurrection, a pure Spirit (free from earthliness) with a heavenly body of glory appropriate to it. As pure Spirit He stripped off, along with the limitations of His earthly existence in general, also the limitation of nationality: the heavenly Christ, the Lord, who is the Spirit, is no longer a Jew, but archetypal man, the first-born of all the sons of God who are called to freedom. And as He has cast off, for Himself, the limitations of earth, of nationality, of the Mosaic law, He works henceforth on those who are His as a liberating spirit who frees them from all those fleshly fetters and unites them into one new spiritual body. This liberating and renewing work of the Spirit of the Lord is not, however, conceived by Paul merely in the moral sense, current among us, of a continued influence of the moral character of Jesus, but in a mystical sense resting upon popular animistic metaphysics, namely, that the individual person of Jesus, now existing in heaven clothed with a body of glory, is at the same time, as a substance or source of power, free from the limitations of space ("omnipresent"), present in all his churches, entering into believers, and as an ethico-religious power producing in them supernatural effects, indeed, a completely new being (a "new creation").[9]

As the eternal Christ is the theme of St. Paul's Epistles and of the Fourth Gospel, so the eternal Buddha is the theme of the great gospel of the Mahayana, the Saddharma Pundarika Sutra—the "Lotus of the Good Law." The Sutra begins, as do so many Buddhist books, with a description of a great gathering of venerable Arhats and other disciples in the presence of Sakyamuni at the Vulture Peak. The Tathagata

[9] *Op. cit.* (Eng. trans., London, 1906), I, 381-82.

is at first presented in something like the Hinayana fashion; he is one of a succession of Buddhas, one who had gone through a long period of preparation as a Bodhisattva, and who had attained enlightenment under the Bo Tree at Buddh Gaya. During his discourse he has occasion to prophesy the future complete enlightenment of several of his disciples there present and their great reward. Many of his hearers request from him a commission to spread the truth. In answer he discloses before their eyes a great cloud of glorious Bodhisattvas, ready to perform the task: and to the astonishment of his hearers he tells them that these Bodhisattvas have existed over countless eons *as his disciples.* At these words his hearers cannot hide their perplexity, which one of their number respectfully voices as follows: "How, O Lord, has the Tathagata been able to perform all this since he left, as a royal prince, Kapilavastu and arrived at supreme enlightenment not far from the town of Gaya, about forty years ago? How has the Tathagata, within so short a time, been able to rouse and bring to maturity for supreme, perfect enlightenment this host of Bodhisattvas, a multitude so great that it would be impossible to count the whole of it even if one were to continue counting for hundreds of thousands of kotis of eons?" In short, "Is not this the carpenter's son?"

And the Buddha's reply to the question might almost be phrased in the words of the Johanine Christ: "Before Abraham was, I am." From all eternity the Buddha has been leading needy beings to the light. Time does not pass for him as for those within the illusion of change. "The Tathagata sees the triple world not as ignorant, common people: He sees things eternally present to him. The Tathagata who so long ago was perfectly enlightened is unlimited in the duration of his life: He is from everlasting." But for the sake of those whose little minds can be touched only by a limited presence of flesh and blood, and who can be made to feel the need of speedy effort only by the seeming death of their teacher, the Tathagata becomes from time to time incarnate, and "without being extinct, makes a show of extinction, on behalf of those who need to be educated."

I am the Father of the World, the Self-born, the Healer, the Protector of all creatures. Knowing them to be perverted, infatuated, ignorant, I teach them final rest, myself not being at rest. Why do I continually manifest myself? When men become unbelieving, ignorant, fond of sensual pleasure, then I who know the course of the world declare, I am the Tathagata: and I consider how I may incline them to enlightenment, how I may make them partakers of the Buddha Law.[10]

In the preceding paragraph I used the word "incarnate" in relation to the historical Buddha. This word does not occur in Kern's translation of the Lotus, but it is important to note that this is the thought embodied in this remarkable Buddhist gospel. In the man Sakyamuni, born at Kapilavastu, the eternal Buddha incarnated himself. The All-one stooped to appear as the son of Maya. It was, indeed, but an appearance; but that appearance was as true as any mere appearance can be. So far as such a thing is at all possible or thinkable, the Infinite Reason became flesh; it came down from heaven and was made man. And this it did for us men and for our salvation. But this it did not once only. In this respect the Mahayana doctrine of the incarnation is closer to that of the Bhagavad Gita than to the Christian. Mankind is repeatedly in need of a new incarnation of the Divine, and so through the infinite ages there has been and shall be an infinite series of Buddhas who in their teachings and their lives show forth the eternal truth. With the Krishna of the Gita, the Buddha might say:

"Though birthless and unchanging of essence, yet in my sway over the nature that is mine I come to birth by mine own magic. For whensoever the Dharma fails and lawlessness arises, then do I bring myself to bodied birth. To guard the righteous, to establish the Dharma, I come into birth age after age."[11]

The monistic and idealistic conception of reality that we have been studying has certain obvious bearings on the nature of Nirvana. In the first place it must be said, the new school of thought takes the word where the Hinayana left it, retaining much of its old significance. Nirvana still means primarily spiritual freedom: freedom from the fires of lust, ill will, and dulness or ignorance. Of these three it is especially the fire of ignorance which the Mahayana would at-

[10] Kern's trans., slightly reworded, *S. B. E.*, XXI, 294-310.

[11] IV. 6-8, Barnett's trans. (*The Temple Classics*, Dent).

tack, for this is fundamental; and it celebrates most joyfully freedom from that form of ignorance which results in the illusion of separateness. "As ignorance is thus annihilated, the mind is no more disturbed so as to be subject to individuation. As the mind is no more disturbed, the particularization of the surrounding world is annihilated. When in this wise the principle and condition of defilement, and their products, with the mental disturbances that flow from them are all annihilated, it is said that we attain Nirvana." [12]

But Nirvana means more than this. It meant more than this to the Hinayana. There it was a state beyond death—Parinirvana—the reality of which the Blessed One had averred, but the nature of which he had not disclosed. The Yogacara thinkers, unwilling to continue the agnostic attitude of the Southern Church, work out from their own metaphysical presuppositions a new interpretation of Nirvana in its full sense. In the first place, Nirvana does not mean nothingness. The writer of the *Awakening* is very emphatic upon this,[13] as is also the Lotus Sutra. At the climax of the vision there depicted which the Tathagata reveals to the eyes of myriads of Bodhisattvas, the stupa of an ancient Buddha, Prabhutaratna, is opened. This Buddha, we are told, has been "completely extinct," has been in Nirvana, for many kotis of kalpas; but when the stupa is opened he is found there "as if absorbed in abstract meditation," and he greets Sakyamuni, and welcomes him to a place on the throne beside him, summons and converses with a distant Buddha and in other ways shows himself both conscious and active.[14] From this and several other passages [15] in the Lotus it is plain that the word "extinct" by no means signifies unconscious or lifeless. The term seems to have been retained from the earlier form of Buddhism and to have reference only to the destruction of those characteristics which to the Buddhist are undesirable. The Buddhas are no longer subject to any form of illusion or self-centeredness. It is in this sense that they may be said to have become extinct on entering

[12] The *Awakening* (Suzuki), p. 87.

[13] Cf. Suzuki's trans., pp. 107-08. For the Madhyamika Nirvana, like everything else, is, of course, nothingness.

[14] Chaps. XI, XXIII.

[15] Cf. pp. 61, 63 of Kern's trans.

Nirvana. Their two less real bodies, the Nirmanakaya and the Sambhogakaya, disappear, though seemingly the second of these may reappear at any time for the edification of the faithful. The waning of these appearances has nothing to do with the real being of the Buddhas and in no way reduces their reality. They are still and ever what always they were, identical with the one spiritual substance of the universe, the Dharmakaya.

And what is true for them is true *in potentia* for every sentient creature. Such a conception makes Nirvana both more universal and more transcendant than it was for Southern Buddhism. In one sense, now are we all nearer our salvation than the Hinayana could have believed; in another, the prize is more lofty and more difficult—and immensely more worth the having—than ever the Hinayana dreamed. To be free from desire, to be extinct in the ordinary sense—compare these sane and earthly hopes with the prospect of becoming Buddha. For nothing short of the attainment of Buddhahood is what Nirvana now must mean. It is this new revelation of what is in store for them that fills the ancient disciples, as depicted in the Lotus, with inexpressible surprise and joy. They had followed the teachings of the Hinayana and had tried to satisfy themselves with its promises. Now they have heard the Lord preach this new secret doctrine, and "were struck with wonder, amazement, and rapture," and kneeling before him they said:

> Lord, we are aged, advanced in years, honoured as seniors in this assemblage of monks. Worn out by old age we fancied that we had attained Nirvana. We are making no efforts for supreme enlightenment. . . . We have conceived no longing after the Buddha-laws. By having fled out of the triple world, O Lord, we imagined that we had attained Nirvana: and we are decrepit from old age. And now, O Lord, we hear from the Lord that disciples also may attain supreme perfect enlightenment. We are astonished and amazed. We have acquired a magnificent jewel, an incomparable jewel. We had not sought nor searched nor expected so magnificent a jewel.[16]

And what was true for these ancient saints is true for all. All shall in the end become Buddha: for all are potentially Buddha now. Nirvana is thus not a place nor a state one

[16] Chap. IV, Kern, pp. 98-99.

shall enter when one dies. From the temporal point of view, to be sure, it is a state that may be progressively approximated. But *sub specie aeternitatis* it is a present condition of all real beings just to the extent to which they are real. "All things from the beginning are in their nature Nirvana itself." [17] For Nirvana is the Dharmakaya. From the metaphysical presuppositions of the Yogacara it could be nothing else. It is the One Reality, the One Soul; not only the Dharmakaya of all the Buddhas but the deepest nature of each one of us. To know it, to realize it, to discover it in ourselves, to live in the light of it, this is the meaning of immortality. The Lotus might have used almost the identical words of the Fourth Gospel: "And this *is* life eternal, to know Thee, the Only true God." To know God, to enter into the Dharmakaya is the aim of all worship and of all life. For the Mahayana Buddhist the only true worship is realization.

This conception forms, in a sense, the central theme not only of the Lotus but of the Surangama Sutra from which I quoted at some length in the preceding chapter. Starting from the common-sense, realistic Hinayana point of view suggested by Ananda's questions, the Tathagata led the thought of his attentive listeners to deeper and deeper insights, and finally to the conception of the Buddha nature that is in all things. And so at last, all the great congregation, including not only the blessed Bodhisattvas but also humble, human Ananda,

> obtained enlightenment. This great assembly perceived that one's Heart is coextensive with the universe, seeing clearly the empty character of the world as plainly as that of a leaf or of any trifling thing in one's hand, and realizing that all things in the universe are but the excellently bright and primeval Heart of Bodhi, and that this heart is universally diffused and comprehends all things within itself. And still reflecting, they beheld their generated bodies as so many grains of dust in the wide expanse of the universal void, now safe, now lost; or as a bubble of the sea, sprung from nothing and born to be destroyed. But their perfect and independent soul, they perceived as indestructible and ever the same, identical with the Dharmakaya.[18]

And in confirming their faith and interpreting their vision the Buddha said:

[17] *Awakening*, Suzuki, p. 121. [18] P. 343.

> The mysterious effulgence (which though one appears as many and lightens all beings) is indeed the secret essence of the Tathagata. It is the universally diffused effulgence of the Divine Intelligence. This unity is boundless, and being boundless yet is one. Though in small things yet it is great: though in great things yet it is small. Pervading all things, present in every minutest hair, it includes the infinite worlds in its embrace. Enthroned in the minutest particle of dust, it turns the great Wheel of the Law. One with the Divine knowledge, it manifests itself as the effulgent Nature of the Divine Intelligence of the Tathagata.[19]

Before closing this chapter I wish to point out two characteristics of the Mahayana which it will be helpful to bear in mind throughout the chapters that are to come and which will follow the story of the Mahayana in the lands to which it journeyed as a pilgrim and a missionary. The first of these points must have been noticed by the reader: the way, namely, in which the compassion of the Mahayana ideal made its way into the very structure of its philosophy. When the Buddha speaks, in the fifteenth chapter of the Lotus concerning his repeated incarnations for the salvation of men, he is not presented as talking symbolism, but literal, philosophical truth. For the Mahayanist, as for the Christian philosopher, at the heart of being there is no mere abstract essence, but an outstreaming compassion.

The second characteristic of the Mahayana I would point out is the inclusiveness of its absolutism. The truth which it teaches is large enough to be compatible with an endless variety of symbols. It is wedded to no literal rendering of any form of presentation and the truth it presents is of such a large and philosophic nature that it would be difficult to conceive of any imaginable scientific or historical discovery which would greatly affect it. If it should some day be demonstrated that Gotama was merely a sun myth this would be a most serious blow to the Hinayana, but the Mahayana would hardly feel it. And as for Darwinian evolution, the spontaneous generation of life, and other scientific hypotheses which have filled the souls of Christian theologians, past and present, with dismay and wrath—your doctor of the Mahayana will snap his fingers at them.

A world view so wide as this will be compatible not only

[19] Pp. 352-53. Cf. the Brihadaranyaka Upanishad.

with many scientific hypotheses, but with many religious symbols. The Tathagata makes use of the teachings of the Hinayana for those who cannot yet behold the larger vision. The "vehicle of the Sravakas" and the "vehicle of the Pratyekabuddhas," once fully understood, lead into the one great "vehicle of the Bodhisattvas," though the Sravakas and the Pratyekabuddhas do not know it.[20] The Tathagata by his "skillfulness" uses many means to lead the ignorant into the true path. Words and definitions and symbols all fall short of an expression of the ineffable truth. "The reason why the Tathagata nevertheless endeavors to instruct by means of words and definitions is to be found in his good and excellent skilfulness. He only provisionally makes use of words and definitions to lead all beings, while his real object is to make them abandon symbolism and enter directly into the real Reality."[21]

These two characteristics, compassion and inclusiveness, equipped the Mahayana to an unusual degree as a missionary religion. Its compassion supplied the incentive, and its inclusiveness made it extraordinarily adaptable to new conditions. It is always ready to admit, even eager to suggest, that the truths of other religions are merely different formulations of its own truth, that the cult objects of other faiths are merely symbolic expressions of its own deeper apprehension of the Real.

By the year 1200, as we have already seen, the Mahayana like the Hinayana had become wholly an exile from the land of its birth. But exile for Buddhism did not mean death, but a new blossoming and a new service. The Hinayana we have watched in its wanderings over the sunny lands of the south. A form of Buddhism which because of its mixed nature we shall not trace in this work spread northward over the frozen regions of Tibet and Mongolia, while a related branch of it invaded the passes that lead into Nepal. Meanwhile the Mahayana had started out on a still more distant mission. We must now trace its fortunes in its long pilgrimage to the far lands of the more remote north.

[20] Cf. the *Lotus*, Chaps. II, III.

[21] Suzuki's trans. of the *Awakening*, p. 112.

THE DYNASTIES OF CHINA

Hsia, 2205-1766 B.C.
Shan or Yin, 1766-1122 B.C.
Chow, 1122-255 B.C.
T'sin, 255-206 B.C.
Han, 206 B.C.-214 A.D.
The "Three Kingdoms," 214-265
The "Period of Darkness," 265-589
Sui, 589-618
T'ang, 618-907
The "Five Dynasties," 907-960
Sung, 960-1280
Kin or Mongols, 1280-1368
Ming, 1368-1644
Tsing or Manchu, 1644-1912

CHAPTER XIV

THE STORY OF CHINESE BUDDHISM

THE Hinayana lands and China seem upon the map to lie in close proximity, with no great barrier between. As a fact, this is far from being the case. The approach to China from the south is not altogether easy today; from the west it is difficult. In the early Buddhist centuries the land of T'sin was cut off from the Indian and semi-Indian lands for all but the most hardy and adventurous. Desert, mountain, and sea had conspired together and presented an almost insurmountable barrier to human intercourse. Upon the west and southwest rise the Pamirs and Himalayas, the loftiest mountains in the world, towering to twice the height of the Alps, with blinding snows and terrific chasms and rushing torrents; while north of them stretches for many hundred miles the Gobi desert, filled with sandstorms and thirst, trackless save for the skeletons of those who tried and failed. This route is still fraught with immense hardship and peril; but for the merchant and missionary of the early days the southeastern route was perhaps even more frightful. For here rage those hungriest and most treacherous of all the earth's waters, the China Seas. The steady surge of its waves, the sunken Paracel reefs, on whose hidden rocks many a junk and many a goodly western ship has pounded to pieces, the typhoons, whose sudden walls of water gleam like white devouring teeth, and before whose unheralded approach the greatest ships seek refuge if they can in some snug harbor on the coast of Annam—these make this section of the ocean still a terror to all but the largest steamships. What the voyage must have been in an ancient Chinese junk it is hard to picture. The waters west of French Indo-China are calm enough; but when one has rounded the Point of Cambodia, the pounding seas driven by the northeast monsoon, blowing for months at a stretch, with the weight of the vast Pacific behind them, the reefs of the coast, the rocky islets, the sudden and tremendous storms, must have been to the ancient mariner, in his small but unwieldy junk, a nightmare indeed. I-tsing who traversed this stretch of the China Seas in the six hundreds has left us a brief word picture of it: "Cutting through the immense abyss, the great swells of water lie, like a mountain on the sea. Joining sideways with a vast gulf-stream, the massive waves like clouds, dash against the sky." [1]

It was over this triple barrier of mountain, desert, and sea, that the Buddhist missionaries forced their way to disseminate the new faith, and that the Buddhist pilgrims from China journeyed out on the long trail to the home land of their religion, and then back again to bring with them a purer faith than the most learned in their own country had ever known.

In many ways China was an unpromising field for the missionary religion. Both Northern and Southern Buddhism are notable for their emphasis on the inner life, and the Mahayana is highly speculative. The Chinese care little for speculation or mysticism and are preeminently a practical and outward-looking people. The scholastic organization of Buddhism, moreover, was an added impediment to its progress; for its praise of the celibate life was out of harmony with one of the most fundamental convictions of the Chinese, their reverence for the family and their belief in the duty of begetting sons. An organization such as the Buddhist Order was, further, a cause of suspicion and antagonism on the part of the Chinese government, which has always looked askance at closely knit groups of individuals within the state. From considerations such as these, a judge of human nature, observing the condition of China in the middle of the Han dynasty, might well have predicted great difficulties for the new religion.

Nor would his predictions have been lacking in justification by the event. Looking back now to that distant point in the past, with all the knowledge that the intervening centuries have given us, we, too, can see that on the whole Buddhism was not very well adapted to the Chinese people. The unfavorable characteristics above recited have steadily worked against its success in China and to them must be laid

[1] *I-tsing's Records of the Buddhist Religion*, trans. by Takakusa, p. xxx.

in large part the present moribund condition of Buddhism in many parts of that great land.

Yet it has had successes as well as difficulties, and these, too, are to be explained by certain of its fundamental characteristics. Most important of these is its elasticity and adaptability. The wise monks who guided the development of Buddhism during its first centuries in China were quick to see the character and customs and the needs of the people, and being bound by no rigid rules or dogmas they were able to adapt their teachings and their services to the new conditions. The monastic order, indeed, could not be given up, but Buddhist monks learned how to make themselves useful to the Chinese family. They adopted into their teaching the Confucian ideal of filial piety, laying almost as much stress upon this as upon the Five Precepts. The Chinese piety toward departed parents, indeed, Buddhism was able to serve in what seemed a much more efficient way than Confucianism, namely, by its masses for the dead; and this did much to enlist the family sentiment in favor of the new religion. Buddhism appealed also to the natural human hope for life beyond the grave. For while neither Confucianism nor Taoism pretended to give any information concerning the condition of the dead, the Indian religion proffered detailed knowledge and a lively hope. It was probably this combination of hope for oneself and knowledge about the condition of one's beloved dead, with the strict moral retribution involved, that did more than any other one thing to bring about the early spread of Buddhism in China. It filled a long-felt need. In the eighth century Buddhist monks added to the appeal of their religion by offering not only knowledge of the future but means of directly affecting it, through the proper recital of sacred verses. From this time on the bonzes were indispensable at funerals and at the later ceremonies for praying the dead out of purgatory. While this rather superstitious and late invention of the Order certainly did much to strengthen the hold of Buddhism on the Chinese laity, it is still true that the chief explanation of the firm position that Buddhism won for itself in China as a whole is to be found in the fact referred to above, that it brought new hope for the other side of death and that it provided a way of salvation by moral effort which appealed strongly to the deeply moral nature of the Chinese people.

In other and lesser ways also Buddhism adapted itself to the Chinese. It found that Taoism had already prepared the soil for its own ideal of inwardness and passivity, in the doctrine of the Tao, as presented in the Tao-te Ching [2] and the writings of Chwang-tse; and it made the most of this situation. Instead of attacking Taoism it almost adopted it. Instead of ridiculing the Taoist deities (which would surely not have been a difficult matter) it took some of them over into the Buddhist cycle as attendants on the Buddhas, some of them it even made into Bodhisattvas. I sometimes wonder, indeed, that it did not adopt Confucius as a Bodhisattva; but perhaps Confucius would have been too big a pill for even a Buddhist monk; and the wise leaders may have seen that such an act would have produced nothing but uncontrollable indignation on the part of the Confucians.

Whether Buddhism had made its appearance in China before the Han Emperor Ming-Ti, in 62 A.D., had his famous dream of the golden man and sent his embassy to the West to learn about him, is a question on which sinalogues disagree,[3] and about which, therefore, I have no opinion. The

[2] Note, for example, the Buddhist and Mahayanist tone of the following from the Tao-Te Ching: "The Tao (that is, the Ultimate) is empty and so is the practice of it. We must not be full of ourselves. When you have accomplished something and thereby gained fame, then let your own self retire into the background, for this is the Tao of Heaven. . . . The reason why the perfect man holds in his embrace the Universe itself and so is the model of all that lives under the sky, is that he is free from self-display and therefore shines bright: free from a selfish existence and therefore is glorious; free from struggling for the sake of himself and therefore performs meritorious works; free from self-sympathy and therefore has superiority. As he does not indulge in struggle with others, no one in the world struggles with him." Nor was Confucianism by any means out of harmony with the moral side of Buddhism, as the following from the Chung Yung (the *Doctrine of the Mean*) will indicate: "When there are no stirrings of pleasure, anger, sorrow, or joy, we call it the State of Equilibrium. When these feelings have been stirred and all in their due measure and degree, we call it the state of harmony" (Chap. I, 4). As the last part of the quotation will show, however, there was a real difference between the Confucian and the Buddhist ideals.

[3] Parker sees no reason to believe that Buddhism was known in China before this time, and discusses the matter at some length on pages 225-31 of his *Studies in Chinese Religion* (London, Chapman and Hall, 1910). Giles, on the other hand, thinks the evidence in favor of such early acquaintance is excellent. See Lecture VI of his *Confucianism and Its Rivals* (London, Williams and Norgate, 1915). Cordier discusses the introduction of Buddhism into China, with many citations, on pages 262-66 of his *Histoire Générale de la Chine* (Paris, Geuthner, 1920). He rejects the story of the emperor's dream as apocryphal. Reichelt accepts the story of the dream and also the view that Buddhism was known in China in the first century before Christ (*Truth and Tradition in Chinese Buddhism*, Shanghai, Commercial Press, 1927, pp. 9-12).

two monks whom the imperial ambassadors found in Central Asia and brought back with them, unloaded at the capital [4] their Buddha image and their books from the back of the horse which had carried them all those weary hundreds of miles, and the Emperor built them a little monastery, named (in typical Buddhist fashion) after the faithful beast,[5] where the great work of translating Sanskrit Sutras into Chinese was begun. One of the monks was an Indian and probably both were. Other monks, some of them Indian, some natives of Central Asia, followed during the next centuries. They made, apparently, no great efforts at proselyting, but spent their time laying the foundations of the future Chinese church in a manner typical of both the great scholarly peoples here involved, the Indians and the Chinese, by continuing the work of translating books. By the time of the downfall of the Han dynasty upward of three hundred and fifty books had been translated. It was not till the period known as the Age of Darkness (265-589) that Buddhism made any noticeable advance among the Chinese people. During this period Buddhism spread rapidly, and according to Brinkley it "became, before the middle of the fourth century, the chief religion of the nation." [6] It seems to have been especially among the small states, in part under Tartar rule, into which China north of the Yangtse was split, that Buddhism made best headway. It was one of these northern rulers (Shih Chi-lung of the Later Chao) who, just prior to 363 A.D., for the first time gave the Buddhist missionaries permission to receive native Chinese into the Order as monks. Hitherto the Chinese converts had been laymen only. From now on they were to become monks as well. This meant an important turning point in the history of Chinese Buddhism—a turning point comparable to that which the Christian church in China is just reaching. After the permission of 363 the Chinese church was to be native, independent, and largely self-guided. This did not mean that it was left without assistance by the mother church in India and Central Asia. Thus in 383 a great reinforcement

[4] Lo-Yang.
[5] The White Horse Monastery.
[6] *China, Its History, Arts, and Literature* (Boston, Millet, 1902), X, 148.

came to Chinese Buddhism in the person of a learned Indian teacher, Kumarajiva, who was captured by a Chinese general in the siege of a city in Central Asia and brought to Chang-an, where he performed a huge amount of work, instructing some three thousand disciples and translating fifty or more books.

One of the books translated by Kumarajiva was the Smaller Sukhavati-vyuha. The Larger Sukhavati-vyuha had been translated into Chinese sometime before the year 186. These two books, with one other [7] which was translated soon after Kumarajiva's time, form the principal scripture of the "Pure Land" form of Buddhism—that evangelical doctrine which promises salvation in the Western Paradise by simple faith in Amitabha, and which naturally made and has continued to make a great appeal to the simpler-minded Chinese. About the time that Kumarajiva translated the Smaller Sukhavati-vyuha, this form of thought and aspiration in Buddhism was crystallized into something that might be called a school or sect, by a Buddhist monk named Hui Yuan, who had been converted from Taoism and who brought something of the Taoist mystic feeling into his adopted faith.[8] The Pure Land or Lotus school of Buddhism is thus the oldest of the present sects of Buddhism in China. Its influence, I should add, was very much greater than the number of its recognized members would indicate; for it eventually permeated to a considerable degree all the other sects. Had not Buddhism been presented in this form it is unlikely that it ever would have been able to get the strong hold upon the Chinese people which the centuries following Hui Yuan's time were to see.

The Buddhist missionaries from India brought with them many things besides their religion. Indian science was well developed by the time Buddhism entered China and the learned monks who brought the teachings of Sakyamuni brought also a considerable amount of the science of their native land. Chinese astronomy in particular was thus enriched by India. It seems probable, too, that the method of

[7] The Amitayurdhyana Sutra, trans. about 424.

[8] For an excellent study of Hui Yuan, the Taoist influence he brought with him, and the Pure Land school in general, see Reichelt, *Truth and Tradition in Chinese Buddhism*, Chap. V.

writing the numerals in accordance with the decimal system was introduced into China from India by Buddhist missionaries. The monks also made the written language of China a less rigid tool, for many Sanskrit names and many Sanskrit terms for which there was no Chinese equivalent had to be presented in some quasi-phonetic fashion. The ingenuity of the Indians and the considerable acquaintance with phonetics that every student of Sanskrit must acquire, enabled them to construct a system of expressing sounds in Chinese characters which the Chinese probably never would have invented but which they were glad to adopt.[9]

For many years, as I have indicated, after the fall of the Hans, the chief successes of Buddhism were won north of the Yangtse. South of the great river, in the region the Tartars had not been able to reach, and where, consequently, the ancient Chinese culture, with its pride and prejudice, its learning and its suspicion of foreign ideas were strong, the two native religions (if so we may call Confucianism and Taoism) made unsystematic but repeated and at times violent attacks upon the teachings of the new faith. In spite of this Buddhism steadily grew in strength on both sides of the river, frequently counting the various rulers, and even the "legitimate" emperor, among its converts. It was during this period that the famous Buddhist travelers Fa-Hien and Sung-Yun made their long and dangerous pilgrimages to India to see their religion in act in its native country, to drink in the truth at its source, and to bring back new books for translation. More important still it was during this period that the great Bodhidharma came from India and brought with him the Dhyana or Contemplative school of Buddhism.

As this is by far the most widespread school of Chinese Buddhism it will be well to pause here and learn something of its nature and history. The western reader, acquainted with a few books on the life and teachings of the Buddha, will probably be convinced on his first acquaintance with the Ch'an Buddhism of China and the Zen of Japan that this strange form of meditative nonsense (as he may regard it) has no relation whatever to the Buddhism of the Founder. As a fact, the seeds of Zen Buddhism, like the seeds of all the

[9] See Edkins, *Chinese Buddhism* (London, Kegan Paul), Chap. VI.

Mahayana, are to be traced back to Gotama. I wish here to deal with Ch'an or Zen Buddhism very briefly, postponing a more detailed treatment to a later time; but even here a few words must be said of its relation to the original Buddhism.

Something happened under the Bo Tree. A new and transforming insight came to Gotama. It is improbable that the tremendous thing that happened in his mind was merely the formulation of the Four Noble Truths and the causal chain. These were doubtless partial expressions of the new experience; but the experience itself was pretty plainly, from the psychological point of view, not a process of ratiocination, but rather belonged to the type of psychical events which in the West we know as conversion. It was partly intellectual, it was partly emotional, it was probably in part volitional. It was a sudden vision of new significance. To use a not uncommon expression which I confess I only partly understand, yet which may give the reader the feeling I am trying to convey, the thing that happened under the Bo Tree was the attainment of a new "level of insight" or a new "depth of life." The Buddha himself felt convinced of this. His disciples and most of those who came into contact with him seem to have felt this insight of his—felt it as something which was the source of, yet transcended, all his specific teaching. His repeated use of Yoga methods for concentration and the instruction he gave his followers in semi-mystical meditation also go to show that what he himself possessed and what he wished to hand on to them was not merely a doctrine and a definable view of life, but an experience of immediate insight. It is this experience of immediate insight that the Dhyana or Ch'an or Zen form of Buddhism seeks to attain, cultivate, and communicate. It was this that Bodhidharma brought to China.[10]

In his authoritative little *History of the Twelve Japanese Buddhist Sects*[11] the great Japanese scholar Bunyin Nanjio writes concerning the Ch'an or Zen sect as follows:

> The general character of the doctrine of this sect is briefly explained by twelve Chinese words which mean "Special transmission independent

[10] See Professor Suzuki's interesting discussion of this matter in his *Essays in Zen Buddhism* (London, Luzac, 1927), pp. 49-61, 107-24, 152-54.

[11] Tokyo, 1886.

of a common teaching and not established on any letter or word." Besides all the doctrines of the Mahayana and Hinayana, whether hidden or apparent, there is, therefore, one distinct line of transmission of a sercret doctrine which is not subject to (i.e., not capable of) any utterance at all. According to this doctrine one is directly to see the so-called key to the thought of Buddha or the Buddha nature by his own thought, being free from the multitude of different doctrines, the number of which is said to reach 84,000. In short, it is truth made apparent to one's own thought.[12]

To illustrate further the nature and the theory of transmission of this "secret doctrine" (which, of course, is not a *doctrine* at all but an ineffable and immediate personal experience), Nanjio relates the following tradition:

When the Blessed One was at the assembly on Mount Guidhrakuta, or Vulture's Peak, there came a heavenly king who offered him a flower of a golden colour, and asked him to preach the Law. The Blessed One only took the flower and held it in his hand, but said no word. No one in the whole assembly (except Mahakasyapa) could understand what he meant. The venerable Mahakasyapa alone smiled. Then the Blessed One said to him: "I have the wonderful thought of Nirvana, the eye of the Right Law, which I shall now give to you." This is called the doctrine of thought transmitted by thought.[13]

According to the tradition of the Ch'an sect Kasyapa thus became the patriarch of the Buddhist Order, after the death of the Founder, and the patriarchate with its mystic insight was handed on by him to Ananda, and on through a long list of famous Buddhist Fathers, including Asvaghosha, Nagarjuna, and Vasubandhu, to Bodhidharma, who, as the twenty-eighth patriarch, came to China and there founded the Chinese branch of the Dhyana school, which is known as the Ch'an. Bodhidharma is said to have come from Southern India, and this is probably the case. India, however, remembers nothing of him, and in no Indian list of Buddhist patriarchs is he mentioned.[14] For China and Japan, however, he is a very great figure, and his landing in Canton in 520 and his arrival at the emperor's court at Nanking was one of the crucial events in the story of Chinese Buddhism. The emperor of the day was a devout Buddhist and eagerly asked his renowned visitor how much merit he might expect

[12] *Op. cit.*, p. 114. [13] *Op. cit.*, pp. 114-15. [14] Eliot, *op. cit.*, II, 95.

from the princely donations he had for many years been making to the Buddhist Order. To this the blunt answer was, "No merit at all." The sacred books which had been translated with so much care, the patriarch said, were worth nothing. No knowledge that is worth anything can be gained by reading, nor is there any such thing as merit gained by good works. The astonished emperor then asked which of the holy doctrines of Buddhism was most important; to which the enigmatical saint responded, "Where all is emptiness, nothing can be called holy." Finally, to make sure of the authority from which such strange assertions came, the emperor asked, "Who are you who thus reply to me?" The philosopher saint responded, "I do not know." One is not surprised in reading Nanjio's assertion that the emperor "was not yet able to understand" Bodhidharma's teaching. "So leaving the capital, Bodhidharma crossed the river Yan tse, and on Mt. Su (in the Shao-Lin temple near Lo-yang) he sat down cross-legged in meditation, with his face to a wall, for nine years." [15]

In Bodhidharma's time Buddhism was growing rapidly. It is said that in the year 530 there were thirteen thousand temples in North China alone. The new mystic school stimulated even more rapid development. At Bodhidharma's death he conferred the patriarchal office on one of his disciples, and thus the patriarchate was handed on, till (in 713) the fifth successor (the sixth patriarch) had died. He appointed no successor, and there has been no patriarch since his day. It was he who left the growing church, if so we may call it, in the north, and carried the new form of Buddhism into the south, and there built up a large group of devoted followers. The Northern school eventually died out, but the Southern school extended over all China. Its influence was particularly great during the later T'ang and the Sung dynasties.[16]

Shortly after the death of Bodhidharma a Chinese monk who had studied the various forms of Buddhism thus far introduced into China and had for a time been a convert to

[15] Nanjio, *A Short History of the Twelve Japanese Buddhist Sects,* p. 116.

[16] For the history of Zen or Ch'an Buddhism in China, see Suzuki's *Essays in Zen Buddhism,* Essay IV.

the Ch'an school, came to feel that Buddhism was larger than any of its sects, and that there was no one exclusive road to salvation. For by this time, as I should have said, there were several schools of Buddhist thought in China, each claiming to possess the truth. These various schools may be classified in three principal types: (1) those who taught salvation was to be gained by knowledge—such as the Madhyamika and Yogacara and some of the Hinayana schools, all of which had followers in China; (2) those that preached salvation by grace and faith (the Pure Land or Lotus sect); and (3) the Ch'an or meditative sect. The monk of whom I have been speaking, Chih K'ai by name, conceived of a form of Buddhism that should have room within itself for all these sects and should do justice to the truth of all without doing injustice to the truth of any. The new school which he founded [17] took its name from the monastery which he built in the group of hills known as T'ien-t'ai, about one hundred and eighty miles southeast of Hang-chow, in Chekiang province.[18]

The T'ien-tai school is thus, in a way, encyclopedic. Yet, while it recognizes the teachings of all schools of Buddhism as true, it differentiates between them, some being more comprehensive than others. In this Chih K'ai was aided by Nagarjuna's distinction of the three levels of truth; and the seemingly opposed teachings and methods of the different schools he harmonized by an ingenious division of Sakyamuni's ministry and teaching into five periods. In the first of these, lasting only a few weeks, the Founder preached the absolute truth in all its lofty perfection to a throng of Bodhisattvas. For simple-minded mortals, however, this, he knew, was much too difficult; hence during the second period of his ministry he put his teaching in the simple words of the Hinayana. "Milk for babes, meat for strong men" has always been a Mahayana principle. In the third and fourth periods he led his disciples farther on the way to real insight. Finally, in the fifth period he taught them the doctrine of the Lotus gospel (the Saddharma Pundarika) which is really inclusive

[17] Chih K'ai is commonly spoken of as the founder of T'ien-t'ai Buddhism; but the members of the sect itself speak of many founders, both Chinese, Indian, and heavenly. See Nanjio, *op. cit.*, Chap. VII.

[18] See Edkins account in Chap. VIII of his *Chinese Buddhism.*

of all the rest.[19] The Lotus gospel is thus the great scripture of the T'ien-t'ai school. It will be seen, therefore, that while this school seeks to be all-embracing, it, too, has its own special form of Buddhist doctrine, which is considered truer than the rest in the sense, at least, of being more inclusive. The T'ien-t'ai, that is, has its own form of philosophy, a philosophy which may be described as a spiritualization of the Madhyamika. I shall deal with its thought more specifically in a later chapter.

Besides the sects I have mentioned there were at the beginning of the T'ang dynasty (A.D. 618) a number of others with which I shall not trouble the reader, since they had no great effect on the subsequent development of Buddhism as a religion, and in fact only one or two of them have lived on into our times. During the T'ang dynasty, however, they were vigorous. In fact, it was during the rule of this dynasty and the first centuries that followed its overthrow that Chinese Buddhism attained the acme of its influence. Both Confucianism and Taoism, to be sure, opposed it and sometimes, when they gained control of the emperor's conscience or judgment, succeeded in having it persecuted. The founder of the T'ang dynasty, a strict Confucianist, closed all but the larger Buddhist monasteries and convents and forced many monks and nuns to return to the world. A second persecution of a similar sort took place about a century later, and a third and particularly severe one in the middle of the ninth century. This last was during the reign of Wu-Tsung, a Taoist, who destroyed 4600 monasteries and 40,000 smaller buildings, confiscated the landed property of the Order, melted down Buddha images, set free 150,000 temple servants, and compelled more than 260,000 monks and nuns to return to the world.[20] These periods of persecution, however, were of fairly brief duration, and as a fervent Buddhist emperor usually succeeded a persecutor, the damage to the religion was in part made good. The persecutions,

[19] For a lengthier treatment of these five periods and their teachings, see McGovern, *Introduction to Mahayana Buddhism*, pp. 124-27, Reischauer, *Studies in Japanese Buddhism* (New York, Macmillan, 1917), pp. 172-73; and Reichelt, *Truth and Tradition in Chinese Buddhism*, pp. 50-52.

[20] De Groot, *Sectarianism and Religious Persecution in China* (Amsterdam, Muller, 1903), p. 69.

moreover, probably did nothing to weaken the hold of Buddhism upon the laity, which seems to have grown constantly stronger during the three centuries of T'ang rule. It was during this dynasty, in fact, that Buddhist monks came to be regarded as indispensable at funerals—a new Buddhist practice which, as we have seen, greatly increased its influence among the laity.[21]

The stream of sacred books from India continued, moreover, to reinforce the learning of the educated Buddhists. This work of importation seems to have been carried on during T'ang times, chiefly not by Indian missionaries but by devout Chinese Buddhists who longed to drink directly from the original spring of their religion. Already Fa-Hien and Sung-Yun had made their pilgrimages to the sacred land, and now, under the reign of the second T'ang emperor,[22] Hiuen-Tsiang made his famous journey, to be followed in 671 by the almost equally famous I-tsing. To appreciate fully the earnest devotion of these early Chinese Buddhists and the strength of their faith one must form some picture of the perils and hardships that faced them on the terrible journey through the Gobi desert and over the passes of the Pamirs, or on frail junks through the China Sea, that most treacherous of waters. Did space permit, it would be interesting to recount some of the trials endured by these dauntless pilgrims in search of greater light and purer truth, but I must content myself with quoting a few words of Fa-Hien concerning the Gobi desert through which his track lay: "In this desert are many evil demons and hot winds: when encountered, then all travelers die without exception. There are no flying birds above, no roaming beasts below, but everywhere gazing as far as the eye can reach in search of the onward route, it would be impossible to know the way but for dead men's decaying bones which show the direction."[23] Many of the pilgrims died on the journey, and those that won through did so, as we learn from the accounts they have left us, only by the confidence they derived from their faith in

[21] Eliot says this was due largely to the influence of a Ceylonese monk who came to China in 719. See II, 264-65.

[22] T'ai T'sung, the great conqueror.

[23] Beal's trans. in the Introd. to his *Buddhist Records of the Western World*, p. xxiv.

the Buddha and Kwan-Yin, to whom they prayed with fervor in all times of peril.[24]

Hiuen-Tsiang brought home with him a library of sacred Sanskrit works [25] which he spent the rest of his life (some nineteen years) in translating. I-tsing brought almost as many and (like his predecessor) spent his remaining years in translating them. The influence of these translations on the development of Chinese Buddhism was very considerable. Hiuen-Tsiang in fact was the founder of a Buddhist sect, or rather it was he who introduced it into China from India. This was the Dharma-lakshana sect, which continued the teachings of Asanga and Vasubandhu. In China it is known as the Fa-Hsiang.[26] On the whole, Hiuen-Tsiang was perhaps the most important Buddhist of all the great and honored Buddhist scholars of this scholarly land.

[24] Cf. especially the description of Hiuen-Tsiang's passage through the Gobi desert during which he prays in all emergencies and with much fervor to Kwan-Yin. At one time he lost his way in the midst of the desert and at the same moment upset his water bottle, losing thus all its contents; but resolutely went on, invoking the merciful Bodhisattva as his only hope. "At this time in the four directions the view was boundless; there were no traces either of man or horse, and in the night the demons and goblins raised fire-lights as many as the stars; in the daytime the driving wind blew the sand before it. But notwithstanding all this his heart was unaffected by fear; but he suffered from want of water, and was so parched with thirst that he could no longer go forward. Thus for four nights and five days not a drop of water had he to wet his throat or mouth; his stomach was racked with a burning heat, and he was well-nigh thoroughly exhausted. And now not being able to advance he lay down to rest on the sands, invoking Kwan-Yin without intermission, although worn with sufferings. And as he addressed the Bodhisattva he said: 'Hiuen-Tsiang in adventuring this journey does not seek for riches or worldly profit, he desires not to acquire fame, but only for the sake of the highest religious truth does his heart long to find the true Law. I know that the Bodhisattva lovingly regards all living creatures to deliver them from misery. Will not my misery, bitter as it is, come to the Bodhisattva's knowledge!' Thus he spoke with earnest heart and without cessation till the middle of the fifth night when suddenly a cool wind fanned his body, cold and refreshing as a bath of ice water. His eyes forthwith recovered their power of sight, and his body being thus refreshed he fell asleep for a little while."

In this sleep he had a dream—a great being [presumably Kwan-Yin] appearing before him. Rousing himself from slumber, he mounted his horse and soon came to an oasis, where his horse had plenty of green grass and where he found a pool of sweet water. The account given in his biography continues as follows: "Now we may conclude that this water and grass were not natural supplies, but were undoubtedly produced through the loving pity of the Bodhisattva" (*The Life of Hinen-Tsiang*, by his disciple Hwui-li, trans. by Beal, London, Kegan Paul, 1911, pp. 22-24). A few days later he was presented with a new kind of peril. The king of the country, a devout Buddhist, received him with every honor, and prized him so highly that he refused to allow him to go on. Hiuen-tsiang succeeded in getting away only by starting a hunger-strike and vowing that he would take no food till the king permitted him to depart. After he had gone for three days and nights without food or drink the king relented, *op. cit.*, pp. 24-29.

[25] Altogether some 657 volumes, carried on twenty horses, *op. cit.*, p. 214.

[26] In Japan known as the Hosso.

Another school of Buddhism introduced into China during the T'ang dynasty was the Chen-yen, or True Word sect —better known in the West by its Japanese name, Shingon. It worships especially the Buddha Vairocana, who stands for both the Dharma and the Sun. This, the last of the Chinese sects, was brought from India about 720 by an Indian named Vajrabodhi, who is reckoned the first of the Chinese patriarchs of this school.[27] His successor (also an Indian) Amogha Vajra by name, is said to have done more than any one else toward the introduction of masses for the dead into Chinese Buddhism. According to Dr. Reichelt, he borrowed from the ritual of the Nestorian missionaries whom he found at the capital much of the material that he used in his masses.[28] It was during the life of the fourth patriarch of this school (Hui Kuo)[29] in 804 that the famous Japanese monk, Kobo Daishi, came to China in search of Buddhist truth and studied the Shingon teaching. Returning to Japan soon after, he founded the Japanese Shingon sect. In this connection it will be well to mention the fact that at practically the same time an equally famous Japanese monk, Dengyo Daishi, came to China to study at Mt. T'ien-t'ai, and returning founded the Japanese Tendai sect. During the T'ang dynasty, therefore, China was a great religious mart, both receiving from India new inspiration and handing on the best it had acquired to Japan.

Buddhism was not the only religion of foreign origin that had some success in China during the T'ang dynasty. It was during T'ang rule that Nestorian Christianity entered China, and at about the same time came also Zoroastrianism and Manichaeism. The two T'ang capitals, Chang-an[30] and Lo-yang[31] were very cosmopolitan cities, centers of great intellectual life. Here representatives of the two native religions and the four foreign ones were defending and expounding their positions and exchanging ideas. Of all these religions probably Buddhism was the most active, for Con-

[27] Nanjio, *op. cit.*, Chap. VIII.

[28] *Op. cit.*, pp. 89-90.

[29] Eliot, III. 317. According to Nanjio, Kobo Daishi studied with the third patriarch.

[30] Modern Sian-fu.

[31] Modern Honan-fu, though the name is now being changed back to Lo-yang.

fucianism is almost necessarily conservative and on the defensive. This was the time, moreover, when the greatest member of one of the Buddhist sects was at the height of his intellectual power and influence, namely, San-tao, leader of the Pure Land sect, known best to history by the name he bears in Japan, Zendo.[32] He was, in a sense, the second founder of his sect, and his influence upon Buddhism in both China and Japan has been immense. The fact that he was living in Chang-an at the same time as the Nestorian fathers is sometimes cited as an argument for the view that the evangelical form of Buddhism of the Pure Land sects in China and Japan is derived from Christianity. But as Professor Moore has pointed out,[33] there are two facts which sufficiently dispose of this argument: first, the evangelical Buddhist view rose long before the Nestorians came to China and is indeed clearly to be traced back to India, and secondly, the Nestorian form of Christianity was not evangelical at all.

But the T'ien-t'ai sect had as great an influence during the T'ang dynasty as the Pure Land and apparently a greater influence among the more educated. For the T'ien-t'ai offered both intellectual explanation and mystic intuition, and the intellectual aristocracy of the capitals seem to have found in it the thing that satisfied their souls. Upon the rising school of Chinese painting, also, Buddhism, and especially T'ien-t'ai Buddhism, had a growing influence. The older, more obvious, less idealistic forms of Buddhism had had their great effect upon Chinese sculpture, in the portrayal of Buddhas and Bodhisattvas; but the more inward, more spiritual, more philosophical teaching of the T'ien-t'ai school needed larger expression. The whole of external nature

[32] It is said that "he had studied all the various teachings of all the sects and was troubled thereby and confused. One day he went into the library of the monastery, and after praying for guidance, he reached out his hand and took up the Amitayur-dhyana-sutra, which tells of Amida and his mercies. When he read this he was comforted and took heart again. This led to further study of this teaching, and for some time he retired to a solitary place. Afterwards he studied with the patriarch Doshaku and emerged from his tutelage as a teacher of the salvation doctrine. It was he who pushed the doctrine to its fullest, and unlike others recognized Amida only of all the Buddhas" ("Honen Shonin and the Jodo Ideal," by Beatrice Suzuki, in the *Eastern Buddhist*, I. 319).

[33] *History of Religions* (New York, Scribner, 1914), I. 136-37. Dr. Reichelt, on the other hand, still insists on a considerable amount of Nestorian influence, *op. cit.*, 131-132.

could now be interpreted as the outer garment and the symbol of the Buddha-life within. Sculpture, with its inescapable limitations, could not present this in visual form. Only painting could do that. It was thus from T'ien-t'ai Buddhism that Chinese painting received its first great inspiration.[34] It was this school that taught the Chinese artists, in the words of Fenellosa, "to image forth the truth in forms of glowing vision, to see the very presences of Buddhas and Bodhisattvas clad with dazzling light, to project angelic groups upon the background of contemplation and to behold the inner circulation of native affinities and sympathies working in intertwisted lives of physical and moral law." [35]

This Buddhist inspiration for Chinese painting was continued and carried further in the later part of the T'ang dynasty and to almost the end of the Sung dynasty by the influence of the Ch'an sect. According to Fenellosa and Arthur Waley, it was the Ch'an declaration of independence from books and specific dogmas and its firm conviction that the Buddha-nature could, by inner search, be found in one's own heart, the Buddha-nature which was in all external things as well—it was these suggestions that led the greatest painters of the T'ang and Sung into those mystical and masterly interpretations of life and landscape that mark the acme of Chinese art and have given to Chinese (and Japanese) painting that peculiar inwardness which marks it off from all the art of the West. As Keyserling puts it:

> Our plastic arts have never expressed what our music and poetry have been able to convey. It is the function of both to give a body to feelings: poetry is a match for articulated feelings, music alone for the inarticulated, the most vital, the profoundest of all. Why is it that these subjectivities cannot be rendered objective in a picture? Because the greatest possible concentration of reason does not lead to the Holy of Holies of the soul. As we have always been rationalists as painters, we have never been able to give direct expression to the "soul" in painting no matter how marvellously we succeeded in doing so in music. . . . That is just what the East succeeded in doing, thanks to which they have produced works by the side of which we have nothing to offer. From the point of view of reason, no work of the East is a match for the art of Greece, but they cannot be judged from the point of view of reason.

[34] See Fenellosa, *Epochs of Chinese and Japanese Art* (New York, Stokes), I. 121-22.
[35] *Loc. cit.*

They spring from the same depth of life that only poetry and music do in our case.[36]

The Chinese painters under the influence of Ch'an Buddhism make no attempt at photographic reproduction, but seek first to absorb the spirit or essence of the landscape or the man or animal they mean to present, and then paint, so to speak, from within outward. If they would present a waterfall they sit in meditation near it for hours, without perhaps making a single sketch; then return home with the feeling of the scene in their hearts, and express the feeling with their brush. In principle this is related to our contemporary "futurism," though in taste, spiritual comprehension, and resulting beauty the two schools are sufficiently far apart. The difference is perhaps largely explained by the fact that Chinese painting under Ch'an influence had the inspiration of a profound religious feeling. As Waley has expressed it:

> The Buddha-nature is immanent not in man only but in everything that exists, animate or inanimate. Stone, river, and tree are alike parts of the great hidden Unity. Thus Man, through his Buddha-nature or universalized consciousness, possesses an intimate means of contact with Nature. The songs of the birds, the noise of the waterfalls, the rolling of thunder, the whispering of wind in the pine trees—all these are utterances of the Absolute.[37]

Another art, if so we may call it, that the Buddhism of the T'ang dynasty has to its credit is the printing of books by the use of wooden blocks—"block printing" it is called. This method of reduplication may have been first invented for the manufacture of charms and very likely by the Taoists; but it was developed into the making of books by Buddhists and in Buddhist monasteries, and it was the Buddhist religion that provided the needed impetus.[38] For upward

[36] *The Travel Diary of a Philosopher,* Eng. trans. (New York, Harcourt, 1925), I, 280-81.

[37] *Zen Buddhism and Its Relation to Art* (London, Luzac, 1922), p. 24. See also Chap. X (in Vol. II) of Fenellosa's *Epochs of Chinese and Japanese Art.*

[38] See Carter, *The Invention of Printing in China* (New York, Columbia Univ., 1925), Chaps. IV, VI. According to Carter, the first books were probably printed in the reign of Ming Huang (712-756). The oldest printed book now in existence is the Diamond Sutra, printed in 868, and found in 1900 by Dr. Stein at Tun-Huang.

of two centuries after the invention of block printing it was apparently only Buddhist monks that made any extensive use of it for the publication of books. Very early in the Sung dynasty, about 972, the Chinese version of the Buddhist canon, consisting of some 1521 works, was printed, "in more than 5000 volumes, and covering 130,000 pages—one of the most monumental works that history records." [39]

Among the arts to which Ch'an Buddhism contributed should perhaps also be mentioned the art of making and drinking tea; for in China and Japan it is hardly less. Here, as in printing, Taoism had been before Buddhism, but the two schools, especially in their feeling for symbolism, were never far apart and the two influences blended. And when in connection with China or Japan one speaks of tea (I had almost written Tea) one must not think of a western "tea," but rather of something more like the unveiling of a statue or the performance of a religious rite. According to Okakura-Kakuzo, "among the Buddhists, the Southern Ch'an sect, which incorporated so much of Taoist doctrines, formulated an elaborate ritual of tea. The monks gathered before the image of Bodhidharma and drank tea out of a single bowl with the profound formality of a holy sacrament. It was this Ch'an ritual which finally developed into the Tea-ceremony of Japan in the fifteenth century." [40]

Buddhism was at the height of its influence during the T'ang and Sung dynasties. In Fenellosa's opinion it was the champion of individualism and progress, while Confucianism was the champion of conformity and conservatism. The struggle of these two religions for supremacy and control of the educational system, was crucial for China. Toward the close of the Sung dynasty Confucianism gained the decided predominance which it has never since lost, except during the rule of the Mongol invaders who followed the Sungs. Even in its defeat, however, Buddhism was not without its great influence on its rival. If it did not contribute directly to the Neo-Confucianism of the "Sung philosophers," it was the indirect cause and stimulus for this new birth of native Chinese

[39] Carter, pp. 62-63.
[40] *The Book of the Tea* (New York, Duffield, 1923), p. 38.

thought; [41] and the last of the great original Confucian thinkers, Wan Yang Ming, who lived under the Ming dynasty, plainly was indebted to the mysticism and idealism of Buddhist philosophy not only indirectly but in very immediate fashion.

The Mongol emperors were very open-minded on religious matters, and most of them seem to have been especially favorable to Buddhism.[42] Yet the revolt which finally drove them from China was largely fostered by the White Lotus Society—a lay Buddhist organization—and much of the strength of the patriotic cause was due to the belief in the immanent advent of Maitreya. The revolt was in fact led by a former Buddhist monk.[43]

It was this ex-Buddhist monk who became the founder of the Ming dynasty. On the whole, both he and his successors were more steady and consistent in their ecclesiastical policy than were the T'ang emperors; and while often personally sympathetic with Buddhism and even favorable to its scholarly development, they were pretty generally suspicious of the monastic order and prevented its spread and often diminished its power. Much the same thing may be said of the policy of the Manchus, though for political reasons they sought to win the favor of the Tibetan and Mongolian Lamaists. Their attitude toward Chinese Buddhism as such was distinctly unfavorable. In one respect, therefore, the foundation of the Republic has proved advantageous to Buddhism: complete religious freedom has been won.

But quite aside from the attitude of the government, the hold that Buddhism had upon the Chinese people seems steadily to have waned during both the Ming and Manchu dynasties and under the Republic. Inwardly, moreover, in both intellectual interest and mystical feeling, it has been pretty steadily losing. But this question of the present condition of Buddhism is one that we must postpone to later chapters.

Before going on, however, to this more important matter,

[41] Cf. W. J. Clennell, *The Historical Development of Religion in China* (London, Unwin, 1917), Chaps. V, VI; also Suzuki, *Zen Buddhism*, pp. 95-101.

[42] It is said that under Kublai Khan there were 42,000 Buddhist temples in China and 250,000 monks (Reichelt, *op. cit.*, p. 19).

[43] See De Groot, *Sectarianism and Religious Persecutions in China*, I. 164-69.

and as a preparation for the chapters that are to follow, I ought to provide the reader with a little further information concerning the supernatural personages of the Buddhist cycle to whom the Chinese look in their moments of worship and supplication—the *dramatis personae,* as I might call them, of Chinese Buddhism. To this not very exciting subject we must, therefore, devote the next chapter.

CHAPTER XV

DRAMATIS PERSONAE

ALL or nearly all of the beings who belong to the cycle of Chinese Buddhism were dealt with in the chapter on the Rise of the Mahayana, but they ought now to be introduced under their Chinese names, with a little further explanation and description. I shall make my account as brief and business-like as I can. The word for Buddha in Chinese is Fo [1] (pronounced in Pekinese as rhyming with *saw*). Of the many kotis of Fos, or Buddhas, China cares for only five or six. The most important of these is Shih-chia-muni Fo,[2] (usually shortened to Shih-chia Fo), that is to say, Sakyamuni. The name Shih-chia-muni Fo (originally Shih-chia-muni Fu-t'o), in fact, represents an attempt on the part of the Chinese to say Sakyamuni Buddha. Almost equal to him in popularity, and rather more popular than he with the adherents of the Pure Land sect, is O-mi-to, the Amitabha of Sanskrit Buddhism. Most Chinese Buddhists know a little about the life of Shih-chia Fo, and some will tell you that O-mi-to also was once a man, though very much longer ago than Shih-chia Fo. Associated with these two is a third Buddha, Yao-shih Fo, the Buddha of healing, whose Sanskrit name was Bhaisajaguru. He once made twelve famous vows to cure all bodily ills and is thought of as the Great Physician. He is also sometimes spoken of as the Buddha of the past; while Shih-chia Fo is the Buddha of the present dispensation, and O-mi-to is to be the Buddha of the future. I have never understood how this conception is related to the anticipation of Maitreya as the future Buddha, but presum-

[1] The word Fo (or Fu) is represented by a combination of the two characters for "man" and "not." "The deep meaning is, evidently, to have gone beyond the sphere of human life with its limitations and entered into the Absolute" (Reichelt, *op. cit.*, p. 34).

[2] He is also sometimes known as Ju-lai (pronounced Ru-lai) and sometmes as Kiao-ta-mo, which of course stands for Gautama.

ably the two ideas have quite different origins and different references.

The two other Fos whom one hears of in China are Vairocana, whom the Chinese call P'i-lo Fo or P'i-lo-che-na, and Loshana (Chinese Lu-she-na). P'i-lo Fo is seldom represented in images and in fact outside of the T'ien-t'ai and Chen-yen (or Shingon) sects, he plays a very small part in Chinese Buddhism. He is closely connected with the sun. Loshana is even more rarely in evidence than Vairocana. Possibly to this list of Buddhas should be added Milei, for though in reality a Bodhisattva, he is regularly referred to as a Fo. He is a popular and friendly figure and much in evidence.

Chinese images of the Buddha seemed to me, on the whole, inferior in artistic merit and religious quality to those of most other lands. Certainly they are much less impressive and less beautiful than those of Burma, Siam, and Japan. Especially is this true of the newer temple images. Ancient bronze Buddhas, cast in northern China during the first centuries after the introduction of Buddhism into the land, have frequently a decidedly Indian tone. The thoroughly Chinese Buddha image of the later centuries is as a rule rather too fat. This, I suppose, is a reflection of the general Chinese love of corpulency. Still there is a certain impressiveness in many a temple Buddha, a real feeling of dignity and calm, though seldom much sense of mystery.

Occasionally one finds a standing Buddha, and occasionally a reclining Buddha—representing Shih-chia Fo's Nirvana or death; [3] but the great majority of Buddhas are seated. They have the usual marks: the protuberance on the skull, the round mark over the bridge of the nose, and (usually) the long lobe of the ear. They are seated with interlocked feet on lotuses, and their hands and fingers are placed in the well-recognized *mudras* or positions, which, to the observer versed in iconography, indicate the acts or functions of the Buddha which the artist wishes here to emphasize. Thus Shih-chia Fo is usually presented with his right arm stretching downward, his palm inward, and his fingers touching the

[3] Notably a very large image of this sort—"The Sleeping Buddha," it is commonly called—at Wo-fo Ssu, in the western hills near Peking.

earth—the attitude of illumination, in which he is calling upon the earth to witness his resistance to Mara and his achievement of enlightenment. Sometimes the hands are raised to the level of the breast, the thumb and first finger of the right hand touching the first finger of the left. This represents the "turning the wheel of the Law," the preaching of the Dharma. There are of course other *mudras,* but I shall not trouble the reader with them.[4] O-mi-to is generally represented in the *Dhyana mudra,* or attitude of meditation, with hands on lap, palms upward, the right above the left. Yao-shih Fo may have several positions, but usually he has in one hand a small jar, to indicate his function as the medical Buddha. P'i-lo Fo is the only Buddha in China who wears a crown. And as for Mi-lei Fo, there is seldom any difficulty in identifying him, as he sits in the entrance gate of the temple, his fat paunch and his jolly look suggesting St. Nick in the poem that all American children know, his legs arranged in some comfortable manner—for he is far too fat to sit as a Buddha should with his legs in a bow knot—and on his face a smile than can never come off. The attribution of this strange form to the "Future Buddha" is said to be due to the fact that about nine hundred years ago there lived in the province of Chekiang a monk whose corpulence was comparable to that of St. Thomas Aquinas, and whose devotion to Maitreya was such that he was thought, especially after his death, to have been an incarnation of that Bodhisattva. There is, I am told, no authority in any Buddhist writing for identifying the rather grotesque figures or "Laughing Buddhas" at the entrance to Buddhist temples with the Future Buddha. But popular thought, both lay and cleric, will have it that these beloved and delightfully fat images represent their dear Milei-Fo. It may be that when Milei comes we shall all be fat![5]

[4] Three fairly common mudras are those of "argument," of "charity," and of "blessing." In the first the arms are bent and the fingers extended upward with palms outward, and one of the fingers touching the thumb. In the "charity" mudra the arm is extended downward, with fingers open and palm out. In the "blessing" mudra the hand is held up, with fingers extended upward and palm out. Sometimes while the right hand is thus extended the left is in the "charity" mudra.

[5] There are some authentic images of Milei in China, corresponding in form to the Maitreya images of other countries. These are not notably corpulent, but usually of immense height.

The Indian word Bodhisattva is far too difficult for the Chinese tongue. The nearest they can get to it is *P'usa.* There are four great P'usas in China; namely, Kwan-Yin (the Indian Avelokitesvara), Ti-tsang (the Indian Kshitigarbha), Wen-Shu (the Indian Manjusri), and P'u-hien (the Indian Samantabhadra). In theory one should add Milei, who is not yet actually a Fo, but only a P'usa; yet as a fact the word Fo has become almost a part of his name in popular speech. To make my enumeration more complete I should also mention Ta-shih-chih, the Indian Mahasthanaprapta, who appears occasionally in a triad with O-mi-to and Kwan-Yin. He is, however, of inferior importance and popularity compared with the four great P'usas named at the beginning of this paragraph.

Kwan-Yin is, as I have said, the Chinese form of Avelokitesvara, the great Bodhisattva of mercy. In becoming a Chinese P'usa, however, the Bodhisattva underwent a number of changes, the most notable of which, perhaps, was the transformation of his sex.[6] Though sometimes presented as a male, Kwan-Yin is usually represented and almost invariably thought of as distinctly a woman. She is known universally as the Goddess of Mercy. It was doubtless the longing of the human heart for something motherly in the divine that was the ultimate cause of this transformation—the same psychological tendency that developed the cult of the Madonna in Roman Christianity, and that prompted the Unitarian Theodore Parker to pray to "Our Father and Our Mother God." Kwan-Yin is the loving mother of all the needy. She watches over those in danger and listens to the prayers of all who suffer or are frightened.[7] She gives children to the childless, and probably is the recipient of more earnest prayers than all the rest of the Buddhist cycle combined. The Chinese have adopted her to a unique degree. They will have it that she once lived in China, as a Chinese

[6] Just when this transformation took place is quite uncertain. Edkins thinks that the worship of Kwan-Yin was introduced into China before the Christian era, but that it was not common to represent Kwan-Yin as a woman until the 12th century, (*op. cit.*, p. 382). Johnston has shown that the transformation of sex must have occurred very much earlier than this, and Poussin thinks it took place in India. See Johnston's discussion of the question in *Buddhist China*, pp. 270-75.

[7] See, for example, Fa-Hien's prayers to her when nearly shipwrecked on his way back to China, Fo-Kwo-Ki XL.

princess, with the name Miao-Chen. This was, says the legend, about 2587 B.C., though more sober Chinese history brings her date down to 696 B.C., "which date," says Miss Getty, "is probably more nearly correct." [8] Her father, the king, wished her to marry but she refused and escaped to the White Sparrow Convent, where the nuns put her in the kitchen. The King, enraged at her departure, sent his troops to burn the convent, but Kwan-Yin prayed, and in answer to her prayer a heavy rain extinguished the flames. Her father, however, had her brought back to the palace, and gave her the choice between marriage and death. The little saint replied, as St. Teresa probably would have done, that she preferred death. She was tortured, but refused to change her choice, and at length strangled,[9] and a local god in the form of a tiger seized her body and disappeared with it into the forest. She herself descended into hell, whereupon hell became a paradise, with gardens of lilies—so lovely a place as to be entirely useless in the judicial system of the universe. In fact, Yen-lo, the king of hell, had to beg her to depart. On her return from hell the Buddha appeared to her and gave her a shining pearl, and advised her to retire to the island of P'uto, off the coast of Chekiang.[10] Some say she was carried thither by a god, some that she floated there on a water lily, while a third account, popular on the island itself, insists that she was born (or born again) on a rocky islet just off from P'uto, connected with it by a short bridge. If the pilgrim to P'uto doubts this story he may himself walk over the bridge and see the little island and its tiny temple and image. At any rate, the island of P'uto has been her peculiar home for hundreds of years, and numberless are the pilgrims who travel there, season after season, in picturesque junks with brown sails and high poop, and a fish's eye painted on the prow.

The little lady Kwan-Yin is one of the loveliest forms of Buddhist mythology. She has not a trait one could wish absent or altered. In the heart of the Chinese Buddhist she holds the place which the Madonna holds in that of the pious

[8] *The Gods of Northern Buddhism*, p. 69.

[9] Another account says beheaded.

[10] For more details see Wieger, *Moral Tenets and Customs in China* (Ho-Kien-fu, Catholic Mission Press, 1913); or Getty, *The Gods of Northern Buddhism*, pp. 73-74.

Catholic. The Catholic conception has the advantage of being based upon a real person who was the mother of the Founder; and it is interesting to ask oneself whether the influence of Kwan-Yin might not have been even greater than it is had it been based upon the historical woman Maya, the mother of Sakyamuni. To the Western mind this seems probable. Yet one must remember how little Buddhism cares for history and how it prizes virginity.[11]

Kwan-Yin is represented in more ways than any book on Buddhist iconography recites. She is made all things to all men that by all means she may appeal to and satisfy the human heart. Sometimes she stands, sometimes she is seated on a lotus. Frequently she holds in her arms a child, symbolic of her power as the giver of children.[12] Often she has the pearl which the Buddha gave her; or she holds in her hand a rosary or a lotus flower with a gracefully bending stem, or a willow branch, or a vase, as in the act of appearing before her supplicating worshipers and pouring upon them the continual dew of her grace. Usually she wears a crown (as do most P'usas), and in this crown is set an image of O-mi-to, to whose Paradise she brings her faithful ones, though refusing herself to enter therein so long as any sentient being is excluded. Sometimes, like the devas of India from whence she takes part of her heredity, she wears forms which to us Westerners seem bizarre or monstrous, but which to the Oriental with his feeling for symbolism are charged with meaning. Thus she may wear a crown of eight or more small heads, or she may have a large number of hands, typifying her all-seeing and all-helping powers. Frequently she rides upon a cloud or on a wave of the sea.

Ti-tsang like Kwan-Yin is the protector of the needy, and like Kwan-Yin again was once a human being whose story is known (i.e., known to Buddhists). He was, in fact, four human beings whose stories are known. That is to say, there are stories about four of his human incarnations con-

[11] The position held by Maya, the mother of Sakyamuni, in Buddhism is interestingly discussed by Johnston, in *Buddhist China*, pp. 277-80.

[12] In this form she sometimes suggests the Madonna and Child of Christian art. Yet the idea intended is, of course, quite different, as in fact may be seen by the way in which the child is held—not nestling in her arms, but as in the act of presentation to the supplicating and barren woman.

tained in a Sanskrit work whose name means the "Sutra of the Original Vow of the Bodhisattva Kshitigarbha." It was translated into Chinese about the year 700. In each of his incarnations Ti-tsang made a vow that he would not become a Buddha until a certain number of suffering souls had been saved. The most famous of these incarnations was a girl named "Bright-eye." After the death of her mother Bright-eye learned from an Arhat that she was suffering in hell for having eaten during life an immense number of fish and turtles. So Bright-eye worshiped the Buddha of that kalpa and gave up attachment to all earthly things, and the Buddha revealed to her that her mother should presently be reborn in her house. Soon after one of the female servants in Bright-eye's house gave birth to a child, and this child spoke and said that she was Bright-eye's mother and had been rescued from hell by her prayers. So Bright-eye made a vow that if her mother might be saved from the Three Evil Paths (or evil forms of existence, to wit, those of animals, hungry ghosts, and inmates of hell), she (Bright-eye) would save all beings in all the hells in all the worlds and in all the Three Evil Paths, and that she would not accept Buddhahood till she had caused all these wretched creatures to attain it. In time Bright-eye died, but in the age of Sakyamuni she had attained to the rank of a great Bodhisattva and was known as Kshitigarbha. To Kshitigarbha, i.e., Ti-tsang, the Buddha intrusted the fate of all beings, especially of those in hell. These are to be saved by his divine power; and in fulfilment of this purpose Ti-tsang continually manifests himself among men in diverse forms and breaks the bars of hell and causes the sufferers there to be reborn in heaven.[13]

In Chinese Buddhism when unmixed with Taoism Ti-tsang's relations with hell seem to consist chiefly in his frequent incursions into that unpleasant region on errands of mercy and the consequent business transactions between him and Yen-lo and the nine other infernal Kings. Taoist writers, however, and writers half Taoist and half Buddhist have made Ti-tsang at times the chief king of hell.[14] This view

[13] See the admirable articles by M. W. De Visser on "The Bodhisattva Ti-tsang (Jizo) in China and Japan," *Ostasiatische Zeitschrift*, II, July–Sept., 1913.

[14] See De Visser, *op. cit.*, pp. 266-79.

has been adopted by some western writers but is uncanonical and quite misrepresents the real nature and function of the gentle and merciful P'usa.[15]

The rescue of the sufferers from hell, through the intervention of Ti-tsang, and their rebirth in heaven is a commentary on the contrast between the Hinayana and the Mahayana. Ti-tsang is a very lovable figure and we all naturally delight in his mercy; but what would Sakyamuni have said of this easy road to heaven, this simple way of evading the consequences of one's evil deeds? It is the old contest once more between divine justice and divine mercy, which we find breaking out in Christianity in quite similar form—the loving Jesus saving sinners from the just punishment of a just Jehovah. The masculine Hinayana stressed justice; the more feminine Mahayana loves better the quality of mercy, and attributes it as the distinguishing character to two of its greatest Bodhisattvas.

For Ti-tsang in China ranks next to Kwan-Yin in popularity. This is owing to his mercy, to his rescue of souls from hell, and his consequent power to aid the dear dead who are now beyond the immediate care of the living, and also to the fact that he stands not only for mercy but for that peculiarly Chinese virtue which Buddhism adopted from Confucianism, filial piety. The story of Bright-eye sufficiently reveals this—as does also the story of one of the three other incarnations of Ti-tsang which I have not recited. It is no wonder that the Chinese love him.

He is usually represented standing, though sometimes he sits, especially upon his mount—the animal sacred to him. Occasionally he is pictured with the ten kings of hell who stand in his presence. He seldom wears a crown but usually has the shaved head of a monk and a round face with a benevolent expression. He regularly carries a staff with which he breaks open the gates of hell, and the jewel of purity by which he lights up its darkness. It is not surprising that all sorts of people, especially the simpler and more devout, appeal to him and crowd in throngs to Chiu-hua, his mountain sanctuary. For most of the pilgrims

[15] See Mr. Johnston's delightful chapter on Ti-tsang in his *Buddhist China.*

he is no phantom, no mere abstraction, but a powerful deity who can and will be a guide and protector of suffering humanity, especially in the dark ways of death. Yet some of the pilgrims know that it is not in images of clay or bronze that they can hope to find the real Ti-tsang and they, while performing all the outward rites that are expected of them, will look for Ti-tsang, not in garnished temple or in curtained shrine, but rather in the secret places of their own hearts.[16]

Wen-Shu is perhaps not quite so prominent in Chinese Buddhism as Manjusri was in the Mahayana of India. Yet he is of great importance, and an object of worship in most of the large temples, and to his special shrine in Wu-tai-shan (in Shansi) thousands of pilgrims make their way every year. His worship goes back perhaps further in Chinese history than that of any other Bodhisattva. Unlike Kwan-Yin and Ti-tsang, he is seldom thought of as having had any earthly or human existence. He had no mortal parentage but sprang from a lotus flower which was miraculously produced by a ray of light proceeding from the head of the Buddha—much as Athena sprang from the head of Zeus. He is emphatically the P'usa of learning and logic. The most characteristic images of him present him holding in one hand a palm-leaf book, in the other the sword of logic. He wears the usual five-leafed crown of the P'usas.

P'u-hien (Samantabhadra) is the P'usa of happiness and of universal kindness. He is often associated in a triad with O-mi-to and Wen-shu. The great mountain Omei-shan, in Szechuan, is his special shrine.

Each of the four great P'usas has his "mount," his element, his spiritual function, and his holy mountain or pilgrimage center. The pilgrimage centers I have already mentioned, Kwan-Yin's being the island of P'uto, Ti-tsang's Chiu-hua (in Anhwei province), Wen-shu's Wu-tai-shan, and P'u-hien's Omei-shan. Kwan-Yin presides over the element water, is characterized especially by mercy, and rides on an animal which is usually called a lion, but which, if one may judge by the presentation given in most temples, looks more like a natural son of the Chinese dragon. Ti-tsang's element is earth; like Kwan-Yin he is characterized by mercy; and he is represented in sculpture as riding another

[16] Johnston, *op. cit.*, p. 206.

rather unrecognizable beast which is sometimes called a tiger but which to Western eyes looks most like a white bulldog. Wen-shu's element is air or ether, his characteristic wisdom, and his mount a lion. P'u-hien's element is fire, his characteristic happiness or kindness, and his mount an elephant. I put these details thus baldly for purposes of reference, and for the use of readers who may wish, in visiting a Chinese temple, to be able to identify the images of the P'usas. The elephant will help him and perhaps the white dog; but unless he has had experience of Chinese lions he may fail to recognize either Kwan-Yin's mount or Wen-Shu's; or at least he may be as much astonished at the appearance of a Chinese lion as Sung-Yun was, in India, at seeing a real one.

In Pure Land theory Ta-shih-chih stands second only to Kwan-Yin, though as a fact he is much less popular than the P'usas just described. His chief attribute is power, and he is known as the Strongest One.

Besides the Fos and P'usas there are a few mythical beings of lower rank who should be mentioned if the reader is to be thoroughly prepared to understand the things he will see in a Buddhist temple. The four Kings—the Kings of the Four Quarters which both Mahayana and Hinayana recognized and revered in India—reappear in China under names which I shall spare all those readers of this book who skip footnotes.[17] Their function is to defend the Dharma, and to reward those rulers who do so. The general of their common army is Wei-to, sometimes identified with the Indian deva Indra. His full name is given as Hu-fa-wei-to, which means, "the deva who protects Buddhism." [18] He is sometimes spoken of as a Bodhisattva. Equally important with these five war-like and rather non-Buddhist figures are the eighteen Lohans. These are the sixteen Arahants to whom, according to a late Sanskrit Mahayana text, Sakyamuni confided the preservation of the Dharma till the coming of Maitreya. The Chinese adopted them and made more of them than ever the Indian Buddhists did, and (probably during the T'ang dynasty) added two more to the number. Just who the extra two are is a matter of uncertainty and disagreement;

[17] Their Chinese names are To-wen, Chi-Kwo, Tseng-chang, and Kwang-mu.

[18] Edkins, *Chinese Buddhism,* p. 240.

but the Chinese are certain there are eighteen.[19] The group of five hundred Arahants who lived in caverns in India during Hiuen-Tsiang's time are also still revered today in China and known as the five hundred Lohans—the word *Lohan* representing the way in which *Arahant* sounds in Chinese ears. Our list of the members of the Buddhist cycle in China might be supplemented by a few more names, such as Yen-lo, the ruler of hell, and his attendant judges, Kuan-ti, the Chinese god of war; the dragon king; Yo Wang, the Pusa of medicine, Brahma and Indra from India, and even Confucius himself. These with a few other mythical beings, some of them borrowed from the pantheons of Taoism or of Chinese popular religion, make up the twenty-four tutelary deities, occasionally represented as a group in Chinese temples. For convenient reference I append to this chapter a list of the principal Buddhas and Bodhisattvas with their Sanskrit, Chinese, Korean, and Japanese names.

These various superhuman beings are taken with varying degrees of seriousness by different classes of Buddhists. To some they are all as real as living men and women; to some they are just possibilities who should not be taken too seriously, yet—it is well to be on the safe side, and after all a little incense doesn't cost much. To the more intelligent none of the lesser beings alluded to in this chapter—none, that is, save the Buddhas and the great Bodhisattvas—are of much importance; and even the greater beings are sometimes regarded as of value chiefly or solely as symbols. To nearly all Chinese Buddhists, however, except the most skeptical, Sakyamuni and O-mi-to and Kwan-Yin are very real beings and very genuine helpers.

This chapter, as I have indicated, is intended only as an introduction—a kind of necessary, dry-as-dust preliminary textbook—to the thing I want to present and which, I take it, the reader is most desirous of understanding: namely, the religion of the Chinese Buddhist in act, as it exists today. To this, our real subject, we may now turn. And we shall seek

[19] See Watters, *The 18 Lohans of Chinese Buddhist Temples*, and De Visser, "The Arahats in China and Japan," *Ostasiatische Zeitschrift*, Apr.-Sept., 1920-21, and Apr. 1922-March, 1923. The names of all eighteen are given by Reichelt, *op. cit.*, p. 191. As Lohans rather than Boddhisattvas they are looked down upon by good Mahayanists; hence the queer and often villainous features given them.

our first acquaintance with it by making a visit to a Chinese temple.

APPENDIX TO CHAPTER XV

Principal Buddhas and Bodhisattvas of China, Korea, and Japan

BUDDHAS

Sanskrit Name	*Chinese Name*	*Korean Name*	*Japanese Name*
Sakyamuni	Shih-chia Fo	Sukka Yurai	Shakamuni or Shaka
Amitabha	O-mi-to	Amida	Amida
Bhais'ajagura	Yao-shih Fo	Yaksa Yurai	Yaku-shi
Vairocana	P'i-lo Fo		Dai-nichi

BODHISATTVAS

Avelokitesvara	Kwan-Yin	Koan-eum	Kwannon
Kshitigarbha	Ti-tsang	Ti-tjang	Jizo
Manjusri	Wen-shu	Moun-sou	Monju
Samantabhadra	P'u-hien	Po-hien	Fugen
Maitreya	Mi-lei	Miryek	Miroku
Mahasthanaprapta	Ta-shih-chih	Tai-sei-chi	Sei-shi, or Dai-sei-shi

CHAPTER XVI

BUDDHIST TEMPLES IN CHINA

ON passing out of the narrow hutung through the red gateway of the Ssu you find yourself in a spacious courtyard, planted with fine old cedars. At the farther end is a small entrance temple, where Milei-Fo and his four friends, the Kings of the Four Quarters, stand guarding the more hallowed precincts that lie behind from the profanation of the evil, and welcoming the honest worshiper with friendly smile. The Milei of Fa Yuan Ssu is one of the few in all China to which I find myself really warming up. He sits there, with a good-natured grin, while a dozen babies clamber over his broad shoulders and capacious paunch, displaying by their unchecked boldness the never-failing good nature and kind heart of the Laughing Buddha. Behind his shrine opens a large court, ending with a broad flight of marble steps which lead up to the main temple; beyond which, in turn, is a maze of shrines, dormitories and courtyards, so that the Ssu (or monastic enclosure) appears a little village in itself.

Most of the larger Buddhist temples in central and northwestern China follow the general plan found in the Fa Yuan Ssu. Nearly all of them face the south. This is not a universal rule, for I have myself found at least four exceptions,[1] and no doubt there are a good manv more. But probably nine temples out of ten are oriented in the regular way. All temples that consist of more than one building—i.e., all but the very smallest—contain enclosures or courts surrounded in part by single walls, in part by some of the subordinate temple structures. Most temples are built of brick, covered over with plaster. In Peking the walls are regularly painted

[1] Namely, the Shan San Ssu in Ichang, the city temple in Chungking, the Kwan-Yin Miao above Chungking, and the temple opposite the Thunder Peak Pagoda on the west lake near Hangchow.

red. The lines of the roofs are usually very pleasing. Scarcely a straight line is to be found. The eaves are very broad and they sway upward toward the corners in a graceful curve. In the north this curve is slight, but in central and southern China it is pronounced, and it ends in what might almost be called horns. In front of the temple entrance, or immediately back of it, is usually to be found a low wall, just longer than the entrance is wide. This is the "spirit screen." Its purpose is to keep evil spirits from getting into the sacred enclosure. Most palaces and public buildings and many private residences are provided with "spirit screens," and the builders of Buddhist temples simply borrowed it from ancient Chinese custom. The belief involved in it—Chinese rather than Buddhist—is that evil spirits can go only in straight lines and never think of turning a corner, hence will bump into the spirit screen but will not have the sense to go around it. The conception seems to be much like that expressed in Goethe's Faust: "*Der Teufel immer ist ein Thor.*"

The portal of the temple is usually a shrine—a building of fair size containing images of some of the subordinate members of the Buddhist cycle. Sometimes one enters the temple precinct through a single gateway; but in this case a portal shrine, as it may be called, immediately faces one, and forms the true entrance to the sacred enclosure. In some of the larger temples of the lower Yangtse Valley this first shrine contains images of two frightful beings known as Hung and Hao—ancient Chinese generals who perform the function which in Hinayana lands and in Japan falls to Brahma and Indra, of scaring away evil spirits. Just beyond the little shrine of the two generals one comes upon the larger temple of Milei-Fo and the four Kings. More commonly the generals do not appear at all and the portal shrine itself is occupied by Milei, whose unfailing smile and jolly appearance welcome and reassure the pilgrim. Reassuring he needs, for even if there has been no Hung and Hao to pass, there are the four very frightful Kings just in front of Milei—two on a side—the Kings of the Four Quarters. The one brandishing the mighty sword is the guardian of the East. The less frightful giant next him playing upon the viol is the guardian of the South. He who holds the flag rules over the North, while the most terrible of all, with the long snake in his mighty hands, controls the West. Just beyond them, as I have said, and in the center of the room, sits the friendly Milei, while behind him and with back turned upon the genial future-Buddha, stands the knightly figure of Wei-to, the gallant guardian of the Law. One comes to be decidedly fond of Wei-to. He seems to represent militant righteousness, ever erect in soldierly posture, clad in full armor, his right hand resting on the hilt of his great sword, which slants downward with point on the ground.

Wei-to regularly stands with his back to Milei, gazing out into the large court just behind the portal shrine. In this court there are sometimes a drum tower and a bell tower, one on each side. Almost invariably a bronze or iron incense burner stands in the center of the court. Sometimes also, and especially if the court be large, one may find here a small pagoda; or the path leading through it may pass between two small pools, with lotus leaves and sacred fish. There are likely to be also two large protecting stone lions in this court, and a stone tablet with a long inscription borne upright on the back of an immense stone tortoise. In any case, at the farther side of the court rises the invariably charming façade of the main temple, with its curving lines and lofty roof. The roof is nearly always covered with green tiles; it is often double; and is usually decorated with dragons or dolphins, and (in the North) with a procession of figurines marching out toward the ends of the projecting horns of the four corners.

The interior of the temple is rather dim. Seldom are there any windows. The doors, however, are very high and are usually kept open, and a fair amount of light is thus thrown upon the central Buddhas. On entering one frequently finds a row of round mats for kneeling and a gong, made of a large piece of wood hollowed out and frequently carved to imitate the head of a fish. Beyond the mats is a long table for offerings, which contains an incense burner, two candlesticks, and two flower vases, sometimes of pewter or of brass or porcelain, and invariably displaying excellent workmanship. Besides these there is commonly a kind of box full of the ashes of incense, and holding several incense sticks —burning or burned out—stuck upward in the ashes, as well as offerings of fruits, flowers, candles, western clocks, vegetables, and other votives of various sorts. Just beyond the altar rises the throne of the Buddhas. There are usually three of these,[2] each more than life size, each gilded, and each sitting cross-legged upon a lotus. The central figure is almost invariably Shih-chia Fo. At his right (the beholder's left) is O-mi-to; while at Shih-chia Fo's left is Yao-shih Fo. In addition to these three principal figures, this central group may contain, immediately at the sides of Shih-chia Fo, his two disciples Kassapa and Ananda—or, as the Chinese call them Yasu and Anan. These, it will be remembered, were the two most prominent disciples at the time of Gotama's death, and it was they who became (in the order named) the first and second patriarchs. Kassapa or Yasu is always depicted as an aged man, with many deep wrinkles, while Ananda has the unwrinkled face of relative youth.

Along the side walls of the main temple are seated the Eighteen Lohans, nine on a side. In the fashioning of these figures the Chinese artists, loosed from the restraints which convention places upon them in modeling the Fos and P'usas, have given free rein to their love of the grotesque and to their ability at caricature. Each of the eighteen is a study in the portrayal of exaggerated individuality, and there is no Western caricaturist but could gain from them astounding revelations as to what may be done with the form of the

[2] In some temples there is but one Buddha in the central shrine. When this occurs the Buddha is usually Shih-chia Fo (though sometimes O-mi-to). He is seldom absolutely alone, but is accompanied by Yasu and Anan, or by the great P'usas P'u-hien on his elephant and Wen-Shu on his lion. In temples specially devoted to Kwan-Yin—and there are a number of them, notably in Chekiang and on the island of P'uto—no Buddha is to be found in the central shrine at all, and his place is taken by the beloved goddess of mercy. In many parts of China—in fact almost everywhere except the northeast—the central images, whether of the Buddhas or of Kwan-Yin, are sometimes so completely swathed in *khotans* or yellow capes as to be almost invisible; or at times they are largely hidden within rather dark recesses, or, especially in the west, fenced off from the observer by glass. As a rule, however, they are in the open, so to speak, and quite accessible to their worshipers, who place incense sticks or candles on the altar, bow or kow-tow or kneel in prayer on the mats before them, or seek to learn their fate or to get medical prescriptions by means of bamboo sticks or other fortune-telling devices. To aid them in this undertaking there is sometimes a kind of office at the side of the entrance of the main temple, where the monk in charge dispenses prophetic papers or medical prescriptions for a consideration.

human head, with the shape and size of the human nose, and with the effect of braided eyebrows reaching to the ground.[3]

Against the rear wall of the temple there are frequently two side shrines, symmetrically placed. These are usually sacred to two of the four great P'usas, especially to Wen-Shu, Ti-tsang, or P'u-hien. In the P'i-lo Ssu in Nanking there is a side shrine to P'i-lo (Vairocana). Kwan-Yin is not so often celebrated in these side shrines because she has a place all her own in every Buddhist temple built upon the regular plan. The throne on which the Buddhas sit in the center of the hall has a high background or screen-wall. The farther side of this wall, facing the back door of the temple, is a very honored place and is regularly sacred to the Goddess of Mercy. Sometimes there is a statue of her, mounted upon her mythical beast, with her back to the wall and facing the rear door. More often the entire wall or screen is decorated with a mythical scene, made of colored glazed tiles in high relief, all in honor of Kwan-Yin. In some of the larger temples, especially along the lower Yangtse, this Kwan-Yin screen is a thing of great beauty and much interest. The lady of mercy, of course, occupies the central position. Her feet rest upon the head of a monster which is just visible above the waves of the green sea. At her sides are usually divine helpers, and above her Wei-to and other defenders of the Faith. Far up toward the top of the screen is Sakyamuni, depicted as an emaciated ascetic

[3] For specially fine examples of them one should visit the Si Yon Ssu at Soochow, or the Pi Yon Ssu in the western hills near Peking; but wherever you meet these eighteen extraordinary Arahats they never fail to be interesting. Occasionally pictures, done in what we should call the poster style, are substituted for images. In two temples, but only two, have I found the original number of Lohans, sixteen, instead of the usual eighteen of Chinese tradition. Sometimes one sees the Five Hundred Lohans in tiny figurines, arranged on shelves high up on the walls over the heads of their more distinguished colleagues.

Besides the Lohans one finds in some temples twenty-four additional figures, ranged along the side or rear walls, and usually divided into two groups of twelve each. These are the tutelary deities to which reference was made in Chapter XV. Some of them are not Buddhist at all but are borrowed from Taoism and Chinese belief in general. They are regarded as friendly to the Buddhas and helpful in keeping off evil and bringing additional blessings. There is nothing narrow about your Chinese Buddhist and he will not begrudge worship to any being of any religion who may by any chance help him. A little incense will do no harm and there is always the possibility it may do some good. There is no reason why in his intercourse with the supernatural world he should confine himself to the rifle; he will use the rifle and the machine gun as well.

(before the enlightenment, I suppose), with a deer and a monkey offering him food. At the sides of the screen, arranged on three levels, are the Eighteen Lohans, standing upon rocks above the waves—nine on a side and six on each level. Then there are innumerable other beings of various sorts, crowned figures, a heavenly girl scattering flowers, sometimes mortals below, and all doing honor to the beloved Goddess of Mercy.

Other deities besides those mentioned sometimes get admittance to the Buddhist temple. Notable among these are Yo Wang, the medicine king, various generals or emperors and heroes, the god of fire, etc. Most of these have been borrowed, like the twenty-four tutelary deities, from Taoism or from some popular Chinese cult.

The interior arrangement of the central hall which I have described is not purely fortuitous nor dictated by convenience. It has a symbolical meaning. Just as the Hindu temple is an earthly representation of the heavenly palace of the deity worshiped, the Buddhist temple is a reminder to the worshiper of the teaching function of the Buddha as the source of all truth. The arrangement of the figures is therefore planned in order to suggest the scene so commonly and lovingly described in many a Mahayana sutra, in which the Tathagata expounds, before a multitude of gods, Arahats, and Bodhisattvas, the sweetness of the Law.

One leaves the main hall of the temple by the rear door, just behind the Kwan-Yin screen, and thus reenters the court or enclosure. Beyond this there are usually a number of buildings, but there is no uniform arrangement among them nor is there any list of these additional buildings which is invariably followed. A dormitory, of course, there must be, and a refectory. The dormitory is usually a large square room with *khans* (low shelves or platforms which serve as beds) about the walls and a small shrine in the center. This room usually functions also as a meditation hall, though a special room for this purpose may be provided. The refectory is a large room with a shrine in the center, facing the entrance, and usually sacred to one of the P'usas, or with an image of the round-bellied Milei (a most appropriate patron saint for a refectory). The tables are arranged in rows facing each other. It goes without saying that near the refectory there will be a kitchen.

Of buildings having a more strictly religious purpose there are frequently several. In the large and rich temples there is sometimes a capacious hall for the Five Hundred Lohans. These are usually represented in life-size figures, and like the Eighteen Lohans, show very considerable ingenuity on the part of the artists. No two of them are alike, and each is a distinct individual—and usually an extremely queer one. Almost invariably the monkish caretakers who show you through will inform you that one of the five hundred is Marco Polo, though frequently they will be unable to tell which he is. Sometimes, when he is found, he is distinguished by a cap or by a dark beard, and in one case I remember, by a very militant appearance, in contrast to the more proper-looking Buddhist saints around him. Not infrequently your guide tells you that one of the five hundred is Jesus Christ; though I have never had a guide that succeeded in identifying him. Special halls are sometimes devoted to special beings. Kwan-Yin sometimes has a little building to herself. Frequently there is a separate hall for the ten judges of hell, with whom Ti-tsang is occasionally associated. The influence of Taoism frequently is seen in the consecration of a separate shrine to one of the long-bearded gentlemen of the Taoist cycle, or to some ancient Chinese hero. In addition to the buildings already mentioned there is sometimes a lecture hall, and sometimes a convocation hall, with a high platform and seats for the three highest monks. There may be also a separate building for the reception of neophytes into the Order. Such a hall contains a high central platform with chairs for the abbot and twelve assistant monks, and a table before which the neophyte kneels. In every monastery there are also reception rooms, and guest rooms, the abbot's special apartments, and sometimes an inner private chapel for the use of the three highest priests and for special services of mass for the souls of the distinguished or wealthy dead. Somewhere in the court there is likely to be a pool for fish—usually carp of enormous size and forward manners. A common method of acquiring merit among the pious laity is to buy live fish at the market and liberate them in one of these sacred pools. In some monasteries in the south there are also enclosures for cattle, pigs, ducks, and other sorts of domestic animals, which have been saved from the butcher and here spend the rest of their lives in peace and quietness. According to De Groot, some monasteries in Fukien province are so consistently Buddhist that they look out for the souls of their animal guests and for their morals as well as for their bodies. In order to save them from the sin of murder they keep the large voracious fish in a pool of their own, separate from the smaller fish; and they prevent the animals from breaking the precept against unchastity by decorously confining the males and the females in different enclosures. The larger monasteries are also provided with infirmaries for their own sick members, where monks from other monasteries are also at times accommodated and cared for. Not infrequently a large monastery will have its own printing press, where various sutras are printed for distribution and sale. Many monasteries have libraries or storerooms for books, one of the monks being appointed librarian. Then there are gardens and little courts, and sometimes, toward the rear of the temple enclosure, a suite of rooms for the solitary confinement of monks who in the pursuit of greater holiness or learning have taken a vow to shut themselves up for a period of years. These rooms are not cells, after the fashion of our Western monasteries, but as a rule very pleasant apartments with plenty of light and comfort; the aim of such confinement being not asceticism but the opportunity which solitude gives for study or for meditation. The Buddhist monk who shuts himself off from his fellows in a solitary room, does so as a rule not for the sake of penance but in order that he may loaf and invite his soul.

Most Chinese temples are very interesting places and many of them possess considerable beauty. They are not, as a rule, very clean places. On the lower Yangtse and in Peking they are usually clean enough, but in the rest of China the Buddhas have no reason to complain of being disturbed by the duster or the broom. The custom of wearing one's shoes anywhere and everywhere in the temple is responsible for much of the dust and mud, and for this and other reasons Chinese temples as compared either with those of Hinayana lands or with Japanese temples, are emphatically dirty. Except in the lower Yangtse, again, and Peking, Buddhist temples in China are likely to be in rather bad repair. Occasionally fresh carving and gilding and painting and patching is done, but outside of the regions specified above, dilapidation as well as dirt is pretty commonly associated with the shrines of the Buddha. One must make up one's mind to these things and not let them spoil the real beauty and the great interest which certainly exist in most Buddhist temples for him who has eyes to see.

Occasionally at the extreme rear of a temple court, less frequently in some other part of the sacred enclosure, is a pagoda. Notable examples of this are to be found at Soochow, Ningpo, Wuchang, Kiu Kiang, Canton, and in two or three temples in or near Peking. Much more commonly, however, pagodas are quite separate and independent constructions, although a small temple or shrine is sometimes added as an appendage to the pagoda—as, for example, at the great twin pagodas of Taiyuan-fu in Shansi. The pagoda itself is usually a shrine, having a Buddha and an incense burner at the entrance, and often additional images in each story.

The pagoda of China is a distinctive type of building, quite different in form and structure from the pagodas of India, Burma, and Japan. It is a striking and really beautiful type of edifice, and one of the most characteristic things in the Chinese landscape. Though I have seen several score of them and though most of them are pretty much alike, I am always ready to go far out of my way to add to my collection. There are a very few round and a very few square pagodas, but nearly all of them are octagonal. They are, moreover, always divided into stories—externally at least. Nearly all are hollow and most of them may be ascended by a winding stair, though in our day the stairway is often no longer to be found, and a few pagodas never had any insides at all, being just solid towers with external divisions suggesting stories which do not exist. So far as I know the number of stories in a Chinese pagoda is always odd. I do not know the reason for this—further than the fact that, like Rorie O'Moore, the ancient Buddhist believed there was luck in odd numbers. There are small pagodas of three and five stories, but in pagodas of any considerable height—say one hundred feet or more—the commonest number of stories is seven. After that nine, thirteen, and eleven follow in popularity in the order named. There are none with more than thirteen stories. The highest pagoda in China is three hundred and sixty feet, and there is a considerable number over two hundred. It is estimated that in China proper, taken as a whole, there are upward of two thousand pagodas of at least one hundred and twenty feet in height.[4]

The pagoda, like so many other things, probably came from India. It was brought with Buddhism, but as I have said, in China it developed into something distinctively Chinese, something quite different from the Indian pagoda or dagoba from which it sprang. The first Chinese pagodas are thought to have been built in the third century of our era, and for many centuries the sole purpose for which they were built was religious.[5] Usually they were repositories for relics, sometimes for images. In any case, they were exclusively Buddhist, neither Confucianism nor Taoism having anything to do with their erection. Under the Sui and T'ang dynasties there seems to have been a wave of pagoda building, distinctly comparable to the wave of cathedral building four hundred years later in Europe. It was an age of great Buddhist enthusiasm, in spite (or was it in part because?) of the occasional persecutions by the state; and many Buddhist temples as well as pagodas were founded at this time. The movement continued under the Sung Dynasty but was stopped under the Mongols. In fact, during the Mongol dynasty many ancient pagodas were destroyed. When the Ming dynasty restored China to the Chinese there was a great new outburst of religious enthusiasm which resulted

[4] For some of the facts used in this and the following paragraph I am indebted to an article by Samuel Couling in Vol. XLVI of the *Journal of the Royal Asiatic Society* (1915), North China Branch.

[5] In 652 Hiuen-Tsiang built a pagoda at Lo-yang for the safekeeping of the precious books and images he had brought from India. "The total height of this structure was 180 feet. It was built after the model of the Indian stupas, and had five stages, surmounted by a cupola" (*Life of Hiuen-Tsiang*, Beal's trans., p. 216).

in the building of many new pagodas and many new temples; and the movement continued into the early Manchu period. The larger part of the pagodas and temples seen today in China apparently date from late Ming and early Manchu times. Pagodas are still occasionally constructed. There is a large one just below Chungking that was completed only in 1885; and even more recent ones could be found. But the motive for the erection of most of these recent pagodas is not Buddhist and not religious at all, but scientific or superstitious, as you may choose. It is, namely, for the sake of Feng Sui—to ward off evil influences of "wind and water." As Feng Sui instruments the new pagodas are more Taoist than Buddhist; for it is chiefly the Taoist priests who specialize in this difficult and important—not to say lucrative—science. There still are, however, a few pagodas constructed for religious purposes; witness the seemingly recent ones crowning the hills that dominate the T'ung-t'ing lake, and erected as votives in fulfilment of a vow or in thanksgiving for rescue from shipwreck.

But to return once more to the temple proper. The description I have sought to give of its general arrangement is subject to many variations and these increase in number and importance as one goes away from the lower Yangtse valley or from Peking. The reader who is interested in the details of Chinese temple planning and architecture will find some account of these variations in the appendix to this chapter. Possibly I ought to end the chapter with this: but I cannot resist the temptation to say a word or two about some of the temples I loved best.

One of these is a mountain monastery up in Szechuan, near Chungking, and named the Lao Chuin Tung. Your way to it—and a narrow way it is, though not a straight one, since in all Szechuan except in the vicinity of Cheng-tu there is hardly so much of a vehicle as a wheelbarrow, and the "roads" are consequently the merest footpaths—your way to the monastery leads between flooded rice fields, each a lake during most of the year, past long stretches of graves on the hillsides, populous with green mounds and occasional cypresses, past wayside shrines sheltered by ancient camphor trees, till the path grows steeper and you climb into a pine wood, and at last pass under a stone p'ai-lou and beyond it ascend a long stairway of green-gray stones that leads you to the lower gateway of the temple. Crossing the threshold you find yourself in a small, out-door courtyard and facing you another stairway—the envy or inspiration it must be of every architect who sees it—rounding out into the courtyard, each step of it a complete half-circle, leading upward toward a wall overhung with banana trees and lace-like bamboo, and so you reach the upper and central court. The temple itself is more Taoist than Buddhist, but if one were to consider only those temples in which pure Buddhism is found there would be little to say of the shrines of western China. The plan of the Lao Chuin Tung is most irregular. The entrance hall stands at the left of the court and in it Taoist deities of frightful mien greet the visitor in place of Milei's hospitable grin. In northern and eastern China one often gets rather tired of Milei, with his "smile that won't come off"; but in the west, where fiend-scaring Taoist images take his place, one rather misses the familiar friendly face and jovial belly. Fortunately Wei-to is still here to make one feel a bit at home. In the principal hall, which Wei-to faces, Lao Chuin—another Taoist deity, but a very venerable one with a long beard—reigns supreme but not alone, for a small Kwan-Yin and a small Shi-chia Fo sit beside him and share the worship of the pilgrims. This arrangement of entrance hall, court, and main hall is the only familiar thing in the entire plan of the temple. The rest of the establishment—and it is very large—is a collection of gardens and shrines, adapted to the steep hillside on which it is built. The gardens, in fact, of these Szechuan monasteries are their most distinctive feature. The Fos and Pusas are sometimes neglected but the shrubs and trees and flowers never. Most of the gardens are little ones, and many of them are tucked away in unexpected places. But the most memorable single feature of Lao Chuin Tung is a small cliff at the back of one of the tiny gardens, the face of which has been covered with bas-reliefs of Kwan-Yin and her worshipers—a collection of carvings as interesting as anything of the sort one will find in China. For here the Goddess of Mercy is seen sending her blessing upon and receiving her worship from every sort of people, and the ancient artist who carved this rock made use of his opportunity to depict a great deal of the life of the upper Yangtse valley. But though human life forms a large part of the rock-sculpture, above all the human scenes hovers ever the sweet Goddess of Mercy, to whom the eye of the observer is constantly directed—Kwan-Yin in many forms, pouring down the heavenly dew to an adoring worshiper, receiving prayers from devoted monks and hermits, saving a man from an immense snake, steering a boat over rough waves, rescuing a monk who has fallen over a precipice—her great hand rising from the rock below to receive him—but most commonly, and it is repeated again and again, pouring down the dew of her heavenly grace upon those who raise their eyes to her. From the level of this cliff and garden one climbs to upper levels and a maze of unexpected corners of natural and artificial beauty, for the whole hillside has been made into a succession of shrines and caves and stairways and gardens, rest-houses, tea-houses, and surprises, all of them charmingly dilapidated, all of them covered with semi-tropical verdure, all of them placed, seemingly, haphazard, yet with a kind of symphonic unity that affects you, once you grasp it, almost as great music does.

Lao Chuin Tung is unique, and so are the great cave temples of Ta-tung Fu in the northwest of Chihli province, on the border of inner Mongolia, with their brilliant robin-egg blue tiles, their rock carving and their immense Buddhas. One who has seen them can never forget them. But as I look back on my China pilgrimage—now "shoved behind me long ago and far away"—the image that most readily returns is that of some of the temples of the Western Hills, near Peking; Wo-fo Ssu, with its famous "Sleeping Buddha"; Pi Yon Ssu and its palatial stairways, pagodas and carvings; Chieh T'ai Ssu on his hilltop, and the great sweep of its view toward the distant Peking plain; and the magic, the fairy loveliness of T'an Che Ssu. We spent the better part of a week in this great monastery, visiting by day its temples and shrines, talking with its monks, attending its religious services, and tramping over the hills that surround it, by night sleeping in one of its courts or wandering through its spacious ways, bathed in moonlight, the like of which, as I believe, has never been elsewhere on land or sea. In a Buddhist temple such as this, one seems transported to another world. The spaciousness of the place with its innumerable buildings ranged in charming disorder up and down a hillside, its gleaming roofs of green and yellow tiles and swaying contours, looking over each other's shoulders from the varied levels of the slope, the stone-paved courts with their great trees and little flowers and alluring vistas, the palatial stairways with their elaborately carved marble railings, the little shrines at unexpected intervals and the solemn temples in whose darkened recesses sit the Buddhas on their lotus thrones —when I think of this and the brilliant blue sky overhead, and the golden light of an October sun, or of the silvery full moon that gave the atmosphere of the place a sense almost of unreality—or of a deeper Real—I feel that only great verse could describe it, something, perhaps, like Keats's lines about

> magic casements, opening on the foam
> Of perilous seas, in faery lands forlorn.

In such a setting the chanting of the Buddha's praises by the monks seems something eternally appropriate. Long before dawn it begins and this early service is followed by others at occasional intervals through the day, the last coming at the end of the evening. About nine o'clock—soon after moonrise—one of the smaller gongs is heard from a little shrine opening on the principal court. This is answered by the deep notes of the great gong near the entrance. Then a wooden gong from another place joins the chorus and the silvery treble of a little bell from a new direction. The gray figure of a monk now appears, crossing the lower court in the moonlight and climbing the broad marble staircase before the temple; others silently follow, coming from different parts of the great monastery, one by one, swimming through the luminous darkness. One of them opens the temple doors, lights the candles on the altar and the incense sticks. The other monks steal in after him through the moonbeams and the shadows. They bow and prostrate themselves before the Buddha and the chanting begins.

I like to think that it continues: that at every dawn and every evening the things of the spirit are not forgotten; that there are many places, even in practical China, where the smoke of incense and the praises of the Blessed One are still streaming upward, through sunrise and cloud shadow and moonlight, as they do at T'an Che Ssu.

Appendix to Chapter XVI

Variations in Temple Arrangement in the South and West

The temples in both the south and the west of China deviate considerably from the fairly regular plan of arrangement followed in the temples of the lower Yangtse valley and in Peking. The principal temple in Swatow, for example, has four shrines or halls, opening out of the court, three of them quite on a line with each other and all facing you as you enter the enclosure. Three of the four have little to do with Buddhism proper, being sanctuaries of gods borrowed from Taoism or from the Chinese popular religion. Only the central sanctuary is fully Buddhist. You enter it through a kind of gatehouse, with no Milei and no kings and no Wei-to. The two guardian gods, or generals, to be sure are present in a sense, but are only painted upon the doors leading into the main part of the temple. The principal shrine is rather small—though it was very busy the morning I visited it. It contained a table for incense and offerings, and beyond this in front was the main altar, piled high with a litter of vegetables, candles, fruit, and more incense. Behind the altar was a space shut off from the public part of the temple and to be entered only through gates which were kept closed. I do not know the purpose of these gates, for they keep no one out who wants to go in. Here, as almost invariably in Chinese temples, any one may go anywhere (except in the personal apartments of the higher monks) without objection or surprise or notice on the part of any one else. There is no holy of holies in a Chinese temple. Knowing this, I opened one of the gates and went into the inner space behind the altar to identify, if I could, the image on the lotus throne. It appeared to be Milei, but it was in so dark a nook, and so hidden by curtains that I could not be at all sure. The monk burning incense before it could only tell me that it was a P'usa and apparently neither knew nor cared which P'usa it might be. His job was to burn incense before it and he was doing his duty. Behind the P'usa's throne and the screen that formed the back to it was a dark passage, with more or less sacred trash lying about, and somewhere in the dimness, by the rear wall, a kind of shelf or altar with a few small brass and porcelain Buddhas in advanced stages of dust. But dust in a Chinese temple must not be interpreted as neglect. It often comes from an excess of incense and candle smoke and vegetable votives, and the dusty or muddy shoes of many worshipers. As a fact, this temple was full of devout worshipers, in addition to three priests actively doing their duty with the incense.

In Canton as well as Swatow considerable liberty has been taken with the temple arrangement. But in Canton, at the time of my visit, at any rate, there were no crowds of worshipers and no busy priests. The one large temple of the city had the usual gatehouse but no Milei welcomed me and no Wei-to was there to guard the Dharma. Even the two heavenly Generals had disappeared. Probably Dr. Sun Yat Sen had carried them off. He needed a general, at that time, in all conscience. Beyond the gatehouse a very dirty walk, littered with orange peel, leads between two slimy ponds to the main temple. This, when I visited it, was locked. But I got the caretaker (no monks were visible) to get the key and let me in. There was a central Buddha with two P'usas, and sixteen Lohans—the two others having been sent away with Milei and the Generals. In place of the Kwan-Yin screen, a Taoist divinity, with an enormous beard, presided amid dust and dilapidation, plainly doing his best to keep up appearances. There were no signs of incense or candles having been offered to any of the inhabitants of the hall for a long time. Behind this building was another large hall with a small pagoda inside it—apparently one used for meditation and probably the dormitory of the monks when there were monks in Canton. It was filled with lounging soldiers when I stepped in. At one side was a third large hall, this one for the Five Hundred Lohans. Here they sat, with eyebrows as long as ever, and though covered deep in dust still screwing up their faces into the same astonishing, sardonic smiles they had worn in happier days. Possibly this was not altogether without reason; for I noticed a little incense had recently been burned to some of them (by the soldiers, perhaps) and in this they certainly fared better than the Buddha. As usual, the caretaker introduced one of them to me as Marco Polo.

Buddhism, with most things Chinese, has spilled over into Annam, and, mingled with the amorphous conglomeration of superstitions and beliefs sometimes referred to as the "Popular Religion of China," Chinese temples of a nameless sort, patronized by the Chinese inhabitants rather than by the native Annamese, are sprinkled along all the way from the Tonquin border to the Cambodian line, beyond Saigon. They have little that is Buddhist about them and little in common with the Buddhist temples of central China. One that I visited several times in Saigon had a most attractive court, a picturesque gateway, a very busy and business-like temple office or shop for the sale of incense, candles and fortune papers, and beyond that an altar with two small porcelain P'usas of Chinese origin. In front of the P'usas were bouquets of paper flowers, incense, fruit, two fresh lotus blossoms in vases, several gongs, three books, many strings of paper money, and a large glass jar of tea. This, however, was the subordinate shrine. The principal shrine was farther on, in the dark recess of the extreme rear, and in it sat a large bearded figure with a gilt crown, called Sing Wong (or King of the City)—a Chinese ruler of many centuries ago. He had a very un-Buddhistic appearance, and I was glad at any rate that he was not sitting on a lotus. At his sides were two trios of protectors, quite black with smoke and dust and nearly invisible (fortunately, I thought) in the deep religious gloom.

There are a few Buddhists among the native Annamese, and these have temples of their own, very different in type from the Chinese temples in Annam. The type is marked by extreme simplicity. Three simple buildings with simple roofs are put together in a row, one behind the other, the inner walls are partly removed, and the overhanging eaves made to project against each other, so that from within the three buildings appear like one long hall. There is no decoration or even plaster on the interior, though the façade has a rude fresco of a dragon. The main shrine, toward the front of the hall, has a Buddha with several attendants, and represents Paradise. A worshiper from Cambodia had somehow added a little Hinayana Buddha, standing on a lotus—as a reminder, I suppose, of home and of the distant West where the Blessed One is revered in the old-fashioned way. The little Cambodian Buddha looked rather homesick among his strange surroundings. Farther back in the large hall are more shrines, a fourteen-handed Buddha on a lotus, the image of an Annamese princess who died a long while ago, and others. There are also many votive Mileis, accumulating dust; but—alas for the transiency of human fame!—the monk did not even know that they were meant for Milei. He had never heard of Milei-Fo. He only knew they were P'usas—and that it was his business to keep an eye on the curious visitor from America lest he should pocket one of the images. I had no great temptation to do so, for Milei is ordinarily no favorite with me; yet the little P'usa looked so unappreciated and forlorn that I almost wished to take him back with me to China.

Western China, as well as Southern China and Annam, has its own variations in temple plan. As one goes up the Yangtse from Hankow, through Hupeh and into Hunan and Szechuan, the type of temple changes. In Hunan and all along the T'ung T'ing lake and the Siang river, the temples commonly have cement side walls of striking shape and often strange coloring, ending at the upper corners in enormous horns stretching outward and upward. The portal and the inner shrines, particularly the central hall, have curving roofs of very accentuated form, even more accentuated than those in Hankow and Wuchung. Many of the larger city temples in Hunan and Szechuan have a theater or elevated stage at the front side of the main court and facing the first of the shrines. These temple theaters regularly have very accentuated roof-horns and many fantastic finials and decorations. Few of these southern and western temples follow the regular arrangement of the north and east. The two guardians are seldom seen and the Four Heavenly Kings are frequently lacking, and even Milei-Fo, though he is sure to appear somewhere, fails to greet the visitor as he enters the first of the shrines. In his place may be some Fo or P'usa, or an image behind glass, so shrouded in yellow cloth that his identity cannot be determined. Wei-to is much more tenacious of his place than Milei or the Kings, and in nearly every temple he will be found in his usual post, at the back of the first shrine, looking into the second court and toward the central hall. And indeed he is needed in these degenerate days. Often he seems a rather forlorn figure, still standing sword in hand, guarding the long-violated Dharma—reminding one sadly of the boy who stood on the burning deck whence all but he had fled. In the central hall are the usual three Buddhas; or more often Shih-chia Fo reigns alone (perhaps with Ananda and Kassapa), while the Eighteen Lohans line the side walls, as they do in other parts of China. Sometimes, however, even these familiar features are lacking, as in the temple at Changsha in memory of the heroes of the Republic, where there is but one large court and one large hall, in which one finds three small gilt Buddhas, perhaps ten inches high, and no other images of any sort.

As one goes farther west, up the Yangtse, the height of the portals is increased. They rise frequently to two, sometimes to three stories, and they often have double roofs with exaggerated curves and out-reaching horns. In Szechuan there is to be found even less regularity in temple plan than in Hupeh and Hunan—owing in part, I imagine, to the great irregularities of the hillsides on which so many of them are placed. Many of the city temples are in such a dilapidated and despoiled condition that it is hard to make out the original arrangement. The No Han Tung, the largest of the Chunking monasteries, is entered through an artificial cave, quite in the midst of the city, with rock sculptures on each side. From the further end of this cave or tunnel the visitor emerges in a court now given over to the oil business, but to the left one finds a hall where Milei-Fo may once have reigned, and where Wei-to—a fine, well-gilded Wei-to, in fact—still stands sentinel. Back of the Wei-to hall is the usual court and the main hall with Shih-chia Fo and his disciples, while the large court behind it is flanked on one side by the refectory, on the other by a hall for meditation, and in the rear by a third shrine, with pictures of the Sakyamuni, Wenshu and P'u-hien over the altar and an image of Milei-Fo. Back of this is still a fourth shrine with a gilded Kwan-Yin under glass and a beautiful marble Buddha recently brought from Siam. If after emerging from the cave-like entrance you turn to the right instead of to the left, you come to the Hall of the Five Hundred Lohans—not quite so well done as those in the great temples of the Lower Yangtse, but on the whole very much like them.

This chapter, even with its appendix, makes no pretension of exhausting all the variations of arrangement in the Buddhist temples of China. But possibly enough has been said to exhaust the patience of the reader, and enough, I hope, to be of service to him should he go to China and try to find his way intelligently around its temples without a guide.

CHAPTER XVII

BUDDHIST MONKS IN CHINA

No one who has read the preceding chapter will need to be told that the original cost of the Buddhist temples in China must have been very great, and that the expense of their upkeep, if we include the support of their resident monks, is considerable. In Peking alone, according to Gamble's *Survey*, there are two hundred and ninety-six Buddhist monasteries and one hundred and sixty-nine convents. For the rest of China I have no figures, but the total number of Buddhist monasteries and temples in the eighteen provinces must be prodigious. Few of the temples of China are new, and most of them, as I have already pointed out, go back to the vanished Ages of Faith. They owe their foundation to the munificence of emperors, viceroys, and rich men, and to the self-denial and faith of monkish founders and devout lay communities. Many of the large monasteries, at their foundation, were endowed with lands, and additional endowments are sometimes made by pious aspirants after merit. From the income of these lands the expenses of the monasteries, including the support of the monks, are paid. T'an Che Ssu, to which I referred at the close of the last chapter, is said to own some three hundred and sixty-five villages with their rice fields and to "devour a village a day." Less fortunate temples, which had no original endowment, or whose abbots have been unskilful or dishonest in the management of the estate, have to depend in whole or in part on the money earned by the monks in chanting at funerals and praying for the departed, or on the gifts of lay worshipers. It is especially pilgrims that may be relied upon to help out the finances. Many a temple encourages an annual pilgrimage to its shrine, during some special week of the year, and counts on the coppers of the pilgrims to carry it through the remaining fifty-one weeks.

Originally many of the temples belonged to the districts in which they lie, and some at least in theory do so still. In strict theory, to be sure, they all belong to the Buddha; but the earthly trusteeship may be in the hands of the village headmen, though almost invariably the real trustee is the abbot. At the foundation of a small temple a priest is secured to take charge of the property and attend to the worship. The priest selects a boy to be his assistant, educates him in the priesthood, and often appoints him to be his successor. Thus young priests come to be regarded as almost the adopted sons of the older ones who gave them their training, and the relation is fraught with much of that respectful and pious affection which the Confucian code inculcates between teacher and pupil, parent and child. It sometimes happens that the priest comes to consider the temple as his own possession, and in this case the pupil-son, to whom he leaves it at his death, receives it with an increased sense of private ownership. An unscrupulous priest in such a position may make evil use of his trust, the more so because he is aware that no member of the lay community, to which the temple really belongs, is likely to interfere. His fellow citizens, as he knows well, are all Chinese and believe that each individual should look out for himself and his family and not meddle with other matters. I heard recently of a Buddhist priest who has been in charge of a village temple in the country districts of Chihli some thirty years, and who has treated the temple and its lands as private property to the extent of selling off nearly all the many acres which belonged to the temple when it came into his hands. The money derived from the sale he treats entirely as his own, and he lives most of the time in Peking. A Buddhist nun recently tried to sell to the missionaries of the American Board the convent over which she presides.

The larger temples and monasteries are, of course, not at the mercy of a single individual. So far as I know there are no constitutional limits to the abbot's power, but here as elsewhere in China public opinion is the real master, and the public opinion of a group of monks would prevent any malfeasance of funds which might affect the rice supply. Neither monks nor abbot can, in theory, own anything individually. The earnings of the monks from chanting services at funerals, etc., are paid into the common treasury. In many monasteries the treasurer doles out to the monks a certain amount of money, twice a year, to buy their clothes and pay the barber, the amount given to each depending on his rank. In matters of discipline the abbot is in theory supreme—but here again he is limited by public opinion resting upon custom. He is largely influenced by the advice of the ex-abbots (who continue to live in the monastery), and as the abbot's term is as a rule but three years, there are frequently several ex-abbots in a large monastery. Buddhist monasteries in China have little of that systematic or hierarchical organization which one finds in Tibet and Mongolia and within the different sects of Japan or even among the Taoist monasteries. There is no Buddhist pope or central committee, though there are occasional conventions or councils made up of representatives from many temples. With few exceptions each monastery is independent, the organization of each sect (so far as we can speak of any such thing) resembling that of the Congregational church in America. Each monastery selects its own abbot without interference from outside. Sometimes the abbot chooses his successor, sometimes the choice is made by the vote of all the monks, sometimes by the ex-abbots and the other elders.

The reader will have noted that I have used the words *monk* and *priest* almost interchangeably. In this I have followed the usual custom of foreigners in China, a custom which is justified by the actual situation. For there is no such distinction between priests and monks as in the Catholic church, nearly all the *religieux* of China being both monkish and priestly in their functions. Those in charge of village temples and those in city temples where the clerics are few and the lay worshipers many, naturally have more of the usual work of the priest to perform than those who dwell in secluded monasteries, or in large city temples with many resident clergy. In such centers as the latter those who wish to spend most of their time in meditation and study may easily do so without being interrupted by professional duties. If the line were a little sharper we might properly confine the name *monks* to members of this latter meditative class and use the word *priest* to designate those whose chief business is to chant, burn incense, make offerings, and perform funeral services. In a general way I shall try to do this, but so large a number divide their work pretty evenly between these two classes that it will be impossible to keep the distinction sharp. Besides, I shall need an English word for the whole body of *religieux*, and for this I shall retain the term I have used in discussing the other Buddhist lands thus far studied, and call them simply the *monks*.

The Buddhist monks of China are divided into four principal sects. By far the largest of these is the Ch'an [1] sect, or Ch'an tsung—the word tsung being the Chinese equivalent of our word sect. This, the reader may remember, was founded about 520 by Bodhidharma, and its chief characteristic has always been its emphasis on meditation. I have never seen any statistics as to the numbers of monks belonging to the different sects, but it would be a fair guess to venture the assertion that eighty per cent of the Buddhist monks of China belong to the Ch'an tsung. It is subdivided into a number of sub-sects, with whose names I shall trouble neither the reader nor myself. Next in importance to the Ch'an sect is the T'ien-t'ai,[2] founded, as the reader may have forgotten, by Chih K'ai toward the close of the sixth century. In contrast to the Ch'an tsung which is the sect of meditation, the T'ien-t'ai tsung is the sect of study. The most bookish and learned monks of China, and also the most philosophical usually belong to the T'ien-t'ai. A third sect is the Lu tsung or sect of the Vinaya, which claims to trace its history back to India—indeed back to Upali, one of the immediate disciples of Sakyamuni, but which, at least so far as China is concerned, was founded in the early six hundreds by Tao Hsuan. It is hardly a sect in the same sense as the others, for it has no special doctrine, but confines itself purely to the training of monks in the monastic discipline. In some sense, all the monks of China belong to the Lu tsung and one may be a member of it and of any of the others at the same time. Still some monasteries are regarded

[1] This is the same as the Zen sect of Japan.
[2] This, of course, is the Tendai of Japan.

as pertaining specially to the Lu, even if their abbots happen to belong to some other order.[3] It is strongest in the coast provinces. The fourth real sect of China is the Lotus, or Pure Land, known sometimes as the Lien tsung, sometimes as the Tsing To tsung. This was founded in the fourth century by one Hwi Yuan[4]—though the worship of O-mi-to and belief in his "Pure Land" go back much further than this.[5]

Possibly for the sake of approximating a complete statement I ought to mention two or three other sects, though they are so small in membership that I had at first intended to omit them, and the reader may well skip them if he likes. One of these is the Hua-yen tsung,[6] which traces its course back to Tibet and ultimately to India, as it is founded on the Atavamsaka Sutra. The exact date of its arrival in China is uncertain, but it seems to antedate the founding of the T'ien-t'ai tsung. At one time it was a very popular and powerful school of thought, but today it has but few members. Like the T'ien-t'ai it is essentially a philosophic sect; and today philosophy is not in favor with Chinese Buddhist monks, and they that do care for it are likely to accept T'ien-t'ai doctrines. I should also mention the mystical school called variously Mih tsung, Chin Yan (or Chên-yen), Yoga, and Tantra—the sect which links the Tantra practices of Bengal and Tibet with the Shingon sect of Japan. It claims to have been founded by an Indian, Vajrabodhi, about the year 730, and is thus the youngest of the Chinese sects. Some of its practices survive in China, especially in connection with All Souls' Day; but as a sect it is at best so nearly dead that the doctors disagree on the question of its continued existence. Eliot calls it "not so much a separate corporation as an aspect of all Buddhist schools."[7] One more sect that I must mention here is the Tsu En tsung or Fa Hsiang tsung, founded by Hiuen-Tsiang, the great traveler, translator and thinker.

[3] This, for example, is true of the Fa Yuan Ssu, perhaps the most important monastery in Peking. The abbot belongs to the Ch'an tsung.

[4] Edkins, *Chinese Buddhism*, p. 171; Reichelt, *op. cit.*, Chap. V.

[5] There is no sect in Japan exactly continuous with this, but in doctrine it is the forerunner of four Japanese sects, namely, the Jodo, Shin, Jishu, and Yutsu Nembutsu.

[6] Corresponding to the Kegon sect of Japan.

[7] *Op. cit.*, III. 317.

In its teachings it goes back to Vasubandhu and Asanga.[8] As a sect of monks it has entirely died out of China but it exists in Japan as the Hosso sect, and several of the most learned and able Buddhists that I met in China, all of them laymen, are carrying on a lively revival of its doctrines.[9]

All of these sects or monastic orders, as the reader will have noticed, are very old. No new sect has been founded since 730. Something approximating a new order, however, is to be founded in the Tsun Lin monasteries. They do not, indeed, constitute a new order or sect in the full meaning of the word, but they do mark a new movement within Chinese monastic life which is worth noting. The aim of the movement is to increase the learning and devotion of the Buddhist clergy by providing monasteries in which earnest and studious monks from any and every order may meet with each other and live together, and where their study and training will not be interfered with by the presence of lazy monks who so often tend to give the tone in the larger monasteries. The necessary financial assistance was secured through the generosity of a Buddhist layman who had not wasted his opportunities as Commissioner of the Salt Gabelle, nor been slothful in looking out for Number One when promoted to be Minister of Finance, and who was glad to exchange a considerable amount of superfluous worldly lucre for an indefinite supply of merit in the other world. A number of Tsun Lin monasteries have thus been founded at different centers in Northeastern China, and monks from the older monasteries, of whatever sect, who desire an opportunity for hard study and rather strenuous devotion may make application to one of the Tsun Lin abbots, and if they seem worthy they are admitted and given a certificate of membership. This certificate gives them the privilege of living as long as they like at any of the Tsun Lin monasteries. The monks in these centers therefore present a considerable sectarian and also geographical variety. No beginners are received by them; only full-fledged monks are admitted. They engage in very little work of a priestly

[8] It is also known as the Dharma-lakshana, and is of course the same as the Indian Yogacara or Vijnanivadin. The founding of it is sometimes attributed not to Hiuen-Tsiang but to a monk named Chich-hsien.

[9] Four other schools besides those named are sometimes mentioned.

nature, seldom participating in funerals or public chanting, but devote almost all their time to study, worship, and meditation.

The level of intelligence in the Tsun Lin monasteries is naturally much higher than that in most of the older religious houses. The general intelligence of the Chinese monk is, in fact, decidedly low. The abbots as a rule know something about their religion, do some reading, teach the novices the necessary minimum, and are able to answer questions about the actual practice of Buddhism and some questions of a theoretical sort that do not go too deep. In every monastery of any size there are usually one or two monks besides the abbot who have a fair acquaintance with the more obvious teachings and practices of Buddhism. But if these be away at a funeral or on some other mission, and if the abbot be indisposed or busy, the inquisitive visitor will have a hard time getting much information. This, at any rate, has been my experience on innumerable occasions. For example, at the Fa Hua Ssu, a rather famous temple on Pao Fang Hutung in Peking, which Li Hung Chang used to make his headquarters when in town, I asked the young monk who (in the absence of the abbot) received me, to tell me about the Buddhas before whom he was burning incense. As to Yao-shih Fo, he could tell me nothing besides his name. When I asked whether Shih-chia Fo (Sakyamuni) had ever been a man and lived on earth he replied that sometimes he comes to earth and some of his time he spends in the Western Paradise. Of India and the historical appearance of Sakyamuni he seemed never to have heard. Looking about for something easy, I asked him the meaning of the prayer "Namu O-mi-to Fo," which he, in common with nearly all Buddhist monks, repeats many hundred times a day. He responded that he didn't know. He only knew that it helped your heart to say it over and over when you were in trouble.

This question concerning the meaning of Namu O-mi-to Fo I made a point of asking in many parts of the country, as a kind of intelligence test for the monks. Namu is from the Sanskrit *Namas*, meaning hail, or adoration to, and the whole phrase is a form of worship, praise, and prayer, by which one gives "adoration to Amida Buddha," or promises devotion or self-surrender to him. I found a good many monks that knew all about it and repeated it intelligently. But I should say about fifty per cent of the monks I asked proved to be as ignorant as the young man in the Fa Hua Ssu. Sometimes they had a dim notion that it had something to do with "surrender," frequently they only knew that they repeated it a good many times a day. The climax is reached in Annam where some of the monks take literally the Chinese characters by which the Sanskrit sound *Namas* is expressed. These characters mean *south no.* So they repeat these pious words over and over, thinking that they mean "The South has no O-mi-to Buddha! The South has no O-mi-to Buddha!"

The whole thing of course seems unutterably silly when thus expressed, but it is not so silly as it seems. As a psychological fact, the literal meaning of a formal prayer contributes but a small percentage of the religious values which its repetition creates for the soul. The devout Roman Catholic may get real spiritual aid from the Latin prayers of the church even though he have but a dim notion how they should be translated. And I think careful introspection of what happens during the recitation of the Litany in the Episcopal church, or of the Lord's Prayer in the Presbyterian, would show that many of those who get most from it give but little attention to the meaning of the separate words as they flow from the lips. The value of most formal prayers—especially of those which, like the *Hail Mary,* or the *Om Mani Padme Hum,* or the *Namu O-mi-to Fo,* are repeated many times—consists in the prayerful or religious mood which they evoke. We may smile at the old Scotch woman who was so helped by "that blessed word Mesopotamia"; but if she found it a blessing it was a blessing. For a similar reason I feel sure that though my young friend in the Fa Hua Ssu could not tell the meaning of the words "Namu O-mi-to Fo," the repetition of it was a truly religious act for him that was not without its value. He was ignorant about the translation; but one thing he knew: "it helps your heart to say it over and over when you are in trouble."

I do not wish to exaggerate the ignorance of the Chinese clergy. There are a number of very learned monks, though these are too busy with their books and their devotions to be seen very often by the casual visitor. One of the abbots that I met was in fact so learned that his knowledge clogged his exposition. He had traveled over the Strait Settlements, India, Burma, and Ceylon in the study of Buddhist history. Though a member of the Ch'an sect (which discourages reading), he had made a detailed study of all the subdivisions of his own Order, and also of the teaching of the T'ien-t'ai and the Fa Hsiang tsung. He looked his part, too, his face a mass of learned wrinkles, and his ancient bald pate shining like a teapot. He received us most cordially and as we took our seats around the table in his private room while the servant brought in the tea and the melon seeds and the candies, I thought the auspices for once were ideal for a most fruitful interview. But, alas, I ventured an unlucky question as to the subdivisions of the Ch'an sect, and the old gentleman started, with a scholar's relish, into a disquisition on the history of each and the distinctions between them, "the eight clubs" and "the four shouts," from which it was impossible to recall him, so that the morning was gone—as were most of the sweets—and we were still immersed in the hopeless bog of endless Buddhist refinements and technical terminology, and getting in deeper with every step and every question.

This old abbot, however, was decidedly an exception. Most Chinese monks are astonishingly ignorant about their own religion. Very few of them, to take a further instance, have so much as heard of the Four Noble Truths or of the Noble Eightfold Path. Not many of them know anything about the important position of the destruction of desire in the teachings of the Founder. The Five Precepts or Vows have quite a different position. Every one knows the Five Vows. But many of the monks seem to have quite forgotten or to be at least a little uncertain as to the additional vows which they took—or should have taken—on being admitted to the Order. Nor is it in learning only that they seem rather below par. Many of them are decidedly dull. A large number of them come from peasant homes or from the coolie class, and are probably inferior to most coolies in intelligence. Life in a monastery does not tend to sharpen the wits.

Nor does life in a monastery automatically transform one into a saint. Some of the monasteries in or near the large cities are said to be retreats for criminals or even worse. As none of the Buddhist monks in China are allowed to marry, there is more or less of the sort of immorality that is found the world over among groups of unmarried men who are living a life artificially deprived of most of the normal interests of hard work and social intercourse.

A monk, of course, may occasionally be found committing almost any sort of crime. A young woman whom I met on a Yangtse steamer told me that on her way up the river she had missed two pairs of her stockings and also a coat and a sweater belonging to her baby. The officers had the ship searched and found all the articles on a Buddhist monk. He was wearing both pairs of stockings, and had tried to put on the tiny sweater and coat, as a kind of vest underneath his arms. As even with the utmost stretching they could not be made to meet, he had tied the ends in front with a string. The occurrence was probably as rare as it was ludicrous. The stories of crimes by Buddhist monks that one hears in the East are to be interpreted in the light of the stories of absconding Sunday-school superintendents that one hears in the West. The fact that the stories are worth so much prominence is a commentary on the rarity of their occurrence.

I have no reason to suppose that the average Chinese monk is any worse than the average Chinese layman; and the average Chinese layman is a pretty decent fellow with a fairly high code of morals. The Buddhist gentlemen of my acquaintance, though they looked down on the monks intellectually, respected them morally, and regarded them as a necessary and useful part of the community. The country monasteries in this respect stand higher than those in or near large towns, and in many of them the level of negative morality is high. Not so much can be said for their positive morality. Most of the monks are lazy. Few of them feel a call to do anything for the community besides chanting prayers for the dead—for which, indeed, their monastery receives a substantial remuneration. They live in a land of great want and are willing to be fed on the rice which others raise, without contributing anything more than they have to toward the spiritual or moral well-being of the community.[10] There are notable and noble exceptions, but the rank and file of the monks get very much more than they give.

In short, most of the Chinese monks lead a rather colorless existence. They do no harm, further than the destruction of a considerable amount of food, and they do little good. They have few positive sins, and few positive and active virtues. But I must qualify this by one further statement. They possess emphatically the virtue of hospitality. To this they are urged by constant repetition in their sacred books. The Sutra which according to De Groot is of more influence in China than any other says, "If a son of the Buddha possesses nothing with which to supply the needs of strangers, he ought to sell himself, sell his sons and daughters, even cut off his own flesh and sell it to supply the needs of his visitor."[11] This command of course is hardly taken literally, but the spirit of it has been fairly contagious in most Buddhist lands. Buddhist hospitality is a very lively virtue. A Chinese country monastery keeps open house the year round. The stranger in need can always find at least a roof and a bowl of rice and a friendly greeting from these rather ignorant and lazy followers of the Blessed One. It would be unpardonably ungrateful of me to write this book and fail to make my testimony to the unfailing welcome I—an utter stranger—invariably received at their hands, whether I came for a ten minutes' visit to the temple, for a difficult interview of hours upon Buddhist philosophy, or for a stay of several nights and days. Their ready smile of greeting, their gentle courtesy, the friendly teacup, always ready for me and always replenished when I emptied it, the good-humored patience with which they bore my unpleasant questioning and did their best to answer me, the candor with

[10] What the Buddha would have thought of a great many Chinese monks today may be pretty clearly seen from a verse in Chap. XXII of the Dhammapada: "Better it would be to swallow a heated iron ball, like flaring iron, than that a bad unrestrained fellow should live on the charity of the land."

[11] De Groot, *Le Code da Mahyana en Chine* (Amsterdam, Müller, 1891), p. 129.

which they admitted their ignorance, and the unmistakable good will toward me with which they shook their own hands (in the Chinese way) or put them together (in the Buddhist way), with many a deep and courtly bow at my departure—these things occupy a conspicuous place in the picture I carry away from China, and I trust I shall not forget them. Doubtless they have their faults, these Buddhist monks—faults chiefly of ignorance and laziness; but they are *good fellows.*

Monkhood is a life-long profession. Most monks become such in boyhood. The motives leading to their joining the Order are varied. A large number of the monks were put into monasteries in their early childhood by their parents. This is sometimes done in conformity to a vow made during some illness, that in case of the child's recovery he should be devoted to the Buddha. Sometimes if the family be large and the parents pious Buddhists they will feel that one of their sons ought to be a monk. Or the boy himself may feel attracted by what he sees of the monks' life and persuade his father to let him join the Order, or even run away from home with this purpose in view. One abbot whom I questioned told me his motive had been the desire always to have enough to eat. There had been a famine in the land during his fourteenth year and he was afraid of starving and so had taken his refuge in the Buddha. A monk at a neighboring monastery said he had joined the Order at eight because he wanted to leave his family. Another told me he applied for admission before he had any belief in the Buddha; he was poor and in trouble and wanted protection and support. It was only after he had been accepted as a novitiate that he learned about the Buddha and believed on him. The pressure of 400,000,000 hungry mouths competing for a limited food supply is so great that it is a wonder more of the Chinese do not take their refuge in the Law and the Order. Professor Hodous estimates that there are in China altogether about 400,000 Buddhist monks, and 10,000 nuns; according to Dr. Reichelt the number of monks and nuns together reaches about 1,000,000. Among those who begin the religious life in mature years there are also other motives than those I have mentioned. Criminals sometimes become monks so as to escape punishment,[12] or (at least they did in Manchu days) in order to lighten their penalty. In recent years there has been a considerable influx into the Order from the ranks of disappointed generals and politicians. Sad experience and blasted hopes have taught these men the truth of the Buddhist doctrine that "this world is all a fleeting show for man's delusion given." These retired politicians are usually able and often educated men, and they sometimes make excellent abbots. Their aim in taking their refuge in the Tathagata may properly be called religious—a felt need for the Buddhist type of life and the help that the Buddha can give. I suppose that occasionally other mature men besides politicians and generals enter the Order, though I have never actually come upon such a case. Two of the monks that I questioned took the vows in boyhood for distinctly religious reasons, to "transcend life and death," to "do what Sakyamuni did." On the whole, however, it must be said that the religious motive is rare (although commoner with nuns than with monks), and that the very great majority of Buddhist monks were either put into the Order by their parents or chose the religious life as an easy and sure way of getting a living.

The attitude of the monks toward their work and their religion is about what one might expect from what has been said of their intelligence and their motives. There is no skepticism among them, so far as I was able to discover, and no hypocrisy. On the other hand there is rather less reverence than I had anticipated. In fact, the rather irreverent bearing of the Chinese in general toward their religions and their supernatural beings and in their temples is one of the things that first strike a foreign visitor. From the great emphasis upon reverence in the Chinese classics I had expected to find this one of the salient characteristics of the Chinese. In matters of worship I know of no other people that has so little of it. One may do anything one likes in Chinese temples—wear one's shoes of course, smoke cigars, shout, feel of the Buddha images, laugh at the Lohans—and no one will protest or even take notice of it. Most of the monks

[12] "Some of these bad characters are in an amazing way changed by the monastic life. They repent and become new men, who with intense fervor concentrate on meditation and worship." Reichelt, *op. cit.*, p. 232.

will not care, and those who are sensitive enough to dislike such conduct will be too polite to mention it. There are exceptional temples, to be sure, especially those which enshrine some sacred relic; but as a rule the contrast between China and other Buddhist lands in the matter of reverence is most striking. The monks are more reverent than the laity; yet even they perform their duties in a mechanical manner which I think would shock a Siamese or a Japanese Buddhist. In one large monastery where we were witnessing a chanting service several of the monks stopped their chanting, left their places near the altar and came to the door to look at the foreigners and talk to us. One of them asked me for a cigarette. This, of course, was extreme, and I never came across anything quite like it elsewhere. And I should of course hasten to add that if there are a few learned monks there are many reverent monks, who take their calling seriously. Some of them are so in earnest in the matter that for years they take the vow of silence, or have themselves shut up in solitary confinement, seeing no one for long periods but the servant who brings their daily food, and devoting themselves to prayer and meditation. This of course is rare; but it is common enough to be a constant influence upon the imaginations of both clergy and laity. Dr. Reichelt, who knows China much better than I, says that "there are many of the monks and their lay helpers who are fired by real spiritual zeal."

As a kind of summary of the strength and weakness of Chinese monks I shall quote here the evaluation of them given by the foremost monk of China—Tai Hsu, the leader of the Buddhist Revival, who understands the monastic life of his country as few others do.

In China the Buddhists have the following shortcomings: First, they are seldom interested in social service or the work of educating the society. The priests or rather monks are generally ignorant, and their services to society are confined to singing of masses or prayers in the funeral services. Secondly, although the monks divide themselves into sects or schools, each pursuing a special object, yet they always fail to accomplish that object. Thirdly, the monks are always religious recluses, taking no interest in the affairs of the community or the country and they are in turn slighted by the Government or the ruling classes. Fourthly, most of the Chinese Buddhist monks lack the necessary modern scientific knowledge and are also ignorant of the current thoughts and ideas in the world. In view of such disabilities, they are unable to preach the doctrines of the Buddha in such a way as to appeal to the minds of the modern people. The Chinese Buddhist monks, however, have also their good points: (1) Most of the devout monks always lead a most austere life of a religious recluse. They remain in inaccessible regions, leave all the vanity and human desires behind and devote themselves exclusively to prayer and contemplation. (2) Although the monks divide themselves into different sects or schools, yet their views are liberal and tolerant. They never engage themselves in religious controversies. (3) The Chinese monks are internationalists. They regard the human society in the world as of the same family regardless of races, creeds, or nationalities. This is the fundamental principle on which the Buddha founded his teachings. (4) Although the thoughts and religious notions of the Buddhist monks in China have somewhat undergone a change during the Sui and T'ang dynasties, yet up to the present they still preserve the main features of primitive Buddhism.[13]

Admission to the Order in China is excessively easy. So far as I could make out there is no universal rule about it, but each abbot uses his discretion. Many members of the staff in some monasteries have never been ordained, and remain novices to the end of their lives. All these assistants need to know is a few prayers. For these there is not even a minimum age requirement, and many a monastery is thus manned chiefly by little boys with shaven heads and priestly garb.

For the external mark of the Buddhist monk in China is a shaven head and a characteristic gown. The gown is long and dark, usually black or gray, and has voluminous sleeves and a V-shaped neck. That is all I should be able to say about it myself; but my Fellow Pilgrim tells me to add the following: The side panels meet in front and instead of crossing straight over the chest as a layman's would, they cross in front, the one from the left shoulder folding over the one from the right, and are cut diagonally downward. The garment has no collar but a stiff band that comes down on a slant, edging the fold of the gown, and fastens under the right arm, being tied there by a small piece of cloth. The sleeves sometimes end in a flowing point. Caps are occasionally worn but these are of various shapes, usually small and black, and often ending in a point such as one sees in the

[13] "A Statement to Asiatic Buddhists," *The Young East*, I. 179-80.

pictures of Tibetan Lamas. The shape varies with the different orders.

Besides having his head shaved and donning the monastic robe, the new monk must also take certain vows on entering the Order. He takes of course the Five Universal Vows of the Buddhist world—not to kill, not to steal, not to be unchaste, not to lie, not to drink intoxicants. In addition to these (which laity as well as clerics are expected to keep), most monasteries require the novitiate to accept the two hundred and fifty monastic rules and to make the five additional vows; though some merely present him with the two hundred and fifty rules which he is expected to obey. The five extra vows are variously stated by various monks—the chief explanation of the divergence so far as I could judge being the differing memories of the different individuals.[14] I am sure, at any rate, that on the ignorant and lazy members of the Order these five additional vows make but slight impression.

In the more careful monasteries, the young novice before being ordained receives not only practical training but some amount of theoretical instruction. This means two or three months of rather severe and concentrated study. At the completion of it he is ready for the first ordination. In monasteries which observe carefully the ancient rules, two ordinations are held. The first is for the novitiates who at this time take the ten vows and accept the two hundred and fifty rules. There is usually but one monastery in a given city or region which has the right (granted by imperial decree) to hold ordinations; and thither the novitiates gather once or twice a year from all the district. It is on this occasion that the young monk receives at the hands of the abbot his robes and that his head is shaved. Some time after this —it may be months or years—when he is thought by his abbot to have progressed sufficiently in the spiritual life,[15] the monk comes up for his second ordination. This begins

[14] The five extra vows or precepts, I will remind the reader, are (1) not to eat at forbidden times; (2) not to dance, sing, or attend plays; (3) not to adorn the person or use perfumes; (4) not to sit on a high seat; (5) not to receive (for one's self) gold or silver.

[15] In some convents the nun is given this second form of ordination at the same time as the first.

with a solemn act of confession and penitence on the part of all the candidates for ordination, and after several earnest invocations to the Buddhas and the Bodhisattvas, the two hundred and fifty rules of the Order are read and the candidates vow solemnly to observe them. This part of the ceremony ends with a period of quiet meditation. But it is not the end of the ordination. A few hours later an additional ceremony is held in which the new monk is given an opportunity to show his devotion to the Buddha by having a number of holes burned into his scalp—a kind of fiery baptism requisite for full membership in the Order. The monk may choose to have 3, 9, 12, or 18 holes, according to his zeal and courage. All the monks whom I have seen have carried either 9 or 12 scars. The holes are made by inserting small pieces of wood into the scalp and setting them on fire till they burn into the flesh—resulting in an honorable scar which the monk carries to his grave. The ceremony is usually conducted with considerable éclat, before a good-sized audience of clergy and laity, and the pain is usually borne with Buddhist patience by the aid of O-mi-to, on whose name the sufferer calls throughout the trying moments.[16] In some of the stricter monasteries a third ordination is held (on the birthday of Sakyamuni) for those monks who aspire to be Bodhisattvas. In this they take the additional fifty-eight vows or precepts of the Sutra of the Thread of Brahma.[17]

The life of the monk, except in a few of the stricter monasteries, is not strenuous. It has, however, certain characteristics which are not exactly comfortable. There is little that one must do but chant and meditate, but these duties must often be performed at such extraordinary hours that to most of us with our Western habits of work and comfort, life in a Chinese monastery would seem a combination of loafing and annoyance. At the great Zin Ssu on the island of P'utow, for instance, the monks rise at midnight and study till two, and are expected to attend service in the temple at 5 A.M. At the Si Yon Ssu in Soochow they rise at two for meditation; at the Nien Hua Ssu in Peking they be-

[16] A careful description of the whole ordination ceremony will be found in Chap. XIV of De Groot's *Le Code du Mahayana en Chine*.

[17] Cf. De Groot, *op. cit.*

gin the day at three, with a prayer service; in the Shi Fang Tsun Lin Ssu at Tsinan fu they read the Lung Yan Sutra from four to 5:30 A.M. This Sutra, if read at that hour, is said to subdue the evil spirits, and I can believe it. In a few monasteries the first service is placed at six.

It will be noted from what I have said of the rising hour that there is no uniformity on this matter throughout China. Each monastery follows its own customs; and it does so not only in regard to the beginning of the day but in all the detail of the day's routine. There are usually three meals a day—the Southern custom of fasting after mid-day being quite disregarded except by a very few of the ascetically minded. Breakfast usually comes at 6 and dinner about 12, with a light supper toward the end of the afternoon. The refectory is usually a large room, with a shrine in the center, and several rows of tables at right angles to the entrance and facing each other. The monks march in and take their places and participate in a short service of prayer and praise. One of their number usually makes an offering of food at the shrine, and then they all fall to. At the mid-day meal each monk finds at his place a bowl of rice, a bowl of soup, and a dish of vegetables. On feast days a greater variety is supplied. Each, as I have said, has his own separate bowls which are filled by the attendants; they do not follow the usual Chinese custom of forming little groups and helping themselves out of a common central dish.

In some of the monasteries which attract earnest monks, the prayer, reading, and meditation are of a rather strenuous sort. Thus at the Si Yon Ssu in Soochow there are two lectures a day, and a large part of the remaining hours are given to meditation during which severe discipline is maintained, infractions of it being punished by beating. At the Tien Tong near Ningpo there are nine periods of meditation daily, each nearly an hour in length, and each followed by a short recess. The meditation periods are measured by the burning of a large incense stick, and the recesses by short incense sticks. The monks are allowed four holidays a month.

Both of these monasteries belong to the Ch'an sect and both are far above the average in earnestness as well as in learning. The meditations in which their monks spend so much of their time is of the usual Ch'an sort, an attempt to empty the mind completely and thus get back as close as possible to the original nature from which they came, the Buddha nature which is within all. It is nearly vain to seek a description of the process from a monk. An old abbot near Ch'angsha told me that he begins his meditation by trying to make himself as much like an image of the Buddha as he can. He takes the Buddha posture and remains motionless. He repeats the "Namu O-mi-to Fo." He cuts himself off from everything. He seeks singleness of heart. If your heart is without distraction you are very happy. Your mind is thus carried upward—this indicated by a gesture, putting his hand to his head and pointing on high. If you should kill him at such a time he would not know it. Further than this in description of his meditation he can say nothing. Whether the soul leaves the body or remains in the body he cannot tell. The answer to all questions concerning the nature of this state of the soul is *Nothing*.[18]

The general run of monasteries make no attempt at forcing their monks to meditate. Usually the abbot tries to do a little of that sort of thing, partly to give a good example to the younger monks, partly for the sake of his soul, partly, I suppose, for the sake of his reputation. The mere monks may meditate if they like; they are not forced to. Most of the monks of China live in easy-going monasteries of this sort; though it is worth noting that the stricter monasteries are sometimes very large, with several hundred inmates. In these monasteries meditation, and a great deal of it, is often required. For the novices the practice is at first decidedly unpleasant. They look forward to the meditation periods with dread, so I have been told, and long for them to be over. One is reminded of Saint Teresa's description of her first years of meditation and how she suffered from it. The older monks—like Saint Teresa in her mature years—find it a great source of joy, and look forward to it with delight. In a few monasteries it is carried to extremes and

[18] For a brief but excellent description of Buddhist meditation see Reichelt, *op. cit.*, p. 281. In general the ancient Indian model is followed: meditation on the vileness of the body, the joy of deliverance, and in addition the Mahayana realization of the identity of the believer with the Buddha.

occasionally results in insanity. This, the monks say, is due to evil spirits and comes about not because one meditates too much but because one uses wrong methods and goes in a wrong direction.

Not all monks meditate and study, but all must take part in chanting the Sutras and some have the special duty of seeing that the offerings are made daily to the Buddhas and their celestial following. Food is offered before the images every morning—and in the morning only, for the Buddhas are better Buddhists than the monks and do not eat after mid-day. Of course no one, probably not even the most ignorant, thinks they eat at all. The offering is like a hymn or prayer, a means of humbling oneself before the Highest. But it would be inappropriate to offer food to the Buddha image at an hour of the day at which the Buddha taught his followers not to eat. Incense and candles may be burned before the Buddhas at any hour of the day. As we have seen, a chanting service regularly takes place early in the morning, though there is no uniformity as to the hour in the different temples. There is almost always a second service later in the day, and sometimes two. The last one comes any time between four and ten. At the close of it, if it be in the evening, the monks promptly retire and the day is done. And high time that it should be, at least in those monasteries where the praises of the Lord Buddha must be chanted again at 2 A.M.

In the chanting service—one might call it the Buddhist mass—the monks take their places not directly in front of the altar, as in Siam, and Japan, but on one side. They sit, either on mats or on low benches, in a line or several lines, usually (not always) at right angles to the altar and facing toward the center of the hall. Sometimes, and especially if a large number of monks are present so that both sides of the temple are occupied, they face toward the rear wall. The service is preceded by ten or fifteen minutes of announcement by bell and drum. Especially in the larger monasteries this call to worship is an impressive affair and its solemnity grows upon one with increased acquaintance. The instruments, if so we may call them, are played with considerable skill and some practice is required to perform the rite properly. When the first streaks of gray appear in the eastern sky one hears the hollow booming of the loud-mouthed drum, or the deep notes of the great bell with the solemn sound, rolling out at intervals of a minute or more—distant, mysterious, reverberating through the courts of the temple, or carried far through the sleeping city. This is followed by the more mellow tones of the gong and by the quicker notes from the hollow wooden fish, leading up to a crescendo of rapid beats. The monks now begin to congregate in the temple. The leader takes his place, the smaller gong by his side is sounded, the monks bow deeply, and begin chanting the praises of the Buddha. It cannot be said that their singing is musical, at least if heard from near-by. At a little distance it is pleasing. There is considerable variation in it, the leader sometimes chanting alone, followed by all the voices in unison. There is no real tune in their hymning, but there is often a decided rhythm. At certain points in the chanting one of the gongs is sounded, either the metallic one or the hollow wooden gong, sometimes alone, sometimes as an accompaniment to the singing. Some services close with a repeated circumambulation by the chanting monks in a solemn procession around the interior of the temple. For some occasions special robes are donned. In the larger temples there may be elaborate services in which fifty or a hundred monks participate, divided into two bodies, with antiphonal chanting, and much bowing, standing, and kneeling. The monks as a rule use no books in these services, but recite the verses without notes; for the passages more commonly used they keep in their memories, or (as they say) "in their stomachs."

Some of the passages thus chanted are taken from the Sutras. These are sometimes in Chinese, sometimes phonetic transliterations from the Sanskrit. The latter are considered the more sacred. They are, in fact, Sanskrit *mantras*, specially sacred verses, and they are retained in their original sounds, without translation, because they are too holy for translation and because a translation necessarily involves personal interpretation on the part of the translator. So holy a thing is therefore best given in its original purity. Of course no one can understand them. They are not Chinese, but neither are they Sanskrit, for a Chinese attempt at phonetic rendering of foreign words is ludicrously inexact. But, as I have already insisted in another connection, ignorance of the original meaning of a prayer or hymn does not necessarily rob it of all religious value. The monk who chants it, if he be a religious soul, may put more of spiritual significance into it than it originally possessed, or may get more religious value out of it than he would if he understood and dwelt upon the literal significance of its words. And I should hasten to add that many of the prayers found in the official prayer books and daily used in the temples are in perfectly good Chinese. They consist of hymns and litanies composed by Chinese Buddhists of various schools and various generations; and they have accumulated and been handed down through the centuries and are used in the temples of all the sects. There are several compilations of these hymns, the favorite being the *Prayers of the Ch'an School for Daily Recitation*, which according to Mr. Johnston,

> include prayers for use by both monks and laymen in connection with all such circumstances of daily life as can be brought into relationship with religious observance. There are, of course, prayers for use on saints' days—that is, on the days specially consecrated to the worship of the great P'usas. There are burial services for monks and laymen, services for the ordination of monks, services in commemoration of pious founders and benefactors and "spiritual ancestors." There are prayers for use before and after child-birth, prayers for fair weather, for rain, for deliverance from plague and famine, for the divine guidance of rulers and magistrates. There are prayers to be used before taking food, prayers for those in danger or difficulty, prayers for those at sea, prayers expressing repentance for sin, prayers for the sick and dying. Such books also contain many superstitious survivals, such as sacred words and charms which are supposed to have a controlling power over the forces of nature, and there are prayers for purely material benefits, such as wealth and worldly prosperity, and rituals which correspond more or less closely with Christian masses for the dead.[19]

Beside the regular chanting services of each day, there are many special services for the dead, at which one, two, or three monks, or perhaps the entire monastic force participate, according to the price paid by the relatives of the de-

[19] Johnston's *Buddhist China*, p. 307. A translation of a large part of the Kwan-Yin ritual will be found in Beal's *Catena of Buddhist Scriptures in China*, pp. 399-409. Reichelt has translated several of the Pure Land hymns, *op. cit.*, pp. 134-40.

parted.[20] There are also solemn celebrations, such as the harvest festival, the birthday of one of the Buddhas or of Kwan-Yin, and services for special emergencies such as drought, flood, famine, pestilence. In a few of the more modern-minded and a few of the more ancient-minded temples there are occasional or regular lectures or sermons. The ancient rules prescribe that there must be preaching on twelve special days of each year—the anniversaries of the birth and the Nirvana of Sakyamuni, the birthday of the emperor, etc., and, in addition, on each day from the fifteenth of the fourth month to the fifteenth of the seventh. Besides this the abbot must preach or appoint a preacher whenever the monks or a delegation of laymen request it. The monastery is rare today, however, in which such request is frequently made or in which the ancient rules are strictly carried out. More attention, I judge from the inquiries I made, is given to the ancient custom of Patimokkha, or the public reading of the two hundred and fifty rules of the Order and the public confession of the infraction of them. Preaching before public gatherings of laymen is much more rare. In De Groot's opinion this is due largely to the traditional attitude of the government, under almost all the dynasties, of discouraging and even forbidding religious activity on the part of the laity. Nowhere, so far as I could discover, is there any such thing as a regular public preaching service, though sometimes one may find an occasional address or a course of lectures lasting several weeks. This is very infrequent, however, and even the occasional sermon or lecture is rare indeed. In indirect fashion, however, the monks do something toward the religious education of the community. There is more or less intercourse between clergy and laity in both the temples, the homes, and the city streets, and in all these ways the monks inevitably disseminate among interested laymen what knowledge of the teachings and hope of Buddhism they may themselves possess. Especially is interchange of ideas on religious matters facilitated at times of pilgrimage. The peasant pilgrims often

[20] According to a dispatch in the *New York Times* for Jan. 27, 1927, the monks and nuns of Hankow and Wuchang "have formed a union demanding union scale for prayers."

spend the night under the hospitable roofs of the temples and this presents an opportunity for questions and conversations on themes of Buddhist belief and practice from which the peasants return to their homes with a little greater knowledge of their religion and considerably greater interest in it than they had on leaving home. Occasionally, also, education of a more direct sort is given in the monasteries, not only by lectures and sermons, but in the training of young boys who are left with the monks with this end in view by pious parents. Not all the boys one finds in Chinese monasteries are destined to become monks. Some are there merely for the sake of receiving several years of education in religion and manners, and at about twelve years of age they return to their homes. I should add that the monks are always ready to go to the homes of the laity to teach the Dharma if invited. To be sure, they are not often invited. They are more likely to be asked to chant than to teach. Sometimes a family will have several monks in to read the Sutras in a series of prolonged services lasting a week. The family is present part of the time—they come in and go out as they like—and the neighbors are invited. The purpose of the reading is not instruction but the acquisition of merit, usually for the benefit of the dead. Instruction, in fact, would be out of the question from such a service, for no one can understand what the monks read. So, at least, I have been told.

Besides giving occasional instruction the monks in a few places and at times of special need serve as dispensers of free food. The rice which wealthy and pious laymen provide for the poor during famines, or it may be in any winter season, is sometimes distributed by lay Buddhist societies, sometimes by the monks of some central monastery. I have heard of one instance in which as many as thirty-one hundred poor were thus "fed with yellow millet mush, cooked in 16 vats about five feet across, and served in any vessel presented by the recipients. There were baskets, pots, pans, tubs, buckets, broken dishes, and Standard Oil tins." [21] Such distribution of free food or, in fact, of any sort of

[21] "The Fleshpots of China" in the Contributors' Club of the *Atlantic* for Feb., 1927.

charity, is rare, and it would be a mistake to picture the Buddhist monastic Order in China as a charitable institution—except in the obvious sense that it lives on charity.

The life of the nun is very like that of the monk. Nothing definite is known as to the number of nuns in China, but Reichelt and Hodous estimate that there are perhaps a tenth as many nuns as monks. The convents are small, and frequently are situated near a monastery, whose elders give it some advice in matters of administration. The nuns "have their little temple hall, etc., where they perform their services and meditations often with great piety. They often go out to the homes of the many lay Buddhists among the women and do a great work both from a religious and a financial point of view. Nobody collects so much money or pulls so many invisible strings as do the nuns." [22] A glimpse into the really beautiful life of one convent is given in the recently translated *Diary of a Chinese Buddhist Nun.*[23] The picture given by this novice in her private journal shows the intimate relations between the nuns and the more religious lay women of the neighborhood, the eagerness with which the monastic life is anticipated, the appeal of the convent's untroubled calm, the intensity of the devotion felt toward the Buddha, the peace produced by the daily meditations, and the spiritual elevation of some of the nuns.

In weighing the contribution of the Buddhist monks of China to the community we must not forget that it is they who keep up the temples and monasteries, and hence whatever of value to the life of China is contributed by these beautiful and often truly religious buildings must be set down in large part to the credit of the clergy. I shall not attempt to assess the value of these monasteries to China; it is among those imponderables that defy quantitative measurement. But I am sure that to any one with esthetic and spiritual appreciation, the thought of a China deprived of its monasteries and temples must be unspeakably dreary. They are gems of ancient beauty, coming from a time long past, amid a land of plains and crops and dirty towns. They are places of refuge for the weary soul from the monotonous

[22] Reichelt, *op. cit.*, p. 265.
[23] Trans. by Y. Y. Tsu, in the *Journal of Religion*, Oct., 1927, pp. 612-18.

materialism of Chinese life. Their hospitable gates are ever wide for whosoever feels the need of a quiet hour and of suggestions from a loftier world. And it is the monks, after all, that keep them going.

Things like these should be kept in mind during those moments (and they are frequent enough) when the meagerness of the direct services of the clergy to the community fills one with impatience at the entire Order. That one able-bodied man in every four hundred of the entire population should spend his life in the lazy and fruitless way I have described, particularly in a land constantly so near the starvation line as China—this is a situation which many Westerners, with our usual views of the importance of economic productivity, will regard as almost intolerable. One frequently feels that the great majority of the Chinese monks should somehow be cleared out and made to earn an honest living. Yet an institution so inextricably interwoven into the life of China as is the Buddhist monastic Order cannot be judged merely by the specific and direct services which it performs for those individuals who seek its aid. As was suggested in the preceding paragraph, it is a part of an entire situation, and its general influence rather than its particular contributions must be the decisive factor in any assessment of its value.

The great contribution which the Buddhist Order makes to the life of China consists in keeping before the minds and imaginations of the people the *fact of religion,* the reality of the spiritual life. Doubtless this great function of keeping the lamp of religion alight is often ill performed by the Buddhist clergy. But as things actually are in China today, and have been for many a century, the clergy, whether worthily or not, are the torch-bearers of religion, and if they should drop their light, it might well be extinguished in the darkness of worldly, unspiritual preoccupation. It is not without value in the life of the Chinese people that they should be constantly reminded of the fact of Buddhism, reminded of it as at least an unfailing potentiality. It is not without value that an Order of men should be consecrated to the lifelong study and service of religion, that buildings of ancient beauty should be devoted to the praises of the highest ideal that China knows, that quiet cloisters should be set aside for the meditation of holy men and of all who wish to meditate. It is not without value that the poorest beggar, the busiest politician, the saddest woman, the most guilty sinner should carry ever in the subconscious regions of their minds the thought that, if they will, they may go any morning or any night to the near-by temple, hear the solemn music of gong and drum and chanting monks, watch the smoke of incense ascend before the image of the Blessed One, and catch some intimation of a higher life, a loftier world, a deeper peace than they have known before.

CHAPTER XVIII

THE BUDDHIST LAYMAN

IN almost any land but China such an expression as the Buddhist layman, the Christian layman, the Mohammedan layman, would have a fairly definite meaning. But who are the Buddhist laymen in China? As we have already seen, nearly every person in the land, except the highly educated Confucianists, is in some sense a Buddhist. He is a Buddhist and at the same time a Confucianist and a Taoist. If we are to define the Buddhist laity of China so as to include all those who have some belief in Buddhism and make some use of Buddhist monks and ceremonies or shrines, we shall have about 350,000,000 to 400,000,000 Buddhist laymen, including in the number nearly all the Taoist laymen and nearly all the Confucianists. If, on the other hand, we exclude from the Buddhist laity the Taoists and the Confucianists, we shall have hardly any one left. It is plain that we cannot divide the people of China on religious lines as we do those of other lands, nor draw fast and sure limits round any collection of them and label this the Buddhist laity. The best we can do is to point out certain groups who are rather more Buddhist than others.

The widest group of those who can in any special sense be called Buddhist is, I suppose, composed of those families who have their funerals conducted by Buddhist monks or employ Buddhist monks to pray for the souls of the dead. There is a general popular belief in Chinese Buddhism that, for the soul fortunate enough to escape all of the hells, forty-nine days elapse between death and his assignment to the Western Paradise or to a new birth. Some say he may be reborn in fourteen, or even in seven days; but forty-nine days is the period usually given. These seven weeks are occupied by his transition through the different stages of purgatory. Sometimes three services are held on each of the first seven days; sometimes one service is held on every seventh day till the expiration of the forty-nine, to give the soul assistance in his perilous journey. This, of course, is expensive, and if the family be poor or the heirs not notable for filial piety, they may take a chance that the virtues of the departed will be sufficient to carry him through the dangers of the next world without constant benefit of clergy; in which case one service, held the seventh day after the decease, may be made to do the work of all seven. These services for praying the dead out of purgatory consist chiefly in the chanting of sacred verses by the monks. The Buddha, I was told by a monk, hears the chanting and saves the soul. Before the funeral there is frequently such a service over the body, prolonged for hours, in the home. Often the chanting service is in the temple. At the temple service for the dead it frequently happens that no one is present, except the monks; though in some cases it is attended not only by the immediate relatives of the deceased but by a large group of family friends, especially of the women. There are also occasional services in which the incidents of the soul's progress through purgatory are dramatically presented, some of the monks personifying evil demons and refusing to let the bier with the tablet of the deceased pass on until appeased by a certain amount of silver.[1]

The Buddhist portion of the funeral service proper frequently consists of two parts, one in the day and one at night. At the former of these,

> Nine or more monks are in charge and the Sutras of the Pure Land (the Sukhavati Vyuha Sutras) are repeated with the accompaniment of music. In the evening the Yoga Tantra is recited, accompanied by the throwing of dice, bread and money (to feed the hungry hosts and supply the needy in hell), the magical finger play (to prevent the dead from being attacked by the evil ghosts) and what is most important, invocations to the compassionate Amitabha, that the dead may be reborn instantly in the Paradise of the West.[2]

It is, I suppose, a smaller group of laymen who not only seek the aid of the Buddha at the time of a death in the family, but who also worship him in less solemn hours by offering

[1] See Hodous, *Buddhism and Buddhists in China* (N. Y., Macmillan, 1924), pp. 35-36.

[2] Leong and Tao, *Village and Town Life in China*, p. 145.

prayers and praises, incense and gifts, in his temple. When one considers the immense mass of China's population, the number of those who frequent Buddhist temples seems very small. The visitor to China, judging by what he sees in the dusty and frequently empty temples, concludes that there are very few Buddhists in China. The appearance of the temples is not so good evidence on this matter as the appearance of Christian churches would be on the corresponding question at home; yet I am convinced that, relative to the population, the number of earnest Buddhists in most parts of China outside of the lower Yangtse valley is very small indeed.

The devout Buddhist layman—and more especially the devout Buddhist laywoman—goes to the temple from time to time to pray and make her vows, to gain assistance, acquire merit, and also to get, if possible, a glimpse into the future. For fortune-telling is inextricably mixed up with worship in most Chinese temples which are popular with the masses. Two methods are commonly used. The simpler, which might be called the yes-no method, is carried on by a combination of petitional prayer with a couple pieces of wood, about the size of a Chinese woman's shoe, and in shape something like a sweet potato that is flat on one side. The pair thus fit, roughly, together. The worshiper holds them to her forehead, utters her prayer before the Buddha, then drops them at his feet. There are, of course, only three possible combinations in the way in which they may alight. Both may lie with their flat sides up, both with their flat sides down, or one in one way and one in the other. I must confess that I am not an expert in fortune-telling and do not know which is the lucky combination, but one of the three means that the petition will be granted, another that it will be refused, while the third is ambiguous. The other method of fortune-telling is more elaborate and is a means of considerable income to the temple. He who would have a look into the future is provided by the priest with a cylindrical box, one end of which is entirely closed, while the other is closed except for a small opening. The box is filled with bamboo rods, each bearing a number. The worshiper who is seeking to know his fortune stands before the Buddha with this box in his hands and manipulates it in such a fashion by a series of shakes that one of the rods makes its way out through the small aperture and falls upon the floor. The worshiper takes it to the temple office and hands it to the presiding monk. This office is usually in a space adjoining the main shrine where, among other things, the presiding monk has at his elbow a filing catalogue, as we might call it —a cabinet with 50 to 100 sections, each of them numbered, and each containing a pile of printed slips of paper, descriptive of fortunes, good, bad, and indifferent. The monk takes the bamboo stick, notes the number which it bears, and (for a consideration) presents the fortune-seeker with a printed slip from the section indicated by the bamboo.

Worship is not always followed by fortune-telling, and in fact the majority of worshipers simply come in, present an offering of incense, candles, paper money, flowers or vegetables, make their prayers and depart, without seeking to unveil the future. I remember a typical scene in a temple in Swatow—the temple swarming with earnest worshipers, mostly women and girls, kneeling with lighted incense sticks, bowing deeply before the draped image, and moving their lips in prayer. Many offered large leaves of gilt paper money. After presenting them with bows before the altar they would put them in a kind of incinerator, provided for the purpose, where from time to time an attendant priest would burn them. There was also a considerable amount of fortune-seeking, by both the methods I have described. One old lady was particularly devout and persistent. She tried the yes-no method several times, apparently with ill success, though she prayed long and earnestly. The pieces of wood persisted in falling in the wrong combinations, spite of her many trials. The bamboo rods she also used more than once, usually with no better success, if one could judge by the anxiety in her old wrinkled face. Her last attempt with it seemed more successful. The kind-faced monk at the office, who produced the red paper fortune-slip, apparently said some reassuring words to her, she returned to the altar, prayed again a long time before the Buddha, tried the yes-no method once more, and after a final prayer, went out of the temple with face smiling and radiant.

I happened into a temple in Saigon on a day of some unusual sacredness and watched for hours the throng of Annamese and Chinese worshiping before the various shrines. One Annamese that I singled out for special attention—man or woman, I know not which—came in with many incense sticks which he or she had bought in the office at the entrance. (The trousers would probably indicate that he was a woman; whereas, the long hair, done up in a knot at the back of the head, would indicate that she was a man.) The incense sticks were carefully lighted at the little flaming lamp on the altar and distributed in front of the many images. She also bowed many times (for the chances are it was she) and mumbled a silent prayer standing before the central altar, now and then drawing a loud sharp breath, suggestive of deep emotion. At the end of her prayer she took off her shoes and knelt four times in succession before the altar, showing much unmistakable reverence and earnestness. As she went out another Annamese with trousers, back hair, and uncertain sex came in and lighted a cigarette at the wick of the altar lamp.

Several Chinese women now began to arrive, each bringing on her arm a large and heavy basket. There was a table in front of the chief altar, and on this table each woman on arriving opened and unpacked her basket. Most of the baskets contained about the same things. The principal object in each was a large roasted goose, done to a turn as only the Chinese can roast a goose, roasted and decked and odorous, so as to make even a P'usa's mouth water. Besides the goose there were fruits, vegetables, a teapot, several small cups, and a bottle of water or of wine. Fortunately the table was large, for each woman put all her goodies upon it. I counted seven roast geese upon the table at once. Each woman would lay out her offering, filling the little cups from the teapot or bottles, then take large bunches of incense sticks and candles, light them and distribute them before the different shrines, bow, pray, and sometimes try the fortune-sticks. After this she would pour the liquid back from the cups into the teapot, or bottle, take the goose away from the poor P'usas, put all the goodies back into the basket, and go out into a little court at the side, where there were four humble but very popular shrines. Arrived at the shrine of her choice, she would unpack her basket once more and lay out all the goodies reverently before the holy place and re-begin her prayers. In this court with its four shrines there happened to be a large turtle, waddling about and making a living from the crumbs and offerings left by the women and the P'usas. While I was watching, this turtle got his eye on the roast goose lying before one of the shrines and made many masterly attempts at it, being warded off just at the critical moment at the point of the umbrella which the woman had brought, perhaps with this in view, and which she used with skill between the phrases of her prayer. At one time she knocked him over on his back, where he lay with paws clawing the air, to the great merriment of several of the women, until their Buddhist consciences got the better of their resentment and their sense of humor, and they righted him; whereupon he recommenced his campaign, sometimes by direct attack, sometimes by strategic retreats and unexpected flank movements. At length the prayers were ended and the woman rescued her goose and her goodies definitively from the turtle, packed them all up in her basket, paid her fee to the attendant at the office, and started home with her now very blessed dinner.

The space I have given the old woman and her goose must not lead the reader to suppose that all lay worship in the temples is as largely external as hers seemed to be. As a fact, I have never seen roast goose offered in a Buddhist temple outside of Annam. There is not infrequently a good deal of earnestness in the worship of the layman—and for that matter, the old woman with the goose was certainly dead in earnest. Sometimes the worshipers are not only earnest and devout but enthusiastic in almost an evangelical sense. I remember seeing one old gentleman in a Peking temple who put on a temple robe and took part with the monks in a service of circumambulation. After the ceremony was over he laid aside the sacred robe and had a long talk with me. I found him devout to the verge of zealotry. Religion was the breath of his life, and it was not a religion of external ceremonies but of inner experience. He had had several visions of the Buddha and believed that the Buddha had conversed with him. Zeal such as his, however, is decidedly unusual in China.

From what I have said it will be seen that the use the average laymen make of their temples is sufficiently different from that which we Christians, and particularly Protestant Christians, make of our churches. The worship of the Chinese layman in the temple is chiefly individual worship. Sometimes, indeed, he is present at the chanting service of the monks. This is often a mere chance coincidence, and not an unusual one, since (as we have seen) the monks have two or three services every day. In some devout Buddhist families, however, it is not a matter of chance; for the more strict families observe the custom of attending the early morning service in a near-by monastery or convent on the first and fifteenth of every moon. On these occasions they first listen to the chanting of the monks—or of the nuns—and after these have finished, the family, with the father at their head, repeats a certain ritual of prayer and praise before the Buddha. The fact that this family service is usually held about four in the morning may help to explain the further fact that the average tourist sees nothing of it and goes home to tell his friends that the laymen in China seldom go near a Buddhist temple. There is a certain type of tourist who thinks a religious service *must* be held on *Sunday* morning, and at half past ten.

It is doubtless true, however, that the number of families who observe this custom of bimonthly attendance at the temple service is relatively small. Most Buddhist families attend the services on behalf of their own dead, and those held on special occasions, and beyond that it is only now and then that they visit a temple. Their attendance at the temple, moreover, as I have said, must not be thought of as the same sort of thing as our Protestant Christian attendance at church. As a rule, when a Chinese Buddhist goes to his temple it is not to hear a sermon nor to listen while some one else prays. He goes there to pray himself. Communal worship is something of which the Chinese have very little conception. It is odd how difficult it seems to be for Westerners to grasp this fact, even when they have resided for some time in China. A missionary describing in a recent number of the

Chinese Recorder [3] a prayer conference that took place at Hang Chow in May, 1924, expresses his surprise that he found no prayer-meeting going on—just individual worshipers reverencing the Buddhas, silently and by themselves, and the monks chanting verses. As a fact, of course, a Chinese Buddhist could hardly conceive of such a thing as a prayer-meeting. It is odd also that this obvious fact is so seldom made use of by Christian missionaries in planning out the services for their newly made converts. These services are almost invariably copied exactly after the pattern of church services at home; and no opportunity is offered the convert from Buddhism and Taoism for that individual worship to which, and to which alone, they have been accustomed since their infancy.[4]

The devout Buddhist layman does most of his praying at home, and many men and women who would call themselves Buddhists and trust in and pray to the P'usas, who look forward to O-mi-to's Paradise and make use of monks at family funerals, seldom go near a temple. As I have said, it is much more difficult to gauge the strength of Buddhism in a given district by the number of laymen one finds in the temples than it is to make a similar estimate with similar methods in Christendom.

The laymen who do come to the temple to pray do so in part because of the opportunity here at hand to make offerings to the Fos and P'usas—both of gifts for the immediate glorification of the Holy Ones, and also of money to aid in support of the Sangha. By these means one acquires merit. Another reason for worship in the temple is that the sacred associations of the place and the presence of the images makes one feel more like praying—puts one in a more religious frame of mind—and presumably the prayer in such circumstances is worth more. Probably the most ignorant directly worship the temple images (whatever that may mean!), but for most laymen the image seems to be merely a sacred representation of the holy Being, who himself is in heaven. Without the image, one Chinese explained to me, it is difficult to

[3] "A Unique Buddhist—Taoist Union Prayer Conference," by Clarence B. Day. *Chinese Recorder* for June, 1925, pp. 366-69.

[4] A few of the wiser missionaries realize this fact and are trying to persuade their fellows that a great tactical mistake has been made.

concentrate one's thought upon the Buddha. One comes to the temple because before the image of the Buddha prayer is easier and more natural.

There are, of course, exceptions to this. In a large temple partly Buddhist and partly Taoist a few miles from Taiyuan fu I found an image of a P'usa to which the peasants pray for rain, and which, in time of specially bad drought, they carry around in a chair so that she may see how dry the land is. This, of course, seems to imply idolatry in the extreme sense. Such an attitude toward images is rare, however, and I think in this case it was due to the influence of Taoism. The P'usa, in fact, was a very local one, and looked more Taoist than Buddhist.

Belief in the efficacy of prayer is fairly general, and is naturally encouraged by the temple authorities. At the temple I have just mentioned there is a large sign reading, "If you pray you will have an answer." In another temple I saw a collection of red cloths left there by worshipers whose prayers had been answered, each cloth bearing the name of the donor and the date of the divine response. As will be seen from this, popular Chinese Buddhism does not share the common prejudice of Southern Buddhism against petitional prayer. Some of the more learned will tell you that there are many things for which you should not make petitions; but the rank and file of the Buddhist laity pray for what they want. They sometimes differentiate between their supernatural friends, moreover, somewhat as Roman Catholics often differentiate between the saints. One prays to Kwan-Yin for rain, for help in danger, for children, for recovery from sickness. One prays to O-mi-to for eventual entrance into the Western Paradise. When visiting a temple in Soochow I happened to mention to the monk that I had a headache; he told me that Kwan-Yin very likely would remove it if I prayed to her to do so. The more spiritually minded pray to the Buddha for peace; or pray that ultimately they may "become Buddha."

The Prayer Conference to which I alluded a few pages back was called, as its name indicates,[5] for the sake of insuring peace and warding off calamity. It was a cooperative

[5] *Kiangsu Chekiang Prayer Union Conference for Peace and Prevention of Calamity.*

undertaking of Buddhist and Taoist clergy and laity. The date at which it was assembled, May 20, 1924, will indicate to the reader who was interested in Chinese affairs at that time, the circumstances that probably prompted it—the civil discord within the province of Chekiang which soon resulted in the war between governors Chi and Lu. It was held in a secluded monastery among the hills west of Hang-chow, lasted for two weeks, and was attended by "groups from widely separated places in the two provinces of Kiang-su and Chekiang, who met for prayer for a common purpose and in a spirit far removed from the warring of the militarists, showing a faith in spiritual forces and their power among men." [6] In addition to peace and prosperity the Conference prayed for the souls of the dead. The bulletin which gave notice of the Conference said: "We must pray for the souls of the dead soldiers lost in the European battles and for the victims of the Japanese earthquake"; "Pray for universal harmony"; "Let every soul heed." The praying, I should add, seems to have consisted in reverential bowing before the Buddha images, and in chanting by the Buddhist and Taoist monks, in four prayer halls. There seems to have been little or no spontaneous petitional prayer. A two-months' session of daily prayer was started in the Lama temple in Peking on June 1, 1927, with the hope "that peace and order may thus be restored." [7]

Prayer conferences of this sort are rather rare occurrences. But it is not unusual in case of drought or pestilence for an entire village or district to demand in a body that the monks of some near-by monastery should seek supernatural assistance by chanting prayers. A description of a service held for this purpose will be found in Hodous' *Buddhism and Buddhists in China.*[8] It consists in symbolic acts and offerings and in set petitions to Kwan-Yin or the Dragon King, to take pity upon the people and remove the cause of their suffering.

As I have indicated, some of the better-read monks and laymen insist that for most things direct petitional prayer

[6] Mr. Day, *op. cit.*, p. 368.
[7] *Peking Leader* for July 15, 1927.
[8] Pp. 24-27.

is useless. If one's father is ill, one monk told me, it is idle to pray for his recovery and one does not do it. For his illness is due to his sin and is the inevitable consequence of his sin; and prayer cannot make this sin less. One may, however, pray directly for one's own growth in wisdom or goodness and also for one's success. One may also pray for the success of other people. The distinction between prayer for other people's success and for their health, the monk did not make plain. He admitted, however, that we might indirectly help a sick man through prayer, by helping his spirit and thereby enabling him to be less sinful. In this case it is the subjective effect of prayer that is relied on. This monk was nearer than most of his Chinese colleagues to the Hinayana point of view.

Offerings of some sort are usually made in the temples in conjunction with prayer. The gift may be of copper cash or paper money. Sometimes it is candles, but most often an incense stick, or several of them. Flowers also are occasionally given, and vegetables.

By no means all the prayer made by the laymen in the temples is petition. Much of it, as with the monks, consists in repeating some form of sacred words. Sometimes they gaze at a Buddha image during the process to keep their minds properly concentrated. Sometimes they repeat sentences taken from some favorite Sutra. Those who know no passages from the Sutras content themselves with repeating many times the Namu O-mi-to Fo, occasionally keeping track of the number of repetitions on a rosary.[9] By this means one acquires merit and also produces upon one's own mind a certain desirable effect. One feels better after doing it. Of course it is not only in the temples that this kind of prayer (or should we call it meditation?) is pursued. It is practiced also in the home or in any solitary spot. Sometimes busy men in need of spiritual repose will devote a few hours consecutively, or a whole day, to this form of prayer, shutting themselves up in their own homes or retir-

[9] The number of beads in a monk's rosary is one hundred and eight (in theory). In the western hills near Peking I was told that the number of beads in a layman's rosary was nineteen. I imagine that there is no uniform usage throughout China, and that many laymen use rosaries with one hundred and eight beads. It is interesting to note that the Vaishnava rosaries in India have the same number of beads.

ing to a monastery. They repeat the Namu O-mi-to Fo from 100 to 5000 times at a stretch, recording the repetitions on a rosary. The practice has, they insist, unquestionable effects in inducing elevation and enlightenment of spirit; and by means of it they find themselves making spiritual progress. Western acquaintances of theirs sometimes testify that if the practice does not make these men more honest, it does seem to make them more gentle.

If the Namu O-mi-to Fo, or a passage from the Sutras, is properly repeated and *if one puts one's mind upon it with deep reverence*, one will thereby acquire merit. The amount of merit thus acquired will depend upon the mental state. Mere mechanical repetition is (in theory) worthless. On the other hand, the repetition of almost any text may acquire merit if repeated with great reverence. The merit thus acquired is transferable (a good Mahayana doctrine, it will be remembered), though a certain amount of it will be lost in the process. Pious women often transfer the merit they have acquired through vows and penances to the members of their family. Most frequently it is to the dead that merit is transferred. The transfer is most economically brought about immediately after the death of the beneficiary—as, for example, when a son causes verses to be chanted for the benefit of his father who has just died.

Just how far the Buddha is involved when one prays is a question on which Chinese Buddhists are no more agreed than are Buddhists in other lands. The popular view is very simple. The Buddha hears and answers prayers, just as do the gods of other religions. So, of course, do the various P'usas. This is a very common belief among both laymen and monks. The more learned Buddhists regard this view as mistaken. Some hold (as we shall see in a later chapter) that the Buddha is quite unconscious. Others will not go so far as that, but say that though the Buddha *may* be aware of our prayers, it is not at all necessary that he should be. For the reverent act itself accomplishes the effect quite automatically. Those who hold this view, of course, discourage petitional prayer and believe only in the reverend and thoughtful repetition or chanting of sacred words. Such chanting or repetition, if done in the presence of a sick father, may benefit his spirit directly (i.e., subjectively); and it also will produce merit which may be transferred to him without the intervention of any supernatural being. Prayer thus works in much the same automatic fashion as in Burma. The doctrine of prayer does not differ greatly among the learned whether their Buddhism be of the Hinayana or of the Mahayana variety.

The more zealous Buddhists, in addition to making offerings at the temples and praying there and at home, make occasional vows of various sorts and for various reasons. A common form of vow is to promise to eat no meat during a given period. For the laymen of China, like the laymen of most other Buddhist lands, are seldom vegetarians. Women frequently take this vow to eat only vegetable food for a certain length of time, either in order to acquire merit (which they share with those they love) or in order to gain some wish explicitly named in the vow, such as the birth of a son, the recovery from illness or the like. Another special means of acquiring merit is the "emancipation of living creatures." It is especially on days fixed by Buddhist custom for this purpose that this pious deed is performed. The devout Buddhist will then buy fish at a market (in China fish are kept alive at the markets) and put them in the pond in some nearby temple compound. Perhaps the commonest vow is to repeat some sacred verse such as the Namu O-mi-to Fo a certain number of times. Just how many times this is to be done may be settled by the divining blocks. The worshiper proposes a certain number of repetitions as the price he will pay for the desired mercy and then throws down the blocks. If they fall in such a way as to mean No, he tries again, offering a larger figure, and so continues till he and the Fo or P'usa have struck a bargain. This done, he has to make sure, by the aid of the rosary or some other mechanical device, to carry out his side of the agreement to the letter.

One of the commonest of vows is to make a pilgrimage to some sacred shrine. The making of pilgrimages is still popular in China. It is of course not only in fulfilment of a vow that pilgrimages are performed. The devout Buddhist makes the pilgrimage for its own sake. And indeed it is not surprising. It is of course primarily a serious religious business; but that does not make it a solemn business. And the Chinese pilgrim, like other pilgrims, has a very good time. It is a joyous as well as an uplifting experience. Sometimes the pilgrims go alone; more often in company. Sometimes they pay their own way; sometimes they are helped by the pilgrim club to which they belong, and which pays the expenses of a certain number of its members every year to go to some famous and sacred shrine. Mat sheds are erected at frequent intervals along the last stage of the journey, and at these free soup, free tea, or free gruel is often provided for the pilgrims, at the expense of some charitable society or pilgrim club. Bands of professional entertainers—*veau de ville* artists as they would be called in the West, sleight of hand performers, dancers—frequently go on pilgrimages and perform for the benefit of their fellow pilgrims without suggesting a remuneration or passing the hat. In short, the whole spirit at many of these pilgrim centers is one of cooperation, good will, and general helpfulness.

There are many pilgrimage resorts in Buddhist China; but four of them are peculiarly sacred. These are, of course, the four mountains consecrated to the four Great P'usas already referred to in a previous chapter, namely, the island of P'uto off the coast of Chekiang, sacred to Kwan-Yin; Mt. Omei in Szechuan, sacred to P'u-hien; Wu T'ai Shan in central Shansi, sacred to Wen-Shu; and Chen Hua Shan in Anhwei, just south of the Yangtse, sacred to Ti-tsang. To each of these, great streams of pilgrims, both lay and clerical, make their way every year, a few almost every day of the three hundred and sixty-five, but in large troops at the appropriate seasons. Nor are these the only goals of pilgrimage. China is dotted with sacred shrines to which religious journeys are made from greater or lesser distances. There are many of them especially near Hang-chow and in various parts of Chekiang. And hardly a day passes in the month before the rice is planted or during the pleasant weather of the autumn after harvest time, but one will find at least two or three peasants in most of these shrines, making the round of the holy places, buying a few incense sticks or candles and placing them reverently before the images of Kwan-Yin or one of the Buddhas, and trudging their weary way homeward with lighter pockets and lighter hearts and a contented smile upon their faces.

These pilgrimages are taken joyously, but, as I have said, also religiously and seriously. Occasionally one meets or hears of ascetic practices carried on by specially zealous pilgrims—walking for three days without food, kneeling or kow-towing every few steps on a pilgrimage of several miles, wearing chains or the garb of criminals, having oneself saddled and bridled like a horse and beaten by an attendant, piercing one's cheeks with a skewer. Extremes of this sort [10] are rare—very much rarer than in India, for example. But even the least zealous pilgrim is careful to conduct himself with propriety. Improper actions and even improper thoughts, he knows, must be avoided or the toil of his rather arduous journey will be wasted. Hence guidebooks are written for the monk and incidentally for the layman to give the pilgrim information as to both geography and conduct which may be useful to him. Mr. R. F. Johnston, in his delightful book on *Buddhist China* translates and paraphrases a considerable section of one of these books, and what he says of its preface in particular seems to me so enlightening as to be worth quoting at this point:

> The short preface urges the pilgrim, in general terms, to cultivate reverent and decorous habits of thought and conduct while engaged in the serious business of visiting the holy mountain shrines of Buddha. From his mind all feelings of vexation, hatred, and ill-will must be eradicated. Gentleness and compassion and humility of spirit must be his guiding principles. When he arrives at a shrine of Buddha let him bow his head and in due reverence worship the Three Holy Ones,—the Buddha, the Law of Buddha, and The Company of the Saints. Let him extirpate all thoughts of worldly ambition and personal gain; let him wholly cease from covetousness and selfish anger. The preface is followed by a page containing four precepts: Hold written characters in respect; Regard all living things with love and pity; Keep your mind from evil thoughts; Let your mind be directed unswervingly towards the Buddha.[11]

Not only guidebooks for pilgrimages are occasionally provided the Buddhist layman: guides for life's pilgrimage, in the form of moral and religious tracts, are frequently

[10] I have been told of one pilgrim who nailed his cheek to the wall of a temple and remained in this position for twelve hours.

[11] From Chap. VII, pp. 151-52.

printed by religious centers such as Hang-chow or gotten out by individuals and distributed gratis in thankfulness for an answer to some prayer or in fulfilment of a vow. These tracts usually proclaim the beauty of some well-known virtue or illustrate it by some shining tale. The virtue most stressed is the Confucian virtue of filial piety and of reverence for the "Five Relations"; after this come the more specifically Buddhist virtues of mercy and purity and the Five Vows, together with the consolations of religion and the hope that it brings. "So by precept and example, by threat of punishment here and hereafter, and by declaration of reward in the future, Buddhism has tried to maintain the family virtues of the Confucian system and has attempted to permeate them with the spirit of sacrifice." [12] Some of the tracts deal not with moral matters but with the delights of the monastic life, contrasting its ease with the toil and discomfort of life in the world.[13] A few tracts purport to have a supernatural origin, or to quote the exact words of some recent revelation, seeking by divine threats to terrify the readers into decency. A rather common form centers attention upon the praises of O-mi-to. One that came into my hands while I was in China was circulated in honor of the birthday of the great Pure Land Buddha, and signed by a committee for the propagation of Buddhism in Hang-chow. It consists of a sheet of thin paper about nine inches long and six wide, bearing on one side a brief account of the life of O-mi-to, and on the other the following injunction, in rather larger characters:

The 17th of the 11th month being the birthday of O-mi-to Fo, we ought to do the following things:

(1) Worship the Fo three times at home,
(2) Repeat the NAME at least ten times,
(3) Promise to pray for the people and the country,
(4) Forbid killing of living things, and refuse to eat meat for one day,
(5) Do philanthropic work according to our ability.

If you do the above five things you will get happiness and do away with suffering.

[12] Hodous, *op. cit.*, p. 34.

[13] Mrs. E. T. Williams, "Some Popular Religious Literature of the Chinese," *J.R.A.S.*, No. China Branch, XXIII. 11.

Besides these instructions there is a list of lecture dates and, in the middle of the page, the six characters of the Pure Land prayer or sacred formula: Nan Wu O-Mi-To Fo: with the injunction after them, "Read Reverently."

A peculiar class of institution that should here be mentioned is the Lay Buddhist Society or the vegetarion sects. Most of these trace their origin back to some of the many epochs in Chinese history when Buddhism has been under the imperial ban, when monastic life was forbidden or repressed, and religious organizations (other than Confucian) were looked upon with suspicion. At these times earnest Buddhists who felt the need of social encouragement in the religious life formed little groups and systems of groups which held secret meetings for the practice of Buddhist training and worship. They were secret societies but in the case of many the chief or only secret thing about them was their membership. They persisted through Manchu times, much to the perplexity and anxiety of the Government which frequently misunderstood their aim and persecuted them when it could. Their aim, I am told, has seldom been political, but it is not strange that the Government failed to realize this fact, considering the number and power of political secret societies that had made trouble for the various dynasties of China. Since the Manchu overthrow these religious societies have enjoyed a fair degree of prosperity, though in the first years of the Republic they were still objects of governmental suspicion. The largest of these societies is known in the north as the Tsai Li, in the south as the Tsai Chow, which means "within the religions"—a name intended to indicate the fact that the society seeks to mediate between the three religions of China. The northern branch (the Tsai Li) has thirty-one subordinate centers or organizations, several in Peking.[14] I have no figures for the southern branch (the Tsai Chow) but I am told it also is widespread and has a large membership.

Almost all the members are from the lower classes. They are rather simple people and they have but little Buddhist learning. They all worship Kwan-Yin and repeat Buddhist verses in the common Chinese way, thus combining prayer

[14] Hodous, *op. cit.*, p. 43.

and meditation. O-mi-to and his paradise plays a large part in their thought and so does Milei and his coming incarnation and regeneration of the earth. They do not frequent the temples and have no temples of their own. In both south and north they abstain from wine, tobacco, and opium, and in the south (though not in the north) they abstain also from meat. In the south a few of the middle class belong; in the north only the lower class. While they all worship Kwan-Yin, they make use of her image in the north, but not in the south. Many of the groups, both south and north, use in their meditation the verse so common in Hinayana lands, *Om mani padme hum,* and they have a theory that each of these syllables comes from a separate part of the abdomen or chest and that the repetition of the words brings them physical as well as spiritual benefit. Plainly there is some distant relationship between this and the breathing methods of the Hindus. Improvement of the health is thus one of the aims of the society, as is also moral and spiritual advancement. Mutual assistance is another of their aims. In most large cities there is a local headquarters for the society, whose location is kept secret from all outsiders, at which members can get help when they need it. I should add that it seemed to be the general impression of both the Chinese and the foreigners with whom I talked that the influence of the society on its members was decidedly of a moral sort, and that it was made up, as a rule, of good and earnest, if simple, men.[15]

[15] My statements concerning the Tsai Li are based on information given me by several Chinese gentlemen of my acquaintance. In his *Chinese Buddhism* (published in 1879) Edkins gives an account of a somewhat similar society (in Fukien province), the Wu-wei-Kiau, which seems to be partly Buddhist, partly Taoist. It is vegetarian, meditative, and non-ritualistic. It teaches that "Religion consists not in ceremonies and outward show, but in stillness, in a quiet, meditative life, and in an inward reverence for the all-pervading Buddha. Buddha is believed in but not worshipped" (*op. cit.*, Chap. XXIII). According to De Groot this sect, known also as the Sien-T'ien was founded under the Ming dynasty, and contains in its teachings a good deal of ancient Chinese and Taoist philosophy, though Buddhist thought is predominant. The members are mostly from the well-to-do classes. At their meetings they "recite fragments of Buddhist Sutras, formulas, and numerous names of Buddhas, or they repeat one name many times. . . . Besides, the meetings are devoted to pious conversation, particularly about the Five Commandments, to the faithful keeping of which they admonish and encourage each other" (*Sectarianism and Religious Persecution in China*, p. 190). Another society rather widespread in southeastern China is the Lung-hwa. This sect is made up of plainer people than the Sien-T'ien, and though it teaches the same mingled Buddhist and Taoist philosophy, and claims the same founder, it makes use of much ritual and of many Chinese gods (mingling on easy terms with Bodhisattvas).

As in most Buddhist lands, the more devout Chinese do more of their worshiping at home than in a group, whether that group assemble in a club or in a temple. In Southern China and in the Yangtse valley most Buddhist homes have an image or two of some member of the Buddhist cycle in their domestic shrines. Kwan-Yin is almost invariably one of these. If one steps into almost any of the house boats on the river front at Canton, in which so many families spend their entire lives, he will see, in what we might call the front room, a little shrine, with the familiar figure of the Goddess of Mercy, and a few other less easily recognizable images. In Chungking, fourteen hundred miles up the Yangtse, one comes occasionally upon a shop with a little shrine hidden away in a corner or on the back wall, holding always a Kwan-Yin and usually a Yo Wang (The P'usa of Medicine). Almost the only time I have ever made a Chinese angry was the occasion on which I asked one of these Chungking shopkeepers for how much he would sell me his Kwan-Yin.[16] The presence of private shrines in these two regions is particularly interesting because Canton and Chungking are notable for the decay of their Buddhist temples. So far as I could find out, the Buddhists of Peking and the north rather seldom have domestic shrines with images of Fos and P'usas in their homes. I have seen a few such home shrines in Peking, but I think they are rare.

The worship carried on in the domestic shrines in southern China consists largely in the reading or reciting of Sutras, or the repetition of sacred verses or the *Namu O-mi-to Fo.*

Like the Sien-T'ien its members are vegetarians and lay great emphasis on the five Commandments. In the variety of its ranks and the glory of the titles given to them, it rivals our own Ku Klux. It has an elaborate initiation ceremony. Sutra reading, usually accompanied by tappings on a wooden gong or a metal bell, forms an important part of their services; and as the members are usually illiterate, the reading is frequently recitation from memory with very slight understanding of the meaning of the words recited. As is the case with most of these lay Buddhist societies, Kwan-Yin is the chief recipient of the prayers. Most of the members are very devout worshipers of her, not only in their group meetings but in their domestic devotions. I should add that her kindly spirit seems to have been contagious, for her worshipers in these societies are said to be very kind and helpful to each other. The lay Buddhist society has broken through family lines and expanded the family affection of the Chinese so as to take in an immensely wider group than most Chinese outside of these sects ever find it possible to love and care for.

[16] It was a sacrilegious question on my part, and I honored the man for being angry with me. As a fact, I made the attempt chiefly to test his religion, and was glad to see him flare up.

This repetition is not very intelligent. The sentiment rather than the thought which accompanies the recital is important. Given the proper sentiment, the number of repetitions is the chief concern. These are counted sometimes on a rosary, sometimes on a "Sutra pagoda"—a roughly printed woodcut of a group of pagodas each made out of a certain Chinese character which by the addition of a single stroke of the brush may be made into the character for 100. Such a stroke is given at the completion of each group of 100 "prayers" or repetitions of a Sutra verse. But

> Sutra pagodas are more than substitutes for memory. By means of a seal of wood or stone they are stamped by the owner in the top corners with his name, and he also inscribes there his address, and any other information he desires to give to the Saints; and they are then forwarded to the abodes of bliss by means of fire, to be entered to his credit in the books of justice or to the credit of the departed for the salvation of whose soul he has done the good work.[17]

There are a good many ways in which the domestic worship may be carried on, varying in simplicity and length according to the zeal of the worshiper. Several of these I find described with some care in a popular little book entitled *A Guide Book for Those Not Advanced in Pure Land Knowledge*. The title sufficiently explains the purpose and nature of the book. It was written three or four years ago by the Tao-yin, or chief magistrate of Ningpo, in simple language and much zeal, for the benefit of those too unlearned or too busy to seek their salvation by the methods of the more sophisticated schools. One of the simpler methods of worship here recommended is the following (I quote the translation made for me by my interpreter):

> Either in the morning after getting up, or before going to bed, wash cleanly your hands, face the West and worship once, or bow yourself. You need only fold your hands and murmur Na-mu O-mi-to Fo, these six Syllables. Don't try to remember the times: also don't limit the number of times—just murmur them at one breath. With a long breath you may repeat the words a dozen times, with a short breath fewer. After reciting Buddha thus in ten breaths, say the names of Kwan-Yin and of three other great P'usas. Also say the "Simple Promise" once; then worship or bow once. That is finished. If you carry out this

[17] De Groot, *op. cit.*, I. 226-27.

method you shall succeed in going to the Western Paradise of O-mi-to. The "Simple Promise" prayer consists of eight sentences, namely:

> I wish to use this merit and virtue
> In the Pure Land of the Solemn Buddha
> To requite the four-fold grace on high
> To deliver the three Ways of Suffering.
> Everyone who sees and hears
> And has a pure heart within him
> And devotes all his body for the sake of his return,
> Shall be born in the Most Happy Land of the West.

The author of this little book makes a great deal of the value of "reciting Buddha," as he calls it; but he insists repeatedly that one must also keep the Five Precepts and "have three kinds of sincere heart." Mere verbal repetition, moreover, is of no value. One's mind should be concentrated and one's heart quiet if the recitation is to be of much value. The author tells us that some Buddhists find such recitation difficult; that when they begin to recite Buddha their hearts begin to feel very uneasy.

> A thought would pop up suddenly and suddenly fall down—so restless in this way. The harder I try to keep my heart quiet, the disquieter my heart becomes. [To such people, the author continues, he would reply as follows:] It is indeed not good to recite with the mouth and to think of other things. But the mind of an ordinary man is generally disorderly. How can he have a quiet mind when he begins practicing recitation? You need only to have a sincere heart, slowly and gradually you are sure to have a quiet mind. Moreover, the disorder in your mind has already been there, and is not due to reciting Buddha. For instance, we cannot see the dust in the air until the shining of the sun. Before reciting Buddha you are not conscious of your manifold thoughts. Reciting Buddha makes you conscious of them, that's all. When you feel that you have many thoughts, your mind has really improved to a quieter degree. You need only be patient and sincere in your recitation—you are sure to improve day by day.

I have quoted this passage because it throws some light on the Buddhist notions concerning prayer, showing, among other things, that the end sought is not merely salvation in the Pure Land but also an immediate improvement in one's own spiritual condition. It is, in short, subjective as well as objective worship. And there can be no doubt that the author evinces considerable psychological insight in his discussion. The subjective effect desired, I should add, is sought not only for its own sake but also because it is considered a step in the great effort toward disclosing and realizing the Buddha nature which, though disguised and hidden, is at least latent in all men.

The reverend repetition of a sacred name or verse or chapter may be of use not only in gaining eternal salvation but in warding off many purely temporal dangers, and should be practiced in all emergencies. In southeast China, it is usually performed before an image of Kwan-Yin. Many devout women, as I have indicated, keep such an image in their bedrooms or on a little household altar. "A common custom is to place a cup with some dry tea upon the altar, and when the recital is over to pour hot water on the tea and drink it, as highly beneficial to health; or else the tea is put away as a medicine for future use." [18] Kwan-Yin is thus singled out for particular and constant adoration for sound empirical reasons. She has repeatedly shown herself merciful by special providences. Your devout Buddhist can tell you of special answers to his own prayers; and some have known of actual visions of the blessed Goddess of Mercy, which she has vouchsafed to devout worshipers who have needed her help.

There is very little attempt among the Buddhist laity at the systematic religious education of their children, or the instruction of adults. There are no Sunday schools and no regular preaching services. The children pick up what they know by imitation and through incidental talks. Consequently, the influence of Buddhism upon the life of the Chinese layman is not nearly so great (if I may judge from what I have seen and heard) as it is upon the laymen of most other Buddhist lands. But so far as that influence goes it is almost unqualifiedly good. The Five Precepts are known by a good many, and especially the first of them, not to kill, is constantly emphasized. And here let me remind the reader once more that Buddhist books and Buddhist teachers when they are true either to the Hinayana or to the Mahayana do not confine themselves to the letter of this first great law but emphasize its spirit. For the true Buddhist it means

[18] De Groot, p. 225.

not merely to abstain from taking life but actively to save the life of all living things. In similar fashion the second Precept means not merely to abstain from stealing but to give what you have to the needy. The practical worldly sense of the Chinese and their family loyalty have prevented Buddhism from making the positive side of these Precepts as influential as they might have been with a people enjoying a wider social horizon. But Buddhism has had its very considerable though diffused and diluted effect. In China as in every other part of the Buddhist world, universal pity is one of the characteristic products of the religion. As usual, moreover, this is emphasized almost as much in relation to the animal world as toward human beings, and sometimes in a way that seems to us bizarre.[19] In some ways this feeling for animals has been most praiseworthy. There can be little doubt that the very general kindness, or even respect, paid to the cow all over China is a result of Buddhism; the ancient books indicate pretty plainly that it was introduced by Buddhism into China from India. It is to be wished that the same thing could be said of the dogs, for whom Buddhism has been able to do but little. One may say, however, that the quality of mercy is appreciated and admired pretty universally, even by those Chinese who do not practice it.

Among the more ignorant not much is known concerning the life and example of the Founder; but O-mi-to's vow and Kwan-Yin's mercy are common property. Especially does the figure of the Goddess of Mercy shine forth in real beauty and purity amid the callousness of the Chinese masses, like a good deed in a naughty world. Few mythical productions can equal Kwan-Yin for real moral beauty or breadth and depth of actual influence. She has a power over the imagination of the Chinese Buddhist world that is of incalculable moral value. Her influence, and that of Bud-

[19] The Kokwa Jichiroku, a Chinese Buddhist book of casuistry, says:

"To rescue one from capital punishment, one hundred goods (or units of merit) for each person rescued. For rescuing the life of horses, oxen, and other animals used by man, twenty goods for each life. For rescuing the life of such insignificant things as gnats, mosquitoes, ants, flies, and minnows, one good for each ten lives.

"To save the life of rats and snakes and other beings which inflict injury, one good for each life saved. Note: If a snake has not yet bitten a man, it does not merit death punishment. However great the injury inflicted by a rat, it never commits a deed sufficient to merit capital punishment" (*Transactions of the Asiatic Society of Japan*, XLII, Part II, 744-45).

dhism in general and its constant inculcation of mercy, is probably responsible for a large part of the charity which Chinese Buddhists have always shown toward certain classes of the needy. Professor Hodous, in his little book on *Buddhism and Buddhists in China*, quotes at some length the reply which a Buddhist preacher in Peking made to the question: "What can Buddhism do for the lower classes?" The reply was as follows:

"For this class Buddhism has the ten prohibitions. Every man has in him ten evils, which must be driven out. Three have to do with evil in the body, namely, not to steal, not to kill, not to commit adultery; four belong to the mouth, lying, exaggeration, abuse, and ambiguous talk; three belong to the mind, covetousness, malice, and unbelief."

"Is not this entirely negative?"

"Yes, but it is necessary, for during the process of eliminating these evil deeds, man acquires patience and equanimity. Buddhism does not stop with the prohibitions. The believer must practice the ten charitable deeds. Not only must he remove the desire to kill living beings, but he must cultivate the desire to save all beings. Not only must he not steal, but he must assist men with his money. Not only must he not give himself to lasciviousness, but he must treat all men with propriety. So each prohibition involves a positive impulse to virtue, which is quite as essential as the refraining from evil."

"What energizing power does Buddhism provide?"

"First, is purgatory with its terrors. The evil man, seeing the consequences of his acts upon himself, becomes afraid to do them and does that which is good. Then there is transmigration with the danger of transmigration into beasts and insects. Again, there are the rewards in the paradise of Amitabha. Moreover, there is even the possibility not only of saving one's self, but by accumulated merit of saving one's parents and relatives and shortening their stay in purgatory." [20]

To the more intellectual Buddhist, his religion means a great deal. In the lives of a number of Chinese gentlemen of my acquaintance Buddhism seems to be the central influence. It apparently dominates their thought and their activity and enables them, most of the time, to live upon a higher level of being. They get from it new insights and larger vistas. To the mystically minded it has much to offer. Professor Hodous, who for sixteen years was a Christian missionary in China, speaks of meeting by chance a Buddhist lady at a temple, in whose heart, he discovered

[20] P. 56.

there was "a genuine longing for God that overwhelmed all the artificial, the material distinctions and devices through which men have limited to particular and exclusive paths their way of search," and who was astonished to learn that Christianity could be as much an inner experience of the heart as Buddhism was to her. He tells also of a convert from Buddhism to Christianity who gradually discovered that he was not being nourished by his new religion and felt his joy slipping away from him, and who finally returned to Buddhism, where he found more of the consolation and inner peace that he longed for than was to be had in the mission church.[21] Another missionary told me of several converts from Buddhism who had become Christian pastors, and who had confessed to him (though they would not tell it to other missionaries) that from time to time they go back to the Lotus (the Saddharma Pundarika Sutra) for the spiritual help and the mystical nurture which somehow they do not get from their adopted religion.

What Buddhism and what the example of its Founder have meant to the real saints of China—and every generation, including our own, has its saints—may be seen from an episode in the life of Hiuen-Tsiang during his journey to India. He had been captured by pirates on the Ganges, who prepared to sacrifice him to Durga, their goddess. They had, in fact, bound him to the altar and were producing their knives for the bloody deed.

> When Hiuen-Tsiang saw there was no escape he spoke to the brigands and begged them to allow him a little time and not to crowd about him painfully, but "let me," said he, "with a joyous mind take my departure." Then with an undivided mind, bent on the Tusita heaven, he thought on Maitreya and earnestly prayed to be born in that place that he might pay reverence to the Bodhisattva and receive from him the Yogachariya-bhumi-sastra, and listen to the sound of the excellent Law. "Then having perfected myself thoroughly in wisdom," he prayed, "may I return and be reborn here below, that I may instruct and convert these bandits and cause them to practice good works and to give up their evil deeds, and thus by diffusing far and wide the benefits of religion, give peace to all the world."

As he thus prayed he seemed caught up into the Tusita heaven, "his body and soul were ravished with joy, he knew

[21] *Op. cit.*, pp. 2, 74.

nothing of the altar on which he was bound and completely forgot the robbers" who were to kill him.[22]

There are, I presume, not many to whom Buddhism means so much as to these deeper souls of whom I have just spoken. Yet Buddhism is a religion of such inwardness, with so little self-advertisement and display about it, that no one can tell the extent of its influence on the inner lives of many individuals who both cultivate and hide a deep spiritual experience under a conventional exterior. Still it would probably be safe to say that such semi-mystical experience is relatively rare in China; among the lower classes it may be very exceptional. For these simpler, less intellectual and less spiritual people Buddhism brings rather a sense of safety and of consolation and of hope, united with a little less callousness and a slightly greater gentleness of spirit. I remember meeting a rather simple old gentleman of the middle class in the rooms of the Fo Hua Shieh, or Buddhist Association, in Tsi-nan Fu, sitting alone, reading and meditating. I learned that he regularly spent hours there in this fashion. He told me he was very happy. He had not always been happy, for he had not always been a Buddhist. He was a merchant and till recently had had but little interest in religion. Some one had told him about Taoism and Buddhism, and had said that the Taoists possessed the ambrosia of life. He had, however, not accepted either religion at first. But on one of his business trips to Tsi-nan Fu he had drifted into the rooms of the Buddhist Association and there had heard some lectures on O-mi-to and the Pure Land. These had made a strong appeal to him, and through them he had become a Buddhist. Since then his life had been very much happier than ever before. Through Buddhism he had got rid of all worldly cares, for he had come to realize that money and possessions and all worldly things are vanity. So he had given up all desire for them and was now in possession of deep happiness.

Probably even this man's experience, though not uncommon, was hardly typical. Probably not many Chinese find

[22] *Life of Hiuen-Tsiang* (Beal), pp. 87-88. Not to leave the reader in permanent suspense, I should add that at this critical moment a tremendous storm arose and so alarmed the pirates that they unbound their victim who thereupon preached to them of the pains of hell and the joys of the Good Law, and so converted them all to Buddhism.

so much in Buddhism as he. But I feel sure that the dullest layman who is at all devout, as he sits rather stupidly repeating on his rosary the Namu O-mi-to Fo, would at least be able honestly to say of his simple Buddhist prayer what the monk in the preceding chapter said: "It helps your heart to say it over and over when you are in trouble."

CHAPTER XIX

THE BUDDHIST REVIVAL IN CHINA

EVEN in distant America one hears a good deal about the Buddhist revival in China. The phrase is becoming familiar and the subject attracts one's interest from afar. One determines, on reaching China, to investigate it, to talk with the revivers, observe their methods, and get statistics as to their results. On landing in China, one discovers that the subject is as baffling as are most things Chinese. A little information at second and third hand one can scrape together if one has good luck, but beyond that the process of investigation is a good deal like stumbling along in the dark. The immensities of oriental space and time get in one's way. One has to be satisfied with a very little.

So far as I can make out, the beginnings of the revival go back to the Boxer times. The anti-foreign and anti-Christian sentiment of those days seems to have roused a new sense of loyalty to the ancient faith which expressed itself among the common people in a greater religious zeal and among the upper classes by a new interest in the intellectual and also in the mystical side of Buddhism. Before 1900 Taoism seems to have been the favorite refuge for those who felt the need of religion; but, for some reason which I shall not attempt to guess, the turn of the century and the turmoil of the times shifted the weight of popularity from Taoism to Buddhism—at least in parts of northern and eastern China. Particularly in eastern Chihli there has been a notable increase of Buddhist zeal. How far this extends in other parts of the country I do not know, but it probably is felt at least slightly through most of the northeast.

A new impetus was given to the movement with the rise of the Republic. Since 1912 politics has been a great game —a game in which every possible kind of help is needed, natural and supernatural, and a game at which many must inevitably lose and which therefore rouses a new sense of world-weariness and a new demand for non-worldly consolation. Hence, it has come about, so I have been informed from many sources, that one of the chief classes participating in the Buddhist revival is to be found among the politicians and ex-politicians. Many men still in active politics find in the mystical side of Buddhism a much-needed relaxation—a kind of warm bath for the spirit—from which they may return to the world of men in both a kindlier and a more rested mood. And if at last they fail and are forced to retire from active politics, they find in Buddhist philosophy the comforting assurance that the game was never worth the candle anyhow, that this world is all a vain show and the winners have really won but a hollow prize; and in the abstractions of the Mahayana Sutras they find their attention pleasantly called away from vain reflections upon an unsuccessful past.

There is thus both a ceremonial, a mystical, and an intellectual side to the Buddhist revival. There is also an active side, seen in the charitable distribution of rice and tracts to poor Buddhists, and still better in the orphan asylums which have been instituted in a few cities and are supported by Buddhist zeal. There is a large one in Peking, connected with the Lung Chuan Ssu, in the southwestern part of the Chinese city. In Ningpo I found two orphanages, both supported and run by Buddhists. The children of these institutions are well cared for, carefully educated in the usual elementary subjects with modern methods, and in addition each is taught a trade. Daily worship in the Buddhist shrine is required, and the fundamentals of the Buddhist religion—especially the five Precepts—are inculcated. According to *The Young East*, a Buddhist monthly published in Tokyo, Shanghai Buddhists

> have recently distributed large numbers of sutras in condensed form among passengers on the Shanghai-Nanking Railway, while regularly holding once every month a lecture class on Buddhism for railway employees. Reformatory works for prisoners according to the principle of Buddhism was first undertaken in Chehkiang Province in 1919 and since that time similar work has been undertaken in the prisons of some other provinces with encouraging results. Succour of the poor also constitutes one of their important works, a remarkable activity being shown for the

relief of starving people in 1921 when North China was overtaken by a terrible famine.[1]

But most of the energy of the Buddhist revival goes into efforts at reform within Buddhism and attempts to propagate it. Not for years, I am told, have there been so many Buddhist books, pamphlets, and periodicals placed on sale and read by the intelligent public. Two new editions of the Chinese Tripitaka[2] have recently been gotten out, or at least started. One of these is merely a new printing of the former edition, the expense of publication being borne by a wealthy Buddhist lady. The other is a photographic reproduction of a really new edition, with modern and scholarly commentary, which is now in course of publication in Japan. But the aim of the leaders of the Buddhist revival is not to reproduce the ancient Buddhism but to purify the religion from the superstitions that have gathered round it, to harmonize it with modern science, and to spread abroad a knowledge of the essentials of Mahayana thought. As to what the essentials of Mahayana thought are the leaders naturally differ, some expounding the abstruse conceptions of the T'ien-t'ai or the Dharma-lakshana philosophies, some teaching the simple faith of O-mi-to and the Pure Land. A few of the leaders of the movement are very bitter toward Christianity, seeing in it, naturally, a great danger to Buddhism, and they attack it with ridicule and invective. This, however, is not commonly met with, Chinese Buddhists as a rule being men of very great liberality of mind. And even the most extreme critics of Christianity save some of their sharpest weapons to be used against the monks of their own religion. Some even go so far as to urge that monks should marry and live and work in the world with the laymen as the Christian clergy do. Even the traditional Mahayana does not always go unscathed, especially its failure to do more for women than it has done being frankly acknowledged and rebuked. The real spirit of the Mahayana, it is said, recognizes the equality of men and women, and for that matter the equality of all human beings. A frequent boast of Chinese Buddhists is that the Mahayana, since it

[1] *The Young East* for Jan., 1926, p. 272.
[2] The canonical books.

levels all differences, is the most democratic of all religions or philosophies.

Propaganda of Mahayana philosophy by means of periodicals is a difficult thing in China, because so few can read articles upon abstruse questions; and also because the Buddhist movement has no funds with which to support such periodicals as are published. Christian periodicals manage to keep the field because they are, as a rule, heavily subsidized. The Buddhist revival is as yet quite unorganized and has but slight funds. In spite of this it has a fair list of publications—as one can see by a visit to the Ta Fo Ssu, in the Eastern city, which is the Peking headquarters for Buddhist publications, and where also religious pictures and images, rosaries and gongs, and other objects of a similar nature are sold practically at cost to the Buddhist laity. There is another publication center in the West city. An organization called the Buddhist Propaganda Party has started work in the south and is publishing a paper, and distributing tracts of a religious and moral nature among the soldiers.[8]

A slight effort toward Buddhist revival is also made by preaching or lecturing services. In some of the larger monasteries in Peking, and especially in the suburbs, occasional preaching services are held. So far as I have been able to find out, there is only one place in the city in which there is a regular preaching or teaching service carried on at stated hours from week to week (namely, in the Kwang Chi Ssu on the street that leads to the P'ing Ts'e Men). Three times a week at this temple a learned layman expounds one of the Mahayana Sutras to a group of laymen. The morning that I visited it, there were in the audience thirty-six men and twelve women. Each was provided with a copy of the Sutra that was being explained, and all followed with evident interest the words of the lecturer.

In Chungking I was treated to one of those surprises which turn up every now and then in the study of Chinese Buddhism and which make one question the worth of all second-hand information concerning this elusive subject. We spent three weeks in or near this interesting city and

[8] *The Young East* for June, 1927.

one of my first undertakings was to visit the Buddhist temples and to question every one I could find as to the local condition of the religion. The unmistakably moribund condition of Buddhism in Chungking is the first impression one gets, and I was assured by a number of resident Americans and Englishmen that nothing further was to be said about the matter. I particularly inquired as to preaching services in Buddhist temples or signs of a revival of Buddhism. An English business man who had spent years in the city and was much interested in the religious situation assured me that there was no attempt at Buddhist revival in Chungking and never a preaching service in any of the temples. Two American missionaries of many years residence told me the same thing. Then, one morning, as I was strolling through the town, I dropped in for a second or third visit to the chief Buddhist temple, and found the place crowded with men and women, listening with great attention to a sermon by a monk. There must have been about three hundred in the audience. One of them told me that preaching services of this sort had been held in that temple every day, except in case of rain, for over three months, and that a genuine revival of Buddhism was taking place.

In Cheng-tu, the capital of Szechuan, a similar revival is being carried on. For most of my information on this subject I am indebted to Mr. A. J. Brace, a Y.M.C.A. secretary in that city, whose campaign for new members in the "Y" was seriously hurt by the Buddhist revival movement. He has kindly written out for me a statement which I shall simply insert without comment.

In the summer of 1922 disciples of the famous Monk T'ai Hsu journeyed from Shanghai to Chengtu in Szechuan Province to bring the modernized message of Buddhism as taught by their master. Their coming was the occasion of great rejoicing, and a real revival of Buddhism was the result. They had been heralded for more than a year and their way prepared by a wide circulation of T'ai Hsu's popular magazine "Hai Chao Yin"—"The Voice of the Sea," or "The Sound of the Tide." Very carefully edited articles had prepared the people for the visit of the missionaries, and the new message found a ready response even before their arrival. It brought a mesage of peace for the troubled days, and the magazine clearly stated that the new message was destined to lift the sublime teachings of the Mahayana Doctrine for the help of the people tossed about in the sea of modern doubt. The message was essentially spiritual and taught, or stood for, three propositions, (1) a real desire to reform monasticism, (2) a plan to reconstruct Buddhist theology along lines of modern philosophy, (3) to use the teachings of Buddha to elevate the people and improve social conditions. On the arrival of the missionaries, they were welcomed officially by the Governor of the Province. The sixteen daily papers all joined in a welcome, and gave columns to the new teaching, thus supplying a liberal supply of advertising. The opening meetings were attended by large crowds who listened attentively to the new program, and large numbers voluntarily enrolled themselves for the daily course to be given. In fact, a real program was gotten out, much like a university course, or a summer school curriculum, and fees charged for the course. Then daily the large hall in the Public Garden of the Manchu City was thronged with auditors to hear the public addresses, and the class rooms were filled with eager students to listen and follow the course throughout. A thorough course was given in the history of Buddhism, what it had done for the world, and how it had become encrusted with many superstitions. Now all was changed. The old simple story of the Enlightened One and how he found the way of salvation was declared. Idolatry was opposed, and in bygone days it was only tolerated as an accommodation to the weakness of the ignorant people. Now education was to be stressed, the priests had always been ignorant. A Buddhist university was to be established. The monks were to be encouraged to be busy as learners and servants of the people rather than follow the lazy lives of the past. The mercy of Buddha was taught and enjoined so that the wicked might be led to kindness, the selfish to righteousness, the hungry to find satisfaction in the doctrine. Most emphasized were the daily hours for fasting and meditation. A real revival was effected along these lines, and many of the foremost business and professional men took the vows and followed the course of meditation regularly. Many men who had not been interested in religion came under the sway of the new-found faith, and personally told me of the value of the hours of meditation and how their faith had been strengthened. The course on reading was followed widely. The students burnt incense daily as they read and meditated. At the meetings singing was indulged in, and often tunes quite similar to Christian tunes were used, and one song used with the refrain, "Take the name of Buddha with you." They even organized a Young Men's Buddhist Association which is going strong.

I was told by another Christian missionary that the Buddhists of Cheng-tu have also recently started several Buddhist schools in which both the Chinese Classics and the Buddhist religion are taught. Following the example of their brethren in Japan they have adopted Christian hymn tunes and put Buddhist words to them, for the school children to sing.[4] In addition to Cheng-tu, Chia-ting is also developing as a strong center of Buddhist revival, and with such success that it is becoming difficult for the Christian missionaries to make converts in that region.

There are two Buddhist organizations which should be mentioned in any account of the Buddhist revival, namely, the Li Shang Hui and the Young Men's Buddhist Association. The Li Shang Hui, or Buddhist Reform Society, antedates the movement we have been considering by a number of years. It was founded under the Manchu Dynasty, and its aim is not propaganda but moral reform. It is essentially what in America we should call a temperance society. Its aim is to prohibit the use of opium, tobacco, and alcohol among its members, and also the eating of meat. Its membership within Peking is said to be 10,000 and it has branches in all the provinces.[5] I asked the intelligent monk who runs the bookstore at the Ta Fo Ssu if he knew anything about the Li Shang Hui and he assured me he knew all about it. He confirmed several of the things I have quoted from Gamble, but added that he had little respect for the society. It is composed, he said, of very low people, and its work is not orthodox Buddhism.

The Peking branch of the Young Men's Buddhist Association was only about a year old when I reached Peking, and was still in a rather amorphous condition. Its headquarters were in one of the rooms of the Kwan-Yin Ssu, near the parliament building, and its equipment at the time of both my visits consisted of a set of teacups. Let not this be misunderstood, for in China especially—and in my personal opinion, all the world over—the teacup is a thing to conjure with. I can imagine no better center for the sort of helpful social intercourse this Young Men's Buddhist Association means to institute than the teacup, symbol of so much warm hospitality, so much intelligent discussion, so much friendly good will. Let no one belittle the teacup in my hearing! As to the membership of the association I must speak with less certainty. On my first visit to the head-

[4] This borrowing, I should add, has not been all on one side. The Christian missionaries have wisely adopted a few popular Chinese tunes which the Buddhists had been using and have fitted Christian words to them.

[5] See Gamble's *Social Survey of Peking*.

quarters I was told that they had two hundred members: on my second that they had five hundred. I do not think the membership really more than doubled during my absence. I think both answers were prompted by hope rather than by statistics, and that at my second visit hope had more than redoubled. For hopes should be mentioned along with tea-cups as a part of the really very useful equipment of the association. The officers of the association, I was told, planned to have several schools, a Buddhist university, and many preaching places. Already, they assured me, the association conducted regular preaching services at the Kwan-Yin Ssu once or twice a week (they were a little vague as to whether it was once *or* twice), and they published a journal, which was supported in part by the emperor and which counted many Japanese among its subscribers. These two were the only activities, they said, which were really started, but they hoped to open some of their schools in the spring. On taking my leave I unfortunately inquired as to the size of the audience at their biweekly preaching service, and was told that in the spring they hoped to have a large attendance; but that as a fact just at that time they hadn't any preaching services at all. Since my visit (I am informed) the association has temporarily disbanded.

The Young Men's Buddhist Association in Hankow—the real headquarters for all China—has much more of solid achievement to show. I speak of it as the Young Men's Buddhist Association though its local name is the Hankow Buddhist Society. It was started in 1921 and has now a large and excellent building of its own, with an auditorium, a temple, a lecture or preaching hall, reception parlors, offices, and a primary school for boys. The Society, I was told, has three thousand members in Hankow. In the lecture hall there is a preaching service every evening. I was not present at the service, as I was a little too early for it, but twenty or thirty men and women had already gathered in the hall before I left. Besides these things they too have their hopes and plans—plans some of which, they assured me, were on the verge of being accomplished. Among these are to be mentioned a middle school, and a high school for poor boys, a nurses' training school, a vegetarian restaurant, men's clubs, and places for the study of the Sutras. They already have a place outside the city where laymen may retire for meditation. They also publish the periodical of the World Buddhist Association, and are the headquarters of the World's Women's Buddhist Association which is just being organized.

There are three resident monks in the headquarters, who lead in the religious services. One of these services I attended, where I found nine laymen and seven boys chanting the Sutras, under the leadership of a monk, with a good deal of unmistakable fervor. The resident monks, I should add, have little to do with running the Association. It is emphatically a layman's movement, and it has evidently a good deal of strength in this region. I was told that across the river, in Wu Ch'ang, there is another branch of the Young Men's Buddhist Association, and that all told the Association has in the Province of Hupeh upward of 20,000 members.

The aspect of the revival movement which I suppose is most in harmony with the Chinese genius is the effort that is being made for the spread of a scholarly knowledge of Buddhist thought. There are two or three Buddhist colleges where serious study is given to the Mahayana Sutras, under the direction of really able scholars. One of these centers is Mr. Ouyang's college in Nanking. The institution is small: at the time of my visit it had but twenty regular students and ten graduate students or investigators. But the work done is of a serious nature and the young laymen that go out from Mr. Ouyang's instruction are well grounded in Mahayana metaphysics, and some of them are qualified to extend to others some insight into the mysteries of this very difficult philosophy. Study of a less systematic but still serious and advanced sort is sometimes carried on by some of the great monastic centers of Buddhism, such as P'utow and Wu-t'ai-shan. In these and similar places learned monks train a few promising young members of the order; and so much of this training as is really sound may properly be classed as a part of the Buddhist revival. The movement as a whole is emphatically a layman's movement, and the average monk, such as one usually finds chanting at funerals or loafing in temples, has no part nor lot in it. Yet if one were asked to name one man as the leading spirit of the present effort to revive Buddhism, there is little doubt what name should be chosen. Nine men out of ten acquainted with the situation would answer the question by the name of the monk T'ai Hsu.[6] T'ai Hsu has earned this distinction by combining in himself, as no one else has done, the intellectual and the religious sides of the movement. Some regard Mr. Ouyang as the sounder scholar and deeper thinker, but Mr. Ouyang's interest in Buddhism is chiefly intellectual. T'ai Hsu is both scholar, thinker, and mystic. He is in the late thirties or early forties, rather under the average height, with shaven head and monk's garb, quite near-sighted and having the quiet prosaic air of the scholar, yet somehow giving one the sense that in spite of his thick glasses he has seen things which the rest of us hardly guess. Some time after entering the order he shut himself up for a period of three years in a monastery in P'utow, with his books and his thoughts and his undisturbed solitude. Since 1914 he has been teaching. At first he taught at Hang-chow; but early in 1922 when ex-governor Li of Kwangtung, an enthusiastic Buddhist, founded a new Buddhist college at Wu Ch'ang, T'ai Hsu was called to be its head. It was there that I met him. After a pleasant interview I was permitted to attend one of his lectures. At the lecture were sixty-three students, all but five of them being monks. T'ai Hsu lectured without notes and very easily, making constant use of the blackboard. Each student had a copy of the Sutra that was being expounded, and followed the lecture eagerly, taking careful notes. I gathered from what my interpreter told me that his lectures were less abstruse than those of Mr. Ouyang. His influence must be considerable. If sixty monks, or half that number, can be sent out every year with his impress upon them, there is still hope for Chinese Buddhism.

At a meeting of Chinese and Japanese Buddhists held in Tokyo, in November 1925, T'ai Hsu outlined his program for a general revival of Mahayana Buddhism as follows:

[6] I am told that in the opinion of many the monk Yung Kuang (originally from Shensi Province), whose headquarters are in P'utow, is quite as influential in the revival movement as T'ai Hsu.

> The first thing we should do is to organize an International Buddhist University to train men for the propagation of Buddhism. In the said institution, there should be two departments: one is to teach the students such liberal subjects as languages, sciences and philosophies and the other to teach the Buddhist sutras, religious disciplines, Buddhist esoteric teachings, etc. Besides the educating of the monks, we should preach Buddhist doctrines to the masses by means of schools, publications, lectures and dramas. The preaching should take place in the market places, on the highways, in trains and on boats, in soldiers' barracks, hospitals, factories and prison wards. Our immediate object should be to teach the masses such good virtues as loving their fellow men, obeying the law of the land, diligence in the pursuance of their daily avocations, muttering of prayers and names of the Buddha, etc., etc. Our social services should be (1) famine relief work, prevention of natural calamities and medical aid to those wounded in war, (2) promotion of industry by establishing factories and encouraging land reclamation, (3) aiding such helpless people as the aged and crippled persons and helpless widows, and (4) to build bridges and roads and provide street lights, free ferry services and such like public utilities for the travelers.[7]

T'ai Hsu summed up his aim, in a conversation with me, by saying that he longed to make Buddhism known as it really is. He is the more hopeful that his effort in this direction will bear fruit because it is in response to a real demand. Chinese students are returning every year from Europe and America, or graduating from colleges in China, and demanding to know what Buddhism is. The question, he insists, must be answered from Chinese sources—from the great Mahayana Sutras—and in a scholarly and philosophical way. His primary aim is, therefore, scholarly and philosophical. Solid knowledge and solid thinking must form the basis of anything lasting in the way of a Buddhist revival. Only indirectly does he hope to spread Buddhism among the common people. I told him of certain degenerate conditions I had found in Shansi Buddhism, and asked him whether he hoped to do anything to regain such regions as this to the Buddhist faith. "Not directly," was his answer. But he wishes to make the truth of Buddhism shine forth, and he believes that once this is done, it is bound to conquer. Had he spoken Latin instead of Chinese he would probably have said, "*Magna est veritas et praevalebit.*"

Yet, as I have already said, his interest is decidedly re-

[7] *The Young East*, I. 181-82.

ligious as well as philosophical, and while intellectual instruction is the weapon upon which he chiefly relies, he uses others as well. In marked contrast to Mr. Ouyang's college, daily worship at the very attractive little temple is a part of the training given at T'ai Hsu's institution, and in this he himself regularly takes part with all his students. He also publishes a religious periodical, and has organized a World's Buddhist Association, which has an annual meeting every summer for lectures and discussions. It is characteristic of his liberal attitude of mind that in 1923 one of the addresses at this Buddhist convention was given, at his invitation, by an equally broad-minded Christian missionary, upon the doctrine of the Logos.

The effect of the revival campaign undertaken by various leaders is beginning to be felt in many parts of China. A few pages back we saw its rather striking success in Cheng-tu—a thousand miles from T'ai Hsu's headquarters. Less startling but perhaps equally lasting results it is doubtless producing in the heart of many a thoughtful and quiet man and woman who says little or nothing about it. Buddhist devotion has a way of hiding itself in unsuspected places. It seldom wears its heart upon its sleeve, and it never does much advertising. The week before we left Peking my Fellow Pilgrim and I were asked to a dinner given at the house of a distinguished admiral, an earnest Buddhist, where we found as our fellow guests a group of thirty young women and girls who constituted a kind of Buddhist school or unofficial convent. Our host, the admiral, explained to us that during the dark days of disillusion that followed the inauguration of the Republic, he and two other gentlemen, appreciating the evil condition of the times, cast about to see what they could do to better them. They decided that the hope of the land lay in Buddhism. Hence they not only deepened their own devotion to their religion, but they founded this Buddhist school or order for their daughters and the daughters of a few of their friends. The girls have entered into the spirit of the enterprise; they study the Sutras diligently and hear lectures, dress very simply, live on plain vegetarian fare, and have decided to live celebate lives of meditation and service. The school had been in existence three years at the time we dined with the girls. It was to me rather significant and rather typical of the Buddhist dislike for publicity that I had spent five months in Peking seeking for just this sort of thing before I happened upon the school, and that the best informed resident Europeans I met—men deeply interested in Buddhism—had never heard of it.

This school of girls was the product of a combination of the ancient monastic spirit and of the modernized form of Buddhism which the revival is stimulating. The same combination of influences I do not doubt is making itself felt in many parts of the land, and hiding itself away in quite as inconspicuous a fashion as in the girls' school. A few years ago one of T'ai Hsu's religious periodicals published a letter written by a young woman to the editor, part of which I reproduce herewith, and which, I expect, represents the aspirations of more than one Chinese girl:

Formerly I was a student at a school, and was not inclined to believe in Buddhism. Later unconsciously my faith sprang up and then I became convinced that the Law of Buddha is the absolute and only true religion, unbounded and most lovable. So at the age of 19, I made a vow before Buddha, that in this life I would never marry but give my life to Him as a nun. I have kept this vow for four years, and many times I wanted to shave off my hair, but was prevented by my parents. I am sorry that I cannot be a nun early in life. I have three friends with the same mind. One is married, but she daily thinks of shaving off her hair and "forsaking the world"; only she is prevented from doing so by her husband. But she is persuading him to become a monk, and I won't be surprised if they two should "forsake the world" together before the end of the year. (For a girl to be able to shave off her hair and be a nun it is the most happy thing. Now-a-days some nuns complain that their lives are unhappy, while the lives of lay-folk are happy. I really cannot understand their way of thinking.) The other two friends were both my school-mates. One is called "Pure-root"; she has no parents, but a brother—none to prevent her—and so she became a nun in the spring of last year. The other is only 18 and yet her determination to "forsake the world" is unusually strong. This year her mother wanted to betroth her to someone, and so she decided to leave home secretly. I recommended her to a certain nunnery. Of us four, two have already realized their wish, leaving my cousin and myself outside the fold. I feel grieved and also envious of their good fortune. At first we thought that by becoming nuns we would escape from the world's misery and sorrow, enjoy peace, and work off by penance some of our sinfulness. Furthermore, by becoming nuns we sisters could live together and never be separated, which is supreme joy. But now after reading Hai Chao Yin, we know that "to forsake the world" is to benefit others, not ourselves. Having known this my will to be a nun has become stronger than ever. I wish that I could now and here shave off my hair.[8]

I am not oversanguine as to the success of the Buddhist revival in China. It is an interesting movement and on the part of many of its leaders and followers an earnest and a deeply religious movement. But it will hardly set China on fire. For the matter of that, China seems to me pretty safely fireproof. We may, however, hope that the Buddhist revival will be one of many influences to check the advance of materialism in thought and life, to hold up a standard around which the lovers of the loftier ideals may rally, and to build up the nobler China that is to be.

[8] Quoted by Yu Yue Tsu in an article on "Present Tendencies in Chinese Buddhism," *Journal of Religion*, I. 510.

CHAPTER XX

BUDDHIST THOUGHT IN CHINA

THE preceding chapter and also the one before it have both dealt, incidentally, with certain aspects of the thought of Chinese Buddhism; but the subject is too large and too important to be passed over in purely incidental fashion. To be sure, Chinese Buddhism believes and thinks in accordance with the general philosophy of the Mahayana which we have already considered. But there are changes and variations of some interest in it, and if the reader's point of view is the same as mine he will care to know the living beliefs and problems of our Buddhist contemporaries in China quite as much as the philosophic doctrines of ancient Sanskrit Buddhism. Unfortunately the subject is as difficult and uncertain as it is interesting. For China is a large place and contains a good many people and a good many ideas; and not only are there considerable diversities of belief within Chinese Buddhism, but much of its thinking is peculiarly elusive to the Western mind. Moreover, while a good deal has been written on the Mahayana philosophy in general, I have been able to find relatively little, in either books or periodicals, about contemporary Chinese Buddhist thought. A large part of this chapter, therefore, will have to be based on material that I managed to scrape together piecemeal, in conversations with monks and scholarly Buddhist laymen and well-informed foreigners. My presentation will thus be necessarily incomplete and must not be taken as in any sense final. Much of importance I shall doubtless leave untouched, and the relative amount of space I shall give to the different beliefs or forms of thought will certainly be out of proper proportion. But what I shall say will, I hope, be worth reading: for, with all its shortcomings, it will at any rate be based largely upon first-hand information.

With so difficult a theme before us it will be well to begin with the easiest part. I shall, therefore, first take up some of the more popular beliefs of Buddhism, such as are held by the mass of half-educated monks and laymen, and go on gradually to the more involved conceptions of the scholars and thinkers. Between these two extremes there is a great variety of views, but all are Buddhist and are recognized as such.

It is seldom that one Buddhist says another Buddhist is mistaken, no matter how he may disagree with him; and it is very rare indeed that one Buddhist will say of another's belief, That view is un-Buddhistic, or It is heresy. In fact, Buddhist tolerance, as a rule, goes out far beyond the fold of Buddhism. I remember being told by the old abbot of T'an Che Ssu that not only Shih-chia Fo and O-mi-to were expressions of the divine revelation, but that the same was true of Confucius and in fact of all holy men. A monk in another of the temples in the Western Hills asked a visiting missionary, who had been brought there by a friend of mine, to burn a little incense to the Buddha. The missionary refused, saying that he and the monk had different gods. To which the old Buddhist replied, "But, sir, there is only one God." In the "Southern Monastery" on the island of P'utow I was discussing with one of the monks the question of the future life. He was impressing upon me the need of faith in the Buddha: but he interrupted himself to add very quickly that Christians who believe in Christ and are good men will go to heaven. Of course there are many heavens—"many mansions" in the Father's house—and Christians can hardly expect to reach as high as Buddhists. Yet a monk in Soochow, noting with delight my interest in his religion, encouraged me to think that in my next incarnation I might be a Lohan (and how I shall enjoy braiding my eye-brows!), and both a Pekinese monk and a monk at Chieh Tai Ssu assured me that all good people whose hearts at death are pure will go even to the Western Paradise of O-mi-to. Yes, this included Christians also; for Christianity, one of the monks insisted, is really a branch of Buddhism, and good Christians are not merely good people morally but are really good Buddhists without knowing it. Not many monks, I think, would go quite this far. But appreciation of what is fine in other religions and honest good will and good hope for all is a universal Buddhist characteristic. Miss Bredon in her book on Peking tells of asking the abbot of the Fa Yuan Ssu why there were tablets on the altar of his temple for the souls of the European soldiers who were killed in the Great War. "Do you not realize," she asked, "that none of these soldiers were Buddhists?" "Yes," he answered; "but may we not admire the beauty of their sacrifice? and are not all faiths fundamentally alike in that they desire the good of all mortals? In your Christian churches do you not pray for the salvation of all and believe in it?" [1] Miss Bredon could not give an affirmative answer to this question.

Most of the more important beliefs of popular and unphilosophical Buddhism I can go over briefly. In the opinion of nearly all the simpler Buddhists, Shih-chia Fo, O-mi-to, and the other Buddhas are existing personalities, who have never merged their being in a Nirvana of the Hinayana type. And not only do they continue to exist: many Buddhists consider them also in some sense active beings. They are working in this world of ours, although invisibly. Sometimes it is suggested that they do their work through the P'usas, to whom (in the form of the Sambhogakaya) they appear and whom they instruct, inspire, and direct. The P'usas, also, are of course conceived as real and blissful beings: and, as we have seen, petitional prayers are often directed to both these classes of divinities (for, as pictured by the simple Buddhist, the non-Buddhistic name *divinity* would fit them very well). The P'usas, on the whole, are much more active than the Fos. Ti-tsang, for example (so I was told by a monk in Soochow) takes various forms for various helpful purposes. He has come so near to Buddhahood that he has stripped off the limitations of particular personality and so is indifferent to all form and also to all place. Certainly he is to be found on his sacred mountain, Ch'iu Hua; but he may also be met with here in Soochow, 1000 *li* away. You or I might meet him at any time and not know it was he. The P'usa Maitreya—Milei-Fo—is somewhat different from the rest. He is in heaven, awaiting the day of his appearance. The Chinese, like the Bud-

[1] *Peking* (Shanghai, Kelly and Walsh, 1922), p. 219.

dhists of most other lands, look forward to his appearance and expect the usual marvelous and delightful rearrangement of the earth when he arrives.

As to man, there is, of course, no such sharp dividing line between him and the Fos and P'usas as exists between man and his gods in most other religions. Many of the Fos themselves were once men—for the matter of that, they were once animals as well—and all men have within them unlimited possibilities. The fundamental Mahayana view that the Buddha nature is in all men has found a ready echo in the minds of the Chinese, who for ages before Buddhism reached their land had been taught by Confucius—and probably by sages long antedating Confucius—to believe in the essential goodness of human nature. I remember visiting a primary school in Nanking—tiptoeing in unobserved, attracted by the hum of twenty boyish voices repeating the lesson aloud, as is the custom throughout the East. When the master spied me he had one of the little fellows recite by memory about half the primer—a book made up of sentences from the classics. The first sentence of all was the following: "In the beginning man was born good." This doctrine the Chinese have always learned in early childhood and have always believed; so it has not been difficult for them to think this Chinese thought in the more metaphysical Buddhist way, and to look within their own hearts, once purified and made "sincere," for the Buddha.

This view of human nature has fitted well with the universalism of the Indian faith. The upward path may be long for some and difficult, but it is never hopeless.[2] The views of the more scholarly and philosophical Buddhists as to the fate of man after death I shall refer to later on in the chapter, for it can hardly be discussed until we have dealt with more fundamental metaphysical questions. The simple beliefs of the rank and file of monks and laymen can be rather briefly recited. If I may trust the various answers I got to my questions concerning the next life, transmigration seems to hold a more prominent place in the thoughts of

[2] So at least nearly all Buddhists believe. I met a monk at Chieh Tai Ssu, in the Western Hills, who said that some unfortunate sinners never get out of hell; but this view is most exceptional.

Chinese Buddhists than in the Buddhism of Siam. Still, heaven and hell are certainly quite as prominent. The usual answer to a question concerning human fate is that the bad go to hell and the good to heaven, while those who are neither very good nor very bad are reborn in this world. Often further information is proffered that after a stay of considerable duration in heaven or hell, the good and bad are born once more as men. One monk made the additional remark that "Heaven is a very dangerous place." It is dangerous because by going there one is likely to be filled with pride; and this great sin will inevitably result in an undesirable rebirth on one of the three evil Paths,[3] or possibly as a man. But if rebirth is a common thought, not many Chinese are very clear about it. One monk, rather better read than the average, told me there were three stages on the upward path. The first consists of seven lives, and if one has been faithful and obedient to the Buddha in all these, one goes on to the second stage, which consists of three lives. This leads to the third stage which is forever. In it we shall go where we please and be free from the senses and leave the body behind. But, he mused, it is difficult to say what one can be thinking about when no senses are left and no body.

In a conversation with a group of monks in one of the large monasteries on the island of P'utow, a leader of the group told me that there were three classes of men: (1) those who disobey the Dharma and do not believe in the Fos; these at death are reborn as animals. (2) Those who believe in the Fos and are not bad, but are not devout and do not work for others; these are reborn as men. (3) Those who have devoted their hearts to the Fo and help other men to come to him; these become Fos and P'usas and live in heaven. At this point in the conversation the small boy refilled our teacups from the pot on the brazier; and either the fresh tea or the remarks of the spokesman stimulated the minds of the other monks who sat around the large table opening melon seeds with their well-nicked teeth. A lively conversation followed, with much writing of imaginary characters in the air, and finally my interpreter told me the other monks did not agree wholly with what had been said concerning

[3] Hell, the animal world, and the world of hungry ghosts.

the fate of the second class: such men as these, they insisted, go to heaven and are not reborn. I had the ill nature to ask what was the difference between the fate of the second class and that of the third, for both apparently go to the same place. This was a puzzler. The best solution they could work out, after some twenty minutes' discussion, was that the men of the second class probably do not stay forever in heaven, but are reborn as men upon earth; whereas those of the third class remain in heaven forever. But it was plain they had never thought much about the subject till I asked them.

One noticeable fact about popular Chinese descriptions of the next life, as compared with what one finds in Southern lands, is the absence of any reference to Nirvana or its equivalent. The nearest approximation to it that I heard from any of my clerical acquaintances was the expression "becoming Buddha." This is common enough. Its meaning is usually left quite vague. One intelligent monk in Soochow, however, whom I pressed upon the subject, gave me a fairly definite answer. The state of becoming Buddha, he said, can be conceived only negatively. We can tell what it is *not* by denying all details. If one attains to Buddhahood there is nothing left of personality. All individual characteristics are gone. What is left is the essence of Buddha and of all the Buddhas. One who has attained this state may take any form, for he has no form of his own.

The followers of Pure Land Buddhism have, of course, a much more vivid and clear-cut picture of the next life than other Buddhists. O-mi-to's famous Eighteenth Vow is well known in China, and thousands are trusting that He will bring to the Pure Land—the glorious Western Paradise—all those who respect his name with faith believing and whose faith has kept them from the worst of sins. O-mi-to's Paradise is pictured, in the Chinese imagination, as a glorified Buddhist temple with elaborate and beautiful grounds. One may find colored pictures of it in various headquarters of Buddhist propaganda. In the center sits O-mi-to, on his lotus throne, with Kwan-Yin and Ta-shih-chih on either side. Surrounding him are the Lohans and many P'usas, while in the large pond before him grow unnumbered lotus flowers and from the heart of each flower is born a redeemed soul. It is faith and the grace of O-mi-to that bring one to this second birth: yet some of the old Buddhist feeling is still preserved in one account of the Pure Land which teaches that if one's sins are great, the lotus in which one is born will not open till after many years.

The repetition of the Namu O-mi-to Fo is at all times helpful. It is particularly so at the hour of death. But, as the *Guide Book for Those Not Advanced in Pure Land Knowledge* [4] points out, it is probable that only good Buddhists who have cultivated right habits and devout thoughts will be able to "recite Buddha" at that critical moment. The habit of devout prayer not only prepares one for the hour of death but it builds up one's stock of merit and makes one's future abode more beautiful. "When a person in this world prays it makes a lotus grow in Paradise. When a person dies O-mi-to and Kwan-Yin and Ta-shih-chih take the lotus his prayers have made and receive him into Paradise. He then grows out of the lotus. But if in this world one begins to pray and then neglects his prayers, his lotus in Paradise will decay, and if he never prays any more his lotus will vanish."

"There is no woman in the Western Paradise: because women who are saved are born there as men. For womanhood implies pain, and there shall be no pain there." "Three ideals characterize all those in the Western Paradise: self-control, unchangeableness, wisdom." "In the Western Paradise there will be no more sorrow, death, or sin." In contrast to it, this world is a sad place. "Man's body is very unstrong [so my interpreter translates]. When it is hurted he will be die." Therefore we ought to realize that the body is very unimportant and pay attention only to character, so as to reach the Pure Land of O-mi-to.

The beliefs thus far discussed in this chapter are those one finds among the less philosophical Buddhists. They are the simple views of rather simple people, comparable in a way to the simple faith of simple Christians, innocent of philosophy. From this point on things will begin to thicken up. My information concerning the opinions of the more

[4] From which I quoted in the previous chapter.

philosophical Buddhists is drawn in part from conversations with a few Chinese thinkers and a few foreign scholars in different provinces, in part from articles in periodicals (English and Chinese), but chiefly from a number of very helpful discussions I was fortunate enough to have with a group of about a dozen Buddhist gentlemen in Peking. We met first on the invitation of my friend, Mr. Yen Te Ching, and dined together at a vegetarian restaurant. Several other philosophical symposia followed, at the homes of some of the members of the group. It was for me a rare opportunity, as it gave me some insight not only into the doctrines of the books and sects but into the working of thoughtful Buddhist minds as well.

All Chinese Buddhist thinkers, so far as I know, accept the ancient Indian view of the two levels of truth and reality. This must be kept in mind when one hears the rather common assertion of Buddhist philosophers that the true and the false, the real and the unreal are one. This assertion refers only to the lower realm—the world of appearance (as we in the West would call it.) On the higher level all is true; hence there are no distinctions within it. (So Mr. Ouyang of Nanking, perhaps the foremost Buddhist scholar in China, explained it to me.) In the lower realm nothing is completely true; so there also no ultimate distinctions exist. But there is a real distinction between the two realms. The higher realm, Mr. Ouyang added, we may reach by intuition after much study. It cannot be reached by either study and logic nor by intuition alone. Since no assertions concerning the lower realm can be entirely true, and all may contain some truth, the characteristic tolerance of Buddhism is logically justified. All sorts of symbols are defensible if appropriate, and different symbols may properly be used with different kinds of people. Your typical Buddhist philosopher not only tolerates but has faith in even the naïve Pure Land teachings. But, as Keyserling would put it, he does not confuse *faith* with *believing to be true*. The loving personal O-mi-to, the brilliant pictures of the Pure Land, all these things are useful symbols of the truth. Already in the Lotus Sutra, Sakyamuni points out his elastic method of presenting the truth as an example of the "skillfulness" of the

Buddhas—the famous "method of adaptation." As Professor Francis Wei puts it,[5] "Any kind of teaching and any way of preaching is Buddhist provided it leads to enlightenment; for when enlightened, one will see the difference between truth and falsehood or rather the non-existence of both and hence the non-existence of any such difference."

This doctrine of the two realms explains to some extent the Mahayana attitude toward morality. Insight transcends morality. Morality is on the lower level and hence is only approximately real or true. The aim of Buddhism is to reach a plane of being that is beyond both the good and the bad—*jenseits von Gut und Böse*. In all this, of course, Western absolute idealists of Mr. Bradley's school would agree. Morality tends ever to transcend itself. Yet the Mahayana, since it deals tentatively with the world of appearance, does not obliterate all moral distinctions. These distinctions are real as far as they go; they are as real as anything in this lower realm can be. Buddhism, said Mr. Ouyang to me, recognizes three things: insight, contemplation, morality. Insight is the aim: but it can be attained only through contemplation, and successful contemplation presupposes morality. This was true even for Sakyamuni in his earthly life. Insight is like pure water which reflects like a mirror. Contemplation makes the water pure, and morality protects it.[6]

On the more fundamental metaphysical problems, the Buddhist thinkers of China are not entirely at one. The Left, as it would probably be called in Europe, expresses itself chiefly in negatives and consciously distinguishes Buddhism from other forms of thought by its insistence upon negating what the rest of the world believes in. Thus Mr. Liang Chi Chao—perhaps the foremost man of letters in China—asserts[7] that Buddhism consists essentially in the denial of personality. What is commonly called personality is really a combination of will, feeling, thought, etc.; or better still, a succession of pulses of consciousness. Each of these

[5] In a letter to me.

[6] This position of Mr. Ougang's is extraordinarily faithful to both Buddhism and the traditional emphasis of China on the value of study and the importance of morality. A typical Indian Buddhist, I think, would have made much less of both these latter things.

[7] In an article in a Chinese periodical, translated for me by my friend, Mr. Millican of Ningpo.

pulses is separate. There is nothing back of them, no substance or subject, nor any sort of permanent entity. Impermanence is the truth. More in detail, the phenomena of mind are analyzed into five parts: [8] (1) Seemingly objective things—colors, forms, etc., which the naïve realist takes for material objects. These are really subjective and must be interpreted idealistically. (2) The power of perception. (3) the power of retaining, recalling, and imagining. (4) Activity of body and of thought, notably discernment and the power of choice; and including all the powers of mind except those set down under (2) and (3). Finally, (5) Consciousness. This is the most difficult of all to explain. It is the ability to experience and differentiate. It is the unity which is the recognizer. But it, like the rest, is impermanent, dependent, with no lasting self-identity, and hence unreal. There is no physical world and the psychical world is made up of appearances with nothing substantive about them. This, in Mr. Liang's opinion, is the essence of the Buddhist classics. It is plain that it is one way of harmonizing Hinayana and Mahayana: for it singles out a point of view common to both and makes it and it alone decisive. It is plain, moreover, that this view is closely related to the Madhyamika of Nagarjuna. In fact, one could find ample justification for it in the Sutras and the Commentaries, not only of the Madhyamika but of several other Buddhist schools. While the tendency of popular Buddhism and of many Buddhist thinkers in China and Japan has been decidedly away from this seemingly nihilistic view, it is interesting to see that it still retains a following in China.

To a considerable extent the monk T'ai Hsu, the leader of the movement for the revival of Chinese Buddhism and one of the representatives of the T'ien-t'ai philosophy, might be set down as belonging to this negative school, though, as we shall see, he has more to say than mere negation. In the periodical which he edits (the Hai Chao In) there were published, a little while ago, a letter from an inquirer and T'ai Hsu's reply, both of which I found of interest. The inquirer was emotionally drawn to Buddhism but his reading of Western science had made it difficult for him to accept

[8] These, of course, are the five *Khandas* of the Nikayas.

the idealistic interpretation of reality. Geology in particular made him trouble: for how explain the world as the product of consciousness during those long ages before consciousness arose? It will shed some light on the Buddhist form of idealism to quote part of T'ai Hsu's reply, as translated for me by Mr. Millican:

> There is not much connection between Buddhist philosophy and any of the Western theories of idealism, materialism, or dualism. The perception theory of Buddhism has a certain importance in explaining the beginning of things, but it must not be taken as equivalent to Western idealism. For if you take perception to be a reality you also take all things as real. All that has been said by Buddhism is for the sake of expelling the creations of a doubting heart. Heart doubt itself is empty, unreal: how can its creations exist? Western philosophies, whether idealism, materialism, or dualism, all first postulate that the men and worlds before our eyes are a reality. Now, to follow this up, What were these men and worlds in their original substance, before they became existent? If you say that originally they were only Mind, or Matter, or a Mind-matter dualism, how and in what manner did they later change into their present form? In thinking of this sort, vagueness and error enter in at the very beginning; hence, howsoever you search you cannot come to the truth. Buddhist teaching is not thus. It teaches, rather, that the appearances known as the world and men are empty, non-existent. And since men and the world are non-existent, why discuss what they were originally? It would be like asking where the horns of a rabbit came from. Men and the world are like a deceptive dream. Blindly they go about acting in their dream. Although it seems to the dreamer that his objects are real, when once he awakens and realizes that it was a dream, not one thread of all these appearances remains. You must first pay some attention to this teaching and then you will understand Buddhism. Now we are in a proper position to understand the Buddhist sayings, "The Three Worlds are only Mind," and "All things are only perception." What are mind and perception? They are the deception of the dream. What are the "Three Worlds" and all things? They also are a dream. In a deceptive dream all is in the end unreal. You must understand that there really is no mind and no perception to differentiate. You cannot postulate a world or a sun. Nearby us there is neither a thought nor a particle which should be considered as if existent. In the distance, in the ten directions and the ten worlds, there is nothing to search for.

The Ch'an sect naturally leads into this *via negativa* quite as readily as the T'ien-t'ai. Three of the Buddhist gentlemen in the discussion group with whom I so often dined in Peking favored the Ch'an form of Buddhism and they all put their chief emphasis on its negations, though at times their negativity led them very near to materialism, at least in words. Two of these men insisted that both matter and mind are indestructible and that they are inseparable, and the word *mind* they used largely as interchangeable with *force*. One of the two added that man's "soul" is only the activity of the material brain, and hence the human mind is inseparable from matter. He added that he did not believe in transmigration. I asked him if he considered himself a Buddhist and he replied that he did: that only the most general outlines of Buddhist thought are necessary for one using that name, and that within these a good Buddhist may think with perfect freedom. I was anxious to see how many of the nine others at the feast would agree with this denial of transmigration and tried to get a vote on the subject. It was not easy—not because of any diffidence on the part of my acquaintances to state their views, but because of the distracting nature of this pleasant non-existent world at the moment. With some twenty dishes full of dainties dotting the large table, with rice bowls before each diner, and ten pairs of shining chop sticks visiting each dish with amazing rapidity and deftness—like bees over a garden of poppies—taking from each a little of its inviting contents to be deposited with wonderful skill on the owner's rice bowl—or on mine, for they were very attentive to their guest and knew the clumsiness of his fingers—with such an accompaniment and at such a moment it is not surprising that it was a bit difficult for my friends to focus their thoughts on transmigration, a subject which though pious could hardly be considered attractive. Eventually, however, I got my vote and found that two besides the speaker whom I last quoted refused to accept transmigration; while the seven others not only accepted it but admitted, when I pressed them, that in their opinion the denial of transmigration was absolutely non-Buddhistic. The man who had denied transmigration continued his discourse on Ch'an Buddhism as he understood and believed and practiced it. Other religions and philosophies and sciences, he said, construct; Buddhism destroys. It nullifies time, space, and all distinctions, including the distinction between right and wrong. Christianity, Confucianism, and the rest have erected sharp distinctions here; Buddhism breaks them down because they are ultimately mistaken. When one attains to the true insight, anger and hatred will be destroyed; and with them love will be destroyed also, and one's power to distinguish between love and hate. All things in this world are one, and when one reaches the higher level where this is realized, one wants every man and woman and every dog and every conscious being to reach it also. It is, he insisted, not love that prompts this wish for others. If he reaches this insight alone then only a part of the One will have reached the higher plane. It is not that he loves others but that he wishes all parts of himself to be perfect too. On the higher stages of realization there is no self, no other, no you, no I, no distinctions. The aim of Buddhism is to reach this realization, to attain to the state of absolute indifference, above right and wrong. All Buddhist sects are really seeking to gain this lofty level, and all are merely means of reaching it. The best means of all is through the point of view and the exercises of the Ch'an sect.[9] So my acquaintance ended up his exposition of Buddhism as he understood it, adding finally that though he himself was seeking the high level of realization he had described, he had not reached it.

Thereupon a friend of the speaker chimed in, saying that he himself had reached the level thus described. The really strenuous part of the feast was now over, the dishes removed (except for the innumerable sweets) and we were sitting over our tea and cigarettes. "Yes," continued the new speaker (also a follower of the Ch'an), "I have reached a pretty high level of indifference to right and wrong, and have attained to a good deal of tranquillity." I asked him whether he had risen to a plane from which he could view the death of a dear friend with indifference. He replied—not quite directly (I hardly expected that he would do that), but at least aiming his remarks at the general theme I suggested—that before he began his Ch'an training he had great difficulty in controlling his emotions. Now he notices a great change: in fact, he now has difficulty in rousing his emotions at all.

[9] Most of this paragraph I have transcribed from a carefully prepared statement which the speaker wrote out for me after the feast.

He used to plan ahead and worry afterwards over many things. Now all this unpleasant anxiety has gone. He takes things as they come, with no worry. Formerly he enjoyed doing certain things while others were distasteful. Now he accepts all things philosophically, not caring what happens. Formerly he admired people better than himself and looked down on those lower than he. Now he does not admire any one, not even Shih-chia Fo, nor does he look down upon even the meanest coolie. All people to him are alike. If he admired Shih-chia Fo, he would look down on bad men. But he has now reached a stage above good and evil. This state of the soul he has reached by the practice of Ch'an meditation. There are several methods of going at this, but the aim of all is to make your mind a blank. This does not mean going to sleep or being unconscious. One may keep one's mind a blank while talking to a friend or doing various things. The point is to get rid of the emotions.

At the highest stage of realization, he continued, the question whether the Buddha exists or does not exist simply does not present itself. As a matter of fact, he believes that Shih-chia Fo has long since ceased to exist. Heaven and hell are merely states of mind. To be a Buddha is merely a state of mind. At the high stage of realization all differences cease, including the difference between existence and non-existence.

Such a view as this is plainly related to the Madhyamika view of Nagarjuna. Nagarjuna's school as such never had any large following in China, and what it had has long since died out. In our little group at the feast, however, was to be found one follower of this ancient Indian school, who in fact prided himself on being the only strict follower of Nagarjuna in China. He was one of the few members of the group who spoke English and frequently interpreted for me. In fact, he repeatedly went out of his way, in truly Buddhist spirit, to do me little kindnesses—as, indeed, did nearly all the members of the group. He usually listened to the discussions and to the assertions of his colleagues in silence and with a certain air of amused superiority. For he was convinced that all the things we talked about were emptiness, vacuity. The thought that everything is empty, that nothing is real, that no assertion is true, seemed to give him peculiar delight. Every statement that one makes is untrue, he asserted; and when I asked whether this assertion of his was also untrue he responded in the affirmative with an air of absolute glee. The material world of course is unreal, the self is unreal, the truth is unreal. One cannot truthfully say that the transmigration doctrine is true or that Nirvana is real. All affirmation is false—apparently because affirmation involves distinctions, but chiefly because all terms are necessarily false, the real being ineffable. I asked whether, then, we reach insight and the ideal state in deep sleep, to which he answered that, on the contrary, after we had come fully to recognize the unreality of all things it would not be like unconscious sleep but like a great awakening. I suppose it follows from this that the True is not nought and that the Madhyamika philosophy is not a form of nihilism. I say I suppose this is the case: but I am sure that had I asked our friend he would have replied with his usual delight that my conclusion was absolutely false. He would say the same thing, and with equal glee, if I should conclude that the True *is* naught and that his philosophy is nihilism; so I think we need not be too much troubled by his assertions of falsity.

The real meaning seems to be that the True is positive and real but not to be put into any form of words. The *expression used*, to be sure, both by Madhyamika books and by their spokesman in Peking, usually makes it appear that all reality is denied and that the philosophy is a pure nihilism. This form of Buddhist thought often seems only a rather absurd way of insisting that *words are not things*. The doctrine that no assertion can be true thus boils down to a paradoxical and striking way of asserting the fact (which no one would think of denying) that the words one uses are not the realities to which they refer. There is, of course, more to the Madhyamika philosophy than this; but what goes beyond this it holds in common with most philosophies of mysticism which deny multiplicity and relations and look beyond and behind them to an ultimate and ineffable unity.

If Nagarjuna has only one strictly loyal follower in China, Asanga and Vasubhandu have not many more. I was told on excellent authority that the Tsu En tsung or Fa Hsiang tsung, brought to China by Hiuen-Tsiang the great traveler and based directly on the Yogacara or Vijnanavadin philosophy of Asanga and his brother, died out soon after the close of the T'ang dynasty, only a few of its Sutras and none of the commentaries on them being left in the land. Both Sutras and commentaries, however, had been carried to Japan, and during the 1880's copies of them were brought back to China by a learned Buddhist scholar named Yang. Mr. Yang founded the first Buddhist college in China for laymen and there taught several forms of Buddhist thought. Three of his students became enthusiastic and scholarly adherents of the Yogacara philosophy of Asanga. Mr. Yang died some years ago and his school went out of existence, but these three men have continued his work, lecturing upon the Yogacara philosophy and publishing some of its texts. One of these three, Mr. Ouyang, to whom I have already referred, has a small Buddhist college in Nanking; while the two others, Mr. Wei and Mr. Kwai reside in Tsi-nan Fu and Peking respectively. I had the good fortune to meet all three of these gentlemen and found them scholarly thinkers and earnest Buddhists. From my many conversations with them I gathered (what they themselves would hardly admit in words) that the school as it exists today in China is divided into a pluralistic and a monistic branch. The pluralistic subdivision is rather ardently opposed to the monistic views of the T'ien-t'ai and Ch'an schools, though it agrees with all the Mahayana in giving an idealistic interpretation to the world. The individual is not lost in the One—to say that it is lost is heresy. (The representatives of this pluralistic school were, I think, the only Buddhists I have ever met who used the word heresy or its equivalent.) Individuals may help or harm each other; they may be united in the sense of sharing the same joy or sorrow; but they are not one in any deeper metaphysical way. I have seldom heard the creed of individualism so explicitly expressed or so ardently advocated as by these Buddhist acquaintances of mine. I should add that they and some Japanese monks of the same school are the only Mahayana Buddhist thinkers I have ever met who championed it at all. The individual is not only independent, say they; he is also eternal. And each one creates his own world for himself; all are dreamers dreaming separate dreams. The material world of each is merely dream-content and ceases to exist when unperceived. These Chinese Buddhists were quite unacquainted with Western philosophy, but they would have accepted gladly Berkeley's phrase that the *esse* of material objects is *percipi*. The fact that we construct our dreams sufficiently alike to have certain common objects is to be explained by the similarity of our natures and of our Karma. If my Karma is to create a world like that of others for fifty years, then it will seem that I live fifty years with them. Most of the objects that I thus create are not under the control of my will—as in a dream. A few of them I can control. Buddhism aims at the increased control over these objects of our own creation.

The real inner self which is the creator of my world is the Alaya-vijnana. There is no universal Alaya-vijnana but a multiplicity of individual ones. It is never perceived, never an object (except as we make it the object of our thought, as at present). It is always the subject, yet cannot even be called the thinker, for it is deeper than this. It is very subtle. We cannot describe or picture it because our thought is gross. The Buddha knows what it is. We add to our understanding of it, however, if we keep in mind the distinction between actuality and potentiality; for the Alaya-vijnana far exceeds all actualities. All our potentialities in fact (and they are far beyond all imagination) are within it. It is eternal and its action is endless and continuous. Nothing else is continuous and eternal. The formation of habit is due to it and presupposes it; for all consecutive things require something continuous and permanent. The world which it creates—the world of our perception—is in constant flux, changing with unimaginable rapidity, faster than the minutest divisions of time. Phenomenal personality changes at the same rate. Even seemingly solid structures are in constant change. The bricks that were brought to build this building, the wheelbarrow in which they were brought, the man who pushed it, all changed many times during their transit and have been changing ever since. Seer and seen arise together. One is not (chronologically) prior to the other. But underneath all this flux is the eternal Alaya-vijnana.

This idealistic interpretation of reality and self has direct bearing on the question of man's fate. Literally speaking, there is no such thing as transmigration; for transmigration taken literally implies a transition from one place to another. As a fact (so teaches this school) the self does not *go* anywhere at death. It is not in space; space is in it. Space is one of its creations. What we call death is really the end of one dream and the beginning of another. An individual Alaya-vijnana creates a world that lasts, say, fifty years, with many things in common with the worlds that certain other individuals create. At the end of that time it will create a new world that will have nothing in common with the people of its present world, but that will have objects in common with others, now unknown. Life was full of constant change, and death is only a larger change. Transmigration, heaven, and hell are thus but changes in one's state of mind. The Western Paradise of the Pure Land sect is real in its way, and one may properly believe in it; but properly interpreted it is not a place to which we go but a state of mind which we create. There is, therefore, nothing to fear in death. It is only a change in a state of mind. As anything more than this it is illusion: it does not exist.

The way of salvation, for this type of Buddhism, is chiefly through morality. Our control over the world we make for ourselves depends at last on the purity of our hearts; and our hearts may steadily be purified by moral training, especially training in the six great virtues: generosity, obedience to the precepts, patient endurance, diligence, meditation, wisdom or insight. The morality of the Mahayana is superior to that of the Hinayana in the same way that a college is superior to a school. It goes farther along the same lines. More in particular it has two great advantages over Hinayana morality. In the first place it is less self-centered and puts more emphasis upon unselfish devotion. In the second place, the Mahayana interprets the moral teachings of the Buddha idealistically, just as it interprets the objective world idealistically. It teaches that it is not the bodily acts that count, but the mental states. Only these can be either good or bad. Thus one of the members of this school with whom I talked tells me that though he considers himself a strict Buddhist he eats meat. The bodily act of eating meat, he argues, is not wrong for the Mahayana. For the Hinayana it is wrong, no matter what one's mental state may be. The Mahayana thus leads to a kind of rational antinomianism, which stresses the spirit and leaves aside the letter; while the Hinayana is bound by the letter and has not attained to the freedom of the spirit. For a Hinayana monk to lie in the same bed with a woman would be a great sin even if he were sound asleep all the time and knew nothing of it: for it would be a transgression of the Vinaya. For the Mahayana it would not be a sin at all. But if a man sleeping alone, wakes in the night and hears a noise in the next room and says to himself, That was a woman's hairpin falling, he sins. For he would not interpret the sound as a falling hairpin but for a lustful thought in the back of his mind.

The power that Buddhism has toward a life of higher morality is partly through the training that it gives and the ideals it sets up; partly through the joy that it induces. Joy is a large part of the motive power of Buddhism, so my friends insist; and they say that those who have followed its training and practiced its meditations will all bear this out.

The Yogacara philosophy of the pluralistic sort of course knows no Absolute. But it recognizes the Buddhas and Bodhisattvas as real and living spiritual beings. These, like ourselves, are in constant change so far as their empirical consciousness is concerned. They also are many and not one. Unlike Asanga, the founder of the school, these Chinese pluralists do not recognize the unity of the Dharmakaya. The Buddhas are superior to the Bodhisattvas in enlightenment, but they have not entered Parinirvana. They have a right to do so, but they prefer to stay in the world and save men. Thus not only in its doctrine of man but also in its theology, these Chinese pluralists might be called *personalists.* With the Buddhas and Bodhisattvas it is possible for us to come into communion. As like elements produce like phenomena we may continuously come to have more in common with them as we grow more like them in character, and thereby may gradually be enabled to perceive and communicate with them, i.e., to have them as a part of our world.

It will be evident to the reader who has clearly in mind the Yogacara philosophy of Asanga and Vasubandhu, as I tried to expound it in Chapter XII, that the pluralistic Chinese form I have been depicting in this chapter is not in all respects identical with the teachings of the founders. This pluralistic form, however, is not the only form under which one meets this philosophy in China. It is sometimes presented with a monistic turn, which the pluralists consider heresy. This is brought about by interpreting the Alaya-vijnana cosmically. In some sense, thus, the inner selves of all merge in one, the *Bhutatathata* of the "Awakening of Faith." This ultimate cosmic Reality, I was told, cannot be got at within experience; yet it is omnipresent and pervasive. In one sense we are within it, yet not in the sense of space, for space is in the world of doubt or illusion, and the One Reality is not. This One Reality is not even to be described as thought, nor yet as not-thought. If it had any qualities it would not be pure Reality. One Chinese philosopher told me it was closely related to the higher Brahma of the Upanishads and the Vedanta philosophy. It is neither the Christian God nor the Chinese Tao. But while it is neither thinkable nor speakable, and while even the Buddhist classics do not describe it, the study of Buddhist philosophy may help one ultimately to get an insight, a revelation of its true being. When one has gained this, one is a Bodhisattva. It is doubtful, so I was told, whether there are at present any Bodhisattvas in the world; though in the past there certainly have been. Certainly words and thought cannot express the Ultimate, but immediate realization would reveal it. Just as we can know a man only by seeing him, or better still by *being* he, so we can know the Real only by immediate contact or union. How, then, I asked, do we who have never had this experience, know that It exists? It is, I was told, a matter of simple logic. Phenomena presuppose a noumenon, a without presupposes a within. This is a matter, therefore, not of faith but of knowledge. There *must* be an ultimately Real.

The name most commonly met with in China, without respect to sect or school, for this ultimate Reality is *Jen Ru.*

A Sinologue would spell it Chen Ju—which would probably not suggest to the reader the pronunciation intended, which is indicated in my spelling. This term is perhaps most associated with the T'ien-t'ai philosophy. For the T'ien-t'ai does not stop with the negations which I cited from some of its representatives in an earlier part of this chapter. According to the best-known spokesman of T'ien-t'ai philosophy in China, the monk T'ai Hsu from whom I have already quoted,

> the word Ru means that which is changeless and ever the same. It is that definite quality and principle in any and every thing or event which never, in any place or at any time, changes. Because of the changelessness of this quality, Ru is also Chen, which means truth. Now although Chen Ru (Truth-Sameness) is not the same as things, yet it is never separate from all things. In short, that quality of changelessness or sameness in all things, places, and events, is given the name Chen Ru.[10]

"It is conceived of as the intangible—not seen, heard, scented or felt; as perfect emptiness, yet an emptiness which is the only reality; as the true Unity without beginning and without end, without life and without death, and the source of all things. It is also conceived of as Nature and as Universal Mind or Spirit." [11] In the letter from T'ai Hsu to his confused disciple, from which I have already quoted, he says:

> Chen Ru is the true nature of all things. Outside of Chen Ru all is imaginary and without reality. Chen Ru is not Mind or Matter: it is not anything. It has no form to grasp, and no activity to effect. There is no time or place which has only Chen Ru and has not mind or matter. And there is no thought and no material particle which is not Chen Ru. Although all things come from Chen Ru as their true nature and Chen Ru is eternally the true nature of all things, it never changes to become all things. So we cannot say all things issue from Chen Ru. Chen Ru is similar to what the scientists call real space. Chen Ru has everywhere an ever-moving spiritual consciousness. . . . You must understand that the differentiations of all things are the result of thought activity, that reality is Chen Ru and that Chen Ru is absolutely without the multiplicity of things which are the creations of thought activity. If you grasp this and also realize that differentiation and multiplicity are due to ignorance and the delusions of vague active thought, then you will see that the world of existence is unreal and that all things melt away and the hidden Buddha nature becomes manifest. Then you will rejoice that Buddhahood has been attained.

[10] "The Meaning of Chen Ju and Ju Lai" in the *Chinese Recorder* for Feb., 1924, p. 119.

[11] F. R. Millican, "Chen Ju" in the *Chinese Recorder*, Feb., 1924, p. 116.

The concept of Chen Ru as held by the T'ien-t'ai philosophy is susceptible of two interpretations; and both these interpretations are justified, in the sense that each of them describes the position of a number of Buddhist thinkers. One of these interpretations stresses the negations of the school and considers its philosophy a form of nihilism. For example, my friend Professor Francis Wei of Boon College writes me:

> I should judge that Chen Ru is *not* conscious, any more than Truth is conscious. Certainly it is not the Idealist's Absolute. A Buddha is one who gets hold of the Truth and he will speak of it in whatever terms may be intelligible to the people of his time and place. He may quite legitimately refer to Chien Ru as the Highest God, for instance, if that should be the most efficient way of preaching in order to enlighten them. . . . Since all paths lead to the Lion's Den it does not matter what track you follow! In fact, it is the opposite of enlightenment to ask whether Chien Ru is conscious or not. When enlightened the question solves itself, for there would be nothing to be enlightened and nothing to raise a question. It is nihilism.

The other school of interpretation understands the Ultimate Reality as something decidedly positive and decidedly spiritual. Thus Mr. Reichelt of Nanking—a man deeply read in the Buddhist scriptures and acquainted on intimate terms with T'ai Hsu and many Buddhists—tells me that in his opinion "the great emptiness" which the Mahayana emphasizes means to most Buddhist thinkers today something far from nihilism or mere indifference or negation. It is for them essentially positive. This is seen in the intense joy with which it fills them. This is for them a very real and positive mystical experience. They describe it by all sorts of negations so as to purify it from all earthly taint. They begin with negatives and pile on the negatives and this tends to mislead the Western listener or reader into supposing that the Reality with which they believe themselves to have come into contact is merely the Void; but as a fact the Reality they have in mind, when finally reached, is positive. The process is comparable to the great Christian truth that one can find one's life only by losing it.

I am more inclined to accept Mr. Reichelt's interpretation as applying to at least many Chinese Buddhists because of the parallel situation in Indian and Western mysticism. More than one student of the psychology of mysticism has pointed out that the ineffable experience of the mystic commonly leads him to attribute to the divine Being with whom he believes himself to have come in contact the same indefinable nature, expressible only in negatives, which characterizes his own mystical experience.[12] In every land mystics who have followed the *via negativa,* and thinkers who have reasoned on the basis of it, have built up a theology which consisted chiefly, so far as words go, in negations. This outcome is the more natural in China because the only form of mysticism commonly practiced there is not one which brings a "sense of presence," but the Ch'an form which seeks to empty the mind; while the whole habit of Buddhist thought is subjective and tends not to interpret the mind through the world, but the world through the mind.

One of the most scholarly Buddhists I met in China, Professor Liang Su Ming of the Government University of Peking, told me that while he had formerly interpreted the Mahayana doctrine in the sense of nihilism, he had, after much thought, changed his opinion, and now interprets it in the sense of idealism. The ultimate Reality for him is spiritual: it is the One Dharmakaya of all the Buddhas. In their Sambhogakaya, as in their Nirmanakaya or historical appearance, the Buddhas are many, but in their ultimate being they are one. Yet in merging their personalities in the Dharmakaya they do not lose their individuality, but still send it forth in various manifestations for the salvation of the world. And we, too, partake of the Buddha nature. The world of matter and sense is unreal; but the Buddha nature within us is real and positive. Salvation consists in being freed from slavery to the body. Immortality is real and means conscious continuance. After shuffling off this body we shall no longer be weighed down by the senses, but we shall still be conscious beings. This consciousness we shall all share, for it is the One. We shall merge our individuality, as the Buddhas do, in Chen Ru, in the Dharmakaya.

[12] Cf. Leuba: "Tendancies Religieuses chez les Mystiques Chrétiens," *Revue Philosophique,* LIV. 480; *The Psychology of Religious Mysticicism* (London, Kegan Paul, 1925), Chap. X; also my book on *The Religious Consciousness,* Chap. XVIII.

While both the negative interpretation and what I might call the spiritual interpretation of Chen Ru are to be found side by side in all parts of China today, and while both will probably continue to have their adherents as long as Chinese Buddhism lasts, it seems to me probable that as Japanese Buddhism and Western idealism and perhaps the Indian Vedanta come to be better and better known in China, the spiritual view of Reality will gain ground over the other. I think it is the opinion of most students of Buddhism that the more idealistic interpretation of the Mahayana has been slowly gaining ever since the religion was transplanted from India into China and Japan.

Taken in this spiritual sense there is something large and appealing in the concept of Chen Ru. It is not Christian, it is not Western; it transcends too completely the personal for that. But it has an inclusiveness, a restfulness, a spaciousness which every one with a cosmic sense must at least acknowledge, whatever he may think of it intellectually. There are minds, at any rate, in the West as in the East, to whom our Western personalism seems at times too active, too efficient, too definite, too restless, and who long for something larger and more cosmic, with a longing as of one who hears afar the distant murmur of the sea. To such an one the concept of Chen Ru may bring the Great Peace of the Buddha—Chen Ru in which all separate things merge and petty distinctions melt and future and past become one in the timeless present: a Spiritual Reality behind the world of action and of striving, in which all differences are reconciled, all discords harmonized, and which has power

> to make
> Our noisy years seem moments in the being
> Of the Eternal Silence.

CHAPTER XXI

KOREAN BUDDHISM

As the reader will doubtless recall, it was during the confused centuries of political division which followed the fall of the Han dynasty that Buddhism won its first extensive victories in China. Especially among the small kingdoms north of the Yangtse it spread with rapidity. Nor did it stop at the Great Wall. As the barbarian invaders had come southward into China, so Buddhism, carrying with it much of Chinese culture, swept northward into Manchuria. No details of its progress are left us, but we may picture the earnest missionaries of the new faith, with a pack animal or two carrying Buddha images and Sutra manuscripts, trudging slowly and inconspicuously, but irresistibly and fatefully, over the flat Manchurian plains, covered perhaps then as now with high growths of sorghum, and broken here and there with sudden outcroppings of rock, rising in cliffs above the level land. Past what is now Mukden they must have pressed, some stopping to spend their lives in missionary activity among the villages along the way, others "carrying on" into the sparsely settled and inexhaustible North, till Parinirvana put an end to their earthly pilgrimage, and still others directing their steps east and northeastward until stopped by the waves of the Yellow Sea, or the tawny flood of the Yalu River. Here for a while they paused and converted to the new faith the little Chinese kingdoms which filled that region, and here they died, handing on to a new generation the task of carrying the torch still farther into regions where as yet the Light of Asia had not shone. The new generation was not slow in taking up the torch, and in the year 369 [1]

[1] According to Frederick Starr. See his *Korean Buddhism* (Boston, Jones Co., 1918), p. 4. According to Bishop Trollope the first Buddhist missionary reached Korea in 372. *Introduction to the Study of Buddhism in Corea*, Tr. R. A. S., Korea Branch, VIII. 12. Griffis also gives 372 as the year of introduction into Northern Korea but adds that "long before this the faith of India was established in Hiaksai" (i.e., Pakche), *Corea, the Hermit Nation* (London, Harpers, 1905), p. 35.

a priest named Sundo, under the auspices of the Buddhist king of one of these little kingdoms, with his images and his Sutras crossed the Yalu and began the work of spreading the Dharma in the "Land of the Morning Calm."

At that time what we know now as Korea, with some additional territory to the north and west of the Yalu, was divided into three kingdoms, called respectively Koguryu or Korai,[2] Pakche or Hiaksai,[3] and Silla or Shinra.[4] Korai was in the north, Pakche in the southwest, and Silla in the southeast. It was probably Korai, the northern (and larger) kingdom, into which Buddhism was first introduced—though according to Griffis the little kingdom of Hiaksai or Pakche received Buddhist missionaries by sea from China before the first priest crossed the Yalu. At any rate, by the year 374, there were two Buddhist monasteries at P'yeng-Yang (the modern Pingyang), the capital of the northern kingdom. These, as is so often the case with Buddhist monasteries, were schools as well as temples, and from them new missionaries went out in various directions, who did their work so well that in a few years Buddhism became the official religion of Korai. In 384 the little kingdom of Pakche sent to China for Buddhist missionaries, and their success was as rapid as that of their brethren farther north. Pakche, in fact, seems to have become the most enthusiastically Buddhist of the three Korean kingdoms, and it was her king who in 552 and again in 572 sent missionaries, images, and Sutras to his friend and ally, the Emperor of Japan. Silla, on the southeast, was the last of the three kingdoms to receive the new religion, which she did in 424.

Buddhism very early became the state religion, not only in Korai but in the two southern kingdoms. It remained the state religion long after Silla (with the aid of China) had conquered and absorbed both her rivals and made Kyun Ju the capital of all Korea. The modern village of Kyong Ju, far from the tourist route, still preserves many impressive remains of its ancient splendor and of the Buddhist zeal[5] of its monarchs and nobility at the time when it was one of

[2] Which the Japanese call Koma.
[3] Kudara in Japanese.
[4] Shiragi in Japanese.
[5] Notably in the near-by cave temple at Sukkul-am.

the world's most cultured capitals. But the great success of Buddhism proved at length its own undoing. So rich and powerful did its monasteries become and so completely did they, during many a reign, control the mind of the king, that the land was burdened with taxes in support of monastic luxury and gorgeous ritual, and the economic productiveness of the country was seriously lessened by the drafting of large numbers of young men into the priesthood. Under some of the kings of the Koryu dynasty, which in 918 overthrew the house of Silla, the ranks of the monks were recruited largely from the nobility, and every family with four sons was compelled by the throne to devote at least one to the monastic life; later this rule was extended to families with three sons.[6] The monks transformed many of their monasteries into fortresses and themselves took the sword, thus making the various monastic centers into great military powers, just as their brethren were doing at the same time in Japan. In spite of the growing strength of the monks, however, and in spite of the continued favor shown by the crown to Buddhism, the military and civil officials were coming under a rival influence—an influence that like Buddhism had come to Korea from China—namely, the Neo-Confucianism of the Sung epoch. The rivalry of these two cultures added to the chaos of the times and hastened the fall of the dynasty.

It was in 1392 that the house of Koryu was overthrown and succeeded by the Yi dynasty, which continued to rule Korea until Korea ceased to be an independent kingdom and became (in 1910) a province of Japan. The 1392 revolution was in part a rebellion against the excessive power of the monks. And though Buddhism was not at first directly attacked by the new dynasty, after some eighty years of alternating indifference and favor, under a young king named Chasan, the government decided to eliminate once for all the danger of monastic interference and rivalry, and drove the monks at first out of Seoul, the capital, and soon thereafter out of all the cities of the land. "The priests took refuge in the mountains and from that time down until these latter days [i.e., till the early years of this century] there have been no Buddhist temples in Korean cities. There

[6] Longford, *The Story of Korea* (London, Unwin, 1911), p. 106.

have only been monasteries in the mountains, often in inaccessible places." [7]

In spite of the expulsion of the Buddhist clergy from the cities and villages, a considerable amount of devotion to the religion lived on throughout the land for many a century, as is shown by some of the Buddhist monuments which neither time nor Hideyoshi destroyed. Thus at Eun-jin there is an immense rock Buddha, whose temple near by, first erected in 1386, was rebuilt (so the ancient inscription declares) in 1581 and again in 1674.[8] It was shortly after the first of these rebuildings that Hideyoshi sent his Japanese on their expedition of conquest and plunder; and during those dreadful days Buddhist monks and their students gave a good account of themselves in the desperate attempt to defend their country.[9] Yet in spite of occasional signs of energy Buddhism was fast losing its hold over the people of Korea. This was, of course, inevitable. With no clergy, no official teachers, no ritual, no temples, the Koreans in all the populous parts of the land eventually forgot their religion. The more educated contented themselves with the teachings of Confucian ethics, while the overwhelming majority drifted back into the animistic nature worship and primitive superstition from which Buddhism, for a few centuries, had raised them. Although the ban upon monks and temples was lifted a few years ago, under Japanese influence, Buddhism was in most of the towns too far gone to be resuscitated.[10] Hence if one

[7] Starr, *op. cit.*, p. 28.

[8] See the account of a visit to it, with a trans. of the long inscription, by the Rev. G. H. Jones, Tr. R. A. S., Korea Branch, I. 53-60.

[9] At the monastery of Yu jom sa, in the Diamond Mountains, is still preserved the banner of the ancient abbot of that temple who once drove back the soldiers of Hideyoshi.

[10] There are still about 185,000 Buddhists in Korea, and many of them are fairly zealous. Dr. C. S. Deming, long a missionary in Korea, writes: "The laity come to seek assistance at the Buddhist shrines in every kind of need. They hire the monks to recite sacred prayers, they fling themselves repeatedly before the altar in prayer, with their foreheads in the dust, murmuring softly the words of supplication, of prayer, of sorrow. Many women go to the temples on New Year's day, taking money or fruit to the monks to solicit their prayers for prosperity during the year. Some also go at the death of relatives to pray that the soul of the departed may not remain long in purgatory but go soon up to heaven. Others pray that they may give birth to children. When the priest offers the prayers for others he first beats a drum or cymbal and with a loud voice prays, 'O merciful Buddha, hear the prayer of this supplicant and grant him prosperity.' If one is rich he brings money and the priest buys fruit and rice with it and then comes before the Buddha and prays." (From an unpublished paper on "Prayer in Buddhism.")

would get acquainted with the Korean Buddhism of today one must forsake the centers of population to follow up some narrow gorge or climb some cliff or wooded hillside. For in many a picturesque and hidden spot the Buddhas keep their ancient places, where monks still feed the lamp of faith and lay pilgrims from distant villages still come to pray.

The most important of these centers of Buddhism is the Kongo-San, or Diamond Mountains, a region of wild peaks and crags, brooks, pools, and waterfalls, in the northeastern part of Korea, resembling the Adirondacks both in latitude, climate, and (to some extent) in formation. The mountains are clad with woods much like those of the Adirondacks, and they rise to about the same height—the highest of them being about the height of Mt. Marcy. They are, however, much wilder than the New York mountains, the brooks are more precipitous, the cascades more numerous, and the peaks much sharper, with many fantastic outcroppings of strange rocks and sudden precipices, reminding one of the Dolomites or the Cullin Hills of Skye. Perhaps the most marked difference of all is to be found in the inhabitants. For there are hardly three villages in all the Kongo-San, and hardly a farm or farmer, almost the only inhabitants being the monks who dwell in the many secluded and picturesque monasteries, which have brought more fame to this region than even its peaks and waterfalls. As early as A.D. 515, it is said, Buddhist monks, with their usual eye for natural beauty and romantic situations, began building temples in this lonely region; and now there are some nineteen temples with their monastic appendages in the Kongo—forty or more if one applies the term Kongo to as wide a territory as is sometimes done.

From Chosen on the Sea of Japan, where, with mingled cursings and thanksgivings, one leaves the precious little steamer, one goes by auto to On-sei-ri, a picturesque Korean village which gets its name from its delightful hotsprings, and which boasts several excellent hotels. One can see typical parts of the Diamond Mountains by making one of these hotels one's headquarters and taking all-day tramps in various directions. But the only way to get the full charm of the region is to commit oneself whole-heartedly to the mountains, and with food and bedding loaded on the shoulders of several stout "jiggy-men," to turn one's back upon the civilization of On-sei-ri and plunge into the wilds. The little trail will lead you along slippery rocks and beside many a precipice, across torrents on felled trees, over high passes and through deep gorges; but it can always be trusted. In the worst places you will find footholds that have been cut in the solid rock for you long, long ago. Great stone Buddhas guard the way, and Chinese inscriptions cut in the cliffs by Korean poets from Shakspeare's time to ours, remind you of the many pilgrims, your predecessors, who have gone safely over this ancient trail before you. Cold water, fresh from brook or spring, is always ready for your use; and it is water that you can drink with no fear of germs—a joy which only those can appreciate who have tramped in oriental lands. When you are ready for your swim a great green pool will offer itself. Such pools as these in the Kongo-San I have never seen elsewhere nor ever quite dared to dream of—so impossibly beautiful are they—green as an emerald, or as the oak leaves that bend above them. And at the end of the day, at the top of some little valley, you come upon the temple, with its group of monastic buildings, where you are to find food and sleep, and (if you are not too stiffnecked) a little religion as well. The jiggy man is already there before you, and the monks give you a real welcome in their decorous and formal fashion, the sincerity of which is unmistakable, even if you cannot understand the words they say. Your bedding and other luggage is unpacked, the brazier is brought out, the kettle put upon it, and a monk fans the charcoal while you make the coffee and warm up the beans which good Mr. Heinz has sent you all the way from Pittsburgh, or while you open up the jam which Messrs. Cross and Blackwell serve indifferently to you in the Kongo-San and to King George in Windsor. Finally out from the refectory comes another monk with a bowl of rice which at home would have served all your family but which in the mountains you now think by no means too large for yourself alone. With it comes a tray of condiments and side dishes which never fail to rouse your interest if not always your appetite. Never is the collection twice alike, but you will probably find bean curd (looking rather nasty and tasting delicious), bean sprouts, dried fish of various sorts, one or two kinds of fried seaweed (crisp and tasty), and perhaps some dark green moss, upwards of a hundred years old, scraped from the rocks in the mountains. The temple is usually situated in a kind of amphitheater among the hills, and, especially as darkness comes, the fantastic rocks on the summits round about take on the forms of Buddhas in all the traditional attitudes—praying Buddhas, sitting Buddhas, standing Buddhas, to many of which the pious monks have given special sacred names—till you feel yourself compassed about by a cloud of supernatural witnesses. And as you lie down in your little room, you hear the deep sound of the gong in the temple, followed by the voices of the monks, praising in unison the Blessed One, while you fall away into slumber.

Buddhist monasteries in Korea, as in Japan and China, contain several buildings, the larger ones suggesting small villages. The roads leading to them almost always lead up some narrow valley or gorge, crossing the foaming stream by picturesque bridges, till at last you come to a kind of alcove in the hill, where the early Buddhist missionaries ended their journey, built a pagoda, and laid the foundations for their temples and their sleeping rooms. There is no regular plan for the arrangement of the monastic buildings—in fact you will find no two monasteries alike, for new buildings are added, through the centuries, as need arises and endowments accumulate; but in general plan there is a certain approximation to uniformity. Almost invariably you enter the monastery enclosure through a monumental portal, with the swaying roof so familiar in both China and Japan, beyond which you come into a court surrounded on the sides by walls or storehouses, and usually containing a great bronze bell. The monks will probably assure you that this is the second largest bell in Korea, or the second largest in the world. I have seen at least five such "second largest" bells. They will also be pretty sure to relate to you the following tale. The maker of the bell could not get from it the desired tone, or for some reason could not cast it at all. On the night when the final attempt at casting was to be made, his daughter—a beautiful maiden—threw herself into the molten metal, and thus assured her father's success. The bell therefore gives out a lugubrious note, which is really the voice of the fair victim, wailing her short life. When you first hear this story it is very touching; but you get used to it after you have heard the incident solemnly attributed to the casting of half a dozen bells in different parts of Korea, as well as in connection with the two big bells in Peking.

Beyond the first court with its big bell is a second entrance gateway, this one containing the gigantic and scowling figures of the Guardians of the Four Quarters, quite as terrific as those in China, who protect the monastery and its temple. Evil spirits cannot get beyond them. You, not being an evil spirit, are not too frightened by their dreadful looks to proceed, and so you go on through the next court to the great temple or central shrine of the monastery. This building is always elaborately carved and decorated, with swaying roof, ornate doors, and artistic inscriptions in Chinese characters; while immediately in front of it there frequently stands an ancient stone pagoda, perhaps thirty feet high, with from three to nine stories, and dating from a thousand years ago. The interior of the temple is usually lofty, rather dark, and with much carving and decoration—invariably two great dragon-heads in wood thrusting downward from the ceiling, and two or more streamers of colored cloth, ten or fifteen feet long, suspended at the sides of the dragons. The central object of interest is, of course, the altar with its image of the Buddha or of several Buddhas with their attending Bodhisattvas.

The most popular Buddhas of Korea (or *Bools* as the Koreans call them) are Sakyamuni and Amitabha—whom they know under the names Sukka Yurai, or Syek-ka-muni, and Amida respectively. The Buddha of healing, familiar in China as Yao-shih-Fo [11] and known to the Koreans as Yaksa Yurai, is also a common object of worship. Less frequently found are Vairocana and Loshana. According to Bishop Trollope,[12] these two, with Sakyamuni, are on the altars of a few temples, grouped in a trinity, in which case Vairocana is interpreted by the learned as standing for the Dharmakaya, Loshana for the Sambhogakaya, and Sakya-

[11] The Bhaisajaguru of Sanskrit: Yaku-shi in Japan.

[12] Tr. R. S. A., Korea Branch, VIII. 19.

muni for the Nirmanakaya.[13] Sometimes reference is made by word or on kakemono, to the "Seven Buddhas"—by which is intended the four Buddhas of the present kalpa and the three Buddhas who preceded it.

Of Bodhisattvas, or *Posals*, as the word is pronounced in Korean, there are six special favorites, namely: Miryek Posal (Maitreya, the Chinese Milei-Fo) ,Ti-tjang Posal (Chinese Ti-tsang P'usa), Kan Seon, or Kwan Sin, or Koan-syei-eum Posal (who is of course Kwan-Yin), Tai-sei-chi Posal (the Chinese Ta-shih-chih, better known under the Japanese name Dai-seishi), Moun-sou Posal (the Sanskrit Manjusri, Chinese Wen-Shu), and Po-hien Posal (the Chinese P'u-hien).[14]

Of these Bools and Posals the four most popular are (as one coming from China might expect) Sukka Yarai, Amida, Koan-eum and Miryek. On the many altars of most temples Sukka Yurai (Sakyamuni) has, as in China, the position of honor at the center, accompanied on the two sides either by Amida and Yaksa Yurai (as in China) or by the two Bodhisattvas Koan-eum and Tai-sei-chi. But in actual worship Amida is more popular than Sakyamuni, and he is, of course, often prominent upon the altar. In fact there is greater variation in the arrangement of the altar in Korea than in China. Sometimes three Trinities are presented on one altar, each consisting of a Buddha with two attendant Bodhisattvas.[15] In general a Korean altar is rather more carefully and

[13] That is the Body of the Law, the Body of Bliss, and the Body of Transformation, respectively. See Chapter XIII.

[14] See list at end of Chapter XV.

[15] There are many other variations in arrangement that might be noted. Thus at the Ma-ka-yön Am (or monastery), the chief place is given to a tiny image of Pakti Posal, or the Law-giving Bodhisattva, kept behind glass; while at Yu jöm sa the altar holds—instead of the usual Buddha seated on his lotus—a miniature tree, with over forty little Buddhas seated in its branches. This rather curious variation is connected with the story of the founding of the temple. Many centuries ago—some say several hundred years before Christ—there were fifty-three little stone Buddhas in the Punjab who decided to leave India and go to Korea. The journey they accomplished in a stone boat, which, in fact, is still pointed out in the "Sea Kongo," a boatshaped rock jutting above the waves at the edge of that rocky coast, where the mountains plunge abruptly into the sea, and the sea sends long arms into the mountains. It may at first seem unlikely that the journey from India to Korea could have been made in a stone boat; but it might well be asked what kind of conveyance would be more appropriate for fifty-three stone Buddhas. At any rate, they arrived and were revealed to the official of the district at the site of the present monastery; for he founded it here in recognition of the divine condescension. Not at once, however, did the little Buddhas succeed in obtaining control of the locality; for nine dragons were already in possession, and they challenged the little visitors to a test of strength. The Buddhas had taken refuge from

artistically arranged and regarded with a little more reverence than is the case with the average temple in China. The walls of the central temple building are usually decorated with pictures of various Posals, not to mention brilliant lotus-covered heavens and terrific hells; and in all the larger temples there are additional buildings devoted to images of Posals and Lohans and other subordinate members of the Buddhist cycle. Notable among these are the Ten Kings of the Ten Hells. The "Temple of the Nether World," as their shrine is called, is especially devoted to the souls of the dead; and lest the Ten Kings should be too suggestive of the fate of the departed, an image of the merciful Ti-tjang—the equivalent of the Chinese Ti-tsang, who saves even from hell—is always associated with the more dreadful figures. Another hall or shrine is commonly devoted to the sixteen chief disciples (the sixteen "Rakan" of Japan, corresponding to the eighteen Lohans of China); or to the greater company of five hundred Lohans, each of whom is given individual representation. There may be also a tiny shrine to the Seven Stars, and one to the Spirit of the Hill. The Bodhisattva Miryek has no such prominent position in Korean temples as Milei-Fo occupies in China; but he has a counterbalancing distinction. Korea abounds in large stones of odd contour that have been roughly shaped into Buddha images. These are commonly said to be images of Miryek; in fact, the word *miryek* or *miriok* has come to be the common noun which denotes these stones. Besides these, there are many gigantic bas-reliefs of Miryek graven upon the face of the cliffs in various parts of the land.

There are two sects of Buddhism in Korea, to one or the other of which all the monks belong. These are the Syen jön, or mystical sect, corresponding to the Ch'an sect of China, and to the Soto branch of the Japanese Zen shu, and the Kyo jön, or dogmatic and "reading" sect, corresponding

the dragons in a tree, and the dragons called down such a terrific wind that the Buddhas fell to the ground; and the wind was followed by such a rain that the little Buddhas were almost drowned. At this juncture they had recourse to the first of the "three refugees." They wrote the name Buddha on a leaf and put it upon the waters; whereupon the waters began to boil at such a rate that the dragons could stand it no longer, and departed for a distant part of the stream (known now as the "Nine Dragon Pool," with a large pot-hole for each dragon) leaving Yu jöm sa to the fifty-three little Buddhas and their adoring monks.

to the T'ien-t'ai. The monks belonging to the first of these —the mystical sect—seem to be much more spiritual and much more in earnest than the Kyo jön monks. The services of the two differ notably. The Kyo jön service consists of the usual prostrations and chanting of Sutras, or repetition of the phrase "Nam Mu Amida Bool" (which of course is the Korean version of Namu O-mi-to Fo) with the accompaniment of bronze and wooden gongs and the burning of incense and candles. This service outsiders may attend with no complaint—but with considerable distraction—on the part of the monks. In many of the Kyo jön monasteries it takes place but twice a day, and at very comfortable hours. Quite different is the practice, and the atmosphere, at the Syen jön monastery. At Yu jöm sa, for example, we were politely requested not to attend the service; for, they said, it is a very spiritual time and they preferred to be alone. At the little Syen jön monastery of Ma-ka-yön—the most remote and in many ways the most attractive that we saw in all the mountains—we were allowed to watch from outside the temple the evening service. After the initial prostrations, each monk took off his outer priestly robe, and knelt upon a cushion facing the wall, the abbot in the outer hall or entrance facing away from the other monks and from the altar. Thus they remained in perfect silence, rapt in meditation, until long after our curiosity was exhausted and we had gone to our beds. At three in the morning the same service is repeated, and again at eight, at 2 P.M. and once more in the evening. In some monasteries each of the first three of these services lasts two hours, and the evening service three; so that nine hours every day are given to kneeling meditation—or, as the Japanese call it, *zazen.*

The two sects are not at all hostile to each other. In fact, at the large monastery of Chang-an Sa I found both sects represented. Until about 1910 the monastery had been exclusively Kyo jön (the "reading" sect), but in that year a group of Syen jön monks had been admitted, and there are now ten of these and twenty-six Kyo monks in the monastery. Each group has its own hall of worship and holds its own services. But the abbot they share in common. He belongs, in a sense, to both sects. When he does zazen with the meditative monks he is Syen jön; when he reads with the larger group he is Kyo jön. To be abbot under such conditions must be a rather strenuous and sometimes even bewildering experience. I use the word bewildering intentionally; for the two sects differ not only in their methods but in some of their rules. Syen monks, for example, must be celibates, while the Kyo monks may marry if they like. I am not sure whether the abbot was already married when he took on the new duties of membership in the Syen jön. If so the alternation from marriage to celibacy and back again several times each day must give him an odd sense of dual personality.

According to Starr, the abbot is usually relieved of the spiritual responsibilities which one naturally thinks of as part of an abbot's task. "He has to deal with the outside world and to oversee everything; he is business manager; he has little to do with spiritual direction but has to settle all quarrels and deal with all the problems that present themselves to the monastery. Next comes the religious head, who leads the services and sees that they are properly observed." [16] At the death of the abbot his successor is chosen by vote of the monks.

In addition to the monks, with their abbot and their spiritual leader, there are in all the larger monasteries a number of acolytes or novitiates, and frequently several orphans. For Buddhist monasteries are the orphan asylums of the land; in all Buddhist countries the care of orphans seems to have been, since earliest times, one of the chief forms of Buddhist activity. Many of the novitiates, naturally, are drawn from the orphan boys who have been brought up in the monastery. In the meditative order the period of the novitiate lasts, in theory, three years, and a certain amount of study is required. The word "study," however, let me warn the reader, must not be taken too seriously. Before one can become a monk one must know how to chant the necessary responses in the ritual, but I gather that not a great deal more is actually required. Some boys enter the monkhood at ten. At the close of the novitiate there is a ceremony of putting on the robes, at which the family of the new monk may be

[16] *Korean Buddhism*, p. 46.

present. At this time the new member of the Order takes the universal Five Vows—not to take life, steal, be impure, lie, or drink intoxicants. They do not take the five further vows which the Founder insisted upon for the clergy, nor are they bound to absolute poverty. They may have a little pocket money if they can get it. They shave their heads once a month. Most of the abbots that I met, in addition to shaving their heads, tried to raise beards. It would be no tax upon one's faith to believe that the hairs of all their beards are numbered.

The rank and file of Korean monks and even of Korean abbots seem to be rather unusually ignorant. Nor are they brilliant examples of morality. Occasionally they, like men of other professions in other lands, are given to vice. Their temples are not always distinguished for the peace and love which the Founder sought to bring. Mr. Starr reports that in one monastery which he and his party visited he noticed that "the head priest lacked a tooth, but we found out only after we had left the place that the most devout of the monks had knocked it out the day before, having had a fight with his superior."[17] But this sort of thing is presumably unusual. A number of the monks we met impressed us as truly spiritual men.

The philosophy or theology of the monks, if so dignified a word may be used in this connection, consists chiefly in a belief in Sakyamuni and Amida and in Maitreya and the Goddess of Mercy. Sakyamuni they know once lived in India and taught righteousness. His aim was to reduce the amount of sorrow in the world, to teach people the laws of health and how to reach old age, and how to have a peaceful, wise and spiritual mind. So I was told by the most intelligent monk I met in Korea. Sakyamuni, I was several times assured, is now living and conscious, and hears our prayers. Of Nirvana I heard no mention. Sakyamuni and all the various Buddhas and Bodhisattvas seem to hold a position not very different from that of the gods of some highly ethical polytheism. So far as I could discover, there was no tendency on the part even of the most ignorant monks to identify the Buddhas with their images—no crass idolatry. The Buddha images

[17] *Op. cit.*, p. 57.

they considered—as Buddhist monks the world over do—merely sacred aids to the religious imagination.

I said just now that I heard in Korea no mention of Nirvana. I mean this both in connection with the Buddha and in relation to human fate. Repeatedly I asked the question what became of men at death, and invariably I was told that the good go to heaven and the bad to hell. By "heaven" the Korean Buddhist invariably means Amida's Western Paradise, pictured so commonly and so resplendently upon kakemonas and temple walls. If you go further with your questions and ask whether the soul may be reborn on this earth, you will usually get an affirmative reply. But it is the thought of heaven and hell that fills the mind of the Korean Buddhist—as it does that of the Chinese and the Southern Buddhist—rather than the thought of transmigration. Not that this Indian idea plays no part. An old abbot with whom I had a long conversation—and whose attention was repeatedly distracted from the profound truths of Buddhism by the fascination of my walking stick and by the migrations of an elusive flea—told me (when the flea had at last been caught) that in the next life he was hoping to be born a rich man. Another monk told me that after the good have been in heaven for a while they will be reborn as noble and high-born men; while the bad, after a term in hell, will be reborn in evil conditions. For his own part, the monk added, he had no special form of hope for the future life in mind: he merely tried to be good. Several monks told me (and no one asserted the reverse) that all good people, no matter what their religion, would go to heaven and have a favorable rebirth; one does not have to be a Buddhist to go to Paradise.

All the monks pray to the Buddha and the Buddha hears and answers prayers. As in China, prayer consists largely in the repetition of sacred phrases, notably *Namu Sukka Yurai*, or most commonly *Namu Amida Bool*. For it is to Amida that most prayers are addressed. Beside prayer there is in some of the more spiritual monasteries a certain amount of confession. So at least I was informed at the Pyo hum Sa. If a monk has broken one of his vows he confesses it to the Buddha at a stated time in the month; and there is a regular ritual of prayer, etc., by which he is reinstated. If his sin is great he may be put out of the monastery. In that case he may sometimes be readmitted by confession to the abbot. A few of the more learned monks have heard of the Four Noble Truths, but these have no practical place in their moral lives. More vital are the Five Vows and Six Paramitas or "means of passing to the other side of the ocean of misery" —namely, charity, morality, patience, energy, contemplation, wisdom.[18]

Bishop Trollope assures me that in the southern part of the Diamond Mountains, which I did not visit, there are a few monasteries with really learned abbots and spiritual monks. Personally, I found in the monasteries I was able to visit no real learning; but I did find what seemed to be genuine spirituality and an earnest effort to cultivate the higher inner life. Naturally the monks of whom this is true are in a minority. Most of the monks are not very spiritual and most of them are very lazy. The monasteries as a rule own rice-lands in the valleys from which they get a steady income. A few are said to receive something from the government. Nearly all, as in China, get some revenue from visiting pilgrims. Thus the monks never have to work for a living. Their isolated position as a rule makes even the chanting at funerals, which constitutes so large a part of the monastic occupation in China, quite out of the question.

There can be little doubt that it is this idle and easy life which attracts a good many of the members of the Order. Of course many come into it because they have been brought up in the temples as orphans. With them it is the natural step. A few join the Order out of truly spiritual motives—leaving the world to find the truth and the peace of the Buddha. This had been the case with some of the more spiritual young monks with whom I talked. But for the rank and file, I fear, especially in the Kyo jön, the chief attraction is a good living with nothing to do. This is certainly true of most of the nuns. At a convent we visited there were ten old monastic ladies, wrinkled as walnuts though giggly as schoolgirls—nearly all of them old enough (and certainly ugly enough) to be the grandmothers of most of the monks in the convent near by. We asked them why they had

[18] See Trollope, *op. cit.*, p. 26.

adopted the religious life. They responded quite frankly that it was because they had become widows and had no one to support them. The convent was really just an Old Ladies' Home.

If the monasteries were simply Homes for Old Men there would be little or no criticism to give. But their membership is largely made up of young men who ought to have something better to do. I asked at every monastery we visited what they did for the neighborhood—whether they had schools for the boys, held preaching services, attended funerals, etc. A very small proportion, I discovered, maintain schools; only one, I think, claimed to hold preaching services—and this one was at a place so remote in the mountains that the congregation could consist of hardly more than the proprietor and servants of a nearby inn, kept for traveling pilgrims. And as to funerals, the monks never take part in them. They instruct pilgrims in the truths of Buddhism if any come and ask for instruction. That sums up the contribution that most of the monasteries we visited make to the welfare of the outside world. Probably there are a few in less remote regions that do a little more. Mr. Starr seems to think so; in fact, he asserts, much more is done for the outside world "than could be expected. At several of the monasteries there is a school for outside children; some have undertaken a definite work of teaching and some others realize that they have a genuine opportunity to aid in the elevation of the country. More and more of the monasteries seem to awake to the existence of these possibilities." [19]

This awakening of Korean Buddhism is not as yet very marked; but it is certain that a real beginning has been made toward a revival of the old religion. In 1918 Mr. Starr was able to write about it as follows:

> Buddhism appears today to be very far from dead in Korea. It shows signs of life and there may be prospects of its future growth and large development. The monasteries of Korea are under control of thirty head monasteries. . . . These head monasteries in 1902 had become greatly reduced in property, membership, influence and splendor. They were estranged from each other. There was no feeling of unity among them. Each monastery was a thing by itself and decay and corruption

[19] *Op. cit.*, p. 64.

were everywhere evident. But about six years ago the priests of these thirty head monasteries came together; they held a great meeting and discussed their common interests; they decided that union was necessary and a forward movement, a thing such as was tried in 1902 and which failed then. It was tried again and has not failed. They elected a president of their commission, with a term of office of one year. His whole time is devoted to the interests of united Korean Buddhism for that year. They bought property in the city of Seoul and erected a central building, partly temple and partly office building. The expenses of this head office are borne by the thirty temples in proportion to their importance and wealth. The monasteries are graded into five groups and each contributes annually a set sum for the advancement of Buddhism in the peninsula.[20]

The headquarters building in Seoul, to which reference is made in the above quotation, is a large and business-like structure, and is emphatically a school and office building rather than a temple. It is known as the Kajo Kwakwan. Its activities are divided among three departments—religious, educational, and industrial. The department of religion carries on nine lines of work (I quote from a recent circular translated for me by a Japanese) namely: "(1) Regular lecture and preaching meeting, (2) Notable men's lecture, (3) Study of Buddhism, (4) Sunday school, (5) Young Men's Buddhist Association, (6) Women's meeting, (7) Concert and amusement, (8) Translation of the Buddhist Bible and publishing of magazines, (9) Employment bureau." The educational department conducts a night school, with about thirty or forty students. The industrial department gives a course in dressmaking and a course in shoemaking. In Seoul there is also a Buddhist "theological seminary" for monks and novitiates from the mountain monasteries.[21]

The magazine referred to under the eighth line of work in the department of religion, as quoted above, started out quite hopefully in 1913, but at the time Mr. Starr wrote his book (in 1918) it had suffered four breaks in publication and had appeared under five different names.[22] It has appeared a few times since 1918, but its latest appearance, so far as I can learn, was in January, 1921. "Since which date," Bishop Trollope observes, "it appears to have flickered

[20] *Op. cit.*, pp. 34-36.
[21] Starr says he found sixty-five students at this seminary.
[22] See Note 6 in Starr's Appendix.

out, and I can not discover that anything has taken its place." [23]

The Y.M.B.A., however, seems to be prospering. According to the Tokyo *Young East* for June, 1925, "it has now upwards of two thousand members. Dividing its work into departments of propagation, education, literature and art, gymnastics and children, and having branch offices in many important centers, it is actively pushing a useful work." A few of the Buddhists of Korea seem to be awakening also to the call for humanitarian service. A "Keijo Buddhist Charity Association" has been formed which though it has not as yet accomplished a great deal may mark by its very existence the beginning of a new point of view in Korean Buddhism. Its name, of course, suggests that the Association is, in part, under Japanese auspices (Keijo being the Japanese name for Seoul). This society recently founded a home for the aged at the capital.[24] A wealthy Buddhist lady (a Korean) has just founded a second "home" for the same purpose on a much larger scale in the suburbs of the city.[25] The great Nishi Hongwanji temple of Kyoto has recently started a school for girls in Seoul, the school to be run on Buddhist principles.[26] A Buddhist college was begun early in 1927.[27] A movement is on foot to collect and publish a number of commentaries and other Buddhist works by eminent Korean monks.[28]

A movement that may well be more portentous for the future of Korean Buddhism is the rapidly increasing practice of sending students to Japan to study the religion in the scholarly Japanese fashion. This movement has been going on for some time, but in the last three or four years it has assumed rather significant proportions. The mountain monastery of Yu jöm Sa at the time of our visit had sent nine students to Japan for this purpose. There are said to be twenty-nine Korean students at the Rissho College (of the Nichiren sect) alone.[29] Some of these Korean youth are distinguishing themselves among their Japanese brethren. One of them has recently been made abbot of a temple in the

[23] "Buddhist Literature in Korea," the *Korean Bookman* (of Seoul), for Sept., 1922.
[24] *The Young East* for March, 1926.
[25] *Ibid.* for Sept., 1926.
[26] *Ibid.* for June, 1926.
[27] *Ibid.* for Feb., 1927.
[28] *Ibid* for Feb., 1928.
[29] *Ibid.* for Nov., 1925.

vicinity of Kyoto, another abbot of a temple in the Tokyo Prefecture and at the same time appointed professor in one of the Buddhist colleges. In another generation, when these students shall have returned to their native land with new insight into the real teachings of their religion and shall have used what they have learned in systematic efforts at revival and reform, it may be that Korean Buddhism will once more become a spiritual power in the land.

I must confess, however, that I am not oversanguine of this result.[30] At any rate it must be admitted that, except for the first few centuries after its introduction, Buddhism has done (and has been allowed to do) but little for the people of Korea. Korean Buddhism, however, did one great thing. It handed on the Light of Asia to Japan. Korea in fact was the bridge by which both the Indian faith and the Chinese culture passed over from the continent to the Island Empire. As one studies the map, the Korean peninsula seems as if built for this express purpose; and an imaginative vitalist who extended his theory from biology to geology might depict Asia, in obedience to the urge of its entelechy, as sending out a great tentacle of land toward the group of islands which lie just beyond its reach. Doubtless this is fantastic, but to the Buddhist pilgrim in these regions, geography itself becomes symbolic. And indeed the wide valleys, majestic rivers, and distant hills of southern Korea, its far-stretching blue-green paddy fields dotted with the brown thatched roofs of tiny villages, and its deep blue skies, put one in the mood for dreaming. One has a sense everywhere of spaciousness and of the sea—the sea which though invisible is always near. One longs to follow in the footsteps of those daring missionaries from ancient Pakche who carried the lamp of their faith to the unknown islands beyond the straits, and to reach the last stage in the long pilgrimage of Buddhism. So one's thoughts press on to the port and to the watery road that leads from the Land of the Morning Calm to the Empire of the Rising Sun.

[30] The religious statistics of Korea, given in the *Young East* for Nov., 1926, show how small a part Buddhism plays in Korea as a whole. A mixture of Taoism, Confucianism and superstition known as Chyondokyo has 2,000,000 followers: Christianity has 350,000; Buddhism 382,000; Shinto 75,000. The editor adds: "Inasmuch as the total population of Chosen (Korea) is 17,000,000, it is plain that an overwhelming majority of the Korean people are without any religious belief."

CHAPTER XXII

JAPAN AND THE JAPANESE

ALL day long the blue sky and the shining sea and the straight, straight line—the mystery of the straight, unbroken line which is yet a circle—where sky and ocean meet. Yet not always unbroken, for now and then a blue opalescent island swims into view, out there on the world's edge: while the westering sun lowers behind us, where China and Korea lie, hidden now in the depths of our past, as the setting sun will soon be in the ocean's waves. Island succeeds island, and the evening comes; and with the dark, scattered yellow lights appear along some distant shore. At first rare and separate, the flashings of isolated beacons, they become more frequent, and gather into clusters, which must be villages along some unguessed coast. New streams of light in the sky, shot upward from hidden cities, lure the imagination; the great ship calls with its tremendous voice for the pilot, like some sea monster frightened at the dark; and we are in the straits of Shimenoseki, with Kyushu to starboard and Nippon on our port, plowing through the jeweled darkness the waters of Japan.

All night we steam through the straits, and with the dawn we are upon the Inland Sea. With seeming uncertainty the ship finds her way through a maze of islands, at times nearly landlocked as she sails down some long avenue of isles with an apparent *cul de sac* at the end. But a sudden turn, sharp and unguessed, brings us once more into the open, and for hours we are again on the broad sea. Then more islands and islets and rocks, and further alternations of narrow channels and open stretches, through this sea of endless fascination and constantly changing beauty.

But the land of Japan is no less beautiful than its Inland Sea. I have known many lands of great loveliness, but none that I know, save Italy alone, and perhaps Greece, can vie in beauty with this empire of the rising sun. It lacks, indeed, the sense of spaciousness one gets in China, and even in parts of southern Korea, and almost everywhere, except in the higher mountains one has a feeling that the land is built upon a smaller scale than most others: that here one is viewing some of Nature's delicate cabinet work, her more minute carving. But as a piece of exquisite beauty, in which Nature and Art have united with one harmonious purpose, Japan has probably no equal. Even from the windows of a rapid express one gets this impression. It seems as if Nature had prepared this land in advance for the possession of a sensitively artistic people, laying it out as a landscape garden with a constant variation of advancing uplands and receding valleys, with a bit of sea or lake or river in the foreground, and ever at the back the irregular sky line of the distant hills. The main island is so narrow and its central rib of mountain range so long that there is hardly a place on it from which one may not see either the mountains or the ocean, and very often both are united in an intricate intermingling or embrace of ravishing beauty. Rarely is there anything commonplace or monotonous about the Japanese mountains. There are few level ridges but a constant succession of peaks and chasms: while almost every little hill seems to feel it his artistic duty to cherish an individuality of his own, or else in shape to imitate and emulate Fuji. In Fuji, as every Japanese knows, Nippon possesses a thing of beauty which, even were the rest of the land a plain, would make it famous. The view from Fuji, to be sure, is not especially beautiful—at least I did not find it so. It is much too distant, much too like a map for beauty. But the view of Fuji at all possible angles and in the constantly varying effects of the Japanese climate of sun and shade, of cloud and mist, reflected in a hundred lakes and streams, or viewed from the far sea, towering above the nearer hills, or hanging, as it so often seems, from the sky with an ocean of cloud beneath, and belonging rather to heaven than to earth—Fuji is rightly felt by all the Japanese to be a joy forever.

The trees join with the mountains in this effort of Nature to make Japan unique. Nowhere else have I seen so many shades of green crowded into one hillside. Many of the trees, too, taken by themselves, are of peculiar loveliness. Foremost, I suppose, stands the giant cryptomeria, shedding about it a sense of almost religious calm and meditative silence, whether one finds it in forest aisles or in long avenues leading up to solemn temples. But the Japanese pine is almost its equal, its parallel branches giving to the hillsides which it clothes something of that bewitching beauty that makes the heart leap up when it beholds a rainbow in the sky. The isolated pine, too, with its knotted arms reaching out at strange angles upon a background of sky or sea, is something never to forget, as the makers of Japanese screens and prints have so abundantly realized. One should mention too the maples with their minutely cut and lace-like leaves (whose glory in the autumn, alas, we did not see), the cherry and plum trees with their wonder of pink blossoms in the spring (which also we missed), the Kiri with its wisteria-like flowers, the generous azalea, the great Icho tree, dominating the courts of so many Buddhist temples, the lustrous chestnut of the mountain slopes, and, loveliest of all trees that grow, the tender, graceful, clustering bamboo.

To all this beauty the climate adds its last poetic touch. For the Sea of Japan on the west and the Pacific on the east send in their clouds to cluster round the mountain peaks, while at their base are festooned white veils of mist, that rise from lake and stream. No one realizes better than the Japanese themselves the value of these silvery curtains, that suggest more than they hide. Japanese painting exults in it. And the earliest writings this sensitive people produced show the same feeling for the added beauty which their climate breeds. In the Nihongi we read that when Izanagi and Izanami had created Japan, "the great-eight-island Land," Izanagi looked down upon their work and said: "Over the country which we have produced there is naught but morning mists, which shed a perfume everywhere." [1]

To the pilgrim fresh from China, among the striking features of Japan are the great uncultivated areas of forest and mountain. Only one sixth of Japan is arable.[2] Economically considered this is doubtless a great pity: but es-

[1] Aston's trans., *Transactions of the Japan Society*, Supplement I, I. 22.
[2] According to R. L. Buell in the *Weekly Review* for Sept. 10, 1921.

thetically it is, of course, an enormous advantage. Not only does it add directly to the beauty of every landscape, but it gives one also a general sense of space and room to breathe and of fresh wildness and relief from too much humanity. The cultivated regions themselves, moreover, are broken up and broken into by invading mountains and long arms of sea, where crops give way to forest, or to fishing villages, white sails, sampans, and the drying of brown nets on the shore. The land has no great rivers, but it is full of mountain streams, riotous with waterfalls and youthful shoutings in their earlier courses, and in the plains harnessed to water wheels or diverted and divided into irrigating ditches to fill the paddy fields. The rice fields of Japan are on the whole less picturesque than those of China, partly because rice cultivation is not carried so high upon the hillsides, partly because the Japanese farmer, with his more scientific methods, drives his lines straight and makes his fields rectangular. Yet even in a square field rice culture cannot fail of interest, while near by the wheat, barley and millet give pleasant contrast in their tones of green, yellow, and brown. On higher levels one finds the dark green of the rounded tea plants and the light green of the mulberry. As everywhere else, the world over, the harvest time—which comes here in late August and September—is full of varied interest; but more varied still are late May and early June. For at this time go on side by side in adjoining fields the harvest of the early wheat and the transplanting of the rice. Terribly hard labor this transplanting; yet somehow in Japan, to the on-looker at least, it seems less dreary and more colorful than elsewhere. It is often done by a group of eight or ten young men and maidens in line, the pink or purple obis of the girls giving a touch of gaiety to the scene, their kimonos tucked up above their stalwart knees, all of them advancing together in a triumphant march over the flooded fields, like children wading in a pool.

One of the most memorable features of the Japanese countryside is its temples. In the hills one finds them, Shinto shrines or Buddhist monasteries, perched on top of some peak or nestling in a glen or beside a waterfall. And in the cultivated plains one cannot go far without seeing a forested knoll or perhaps just a little round grove on the level—a kind of island in the midst of sunny rice lands—with a torii or gateway before it, and a temple roof dimly suggested within the branches and shadows of the tree-tops. Nor are these fanes deserted or ruinous, as country temples in China are so apt to be. Enter them and you will find them ancient but well kept up, clean as if a New England housewife had just been at them with brush and broom; and it will be strange if you do not discern a peasant bowing in front of the central shrine, throwing down a coin and mumbling a prayer or two before he goes away. On the edge of every village or at its center the same tale is repeated—a simple Shinto shrine with its round mirror in lieu of idol, perhaps a pair of stone foxes guarding the entrance, or a Buddhist temple with its meditative Amida or Kwannon the Merciful One, or the loving Jizo who saves little children.

A Japanese village as yet untouched by Western architecture—especially if it be on a hillside—is a thing of beauty hardly to be surpassed. I remember one in which I spent the evening of a fête day. All the houses were adorned with paper lanterns, and through the winding streets, up the crooked stairways, under the projecting roofs, streamed the children of the village, each little boy and little girl carrying a red lantern, while the older young people, in serenading groups of six or eight, filled the night with music and happy voices.

The rural cottages of Japan seem to have been planned to fit the landscape. Their curving lines, high thatched roofs of a rich brown or covered over with splashes of many-colored moss, are no intrusion upon mountain and meadow. Unfortunately the same cannot be said of the modern type of Japanese building. Particularly—and painfully—striking is this intrusion of the new upon the old as one travels eastward toward Tokyo. Most of rural Japan is still but slightly marred by the West; but as one enters the zone devastated by the recent earthquake the contrast and clash of the two cultures becomes almost tragically evident. Interspersed among the ancient houses, with their swaying lines and their lofty thatch, are numbers of modern structures, put up to take the place of the older buildings the earthquake leveled.

These new houses are wooden shacks, with straight lines, right angles, and low roofs of corrugated iron.

The immediate occasion of this substitution of the ugly for the picturesque is, of course, the earthquake and grim necessity. But the deeper cause is the invasion of Japan by Western culture. It had made itself felt in the cities long before September, 1923. If rural Japan is unsurpassed in beauty, the westernized Japanese city is, and for years has been, unsurpassed for ugliness. The Yokohama of the pre-earthquake days was notable among the ports of the world for deadly commonplace and for the mingling of just the worst features of East and West. And as for Tokyo, the capital of the Empire, the metropolis of Asia—where is there another city remotely approaching it in size so lacking in distinction? Name three temples, two parks, and a few tombs, and you have told all there is that raises itself above the dead monotony of this endless straggling village—this village that is neither East nor West. So it was before the earthquake. Since then it has, of course, the distinction of a great tragedy. Not that any desolate spaces are left or any noble ruins. There was nothing architecturally noble to ruin, and the great central section that was swept clean by the fire was quickly rebuilt with little wooden shacks, so that, when I last saw it, this part of the city presented the appearance of a western or southern American town where they have recently discovered oil.

Fortunately, not all Japanese cities are like Tokyo and Yokohama. In fact, no others are. Osaka is fast becoming in appearance an up-to-date Western town, with broad, straight streets, and brick and stone business blocks. Kobe is mostly Western, with a few attractive Japanese streets in the native section. There are still some cities which the West has but slightly touched, and these retain considerable charm. Notable among them is, of course, Kyoto, one of the most attractive towns in the world, with its colorful streets, its little river lined with gardens, lanterns, and gay tea-houses, its parks and palaces, and the fringe of great temples with their exquisite gardens that surrounds the whole city, and farther out the rim of hills and mountains that look down upon it from every side.

It might be said of most peoples that in some respects they seem to fit the lands in which they dwell. Of none is this more notably true than of the Japanese. Their land seems made for them and they for it. I have already pointed out that everything in Japan except Fuji and the cryptomerias seems built on a smaller scale than one finds in most countries, and the inhabitants are no exceptions to the rule. That is usually the first thing the foreigner notices about them. On further acquaintance this characteristic is increasingly brought home to one. One's first introduction to a Japanese sleeper fills one with mingled amusement and dismay—this double row of tiny berths, too low to put anything under them, too short for most Westerners to stretch out in, this aisle too narrow for any luggage, yet in which all the luggage must be put, these wash-stands so low one must bend double to reach them. In a Japanese house there are, of course, no beds nor chairs, but they have dining-room tables, which are perhaps four inches high, and within the "honorable recess" there is usually a still smaller table supporting a full-grown pine tree which from root to topmost branch may reach to eighteen inches. Most Japanese automobiles are of foreign make; but there are some home-made ones a trifle larger than rickshaws and noticeably larger than Western baby-carriages. Not only do the Japanese find little things useful: they have a great love for the tiny as such. Dwarf trees are their delight, and with marvelous skill they grow minute specimens of many a forest giant. A space in a backyard that most of us would consider too small for anything but a garbage can they will make into a garden, with ponds and streams, stone arched bridges, lanterns, flowers and a forest of dwarf trees. In such a land an ordinary American feels like Gulliver in Lilliput.

Next to the small size of the Japanese and of much of their work, the thing that is most likely to strike a casual visitor is the fact that many of the things one has been told about this interesting people are palpably untrue. This is notably the case on the question of honesty. Which of us has not been credibly informed by innumerable persons that the Japanese are so dishonest that all cashiers in Japanese banks—but I refrain from repeating what every one has heard. One lands in Japan ready to be cheated, fleeced, and robbed. One soon learns, to one's enormous astonishment, that there is not a land in West or East where one's property is safer. I have been told, to be sure, by American and British business men that Japanese merchants do not live up to the spirit of a contract so thoroughly as Chinese merchants, that the goods they furnish are not always certain to be up to specification, that their word is not so uniformly equal to their bond as is that of the Chinaman. Of these things I know nothing. But I know I have never been in a land where the tradesmen seem farther removed from sharp practice, where the proper change is so regularly returned to one, where so little advantage is taken of the stranger's ignorance, where one can with impunity be more careless of one's luggage and one's valuables. Honest as is the Chinese merchant, one feels always that he is honest because he is keenly aware that honesty is the best policy; and that alongside of his honesty there goes a certain—let us say—*financial* point of view. With the Japanese merchant I do not have this feeling to anything like the same extent. His attention does not seem to be so steadily glued to the main chance or to the financial aspect of life. His honesty is a little less that of the merchant, a little more that of the gentleman.

Both peoples have the morals that have grown out of their cultures and their histories. Both have developed intensely the virtues of the Oriental family and of the conventional Confucian morality. Beyond that the Chinese have particularly emphasized the morals of the merchant, while the Japanese have been trained in the virtues that grow out of the soldier's life and out of the feudal relationships. Furthermore, Buddhism, which has been taken so much more seriously in Japan than in China, has had its noticeable effect in imparting to the Japanese mind a certain other-worldly point of view, a way of disregarding and even scorning the good things of a materialistic common sense, which would be quite incomprehensible to your average Chinese. Spread quite widely among the Japanese people there is a desire for self-discipline, a Nietzschian love of hardness toward oneself, which is largely traceable to Buddhist stoicism and especially to the Zen training and ideal, and which one would seek for in vain among the eminently sensible Chinese. The exigencies of their history and their social organization, moreover, have developed in the Japanese a sense of loyalty to the social group which is notably lacking in individualistic China. The glories of Bushido have, no doubt, been greatly exaggerated and Japan's feudal age has been idealized by both native and foreign writers past all historical recognition; yet there is no denying the fact that in those centuries of civil war and feudal allegiance and Buddhist training, the upper classes of Japan did work out a form of morality that was rather noble, and that was notably different from that of the rest of Eastern Asia.

But if we of the West have underestimated the honesty of the Japanese, most of us have certainly overestimated their cleverness. We have built up, and are still adding to, a myth that the Japanese possess a kind of uncanny or superhuman cleverness. We often picture them as almost miraculously efficient and almost diabolically astute. One does not have to know the Japanese very well to discover that this whole point of view is another illustration of the adage, *omne ignotum pro magnifico.* The Japanese are undoubtedly efficient and astute, but not more so than many other peoples. They have particularly "backed themselves" to learn the German art of war, and they have succeeded very well. The astuteness of their diplomacy has been greatly exaggerated. Their diplomats have often been free from political idealism of the Gladstonian, Wilsonian type, and so have won the admiration and applause of many little-minded on-lookers. But if they have seen clearly certain small things that others overlook, they have failed to see certain large things in human nature and the life of nations which in the long last are more essential to sound policy than are the innumerable brilliant little *coups* of a cynical and disillusioned *Realpolitik.* And in matters industrial and mechanical they are imitators only, and frequently rather stupid imitators at that. Outside of their unquestioned artistic qualities, they have as yet shown small sign of becoming in any sense rivals of the Western peoples. One of the things that most strikes a visitor to Japan is the cheapness and flimsiness of many of their productions.

Yet I hasten to add that the Japanese are certainly a very intelligent race. Only an intelligent race could assimilate so much of an entirely foreign civilization as they have done in the last fifty years. They are great learners. They are omnivorous readers.[3] I have never seen a city in either Europe or America in which there were one quarter as many bookshops as one will find in Tokyo: and the other cities of Japan are not far behind the capital in this respect. Japan has an immense reading public, filled with a great intellectual curiosity; and this fact is bound to tell in many ways.

Like the Chinese, the Japanese are a very industrious people. They work long hours, and, like the Chinese again, they seem to enjoy their work.

But the quality that has struck me most forcibly in the Japanese is their restraint. It goes through a large part of their lives and comes out in all sorts of unexpected ways. It is, of course, very noticeable in their courtesy. A large part of all courtesy, for that matter, is restraint—restraint of impulses that might prove unpleasant to others. But the Japanese seem to carry this farther than most peoples. They train themselves to inhibit not only such actions as would give offense, but all expressions of emotion that might sadden others. Long faces and sorrowful words are taboo. Shortly after the earthquake I asked a Japanese whom I met on a train whether he had lost any of his friends in the catastrophe. He answered with a forced laugh that his children had all been killed. One would have thought he regarded it as a good joke on himself. I am sure the man's heart was torn as any father's would have been, but he had been trained to laugh at whatever happened, so as not to force his private woe on others.

> Laugh and the world laughs with you—
> Weep and you weep alone.

This, thinks Japan, is as it should be.

But Japanese courtesy goes deeper than this. It is not merely a matter of restraint. It is not merely negative. The Japanese are, I believe, the most courteous people in the

[3] According to the *Young East*, during the year 1925 Japan published more books than any other country save only Germany.

world, and their courtesy is more than superficial. It does not come merely from the desire to keep up appearances—though doubtless this desire contributes largely to it. It comes in part also, I am convinced, from genuine good will and honest kindliness. One sees it in their eyes and in their actions. It is a kind of impersonal kindliness—a readiness to look out for human beings as such. Foreigners traveling in the earthquake zone just after the catastrophe unanimously testified to the positive kindness they received from all sorts of people—men and women of all classes going out of their way to help the foreigner and if they had no more, sharing their last crust with him. Of course if the mob spirit gets hold of them, the Japanese like other peoples can lose their courtesy and lose their heads. After the earthquake Japanese mobs treated many Koreans almost as cruelly and madly as our American mobs treat the negroes. But it is very rare, this sort of thing, in Japan, and even a national insult is not enough to break down the deeply rooted habits of courtesy. We were in Japan at the time of the passage of the Exclusion Act by the American Congress, and could see how deeply hurt all classes of society felt at what they regarded as an incomprehensible slap in the face. Yet never even in the most exciting moments did we see or hear of a discourteous act toward an American. On the contrary, we repeatedly were treated, by all sorts of people, with positive and uncalled for kindness. It seemed as if the Japanese as a whole had made up their minds to show Christendom what it means to love your enemies.

The courtesy of the Japanese has still another source than those I have mentioned. It is the product not only of carefully practiced restraint and genuine kindness of heart: in seeking to explain it one must refer also to the peculiar gentleness and refinement native to the race. The Japanese are an extremely sensitive people, on whom bad taste in conduct or in art rasps unpleasantly. This may seem inconsistent with what I have said of the hardness which they cultivate toward themselves and the callousness toward suffering which I shall have to mention later on as one of their characteristics. But he who expects the character of the Japanese people, or of any other people, to be free from contradictions must have had but small acquaintance with human nature. I do not say that gentleness is native to them in the sense of being a biologically inherited trait. I am not here distinguishing between biological and social heredity. It is quite probable, I think, that the gentleness of which I speak is a racial characteristic, both in the biological sense and as a socially inculcated habit and ideal. The Japanese are naturally gentle except when there is a call for aggressive action. They love gentleness and inculcate it. It is very rarely that they lose their temper, very rarely that they raise their voices. One could live years in Japan without seeing a quarrel. All classes of society show a deep-lying refinement of manners and of taste which is very striking indeed.

This refinement and gentleness are particularly noticeable among the women. Their gentleness begins with their attitude toward their own children and is carried on to all the world. There is none of the bawling at naughty children so common in Europe, no loud-voiced threats, and very little corporal punishment. Probably there should be more than there is, for Japanese children are sometimes spoiled. Yet they seem to need active and violent control less than Western children; for they, too, are, in most cases, astonishingly gentle, and consequently easy to govern. Probably they acquire the characteristic by imitation from their mothers. And with the gentleness of the Japanese mother there goes also a great patience, a beautiful humility of bearing, and the usual unselfishness which regularly characterizes the women of the East.

Yet with all their gentleness, the Japanese are essentially and notably a brave people. In a sense, of course, all peoples are brave. Courage is one of the commonest and cheapest of the virtues. But the courage of the Japanese is not merely of the common sort. Theirs is the courage of endurance, the courage of self-repression, the courage of restraint. Here, once more, I think we may see the influence of Buddhism, with its reiterated lesson of killing out the thought of self. The peculiarity of the Japanese soldier in the Russian War was not the courage of daring, in which the Westerner quite equals him. It was the courage of selflessness: the willingness of the individual to lose himself as an individual in the whole;

not merely to die gloriously, but just to go out quite namelessly and with no memory. The same courage of restraint, the same persistent endurance came to the surface again in the presence of the great disaster of September, 1923. The survivors of Tokyo and Yokohama, and in a sense the whole nation, faced the situation with a kind of stoical calm and quiet unsubduable persistence that must wring admiration from even the most prejudiced.

It may be in part owing to this constant undertone of restraint that one feels the Japanese to be at heart a somewhat sad people. Not that they are lacking in smiles and laughter. On the contrary they laugh by far too much. One quickly becomes very weary of their recurrent laugh, regular as clockwork, whatever be the subject of conversation. It is even difficult at times not to lose one's temper and cry out, For Heaven's sake, be serious! But as I have already pointed out, the laugh of the Japanese is not a token of inward gaiety, but a part of deliberate courtesy, consciously inculcated. It has not the merry and whole-hearted ring of Chinese laughter; and underneath this smile that refuses to come off there may beat a very heavy heart. It reminds one of the smile on the faces of archaic Greek sculpture—of the heroes of the Aegina marbles who have been smiling now these 2500 years with a sword piercing their vitals.

The constant restraint which goes so deep in Japanese life has its unpleasant as well as its attractive features. Most foreign residents of Japan from Lafcadio Hearn down will tell you that nearly every Japanese keeps his true self forever hidden behind a wall of reserve which no outsider can ever break through. Their outer lives seem to possess no privacy, and their inner lives have nothing else. This constant self-restraint, so deliberately inculcated and practiced, means, of course, a constant self-consciousness which results in a certain stiffness of manners that I have never noticed to the same extent in any other people. Those, indeed, who have been educated abroad are frequently free from it, but there are very few Japanese who have grown up entirely in their own land who seem able to throw it off. With a group of Chinese gentlemen one may soon feel as much at ease as with a group of Americans. There is a suppleness, an easy largeness and naturalness about them that gives them at once the air of men of the world. They seem cosmopolitan and to the manner born. Your Japanese gentleman seems hopelessly incapable of losing himself.

Restraint, once more, is the chief secret of what is most characteristic in Japanese art. Not that it is by any means their only artistic quality, for they have all sorts; they are, in fact, possibly the most thoroughly artistic people of our times. But the characteristic which most completely differentiates their art from the art of the West seems to me just this ability to deny themselves the satisfaction of going the whole distance, this knowledge of when to stop, this surprising temperance in expression, this insight into the enormous emotional appeal that results from leaving to the imagination of the beholder the climax of the entire piece. In sculpture, to be sure, there is little chance for this, but in Japanese architecture at its best (which unfortunately is not Japanese architecture at its latest), this noble restraint is as obvious as in Greek temples of the Periclean age. It is, however, in painting and in poetry that its effects are best observed. On many a screen the glorious pine tree rises, marked out sharply from its golden background, and as the eye follows its fascinating lines toward the glory of its full-branching development, a cloud intervenes, or there is an absolutely blank space, behind which, or in which, the imagination may guess at forms more beautiful than any brush can paint. The landscape leads out to widening and enticing vistas, but just as the full promise is about to be attained, a mist closes in. So in the No plays, the tragedy on which the Western playwright would lavish the greatest pains and to which the whole play has led up is only vaguely hinted. *Rien de trop* is the great canon of taste for the Japanese artist. It is characteristic of this people that they have developed the arrangement of flowers into a professional art, and that never more than five sprays are used in a bouquet.

In saying that the Japanese are perhaps the most artistic people of our times I am only quoting the opinion of many who are much better judges than I. Certainly they seem to be in love with beauty as hardly any others. They carry ever with them the fresh eye, prepared to see beauty wherever it exists. They feel a need for the constant enjoyment of the beautiful of which we in the West have little conception. We fill our houses with beautiful things—and seldom look at them. If one disappears we note its absence, but its presence is taken for granted. This is partly because we have become accustomed to it, in its regular place, partly because it is mixed in our rooms with a quantity of other beautiful things. We want to have beautiful things around us: the Japanese want to enjoy beautiful things. To bring this about they keep in a room but one picture or one bunch of flowers at a time and as soon as the eye grows familiar with it they take it away and put a new one in its place. They consider it almost as difficult to enjoy two pictures on one wall as to enjoy two pieces of music played at the same time. They really want to enjoy the beautiful. And they really do so.

They not only love beautiful things: they produce them. As a people they show extraordinarily good taste—except, indeed, when they imitate Western architecture or Western fashions: for then they can unconsciously turn out as ugly things as the mind of man ever devised. But when working along their native lines they still produce, as they always have, innumerable things of exquisite charm. It is, for instance, most instructive to compare a modern china shop in China with one in Japan. The Chinese cups and saucers, plates and jars, are almost uniformly ugly in both shape and color and type of decoration—at times extremely so. A Japanese china shop, on the other hand, is full of exquisite things, almost every one a work of art in its way. They may cost only a few sen but they are things of beauty. Everything that the Japanese uses he insists must be beautiful; and he usually sees to it that it is so.

In loving the beautiful the Japanese loves the world not as it is but as it ought to be. This tendency of his is, perhaps, not unrelated to a quality that has often been pointed out and is indeed extremely obvious. The thing I have in mind is a certain unreality, a certain lack of realism, a kind of universal conspiracy and agreement to shut the eyes to undesired realities and to substitute fancy for fact. Mr. Gulick in his excellent work on the evolution of the Japanese has given a name to this quality: he calls it "nominality." The Bishop of Southampton evidently is thinking of the same thing when he says, "The Japanese can pretend longer than most." We must not be too surprised at the power of pretending nor regard it as peculiar to the Japanese. We peoples of the West are also pretty good at it. Most of us cherish certain pious fairy tales—of a political, economic, moral or religious nature—which we know are not true but which we agree to respect, and somehow we repeat them to each other with straight faces. The Japanese are merely like the rest of us in this, with the single difference that, as the bishop says, they can pretend longer than most. The quality comes out in all sorts of ways, but is, perhaps, most striking to us Westerners in the strictly official attitude which almost all Japanese take on the myth of the divine descent and of the divine nature of the imperial family.[4] Their ability to keep their faces straight when talking on this subject ranks them one grade higher than even the Roman augurs.

Their ability to cherish a living belief in one half of their mind which in the other half they must know to be purely fanciful is due in part to the fact that, with all their realism, they live their lives largely in an ideal world. In international relations they admire *Realpolitik*, but in a large part of life they are sentimentalists and idealists. They have in them a good deal of the mystic. It is not the mysticism of St. Teresa nor that of the emotional revival meeting, but it is mysticism none the less. It is partly due to this that they may properly be called a religious people. They are by nature much more religious than the Chinese. In

[4] Cf. the following Suggested Solution for World Peace:—"To preserve the world's peace and to promote the welfare of mankind is the mission of the Imperial Family of Japan. Heaven has invested the Imperial Family with all the qualifications necessary to fulfil this mission. He who can fulfil this mission is one who is the object of humanity's admiration and adoration and who holds the prerogative of administration for ever. The Imperial Family of Japan is as worthy of respect as God, and is the embodiment of benevolence and justice. The great principle of the Imperial Family is to make popular interests paramount—most important. The Imperial Family of Japan is the parent not only of her sixty millions but of all mankind on earth. In the eyes of the Imperial Family all races are one and the same; it is above all racial considerations. All human disputes, therefore, may be settled in accordance with its immaculate justice. The League of Nations proposed to save mankind from the horrors of war can only attain its real object by placing the Imperial Family of Japan at its head, for to attain its object the League must have a strong punitive force of a superracial character, and this force can only be found in the Imperial Family of Japan." Trans. from the Japanese paper "Niroku" and published in the *Japan Advertiser* of May 6th, 1919.

fact, I am inclined to think that among the peoples of the East they stand in this respect second only to the Indians. Not only have they a decidedly strong mystic vein: they have also a great interest in and feeling for the cosmic. And not only have they a feeling for the cosmic: they have, in my opinion, a really philosophical attitude toward the ultimate problems which religion presents. I cannot at all agree with Keyserling that the Japanese are a superficial people, that they fail to understand their own religion, that they are lacking not only in appreciation but even in seriousness.[5] The thinkers of Japan have taken their Mahayana Buddhism seriously, have written many books in the exposition and defense of it and made some progress in developing it. Those that I have met are able to discuss it and its problems with real intelligence. And certainly they have adorned their religion with a feeling for beauty so that the charm of it is beyond almost anything that we know.

The Japanese, like the rest of us, have their faults, and some of them I have tried to indicate. To be sure, the faults that we of the West most often attribute to them are hardly of the sort that can be properly called racial or national faults at all. The fact that they live simply and cheaply and work hard is scarcely a reproach, although of course these qualities of simplicity and industry may make them unpleasant competitors. That their government has pursued an aggressive, imperialistic and at times unscrupulous and tyrannous policy is a grave accusation against the government. That this policy has usually had the approbation of the Japanese people is a grave accusation against the people and one that justly makes other nations look at Japan with a certain amount of uncertainty, not to say suspicion. These facts, however, are hardly surprising and need no reference to racial dispositions to explain them. They are sufficiently explained by the political situation of the times, the example of Western nations, and the short-sighted views that necessarily go with a youthful and enthusiastic nationalism. They are events, policies, and do not go deep enough to be called national qualities. What may justly be described as a national quality—whether due to biological or to social heredity, or to

[5] *The Travel Diary of a Philosopher*, II. 158f.

both—is a certain indifference to the welfare and a callousness to the sufferings of others, especially when these others are not immediately visible, which the Japanese, in common with the Chinese, not infrequently display. The ruthless violence with which the Japanese government put down the insurrection in Korea was short-sighted and unscrupulous policy; but the almost universal indifference on the part of the Japanese people—Buddhist, Shinto, and Christian alike—toward the aspirations and the sufferings of the Koreans showed that this policy was not merely an isolated event but the cropping out of a truly national characteristic.[6] For the attitude of the Japanese people during the recent Korean persecutions was not an isolated affair. It must be read in the light of history. One must recall the outrageous ruthlessness of the Japanese soldiers in Hideyoshi's invasion of Korea three hundred and fifty years ago, and the martial hardness and indifference to suffering to which so large a portion of the people trained themselves during the centuries of medieval civil war. In making up one's picture of the Japanese people one must not stop with Lafcadio Hearn's *Glimpses of Unfamiliar Japan.* One must not think of them merely as a race of charming and beautiful little fairies flying about in kimonos and on butterfly wings. All that indeed should go into the picture. In ordinary circumstances they are a people of wonderful courtesy and of genuine kindness. But one should remember also Hideyoshi's ear mourned in Kyoto and the iron heel shown in Korea in our own times.

But where is the people that have no faults? And in spite of those I have mentioned I cannot close this chapter without testifying to the fact that personally I found the Japanese immensely more likable on the whole than I had anticipated. Nearly every American who lives among them for any length of time comes to be fond of them. The fondness is not as a rule so great as that which the residents of China feel for the Chinese; for, as I have pointed out, there is an aloofness about the Japanese character which usually prevents close intimacy, a certain stiffness which seldom

[6] Again I wish to draw the reader's attention to the fact that when I say national I do not necessarily mean racial, i.e., in the biological sense. I am not committing myself one way or another in the difficult theoretical question here involved.

allows personal relations between them and foreigners to get beyond the formal stage. Yet one can hardly help feeling, however one likes or dislikes them, that they are a nation of gentlemen. On the whole it must be said they are a brave, courteous, admirable people, an efficient, intelligent, sensitive, and likable people, and a people to whom we of the West, and especially we Americans, have in recent years done but scant justice.

It was to this able and gifted people that Buddhism came in the sixth century of our era. That some of the qualities of the modern Japanese are due to Buddhism is undoubtedly true—as in fact I have already pointed out. But, on the other hand, the development that Buddhism has had in Japan is in part due to the qualities which it found in the Japanese people. The Japanese are often spoken of as mere imitators because they received the essential elements of their religion and their art from China and Korea. But, as we shall see, the Japanese were no more content with merely imitating Chinese Buddhism than with merely imitating Chinese art. When Buddhism and Art came, it must be remembered, the Japanese were still in the formative stage of their racial life. Their condition was quite comparable with that of our own ancestors at the same time. They accepted Buddhism and Chinese civilization from abroad, just as our English, French, and German ancestors accepted Christianity and Roman civilization; and in both East and West a somewhat parallel development went on. In fact, the Japanese were Buddhists before most of our ancestors were Christians. Buddhism came to Japan before Charlemagne had civilized the Franks and Christianized the Saxons, and before Hengest and Horsa had landed with their pagan hordes on the shores of Britain.

The story of Japanese Buddhism is therefore a long one, and some acquaintance with it will be necessary to an intelligent understanding of the Buddhism of modern Japan. To this historical and introductory study we must therefore turn in the following chapter.

PERIODS IN JAPANESE HISTORY

Mythical, Traditional, and Pre-Buddhist Period, 660 B.C.—522 A.D.

Introduction and Early Spread of Buddhism, 522-709.

Nara Epoch, 709-794.

Heian Epoch (Fujiwara and Taira Supremacy), 794-1192.

Kamakura Epoch (Minamoto and Hojo Supremacy), 1192-1335.

Muromachi Epoch (Ashikaga Supremacy), 1335-1573.

Nobunaga, Hideyoshi, and Iyeyasu, 1573-1616.

Tokugawa Shogunate, 1603-1867.

Restoration and Rule of the Emperors, 1867 to the present.

CHAPTER XXIII

THE STORY OF JAPANESE BUDDHISM

THE immediate source of Japanese Buddhism was Korea. The original source of it was, of course, the teachings of Gotama. Yet if we should confine ourselves to the contributions made by Gotama and by Korea we should have to leave out of account immense portions of the Buddhism of Japan. As we have seen, before Buddhism left India on its long pilgrimage to the northeast, it levied heavily upon all that India had to give of stored-up spiritual treasures. The Founder himself was not merely a founder but also a transmitter, and much of the wisdom of the Vedas and possibly of the Upanishads, and many a concept from the Samkhya and Yoga he welded into his rich and composite teaching. His successors, in spite of their earnest orthodoxy, added much. The developing Vedanta philosophy and the Bhakti schools made their contributions. Hindu mythology wove its festoons around the growing religion, Indian logic, mathematics, astronomy gave all they had, and Indian architecture, sculpture, painting and poetry decked out the whole. Nor was this all. Before Buddhism started out for China it drew upon the resources of central Asia, it borrowed incidental ideas from the Persian Zoroastrians and perhaps from other peoples, and in visualizing its thought of the Buddhas and Bodhisattvas it took all that the Greek sculptors of Bactria had to give. It was this magnificent procession from the Indian world that came to China in the first part of the Christian era, taking (to borrow a current phrase) several centuries "to pass a given point."

I spoke of its entrance into China as if it had been one long procession. It was not one procession but many. Different pilgrim bands took different routes. Each caravan found fresh recruits and fresh treasures on its long way. From Khotan they came, from Tibet, from Mongolia and the

Himalayan states, from the islands of the sea. All these pilgrim caravans converged on China and there unpacked their treasures and poured them into the common melting pot. Then the Chinese brought from out their store new contributions, things both new and old, and added them to the common hoard. A few of these things must be here specified. One of them was the feeling for the communal life, always so strong in China, which, though it may not have changed a line in the writings of any Buddhist philosopher, surely did soften down and mellow the rather sharp and hard individualism which was one of the aspects of the original teachings of the Founder.[1] Confucianism added its concept of filial piety and family loyalty and its large store of practical morality, while Taoism brought its mystical insight and poetical feeling. Chinese learning and poetry and art merged themselves in the rich store. New treasures poured in also from central Asia, once Buddhism was well at home in China—central Asia, that mart of ideas through the long centuries now so dark to us, where East and West, Hindu, Confucian, Manichæan, Zoroastrian, Buddhist, Mohammedan, Greek, and Christian exchanged religions and philosophies with their wares. Thus enriched, Buddhism swept up into Korea, and gathered what this poetical and artistic people had to offer. So at last it was ready for its pilgrimage across the straits into the island empire of Japan.

When we say, therefore, that Buddhism began to be carried over to Japan in the sixth century, we refer to very much more than simply the teachings of Sakyamuni. In a sense we might say that most of eastern and central and southern Asia rose up and marched across the straits. Nor does the story of the enrichment of Buddhism end here, for the Japanese people had also their contribution to make. As we shall see, this gifted people have done with Buddhism what they have done with everything else that has been brought them from abroad. They have accepted it simply, humbly, in sincere and almost childlike fashion, and then they have laid the stamp of their own transforming genius upon it.

One further remark of a general nature let me make be-

[1] Cf. Okakura, *The Ideals of the East* (New York, Dutton, 1905).

fore we proceed to the more detailed story of Japanese Buddhism. I have spoken of the many accretions to the religion and the many developments within it after the lips of the Founder were mute. The interesting thing to note here is the fact that these many and multiform additions, with the exception of certain superstitions and externalisms, have been so transmuted by adoption, have been so thoroughly assimilated, that foreign as they at first appear one is constrained, on further examination, to say, Yes, these are thoroughly Buddhist after all. Within the original form of the religion there seem to have been quite literally innumerable potentialities that required only the touch of new conditions and new human needs to bring to light. The Buddhist religion had no little hard kernel of sharply definable selfhood to prevent it from merging and mingling, absorbing and assimilating, adapting itself with wonderful elasticity to all sorts of new situations and identifying itself fearlessly with many a spiritual force that seemed on the surface foreign and antithetic. The Anatta doctrine could hardly find a better exemplification than in Buddhism itself.

I have said that Buddhism came first to Japan from Korea. That is true in the sense that the first successful landing, so to speak, of the great Pilgrim was made by the help of Koreans and from Korea as a base. But the first attempt to carry Buddhism into Japan was made by a Chinese monk, one Shiba Tachito as the Japanese learned to call him, who in 522 reached Yamato and built a temple there, enshrining an image of the Buddha. Whether he made any proselytes is unknown; but he abode steadfastly at his shrine, worshiping the Buddha through long years with the patience of an oriental and the confidence of an unshakable faith. The more spectacular beginning of Buddhism in Japan took place some thirty years later (552) when the King of Pakche —the southwestern division of the peninsula, called by the Japanese Kudara—sent to Kimmei, the emperor of Japan, a copper image of the Buddha (probably Amida) plated with gold, together with several Sutras, some flags and umbrellas, and a royal letter, which read, in part, as follows:

This doctrine is among all most excellent. But it is difficult to explain and difficult to understand. Even the Duke of Chou and Confucius did not attain to comprehension. It can produce fortune and retribution immeasurable, illimitable. It can transform a man into a Bodhi. . . . Moreover, from farthest India to the three Han, all have embraced the doctrine and there is none that does not receive it with reverence wherever it is preached.[2]

The emperor seems to have been pleased with the image but not to have known what to do with it. Rather characteristically the military members of the council, and those closely connected with the ceremonials of the native religion, Shinto, were decidedly opposed to the acceptance of the gift and the introduction of the new religion; they, therefore, urged the emperor to take no chances on the anger of the native *Kami* or deities, but to reject the gift outright. Some of the civil officials of the court, on the other hand, under the leadership of the Soga family advised the emperor to take the more daring course and put Japan in line with the more advanced and cultured nations of the world, namely, Korea and China. The emperor finally decided to "play safe," and adopted the experimental course of trying out the image on the family that had urged its acceptance. The bronze Buddha was accordingly intrusted to the Soga chief, with the command that he must worship it.[3] He of course obeyed and courageously made his house into a temple for the new god; and the court and capital waited to see what would happen. The experiment turned out very ill for the Sogas and the new religion; for the first thing that happened was a pestilence, which was of course taken as a token of the anger of the Kami. The image was accordingly thrown into a canal, and for twenty years nothing more was heard of Buddhism, except near the little shrine of Shiba Tachito (the Chinese monk), where the sound of bell and gong and chanted prayer rose as regularly as morning and evening.

By 572, when the emperor and all his ministers had died, the king of Pakche made a second attempt, sending this time to the imperial court "two hundred volumes of sacred books, an ascetic, a yogi, a nun, a reciter of mantras, a maker of images, and a temple architect." [4] The Koreans were per-

[2] Nihongi XIX. 33, 34. In Aston's trans. (London, Kegan Paul, 1896), II. 65-66.
[3] Nihongi XIX. 36, Aston, II. 67.
[4] Brinkley, *A History of the Japanese People* (London, Encyclopædia Britannica Co.), p. 132.

mitted to build a private temple in what is now Osaka, and other Korean missionaries soon followed. The Soga family, still faithful to the new religion, once more took it under their protection and built a new private temple for the new images. They also hunted up Shiba Tachito at his shrine, and with his assistance found one other Buddhist in Japan, a Korean priest. Shiba Tachito now dedicated his daughter to the holy life, and the new-found priest ordained her a nun, with two other girls. So the religion was given a new chance. Once more, however, the pestilence broke out and once more the images were thrown into the canal. But as the pestilence grew worse instead of better, the Soga family argued that it might mean the anger not of the Kami but of the Buddha. So the new religion was allowed to remain.

The next emperor, who ascended the throne soon after the end of the pestilence, was a nephew of the head of the Soga family, and it is recorded of him that he "believed in the law of Buddha and reverenced Shinto"; and during his reign the new religion apparently enjoyed imperial favor and flourished correspondingly. At the emperor's death (in the arms of Buddhism), the opponents of the new religion led a revolt which was put down by the combined exertions of the Soga family and the son of the late emperor, a youth of sixteen, whose name was destined to be one of the brightest in all the annals of his religion and of his country, the prince Umayado, known to history as Shotoku Taishi.

New bands of Buddhist missionaries from Korea now followed each other into Japan and the faith of the Buddha began to spread among the common people. The lasting success of the new religion was made certain when, in 588, Suiko became empress and Shotoku Taishi, her nephew, was nominated prince imperial and regent. The prince did not live to become emperor in his own right;[5] but he wielded the power of an emperor during his life, for he and the empress were apparently of one mind in all matters of importance.

Shotoku Taishi has been called the Constantine of Japan. It would be more fitting so call him the Asoka. In more ways than one he emulated (whether consciously or not) the career of the great emperor of Magadha. He was an able

[5] He died in 621; the Empress Suiko, in 628.

administrator, a devoted servant of his country, and a reformer of its laws; and he and the empress bent their united efforts toward spreading the faith in which they profoundly believed, and encouraging the rapid introduction, from Korea and China, of the art and culture that seemed an inextricable part of the new religion.

It was Shotoku Taishi who built the first public Buddhist temple in Japan.[6] His most famous construction was the great religious institution (one can hardly call it less) at Horyuji. The heart of this institution was the temple which still survives—filled today with noble art treasures produced in the Suiko epoch or shortly after it, and some of them said to be the work of the great prince himself. The temple was surrounded by many other buildings, for this was not merely a place of worship but a place of learning, a small university for the study of Buddhist thought and the art of music, and a place of human helpfulness as well, with a hospital, a dispensary, and a poorhouse, where the Buddhist ideal of universal love was put into actual practice. "The whole foundation thus served as a focus of the Buddhist religion, morality, and art, which now became integral parts of the national life."[7]

The national life, in fact, interested Prince Shotoku quite as much as the Buddhist religion; and it was largely for the sake of the national life that he did so much to spread and deepen the faith of his adoption. He regarded it as a pillar of the state and as a means for harmonizing and unifying the social life of the people. It is important to realize this fact. Even in its earliest days in Japan Buddhism was regarded by the leading men who adopted and taught it, not as a religion for the lonely individual, or at least not only for him, but as a religion possessed of great potentialities for social solidarity. It was for this reason that the second article of the famous "Seventeen Article Constitution" which Shotoku Taishi promulgated, begins thus: "Reverence sincerely the Three Treasures. The Three Treasures—viz., the Buddha, the Law, the Order—are the final refuge for all generated

[6] Dedicated to the Shi-Tenno, or Four Guardian Kings. It was built in 587, in the province of Settu. See Brinkley, pp. 137-38, and the Nihongi, Aston's trans., II. 123.

[7] Anesaki, *Buddhist Art* (Boston, Houghton Mifflin, 1915), p. 21.

beings, and the supreme objects of faith in all countries."[8] It is significant that of the three Buddhist works on which Shotoku Taishi wrote commentaries, one was the Vimalakirti Sutra,[9] the whole aim of which is to praise the helpful active life, not of the monk, but of the devoted layman.

It is not surprising that with the stimulus given by the Empress Suiko and her able regent Buddhism grew with rapidity, and that before her death there were forty-six Buddhist temples in the land, eight hundred and sixteen monks, and five hundred and sixty-nine nuns.[10] Additional reinforcements continued to stream in from Korea during the years that followed Suiko, many Buddhists also came from China, and at least one noted Buddhist saint from India. This man is known by the Japanese name Hodo. He is said to have healed the Emperor Kotoku in 645, and to have preached among the people with great success.[11] The example of Suiko and Shotoku Taishi was emulated by many of the monarchs that followed the Suiko era, and particularly by the ladies who occupied the imperial throne. This was the beginning of an age of temple building quite comparable to the eleventh and twelfth centuries in western Europe.

The reasons for the rapid spread of Buddhism during this period were numerous, for the new religion appealed to various parts of human nature, some of them lofty, some decidedly commonplace.

> To Shotoku Taishi Buddhism was evidently a religion of the rational moral sense—a religion not only of obligation or of fear but of gratitude for the receipt of blessings, if not unsought for at least undeserved. But to most of his contemporaries, Buddhism was simply a splendidly easy device for obtaining temporal and perhaps everlasting prosperity, for dodging the Devil or Devils, and escaping the pains and penalties of the various Hells. . . . Buddhism made its appeal to the ignorant vulgar by its magicians and exorcists, by its living saints in the flesh who were supposed to possess strong court interest with the dignitaries of the ghostly world, by the gorgeousness of its temples and the solemn pomp of its ritual observances. Yet in spite of all this it held in its embrace

[8] Nihongi, Aston's trans., II. 129.

[9] The reader may recall the long quotation from this Sutra toward the close of Chapter XI.

[10] Brinkley, p. 144.

[11] See Takakusa, "What Japan Owes to India," *The Young East*, I. 74-75.

higher and loftier elements that could do, and did do, much for the culture and civilization of Japan.[12]

It seems probable that during the period following Shotoku Taishi Buddhism gained not only in extension but in depth. The school of Buddhist philosophy founded by the great prince for the education of an intelligent priesthood, together with the advent of large numbers of Korean and Chinese scholars, can hardly have failed to have an influence. Some evidence of the same conclusion would seem to be furnished by art. There are at Horyuji two small bronze Buddhist trinities, both from this early period but one of them produced about sixty years after the other. A comparison of the two shows, as Fenellosa has pointed out,[13] a marked superiority of the later over the earlier work in spiritual expression and religious value. This means chiefly, of course, a gain in technical skill; but it suggests also a deepening influence of the religious ideal within the spirit of the artist. This finer side of Buddhism speaks out especially in the many images of the Bodhisattvas, the visible manifestations of the Buddhist virtues—Kwannon personifying mercy, and Jizo also quite as loving, Monju typifying wisdom, Bisjaimon courage, and others like them. "The simple attitude of the Suiko and Nara congregations," writes Fenellosa, "may be said to have regarded these virtues and graces not as ethical abstractions in their souls, but as living and gracious spiritual presences, with just personality enough to pray to. It is the idyllic deification of all the good in man and society." [14]

The rapid importation of ideas and arts from China, now at the height of its military power and of its artistic achievement under the early T'ang dynasty, had an immense effect upon young Japan. In 709 the Emperor Shomu made Nara his capital, and the city developed rapidly into a large metropolis embellished with the new culture and devoted to the new religion. Not content with building temples, this devout Buddhist monarch resolved to outdo all his prede-

[12] James Murdoch: *A History of Japan*, I (Yokahama, Kelly & Walsh, 1910), pp. 174-75.

[13] *Op. cit.*, I. 69.

[14] *Op. cit.*, I. 107.

cessors by building a stupendous image of the Buddha Vairocana (known by the Japanese as Dainichi). This immense figure—the largest bronze statue in existence—was paid for in part out of the emperor's treasury,[15] in part out of voluntary contributions from large numbers of enthusiastic Buddhists of all classes. Before the completion of the work the emperor abdicated to become a Buddhist monk.

The Dai Butsu, as the great image is called, was only the most striking of innumerable expressions of Buddhist zeal during the Nara period. Several large temples were founded at the capital, and the provinces did not remain far behind. Twenty years or more before the beginning of the Nara epoch an imperial rescript had ordained that every household in the land should provide itself with a Buddhist shrine and place in it a Buddhist image. This did not mean an attack upon Shinto, for the emperors themselves were usually—in one sense always—pious Shintoists and all their subjects were expected to be the same. There was some dogged and passive opposition to Buddhism on the part of some of the conservative members of society, but apparently until the nineteenth century there was very little open antagonism between Buddhism and Shinto such as prevailed so frequently at the Chinese Court between Buddhism, Taoism, and Confucianism. The loyal Shinto sovereigns of Japan, who believed themselves lineally descended from the Sun Goddess, and counted many of the other great Shinto deities as blood relatives, thought it in no wise inconsistent both to build Buddhist temples and to carry on ardent works of Buddhist propaganda. As early as 695 Buddhist missionaries were sent under imperial sanction to the distant island of Yezo where many converts were made; and at the same time an imperial decree directed "that a certain Sutra should be read during the first month of every year in each province."

During Mommu's time (697-707) Buddhist hierarchs were appointed to the provinces. Their chief functions were to expound the Sutra and offer prayers. The devout Shomu not only distributed numerous copies of Sutras, but also carried his zeal to the length of commanding that

[15] "The wealth of a great and growing empire had literally been cast by Shoumu into this proud creation of a colossus. For it special taxes from provinces a thousand miles away and recently wrested from the Ainus, and stores of copper and gold from Japan and Corea had been amassed in monasteries." *Fenellosa*, I. 110.

every province should erect a sixteen-foot image of Shaka (Sakyamuni) with attendant Bosatsu (Bodhisattvas) and, a few years later, he issued another command that each province must provide itself with a pagoda seven stories high. By this last rescript the provincial temples were called into existence and presently their number was increased to two in each province, one for priests and one for nuns. The *kokushi* attached to these temples labored in the cause of propagandism and religious education side by side with the provincial pundits whose duty it was to instruct the people in law and literature; but it is on record that the results of the former's labors were much more conspicuous than those of the latter.[16]

As I have said, this elaborate propaganda of Buddhism was not regarded as in any way an attack upon Shinto: for the very good reason that it really was not an attack upon Shinto. This lack of destructive animus against other religions is regularly one of the distinctive marks by which Buddhist missionary work is differentiated from the work of Christian and Moslem missionaries. The Christian-Moslem view has usually been (it is not *universally* so any longer) that destruction must precede construction, or at any rate that the two must go hand in hand. The Buddhist aim has usually been to do no destroying and to put all the emphasis on the constructive and positive side. Hence Buddhism was quite generally accepted in Japan from the first as an additional insight, and the Buddhas and Bodhisattvas were simply united with the native Kami as proper and helpful objects of reverence or worship. Shinto shrines and Buddhist temples were spoken of in one breath as forming a kind of religious unity—the "ji-sha" or "temple-shrines." In some, and probably in many places, the two religions (which were not recognized as two religions in our sense) tended to merge within the same sacred precinct. Practically speaking, this was the beginning of *Ryobu Shinto*, or the mixed Shinto, which was destined to be the religion of the masses of Japan for so many centuries.[17]

A further step toward the amalgamation of the two religions was taken in the reign of the devout Shomu—the imperial descendant of the Sun Goddess who inaugurated the immense image of the Buddha at Nara, and then became a

[16] Brinkley, *op. cit.*, pp. 194-95.
[17] Cf. Brinkley, p. 195.

Buddhist monk. This further step was taken under the guidance of a great Buddhist preacher of the day, Gyogi by name. It is said that before beginning the work of construction on the Dai Butsu the emperor Shomu, uncertain how the native Kami would feel toward so great an honor being paid to Vairocana, sent Gyogi to the shrine of the Sun Goddess at Ise to inquire what was her good pleasure. Gyogi returned bearing an answer that was not only favorable toward the particular task, but which went much further and declared that the Buddha Vairocana (Dainichi) was none other than her own very self. This identification of the emperor's favorite Buddha with the divine ancestress of the imperial house and head of the Shinto pantheon was as natural and logical as it was effective. For Vairocana is the Buddha of the central sun, and hence to a liberal religious mind was rather obviously not other than a new name for the Sun Goddess. We need not, therefore, ascribe this identification to astute political insight on the part of Gyogi as if he were a clever schemer and had devised a subtle method for advancing his own religion. It is enough to say he was a Buddhist: that he shared the almost universal disregard of mere names which Buddhism has shown in every land, its universal willingness to see the truth under many different forms, and to accept the symbols of other religions as fitting and admirable provided the underlying significance be really valid. The Sun Goddess was for Gyogi a Japanese name or symbol for the Reality in which he believed, and I think it probable that he was convinced the Ise shrine really gave, or at any rate meant, the answer he brought back to his imperial master. It is recorded that the emperor, a few nights later, had a confirmatory dream in which the Sun Goddess appeared to him and again identified herself with Vairocana. This was the beginning of the theoretical side of Ryobu Shinto, which eventually resulted in the identification of the Kami with the members of the Buddhist cycle.

This identification, however, showed only its faint beginnings in this early age. As yet, for the most part, the Shinto deities were conceived as holding the same relation to the Buddha as that attributed in the Mahayana Sutras to the ancient Hindu gods of India. They were attendants, guardians, worshipers, hearers, but by no means identified with the Buddha and his glorious Bodhisattvas. Apparently it did not enter the heads of the Kami at this time that they could aspire to anything so sublime as Buddhahood. Two very early cases are reported of Kami expressing their desire to receive Buddhist instruction, so that they might hope for ultimate salvation—they were tired of being merely gods.[18] It was not until the Fujiwara and Kamakura periods that the identification of the Kami with the Buddhas became explicit and general.[19]

This relationship of friendliness between Shinto and Buddhism of course made the spread of the new religion immensely more easy. Nor was it merely new names for old deities and new forms of ecclesiastical art that the Buddhist missionaries carried with them. It was new ideas, new aspirations, new insights, and a new attitude of justified sympathy for all one's fellow creatures. Not that the Buddhism preached in Japan laid its emphasis on moral questions to anything like the extent to which the Founder had laid it. From the moral point of view the Mahayana as at first taught in Japan was inferior to the early Hinayana and inferior also to the form of Confucianism which was being introduced into Japan at almost the same time as Buddhism.[20] The emphasis sometimes laid upon mere externals of an almost magical sort—entirely out of keeping with the original teachings of the Founder—is seen in the fact that the first printing in Japan consisted of a million charms, in Chinese characters transliterating Sanskrit sounds, made by the order of the pious empress Shotoku in 770—she having read in a Buddhist Sutra that whoso made a certain number of these charms and placed each in a pagoda should secure long life and forgiveness of sin.[21] Yet moral emphasis was by no

[18] See Coates and Ishizuka, *Honen Shonin, the Buddhist Saint* (Kyoto, Chionin, 1925), pp. 17-19.

[19] *Idem*, see pp. 13-14, 33.

[20] Cf. S. L. Gulick, *The Evolution of the Japanese* (N. Y., Revell), p. 269.

[21] See Carter, *The Invention of Printing in China*, Chap. VII. While this use of charms by early Japanese Buddhists indicates a most unintelligent and even superstitious attitude, we should remember that this attitude is common to large numbers of the pious followers of every religion. It is interesting to note that the earliest extant

means wholly absent in early Japanese Buddhism, and while one hears nothing of the Four Noble Truths, the ideal of universal sympathy went with the Buddhist propaganda, as it always has. And it went not only in theory but in practice. Not only were temples built, but educational, medical, and other philanthropic and humanitarian institutions were founded. Physicians as well as preachers were sent about. The empress Komyo, during the Nara period, founded (under Buddhist influence) one of the first leper hospitals in the world. It is said that as an example to her people and in order to dispel their terror of leprosy and abhorrence of those suffering from it, she bathed a leprous woman and ministered to her; whereupon the Buddha himself appeared and gave the empress his blessing.[22] In addition to their labors of propaganda and helpfulness, the Buddhist leaders were also frequently foremost in the dissemination of Chinese and Korean applied science. They built bridges and ferries, harbors and roads.

> Among the various industries introduced into Japan by the religious fervor [of Buddhism] [writes Count Okuma] the following may be mentioned: the carving of images, building of temples, painting and the manufacture of tiles, concrete, lacquered and earthen wares, woven goods, embroideries, paper, ink, and dyeing materials. It was also through Buddhism that calendars, music and useful plants were brought into the country, and by means of their philanthropic work medical art was improved, schools and orphan asylums built, and hot springs discovered. . . . From this array of facts we can safely conclude that the civilization peculiar to Japan and existing before the Restoration undoubtedly had its source in Buddhism.[23]

Christian missionaries are not only Christian: they are also Protestant or Catholic—Congregational, Presbyterian, Methodist, Baptist, or members of some other denomination —and inevitably, after the first large foundation of the

European block print (other than playing cards) is an image of St. Christopher with the inscription:

> "In whatsoever day thou seest the likeness
> of St. Christopher,
> In that same day thou wilt from death no
> evil blow incur."

This print was made in 1423, some six and a half centuries after the Empress Shotoku's quite similar charms. See Carter, *op. cit.*, Chap. XXI.

[22] From an article by W. M. Dannor in the *Seoul Press* for Dec. 16, 1925.

[23] *Fifty Years of New Japan* (London, Smith, Elder and Co., 1910), pp. 71-72.

Christian church in the new lands are laid, they teach the form of Christianity which their own denominations stand for. The same thing had to be true of Buddhist propaganda in Japan. The first Korean and Chinese missionaries had preached Buddhism in general; but after a start was made and native monks had to be instructed in the philosophy of the new religion each missionary necessarily taught that of the sect to which he belonged. Thus it came about that before the end of the Nara period six of the Buddhist sects of China had established themselves in Japan. Three of these six no longer exist in Japan, so I shall not trouble the reader with their names.[24] The three that still continue were the Hosso (Dharma-lakshana, or Tsu-en tsung of China), the first of all the Chinese sects to reach Japan (it came about 650); the Kegon (the Hua-yen tsung of China) which arrived in 736; and the Ritsu (the Vinaya or Lu tsung of China) which was the last of the six sects to reach Japan (in 754). All three of these survivors of the early six are at present in a moribund condition. In fact, the Ritsu shu is sometimes said to have disappeared long ago. I found it still existing, however, or at least claiming to exist in the Nibudera temple in Kyoto and claiming to have its headquarters still at Nara.[25] If not actually deceased it might almost as well be if one can judge by its present condition. And while Hosso and Kegon are decidedly stronger than Ritsu, they have but few temples and few monks and little direct influence on the laity. In the eighth century, however, these with the three other sects long since disappeared, known conjointly as the six Nara sects, were a great power in the land. Their monastic establishments were enormously wealthy, their monks numerous, and their influence extended not only throughout matters religious but into politics as

[24] For the reader who reads footnotes I shall here append the names of the three dead sects, and the dates of their arrival in Japan:

Sanron (Madhyamika) 625
Jojitsu (Satya-siddhi-sastra) 625
Kusha (Abhidharma-kosa-sastra) 658

Both the Jojitsu and the Kusha are regularly spoken of by Japanese and Western students of Japanese Buddhism as Hinayana sects. They were not Hinayana in the sense of this volume, and in fact I think it very doubtful if the Indian Hinayana has ever had a footing in Japan. A list of all the principal sects of Japan with the names of their founders and their dates will be found in a note on page 519.

[25] In the To-sho-dai-ji.

well. It is said to have been partly on account of the hampering influence of the monks of these great orders that in 784 the Emperor Kwammu decided to change the site of his capital. A new capital city was built on the site now known as Kyoto, and in 794 the court took up its headquarters there. From one of the names early given to the city, *Heian-jo* (castle of peace), the next period of Japanese history (794-1192) is usually referred to as the Heian epoch.

In advance of the emperor came the monk. Not quite that either: for young Saicho had not as yet taken holy orders. He was a deeply religious youth, this Saicho, who was destined to have so large a share in shaping the religious history of his country. The externalism and political meddling, as well as the philosophy of the Nara monks—particularly of the Hosso monks—displeased him, and in order to deepen his religious life, instead of entering one of the monasteries of the capital, he left Nara and built himself a hermit's hut on the side of Hiei-san, the mountain that looks down upon the valley of Kyoto from the east. Whoever has tramped over its broad shoulders or climbed its twin peaks and roamed through its forests of giant cryptomerias and graceful bamboo, must almost envy the young hermit and wish for at least one look through his eyes upon the scene that lay before him when the forest paths were almost untouched by human feet, when Kyoto was not yet begun and the mountain dreamed across the green valley to Nishiyama on the west and gazed on the east upon the blue waters of Lake Biwa, perhaps still surrounded by virgin forests. It was in his nineteenth year that Saicho, or Dengyo Daishi (to use the name by which he is best known to history) began his solitary vigils on Mount Hiei. Here he stayed for some years. In 788 he built a small Buddhist temple on the mountain [26] and divided his time between serving in the temple, watching the new city come into being in the valley below him, and studying a new form of Buddhist doctrine which a few Chinese missionaries had recently introduced into Japan, the famous T'ien-t'ai doctrines, now at the height of their influence in China. Meanwhile the fame of

[26] This became the great mother monastery of the Tendai Order, under the name Enriaku-ji.

the young hermit's sanctity was spreading, and the emperor Kwammu, who apparently had known of the little temple on Hiei-san and may even have encouraged its construction, came to feel that Dengyo was just the man he wanted to give the new capital and the new venture in government the kind of religious assistance that it needed. The two men seem to have understood each other and cooperated in the task of establishing the imperial government on a firmer basis, away from the influence of meddling, worldly monks, and of renewing Buddhism on a more spiritual level. When the capital was moved from Nara to Kyoto, in 794, Dengyo was chosen as the celebrant of the high mass at which the emperor was present.[27] The emperor also sent him about preaching the new doctrines of T'ien t'ai and expounding the truths of the Saddharma Pundarika Sutra—the "Lotus Gospel"—on which the new sect was so largely founded. But Dengyo felt his knowledge of the great subject insufficient and he longed to complete his studies by going to the fountain-head—the monastery of T'ien-t'ai itself, in distant China. He wished also to get ecclesiastical authority from the sect in China to found it in Japan, for as yet the sect had no official representatives in the island—like others of his time and of every time he felt the value of apostolic succession. At this period the culture of the T'ang dynasty was still flowing rapidly into Japan, and the emperor was no less eager to learn from China than was the monk. His new capital in fact was being laid out in imitation of Ch'ang-an. So in 802 he sent Dengyo to the T'ang capital, in the train of the Japanese ambassador.[28] This middle period of the T'ang, it will be recalled, was one of great intellectual and spiritual activity in Chinese Buddhism. Arrived in China, Dengyo went at once to the famous mother monastery of the sect of his choice on the T'ien-t'ai mountain in Chekiang. After a few years of study here, he returned, rich in new ideas and experiences and with many volumes of Buddhist lore, and, perhaps most important of all, the longed-for ecclesiastical authority from the mother sect in China.

[27] Cf. Arthur Lloyd, *The Creed of Half Japan* (London, Elder, 1911), p. 230.

[28] Brinkley, p. 228.

Thus Dengyo Daishi became the founder of the Japanese sect of Tendai—the Tendai shu (*shu* means sect or denomination). The philosophy taught by this school of Buddhism will be discussed in a later chapter. Here it will be sufficient to point out its two leading ideas—namely, the liberal view that all the varied forms of all the Buddhist schools were merely symbolic ways of expressing the same truth, and the more specific doctrine that the heart of Buddhism was to be found in the Saddharma Pundarika Sutra and its teaching that the Buddha nature is in all men. It was on this point particularly that Dengyo attacked the Hosso monks of Nara who taught that only a limited few could ever become Buddha, and that most men were forever excluded from Buddhahood.[29] All men, Dengyo taught, were potentially Bodhisattvas—or Bosatsus, as the name is called by the Japanese—and the members of the new, or transplanted, Order were expected to act as such. Their first duty was devotion to the community, and in the early days the Tendai monks seem to have been earnest servants of the state and eloquent popular preachers of the Buddhist religion.[30] The influence of the sect throughout Japanese history (both ecclesiastical and political) has been enormous. Out of it have come, directly or indirectly, nearly all the later sects of native origin. And the philosophy of the Tendai and Kegon combined (they are on fundamentals almost one) may be called the very keel of all serious Buddhist thinking in Japan.

Two years after Dengyo Daishi went to China to complete his studies, a friend of his, several years his junior, followed him on a similar errand. This was Kukai, better known to history as Kobo Daishi. Stories are told about his childhood similar to those our Christian Middle Ages loved to tell about great Christian saints and mystics: his childhood piety, his exhaustless devotion, his precocious intuition. Certainly he was one of the greatest minds and one of the greatest men Japan has produced. His chief philosophical work he composed at the age of twenty—a treatise in dialogue form, presenting the arguments of a Buddhist, a

[29] See Bruno Petzold, "Dengyo Daishi and German Theology," in the *Eastern Buddhist*, II. 352.

[30] Petzold, *op. cit.*, pp. 353-55.

Confucian, and a Shintoist,[31] and showing in the end that only a doctrine founded on universal truths such as the Mahayana can form a trustworthy religion.[32] In China he studied especially the teachings of the Chen-yen, or True Word, sect, which in Japan is known as Shingon. This sect, it will be recalled, had been brought to China from India in 720. Its fourth Chinese patriarch, Hui Kuo by name, was living at this time, and he received young Kukai and saw at once the promise of his mind. Tradition says that when the patriarch first saw the young Japanese he said to him, "I have been waiting for you a long time," and that at the end of four months' instruction he gave him ordination, and commissioned him to spread the esoteric doctrine of the True Word in Japan.[33] In its philosophy Shingon is very nearly in agreement with Tendai, though differing in details. To be exact, its philosophy is nearer to that of Kegon than to that of Tendai. But its distinguishing character is to be found in its elaborate use of outward and visible signs, among the ignorant approaching almost to the magical, and in the detail and beauty of its ritual. It is sometimes called the high church of Japanese Buddhism.

For many years after his return to his native land Kobo Daishi devoted himself almost entirely to missionary journeys, especially in the uncivilized north. He preached everywhere the Shingon version of the central Mahayana truth which Dengyo Daishi was also preaching in the Tendai fashion—the essential unity of all men with the Buddha. Like Dengyo Daishi, Kobo felt it necessary to hand on his teachings in a regularly ordained order of monks. For a suitable site for the mother monastery and temple of his new order he searched (under supernatural guidance, says tradition)[34] and finally decided upon the lofty summit of Mount

[31] Or Taoist, as is sometimes said. The Japanese on first learning of Taoism seem to have regarded it as equivalent to their native Shinto.

[32] See the address of Prof. Tomeri Tanimoto of the Imperial University of Kyoto, on the occasion of the 1134th anniversary of the birth of Kobo Daishi, published in pamphlet form by the *Japanese Chronicle* of Kobe, in 1907.

[33] Ryanon Fujishima, *Le Buddhisme Japonais* (Paris, Maisonneuve, 1889), p. 81.

[34] Just before embarking from China on his return home, "standing on the sea-beach he threw his *vajra* [a bronze instrument used in the Shingon ritual] toward Japan," It disappeared from view in the distance. After reaching his native land, while searching for a suitable site for his temple among the mountains of Kii province, "two dogs, one white and one black, and a hunter came to show him the way, and brought him

Koya, covered with a silent forest of cryptomerias. Here, far from Kyoto and its court, far from Nara and its politically-minded monks, he founded his first temple and his little hermitage. Later on, the emperor, feeling the need of this new form of really spiritual religion and its great leader within the capital, induced him to come to Kyoto for a few years and inaugurate a great Shingon temple there. This temple, Todai-ji by name, the emperor built for the saint. Here, and on further missionary journeys, Kobo Daishi led an active and useful life, devoting himself not only to the spreading of his form of Buddhism but to the extension of learning, art, and applied science.

It was the united influence of Dengyo Daishi and Kobo Daishi that produced the completed form of Ryobu Shinto—the amalgamation of Shinto with Buddhism through the (theoretical) identification of many of the greater Kami with the Buddhas. This conception was a natural outgrowth of the Tendai and Shingon philosophies, with their insistence upon identity, their denial of ultimate separateness, and their monistic idealism. The marriage of the two religions was in many ways unfortunate for Buddhism.[35] It enabled it to make rapid strides at first, and to take nearly all the inhabitants of Japan into its fold; but it made this gain only at the price of losing much of its distinctive character. The results have not been so evil as were the results of the partial union of Buddhism with Taoism in China—although the Japanese union was for a long time much more complete than the Chinese—because of the superiority of Shinto to the degraded form of later Taoism. Shinto is lacking in profundity, but it has a certain charm, and especially the nature side of it has retained much of that ancient beauty

to a place where there had once been the shrine of an ancient Buddha." This place was Mt. Koya, and the god of the mountain appeared to him and "offered him that place until the coming of Maitreya, in order that the land might be blessed." Thereupon the saint found his *vajra*, lodged in a pine tree, where it had been ever since he threw it across the sea from the shores of China. This was another sign that Koya-san was the place for his mountain monastery. If one doubts the story one can still see on the summit of the mountain the very tree in which the *vajra* was found! (The sentences quoted in this note I have taken from the Namu-daishi, a Japanese poem on the life of Kobo Daishi, trans. by Arthur Lloyd as Chap. XXI of his *The Creed of Half Japan.*)

[35] And in some ways fortunate for Shinto. Dr. Kato points out that Buddhism did much to deepen Shinto, making it moral and spiritual, *A Study of Shinto* (Tokyo, Meiji Society, 1926), p. 182.

that the poets have found in Hellenic Paganism. Most of us, I suspect, feel now and then a certain wistfulness in looking back at the nature-worship of the ancients, at the times when every spring had its nymph, and every wood its satyr. Our modern western religion has become so largely a matter of moral acivity for social betterment that in moments of weariness or relaxation we feel with Wordsworth that "the world is too much with us," and almost wish ourselves pagans once more,

> Suckled in a creed outworn.

Now Shinto is the last remnant among a civilized people, in our scientific and sophisticated age, of the common paganism of the ancient world. For it the earth and the fulness thereof is still effulgent with deity. For it the fountains are mysterious and the waterfalls doubtless the haunts of the Kami. In a Shinto shrine, by the side of some torrent or on some mountain side, one feels like singing the Song of the Holy Children:

> O ye mountains and little hills,
> bless ye the Lord; praise him and magnify him forever.
> O ye fountains, bless ye the Lord:
> praise him and magnify him forever.
> O ye seas and rivers, bless ye the Lord:
> praise him and magnify him forever.

In nature worship such as that of Shinto the poet and the philosopher can gladly join. And the attitude of the great Japanese thinkers who adopted Shinto into Buddhism was that of the philosopher and the poet. In this simple worship of their fellow countrymen these pantheistic mystics recognized a simple and symbolic way of expressing a great truth. Yes, they said in effect, the Shinto view of Nature is true. There is a divinity in mountains and streams; all these are shadowings forth of the One divine nature in a million forms. It is the truth, though put in children's language. Therefore let us not deny it, not destroy it, not oppose it; but adopt it.

Of course it was not in this philosophic sense that the rank and file of Japanese Buddhists adopted Shinto. For them—and at times even for Kobo Daishi himself—the Shinto Kami were very much more than names or symbols for a deeper reality. Within this phenomenal world they were as real as they ever had been. Even the War God Hachiman (a most unBuddhistic figure) had been admitted to the great Todai-ji temple in Nara in 749; before long he was recognized as a Bodhisattva,[36] but a Bodhisattva of surely a peculiar sort, and one that hardly added greatly to the ethical value of Buddhism. In spite, therefore, of the poetic beauty of many Shinto shrines, I cannot but feel that the amalgamation of the two religions was a loss to Buddhism, and that in bringing it about Kobo Daishi did rather more harm than good to the faith of Shaka.

In matters of art Kobo's influence was of less ambiguous value. Like Shotoku Taishi he was a sculptor of preeminent ability. It was he who introduced into Japan the conventional iconographic forms for the representation of the various Buddhas and Bodhisattvas.[37] He was also a master of chirography, a great grammarian and linguist, and something of a poet. He is said to have been the first to introduce a knowledge of Sanskrit in Japan;[38] and the invention of one of the phonetic syllabaries, by which writing has been made so much simpler for the Japanese than it is for the Chinese, is usually attributed to him. Besides all this he planned roads and bridges, promoted the newly introduced culture of the silkworm, and founded a great school in connection with his Kyoto temple, the first school in Japan for giving common education to the children of the masses. With all his active tendencies and practical powers, the mystic in him was strong; and when old age approached he left his great temple

[36] Coates and Ishizuka, *Honen*, pp. 16, 23.

[37] According to Prof. Tanimoto, *op. cit.*

[38] According to Professor Tanimoto. This, however, is far from certain. There is pretty good evidence that, in the reign of the Emperor Shomu (who made Nara the capital and inaugurated the Dai Butsu), an Indian Buddhist monk named Bodhi-Sena was living in Nara, and that he was a friend and colleague of the famous Gyogi. It is said that he taught Sanskrit to the Nara monks. (See Takakusa, "What Japan Owes to India," *Young East*, I. 107-108.) It is quite likely, however, that Kobo Daishi had a good deal to do in spreading Sanskrit in Japan and quite possible also that he reintroduced it. His influence in turning the thoughts of Japanese Buddhists not only to China, but to India may be indicated by the belief that Kongo Sammai, the first Japanese Buddhist to make a pilgrimage to India (in 818) was a disciple of Kobo Daishi, and by the fact that the second Japanese to start on a pilgrimage to India was a Shingon monk who had studied on Koya-san. This was the Imperial Prince Takaoka. Unfortunately he died on his way to India, somewhere in the Malay Peninsula. See Takakusa, *op. cit.*, pp. 37-39.

in the city and retired to his remote mountain sanctuary on the summit of Koya, where in 835, surrounded by his monks and his silent forests, he died, and where his followers believe he is still sitting in his tomb, waiting, like Mahakassapa in India, for the joyous coming of Maitreya.

Both Dengyo Daishi and Kobo Daishi, we have seen, eagerly cooperated with the emperor in the spread of the new civilization and in support of the government. Once before in this chapter I have referred to the great contrast between Japanese Buddhism and the early Indian Hinayana in this matter of social cooperation and the effort not to escape from the world but to make this world a better place to live in. Buddhism did not cease in Japan to be a religion for the spiritual cultivation of the individual, but it became also a religion for the elevation of the social life of man. This was the logical outcome of the Mahayana Bodhisattva ideal, and of the fundamental conception that one nature exists in all men. While this interest in society and in the life of the world is doubtless a source of strength in a religion, it is a source of danger also, as both the history of Christian and the history of Buddhist monasticism sadly show. The great Tendai monasteries in Hiei-san and Lake Biwa, the great Shingon monasteries at Kyoto and on Koya-san rapidly grew into centers of immense wealth and power; and in the centuries that followed began to mix in politics in the worldly fashion that had characterized the Nara sects in the earlier period—and, for that matter, still continued to characterize them. It was not only in politics that these great monasteries began to mingle, but in actual war. Many a temple became a fortress, and three of them in particular [39] came to be centers of armies of ruffians and professional soldiers, employed by the monks to enforce the interests of the sect. At times the monks themselves did not hesitate to violate the whole spirit of their religion to the extent of taking arms in their own hands and joining in battle and in plunder. Some of them had wives, built houses, cultivated lands.[40] They often controlled the policies of the court, and

[39] Enryakuji on Hiei-san, Miidera on Lake Biwa, and Kofukuji at Nara.

[40] Cf. the memorial presented by Myoshi Kiyotsura to the emperor in 914. See Brinkley, p. 245.

through their influence superstitious and prodigal emperors wasted the wealth of the land, wrung from the populace by heavy taxes, upon thousands of superfluous temples, images, pictures, and pagodas.[41]

The state of the laity seems not to have been much better than that of the clergy. Not that they were losing their faith in Buddhism—far from it. Never had its temples been more crowded, never had its ceremonies been more magnificent. But the trust of the people was in its ceremonies and in various external practices not far removed from superstition, and the noble moral and spiritual sides of the religion were being largely forgotten.[42] Though the period was filled with enthusiastic reverence for the Buddhas and their train, it marks one of the lowest levels to which Japanese Buddhism has ever sunk. But it seems to have possessed one element of promise, namely a deep longing for something better.

It must not be supposed that all the monks were politicians and soldiers or all the laymen superstitious worldlings during these degenerate days of the later Heian epoch. In the Tendai school of philosophy connected with the great monastery in Hiei-san there were many devout as well as learned scholars; and in the subordinate sanctuaries and cells that covered both sides of the mountain there were still a few—and perhaps more than a few—earnest souls in whom the old spirituality still burned with all its former intensity. Men such as these felt great dissatisfaction with the degenerate condition of Buddhism in their day. Particularly did they feel the need of some simpler form of religion than was provided by the philosophy of Tendai and the Nara sects or by the elaborate ritualism of the Shingon. It was natural that this feeling should turn their thoughts toward the simple teachings of Pure Land Buddhism and the worship of Amida. A learned Tendai monk and teacher on Hiei-san, Genshin by name, did much to make this form of Buddhism

[41] The ex-emperor Shirakawa, who, though he had retired (in 1086) from office and taken the tonsure, still continued to wield the imperial power, ordered the construction of 21 large pagodas, 446,630 small ones, 6080 images, 5470 Buddhist pictures, and 127 statues, each 16 feet high; he also forbade the taking of animal life, and to enforce his edict had 8000 fish nets destroyed, which involved suffering upon thousands of families who depended on fishing for a living.

[42] Cf. Coates and Ishizuka, *Honen*, Hist. Introd., Chap. II.

—as yet quite ill-defined in Japan—into a specific doctrine. He did not attempt to establish a new sect, and remained within the Tendai fold to his death; but his influence had much to do with the formation of the new sects that began to spring up in the next generation. Another student in the Tendai university (if so we may call it) on Mount Hiei, whose name was Ryonin (1072-1132) and who, largely through Genshin's influence, had come to a view similar to his, was convinced that the new and simpler way of salvation through the grace of Amida needed a new and simpler church for its propagation. Hence he founded the first native Buddhist sect in Japan—the Yutsu Nembutsu shu (*shu,* it will be recalled, is the word for sect or denomination). The name means "Society for Mutual Benefit through the Nembutsu." Nembutsu is the name for the great Pure Land prayer or meditation formula, "Namu Amida Butsu," which, under the form "Namu O-mi-to Fo," we have seen so popular in China. It means, of course, "adoration to Amida Buddha," and it is also considered a name of Amida. Ryonin had been greatly impressed by the famous vow of Amida, recorded in the Larger Sukhavati Vyuha, in which He promises that all shall be saved who with faith repeat his name. Hence he taught that neither knowledge nor works was needed for salvation, but simply the repetition of the Nembutsu, with a heart concentrated upon Amida. He himself made a practice of repeating it some 60,000 times a day.

The Yutsu Nembutsu shu is still in existence. But it is small and has never had any great influence. Pure Land Buddhism became really important in Japan only through Honen Shonin and the Jodo shu which he founded in 1175.[43] Like so many of the other pious and promising Japanese lads who afterward became religious leaders, he was sent from his native village to study Tendai Buddhism at the great Hiei-san school.[44] The Tendai doctrines, however, did not fully satisfy him. We have, fortunately, his own account

[43] According to Suzuki the Yutsu Nembutsu sect can hardly be classed as a Pure Land sect in the full sense of the word as it is based on the Atavamsaka Sutra, *Eastern Buddhist,* III. 288.

[44] He was a boy of such promise that the monk who had been his teacher sent with him to the university the message, "I am sending you a little Manjusri" (Coates and Ishizuka, *Honen,* p. 125).

of his conversion to a simpler and more evangelical faith.

> Having a deep desire to obtain salvation and with faith in the teaching of the various scriptures, I practiced many forms of self discipline. . . . But the fact is I do not keep even the precepts, nor do I attain to any one of the many forms of meditation. . . . Unless one get free from evil conduct and evil passion how shall he obtain deliverance from the bondage of birth and death? Alas! alas! What shall I do? What shall I do? The like of us are incompetent to practice the three disciplines of the precepts, meditations, and knowledge. And so I inquired of a great many learned men and priests whether there is any other way of salvation than these disciplines, but no one could either teach me the way or even suggest it. At last I went into the library where all the Scriptures were, all by myself, and with a heavy heart read them all through. I hit upon a passage in Zendo's [45] Commentary, which runs as follows: "Only repeat the name of Amitabha with all your heart, whether walking or standing, whether sitting or lying: never cease the practice of it for a moment. This is the very work which unfailingly issues in salvation; for it is in accordance with the Original Vow of Amida Buddha."[46]

This passage from the great Chinese teacher seemed to answer all the young man's questions, and by following the injunction contained in it he gained the peace of soul and assurance of salvation for which he had longed. And in order to help others to find the same simple road into the Western Paradise he founded a new sect, the Jodo.[47] Japanese Buddhists recognize two ways of salvation: *Shodomen*, or "Holy Path" which leads to salvation through self help, and *Jodomen*, or "Pure Land" which brings salvation through the aid of Another. The Jodo shu taught nothing essentially different from the Yutzu Nembutsu shu (it made the recitation of the Nembutsu perhaps a little more simple, with less of meditation), but it succeeded where the other had failed in extending to large numbers of Japanese the hope of salvation through faith and divine grace and the simple practice of the Nembutsu.

The new evangelism took quick hold not only upon the masses, but upon many of the more religiously minded members of the aristocratic and intellectual circles. It had a

[45] The great Chinese teacher of the Pure Land doctrine, who had been converted to it in a similar fashion. See page 287 of this book.

[46] Coates and Ishizuka, *op. cit.*, pp. 185-87.

[47] It was not generally recognized as an entirely independent sect until the beginning of the Tokugawa Shogunate (Coates and Ishizuka, pp. 59-62).

notable effect upon the art of the day, in the later Heian and early Kamakura times.

> The mystic vision of the reformers wished to discard the elaborate rituals and focus all force into the invocation of the central Amida, the Buddha of boundless light, who was seen in ecstasy as a form of dazzling light surrounded by a gorgeous company of Bosatsu, all equally luminous.[48]
>
> Throughout the 11th, 12th, and 13th centuries this gentle and beautiful art kept pace with the spread of Amida worship. Vigor gave place to meekness, sweet harmony became more conspicuous than virile inspiration, and the artists worked in ecstasies of tender piety and self-forgetting devotion.[49]

Upon the literature as well as the art of the Heian and Kamakura periods Buddhism had its considerable influence. Japanese poetry is seldom upon religious themes, but many a verse in the colorful, picture-like four or five-line poems that come to us out of the Japan of a thousand years ago, bears unmistakable evidence of the deep imprint that Buddhism had made upon the minds of the writers. The recurring note of sadness with which Buddhist thought brings home the transciency of all earthly things found a quick echo in the native melancholy of the Japanese mind. As in these verses from an anthology collected in 905:

> Even as this passing life of ours
> The cherry-blossoms fair display.
> Scarce have we gazed, in fragrant showers
> Of petals, from the wind-tossed spray,
> The blossoms' beauties pass away!
>
> See the red maple-leaves that swirl
> In Autumn storm winds! Brief their span.
> Into the outer dark they whirl.
> More fleeting still the life of man.[50]

The sorrow that came to so many families during the civil wars between the Tairas and the Minamotos (1159-1185) and the rapid rise and even more rapid fall of the Taira clan seem specially to have impressed the imagination not only of contemporaries but of many successive generations, and to

[48] Fenellosa, I. 163.
[49] Anesaki, *Buddhist Art*, p. 28.
[50] Trans. by Clara A. Walsh, in *The Master-Singers of Japan* (London, Murray, 1910), p. 60.

have made more intense the Buddhist feeling for the transciency of worldly glory. The Taira Atsumori, in the No play that bears his name, has come back to earth some years after the great battle in which he was slain, and is made to say:

> Now the clan of Taira, building wall to wall,
> Spread over the earth like the leafy branches of a great tree.

And the Chorus responds:

> Yet their prosperity lasted but for a day:
> It was like the flower of the convolvulus.
> There was none to tell them
> That glory flashes like sparks from flint-stone.
> And after—darkness.
> Oh wretched life of men!

All is not sadness, however, for, as the Chorus reminds us,

> The Buddha bids the flowers of Spring
> Mount the tree-top that men may raise their eyes
> And walk on upward paths;
> He bids the moon in autumn waves be drowned
> In token that he visits laggard men
> And leads them out from valleys of despair.

And at the end of the play, when Atsumori recognizes in a Buddhist priest who has prayed for him Rensei (the Minamoto chief who had killed him in the battle) and rushes at him, sword in hand, to take his vengeance, the Chorus tells us:

> . . . the other is grown gentle,
> And calling on the Buddha's name
> Has obtained salvation for his foe:
> So that they shall be re-born together
> On one lotus-seat.
> "No, Rensei is not my enemy,
> Pray for me again: oh, pray for me again!"[51]

It is plain that the twelfth century was a time of great searchings of heart among large numbers of Japanese. Honen Shonen founded his evangelical denomination in the midst of the Taira-Minamoto wars, and it made an immediate ap-

[51] These quotations I have taken from Arthur Waley's trans. in *The No-Plays of Japan* (New York, Knopf, 1922).

peal to large masses of earnest people. The same longing for greater inwardness, which with simpler souls found its satisfaction in Amida's grace, showed itself in profounder minds in increased practice of those methods of contemplation which have been the common property of Buddhists in all lands and which were specially developed by the Ch'an sect in China. Representatives of this sect had been in Japan for centuries [52] and many Tendai monks had adopted some of the Ch'an practices and ideas; but as a distinct sect it had never been established in Japan until, in 1191, a devout member of the Tendai sect named Eisai, who had studied on Hiei-san, returned from China where he had investigated the doctrines of the Southern Ch'an school. This marks the beginning of the Zen sect (for so the word *Ch'an* was understood in Japan). In 1202 Eisai founded a temple of the new sect in Kyoto, but the monks of the older sects got the emperor to drive him from the capital; so he went to Kamakura (the headquarters of the Bakufu, or military administration which, under the able Hojo family, really ruled Japan). The Hojos protected him and, with many of their followers, became ardent adherents of Zen. It was probably the virility and self-reliance and spiritual discipline of Zen that made it appeal to the soldiers of the Bakufu in the great military camp that Kamakura then was. But an incidental advantage was to be found in the fact that it despised books and learning, maintaining that truth could be transferred from heart to heart without the intervention of words: this surely must have appealed to the rude soldiery of the times, hardly one of whom could read.[53]

The particular division of the Chinese Ch'an sect with which Eisai had been connected is known as the Rinzai: so it was this school of Zen which he founded in Japan. Another of the subdivisions of the Chinese Ch'an sect, *Soto* by name, was brought to Japan by Dogen about 1225. A third, called *Obaku,* was brought over from China much later,

[52] It is said that Hiuen-Tsiang taught the Dhyana form of Buddhism to a Japanese monk named Dosho, who came to China to study with him, and that Dosho taught the practices of the Dhyana school on his return to Japan, but did not found a branch of the sect in any ecclesiastical or authoritative sense. See Takakusa, *What Japan owes to India,* I. 106.

[53] Cf. Murdoch, *History of Japan,* I. 485, 487.

about 1654. Thus the Zen shu in Japan includes three subdivisions, each of them ecclesiastically independent, namely Rinzai, Soto, and Obaku.[54] They differ but little, save that the Soto makes rather more of Buddhist learning and literature than Rinzai, while Obaku mingles with Zen training the worship of Amida.[55]

In the same year that Dogen introduced the Soto branch of Zen into Japan, a new evangelical sect developed out of the Jodo, and one that was destined to become in the number and activity of its members, the largest and most powerful of all the sects in Japan. This was the Shin-shu, founded by Shinran Shonin. Shinran was born in 1173, a member of the great Fujiwara clan, and thus connected with the highest court aristocracy. He was a deeply religious and thoughtful lad and was educated for the priesthood, studying for many years at what I have sometimes referred to as the Tendai University on Mount Hiei. A very large part of this great ridge between Kyoto and Lake Biwa was, by Shinran's time, covered with monasteries and monastic schools—some three thousand monasteries altogether there were, each with its abbot, and all under one chief abbot. The great Tendai establishment had thus become a city of monks; and while some of these monks were politicians and some were soldiers, there were also many who were scholars and at least a few, I presume, who were "called to be saints."

Among these Shinran, in the course of years, came to have a great reputation for learning and piety. But neither his piety nor his learning gave him satisfaction, and he sought in vain for the deep peace of mind that religion had brought to so many others but not to him. One day in his twenty-ninth year, while still searching for the insight that he lacked, he came down to the capital and worshiped in the little Shingon temple Rokkaku-do.[56] Here he had a vision of Kwannon, the Goddess of Mercy. This seems to have been one influence of several in turning his thought away from

[54] Each of these originated in China, and all are descended from the Southern school of the Ch'an sect. This school very soon after its origin divided into two subdivisions, namely the Rinzai and the Soto. The Obaku school is a later subdivision of the Rinzai. See Kaiten Nukariya, *The Religion of the Samurai* (London, Luzac, 1913), p. 49.

[55] See Kaiten Nukariya, p. 49.

[56] An interesting octagonal temple just east of Karasmaru, still very popular.

the salvation through "self-strength" of Tendai to the salvation through "another's strength" of Jodo; and soon after his vision he went to hear Honen Shonin propound evangelical Buddhism, in the eastern part of the city. This was the last influence needed, and Shinran found the light and comfort he had been seeking. He became a disciple of Honen and eventually his ablest and most promising disciple. Honen had long been doubting the value of the Buddhist law of celibacy for monks. He may have felt that it set a bar between clergy and laity; more likely he felt that it was a remnant of the older doctrine of salvation through works which he and his Jodo church had thrown off. At any rate, he urged Shinran, as one of the most prominent members of the new sect, to give an object lesson to the world by entering into the state of marriage.[57] Shinran saw the point and obeyed his master's command. He not only married but he ate meat and lived in the world, while still devoting his entire time to the spread of the new Gospel. This act of Shinran's marks a further step in the secularization of Buddhism, begun away back in India when the Mahayana was first formulated as a distinctive attitude toward life. The two leaders of the new movement, master and disciple, had great success in spreading this new conception of what the Buddhist life might be. Much hardship, however, was before them. Through the jealousy of some of the old Nara sects they became objects of dislike in court circles. Honen, now 77 years old, and his disciple Shinran, were both exiled, and to distant and widely separated parts of Japan.[58] Shinran made use of his misfortune to spread the new evangelical Buddhism in the land of his exile. When the decree of banishment was repealed he carried on missionary activity for some years in various provinces of the East, and finally returned to Kyoto. Honen Shonin was now dead and his followers were divided into two schools, the more conservative retaining the name Jodo shu, while the more advanced

[57] The immediate suggestion to Honen Shonin was made by one of his lay disciples, a member of the Fujiwara family. See Lloyd, *Shinran and His Work* (Tokyo, Kyobunkwan, 1910).

[58] Honen to Toso Province, in the Southwest, Shinran to Echigo in the Northeast. See a little booklet with a Life of Shinran, published by the Otaniha Hongwanji in Kyoto, entitled *Principal Teachings of the True Sect of Pure Land*.

followed Shinran in founding the "Jodo Shin shu," or True Pure Land Sect, commonly referred to as the Shin shu. This differed from the more conservative Jodo in giving up the ancient Vinaya discipline which the Jodo retained, allowing its priests to marry, eat meat, and live as laymen, and in laying relatively little stress on the repetition of the Nembutsu, but trusting for salvation solely to the grace of Amida and to faith in him. As many writers have pointed out, Shinran was thus the Martin Luther of Japan, both in leading the way out of the monastic life and in preaching salvation through faith alone. The attitude today of the great Shin sect toward him is indicated in the following passage, which I take from a little book authorized and circulated by the Sect headquarters.[59]

> The Shonin was apparently a manifestation of Amida-Butsu, he was indeed a saving light who came among us some seven hundred years ago to dispel the darkness of this world. His life of 90 years on earth was an imprint eternally engraved on the hearts of sinners not yet freed from impurities. He lived among us to typify the life of a sinful soul who could yet be saved through his faith in the boundless love of Amida.

It was in 1192 that Minamoto Yoritomo became shogun and established his capital at Kamakura (which must be distinguished from the capital of the emperor at Kyoto.) He seems to have felt that his success was in part due to divine assistance, and the sentiment of gratitude that he and his followers felt toward Buddhism showed itself in many ways. It was he who planned the great image of Amida at Kamakura, perhaps the most majestic image in the world, a work showing both artistic ability of a high order and real religious feeling. Kamakura became in fact a religious as well as a political and military center. It was particularly the Zen type of Buddhism that flourished under the Minamotos and their successors at Kamakura, the Hojos. For Zen made a great appeal to the soldiers of these centuries, and thus a new and knightly element developed in the religion which had seldom been guessed before. It was largely this Zen Buddhism which gave the Hojo regent and his knights the calm courage to defy the seemingly irresistible force of Khubla Khan and his Mongol host, when in the latter part of the

[59] *Principal Teachings of the True Sect of Pure Land.*

thirteenth century they threatened to engulf the little island empire.[60]

The very success of Zen, Jodo, and Shin during these years aroused a certain amount of antagonism in the older sects, but this antagonism got its most forceful expression not in a conservative but in a fiery and radical spirit who became himself the founder of a new sect. This was Nichiren. He studied for a time in a Shingon temple, but like so many of his spiritual predecessors he received the major portion of his education in the Tendai school of philosophy on the slopes of Hiei-san. The influence of Tendai thought he never lost. His philosophy to the end remained essentially that of his teachers, and he took from Hiei-san especially the profound reverence for the Lotus Gospel which has always been the basis of Tendai thought. He was not willing, however, to spend his life in philosophic contemplation on Mount Hiei. The center of religious as well as temporal influence had in his time shifted to the region of Kamakura; and Nichiren, essentially a man of action, on completing his education began his preaching in and near the Shogun's capital. The burden of his impassioned sermons was the evil of the times, both religious and political. The greatest offenders, in his eyes, were the monks of the Jodo and Shin sects who had deserted the great teachings of the Lotus Gospel and had set up in the place of Sakyamuni the imaginary being Amida. The Zen sect was attacked almost as hotly, and even Shingon was ridiculed for its superstitious rites and practices. The government, too, came in for its share in the general denunciation, and predictions of evil for the land, like those of Amos, were published abroad.[61] The government responded as had the High Priest of Bethel to Amos' thunders, by having Nichiren banished, and at one time almost had him executed. In spite of which Nichiren thundered on.

But he was not merely a denouncer. The positive note in his sermons and writings, the cure which he offered for the evils of the time, was a return to the teachings of Sakyamuni. To Nichiren, however, we must realize, to Nichi-

[60] See Brinkley, p. 361.

[61] Nichiren predicted even foreign invasion—a prophecy which was, in a sense, fulfilled a few years later, when the great power of the Mongols sought to annex Japan as it had China and did get an insecure foothold on some of the outlying islands.

ren who knew nothing of the Pali Scriptures, the cry "Back to Shaka" (Sakyamuni) meant "Back to the Sakyamuni of the Saddharma Pundarika Sutra"—the Lotus Gospel of the Tendai sect. It was, thus, neither a more scholarly form of historical research nor a new philosophy that characterized the new sect which in 1253 Nichiren founded, but rather a greater zeal, a tremendous devotion to the Lotus Scripture, and a literal acceptance of the prophecies given in the later part of that Sutra.

Concerning this question of prophecy a few words must be said. As we have seen, an old Buddhist tradition, accepted in both Hinayana and Mahayana lands, had from early times pointed to a gradual decay of the Dharma. In Japan this general expectation had been made more definite, and the centuries of degeneration after the death of the Founder had been divided into three distinguishable ages. These were the Age of the Perfect Law, in which the Dharma was strictly observed and which covered the first thousand years after Shaka's Nirvana; the Age of the Copied Law, the second thousand years, in which faith and morals declined, but piety was still to a considerable extent preserved; and the Age of the Latter Law, which was to last ten thousand years, a time of evil and war. "Though there were minor variations in the tradition as regards the time divisions, all Japanese Buddhists believed in the apocalyptic legend as a whole. And since they put the Buddha's death in 949 B.C., they believed that the last of the three ages began in the year 1052 A.D." [62] The wars and moral degeneration of Nichiren's day seemed to tally very exactly with the nature of the Age of the Latter Law as predicted, and it was plain to Nichiren, living two centuries after this third age should have begun, that they were well within the evil time. With this commonly accepted view Nichiren connected a prophecy which he took from the fifteenth chapter of the Saddharma Pundarika, in which the Buddha shows to his human followers a great band of celestial helpers under the leadership of four great Bodhisattvas who are destined to keep alive and spread the true Dharma in future ages. The first of these four was named

[62] Anesaki, *Nichiren, the Buddhist Prophet* (Harvard University Press, 1916), p. 4.

Visista-caritra; and as Nichiren found himself, through years of persecution, standing almost alone for what he considered the pure Dharma, it was borne in upon him that he himself was a reincarnation of this great Bodhisattva, and that he thus had a peculiar mission to restore the truth of the Lotus Gospel.[63] As he had implicit faith in his own mission and in his ultimate success, he substituted an optimistic view of the future of Buddhism for the pessimistic one prevalent in most other sects.

The little band of followers whom Nichiren gathered round him naturally accepted this saint and prophet at his own self-evaluation, and their many successors have ever since regarded him as a great Bodhisattva who was born in the darkest days of Japan's history with a special and divine mission to perform. The Nichiren sect is still one of the most influential and active of Buddhist denominations. Its appeal is chiefly to the common people and it retains a good deal of the energetic and contentious spirit of its founder.[64]

But the last sect of Buddhism to be found in Japan was of the Pure Land or Amida type which Nichiren had so strenuously opposed. In the later years of Nichiren's life, an earnest monk of the Jodo sect, who had originally been a Tendai monk, and who felt that new impetus should be given to the Pure Land doctrines, went through many provinces on long missionary journeys, probably in part to counteract the influence of Nichiren, preaching everywhere the glory of Amida's love, and the simplicity of salvation through his grace. This monk is known to history as Ippen Shonin (1239-1289). In 1275 (seven years before the death of Nichiren) he left the Jodo shu and founded a new sect—

[63] The reader will be reminded of the somewhat similar yet characteristically different belief which was being taught in Christendom by almost a contemporary of Nichiren, Joachim de Flore (born in 1132, ninety years before Nichiren's birth). This Christian theory, like the Buddhist, divided the centuries of faith into three Ages; but unlike the Buddhist triad they were ages not of steady degeneration but of steady advance—the Age of the Father, dating from the Mosaic dispensation till the coming of Christ, the Age of the Son, extending to Joachim's time, and the Age of the Spirit, which was then to begin and was to last till the end of the world. See Gebhart, *L'Italie Mystique* (Paris, Hachette, 1893), Chap. II.

[64] For us Westerners, ignorant of Japanese, acquaintance with Nichiren, Honen, and Shinran is easier than with most of the other leaders of Japanese Buddhism, owing to Professor Anesaki's interesting little book, *Nichiren, the Buddhist Prophet,* the great Life of Honen Shonin, edited by Coates and Ishizuka, and Lloyd's *Shinran and His Work.*

the last Buddhist sect to be founded in Japan—which is called the Ji-shu.[65] Ippen's teaching differed only in slight details from Honen Shonin's. He seems to have stressed the necessity of rejecting self-help and of mere reliance upon Amida, and to have been influenced somewhat by Zen thought. The chief reason for his founding a new sect, however, was his conviction that he had received a special and immediate revelation from Amida (in the form of the god of the Kumano shrine). The influence of the Ji-shu has never been very great, and it is today, like the Yutsu Nembutsu, in a rather failing condition. The great prosperity of Jodo and Shin leaves little room or need for the two smaller Pure Land sects, which indeed have nothing of importance to differentiate them from their larger sisters.

Except for the importation of the small Obaku branch of the Zen, brought by Yin Yuen from China, in 1654, there have been no new sects of Buddhism in Japan since 1275. The story of Japanese Buddhism for several centuries after that date is principally the story of the steady permeation of Japanese society by the four more recent sects—Jodo, Shin, Zen, and Nichiren—with the Tendai philosophy as the intellectual background of the whole. Hiei-san and the other great monastic institutions continued for centuries to send out the great scholars of the times, who kept up the cultured life of the capital.[66] The mass of the people were illiterate but it was the Buddhist monks alone who made any effort to educate them. The example which Kobo Daishi had set early in the ninth century by founding a school in his great temple in Kyoto was followed by many temples in various parts of the empire, where instruction in learned subjects was given by learned monks. "It stands to the credit of these bonzes that they made no attempt to monopolize erudition. Their aim was to popularize it. They opened temple-seminaries and exercise halls where youths of all classes could obtain instruction and where an excellent series of textbooks

[65] See Reischauer, *Studies in Japanese Buddhism*, p. 128, and Coates and Ishizuka, *op. cit.*, pp. 54-55. The name Ji-shu means the Hour sect, or the Now sect, indicating the founder's belief that his sect was the one needed by the men of his time.

[66] Cf. Yoshitaro Yamashita, *The Influence of Shinto and Buddhism in Japan*, Transactions of the Japan Society, IV (1897-98), 260.

was used." [67] One of the chief aims of these textbooks was moral education; and if one may judge by the quotations given in Brinkley's history, the virtues taught were not peculiarly Buddhist in type—except for the emphasis they put upon generosity.

Of all the schools of Buddhism it was probably the Zen that had the most influence during these centuries on the cultural life of Japan. It was especially the Zen monks who became the most zealous educators. As in China, it was Zen Buddhism that had the greatest influence upon painting. The great school of mystical landscape painting which had flourished in China under the Sung dynasty scarcely touched Japan until the times of the Ashikaga Shoguns (1335-1573); then it united its influence with Zen Buddhism, and the school of Japanese landscape painting was the result.[68]

> As a method of achieving a union of the individual soul with the cosmic spirit, Zen training manifested itself in art of a transcendental kind. Naturalism and intuitionism enabled Zen not only to absorb the serenely transient beauty of nature, but also to express it, distinct from human passions, in placid dignity and pure simplicity; while individualism, a necessary consequence of Zen practice, found expression in a vigor and freshness of artistic treatment always implying a touch of original genius. . . . The influence of Zen pervaded the lives of the people and moulded their perceptions in every branch of art—in the composition of poems, the building of houses and furnishing of rooms; in methods of flower arrangement, of gardening, and even of preparing and drinking tea. Indeed, there is in Japan hardly a form of thought or activity that Zen has not touched and inspired with its ideal of simple beauty.[69]
>
> Fans, kakemonos, calligraphy, the Japanese smile, the sternness of expression, everything now known as peculiarly Japanese was the product of Zen, directly or indirectly.[70]

But in recalling what the Buddhism of Kamakura and Ashikaga days did for Japan we must not forget the other side of the picture. The great Tendai and Shingon and Hosso establishments continued their political and military meddlings, and the new sects too often followed suit. In fact, the Tendai power on Hiei-san became so menacing to the state that in 1574 Nobunaga attacked it with his army, burned down its 3000 monasteries and temples, and put to the

[67] Brinkley, p. 448.
[68] Cf. Fenellosa, Vol. II, Chap. XII.
[69] Anesaki, p. 53.
[70] From a lecture by Professor Anesaki.

sword most of the monks who had not already perished in the flames. Under the Tokugawa Shoguns the mountain was restored to the Tendai shu and a few new monasteries were built on the ruins of the old ones; but the political and military power of Tendai never reappeared. And for that matter, under Nobunaga and his strong successors all the Buddhist orders ceased to be centers of political influence or military force.

It was in Nobunaga's time [71] that Christianity was introduced into Japan by Francis Xavier and his Portuguese Jesuits. The missionaries were kindly received by the Buddhist monks of the region in which Xavier landed. The abbot of the Shinshu monastery in Kagoshima, and other monks, spoke of the newcomers in most favorable terms. [72] After a few weeks, however, the fiercely exclusive and even violent form of the new religion forced the Buddhists to change their opinion of it and their attitude toward the missionaries. In the course of a few years these earnest but narrow Jesuits, and their less politic followers, the Franciscans and Dominicans, had forced the government to feel that Christianity was a menace to the Japanese nation; and finally in 1635 it was expelled and forbidden.

Twenty years after the arrival of the Jesuits they had succeeded in founding a mission in the capital (Kyoto) and one of them, Froez by name, has left us his impressions. It is interesting to note that he was struck with the high moral level of the people and seems to have attributed it in part to the teachings of the Buddhist monks. "After describing and praising a sermon by a bonze he heard in a Kyoto temple, Froez tells us that he ceased to wonder how it was that Buddhist priests were held in much respect and reverence by the people; and he adds, 'In truth these people both in goodness of nature and excellence of wit surpass many nations of our Europe.'" [73]

The Tokugawa Shoguns (1600-1868) adopted a paternal attitude toward Buddhism; they protected, patronized, and controlled it. They endowed many of the temples richly, often pampered the priests and made them financially in-

[71] In the year 1549.

[72] Murdoch, *History of Japan*, II. 65.

[73] *Idem.*, II. 150, note.

dependent of the people. The result was very deleterious to the priesthood, and, through them, to the religion. Buddhism became practically a state church. By command of the third Tokugawa, in order to make sure that Christianity could not reenter the land, a census of the population was taken, under the supervision of Buddhist monks, and it was decreed that every inhabitant must be registered as belonging to some specific Buddhist or Shinto parish, and Buddhist and Shinto temples were ordered to keep accurate lists of their parishioners and of the births and deaths in their families. Every *daimyo,* moreover, was required to adhere to some specific sect of Buddhism.[74]

The paternal attitude of the Tokugawa Shoguns toward Buddhism did not mean that they sought to propagate Buddhist thought, as the early emperors had done, or that they protected it from rival teachings. On the contrary they cultivated Confucian philosophy, and endowed schools for the spread of it. During the last part of the Tokugawa régime Confucian scholars had quite wrested the intellectual and moral leadership of the land from the Buddhists, and the upper classes largely ceased to be interested in Buddhism. The financial backing of Buddhism by the government still continued, but the chief effect of this was to keep the clergy in a state of passive satisfaction, saying masses, chanting at funerals, and living lives of elegant inactivity. These late Tokugawa years thus resembled in some ways the period of moral slump that Buddhism went through in the century prior to the rise of Jodo and Zen. They constitute the second low-water mark of the religion.

During the last century of the Tokugawas a new rival arose to offer unexpected opposition to Buddhism: namely its old ally, Shinto. For Shinto had at last become self-conscious, and rebelled against its partial absorption into Buddhism in the form of Ryobu Shinto. This revival of pure Shinto, by scholars and patriots, was one of the chief influences in finally overthrowing the Shogunate and restoring the emperor to power. It was in part for this reason that at the restoration Buddhism was disestablished and

[74] Brinkley, pp. 578, 583; also Anesaki's lectures.

Shinto was made the state church.[75] The government withdrew its financial support from Buddhist monks, appropriated much of the landed property belonging to Buddhist temples, and for a time even entered upon a mild attempt at persecution. Some temples were stripped of their treasures, their monks driven out and forbidden to teach. It was, to be sure, for only a short time that the government—so eager to be modern—continued this most unmodern procedure, but its attitude toward Buddhism was still notably hostile. At the same time it opened the country once more to Christian missionaries, who flocked in and soon had made large numbers of converts, not only among Shintoists but among nominal Buddhists.

These events came as a stunning blow to Buddhism, from which at first it seemed almost impossible that it should recover. But as one looks back now through the sixty years or so that have elapsed since then, both the withdrawal of government support and the entrance of Christianity are pretty plainly seen to have been blessings in disguise, not only to Japan but to Buddhism itself. The patronage and control of the religion by the Tokugawa government had been a great spiritual handicap, whose withdrawal was like the lifting off of a heavy weight; while the presence of an active and noble spiritual rival has proved to be just the stimulus which Buddhism most needed. How much life there is left in the old religion, and how much soundness of heart and of head, will, I trust, be made clearer by the following chapters.

[75] Government officials and many Japanese Shinto scholars will insist that this statement is unjustified. The term, I acknowledge, is not exact, but in a rough and general way it expresses the actual situation. Cf. Holton, "The Political Philosophy of Modern Shinto," *T.A.S.J.*, XLIX (1922).

CHAPTER XXIV

THE BUDDHIST CYCLE IN JAPAN

All or nearly all of the more important beings reverenced and worshiped by the Buddhists of Japan are already familiar to the reader, under slightly different names—provided, at least, that he has read the chapters in this book that deal with the rise of the Mahayana in India and the *Dramatis Personae* of China. There is, however, in Japan a slightly new attitude toward some of them and a different relative emphasis among them, and there are, besides, a few actual additions to the familiar list; so that for the sake of the intelligibility of the following chapters it seems best to set down here a few remarks about the cycle of Buddhas and Bodhisattvas in Japan, which will be useful for reference if not for reading. The result, I fear, will hardly be worthy of the name *chapter*, but will degenerate, rather, into something scarcely distinguishable from a mere list.

The word for Buddha in Japanese is *Butsu;* that for Bodhisattva is *Busatsu.* As is so often the case in Japanese, the last syllables of these words are barely sounded. There are four Butsu and six Busatsu of primary importance in the religious life of the Japanese Buddhist. These ten great beings are the same as the great ten in China, and their names in Sanskrit, Chinese, Korean, and Japanese, will be found in the list on page 304. From the Japanese point of view a slight change should be made in the list. If we are to arrange it in the order of importance, Amida should be at the head, taking precedence of Shaka (Sakyamuni).

Concerning the four Buddhas of this list little further need here be said. The orthodox members of the Pure Land sects believe that Amida was once a man, Hozo by name (in Sanskrit Dharmakara) and that it was as Hozo he took the famous vows to save mankind. In art Amida is usually presented with the first finger of each hand pressed against the thumb. The first finger represents man, while the thumb means the lack of all separateness; so that this attitude symbolizes the identity of man with the Ultimate. Amida is usually accompanied by the Busatsu Kwannon and Sei-shi. Dainichi wears a crown instead of the usual cephalic protuberance; but a crown more lofty and ornate than that of the Busatsu. The first finger of his left hand is usually held upright and grasped by his right hand, in such a way that the tips of the two first fingers touch. According to Shingon symbolism, the right hand means the Buddha, the left-hand man, and the touching of the two fingers means, as in the case of Amida, the union or identity of the two. Shaka (Sakyamuni) is commonly accompanied by Monju and Fugen, while Yaku-shi has for his attendants the Sun (Nikko) and the Moon (Genkko). I ought to note here in passing that the Buddha images of Japan rank with those of Siam as the finest product of Buddhist religious sculpture. Some of them, of course, are unsuccessful, but the average level is high, and the Japanese Buddha at its best is one of the most spiritual creations of religious art.

A little more should here be added to what I said in Chapters XI and XV on the great Bodhisattvas. Monju and Fugen often accompany not only Shaka but also Dainichi. This fact makes them rather prominent in art, but as religious objects they have lost in importance and popularity in coming from China to Japan. In character and function they have not notably changed. Neither, for that matter, has Kwannon (Kwan-Yin). Here as in China, the Goddess of Mercy is extremely popular; and as an object of worship among the less intelligent masses she is second only to Amida in importance. She is represented in many forms, often as a youth with the usual crown bearing an intaglio of Amida; generally she (or he) carries a lotus. Then there is the eleven-headed Kwannon (wearing a crown with ten small head-like decorations), the horse-headed Kwannon (with the picture of a horse's head in her crown), the forty-handed Kwannon (called the "Thousand-handed Kwannon"), and many other forms too numerous for mention in this place. The Butsatsu Sei-shi has notably gained in popularity since leaving China. This, I expect, is due to the great extension of Amida worship in Japan and to the fact that Sei-shi is regularly joined, in artistic representation, with Kwannon as one of the two attendants or companions of Amida. Among his functions (or hers?) is the important one of coming with Amida and Kwannon to meet the soul after death. As Kwannon is the personification of the mercy of Amida, Sei-shi personifies his wisdom, and thus trenches upon the function of Monju.

Concerning Jizo more should be said. For Jizo occupies an even more important place in Japan than Ti-tsang does in China. As in China he delivers souls from hell, but he has also acquired a number of other specific functions, most of them connected with his quality of mercy. He helps women in childbirth and is (like Kwannon) the giver of healthy children.[1] He drives away the demons of disease and calamity. Sometimes he is regarded as a kind of sixfold deity—the "Six Jizos"[2]—and as such is the object of a special and popular cult. Like Kwannon again he is at times (especially in the Jodoshu) associated with Amida, and has the function of leading souls to the Western Paradise. In a special way he is the protector of travelers and pilgrims. But most of all he is the loving guardian of little children. And not only of living children but of dead children as well. This conception seems to be of purely Japanese origin. Parents who have lost their little ones make a special point of worshiping Jizo; the toys of their dead children are offered in his temples, their diminutive kimonos are hung up before him, and their little red bibs festoon many a rough stone Jizo in temple courts or along country roads. An ancient Jizo image by the roadside, with from one to twenty little bibs around its neck, is at first sight a rather ludicrous object; but when one understands all that it means it becomes a symbol full of pathos to the

[1] He has in part taken the place of the Shinto phallic deities of fecundity.

[2] De Visser suggests that this may be due to the fact that in the Sanskrit Sutras dealing with him (under the name Kshitigarbha) he takes many bodies to save all beings in the "Six Paths." The Chinese Sutra of the Ten Kings refers to the six Ti-tsangs; but there never was a popular cult of the six Ti-tsangs in China as there is of the six Jizos in Japan. This Japanese cult is said to date from the ninth century. See De Visser, "The Bodhisattva Ti-tsang in China and Japan," *Ostasiatische Zeitschrift* for 1913 and 1914.

unbelieving, and doubtless of hope and comfort to the bereaved but faithful heart. For, as many Japanese believe, the souls of little children at death go to a land beside the sea [3] where they amuse themselves by piling up little towers of stone. No sooner have they made their little towers than a terrible red devil rushes forth, knocks to pieces the piles of stones, and terrifies the children. And then, as though in answer to their cries, great, calm, tender Jizo, strong and loving, appears and drives off the devil, while the little ones take hold of his staff or hide in the folds of his garment. So he rescues them and (presumably) takes them back with him to Amida's Paradise.

But it is not only the children whom Jizo aids. Whoever is in need and calls upon him receives his help. He heals the sick; he substitutes himself for the heavy-laden and does their work for them; he suffers with and for his worshipers; he even takes the place of animals who are threatened or killed by hunters. Many miraculous deeds are attributed to him, and many stories are told of his guidance or of his actual appearance to the eyes of his worshipers; as, for example, the following.

Myogwan, who lived in Hoki province about the year 775, had a great longing to see the living Jizo. "For many years he had been a devout believer in Jizo and every morning at daybreak he opened the window looking out to the south and recited Jizo's holy name, with almost closed eyes and quieting his heart, in the hope that the Bodhisattva might appear. But he always looked in vain." Then he was told in a dream that if he would go to Mount Iwafune in Shimotsuke, Jizo would appear to him. So he made a pilgrimage to the mountain. "When Myogwan arrived at the foot of Iwafune, the dusk was falling and he was hospitably received by a Buddhist monk who lived in a lonely dwelling far from the mountain village." The monk assured him that if he would wait till the eighteenth of the month and then go to the top of the mountain his great wish

[3] Some think that the children's souls go to a remote part of the Japanese coast and it is here Jizo rescues them. See Lafcadio Hearn, *Glympses of Unfamiliar Japan* (London, Kegan Paul, 1894). A variant of this myth has it that the little souls go to hell where an old hag forces them to build towers of stones; and then Jizo comes and rescues them. De Visser, *op. cit.*, sec. III.

would be granted. So Myogwan waited, staying as a guest of the monk. "During these days he observed that the monk was called Jizo bo (priest Jizo) and that he helped the people in all kinds of work. During the night he heard old men and women knocking at the door and calling Jizo bo, whom they begged to assist them the next day in plowing or thatching a roof or digging a well, and the good monk always consented. Myogwan saw him actually engaged in all these kinds of work during the daytime. On the morning of the eighteenth the mysterious monk led Myogwan part way up the mountain and pointing to the peak he said: 'That peak is Mount Iwafune. Go there and joining your hands look up to the top of the mountain with a heart filled with devotion: then Jizo's shadow is sure to appear.' After these words he vanished." Myogwan did as he had been directed and soon saw a gigantic golden shadow of Jizo rising over the mountain peak. When the vision had passed the mysterious monk returned and said, "Today your prayer has been fulfilled; now you may return to your native village." Thus they descended the mountain together, and on the way the monk expounded the Law to Myogwan in wonderfully clear and subtle fashion, and at the foot of the mountain bade him farewell. And Myogwan realized that the monk was none other than Jizo himself.[4]

Jizo is almost always represented as a monk, with shaven head. Usually he stands, bearing in his right hand a pilgrim's staff, in his left a pearl. The staff is of the sort commonly carried by Buddhist pilgrims. At its upper end there is a metal ring from which hang six other rings. These six rings are symbolic of the virtues of charity, discipline, perseverance, effort, meditation, and wisdom.[5] The pearl too—in Jizo's left hand—has its significance, in fact both a shallower and a deeper one. The shallow meaning is that all blessings are contained within the jewel and Jizo can give any of them in answer to prayer. The deeper meaning is Pure Mind: and this may be interpreted to mean whatever

[4] De Visser, *op. cit.*, II. 397-98.

[5] These, of course, are the six Paramitas or cardinal virtues of the Mahayana: see Chap. XI.

virtue the worshiper most longs for in himself. This virtue can be obtained by earnest prayer to Jizo.

Of the remaining members of the Buddhist cycle in Japan little need be said, and what I shall set down here will be of value chiefly as a matter of reference. One more Buddha should be added to the list given at the beginning of this chapter, namely, Ashaku, in Sanskrit Akshobhya, one of the five Dhyani Buddhas referred to in Chapter XI. The Shingon sect in Japan makes something of Ashaku,[6] but elsewhere he is of no religious importance. Another Bodhisattva should also be mentioned who plays some part in Shingon Buddhism, though little elsewhere. This is the Busatsu Kokuzo. His Sanskrit name is Akasagarbha, and he represents the ether and is one of the group of eight prominent Bodhisattvas. Like Monju and Sei-shi, he personifies wisdom.[7] A more prominent religious figure is Fudo. Like the two just named he is of importance chiefly in the Shingon sect. Many scholars think he is derived from the Sanskrit *Acala* or *Achala,* and for this reason is known as the Immobile. However this may be, he is for the Japanese Buddhist a form of Dainichi. It is said that he was incarnated as a slave in order to serve all beings and that he took a vow to destroy all evil in the world. He is one of the few frightful-looking members of the Buddhist cycle. In his right hand he holds a sword to smite the wicked and in his left a lasso to catch and bind them.[8] His face and arms are usually a deep livid blue, and behind him rises a mass of red flames. Like most frightful beings in religions derived from India, he is terrible only to the wicked, and is the friend and protector of those who are really striving to live the decent life.

Fudo is not spoken of as a Busatsu, but as a form of Dainichi he seems to rank as one. The level below that of the Bodhisattvas is, I suppose, in theory, that of the great Arahants. It will be recalled that the early Mahayana rec-

[6] He is one of the five Buddhas in the Vajra-dhatu Mandala, and one of the thirteen celestial beings used in the funeral ceremonies of the Shingon sect. See Getty, pp. 30, note, 33-34.

[7] He also belongs to the thirteen celestial beings of the Shingon funeral ceremony. Kobo Daishi considered Kokuzo his personal protector.

[8] Cf. Getty, pp. 33-34. See also Anesaki, *Buddhist Art,* p. 34.

ognized sixteen of these as of special importance, and that the Chinese raised the number of "Lohans" to eighteen. Japanese Buddhism went back to the orthodox number and recognized sixteen "Rakans." Of these sixteen only one is singled out as a figure of independent importance, namely, Binzuru. According to Miss Getty, Binzuru is a popular form of Yaku-shi, the Buddha of healing. Certainly Binzuru is one of the gods of healing, as a glance at his image on the external wall of many a popular temple will indicate. I have said that only Binzuru is singled out among the Rakan as of special importance. I should add that sometimes one finds Dammo (Bodhidharma) represented as one of the Rakan (especially on Zen scrolls), and wherever Dammo is present he is, for the Zen followers, a very important figure. He is regularly represented as clad in brilliant red, and is a favorite theme not only with the makers of Zen kakemonos, but with the woodcarvers of Nara.

Below the rank of Rakan stands a long list of beings borrowed from Indian and Japanese mythology, and added, by the liberal interpretation of Buddhist thinkers and the superstitious tendencies of the Buddhist masses, to the Buddhist cycle. Prominent among these are the Ni-O, or two Deva Kings, Indra and Brahma,[9] who often guard the outer entrance to the temple; and the Shi-Tenno or Kings of the Four Quarters, familiar in both Sanskrit and Chinese and Korean Buddhism. One of these Four Kings, Bishaimon (Sanskrit Vaisravana) is singled out for special attention in Japan, as one of the seven gods of luck. He is thought to be connected with the Chinese god of wealth. Decidedly important is Hachiman, commonly called the god of war, whom Buddhism in an unBuddhistic moment borrowed (with the blessing, apparently of Kobo Daishi) from the patriotic hero-worship native to Japan. According to Anesaki his name is Buddhist in origin, meaning the Eight Symbols, or eight perfect ways or morality. He is generally said to be the deification of the son of the war-like empress Jingo, who invaded Korea in the third century and left

[9] This is the common interpretation. Professor Takakusa thinks they are two aspects of Narayana, a name for Vishnu. See "What Japan Owes to India," in *The Young East*, I. 147.

behind her not only one war god but a progeny of war lovers in all lands and all centuries who most appropriately bear her name. Another Shinto deity who has crept at least part way into Buddhism is Inari, an ancient rice god, somehow associated with the fox. Little Inari shrines will be found on the outskirts of many a Buddhist temple.

Four of the seven (or eight) gods of luck possessed by the Japanese came in the train of Buddhism from India. One of these is Bishaimon, already referred to. A second is Daikoku, originally a form of Shiva; a third is Benzai, derived from the Indian goddess Sarasvati; while the fourth is Kichijo, who originated with Lakshmi. Emma-O, the regent of hell, and known in China as Yen-lo, is a direct descendant of the Vedic Yama. He has, as in China, several assistants and doubtless he needs them. I add in a note a few other Indian deities who have found a new home for themselves, under new names, in modern Japan.[10]

To this list of objects of Buddhist reverence should be added a few historical Japanese Buddhists, such as Shotoku Taishi, Gyogi Busatsu, and the founders of most of the great sects. All these names combined make a formidable list. It would be a misunderstanding, however, to take them as "the Gods of Japanese Buddhism." The uneducated Japanese Buddhist regards them in much the same way as the uneducated Roman Catholic regards the saints of his calendar. The Buddhist who understands his religion smiles at many of these popular figures, reverences a number of them, and realizes that even the greatest and highest of them are but representations, symbols, visions of the Buddha nature which is in all things.

[10] Sho-ten, derived from Ganesa; Kompira, whose derivation is uncertain; Sui-ten, who is Varuna; Taishaku, who is Indra; Bon-ten or Brahma; Kojin or Rudru; Ucchushma, an aspect of Agni. I take these names and their derivations from Professor Takakusa's article already referred to, pp. 144-145.

CHAPTER XXV

BUDDHIST TEMPLES IN JAPAN

If the pilgrim to Japan makes Kyoto his first stop, his attention immediately upon alighting from the train will be called to the great roofs of the Higashi Hongwanji, the immense temple of the Shin sect near the station. The majority of Buddhist temples in Japan follow the Chinese custom of facing south; but there are exceptions aplenty, and this is one of them. Like many of the Shinshu temples it faces the east. Three monumental portals pierce the front wall of the sacred enclosure, the central one a gigantic gateway with a high double roof, rich with elaborate carving. Passing through this, one finds oneself in a spacious court. A small shrine is at one's left, with a kind of pavilion before it in which a few old or weary people are always to be found, resting in the shade and chatting pleasantly with their neighbors. Beyond this is the southern gateway and a bell tower. A fountain is playing in the court, made in the form of a huge lotus bud, and in another place there is a large bowl with running water, roofed over for the protection of pilgrims who often wash here before worshiping. One sees also a few large bronze lanterns. But at first these things are hardly noticed, for one's eyes turn irresistibly toward the two great halls on the western side of the court. The northern and larger of these is the *hondo,* or founder's hall, with a double roof, and the smaller *Amida-do,* to the south, with a single roof, is connected with the larger building by a covered corridor. Along this corridor are piled several huge coils of rope, many inches in thickness and made of human hair, donated for the purpose by zealous Buddhist women at the time of the building of the temple. It was with these ropes that the great beams of the temple were carried and hoisted into place. The roofs of both the main halls are too high and steep to give that sense of perfect proportion which the earliest Japanese temples possess; but the curve of the roofs and the tilt of the eaves, rather less pronounced than those of Chinese temples, is exceedingly graceful. And what the exterior lacks in beauty, as compared with the few extant specimens of early Japanese architecture, is more than atoned for by the impressiveness of the interior.

To one whose acquaintance with Buddhist temples is confined to China and Korea, these great Shinshu interiors will come as a revelation. Here no confusion of tawdry decoration and cheap votives, no burning of paper money or even of incense, no dirty floors or fantastic Lohan images; just a great, cathedral-like open space (in this case 42 by 66 feet) covered with matting and immaculately clean, a rail dividing the hall in two unequal parts, and behind it a rich but not confusing altar, and a single image, executed in exquisite taste. The standing Amida in the Amida-do is particularly beautiful and reminds one at once of the Madonna in some Italian cathedral. The worshipers, as well as the building, present a striking contrast to those one has become accustomed to in China. As I have said, there is here no burning of paper money, no fortune-telling, but just little groups of silent, earnest worshipers, coming in, kneeling a few moments before the shrine in earnest prayer, and silently departing. The whole atmosphere of the place is unmistakably religious; and he who cannot worship his God (whatever that may mean to him) in this shrine of Amida must, I think, be somehow lacking in spiritual susceptibility.

The Higashi Hongwanji temple of Kyoto is typical of nearly all the large temples of the Shin sect and fairly representative of many Jodo temples as well. It can hardly be said to represent all Japanese Buddhist temples, for the Buddhist temples of Japan have no such regularity of plan as that one finds in most Chinese temples. So far as I know there is only one Japanese temple laid out on the regular Chinese plan—the large headquarters of the Obaku division of the Zen sect at Uji, built in 1650 by Chinese Buddhists and kept for many years after its founding in the hands of Chinese monks. Some of the larger Zen and Shingon temples, while not following at all strictly the Chinese pattern, follow the general scheme of having a large portal, with guardian gods, and back of it, in a spacious enclosure, a succession of two or three large temple-halls, with the buildings for the monks at the rear and on the sides. This, however, is not very common, and, as I have said, there is no regular plan for either the exterior or the interior of a Japanese temple. Yet certain things are fairly constant. Most constant of all, perhaps, is the universal cleanliness and excellent repair—a characteristic of nearly every temple I have visited in Japan. Nearly all Buddhist temples have a court or enclosure, though I have seen one or two without anything of the kind. The enclosure is usually entered through a roofed gateway in which are often enshrined the gigantic and terrible Ni-O—the two Devas, Indra and Brahma. These are genuine objects of popular worship, as the many little "spit-balls" of paper sticking to the wire netting in front of the gods clearly show.[1] In place of the Ni-O one may find the Kings of the Four Quarters, so familiar in China and Korea. Sometimes the temple enclosure is entered through a torii (of the more artistic and less archaic variety),[2] borrowed, of course, from Shinto in the days before the Restoration, when the two religions were practically one. Sometimes just within the gateway is a tiny Shinto shrine, especially in temples of the Shingon and Nichiren sects. There may be also a pagoda, with two, three or five stories. In some temple grounds, especially in those of the Shingon sect, one will find a *sotoba* or stone monument made up of five parts, symbolizing the five material elements. The lowest part is a cube or parallelopiped signifying earth; the second a sphere signifying water; the

[1] It is a popular belief that one may tell whether or not one's prayer to the Ni-O will be answered by chewing a bit of paper, making it into a "spit-ball," and throwing it at the wire grating. If it sticks, the prayer has been heard.

[2] There are two forms of torii, one with straight cross beams and of rather ponderous appearance; the other much more graceful, with cross beams that have swaying lines and an upward tilt at the ends. The straight and ponderous kind is thought to be the more ancient form, while the graceful type is by far the more popular. The archaic style of torii is found only at a few Shinto shrines (never at Buddhist temples) and is always the token of a self-conscious effort to revert to pure Shinto uncontaminated with Buddhist or Chinese influence. It is found, for example—characteristically enough—at Ise, where the government sees to it that everything is as it was in the beginning, at the historical moment when Jimmu Tenno descended from the skies. The great majority of Shinto shrines have clung to the more graceful form of torii.

third a cone with broken apex, signifying fire; the fourth a crescent signifying air or wind; and the uppermost a ball ending in a tip or flame-like point, signifying ether. A few temples have, in some part of their grounds, a peculiar cylindrical metal column known as a *sorinto*. The upper part of the shaft is surrounded with nine metal rings and usually surmounted with a lotus carrying a pointed ball, like that on the summit of the sotoba.

The court or enclosure of a Buddhist temple is one of the loveliest things in Japan. The stone lanterns, the ancient pine trees, the wonderfully wrought brazen dragons that spout water in a fountain, the stone Jizo, wrapped about with votive cloths presented by devout worshipers whose little children have gone to the far land where now only Jizo can help them, the bell tower, the façade of the temple itself with perhaps half a dozen smaller structures standing about it, the lotus pond with its gold fish, the many pigeons that fly about the court, owing their living to the kindness of the pilgrims, and most of all the glad looks of the worshipers who have come in their best kimonos to do homage to the Buddha, and the joyous faces of the many children almost invariably found here, make it a scene not to be forgotten. For the temple courts are the playgrounds of Japan. They do not merely happen to be playgrounds. The children are desired. Many temple courts are provided with swings and various simple games; and the children love the place and learn thus early to associate religion with delight. A very large proportion of the men and women of Japan must look back upon some Buddhist temple as the scene of their happiest hours. Besides the children there are tired mothers with their babies on their backs, and weary people of various ages. Some have come here with their grandchildren to watch them play, some have come for an hour's chat with old friends, in the shade of a great tree or beside the fountain, some, still in the midst of life's work, have fled here for a moment's refreshment and worship, spent in part before the calm image of Amida in the shrine, in part out here in the fresh air of the courtyard filled with the cooing of doves and the shouts of children.

Many of the tenderest memories and most significant

moments of life thus cluster round the Buddhist temple. Not only the children but at times people of all ages find the temple court a kind of playground. Many a temple has a monthly fair, when for a whole night the sacred enclosure is luminous with colored lanterns, and filled with booths at which you can buy all sorts of pretty things, and the air is musical with the notes of the temple gong, the chanting of priests, and the voices of young people.

But the temple enters also and of course into the solemn hours. Here the funeral service is held, and the memorial service for the dead. Here the tablets of many of the departed are preserved and sometimes a portion of their ashes,[3] and around many a Buddhist temple lies the ancient "churchyard," as we should call it—its gray stones clustering about the sacred walls, just as they so often do in New England—and Old England.

The main hall of the temple, in some of the Buddhist sects, is not infrequently closed. But except at night the temple inclosure, and at least one of its shrines, central or subordinate, is always open, and worshipers enter and depart during any hour of daylight. If one is tempted to criticize the enormous amount of capital that has been expended on Buddhist temples in Japan, saying that all this money might have been invested in more profitable ways, this answer may at least be given, that hardly anything in Japan is in more constant use than her temples.

The temple proper—the building itself as well as all the subordinate buildings belonging to it—is, like everything else in Japan, made of wood—of wood and paper. Frequently portions of the roof and the ends of the overhanging beams are elaborately carved. There is usually no great front door, as in Chinese temples, but just many sliding screens, mostly of paper. A familiar figure just outside the door of many of the larger temples is Binzuru, one of the sixteen Rakans, who, the story goes, once looked after a woman too curiously and thereafter was forbidden to enter the sacred building. This punishment (or was it his sin?)

[3] In the Shi-Tenno temple at Osaka the ashes of the dead are sometimes mixed with clay and made into small Buddha images, which are deposited in one of the shrines, a rather striking symbolization of the hope that the departed one has "become Buddha."

seems to have resulted in making him more popular than all his brethren. Tradition has endowed him—or his image—with a miraculous power of healing. The worshiper who is ill has only to rub his hand upon the part of Binzuru's image corresponding to the diseased part of his own body and then to rub his hand upon the infirm member; if he does this with sufficient faith he will be healed. So firmly planted is this belief in large numbers of temple visitors, that the legs and arms of most Binzuru images are half rubbed away. The Binzuru at the Asakusa temple in Tokyo has healed so many parts of so many ailing bodies that there is hardly anything left of the poor fellow. The government at times has had to lock up Binzuru images to prevent the spread of disease through their miraculous touch.

The other Rakans are seldom seen. There are two or three temples in Kyoto, and one in Nagoya where they are carved in the round though of smaller size and less fantastic in shape than in China, and so far as I know they never (except at Obakusan) occupy the position in the central temple which Chinese custom assigns them. Usually one sees them, if at all, represented not in carving but painted upon kakemonos, hung up in the exhibition rooms of the temple, or (quite as often) in some museum. For the Rakans in Japan are of antiquarian and artistic interest chiefly and (except for Binzuru) form no part of the real life of the religion.

The interior of the temple is arranged in various ways with little that is absolutely uniform. There is, of course, always a central shrine or throne—more commonly a shrine with doors that may be, and often are, closed. Within this shrine (or on the throne if there be one) usually sits or stands an image of one of the Buddhas, Bodhisattvas, or founders, although a tablet may be substituted for the image, bearing a name upon it, or (as in some Shinshu temples) the sacred formula Namu Amida Butsu. As I have indicated, the shrine is quite frequently closed and the image may be shown only at certain times of the day or, it may be, only at intervals of many years. In front of the shrine stands the altar, a long and narrow table which usually contains a large incense burner in the middle, two candlesticks, one on each side, and at each end a spray of lotus leaves gracefully carved of wood and gilded. The candlesticks may be of brass or lacquer; the incense burner is usually of bronze, though it may be of lacquer or of porcelain. Usually the altar contains little or nothing else besides these five things, though at times one finds it crowded with offerings of food, flowers, and candles, as in China. Among the votives frequently placed on or near the altar (sometimes in the shrine itself), the Shinto mirror is not uncommon (especially in Shingon, Kegon, and Nichiren temples). In the larger temples there are usually two subordinate shrines at the right and left of the central shrine and further back—close up against the rear wall. These are usually sacred to Kwannon or Jizo, or Fudo or Monju, or to the founder of the sect or some distinguished abbot; or one of them may be devoted wholly to the tablets of the dead.[4]

Besides the shrines and altars I have mentioned, a Buddhist temple may contain all sorts of things; and in fact its irregularity of plan and the almost endless variety which it may present constitute a large part of its unfailing fascination. In a large and popular city temple like that of the Shi-Tenno in Osaka there are any number of little side shrines to all sorts of Buddhist and Shinto nobility (if I may use the phrase), with votives of every kind from the odd to the pathetic—from pictures of mothers with breasts spouting streams of milk, to little kimonos that once belonged to children now dead, and presented by their parents to Jizo in the hope that somehow he may clothe them. Many Buddhist temples have long rows of show apartments which are in fact museums and in which are to be seen some of the choicest specimens of Japanese painting at its best. All monastic temples of course possess dormitories and a refectory, and most of them have offices as well. The larger temples thus form a maze of buildings, with hundreds of occupants. Sometimes one finds a round or octagonal building erected to house the Buddhist scriptures. Occasionally these round library buildings are so constructed as to revolve

[4] For description of the temple interiors of the different sects see appendix to this chapter.

when sufficient force is applied—the idea being that by whirling the building and its contents around several times one may in economical manner acquire the merit of reading all the books. The idea may seem superstitious, but it is probably true. One rather interesting feature—unique so far as I know—is to be found in the great Zenko temple (of the Tendai sect) in Nagano, up among the central mountains. A steep dark stairway in the main hall leads down into a passage running beneath the central shrine. One gropes one's way in absolute darkness, turns two corners, and under the holy of holies one's hand (guided by a long depression on the wall) comes in contact with a key, the touch of which has some miraculous quality. Then one pushes on past two more corners in the same Stygian darkness and clambers up another stairway to the light. It is indeed an act of faith; and faith, let us hope, never goes without some reward.

But I fear that my attempt at description, overloaded as it probably is with detail, has failed to transmit to the reader any suggestion of the charm possessed and exhaled by the Buddhist temples of Japan. It is upon the temple that the people lavish their greatest care. Nothing is too good or rich for it. Their own houses are often tiny shells, but the house of the Buddha is lofty and full of that restrained beauty for which the Japanese have so sensitive a feeling. In all their lovely villages and towns the temple is the loveliest thing of all. But to see it at its best one must desert the towns and cities altogether and thread one's way up some ravine or climb to the forest solitudes of some mountain side, where, far from the haunts of men, the Buddha and a few of his chosen monks dwell apart in a monastic shrine whose curving roofs and ancient thatch and lichen-covered lanterns and images seem to be as much Nature's own as the peaks and glades that surround them. Up some deep gorge you take your way, as at Komoro, among the central rib of mountains near Samayama, following a rushing stream whose many waterfalls shout the praises of the Kami and the Buddhas, greeted now and then by an ancient image of Dengyo Daishi partly covered over with ivy, and further along you climb a crag commanding a wide panorama where you find a shrine with ancient images, at the feet of which space opens below you for a dizzying distance. The little path beyond it leads you past a few gray stone figures, and on to the Tendai temple, at the top, where in unbroken calm Shaka in his golden shrine grants peace alike to monks and pilgrims.

Sometimes an entire mountain top of many square miles extent is given up to temples—*is* in fact one great temple enclosure. Notable especially is Hiei-san, the mountain near Kyoto, once covered with over three thousand monasteries of the Tendai sect, until Nobunaga's fires and his soldiery brought destruction to nearly all. Early in Tokugawa times some of them were rebuilt on the old foundations, and though the glory of Tendai on Hiei-san never returned, the forest glades and the summit and sides of the mountain have still many a noble shrine to the Buddha and his great Japanese disciple. Impressive these woodland temples are and captivating to the eye and to the imagination quite beyond any power of words to express. Down long avenues of giant cryptomerias you tramp, and suddenly through the trees a vista of forest aisle opens up ahead with a gateway and the swaying lines of a temple roof at the end of it. The Japanese nightingale among the leaves heralds your approach with his unforgettable song, strangely tentative in its beginning, and prolonged into a trill of unimaginable sweetness. But the temples are silent and the woods are silent with a silence that seems musical, and that speaks of awe and reverence and centuries of meditation. Behind one of these forest temples lie the ashes of Dengyo Daishi, and before the central shrine burn two lamps whose fire, tradition says, goes back to him—well over a thousand years ago. Through the woods comes the boom of some distant temple bell. And occasionally through a forest window on the mountain slope you catch a vista of Lake Biwa, in the valley below you, stretching off far to the northeastward, and other mountains beyond it, and the rest of the world out there—the busy, struggling world out there, while you and the monks and the ashes of Dengyo Daishi and the fire which he lighted are still here in the shadow of the great cryptomerias, where the monks chant their praises to the

Buddha at dawn and evening, and where a day seems as a thousand years, and a thousand years as a day.

But most impressive of all the sacred places in this land of the gods is Koya-san—Koya-san the headquarters of the Shingon sect, and the center of pilgrimage from all over the empire, Koya-san with its more than fifty monasteries suspended between earth and sky, whose venerable forests, silent temples, and sacred graves speak of eleven hundred years of unbroken and deeply reverent worship. So remote is this center of ancient religious life from the world of the plain below it, and from all our twentieth-century thought and activity, that to the pilgrim who has gained its summit the ages somehow seem telescoped, and one feels only just too late to hear the echo of Kobo Daishi's footfall as he followed the ghostly lead of his supernatural monitor when first he explored this mountain top and laid the foundation of his spiritual community.

The pilgrimage up the mountain side from the village of Shiba is still unprofaned by trolley or motor car or carriage.[5] One must go on foot, as a pilgrim should, or be carried up in a basket. And every day the pilgrims come, especially from Shiko-ku, which was Kobo Daishi's birthplace. For the zealous Buddhists of that island, in imitation of their great saint, hold it a special means of grace to make the round of sacred places in their own land, as Kobo Daishi is said to have done, and to complete their long pilgrimage by climbing Koya-san. The journey up the mountain is one of increasing beauty and impressiveness. For a considerable distance upward from the river one is accompanied by terraced rice fields. Then the woods begin, and soon one is in an unbroken forest of lofty cryptomerias, varied with pines, chestnut, and bamboo. Not for a moment can one forget that this is no ordinary mountain. Little shrines are passed at frequent intervals, now and then a tea-house for the rest of pilgrims, where rosaries and images of Kobo Daishi may be purchased for a few sen, ancient stone Jizos guard the pathway, while fellow pilgrims are seldom far from

[5] I am informed that this is no longer true: that a cable-car line is being installed to carry passengers up the mountain. Thus one more step has been taken toward the Americanization of the world.

sight, clad in abbreviated kimonos or short coats and tight-fitting leggings, with broad-brimmed straw hats, and often carrying long pilgrim staffs, like the one Jizo uses, and little wooden boxes that contain certificates from various holy places to which they have already journeyed. The sacred precinct occupies most of the broad mountain top, and one enters it under a great stone torii, with a fine bronze Jizo on one's right and an even finer Kwannon on one's left. Within the enclosure the path still leads nearly a mile more through forest, then past temples and monasteries, along a village street lined with shops almost wholly devoted to the sale of religious objects, on to the most wonderful cemetery that man and Nature and Religion ever combined to make glorious. Lofty aisles of giant cryptomerias, ancient monuments of gray stone, lichen-covered bridges over little streams, unguessed depths of mingled forest and graves, images of Jizo and symbols of the unity of God and man—a place, in short, so filled with light and with deity that if one knew one were to be buried here one might well look forward with impatience to that last long sleep. The stone-paved avenue that leads through the Necropolis finally crosses a last arched bridge and leads up a flight of broad steps to the temple of Kobo Daishi; and the climax of the seven-mile pilgrimage is reached in the rear of the temple, where, beyond a simple rail, past which one may not go, one catches a glimpse of the grave of the Saint and Founder. On one side is the temple, on all other sides the deep forest, whose tall trunks, straight and aspiring, lift the pilgrim's eyes to the sky and his thoughts to heaven. For the whole atmosphere of the place is such that here surely, if anywhere, one may feel that serene and blessed mood,

> In which the affections gently lead us on,—
> Until the breath of this corporeal frame
> And even the motion of our human blood
> Almost suspended, we are laid asleep
> In body and become a living soul;
> While with an eye made quiet by the power
> Of harmony and the deep power of joy,
> We see into the Life of things.

In such a place one finds religion in act; not religion in its more active and efficient form, to be sure, as in its crusade against evil, but the religion of the heart, the religion of the cosmic sense, the religion of meditation, from which, indeed, so much of the more active life is fed. Even the memory of that summit of Koya-san is enough to bring back some of the haunting sense the place inspires as

> . . . of something far more deeply interfused,
> Whose dwelling is the light of setting suns,
> And the round ocean and the living air
> And the blue sky, and in the mind of man.

It is with a sense of things like these that I look back upon the forest vistas of Koya, with their solemn trees, the large bronze lanterns with their golden Chinese ideographs scattered among the trunks of the cryptomerias; the incense burner in front of the rail, from which during most of the day a cloud of fragrant smoke is constantly rising; the little group of earnest worshipers about it; half a dozen monks in the background, by the temple wall, murmuring a prayer; two kneeling figures, reading from the Sutras, close by the rail; and beyond it, guessed rather than seen, somewhere among the trees and shadows, the ancient grave.

Appendix to Chapter XXV

Characteristic Temple Interiors of Various Sects

Nearly every Japanese sect has its own special way of arranging the interiors of its temples, so that it is usually possible to tell the sect of a temple by scrutinizing its interior. For the benefit of those who may be interested, particularly of those intending to visit Japan, I shall set down here some of the points of temple arrangement characteristic of the different sects, which I collected by examining closely a large number of Japanese temples.

In Tendai temples—and in many others for that matter—there is usually a railing right across the hall, dividing it into two unequal parts, the one nearest the entrance being perhaps ten or fifteen feet wide. All the worshipers are admitted to this and here most commonly they kneel or stand, saying their prayers and gazing up at the shrine and altar. The larger space, beyond the rail in Tendai temples, is usually covered with matting, but in the middle part of it, immediately in front of the altar, there is a good-sized square space with no matting on it—just the polished wooden floor. Sometimes this is further marked off from the rest of the interior by a row of Sutra boxes on each side for the use of the monks at the chanting service. The temple interior is thus divided into four sections; the part outside the rail, the central square, with its bare floor, and the two wings, which are also beyond the rail and lead back to the rear and side walls. In the center of what I have called the square space there is a chair or throne for the chief priest to sit during the service: not a Western chair but a kind of platform, four or six inches high. In front of this, i.e., between it and the altar, is a low table, on which there are a number of ceremonial objects—usually a few bowls for offerings and vases for flowers. Sometimes the table is square and contains in the center a reliquary in the shape of a tiny pagoda and four bunches of artificial flowers, each bunch containing five flowers of different colors. Over the seat and table is suspended a gilded baldaquin, usually square, and at its sides or at each of the corners there usually hangs a *do-ban.* The do-ban was originally a collection of hanging banners or strips of cloth. Those one finds today are of two kinds: the commonest are made of carved wood gilded, the less common of cloth, usually *obis,* the gifts of zealous women. The do-ban hanging over the central square, to which I have referred, are of the gilded wood variety. If the temple is small, there will be but two of these, one on each side of the canopy; if it be large, there will probably be four of them and several cloth do-bans suspended in the wings at the sides. The central image in a Tendai temple may be almost any of the distinguished members of the Buddhist cycle—especially Shaka, Amida, Yakushi, Dainichi, Kwannon, or (not infrequently) Dengyo Daishi.

A Shingon temple has much the same interior arrangement as the Tendai, but is distinguished by means of its central table from all other sects (except Kegon and Ritsu, which in form of service are nearly identical with Shingon). This Shingon table is always square and contains invariably certain ceremonial objects, more numerous and more complicated than those on the Tendai table. In the center there is a reliquary in the shape of a small brass pagoda. Close to the pagoda is a bouquet of five artificial lotus buds, and at each corner of the table stands another bouquet, all of them similar, except that the five bouquets are of different colors. Behind the square table is a seat for the priest, and on the table in front of him are ranged eleven objects, viz., a central incense burner, signifying effort (from analogy of the smoke which is ever ascending); two water bowls, symmetrically placed on the sides of the incense burner and symbolizing love (since water seeks its level and levels all things and makes the low high and the high low); two bowls holding a sweet powder and signifying discipline and obedience; two flower vases meaning perseverance; two lamps, meaning wisdom; and two bowls for food offerings, symbolizing meditation. Beyond this row of bowls is a tray holding a bell and a peculiar Shingon sacred implement known as a *goku*—a rod with five points on each end, symbolizing the five kinds of potential and actual wisdom, and held by the chief priest during certain parts of the service. Over the table and the seat of the priest there is frequently, though not invariably, suspended a gilded canopy. The central image in Shingon temples is usually Dainichi, Shaka, Amida, or Kobo Daishi. In most Shingon temples of any size, in addition to the central shrine there is likely to be (as in some Tendai temples) a shrine at one side to Fudo, with a square table in front of it for use in the fire ceremony.

Every Zen temple, except the smallest, is supposed to possess the following seven buildings: (1) gateway, (2) Buddha hall, (3) lecture hall, (4) meditation hall, (5) residence of the presiding priest or abbot, (6) bell tower, (7) bath hall. The central or Buddha hall of the Zens is distinguishable from the main hall of other Buddhist temples by having in its center a high platform, accessible by three stairways. Some Shingon and Kegon temples have halls with similar platforms, but these are for lectures or ordinations, and do not constitute the temples' central shrines. The

Buddha hall in the Zen temple is used only on great occasions, the daily worship of both monks and laity being performed in the modest chapel in one of the buildings farther to the rear. These Zen chapels which form the real center of devotion are distinguishable from temples of most other sects by their notable, almost severe, simplicity. The image before a Zen altar is usually Shaka.

Jodo went out from Tendai, and the interior arrangement of a Jodo temple is hardly distinguishable from that of the parent order except in being rather simpler. It has the same division of the main hall by a long rail, the same central unmatted square, the same seat for the priest with a small table in front of it. This table is smaller in Jodo than in Tendai and has fewer things upon it. A gilded canopy is suspended above it and gilded do-bans hang at its sides. The central image in the main hall of Jodo temples is usually Honen Shonin, though it may be Amida. Larger Jodo temples usually have a Founder's hall and an Amida hall, and sometimes a Shaka hall as well.

As we have seen, the Shin sect went out from Jodo, and as we might expect, its temples are much like those of the parent sect, with variations in the direction of still greater simplicity. Almost all Shinshu temples have two halls of worship—the Hondo and the Amida-do—the Founder's hall and the hall of Amida. The Shin temple is said to have developed in part out of the tomb of Shinran; which explains the importance of the Hondo. The Amida-do was added later as an afterthought. The central image in the Hondo is of course that of Shinran; while that in the Amida-do is Amida. Shin temples never possess a Shaka-do, nor even any image of Shaka. The interior of these temples is very simple in arrangement. They have retained the long rail of the Tendai and the Jodo, but have done away with the square unmatted space and its seat for the priest, and have substituted for baldaquin and do-bans merely a few hanging lanterns.

The distinguishing feature in a Nichiren temple is the drum. This drum is of a characteristic shape, usually about eighteen inches or two feet in diameter and perhaps four inches thick. Its place is on one side of the central square, which is marked off in Nichiren temples much as it is in those of Tendai and Jodo, and over which is hung a gilt canopy. There is usually also a peculiar kind of gong—a gong in the form of a large bronze bowl placed upon two red silk cushions which rest on a pedestal. The central image in a Nichiren temple is sometimes Nichiren, sometimes Shaka. Rather oddly—considering the Protestantism of the Founder—Nichiren temples frequently have about them many traces of Shinto, notably a mirror or two in or near the central image and in the court several tiny Shinto shrines.

CHAPTER XXVI

BUDDHIST SECTS AND CLERGY

EVERY Buddhist monk in Japan belongs, as a matter of course, to one or another of the great sects or denominations into which the religion is divided. If you ask an orthodox Japanese Buddhist how many sects there are he will, in all probability, answer "Twelve." Just why he should answer twelve I do not know. For if one disregards subdivisions and counts only the main sects there are at most but nine; while if one counts all the sub-sects recognized by the government there are over fifty.[1] In spite of which, the usual answer you will get is "Twelve." We can hardly attribute this fondness for twelve to the number of the apostles nor of the tribes of Israel; nor can it be explained by the motive which led the little cottage girl to answer "We are seven," for the dead sects are no longer included in the enumeration. In fact, if we should count all the sects of Japan, both the quick and the dead, we should have not twelve but fourteen.[2] In spite of which the old answer holds. So authoritative a source as the Japan Year Book, for example, enumerates just twelve sects. To do so it has to call each of the subdivisions of Zen a separate sect, refuse to recognize the subdivisions

[1] Reischauer, *op. cit.*, p. 129.

[2] I append here a list of the sects (including the three sub-sects of Zen) in the order of their introduction or foundation, together with the names of their founders (or introducers) in parentheses, and the date of their introduction. If Zen be counted as but one sect, we shall have fourteen, as suggested above.

Sanron (Ekwan) 625
Jojitsu (Kwan-roku) 625
Hosso (Dosho) 650
Kusha (Chitsu) 658
Kegon (Do-sen) 736
Ritsu (Gan-jin) 754
} The six Nara sects

Tendai (Dengyo Daishi) 804
Shingon (Kobo Daishi) 806

Yutsu Nembutsu (Ryonin) about 1100
Jodo (Honen Shonin) 1175
Rinzai division of Zen (Eisai) 1191
Soto division of Zen (Dogen) 1225
Shin (Shinran) 1225
Nichiren (Nichiren) 1253
Ji (Ippen Shonin) 1275
Obaku division of Zen (Ingen) 1654

of other sects as separate, and leave out the Ritsu sect[8] altogether.

The statistics concerning the temples and monks and lay members belonging to these sects, as given out by the Federation of the Buddhist Organizations for Children, may be of some interest to the reader as a matter of reference, and I therefore copy them down here for his convenience. They are for the year 1919.

Name of Sect	Hosso	Kegon	Ritsu	Tendai	Shingon	Yutsu Nembutsu
Temples	43	32	23	4,548	12,290	361
Preaching Stations	13	3	..	203	1,001	3
Monks, Teachers, etc.	463	30	33	10,070	17,208	472
Lay Adherents	10,286	21,211	18,948	2,093,903	16,025,463	30,421

Name of Sect	Jodo	Rinzai (Zen)	Soto (Zen)	Shin	Nichiren
Temples	8,350	6,068	14,228	19,661	5,009
Preaching Stations	405	238	640	2,236	999
Monks, Teachers, etc.	10,418	9,391	25,218	40,008	8,452
Lay Adherents	3,116,840	2,397,924	5,887,429	13,089,890	2,810,987

Name of Sect	Ji	Obaku
Temples	495	523
Preaching Stations	8	14
Monks, Teachers, etc.	613	629
Lay Adherents	256,011	60,495

I have given these sects in the order of their foundation or introduction. If I had arranged them according to their size and influence the order would have been very different. As the reader will observe, if we list them according to the numbers of their clergy (and combine the three sub-sects of Zen) the six largest would stand in the following order: Shin, Zen, Shingon, Jodo, Tendai, Nichiren. If we list them according to the numbers of their (reputed) lay adherents, the same sects would stand as follows: Shingon, Shin, Zen, Jodo, Nichiren, Tendai. Neither of these lists properly represents the relative influence of the sects with the people of Japan. Particularly should the figures given as to lay adherents be taken with no great seriousness. They represent the traditional alignment of Japanese families, inherited from Tokugawa days, and mean very little as to the actual conditions of contemporary Buddhism. There is no doubt that

[8] Which on the preceding page it had referred to as one of the present sects.

the Shin shu stands first in the number of its earnest lay adherents, and its hold upon the masses. The Nichiren sect also, which expends most of its efforts among the lower classes, naturally has a larger popular influence than Zen. In the aristocratic days before the restoration Zen was chiefly the church of the Samurai, and its adherents today are largely the descendants of the old Samurai families. Jodo also is rather more aristocratic in its membership than Shin or Nichiren. Shingon makes, in some ways, the same varied appeal to high and low as does the High Church of England. It is hardly so active, however, as are Shin, Nichiren, and Jodo. The Tendai shu never fully recovered from the terrific blow dealt it by Nobunaga, when all its monasteries on Hiei-san were destroyed. The majority of observers will tell you that the most active and influential of the sects today are Shin, Zen,[4] Nichiren, and Jodo.

All or nearly all of the sects (or of the sub-sects when the sect is split up) have a chief temple or monastery which is the official headquarters and which transacts the executive and disciplinary business of the sect. This temple is called the Honzan or "Main Mountain." The abbot of the Honzan is usually *ex officio* head of the sect and its official spokesman —the patriarch or bishop as we should probably style him. Usually he is elected by the abbots of the subordinate monasteries. In the two great branches of the Shinshu the patriarchal office is hereditary in the Otani family. There are ten sub-sects of Shin, but only two of them, known as the Eastern and Western Hongwanji, are of large importance. For three centuries and a half after the death of Shinran, the founder, these two were one, and were presided over by the descendants of Shinran's daughter, the Countess Otani. In 1602 the Hongwanji was divided by Iyeyasu into an Eastern and a Western division,[5] and the office of bishop or patriarch was made hereditary in two branches of the Otani family. Against this monarchical form of rule in perhaps the most popular branch of Japanese Buddhism there is considerable complaint; the "Kingdom of Hongwanji" is not liked, and

[4] Especially the Soto branch.

[5] The Higashi Hongwanji and the Nishi Hongwanji, so called because of the relative position of their headquarters temples in Kyoto.

rebellion may break out at any moment. Each of the two Hongwanjis is divided geographically, for administrative purposes, into about thirty chief dioceses, and these into some four hundred or more subdivisions, each with its chairman or administrator. There is a Central Conference (or Diet), the legislative authority of the sect, which is composed of representatives elected by the thirty or more dioceses, and a few other members appointed by the bishop. It meets once a year.

The Hongwanji divisions of the Shin shu are, so far as I know, the only sects whose heads are hereditary. The patriarch or bishop of Jodo is chosen by the votes of all the active monks from among the four great abbots of secondary rank; and he becomes *ex officio* the abbot of the Chionin temple in Kyoto, the headquarters of the sect. Jodo divides Japan into eight large dioceses, the head of each of which is appointed by headquarters (the Honzan). Each diocese is divided into smaller sections of which there are, altogether, forty-eight. Each of these elects a member to represent it in what might be called the control committee at headquarters. This body, constituted of these forty-eight representatives, is the ultimate authority of the sect. Most of the other sects are organized in some such manner as Jodo. The abbots of the subordinate temples (or Matsuji) are usually appointed by the patriarch (the abbot of the Honzan), due consideration being given to the wishes of the local monks; and when he dies, the abbot of the various Matsuji elect his successor.

During the Tokugawa Shogunate a large part of the funds for the support of Buddhist temples came directly or indirectly through state assistance. Almost all of the greater and more ancient temples owned extensive lands and thus had stable incomes in addition to the contributions made by lay members. At the restoration state support was withdrawn from Buddhism and many of the landed endowments of temples were seized by the crown. Some temples still own lands and derive from them a steady income. I remember one Zen temple on the outskirts of Kyoto which owned several lots in its immediate vicinity and rented the lots to a moving-picture company. The aggregation of Japanese actors and actresses, in striking and gaudy costumes, posing for a new film just outside the gray old walls of the rather somber Zen temple was an interesting sight. Most temples, however, have to depend on the contributions of their lay members. A great many Japanese families are still listed as belonging to certain specific temples, and from these a definite annual sum is expected, which amounts almost to a tax. The Honzan or headquarters temples of the various sects have no such lay members, and therefore, for their own support, they levy a certain tax upon branch temples, which is raised from the lay members of these branches. Something, moreover, is added to the income of each temple by the gifts of pilgrims and occasional worshipers and (in the branch temples) from funeral services and masses for the dead. The Asakusa temple received last year from these incidental sources 160,000 yen. The expenditure of the temple funds is in the hands of the abbot.

The religious and secular duties of the abbot are sometimes divided, especially in large Zen monasteries, a spiritual director having charge of the culture of the religious life among his clergy, while the abbot attends to the administration of the more worldly affairs of the temple.[6] The Tendai shu has for centuries recognized fourteen grades within the priesthood, and most of the sects have adopted the Tendai system. Shingon, I believe, has sixteen. Promotion from one grade to another is made by headquarters on recommendation from the abbot of the local monastery, on the basis of conduct, life, and discipline. Zen makes a distinction (in an informal way) corresponding to that in Christian monasticism between monks and priests; for some of their monks live together in monasteries, beg their food, and give themselves up to a life of meditation and study, while others are entrusted with the more active duties of administering small temples.

A considerable number of monks in nearly all the sects are married. This innovation, as we have seen, originated with Shinran, and the Shin monks have regularly followed his example. In some of the other orders marriage has long been permitted in a few exceptional cases.[7] But until the

[6] This, at any rate, I found to be the case at the Shokokuji temple in Kyoto, and I suppose it is not unique.

[7] In Tendai, for example.

restoration these cases were rare, and Japanese monks pretty generally held the same attitude toward family life as their brothers in other Buddhist lands. A monk, presumably intended to be typical of the fourteenth century, in the No Play called Komachi [8] is made to say:

In a dream-lull our lives are passed; all, all
That round us lies
Is visionary, void.
Yet got we by rare fortune at our birth
Man's shape, that is hard to get;
And dearer gift was given us, harder to win.
The doctrine of the Buddha, seed of our salvation.
And me this only thought possessed
How I might bring that seed to blossom, till at last
I drew this sombre cassock across my back.
And knowing now the lives before my birth,
No love I owe
To those that to this life engendered me,
Nor seek a care (have I not disavowed
Such hollow bonds?) from child by me begot.
A thousand leagues
Is little road
To the pilgrim's feet.
The fields his bed
The hills his home
Till the travel's close.[9]

With the rapid westernization that commenced when Japan was opened up to the rest of the world, this traditional monastic view of the ideal life has begun to wane. Soon after the Restoration, various sects rescinded their prohibitions upon matrimony and monks were allowed to marry if they chose. In most of the sects except Shin, Jodo, and Nichiren, however, there is a decided feeling against it, and the highest positions are filled by celibates. To take a wife is considered a mark of weakness and of yielding to the flesh, and the more spiritual monks, it is thought, are those who remain single. In some sects marriage is likely to stand in the way of promotion within the priesthood. None the less, as I have said, many of the priests marry. These as a rule live at their homes with their families, and come to the temple in the

[8] By Kwanami, who died in 1384.
[9] Waley's trans., *op. cit.*, pp. 114-15.

morning for their daily work, returning in late afternoon or evening.

The majority of the monks remain celibate. They live, of course, in the monasteries, sleeping in a common dormitory and eating together in a refectory. In the dormitory the sleeping spaces are arranged along the walls. All Japanese, of course, sleep upon the floor, and in the monastic dormitory, as in most homes, the floor is covered with thick matting. On the wall, at the end of each of the sleeping spaces, is a shelf or locker where during the day the blanket or comfortable is stored. In Zen monasteries and in others where the monks meditate, the dormitory is often used in the daytime for a hall of meditation. Sometimes only one blanket is provided for each monk, and at best the bed is hard and often cold.

The abbots and vice-abbots naturally have more pretentious apartments. The vice-abbot of a large Zen monastery which I visited near Tokyo, received me in his private quarters, at once study and bedroom. The room was small and nearly square, with immaculate matting-covered floor, sliding doors at each end of the room, and a row of windows on one side. On the other side was of course the "honorable recess," raised some three inches above the rest of the floor and containing a small table or stool—perhaps eight inches high—on which were two bowls and some papers. Beside it stood two potted dwarf trees. On the wall was a scroll bearing a few artistic Chinese characters and in the corner was hanging a kind of wand, looking like a fly-flapper—a token of authority carried by the higher clergy in certain ceremonies. Beside the things named there were in the room three cushions, on one of which the vice-abbot was sitting when we entered, the two others being intended for my interpreter and me. At the side of our host was a large porcelain charcoal brazier, with the never-failing hot-water pot upon it, so that tea might be prepared for every emergency. The patient teapot and the vice-abbot's teacup were sitting on a tray close by, and near it was another tray containing writing materials. A young monk followed us in and after prostrating himself made tea and placed a cup of it before each of us; and also a tray with sweets, a box of cigarettes, and a small brazier with a spark of smoldering charcoal to light our tobacco.

While I am on the subject I might add (for it was typical of Buddhist hospitality) that when, after an hour's interview, I started to go, the vice-abbot insisted upon our staying to lunch and would take no refusal. So after a little stretching of my poor legs about the room I curled them up again on my cushion, seeking to look as much like a Buddha upon a lotus as I could—which, for a Westerner, is no easy thing to do. The lunch was served to us where we sat, and a dainty and tasty lunch it was. During our conversation over the rice and vegetables I heard the sound of a telephone; and remarked that it seemed to me somewhat incongruous in a Buddhist monastery. Whereupon my host informed me that they had sixteen telephones in the monastery. He also added that the cooking for the monks was done by electricity.

The reader will judge from these last details that Japanese Buddhism is much more "up to date" than it is usually pictured in the West, and that the life of the higher members of the clergy in the city temples is far from that of the traditional hermit. The same impression is given by the homes of the married clergy. A Nichiren abbot whom I called upon had a really luxurious and beautiful Japanese house, with a large suite of three interconnecting rooms for the reception of his guests. The abbot was out walking when we arrived, and we were asked to await his return, and meanwhile were served with tea, sweets, cigarettes, and a charcoal brazier. There were, of course, no chairs nor tables, but cushions, and the honorable recess; and upon the walls were two Chinese scrolls and a painting. Through the windows we could see a very pretty Japanese garden, with a lotus pond, dwarf trees, and the usual miniature river and wood, which never fail to delight the Japanese and me. When the abbot returned he approached us in courteous fashion on his knees, bowing to the floor; although (as I discovered during our conversation) he was by nature a rather abrupt man, with much self-confidence and ready learning—in short, one who was and felt himself to be every inch an abbot. At the close of our interview he offered to send us to the railroad station in his rickshaws (of which he had two); but then consulting his watch he said, "No, there is hardly time for that; I will send you in my car." So he issued orders and his chauffeur whisked us off through the crowded streets to the train.

It is, I gather, a rather small minority of the monks who have homes of their own; and the life of the celebates who live in the monasteries has much of the monastic routine followed by the monks of China and Europe. The day opens with a chanting service before the Buddha, at an early hour, seldom later than five, sometimes as early as three. This service is usually followed by breakfast, after which they have an hour of reading and study. A large part of the morning is devoted to the business of the temple, funerals, distribution of help to the poor, in some monasteries a lecture, preaching services for the laity, and in temples that are sect headquarters more or less secretarial and administrative work. Or there may be special addresses to groups of pilgrims or special masses for the dead. In many temples, I doubt not, there is a certain amount of loafing. Frequently there is another chanting service just before lunch; which comes about eleven. In the afternoon, there is more study and business, and some free time, with supper about six; and sometimes a third chanting service before bedtime. In Zen, which concentrates more than the other sects on the cultivation of the inner life, the monastic day is more minutely systematized. Zen monks live a rather simpler and more strenuous life than do those of other sects; they do nearly all their own work, gardening, cooking, cleaning, and even begging some of the rice for their meals in Hinayana fashion. In some monasteries they rise at three and do an hour of zazen [10] before breakfast. After breakfast they clean and put in order the various shrines, and from nine to ten they do zazen once more. In some monasteries there is a lecture for the monks every morning, given by the abbot or director; and the monks may have personal interviews with the director concerning their progress and their difficulties in the spiritual life. Special calls may also come from the laity for funeral services or masses for the dead. About ten-thirty they celebrate mass—i.e., perform another chanting service—before the Buddha. Dinner comes about noon, and after it each

[10] The Zen form of meditation.

monk cleans up his chopsticks and his three bowls. This is followed by an interval of rest and by a period of study. Or in place of the study there may be a special lecture for the laymen which the monks also may attend. At four there is another service of prayer before the Buddha, and at five-thirty they have supper. It will be noted that the monks of Japan, like those of China, disregard the rule so strictly observed in Hinayana lands against eating after midday. A few very strict monks of the Shingon sect observe this rule but I do not know that any others do. The day closes, in a Zen monastery, with a third period of zazen, from seven-thirty to nine, after which the great bell rings and they go to bed.

Possibly something more should be said at this point concerning the method of doing zazen. It is described in a series of directions written by the founder of the So-ji-ji temple, the headquarters of the Soto sect, and though these directions were written about five hundred years ago they are observed fairly well even today. They read in part as follows:

> There are two postures in Zazen—that is to say, the crossed-leg sitting, and the half crossed-leg sitting. Seat yourself on a thick cushion, putting it right under your haunch. Keep your body so erect that the tip of the nose and the navel are in one perpendicular line, and both ears and shoulders are in the same plane. Then place the right foot upon the left thigh, the left foot on the right thigh, so as the legs come across each other. This is the posture called the crossed-leg sitting. You may simply place the left foot upon the right thigh, the position of the hands being the same as in the cross-legged sitting. This posture is named the half crossed-leg sitting. Do not shut your eyes, keep them always open during whole Meditation. Do not breathe through the mouth; press your tongue against the roof of the mouth, putting the upper lips and teeth together with the lower. Swell your abdomen so as to hold the breath in the belly; breathe rhythmically through the nose, keeping a measured time for inspiration and expiration. Count for some time either the inspiring or the expiring breaths from one to ten, then beginning with one again. Concentrate your attention on your breaths going in and out as if you are the sentinel standing at the gate of the nostrils. If you do some mistake in counting, or be forgetful of the breath, it is evident that your mind is distracted.[11]

The regular daily routine of the monastery described two paragraphs back is broken into at various seasons by special

[11] I take this from Kaiten Nukariya's *The Religion of the Samurai*, pp. 189-90.

services. There may be a series of public lectures, or, in Zen, protracted periods of zazen. In some temples there are especially long hours of prayer on the first, fifteenth, twenty-second and twenty-ninth of each month. The Rinzai division of Zen sets aside six periods of a week each, during the year, in which the monks are required to do zazen many hours every day. In some Soto temples there is only one such week of protracted meditation, but it is extremely severe, the monks getting only two hours of sleep each night. In ordinary times each Zen monk who is seriously studying goes to his spiritual director perhaps once a day or less often; but during this period of intensive effort he frequently goes three times daily, in order to talk over his difficulties and report on the progress he has made. During these weeks of "retreat," moreover, the director preaches every day.[12]

In addition to performing funeral services and celebrating masses for the dead, the monks occasionally visit the homes of some of their lay parishioners. This is usually in response to an invitation, but at times the initiative comes from the monks. There are many modern-minded young men in the monasteries of Japan, and some of these are beginning to take an active part in the life of the laity. A monk whom I met in the great Tendai temple at Nagano—up among the mountains of central Japan—was the leader of a boys' club which he had organized, and it was difficult to determine whether he was most enthusiastic over Buddhism or baseball. He had spent two years or more in America studying electrical engineering, whence he had been recalled by his brother who was a priest in the Nagano temple. He was glad to come back, for he wants to be saved by Amida—though, he added, he might have been saved had he stayed in America and turned Christian, for good Christians are saved just as Buddhists are; but he is glad to be saved by Amida. His American training has not been wasted, however, and he is putting into the service of the Buddha a breeziness and active energy which one associates rather with the American engineer than with the monk of the Orient. While in California he attended a Christian Sunday school, and though

[12] According to Schuej Ohasama, in his little book, *Zen, der lebendige Buddhismus in Japan* (Gotha, Klotz, 1925), p. 16.

the teaching he received did nothing to undermine or weaken his enthusiastic Buddhist faith, he did get from it—or from somewhere—a vivid conception of efficient social service, and this he is applying in his new job. Not only does he perform his share of the temple ritual with contagious enthusiasm, and preach to bands of pilgrims ten times every month; he has, as I have stated, formed a boys' club and taught the boys to play baseball and tennis; he takes them on trips to compete in athletic games with other clubs; he has even gone into the politics of the town and succeeded in getting a large lot set aside for the public sports of the town children. This priest is, of course, unusual—in part because of his American experiences. But he is by no means unique. Many Japanese monks have been in America, or Europe, and many who have not have a full share of the Western spirit for efficient social service. According to the *Young East* for January, 1928, a new mode of helpfulness has been devised by Buddhist monks in Hiroshima and a few other prefectures. "It is to make use of part of the temple premises as a sort of kindergarten for the benefit of peasant women during their busiest season, when they have little time to look after their young children. In other words, the priests will take charge of the young ones while their mothers are busy at work on the field." A Japanese newspaper not long ago gave an account of a group of young monks in a village temple organizing a dramatic club among the young people of the village, and planning to give a Buddhist pageant in the interests of Buddhist foreign missions. The abbot of their temple was of the old school and vetoed the proposal. Whereupon seven of the young monks went on a strike, leaving him to do all the work of the temple, while they reorganized the dramatic club. During our stay in Kyoto there was a very serious strike on the car lines of Osaka. Both sides at length appealed to the Shingon monks of Koya-san, who acted as mediators and arbitrators, and successfully ended the strike.

It is plain that the Buddhist monks of Japan are very much more active than are their brothers of China. They are also better educated and more wide-awake in their interests. On the other hand, they are, at least outside of the Zen sect, less meditative, less "monastic." One hears occasionally of a specially zealous monk whose religious devotion requires some special outlet for its expression—such as fasting after midday, or having only one clete in one's zori.[13] Most monks frequently find the monastic life sufficiently ascetic without any such additional forms of self-denial. The dormitories, for example, are often very cold in winter, and frequently the blankets provided are quite inadequate. No matter how cold the monks may be, they are never allowed to sleep together and thus keep each other warm. But the suffering in summer nights is often worse than that in winter, as every one will believe who has spent a summer in Japan, outside the mountainous regions. I do not refer to the heat, though this is bad enough, but to the mosquitoes. Monasteries are seldom provided with mosquito netting—never, so far as I know; and for the monk it would be a great sin to kill a mosquito. To do zazen several hours a day and keep awake and strenuous at the process, after having fed the mosquitoes during a large part of the night forms a sufficiently ascetic life for most Japanese monks. Rarely do they shut themselves up for years of solitary confinement as do the more zealous monks of China;[14] but few occidentals, I fancy, will blame them for this omission.

The Japanese nun has, naturally, fewer outside activities than the monk. I have no statistics as to the number of nuns in Japan, but it is very much smaller than that of the monks. It is especially the Jodo order that encourages them; and at the Jodo headquarters—the Chionin temple in Tokyo—there

[13] Apparently to avoid taking insect life when walking.

[14] Some of them, however, live relatively isolated and very simple lives. Thus a monk whom the people refer to as "Saint Fruit-eater" (Mokujiki Shonin) has lived for more than thirty years in a small temple in the suburbs of Tokyo, who in his love of frugality is typically Buddhist and in his love of beauty typically Japanese. I quote from the *Young East* (for July, 1927) concerning him. "As his nickname indicates, he has subsisted on nothing but fruit, barks of trees, roots of grass for nearly half a century in the past. Having no desire after worldly pleasures, he has had no need of money for his own use. And almost all the offerings presented to him in money have been kept in a wooden box. Sometimes he bought towels and other small necessities for poor beggars and laborers thrown out of jobs. When he counted his money recently, however, he found that there was more than one thousand yen in the box. He thought the money should be spent in such a way as would please the public for all the time to come. After a careful consideration, he spent his money in purchasing azaleas, pine trees, arbor vitaes, and a few other kinds of trees, bearing beautiful flowers. And without the assistance of other people, he has planted them on the embankment of the railway track near his temple. The azaleas, which he has planted there, bloomed beautifully in June and delighted the weary eyes of railway passengers and of all the people living in the neighborhood."

is a convent with about sixty nuns and a school with about three hundred girls who are preparing for the religious life. The daily routine of the nun is much like that of the monk, except for the slighter emphasis on outside activities. At some convents the first chanting service begins at four-thirty, followed by breakfast and various duties about the temple. A second service takes place at eleven, followed by the midday meal; while a third service is held after supper. The nuns sometimes sit up as late as ten. The religious vocation is still regarded as an honorable career for the daughters of the aristocracy. Thus the office of lady abbess of the Che-gu-ji convent at Horyuji is always given to some nun from a family of the nobility; and the same position in the Jodo convent at Nagano is filled by an imperial princess. The Japanese nuns that I have seen appear greatly superior to the nuns of China and Korea, in both intellectual, spiritual, and social qualities. Many of them are earnest students of Buddhism and devoted servants of the Dharma or Amida.

Both nuns and monks at ordination take the tonsure, which means having their heads completely shaved; and keep their heads in this condition of artificial baldness to the end of their lives. There is no ceremony of burning holes in the scalp as in China, and the ordination service is a rather simple affair. Candidates are admitted to the Order at about twenty years of age. In most sects there is a novitiate of a few years, beginning at about fifteen. On entering this the boy (or girl) takes the usual ten vows of the Buddhist clergy, and on being admitted to the full rank of monk (at twenty) he adds the traditional two hundred and fifty vows having to do with the special rules of the Order. According to Lloyd, "When a Buddhist priest is ordained, he receives 'letters of orders' on which are given the principal names of the priests through whom the succession has come down to him from the Apostles of Sakyamuni." [15]

After being ordained the monk assumes the regular priestly garb. This varies somewhat among the different sects, but I am told that there is a general similarity in the

[15] *The Creed of Half Japan*, p. 234, note. The Yutsu Nembutsu sect is an exception to this rule which traces back only to its founder in the twelfth century.

garb of all the monks which is quite sufficient to strike the eye of any woman. Unluckily when I try to recall details like these my mind reverts to the condition of the Alaya-vijnana or even to the original Buddhist Void; but here, as usual, my Fellow Pilgrim comes to my rescue and furnishes me with the following description. The monk, it seems, wears a kimono, like any other Japanese, except that in his case it is usually white. Over it is a *hauri* or coat of special cut. Like the hauri of the layman it comes down to the knees; but there is attached to it a kind of flounce in pleats—not gathers (I am particularly instructed to insist it is not gathers, though personally I could not possibly tell a gather from a pleat)—and this flounce extends below the knees some eight or ten inches. This hauri or coat is usually made of a fine grenadine material, varying in thickness with the season. It is sheer and dressy so that you can see the white undergarment or kimono through it. It is frequently black but it may be green, plum, or some other color. It is sometimes made of silk grenadine and gives an elegance and distinction to the wearer. Over it is the chasuble, a long band several inches wide hung around the neck and coming down in front on both sides. This is usually of silk damask in lovely colors, adorned with in-woven peonies, azaleas, and other flowers. Suspended by a band around the neck, like a child's book-bag, is a square piece of damask about sixteen inches on a side, patched together from several pieces (reminiscent, I will add, of the patched garb of the first followers of Shaka). It is often decorated with flowers or gold woven into the damask and is worn on the left hip or in front.

Before being admitted to the priesthood the candidate must pass an examination; but in most of the sects except the Shinshu this offers but slight obstacle to ignorant piety. Sometimes all that is required is ability to read a few Sutras in Chinese; sometimes committing to memory these Sutras is sufficient, with no unpleasant questions asked as to what they mean. Many Japanese monks are still very ignorant. Fifteen or twenty years ago Professor Inonye Tetsujiro of the Tokyo Imperial University wrote as follows: "Buddhist priests, in spite of a few notable and brilliant exceptions, which only serve to make the general darkness more visible, are behind the rest of the world in education, character, morals, and influence." [16]

To give a trustworthy picture of the situation, however, one should add that since these words were written the "notable exceptions" have become more frequent, and that the ignorant condition of the priesthood is being rather rapidly remedied in all the more advanced sects. As we shall see, all of these sects have universities or advanced schools for the training of their priesthood, and while it is still possible to enter the order without going to any school, a larger and larger proportion of the clergy is being recruited from among the graduates of these educational institutions. Many of the monks of Japan, as I have said, are still ignorant, but a fair number are learned, and the proportion of those with an intelligent apprehension of Buddhism is steadily increasing.

The same charges are brought against the morality of the Buddhist clergy that one hears against the morality of the clergy in most lands except Protestant Christendom.[17] The truth seems to be that the Buddhist monk is decidedly inferior in moral earnestness to the Christian preacher; but that he is by no means worse than the average Japanese layman. So far as negative morality goes he is probably a good deal better. One hears of scandals among Buddhist monks for the same reason for which one hears of scandals among American Sunday-school superintendents. They are human, and if in exceptional cases they commit some striking offense every one is interested in publishing the fact. The chief accusation that can properly be brought against them is the lack of some of the more positive virtues. Many of them are lazy and many of them are satisfied to serve the community which supports them in no other way than chanting at the funerals of the dead—for a consideration.

On the other hand, as we shall see in the next chapter, many monks, and an increasing number of them, do a good

[16] Quoted by Reischauer, *op. cit.*, p. 316. Dr. Armstrong also has a very poor opinion of the old school of priests, but admits that "an increasingly large number" of of them are trying to reform "the almost hopeless system"—*Buddhism and Buddhists in Japan* (New York, Macmillan, 1927), pp. 75-77.

[17] These words were written before the appearance of *Elmer Gantry*.

deal of active service among the laity, and lead useful lives of helpfulness. And not only of these more efficient members of the Order but of nearly all it may be said that they exemplify, as their colleagues and predecessors in all Buddhist lands have regularly done, the virtues of mercy, generosity, hospitality, and every sort of liberality. A recent number of the *Outlook* reports the experience of a Christian colporteur in trying to sell a Bible to two women in a Japanese house where he was calling in the course of his business rounds. From the next room he heard the voice of a monk loudly repeating Buddhist prayers. The women hesitated to buy the Bible; whereupon the monk stopped his praying long enough to urge the women to make the purchase; adding, "Books like that are good to have. All religious books are helpful." [18] Tokichi Ishii (a murderer converted to Christianity while imprisoned awaiting execution) tells in his journal of an interview with the Buddhist chaplain of the prison, shortly after his conversion. On learning that Tokichi had been converted to Christianity and that Christianity had changed his heart, the chaplain said, "Then your religion is an admirable thing. There is no better than the teaching that changes a man's heart." [19] On another page of his diary Tokichi writes:

> Today the head chaplain came to my cell and made enquiries about the state of my mind. He knows that I believe in Christ but still he comes once every week or two to talk with me. Being a Buddhist himself, he would naturally think he would talk about Buddhism; but never once has he done so. He has never suggested that it would be well for me to believe in Buddhism. He simply encourages me to believe more deeply in Christianity. Not only that, but he has lent me Christian books to read. I have a very great admiration for this chaplain.[20]

The Japanese monks are pleasant and agreeable gentlemen, not very learned as a rule but on the whole intelligent, and almost without exception, kindly, hospitable, generous. As a rule they have little enough to be generous with except

[18] *The Young East*, I. 171.

[19] See Caroline Macdonald's delightful translation of Tokichi's journal, under the title, *A Gentleman in Prison* (Doran, 1922), p. 88.

[20] *Op. cit.*, p. 154.

time, and it would be ungenerous of me if I, who have taken so much of their time, should fail to testify to their generosity with the one thing they have to give. I can imagine few things more delightful than to start out morning after morning, as I did during several months, accompanied by my Fellow Pilgrim and my interpreter, and armed with notebook, pencil, and shoehorn, to take our way, by rickshaw or on foot, through the colorful streets of Kyoto or of some other city, crowded with courteous people in fresh kimonos, and lined with little shops whose wares are always beautiful, out through the larger spaces of the suburbs, and on through some ancient monumental gateway guarded by gigantic Ni-O and the Four Kings, into the peace of a temple enclosure, and up to the office of the monastery, there to send in our cards, take off our shoes, and spend a quiet hour with some courtly abbot of princely bearing or some modest but earnest monk, sipping endless tea and discoursing on the deep things of the Mahayana. One of these visits, I should add, a visit of three days and nights on the summit of Koya-san, stands out in the memories of both of us as among the great intellectual and religious experiences of our lives. The unimaginable beauty of the place, the almost incredible kindness and courtesy of every one there, the intellectual banquet offered us by the reverend professors of the Koya-san Daigaku, the impressive interview with the Lord Abbot (the Bishop of Shingon), the earnest attitude of the hundreds of college students preparing for the Shingon priesthood, the atmosphere of monastic calm, of cosmic security, of spiritual serenity—influences like these gave us the feeling that few places on earth can be so near to heaven as this monastic center on the summit of Mount Koya.

Koya-san is probably unique, and not all the Buddhist monks of Japan are like those on its summit. Many are ignorant, many are lazy, many I presume are selfish. Some are certainly immoral. Yet, on the whole, they are a likable lot. In comparison with the monks of China (and all human praise and blame must be largely a matter of contrast) the Japanese monk is perhaps a little less congenial, a little less easy, a little more formal; but he is notably more intelligent, more enlightened, more active, and useful, and perhaps more deeply religious.[21] Like most of his brotherhood he has caught a good deal of the Founder's catholicity of spirit and liberality toward every formulation of the truth. He shares, as a matter of course, in the beautiful courtesy of his nation. He has his faults; but one can hardly deal with him without feeling that he honestly and deeply wishes well to all sentient creatures.

[21] It may be well to append here the opinion expressed by Tai Hsü, the leader of the Buddhist revival in China, concerning the merits and failings of the Japanese monks. "Of their good points there are four: (1) They organize themselves into bodies, which by cooperation are capable of doing public charity work or carrying out large scale education campaigns for the benefit of the public. (2) Japanese monks are better trained for the work of propagating the Buddhist religion. (3) They are patriotic and oftentimes render useful, though worldly, services to the country and the community. (4) Their minds being more susceptible to western thoughts and ideals, they are capable of making the Buddhist teachings acceptable to the modern mind. Regarding shortcomings, (1) they are less devout in their religious life and unable to undergo the austerities of a religious recluse as their brethren in China and Tibet can do, (2) they are more sectarian and have no unity among the different sects and (3) they are too patriotic and nationalistic to pay much attention to the Buddha's teachings of universal brotherhood, (4) they learn so much of modern scientific studies as to tinge the Buddhist teachings they preach with a touch of Modernism." *The Young East*, I. 180.

CHAPTER XXVII

THE JAPANESE LAYMAN

In Tokugawa times, the head of every Samuraï clan had to be registered as a member of one or another of the Buddhist sects, and every family in the land was listed as belonging to some particular temple or shrine. As nearly all Shinto shrines were then of the Ryobu-Shinto type, and as the census-taking was put into the hands of Buddhist monks, the result was that nearly every family in the land was in theory assigned to some Buddhist or semi-Buddhist temple. Since the time of the restoration, when Buddhism was disestablished, this custom of religious registration has no longer been enforced by the state, but a large number of families have allowed their names to remain on the temple books and have continued to support these temples and make use of their priests at funerals. Thus there is something in Japanese Buddhism distantly corresponding to church membership in Christianity. Only it is not individuals but families that are the church members, and so far as an individual can be called a member, it is not by voluntary act but by heredity. Members of what we might call registered families have an hereditary right to have their funerals celebrated in the temple of their registration, and in some sects to be buried in the temple graveyard. They may also have the right to have the third and seventh anniversary of their deaths celebrated in the temple, and sometimes to have their tablets placed within the sacred building. Registered members are expected, at least in several of the sects, to aid in defraying the temple expenses. Beyond these funeral rights and financial duties, temple membership means little. It does not necessarily imply worship in the temple of registration, nor any special kind of belief. No one cares what a member believes, but one cares what priests conduct the funeral services of the family. If a member of one temple is buried by the priests of another temple, the priests of the temple of his registration will refuse to act for his family at future funerals. Of course, for the more devout, membership in a temple may and does amount to much more than this. An earnest layman may worship regularly in his family temple, aid it financially, attend its preaching services and receive frequent visits from its clergy in his home. But all this he might also do though not registered as a member of any temple. There are large numbers of simple believers who worship devoutly at temples of their choice and help support them but who are not registered anywhere and have no special temple rights.

The headquarters temples of the various sects have no members: it is only the branch temples that have registered members. Most Japanese, as I have said, inherit their membership and go through no ceremony of baptism or confirmation. The Nichiren sect alone, so far as I know, has a rite approximating that of baptism. The new-born child is brought by his father or nurse to the priest of the temple in which his family is registered, and the priest touches his head with the sacred scripture (the Hokkekyo, or Saddharma Pundarika Sutra). If an adult who has no hereditary connection with the Nichiren sect wishes to join it he goes to one of the branch temples, has his name registered, and the priest gives him a rosary and touches his head with the Hokkekyo. In the other sects, so far as I could learn, there is no rite even of this simple sort for joining the church. If a man is converted to a given sect to which his family does not belong, he simply goes to a branch temple of that sect and has his name enrolled. The branch temple will thereafter see to the funeral rites of his family, and it hands his name in to the headquarters temple.[1]

While there is no sacrament of confirmation for the Buddhist layman, some sects have a rite somewhat comparable to it for the benefit of the more zealous. It is a purely voluntary and individual matter, and takes place on certain special occasions. Thus Jodo has at times a series of what

[1] A distinction is made in some sects between those whose families have belonged to the sect since Tokugawa times and those recently converted. Thus the West Hongwanji has on its rolls some 1,450,000 families with an aggregate of 7,209,755 individuals, and in addition some 143,427 individuals who have been registered as converts since the restoration.

evangelical Christians might call "protracted meetings," lasting a week, in which the "five-fold instructions" are given to whosoever wishes to receive them; and at the close of the period the lay participants may take the Five Vows, for a limited period or for life, and go through the form of having a razor put to the hair, as if they were to take the tonsure, a symbol of joining the Order as it were. The Shinshu also has a similar ceremony of the "shaving of the head," and many of the more devout go through it. It is merely a way of expressing their greater zeal. A new name is given the believer at this "conversion ceremony" and a small contribution—perhaps a few yen—is made by him. Those who have had this rite of confirmation, as we might by analogy call it, may wear thereafter a badge of distinction (usually a piece of silk, green or some other color, thrown over the shoulders), and have the privilege of sitting inside the rail at religious services. Zen also has a special ceremonial, suggesting adult baptism, for the more devout.[2]

A large number of the laymen registered as members of Buddhist temples have little knowledge as to the beliefs of the Buddhist sects or of the differences between them. To many of these nominal Buddhists their religion appears to mean hardly more than that they remember playing in Buddhist temple courts when they were children, that they occasionally attend a Buddhist festival in some temple precinct, and that they expect to be buried by Buddhist priests when they die. It goes without saying that a large proportion of them never look into any of the Buddhist scriptures: this goes without saying because it is a characteristic which the Japanese "Buddhist" shares with several European and American "Christians." One Buddhist I met in Nikko (a curio dealer) told me he was a member of the Zen sect. I asked him to tell me about zazen and he replied he had never heard of it. He was a member of Zen, I discovered, only in the sense that he admired the simplicity of Zen temples and the self-control of Zen members and that he had some Zen utensils of ritual in his home shrine. He also said that he regularly read from the Buddhist scriptures. When I asked

[2] The reader will find a brief account of this in Armstrong's *Buddhism and Buddhists in Japan*, pp. 47-49.

him the name of some of these scriptures, he said he would have to go and ask his wife. Another Nikko curio dealer with whom I talked called himself a member of Tendai. Personally, he said, he prayed to Amida—every one in Nikko prays to Amida. All the Buddhas, he said, are one. But then, he suddenly added, Amida and all the other Buddhas are just imagination. In spite of which he continues to pray to Amida and teaches his children to do the same. He also prays to his ancestors. But he believes his ancestors are all annihilated. Buddhism teaches paradise and hell, but personally he believes that when a man dies it is all over with him. Buddhism, he said, is just imagination and the teaching of mercy and wisdom. But he keeps on praying to his ancestors and to Amida just the same. Most Buddhists under fifty, he asserted, believe as he does. It is chiefly the older people who really believe in the Buddhas and in the immortality of their ancestors.

This man's knowledge of his countrymen was confined chiefly to Nikko; and if applied to the inhabitants of Nikko only, what he said may possibly be true. Nikko is, of course, a Shinto rather than a Buddhist center, and I am told there are few places in Japan where Buddhism is so weak. Probably the attitude of the Nikko curio dealer toward his religion could be duplicated in many other places; but it is characteristic not of Japanese Buddhists but of Japanese skeptics. And there are many of both. It is, however, the Buddhists we are studying; the mind of the skeptic is pretty much the same the world over.

The religious books read by the more devout and intelligent Buddhists vary according to the sects. Of the ancient and canonical books the most commonly read are, perhaps, the following: the Saddharma Pundarika (called in Japanese the Hokkekyo), the Vajrakkhedika or "Diamond Cutter," the Prajna-paramita-hridaya (popularly known as Shingyo) and the Vimalakirti. In theory the Larger and Smaller Sukhavati Vyuha are of primary importance for the four Pure Land sects, but their chief use is for ritualistic purposes. Jodo followers read chiefly the letters of Honen Shonin, the Shin followers the letters of Shinran and Renyo. Zen members read the Goruku, or sayings of the Zen masters. There is, beside, a growing mass of modern religious books, magazines, and pamphlets which probably have a larger reading among many classes of religious people than the canonical and semi-canonical books.

Reading from the sacred books occupies a less conspicuous place in the life of the devout Buddhist—as it does in the life of the devout Roman Catholic—than is usually given it by the old-fashioned orthodox Protestant Christian. Prayer, praise, and the presentation of offerings are more important for the Buddhist than reading. The devout member of the Shinshu practices five different ways of "nourishing his faith," which are expounded in the Catechism of the sect as follows: "The best way is to recite the Nembutsu [Namu Amida Butsu]. Second, read with appreciation the Scriptures. Third, cultivate joy in the heart by dwelling in imagination upon the enlightenment of Paradise. Fourth, worship and adore the images of Amida. Fifth, meet with like-minded believers, praise the merit of Amida and talk about his Law."[8]

The injunction "to meet with like-minded believers" is characteristic of the Shin sect rather than of the other divisions of Japanese Buddhism. As in other Buddhist lands, much the greater part of worship in the temple, as well as in the home, is individual rather than communal. The regular morning and evening chanting services of the monks, in most of the sects except Shinshu, is seldom attended by laymen. Most of the layman's worship is carried on in his home; and the major portion of his temple worship he performs by himself and at times when the monks are not carrying on their services. As in other parts of the Buddhist world this individual worship of the layman is a very simple matter, and there is an immense amount of it. One seldom enters a Japanese temple of the more popular sects without finding at least a solitary worshiper, standing in silent prayer before the Buddha—silent except for the long sibilant indrawn breaths with which the Japanese regularly express the emotion of reverence, or the softly repeated prayer, "Namu Amida Buts(u), Namu Amida Buts(u)." Sometimes the

[8] "A Catechism of the Shin Sect," trans. by A. K. Reischauer, *Tr. A. S. J.*, XXXVIII (1912), 385.

mode of worship seems a bit cavalier and quite lacking in inwardness. A casual visitor to a Japanese temple may thus naturally enough come away with the conviction that Buddhism means very little to the native worshipers. My own first impression amounted to as much. The first Japanese temples I visited were in Kamakura, and I find in my early notebook the following entry:

> At the Hachiman temple and before the great Kwannon the worshipers clap their hands three times and toss a coin into a receptacle for offerings and that is about all. Some stand a moment repeating some very brief prayer, some do not do so much. A group of eight or ten pilgrims visited each of these shrines at the same time with us, and did as above described. By them as by all the others whom I watched, with the exception of one earnest old woman, the Kwannon image seemed to be taken in much the same way as we took it—as an object of artistic and archæological rather than religious interest. I think I felt quite as much real reverence as any of them showed. As to the clapping of the hands three times, this I note is what the maid does when she comes to our door, instead of knocking. Before the great Dai Butsu—a really religious and imposing statue—I think I was more reverent than any of the Buddhist visitors whom I saw. In fact, though I was as "gentle" as Kipling could have wished, I saw no "heathen" praying before the Buddha of Kamakura.

This was written on my first day in Japan; and I should hasten to add that before I had been long in the country I had to revise very considerably my opinion as to lay worship in the temples. There is much superficial and purely external worship in Japanese temples, but also much that is unmistakably fervent; and when one gets acquainted with the mask of external gaiety by which almost all Japanese hide their inner feelings, one comes to the conclusion that some of the worship which seems to the onlooker purely formal may have behind it an unsuspected depth of meaning. The extravagant expression of religious emotion which one used to find at an old-fashioned American prayer meeting would seem to most Japanese an indecent exposure of soul.

The mode of individual worship at the temples is, as I have said, very simple and resembles in many ways what one finds in China and even in Southern Buddhist lands. In many of the smaller temples there is a bell over the entrance, with a rope attached by which the bell may be sounded. The worshiper on entering sounds this bell, or claps his hands and usually throws a coin into the coin receptacle, and there stands for some moments in prayer, making low bows or prostrations at the end. Family parties appear, father, mother, and several children: they kneel, intone prayers, and pass out. An old woman has been sitting as near the altar as she can get for a long time, mumbling the Namu Amida and recording its repetitions on a rosary. A man is reading a Sutra to himself in an audible voice—in Nichiren temples sometimes accompanying the reading by gently sounding a wooden gong. Outside, a specially zealous devotee is apparently carrying out a vow by circumambulating the temple a great many times, repeating prayers as he goes. The impression one gets at a great city temple like the Asakusa in Tokyo, from the unceasing procession of worshipers, arriving, praying, and departing, is very considerable. Possibly more impressive is it to step into some smaller shrine and find it quite empty save for the merciful Amida and one lone worshiper, a woman, sobbing out her broken heart before him.

The chanting services of the monks vary considerably between the different sects. In the Tendai, Shingon, Jodo, and Nichiren sects, the abbot or an appointed leader takes his seat on the low platform in the middle of the central square, with his monks seated in two rows at his right and left, facing each other and him, while he faces the altar. The service in all the sects consists, as in China, principally or entirely of chanting, sometimes by all the monks, sometimes by the leader alone, and at various tempos, sometimes slowly and with much solemnity, and again hastening on with rapid beating of the gong or bell to an exciting presto. The Shingon services are the most elaborate and ornate, and include besides chanting various movements of the *goku*,[4] and the presentation of symbolic offerings by the celebrant.

[4] The *goku* or *vajra* is a symbolic implement, usually of bronze and about four to six inches long. It seems to have originated from the trident of Siva, but it has been greatly modified on passing from Hinduism to Buddhism. Instead of having three points it has five—five on each end. Four of these are arranged about the fifth or central one, and these four outer points are at the extremity turned inward, so that all five tips meet. It is largely used in Tibet. According to the Shingon interpretation the five points on one end symbolize the five kinds of *a priori* or innate wisdom possessed in actuality by Dainichi and potentially by all beings; those on the other repre-

While the major portion of the layman's worship is, as I have said, individual, a small group of the more zealous laity is sometimes found at the chanting services of the monks, which thus come to take on something of the aspect of communal worship which all our Protestant services present. In some Shingon masses there is an opportunity for the laymen present to participate if they wish, by going, at a certain point in the service, to a side shrine and there making, with great reverence, a simple symbolic offering of a few grains of incense. In Tendai temples, especially in those which are the resorts of pilgrims, laymen sometimes kneel in considerable numbers outside the rail and follow with reverence and with prayer and bowing the chanting of the priests. An impressive service of this sort we witnessed at the great temple at Nagano, where a curtain, behind the altar, ordinarily hides the sacred image. At the climax of the mass this curtain was dramatically drawn, and exposed for a few moments the Buddha in the darkened recess behind.

The Nagano temple is peculiar in being used for both Tendai and Jodo services. It belongs to the Tendai shu, but just outside of the monastery grounds there is a convent of Jodo nuns, and these are allowed the use of the great temple for their morning service—which follows the Tendai service at an interval of a few minutes. This Jodo service was one of the most memorable I have seen, for the celebrant was peculiarly reverent and chanted what might be called the solo portions of the service with great impressiveness and with a voice of unusual charm. At first I thought the celebrant, with close-shaved head, was a very young monk; and then I realized it was a nun—the lady prioress of the convent, the imperial princess to whom I referred in the preceding chapter. I shall not soon forget the depth of reverent feeling and the sense of significance she put into the words, "Namu Amida, Namu Amida." The little lady—she was twenty-two—looked every inch a princess, and bore herself as such. After the service there was a kind of recessional

senting the five kinds of *a posteriori* wisdom. Members of the Shingon sect make much use, during meditation, of one of the Sanskrit characters corresponding to our vowel A. It symbolizes identity and difference.

through the temple grounds to the Jodo convent, and as she led the way, followed by her nuns and attendants, the pilgrims knelt in a long line and she touched the head of each with her silk tassel in blessing.[5]

Services somewhat more like our Protestant type are to be found in the more popular sects, Nichiren and Shin. The Nichiren services are often held not in the main temple but in some smaller and less sacred building within the temple enclosure. Forty or fifty people may collect in such a room, with one or two priests to lead them, and conduct a rather noisy service of praise in which all take part, with considerable assistance from the drum. The drum is one of the chief characteristics of the Nichiren sect, as only the members of this sect make use of it. In a Japanese city one may hear the booming of the drum from some far-distant Nichiren temple, and know that an enthusiastic service of prayer and praise is going on. Young laymen as well as priests are taught to beat it, which they do with great skill and with a peculiar rhythm. The noisy cadence thus produced is said to be helpful toward inducing the spirit of praise and prayer.

The daily morning service of the Shinshu (about 5:30 A.M.) is attended by a considerable number of laymen, and once every month, on the monthly celebration of the death of Shinran, the service is especially elaborate and the attendance especially large. At one of these services which I attended in the Higashi Hongwanji in Kyoto there was an audience of about six hundred. All of these but about a dozen sat outside the rail, which divides the temple into two unequal parts. Within the rail were twelve or more laymen who had gone through the rite of having the razor put to the hair, and who wore, on this occasion, the badge of honor, a piece of colored silk over the shoulders. These sat at the sides. In the central space within the rail and in front of the enclosure containing the altar were the monks—seventeen in number. Back of them, near the altar, sat the abbot and bishop of the sect (the head of one branch of the Otani family), with three or four other dignitaries, and still farther back, on a throne facing the altar was the celebrant, a young monk, nephew of the abbot. The service began with a chant by

[5] Two of the kneeling pilgrims thus blessed were Americans.

the chorus of monks—each line of their chant being first intoned by their leader. This first chant, I was told, was from a Chinese hymn by Zendo. The celebrant then intoned part of a prayer by a grandson of Shinran, sounded a gong and burned incense, while the priestly chorus intoned the Namu Amida Bu(tsu). A period of deep silence followed during which (as every good Shinshu member would know) the celebrant read to himself the rest of the prayer by Shinran's grandson, and the audience appeared to be worshiping. After this the celebrant descended from the throne, bowed three times toward the altar, and slowly circumambulated it, taking his seat near the abbot, while the chanting continued, fell to a pianissimo, and died. A gong was twice sounded and the abbot read a poem of Shinran, line by line, the chorus repeating each line after him—a poem in praise of the seven patriarchs beginning with Nagarjuna.[6] This was followed by another intoning of the Namu Amida Bu, interspersed with some of the *Wasans* or Psalms of Shinran, begun by one of the higher dignitaries and taken up by the priestly chorus. Buddhist chanting resembles somewhat the intoning of the Anglo-Catholic church: it is on various notes though hardly a tune or song. At the end of the last *Wasan*, a gong was sounded three times, the abbot bowed toward the altar, the higher dignitaries bowed in the same way, the chorus of priests bowed, and last the audience bowed. Most of the clergy retired but nearly all the lay congregation remained and continued their individual worship, after which many of them went to one of the larger halls of the temple where a preaching service was held.

If one compares this Shinshu service with the masses said by the monks in the older sects (no lay congregation being present) and also remembers that it is Shinshu more than any other which marks the direction in which Buddhism is developing, it will be plain that there is nothing fixed or unduly conservative in Buddhist cult, and that the tendency is steadily toward larger participation by the laity and a form

[6] The reader may find this in part translated in a little book by S. Yamabe and L. Adams Beck, entitled *Buddhist Psalms*, in the *Wisdom of the East Series* (London, Murray, 1921). A large part of the West Hongwanji ritual translated into English, together with descriptions of many special ceremonies, may be found in a little book, *The Vade Mecum*, by Rev. and Mrs. Ernest Hunt and A. R. Zorn.

of public worship more like that of Protestant Christianity. This tendency and also the flexibility of the Buddhist cult become the more noticeable if one visits the temple recently built by the Shinshu as a mission chapel in Honolulu. The exterior, I regret to say, has little of the beauty of the Buddhist temple in Japan, and the interior, except for the Buddha in his gilded shrine, might easily be taken for an American church. There are pews, pulpits, and organ, and they have a service every Sunday with a choir and a sermon. It is to be hoped that Buddhist worship will not become too much like ours. I am afraid it will. Japanese converts to Christianity, I am told, usually prefer a non-liturgical and simple service. They also say they dislike the dimness of many Buddhist temples—it makes them sad. Probably we shall have to make up our minds to the Americanization of a good deal of the world. Shinshu and Jodo theology is already quite evangelical and it may be that their cult and their architecture will follow suit.

In addition to the kind of temple services I have mentioned, the special masses for the dead play a large part in the religious life of the Japanese layman. These services are held in the main temple or in some of its subordinate shrines, and vary through all degrees of simplicity and elaborateness. The members of the family attend and sometimes take part, coming forward, one by one, at a certain point in the service, burning incense, kneeling and praying before the altar.

The funeral ceremonies of Buddhist families—unlike marriages, with which the Buddhist clergy, until recently, have had nothing to do—consist largely of prayers by the monks. These masses for the dead are held on the day of cremation and burial and (as in China) at intervals over seven weeks after the burial. Seven days after the death of the departed a special ceremony is held in the home and one in the temple, and at the end of every week till forty-nine days have passed a priest is employed to read the scriptures for the dead. During this time the soul is supposed to remain in purgatory. Some of the rites connected with these sad weeks will seem to the reader both superstitious and touching. As for example, the following, which I take from Lafcadio Hearn's *Unfamiliar Japan:*

When a child dies, the mother buys a small wood-cut of Jizo and with it prints an image of the divinity upon 100 little papers. And she sometimes also writes upon the papers words signifying, "For the sake of . . . ," inscribing the soul name which the Buddhist priests have given to the dead child and which is written also upon the little commemorative tablet kept within the Buddhist household shrine. Then upon a fixed day (most commonly the forty-ninth day after the burial), she goes to some place of running water and drops the little papers there, one by one, repeating as each slips through her fingers the holy invocation, *Namu Jizo Dai Bosatsu.*[7]

In most sects except Shinshu tablets of the dead are kept in the temples to which the family belongs as well as in the homes. Almost universally the Buddhists of Japan practice cremation. The greater part of the ashes are left at the place of burning, but a portion are usually buried in the Buddhist graveyard. An interesting custom is followed in Osaka—and it may be in several other places so far as I know—some of the ashes of the dead are brought to the great Tenno-ji temple and there mixed with clay and molded into an image of the Buddha, which is thenceforth preserved in the temple. Thus the body as well as the soul "becomes Buddha."

This same Tenno-ji temple exemplifies in extreme fashion another aspect of the Buddhist cult which is far less attractive than the temple worship I have been describing. One who wished to make a case against Buddhism and charge it with superstitious and absurd practices would do well to spend some time in this immense and ancient temple. Long ago it became a center of the worst mixture of Buddhism and Shinto and this it still retains. It does but little to stimulate the religious sense but it seeks to offer a magic refuge from fear and disease and is run chiefly for the benefit of the sick and the dead. The fox cult, the monkey cult, the sale of charms, the rubbing of diseased members on the corresponding member of the Binzuru image (which thus becomes an efficient spreader of disease germs [8] and is nearly rubbed out of recognition), more healing by the touch of magic paper, the writing of one's name on a lucky strip of wood-shavings with a prayer stamped on it (which one procures for a consideration) and

[7] *Op. cit.*, I. 169.

[8] The government has now locked up the Binzuru of Tenno-ji within an iron grating so that it may be seen but not touched.

the presentation of it to a stone turtle in a pond, so that he may take it to the next world—things like these make the immense enclosure a busy scene of which Kobo Daishi might have approved but which would have shocked Honen and Shinran and enraged Nichiren, and would have made Sakyamuni feel that the Dharma had nearly disappeared from the earth and that it was high time Maitreya should descend from the Tusita heaven.

Possibly I have maligned the great Kobo Daishi (for whom indeed I cherish deep respect), but the superstitious attitude of the masses (not of the intelligentsia) of Shingon partly justifies my guess. As every extremely ritualistic church is in danger of doing, the Shingon sect encourages its uneducated followers to lay great stress on the spiritual value of form and ritual. These in Shingon consist of finger attitudes,[9] sacred implements, and other externalisms of various sorts. Nor are they alone in this. Fortune telling [10] such as one finds in Chinese temples is common enough, not only in Tenno-ji, but in other large city temples such as Asakusa in Tokyo (a Tendai temple) and Todai-ji in Kyoto—especially in the Kobo Daishi shrine. Other things of the same sort might be mentioned. But it would be as unfair to call this Buddhism as it would be to describe the doings at and near the church of San Isidro in Madrid and call it Christianity.

A more truly Buddhist expression of religious zeal on

[9] These various arrangements of the fingers, or *mudras*, are used in prayer and worship, each of them being symbolic of some truth of the Shingon teaching. There are twelve of these *mudras*, such as pressing the palms tightly together with the fingers slightly open, placing the palms loosely together with the ends of the fingers touching each other, etc., etc. The thumb symbolizes the Void, or the Buddha, the first finger man, and the two when joined stand for the truth of the unity of the divine and the human. Or the four fingers may symbolize the four elements air, fire, water, earth, and the thumb may stand for the Sanskrit A and its mystic meaning, Ultimate Reality.

[10] The method is the same as in China. He who would interrogate the future is provided with a box containing one hundred small sticks or rods, each bearing a number. He shakes one out before the altar and presents it at the temple office. There are ten types of request represented by the sticks, such as recovery of the sick, the return of absent ones, a happy rebirth, etc. To each of these there are ten answers: that is a total of one hundred possible answers. These one hundred answers are printed out on little slips of paper arranged in the office in a kind of filing case, and each bearing a number corresponding to the number on one of the sticks. So when a stick is presented at the office, the monk in charge gets out from the filing case the corresponding paper slip. Of each ten answers to any one of the possible ten questions or requests, seven are good and three bad. Out of one hundred answers there are fifteen utterly and hopelessly bad ones. But if you draw one of these you may wait a while and try again.

the part of laity and clergy alike is to be found in the joyful practice (which Buddhism shares with Shinto) of making pilgrimages to various sacred shrines. As in China there are many pilgrim clubs which pay the expenses of one or more of their members each year on some pilgrimage. The undertaking is usually either an act of thanksgiving or one of penance. The pilgrims "come almost exclusively from the peasant and artisan classes and wearing a special garb, go on foot in twos and threes, begging for alms from house to house and chanting songs in melancholy tone as they trudge wearily along the country road. Thirty-three temples in the districts around Kyoto (including Koyosan) and eighty-eight in the large island of Shikoku are the goals of their piety."[11] Most of them carry a long staff like that borne by Jizo, adorned at the top with a circular metallic band to which are attached six rings. They wear a white *hauri* or coat (here my Fellow Pilgrim again comes to my aid), which is usually white, or of some color adopted by the pilgrim club to which they belong. Many of them have the official seals of the various shrines which they have visited stamped upon their *hauri,* and when they die they are clothed for their graves in this coat adorned with the evidences of their past piety. They usually also receive from each shrine a certificate (a paper stamped with the seal of the shrine) testifying to their pilgrimage. Some also carry, strapped upon their breasts, a box in which donations from the generous may be placed. They never beg; but if one wishes to help them out with a few sen and thereby acquire an indefinite amount of merit for oneself, there is the box! This, with a long rosary around their necks, a white band round their heads, and an immense straw hat, ending in a peek and large as an umbrella, completes their costume.

Many of the pilgrims are broken men and women suffering from disease and seeking cure; and it is the belief of some who watch them that the venture of faith is by no means always in vain. A pious Buddhist woman who has given her life to aiding these processions of needy and hopeful people says, "It is not rare that a pilgrim suffering from evidently incurable ailment comes back completely

[11] F. Kawabata in "A Friend of Pilgrims," *The Young East,* I. 85.

restored to health. On such occasions I cannot but feel grateful for the mercy of Buddha."[12] This woman, by the way, is a beautiful example of Buddhist piety and pity. Though with no resources of her own she collected about 50,000 yen and with it erected a group of buildings in a desolate corner of Shikoku, between wild mountains, situated on one of the most important pilgrim routes. Here she has spent her life, welcoming and succoring thousands of pilgrims and supplying their needs. The money for this purpose was raised chiefly from poor people who gave what they could—one gift of seven thousand yen coming from a village of peasants who live on millet and accumulated the money for their donation by saving a few sen a day.

Each Buddhist family has a household shrine. Some of these are exceedingly simple affairs, hardly more than shelves; some are very elaborate with much carving and gilding. The shrine, whether simple or ornate, contains at least one image of some member of the Buddhist cycle. In Zen families the image is likely to be Shaka—though the red-clad Dammo (the Bodhidharma of China) is usually somewhere in evidence. Shinshu families use no Shaka images but substitute a picture or image of Shinran or of Amida, while Jodo families may have representations of Amida, Zendo, and Honen, and occasionally Kwannon and Seishi. The more intelligent members of the Nichiren sect insist that Shaka should be the central image of the household shrine and of the temple; but very often his place is taken by Nichiren himself. Besides the shrines, scrolls with religious pictures or inscriptions will be found in many a pious home, representing one of the Buddhas and his chief Bodhisattvas, the Western Paradise, Jizo saving little children, a death-bed scene with Amida receiving the departing soul, a Buddhist pursued by monsters and enemies representing sins, and walking across a bridge between this world and the next, spanning fire and a hungry sea, guided and sustained by the warning voice of Shaka and the beckoning hands of Amida.

Worship is performed before this household shrine in all the more zealous families morning and night. By much the larger part of Buddhist worship is in the homes and hence

[12] Quoted by Kawabata, *op. cit.*, p. 86.

quite unseen by the outsider. Once a month in many families, a monk is invited to the house to give advice and to pray.

In addition to this home worship of the Buddhas should be mentioned the cult of ancestors: for, in contrast to the conditions in China, Japanese Buddhism has incorporated this as a part of itself. It found a rather primitive ancestor worship when it arrived, already being molded into definite form through the rapid invasion of Chinese influence. As the Reverend James H. Addison has pointed out, the adoption of this Chino-Japanese custom by Buddhism necessarily affected both its external forms and its inner meaning.

> Buddhism, in the first place, could supply a definite picture of the future state of the departed. Its heavens and purgatories offered vivid pictures of a life beyond death which had hitherto been devoid of color or detail. So far as Buddhism was true to its own teachings, its tendency was to minimize the power of the dead to aid the living, and to magnify the needs of the departed and the power of the priesthood to aid them. Its doctrines operated to encourage prayer offered for the dead rather than addressed to the dead. But with that inveterate tolerance so characteristic of Mahayana Buddhism, it found a place for all the older beliefs; and if it did not call the ancestors *kami*, it conceded to them as *hotoke* the power to exercise "a calm tutelary protection over the living descendants." And the spirit of gentle charity, so essential in every type of Buddhism, permeated the rites with the atmosphere of affectionate tenderness, and colored them with compassion.[13]

The ancestral tablets or *ihai* of a Buddhist home are placed beside the Buddha images in the *butsudan,* or Buddhist shrine. They vary in size and shape but are usually from four to twelve inches in height and are mounted on a base carved like a lotus, are lacquered and gilded, and inscribed with the posthumous names of the dead. "The first religious duty of the morning in a Buddhist household is to set before the tablets of the dead a little cup of tea made with the first hot water prepared. Daily offerings of boiled rice are also made; and fresh flowers are put in the shrine vases; and incense is burned before the tablets." I take this from Lafcadio Hearn's description.[14] In a particularly elaborate shrine in the house of a priest whom I met, there were two

[13] "Religious Life in Japan," by J. H. Addison, *Harvard Theol. Rev.*, XVIII. 332.
[14] *Unfamiliar Japan,* II. 407-408.

lighted candles before the Buddha images and many fresh peaches before both Buddhas and ancestral tablets. There are special celebrations for the more beloved dead on the monthly and on the yearly return of the day when they died, with special offerings, and frequently with special prayers by a priest, who is invited in for the occasion: and on the *Bon* festival, or Feast of Souls (which comes in August) the butsudan is gayly decked and the whole house is made beautiful with flowers, food, and lanterns.

In Buddhist families a distinction is made between those long dead and those who have recently died. To these latter one seldom prays or cries for help—rather one prays for them, at least to the extent of uttering the formula, "O Lord Amida, vouchsafe augustly to welcome this soul." But real prayers are addressed to the Hotoke, the souls of those long dead. Lafcadio Hearn gives the following examples: "That our family may be preserved!" "That we may enjoy long life without sorrow!" "That the perpetuity of our descent may be assured." Besides these formulae, any prayers prompted by the heart, whether of supplication or of gratitude, may be repeated.

In the temples as in the homes, the rank and file of the less learned Buddhists, outside of the Jodo and Shin sects, make petitions to the Buddhas and Bodhisattvas—and in fact to almost any of the Buddhist cycle—for all the various things that the human heart longs for.

> Everywhere at shrines and temples people write their prayers on little pieces of paper and present them to a god or temple. These prayers reveal the heart of the suppliants and the common need. Men pledge themselves to abstain from wine and women for definite periods of time. Some promise to give up gambling and others who are diseased promise that if they are cured they will make a thank-offering. Lovers pray that the object of their love may be led to them or that peace and harmony may be established. Before the Jizo shrine women pray for many things. Some are happy in expectant motherhood and seek blessings relating thereto: others are sick or troubled and seek relief. Before Yakushi, the Buddha of healing, a woman troubled with warts on her face prays for their removal within two weeks; a man prays for restoration of his hearing; and a weary mother prays that her peevish child may cease crying in the night and that her own swollen limbs may be healed.[15]

[15] R. C. Armstrong, in the *Year Book of Christian Work* for 1922, p. 101.

Much of the prayer of the less spiritual Buddhists—as much of the prayer of the less spiritual in all religions—is of a rather mechanical nature. Many laymen doubtless have no more real belief in the reality and present power of the Butsus and Bosatsus than my Nikko curio dealer, and yet continue praying to these beings out of mere force of custom, and because of the unreasonable discomfort which neglect to do so would bring. But among the many laymen to whom the sacred beings of Buddhism are realities prayer also is very real. As in China, a large part of the praying is done through the reverent repetition of sacred formulae, such as the *Namu Amida Butsu* (which, of course, means, Reverence to Amida Buddha!),[16] or the *Namu Jizo Dai Bosatsu* (Reverence to Jizo the great Bodhisattva!), or the common prayer of the Nichiren sect, *Namu Myoho Renge Kyo* (Reverence to the Lotus Sutra of the Good Law!). Members of Shingon use the mysterious syllable *Abiraukein* in much the same way as Jodo, Nichiren, and other sects use the three prayers or formulae just named. This is for Shingon a highly symbolic word, and its reverent repetition signifies belief in Dainichi and in our identity with him.

The monks of the various sects insist, and teach the laity, that the repetition of prayer formulae is valuable only if one's mind be in the right state. Mere repetition by the lips is of little use. When one says the *Nembutsu,* so a Jodo monk told me, one must also will to do right. If one repeats the prayer with a bad will no benefit will result: but if one says it with a heart full of true devotion one will be led to the right kind of living, and saving grace will be received in the soul. The *Namu Amida,* it will be observed, is neither a petition nor a formula of meditation, but, at its best, is a means of prostrating oneself before the Divine, a pouring out of one's soul in the pure feeling of devotion, a rushing forth of the impulse to worship, a vent for what Otto calls the emotion of the numinous.[17] That it is just this to many

[16] The Shinshu gives several translations to this phrase. Most commonly members of this sect regard it as simply the full name of Amida. The semi-official "Catechism of the Shin Sect" renders it "The Glorious One who has Boundless Life and Truth," and "The Glorious One from Eternity whose Light Radiates Freely in all Directions," Reischauer's trans. in the *Tr. A. S. J.*, XXXVIII. 361.

[17] *The Idea of the Holy* (Oxford U. Press, 1924), Chaps. II, III, IV.

a devout Buddhist can hardly be doubted by any one who has intelligently watched what goes on in Japanese temples.

This may be as good a place as any for a last word on the matter of prayer. Much might be said in favor of the Buddhist view that prayer should seldom be petitional. Petitional prayer for particular things involves a theory of the universe which is becoming increasingly difficult today. The very act of making petitions, moreover, fastens the mind on the finite things for which request is made rather than on the Divine, and thus begets a mental state which is hardly the most religious. If petitional prayer be given up, prayer may still be retained as thanksgiving, and as such it has a real and permanent place in the life of the soul. This, however, is hardly the chief office of prayer. More important is prayer as *realization* or perhaps as spiritual discovery, a voyage of the soul in realms beyond the physical. For the mystically minded this may be a useful exercise and at times even a great experience. Much the same may be said of prayer as an inner listening for the voice of the spirit, an emptying of the mind so that the Divine may fill it. Both of these last-mentioned uses of prayer are helpful and admirable for those more adept in the spiritual life; but for the rank and file of earnest but not deeply mystical men and women they will often prove of little value, and will sometimes result in bewilderment and even boredom rather than benefit. There is, however, one use to which prayer may be put of which all earnest souls may avail themselves, and that is the active debasing of oneself before the Divine, the August, the Overpowering, the immediate sensing of the contrast between one's own finiteness and the infinitude of the Eternal, the pouring forth of one's soul in deep humility and reverence before the unspeakable Whole of things which is never far away. For this each of the great religions has its formula of expression, a form of words that both pours forth and reinforces the numinous emotion. Judaism has its "Holy, Holy, Holy," Islam its muezzin's cry, "God is Great, God is Great, there is no God but God," Hinduism its Gayatri or address of reverence to the Source of light and life, the Hinayana its "Om Mani Padme Hum." The form by which this emotion gains at once its vent and its rekindling matters not greatly, but I doubt if any verbal formulations for it are really more effective than the Namu Amida of Mahayana Buddhism.

The worshiper who repeats this sacred formula usually knows what the words mean: but that is of relatively slight significance. The important thing is that he knows what *he* means, and the words help him to realize this meaning in his own mind. The repetition of the vernacular words which mean "reverence to Amida" could hardly bring him the same religious emotion as do these more sacred sounds. Words in his own language would get in the way of the meaning of his soul. For he means very much more than any verbal assertion can express. Forever

> . . . words are weak
> The glory they transfuse with proper truth to speak.

It is this essential inadequacy of language to the inner life which explains the very real advantage which a foreign and sacred tongue so often possesses in the expression of religious emotion. These reverend sounds, which are to the worshiper both less and more than words, do not compel him to sign on any dotted line or to confine his meaning to any statable proposition. They suggest but do not hide. They are like music.

The *Namu Amida,* therefore, instead of being, as at first it seems to many of us, a superstitious and meaningless repetition, has, as a fact, profound justification in human psychology. Doubtless it is often misused as a mere mechanical contrivance for acquiring merit—as is the Lord's Prayer. But we should not judge its nature or its value by its misuse. As used by the more intelligent and spiritual Buddhists it is a psychological means of producing really desirable results. One can easily understand how for the simple-minded "it helps your heart to say it over and over when you are in trouble," while with the more spiritual it may play the same part as that prayer which the Fioretti tells us St. Francis used to repeat for hours in the night, "O my God! O my God!"

In the repetition of the various prayer formulae of Buddhism a rosary is frequently used [18] as in China. The habit of repeating these prayers, begun in childhood and continued through many years, naturally sinks deep into the mind and they rise to the surface at all sorts of emergencies. Even complete abandonment of Buddhism and conversion to an alien religion cannot put an end to this. A missionary friend of mine told me of an old woman who, four years after her conversion to Christianity, complained that she still found her old Buddhist prayers coming up into her mind at frequent intervals. She felt that it was a kind of sin and thought it must be due to a fox spirit, or perhaps a badger. She had no trouble in giving up liquor; but tobacco and Buddhist prayers were habits that she found difficult to conquer.

On the question of the manner in which prayer works and the appropriateness of petitional prayer there is much the same divergence of opinion as in China. To the masses, as we have seen, prayer is as simple a matter as in most other religions: one prays to the Buddhas, or to any member of the Buddhist cycle, for anything that one wants, and the Being thus addressed hears and answers. The theory of the Nichiren sect about prayer is not essentially different—except that prayer should be directed to Shaka—or to Shaka through Nichiren. If one's father is ill (so I was told by an abbot of the Nichiren sect) one prays earnestly to Shaka, either by means of a sacred prayer formula, or by a direct petition, and Shaka hears and answers. In the Hosso sect also direct petitional prayer is approved—though the repetition of a

[18] Each sect has its own type of rosary, and one familiar with the matter can therefore tell by seeing a Buddhist's rosary to what sect he belongs. In most sects the rosary is used chiefly as in Catholic Christianity to keep track of the number of formal prayers repeated. In this, as in most things, Shingon is rather more elaborate and symbolical than the other sects. A Shingon rosary contains 108 beads (as do so many rosaries in China and India) because, say the Shingon authorities, there are 108 Buddhas. (There are, of course, an infinite number of Buddhas, but this is not inconsistent with the statement that there are 108.) So in saying the rosary one names the 108 Buddhas. But there is another and a better reason for the number: the steps of the Bodhisattva's path in attaining Buddhahood are 54; and twice 54 is 108. One says the 54 beads meditating upon the 54 steps and so reaches the 54th bead, which is of glass or amber, or in some way made more glorious than the others. This symbolizes Buddhahood. Inasmuch as it is impossible to go beyond Buddhahood, on reaching the 54th bead one reverses the rosary and says the 54 again in the reverse order. The first time one says the 54 beads it is for his own sake, the second time is for the community, and so on alternating. This is because in helping others one helps oneself, and in helping oneself one helps others.

Sutra is the more common method—and the Buddha hears and answers. The great temple of Horyuji was built in fulfilment of a vow that was made in connection with a petitional prayer for recovery from illness. Among most of the other sects there is a feeling on the part of the more learned against direct petitional prayer. A Tendai monk told me that while the common people in his sect pray for all sorts of favors, he himself did not approve of that sort of thing and never practiced it, and did not believe that petitional prayers were answered. Prayer, he said, should be only reverence and praise. The Shingon theory is much the same, though characteristically more complicated. The learned Shingon monks do not believe that the Buddha hears and answers prayer. For them prayer is primarily meditation. More specifically it is meditation upon the identity of the Buddha, the maker of the prayer, and the object of it. By meditating upon this truth one becomes both the Buddha and the person for whom one would pray. Thus if I would pray for my sick father I meditate on our common union or identity with the Buddha, and my praying thus *is* my father praying. He prays if I pray, once I have reached in meditation the unity of myself with him and with all things in the Buddha. For by such deep realization one gets back to the real world where there are no differences. It is only in the phenomenal world that such things as illness exist, and this is due to ignorance and illusion. By destroying this illusion one gets rid of illness.

Jodo and Shin are less mystical in their theories but none the less insistent (in fact very much more insistent) that direct petitional prayer is useless. Not only is it useless. Both Honen Shonin and Shinran regarded petitional prayer as almost sinful. One should repeat the *Nembutsu* over and over again with a heart full of devotion to Amida, and with simple trust that He knows best.

Though Japanese Buddhism clings persistently to the Anatta doctrines—the denial of a substantial soul—the uneducated Buddhist layman probably does not make a great deal of it. At any rate, the rank and file of the four Pure Land sects expect at death to go to the Western Paradise of Amida, much as the simple Christian expects his soul to go to heaven. Amida for them is really a personal God, though there is doubtless in the back of their minds at the same time a recognition of the teaching that somehow all the Buddhas are one and that all beings are one. Many members of the Tendai and Shingon, and some members of Zen, have much the same attitude toward Amida (or Dainichi) and toward the problem of immortality. Ask one of them what he expects will become of him after death, and he will probably reply, "I shall become Buddha." But what he means by this neither you nor I nor he can tell. Doubtless the Buddha knows.

In Japanese Buddhism as in Chinese Buddhism there is less relative emphasis on morality than there was in the original teachings of the Founder, probably also less than there is in contemporary Siamese Buddhism. One reason for this is, of course, the fact that Japanese Buddhism includes so many more doctrines of a metaphysical nature, it has so many other things to emphasize, than the Hinayana, whether ancient or modern. The type of morality taught is also different. There is little reference to the Four Noble Truths, and in fact little knowledge of them. A learned Hosso monk in Nara whom I questioned had never heard of them. One of the few Japanese references to the Four Noble Truths I have ever come across is in a little pamphlet published by the Federation of Buddhist Organizations for Children, and entitled *The Mahayana Buddhists.* Under the heading, "What are the Fundamental Teachings of the Buddha?" it gives the following astonishing version of the "Fourfold Noble Truths": (1) Life is pain; (2) This is the result of past deeds; (3) In order to obtain a release, an end must be put to all that; and (4) finally, there is the way to do this." The reader will have noted that the original Second Noble Truth (the cause of sorrow is desire) has been entirely omitted and a reference to former lives substituted. This is altogether typical of Japanese Buddhism. It is extremely rare in Japan that one comes upon any recognition of the evil of desire as such. Broadly speaking, the Buddhism of modern Japan makes absolutely no attack upon desire but distinguishes, much as Christianity does, between desires, some of which are bad and some good. There are many good desires, and the Mahayana does not urge that these should be destroyed.

Like Chinese Buddhism, the Buddhism of Japan has to a great extent adopted the Confucian morality; in fact, so far as ethics is concerned, the impress of Confucius is quite as obvious as that of Gotama. Filial piety, loyalty in the various relations of life, truthfulness, and the social virtues it emphasizes in no different way from Confucianism. Its more typically Buddhist coloring is seen chiefly in its greater emphasis upon mercy and kindliness. The Bodhisattva ideal of self-sacrifice for the sake of others gives its good will a certain intensity and extensity [19] that the more conventional and limited Confucian teaching and practice does not possess. In common with the Buddhism of all other lands it emphasizes the Five Precepts; and in good Mahayana fashion it adds to its ideal the Six Paramitas, or virtues of perfection, namely, generosity, discipline, patience, energy, meditation, and wisdom or insight. These moral precepts and ideals are taught in various ways. The children learn them from their parents and teachers and from the monks. In some of the temples one finds ethical ideals engraved or written upon the walls in prominent places. As we shall see in the next chapter, the sermon and the Sunday school are becoming efficient tools for the propagation of moral as well as other teachings.

No one, I think, would deny that Buddhism has had and still has an immense influence on the character of the Japanese people. In spite of their martial disposition they have imbibed a great deal of the gentleness of Gotama and much of his sympathy, generosity, and liberality of view. The Nichiren sect alone is sometimes accused of having lost this almost universal Buddhist virtue of tolerance. But I know that both monks and laymen in that sect may be thoroughly liberal in their views toward other sects and other religions.[20]

[19] Kindness toward animals is sometimes carried to an extent that seems to Westerners almost grotesque. Pet dogs are not infrequently buried in temple grounds. According to Dr. Armstrong, "The Young Men's Buddhist Association in Kyushu recently held a memorial service for 34,000 frogs, 7000 rats, 1000 hares, 500 dogs, 500 cats, 300 hens, and 500 doves dissected in the study of anatomy in Kyushu University" (*Year Book of Christian Work* for 1922, p. 94).

[20] A Nichiren monk told me that good Christians, like good members of the Nichiren sect, would "become Buddha" after death. One of my interpreters had been brought

Against the other sects I have heard no accusation of intolerance. From early times, moreover, and up to the present day, it has not been uncommon for earnest Buddhists in time of war to pray for their enemies.[21] Masses are often said and occasional monuments erected for the repose and the memory of friend and foe alike. The Japanese are good soldiers but the better Buddhists among them do not forget, even in the excitement of war, that the Buddha nature is in all men.

But while the ancient Buddhist virtues of sympathy, generosity, and liberality have been maintained, Japanese Buddhism has taken on some of the active and (at times) even knightly qualities of the Japanese. Zen Buddhism was for centuries the inspiration of the Samurai, and the Nichiren sect makes much of the teaching of patriotism. As we saw in the historical chapter, from the very first introduction of Buddhism into Japan the leaders of the new religion distinguished themselves by active propaganda, by energetic efficiency in humanitarian and cultural undertakings, and even by participating prominently—at times all too prominently—in the public and political life of the nation. Japanese Buddhism has always had and still retains a good deal of other-worldliness; but it has been but seldom characterized by that renunciation of the world, that fleeing from the world, that disregard of the welfare of human society which is so often found in other Buddhist lands.

In its relation to human happiness as well as to human

up in the Nichiren sect, his mother being an ardent worshiper of Nichiren. But when at eighteen he started going to a Christian Sunday school and chose Christianity instead of Buddhism his mother did not object, for she thought that both Christianity and Buddhism were good for life.

[21] An interesting case of requiting one's personal enemy with good is reported in *The Young East* for July, 1927. In May of that year "the chief priest of a Buddhist temple in Fukushima Prefecture, his mother, an acolyte and a maid servant were murdered by an armed burglar, who was later arrested and was identified as a desperate old offender. He was condemned to death. Now this man has two children, a daughter of 11 and a son of 7. The girl was adopted by a remote relative, but the boy was left wholly helpless, none caring to adopt the son of such a ruffian. Hearing of this, a man and his wife have come forward with a proposal to adopt the poor orphan. They are Mr. and Mrs. Shoten Aoyama of the city of Toyohashi, and Mrs. Aoyama is the sister of the murdered priest. For some years past Mr. and Mrs. Aoyama have been engaged in social service in their city, chiefly taking care of orphans and depraved boys and girls. 'I am not sure to what extent the poor father of the boy is to blame for the crime he committed. We must remember our society is still so imperfect,' said Mrs. Aoyama. She proposes to console the souls of her mother and brother by bringing up the boy as her own and making him an honest man."

morality Buddhism has gradually changed since entering Japan. As I have pointed out in an earlier chapter, it is hardly correct to describe Buddhism in its total world view as pessimistic. But the picture which early Buddhism draws of *this world* and the life of the worldly (abstracted from its total setting) is certainly dark. That is the whole point of the First Noble Truth. Hence in all Buddhism there is at least a certain gentle melancholy which perhaps will never disappear. As I suggested in another connection, Buddhism did not lose this quality in coming to Japan; its partial sadness struck a note to which the Japanese heart quickly and naturally vibrated. The very love of beauty so deeply implanted in these sensitive people gives a certain poignant quality to beautiful objects which mingles with the Buddhist sense of the transitoriness of all things earthly. The cherry-blossoms and the autumn leaves—what more lovely, and what more perishable? And such, the Buddha taught, is this life of man.

> What of our life! 'Tis imaged by a boat:
> The wide dawn sees it on the sea afloat:
> Swiftly it rows away,
> And on the dancing waves no trace is seen
> That it has ever been.[22]

But while the tender melancholy of Buddhism has been felt by the Japanese, I do not think one can justly say that it has made them a sad people. Surely little of this melancholy is found in the modern teachings of Jodo, or Shin, or Nichiren. And in the other sects Buddhism has at least given as much of joy as it has taken away. The childlike lightheartedness of Shinto Buddhism has indeed modified. But if superficial and thoughtless delight in the things of this world is no longer possible for one who has gained a taste of Buddhist feeling, a certain deeper joy has been made possible by its deeper thought and its more lasting promise. Shinto has little to say of death, Buddhism much. But Buddhism not only faces death: it gives a hope for something beyond death, a conception of a point of view transcending death, of which Shinto never dreamed. Buddhism has not made life more

[22] From a compilation of Japanese poems made in 922, trans. in Clara A. Walsh's *The Master Singers of Japan*, p. 61.

gay for the Japanese, but it has made it immeasurably more significant. It has perhaps taken away a certain amount of gaiety but it has given peace, joy, and depth. As I think over the Japanese Buddhists I have known they do not seem to me a sad people. The less educated were filled with a steadfast hope based upon the love and promises of Amida and the grace of Kwannon and Jizo. And the more intelligent were living lives colored by an idealistic philosophy and a noble mysticism, and filled with a certain calm confidence in the universe which if it be not joy is something more than peace.

Another modification which Buddhism has taken on from this land of its last pilgrimage is a peculiar charm, the characteristic beauty of Japan. Charm, indeed, Buddhism has possessed to an unusual degree in every land where it has dwelt. It has allied itself spontaneously with the native forms of beauty wherever it has gone. But just because of the peculiarly artistic nature of the Japanese it is in Japan that Buddhism has attained a level of charm which is quite unique. Keyserling, who has no very high opinion of the depth of the Japanese mind, has felt and expressed this unique character of their Buddhism so well that I must quote a few of his words.

> Japanese religiosity has created realities in the domain of sensibility and in the realm of moods which belong to the most priceless treasures of the human race. . . . In the realm of sensibility the Japanese stands, perhaps, higher than all other men. No wonder therefore that in spite of his essential superficiality he excels everyone in the power of religious sensibility. . . . The Japanese objectification of spirit is artistic in the highest degree; her forms are never allegories, always symbols, and they have all the advantages of an expression whose elements are born of feeling. . . . In so far as Confucius is right, the Japanese Church may be regarded as the crown of Indian wisdom. Kung Fu Tse taught that only such wisdom was to be regarded as perfect which appeared in the form of charm: this has happened here. It is the genuine spirit of Mahayana, all-embracing, earnest and profound, which animates this form of Buddhism—but its appearance is pure beauty and charm.[23]

There is no form of Japanese Buddhism which this charm has not touched. Its temples, its images, its religious paintings, its ritual, are things of beauty: and even its philosophy

[23] *Travel Diary*, pp. 160, 157.

and its myths and its ways of expressing abstract truths are wreathed about with a certain wistful and suggestive loveliness. Let me close this chapter with one further illustration of the sort of thing I mean.

The Emperor Go-Mizuno-In, an ardent Buddhist, who abdicated in 1629 and later on became a monk, wished to write a little book which would teach the lessons of the world's transitoriness and the Buddha's comfort, and he put it in the form of a story, typically Japanese and Buddhist in flavor. There once lived near the capital, so the story began, a man of meditative disposition who never married but devoted himself entirely to the care of his mother and to the cultivation of the flowers in his garden. With such loving care did he tend these that the neighbors gave him the name Kocho, which means Butterfly. In time his mother died, and his heart was filled with woe; and as he walked through his garden, filled with sad thoughts, he noticed that his flowers too were fading and falling and strewing the earth with their petals. It was not unnatural that these events impressed upon his mind the Noble Truth of Sorrow and Transitoriness; and he soon took his refuge in the Buddha and became a hermit in the wild recesses of Kitayama. After dwelling alone for many years, it happened that one stormy night, when he had been for hours rapt in meditation, there came a knock upon the door of his hermitage, and he heard the voice of a woman asking instruction in the way of the Buddha. The hermit at first hesitated to admit a woman to his cell, but so urgent was she in her supplications that he had not the heart to deny her request, and so admitted her. She was an old woman and apparently a nun, though clad in a light green robe. No sooner had she entered than two young girls, of about 16, dressed in willow-colored robes with purple hoods, came gliding into the hut; and after them other girls and young women, all beautiful, all brilliantly clad, and all earnestly beseeching instruction in the Buddha's Law. So Kocho preached to them a Buddhist sermon, emphasizing the vanity of this world's pleasures and the dangers of its temptations, but holding open the door of hope to all who would put their trust in the grace of the Buddha. By this the ladies, young and old, were filled with joy, realizing that the mist of blind attachment that had bound them to the wheel of birth and death was now cleared away and that the Moon of Truth had been revealed to their hearts. So, moistening the sleeves of their kimonos with their joyful tears, they thanked the hermit and arose to go. For a moment he detained them, asking that they would tell him who they were. To this they responded: It is very right that you should know. We are the spirits of the little flowers that you tended, long ago, in your garden.[24]

[24] This little story has been translated into English by A. L. Sadler and published by the Meiji Society of Japan under the title *Kocho* (Tokio, 1922).

CHAPTER XXVIII

PROPAGANDA, EDUCATION, AND PHILANTHROPY

At the close of the Tokugawa régime, Japanese Buddhism was in a moribund condition. It was, to be sure, largely supported by the government, but it was also largely controlled by the government, and the great majority of its clergy had settled down into a condition of comfort and complaisance, feeling they need make but little effort toward the preaching of their religion, and none for its purification, and well satisfied with themselves and with the *status quo* since the cult was duly performed and nothing interfered with the rice supply. Thus they were ill prepared for the rude shock of disestablishment and even mild persecution that came with the restoration. Fortunately for Buddhism, not all the clergy were of this complaisant and lethargic sort, and a few of the leaders were gifted with both insight and imagination, and therefore able both to cope with the present and anticipate the future. Prominent among these men was Count Kozon Otani, the bishop of the West Hongwanji division of Shinshu. Soon after the ban upon foreign travel was lifted he sent a commission to Europe to study religious conditions and Christian methods, and on the basis of its report the West Hongwanji adopted new forms of religious activity.[1] East Hongwanji very soon followed suit, and it was not long before the other more important sects began at least to wake up from their former lethargy.

But it was chiefly the inrush of Christian missionaries and the whirlwind campaign they carried on and the astonishing initial success they won that roused Japanese Buddhism from its sleep. Christianity was carried into Japan on the tidal wave of Western prestige, which threatened to overthrow most of the older forms of culture and thought

[1] Cf. Addison, "Religious Life in Japan," *Harvard Theol. Rev.*, XVIII, 333-34.

and, up to the late eighties, seemed to be carrying all before it. Throughout the nineties came a reaction, with a new appreciation of ancient Japanese culture and the cry "Japan for the Japanese." Just as Christianity had profited by the early fad for everything foreign, so Buddhism now profited by the revival of love for everything native. But this was not all. As Buddhism began to pull itself together after receiving the double blow of being thrown off by the government and faced with a new and active rival, its leaders discovered that the lessons of adversity need not be altogether bitter, and that in fact it might be posible for their religion to profit by both its seeming misfortunes. For disestablishment brought spiritual freedom and the presence of a rival brought spiritual stimulus, and the study of Christian methods in both Europe, America, and Japan suggested new ways of strengthening the hold of Buddhism upon at least a portion of the population. This movement of revival and reform, begun, in one sense, as far back as 1870, and showing its effects throughout the nineties, has been continued with steadily increasing strength ever since, and particularly in the last ten or fifteen years has assumed proportions such that no study of modern Buddhism can overlook it.

One of the things which Japanese Buddhism has learned from Christianity is the value of preaching. Of course I do not mean by this that there were no Japanese preachers until the Christian missionaries arrived and set the example. Buddhism was spread throughout Japan in Shotoku Taishi's time and before by means of preachers; and if we go back to ancient and Indian Buddhism, the Founder himself was primarily a preacher and teacher. Long before the restoration, however, preaching had come to play a decidedly unimportant rôle in the actual life of Japanese Buddhism. For that matter, if we compare Buddhism with Protestant Christianity, preaching plays a decidedly secondary rôle in Japan still. But a start, at least, has been made in the more active sects toward something like the Christian methods. If we compare Japan with America it appears to have very little preaching; if we compare Japan with China it has a good deal.

There is quite as much difference between the various

Buddhist sects on this matter as there is between Buddhism and Protestant Christianity. The Hosso sect sends around an itinerant monk at times to do a little work of propaganda, but it seldom if ever has a preaching service or a lecture (for laymen) at one of its temples. Kegon also has no regular preaching services: but at the Todai-ji temple in Nara they occasionally have a public lecture on the life of Dosen (who introduced the Kegon sect into Japan), and illustrate it with moving pictures. Only a few Shingon temples hold preaching services, though the number of those that do is slowly increasing. Tendai is in much the same condition as Shingon. At the Shoren-in temple in Kyoto, for example, there is a sermon once a year; at the Dai-ko-do on Hiei-san a sermon is preached once in five years—and this for monks only (so at any rate one of the monks at the temple told me). At the great Tendai temple in Nagano, on the other hand, they hold preaching services for the pilgrims several times a week. In the Asakusa temple, in Tokyo, also there are evangelical meetings (with a sermon) very frequently. In fact, one of the Asakusa priests assured me they held a service of this sort every evening. I believe he believed it, but my experience with Oriental monks has made me realize that the ideal world is so real to them it occasionally gets substituted for the actual. It is, however, probably safe to say that they hold frequent evangelical services at the Asakusa temple. My informant added that their audiences varied from three hundred to a thousand. I take it this should not be construed to mean that they never have less than three hundred. The Asakusa and Nagano temples, however, are exceptional in Tendai; and it may be said of all these older sects, from Hosso to Shingon, that they still make very little use of preaching, though sermons are commoner than they used to be.

When we turn to the younger sects the situation is markedly different. Zen naturally trusts less to the "foolishness of preaching" than the other members of this group, but there are many Zen temples that make a good deal of it. At the Obakusan, the headquarters of the Obaku division of Zen, there are six preaching services a month, in the hall at the rear of the temple. The other Obaku temples, I understand, do very much less. The Rinzai branch of Zen—conservative of the old Zen traditions and skeptical of the value of instruction and of books—naturally preaches but little. Rinzai temples are for the cultivation of the mystical and monastic life. They have lectures, in some cases as often as six times a month, and laymen are admitted to them if they choose to come; but the lectures are not sermons. They are intended primarily for the monks, and have to do with the technique of zazen and other things of little interest to the average layman. In the Soto branch things are different. Soto is less conservative than Rinzai and believes in the utility of modern methods of instruction. In many Soto temples popular sermons are preached for the benefit of the laity at intervals of a week or ten days—at six A.M. The preacher points to the heart and tells his hearers that it is there the Buddha is to be found. He urges them to bring their hearts to the temple, and their wishes whether good or bad, to get rid of evil and especially of worry and anxiety. This he helps them to do by instructing them in the ultimate identity of all Reality and in the non-existence of separate selves. At some temples Sunday is chosen as the day for the sermon and they have one every week. In the So-ji-ji at Tokyo I was told they have an audience every Sunday of about one hundred and fifty. In addition to these there are special sermons for special occasions; and noted preachers or distinguished abbots sometimes make preaching tours in various parts of the country.

The Nichiren sect has always done more or less preaching. Its constituents have regularly been drawn largely from the common people, and the founder of the sect gave an example of intense, almost violent street preaching which has never wholly lost its effect among his followers, and is still sometimes imitated. In many Nichiren temples there is a sermon every Sunday or at less regular but equally frequent intervals, and itinerant preachers are also sent about. In their sermons they seek to put a few philosophical ideas in very simple terms, to inspire loyalty to the nation and loyalty to the Nichiren sect, and to depict the more picturesque incidents in Nichiren's life, especially the sufferings he went through during the many years of his persecution, thereby eliciting the emotions and warming the faith of the hearers.

Jodo, I gather, is about on a par with Nichiren in its use of preaching. At the great headquarters temple in Kyoto, the Chionin, there is a sermon every Sunday with an audience of about thirty or forty. At the Kurodani, also in Kyoto, they have preaching services twice a month. Of course there are many temples in Jodo and in all the sects, except perhaps Shinshu, which have preaching services but seldom. On the other hand, Jodo, like Nichiren, sends out evangelists in the autumn, winter, and spring, to preach in those districts which otherwise would be neglected. Jodo sermons, as might be expected, are devoted largely to the grace of Amida, the glories of his heaven, the value of the Nembutsu, and the edifying events in the life of Honen Shonin.

It is the Shin sect which has made and is making the greatest use of preaching. Every Shin temple, I have been told, holds preaching services, and nearly all of them at least once a week. The two great Hongwanji temples in Kyoto have one every day, and frequently two—morning and evening. In many places where it has no temples, Shinshu has established preaching halls—the West Hongwanji has 248 of these and East Hongwanji about as many. It will be noted from the statistical table given on page 520 that in addition to its temples and halls Shinshu possesses 2236 preaching stations, scattered through the land. Both branches of Shin also do a good deal of work in the army and navy, West Hongwanji having seventy-four preaching centers of this sort, each in charge of a priest who on Sundays or Saturdays preaches to the soldiers and sailors and distributes tracts and pamphlets. Shinshu has also established missions among railway employees. Several Japanese sects provide preachers for the prisons, but it is Shinshu that does most of this work. The custom of preaching to prisoners is a very old one in Japanese Buddhism. It is said that a Buddhist monk named Shuncho, who lived many centuries ago, being refused admission to the prisons, committed theft seven times deliberately in order that he might be imprisoned and attempt to reform and comfort his fellow prisoners through exhortation and instruction. The prison authorities of our day are of course glad to have prison chaplains and preachers, and many Shinshu priests avail themselves of the opportunity thus offered. The West Hongwanji alone furnishes one hundred and fifty-nine preachers for this service, who work in eighty-nine prisons; the East Hongwanji has seventy-one chaplains in forty-seven prisons. In November 1926 a special three-weeks' course of lectures was given for the benefit of the prison chaplains in Tokyo.

In this last paragraph I have given a number of statistics, and as I foresee that during the course of the chapter I shall have to give a good many more, I will take this opportunity to warn the reader against taking my figures too seriously. I do not vouch for their exactness. Some of them are drawn from the year 1919 and are therefore no longer exact, and some of them I fear never were exact. The Oriental is not greatly impressed with the importance of a meticulous nicety in statistics—and there are some of us who sympathize with him. While the statistics of this chapter, therefore, may not be as exact as they would probably be if drawn from Western sources, they are, I believe, trustworthy in a general way, as giving a fair idea of the sort of work modern Buddhism is doing.

The Buddhist leaders do not confine their efforts at propaganda to preaching in the temples and prisons. Various other methods are used. I have mentioned street preaching, especially in the Nichiren sect. A Buddhist Salvation Army has been started in Tokyo. Various organizations and societies have recently been founded by energetic and loyal Buddhists for getting hold of different classes of people and doing something for them in the way of spiritual guidance.[2] Prominent among these are the Young Men's Buddhist Associations and the Young Women's Buddhist Associations. I use both these terms in the plural, for there is no united Y.M.B.A. or Y.W.B.A. such as our Y.M.C.A. and Y.W.C.A.; instead, each of the more active sects has its own association, or (as in the case of Shinshu) it may have two of each. It is,

[2] The most recent I have heard of are the "Eastern Buddhist Association" and the "Buddhist Union to Reform the Buddhist World," both started in Tokyo in 1926, and the "Liberal Buddhist Association," organized in 1925 by a philanthropic Buddhist physician, with the purpose of "initiating human beings through religious faith and scientific help into noble happy life."

of course, the Shin Associations (belonging to the West and East Hongwanji) that are by far the largest and most active, the one belonging to the West Hongwanji having upward of 100,000 members (on paper), with centers in sixty different places. The Tokyo center is the largest, and here they have just completed a new building for the benefit of the students in the Imperial University. There is a Y.M.B.A. closely associated with nearly every university in Japan. The activities of the Y.M.B.A. and of the Y.W.B.A. are in part evangelical, in part social. In the Central Tokyo Y.M.B.A. (belonging to the Shin sect) the Social Department runs a dormitory for boys and young men in need of a home, at which about twenty-five are accommodated, and a sleeping place for transients, which takes care of about forty-five a night. This department also has a Bureau for Consultations on Personal Problems and a Women's Employment Bureau which finds places for needy young women. The Evangelical Department carries on a Sunday school for children and conducts a series of Saturday evening evangelical services, at each of which a lecture or address is made by some priest, professor, or learned layman. The audience, I was told, averages about one hundred, and the subjects of the lectures are such as the following (I take them from the 1924 list): "The Mind of the Buddha and Mind in General," "Concerning Primitive Architecture," "What is Human Life?" "The Dignity of One's Native Land," "The World Religion," "What is Shinshu?" "Death, Love, and Peace," "Social Activities of Believers in Shinran," "Shinran as the Incarnation of the Law."

The Y.W.B.A. is much like the Y.M.B.A., though smaller. Its membership in Tokyo is about two thousand. It carries on both evangelical, educational, and social work, publishes a journal, sends, occasionally, some of its members to Korea to propagate Buddhism, and has recently initiated a campaign for woman's suffrage.

There are several other societies of Buddhist women, besides the Y.W.B.A., which carry on various sorts of evangelical and philanthropic work. For example, in the East Hongwanji, the Fujin Howakwai, or Society of Women for the Deepening of Devotion, which has two hundred and forty-six branches and a membership of about 190,000; a similar society of women in the West Hongwanji with four hundred and seven branches; the Fujin Seineukai, or Young Women's Society which combines the study of Buddhism with training in the manual arts; a school in Tokyo for young women about to be married, the aim of which is to teach them some of the things they will need to know in order to be good wives. The Buddhist women of Japan are fairly active and do their share in the Sunday schools, kindergartens, orphanages, nurses' schools, and other social institutions which the new spirit of Japanese Buddhism is initiating.

This new spirit of Buddhism is new in more ways than one. Not only is it an expression of the revival of the spirit of the Founder and an application of it to new lines of activity: its leaders, in typical Japanese fashion, sometimes make a special point of utilizing the very latest methods and devices in carrying out their efforts at propaganda or service. No one can accuse them of being behind the times. Every year on April 8, the birth of the Buddha is celebrated —the Lumbini Festival it is called—with lectures, evangelistic meetings, and dramatic representations of the life of Shakamuni, etc. The following account of the Lumbini Festival in 1926 is typical:

> As usual the birthday of Buddha, April 8, was celebrated with great rejoicing throughout Japan. A recent welcome sign in connection therewith is that whereas in former days the festival was held in Buddhist temples only, it is now a popular event and the felicitous day is observed as children's holiday in many homes. In Tokyo this year, the festival was ushered in with a great meeting held on the evening of April 4 in the auditorium of the *Hochi,* the daily journal enjoying the largest circulation in the metropolis. At this meeting music and dancing were given, besides lectures on Buddhism and its founder by Prof. Taiken Kimura and a few other eminent Buddhist scholars. The day preceding Buddha's birthday members of the Y.M.B.A. conducted an evangelistic campaign at ten different places in Tokyo, and the same evening the Tokyo Radio Office broadcasted a story for children of the birth of Buddha by Mr. Takaaki Iwano. Mr. Sazanami Iwaya, Japan's foremost writer of fairy stories, also sent on the air an account of a Lumbini festival observed by Japanese residents in Berlin twenty-five years ago, the first ever held by Japanese abroad, and the Lumbini Chorus [3] rendered hymns in praise

[3] The Lumbini Chorus is a new organization whose aim is to produce new Buddhist hymns and sing them. It plans to publish new hymns every two months.

of Buddha. During the night Buddhist believers held parties in many places appropriate to the occasion. The following morning four aeroplanes flew over the capital raining millions of petals of lotus flowers made of gold and silver colored paper. The same day ceremonies in celebration of the birth of Buddha were held in Hibiya Park, at which not less than 10,000 Buddhist devotees were present. In the evening lectures on Buddhism were given at the Tokyo Imperial University Y.M.B.A. building and other places. The same day the Radio Office broadcasted a lecture by Mr. Motosada Zumoto on "The Significance of the Birth of Buddha" and another by Dr. Junjiro Takakusu on "Buddha's Birth and Art." For the benefit of foreign residents Mr. Zumoto specially spoke in English. In the evening Mr. Fukuo Kishibe, President of the Tokyo Girls' School, talked to children on the birth of Buddha and Dr. Masataro Sawayagi to the general public on the Lumbini festival. Selections of Buddhist music were then given, including a chorus by boys and girls of Buddhist schools. Several books and pamphlets in commemoration of the day were published and widely distributed.[4]

At the second anniversary of the recent earthquake Bishop Shuikyo Michishige of the Jodo sect, who is seventy-one years old, "boarded an aeroplane in Tokyo, early in the morning, and after visiting Yokohama and saying mass for the victims there, flew back to the capital and circling over the ground of the Military Clothing Depot (the place where upward of 30,000 people perished in the flames) dropped 300,000 pamphlets and paper lotus flowers."[5]

For the sake of more efficient extension of the work of Buddhism, some of the more alert leaders have felt the need of greater cooperation between the different sects. A dozen years ago, or more, a union preaching hall was built near the Asakusa temple in Tokyo—with but little influence, it must be said.[6] The sect leaders are quite as sectarian as the leaders of some of our American denominations were a few years ago. Unsystematic efforts at cooperation are made occasionally and rather more frequently than in former years. The adventurous old Jodo bishop who went up in the aeroplane to say mass and scatter lotuses, has shown his modern spirit in possibly more effective if less spectacular fashion by entering on a campaign of joint propaganda with the bishop of the Soto branch of Zen. The Jodo, Tendai, and Shingon sects in Tokyo have recently joined hands to found a "United

[4] *The Young East* for April, 1926, pp. 370-71. [5] *The Young East* for Sept., 1925.
[6] *Reischauer*, p. 313.

Buddhist University."[7] Perhaps the most hopeful effort in the direction of union and cooperation is to be found in the Kakushu Rengokai, or Interdenominational Association, organized in 1918.

Though far more loosely knit, it corresponds in certain respects to our Federal Council of the Churches of Christ. Representing all the leading sects except the irreconcilable Nichiren, it speaks for the Buddhist church and the Buddhist community, especially in regard to public affairs or matters involving relations with the imperial government. During the past few years, for instance, it has been working to secure the passage of the new universal-suffrage bill; and on one recent occasion it combated successfully the proposal to receive at court a permanent papal envoy.[8]

This Interdenominational Association aims at doing more than producing cooperation between the Buddhist sects of Japan. It wishes also to unite, in spirit and in effort, the whole Mahayana world. With this purpose in view, a few years ago, it invited the Buddhists of China, Korea, and Formosa to send delegates to a "Far Eastern Buddhist Conference." This conference was held in Tokyo on November 1, 2, and 3, 1925, twenty-one official delegates from China being present, three from Korea, and three from Formosa. A large number of people ("1300 persons including many ladies") attended the open meetings. Many papers were read and many resolutions passed, as is the custom with conferences East and West. The resolutions must not be taken as necessarily prophetic, but some of them will be worth reporting here, to show the sort of thing modern Buddhists are interested in and would like to do. I jot down a few, copying them from the columns of the *Young East*.

That Buddhists of Eastern Asia shall coöperate for worldwide propaganda, so that all the nations on earth may eventually bask in the boundless mercy of Buddha. To attain this object it is planned to publish Buddhist books and magazines in several Occidental languages, to send missionaries abroad and to establish a mission school either in Tokyo or Peking by coöperation of Japanese and Chinese Buddhists.

That in connection with general education, plans shall be framed and considered for fostering in the minds of children religious sentiment.

Education during holidays (Sunday Schools and Summer Schools)

[7] *The Young East* for Jan., 1926.

[8] Addison, "Religious Life in Japan," *Harvard Theol. Rev.*, XVIII, p. 338.

shall be made a regular annual function following the methods taken by early Buddhists of India.

That fundamental principles shall be fixed in Buddhist education.

That plans shall be framed and considered for spreading social educational work.

That kindergartens, primary schools, middle schools, girls' higher schools, colleges and universities shall be made complete.

That women's education shall be advanced to the level of men's.

That plans shall be framed and considered for completing Buddhist text-books.

That a Buddhist primary school shall be established in England.

That a federation of Buddhist social welfare works shall be brought about.

That endeavors shall be made to do away with all evil customs which are at variance with the respect of personality of women and children as well as to complete arrangements for their protection.

That works for giving free medical treatment and free medicines to the poor shall be extended.

That aggressive and vigorous movements for the suppression of drinking and opium-smoking shall be started.

The next meeting of the Far Eastern Buddhist Conference is to be held in Peking, at the call of the Buddhists of China. It is possible that this movement in conjunction with Tai Hsu's World Buddhist Association may succeed in uniting and increasing the activity of the Mahayana world in its efforts to deepen the spiritual life and elevate the intellectual comprehension of its followers. But the leaders of Japanese Buddhism are not satisfied with this aim. They would like to unite, if they could, Southern with Northern Buddhism. And some of them are eager to extend the blessings of Mahayana Buddhism to the whole world. Not infrequently one sees the statement in some Japanese publication that universal peace and the solution of the world's woes are to be looked for only through the spread of the Mahayana conception that all men share in the Buddha nature and are therefore brothers, and in the acceptance of the Bodhisattva ideal of self-devotion and loving service.[9]

[9] An organization called the Federation of Mahayana Brotherhood has recently been started with the purpose of aiding the movement toward universal peace through the spread of Mahayana ideals. The "manifesto" of its organizer begins thus: "Love of mankind as taught by Mahayana Buddhism does away with social discrimination and with international differences. Still more it makes us forget individual differences in respect to wealth, position, intellect, and character. When people once awake in the great spirit of Mahayana brotherhood all races, nations, and communities of the world will enjoy the glory and happiness of coexistence and mutual prosperity." Reported in *The Young East* for Dec., 1925.

The more active sects are not satisfied with pious wishes that Mahayana Buddhism might be carried to other lands: they have undertaken a certain amount of foreign missionary work. Much the larger portion of this is hardly on all fours with what Christianity knows as foreign missions; for the major portion of it is carried on among Japanese families who have left Japan, and nearly all the rest is in lands which are nominally Buddhist, at least in part. The mission field, thus understood, includes Korea and Formosa (both now parts of the Japanese Empire), Siberia, Saghalien, Manchuria, China, Singapore, a few of the South Sea Islands, Hawaii, the Philippines, and the western coast of North America. Statistics on Japanese missions are somewhat difficult to interpret, because of the contradictory statements which one finds, which may be due chiefly to a varying use of terms. Thus the most recent report by the Japanese government gives the following figures for China (including Manchuria), America (including our western states and British Columbia), Hawaii, and the South Seas (Sumatra, Singapore, the Philippines):

	No. of Priests	Chapels and Preaching Halls	Followers
China	45	22	45,608
America	36	136	7,357
Hawaii	44	41	64,750
South Seas	5	3	218

According to a pamphlet put out in 1920 by the Federation of the Buddhist Organizations for Children, there are 87 Japanese Buddhist "missionaries" in China (note the government statistics specified 45 "priests"), 77 in America, 86 in Hawaii, and in Korea and Formosa together 306. There is no real contradiction here, as only a portion of the missionaries are priests; but probably neither of the lists is absolutely exact. The West Hongwanji in 1927 announced that it had eighty missionaries in America, and desired to send two or three hundred.[10]

Five of the sects carry on this missionary activity, namely, Shin (including both the Hongwanji's and four of the small

[10] *The Young East* for April, 1926.

branches), Jodo, Nichiren, Zen (both Soto and Rinzai), and Shingon. By far the largest part of it is done by the two Hongwanji divisions of Shin, which taken together support 126 missionaries in Korea, and 74 in China.[11]

The need of Buddhist mission work in both Korea and China will, I trust, be plain to any reader of this book. Its aim is, of course, largely to look out for the unchurched Japanese who have emigrated to these lands; but an effort is also made toward propaganda among the native Koreans and Chinese. In the other mission lands the effort of the missionaries is confined almost exclusively to work among Japanese, and Japanese subjects.[12] In the United States and Hawaii a few converts have been made among Americans and Europeans and, according to an article in the *Young East*,[13] "some Europeans and Americans in Hawaii and California have erected at their own initiative Buddhist halls and hold regular weekly meetings. Three of such persons have become priests of Nishi Hongwanji missions, and ten others, including some ladies, preachers." On the whole, however, Japanese missionaries are too sensible to spend much of their time trying to convert Americans, and believers in the Yellow Peril and haters of the "heathen" need not be greatly terrified by Buddhist propaganda on American soil.[14]

The sort of work done by these Buddhist missionaries when at its best may be seen by an analysis of the activities of the Hawaiian mission. There are over forty Buddhist missionaries in the islands and these together hold some 660 preaching services a month; besides giving lectures, making visits, and distributing tracts. The principal temple in Honolulu has a membership of 2000, with 700 children in

[11] According to the pamphlet of the Federation of Buddhist Organizations for Children the Shingon sect sends out 68 missionaries, Jodo 158, Rinzai 5, Soto 153, West Hongwanji 245, East Hongwanji 125, other branches of Shin 12, Nichiren 73. This, it will be noted, makes a total of 839 missionaries.

[12] For example in Formosa where the West Hongwanji has a few missionaries, and where it is planning to send some young native Formosans whom it is educating for the purpose in Japan. In the Palao Islands, held by Japan as a mandate under the League of Nations, the East Hongwanji has a few missionaries, and is now introducing modern Sunday-school methods.

[13] For Dec., 1925.

[14] In 1924 there were in the United States and Canada "twenty-seven Buddhist churches with forty priests. The membership numbers over 8000, and the church property is valued at from $450,000 to $500,000 (*Buddhist Annual of Ceylon* for 1924).

the Sunday school. In the Hawaiian Islands as a whole there are thirty-three Buddhist Sunday schools with about 8350 children and 200 teachers. They have a Y.M.B.A., with 26 branches, doing the same general kind of work as the Tokyo Y.M.B.A.; and they have also a Y.W.B.A. with a few branches. They publish a religious monthly known as *Dobo* (or Brotherhood); and besides this Honolulu magazine there are five other Buddhist monthlies published in other parts of the Islands. They also print and distribute tracts in both Japanese and English. A Buddhist middle school is supported at Honolulu and another at Hilo, each with a six-year course and having at present 340 and 65 students respectively. These are for boys; but there are also two schools for girls, in the same cities. Twenty-three primary schools and a few kindergartens complete the educational activities of the mission. There is also a Buddhist Women's Society with nearly 50 branches and 3500 members; and a Propaganda Association whose object is to train missionaries in English for work among American-born Japanese.[15]

The work in Hawaii seems to be done with efficiency. Some years ago the younger generation of Japanese, born in the islands and speaking their parents' tongue but slightly, were found to be falling away from Buddhism because they could understand but little in the Buddhist temples and were attracted by the English preaching in Christian churches. To put a stop to this disadvantage an English Buddhist of scholarly distinction, who had already become a monk—the Reverend M. T. Kirby, Ph.D.,—was induced to come from California and preach, or lecture, every evening in one of the Buddhist temples. He attracted and kept large audiences right up to his recent departure for Japan. How his place will be taken in Honolulu I have not heard, but I have no doubt that modern methods and lectures in English will be continued. A recent writer in the *Young East*, who was born and had spent his whole life in Hawaii, has just given his impressions of his first visit to Japan: and his chief impression is that the Buddhist Sunday schools in Japan and the

[15] These figures I take from an article in the *Young East* for July, 1925, and from a pamphlet published by the Hongwanji Mission in Honolulu entitled *A Short History of the Hongwanji Buddhist Mission in Hawaii, 1897-1927.*

methods of making Buddhism appeal to the young are far inferior to those used by the partly Americanized Buddhists of the islands.[16]

From this summary of the work of the Hawaiian mission, it will be seen that a large part of the activity of aggressive Buddhism in the foreign field is devoted to education. The same thing is true of aggressive Buddhism at home. It will be recalled that the first school in Japan was founded by Kobo Daishi, in connection with his great Shingon temple in Kyoto. The example thus given was followed here and there in other temples, and in the thirteenth century the "Terakoya" system of "temple schools" was officially adopted and the education of the common people put into the hands of the Buddhist clergy. The system was something like the educational system of Burma. Boys from ten to fifteen went to the monasteries and were taught the elementary subjects by the monks. In 1873 these Terakoya schools were given up, having been replaced by government schools. After this event and until nearly the end of the century but little was done by Japanese Buddhism toward specifically religious education of a systematic sort for its young people; and except in those centers where Buddhist Sunday schools exist, the same condition still obtains. Even in a pious Buddhist home it is rare indeed that there is anything corresponding to that systematic Bible reading which used to be so common in Puritanical England and America—and which is becoming so uncommon today. Japanese children watch their parents worship at the home shrine, and are taken with them occasionally to the temple, and learn to imitate what they see. The parents show them how to bow before the Buddha and how to place their hands and how to repeat a few sacred formulae. As we have already noted, even skeptical parents usually teach their children to pray though they themselves have ceased to believe, in theory, that prayer is of any use. Children of zealous parents get a little more than this. I have already referred to one of my interpreters whose mother had been made a zealous Buddhist by Kwannon. When the boy was born she had been unable to nurse him and had besought the Goddess of Mercy to give her milk for her child.

[16] *The Young East* for March, 1926.

The gracious Kwannon had answered her prayer, and she became an ardent member of the Nichiren sect, and brought up her little son religiously. She instructed him in various moral precepts such as honoring his parents, and taught him the story of Nichiren's life—though nothing about Shaka—and trained him to pray to Nichiren. For three years—from the time he was fourteen till he was seventeen—she took him with her every morning to the temple to pray, and had him learn how to beat the temple drum in connection with the prayer: and she urged him never to forget that whenever he was in trouble he should pray. The temple priest taught him also a little about Shaka. This constituted the sum of his religious education until he was eighteen, when his uncle induced him to go to a Christian Sunday school. I expect that his Buddhist education was much more systematic than that of most Buddhist boys.

But there are thousands of Buddhist children today who are receiving a fairly systematic religious education. This is owing to the organization of Buddhist Sunday schools—obviously and confessedly imitated from the Christian Sunday schools. The new movement was begun about 1890 when several "religious associations" of children were instituted, and after a short time these were organized into Sunday schools after the Christian model, with the usual adaptations to the Japanese conditions which the Japanese know so well how to make. The older and the inactive sects of course are only now beginning to take up this new and Western form of religious activity. Hosso has as yet no Sunday schools at all. Kegon, Tendai, and Zen have very few. The Shingon and Nichiren sects have Sunday schools in the principal temples of the principal towns. Jodo has rather more and is rapidly increasing its numbers (so, at least, I was informed by President Mochitzuki of the Jodo University in Tokyo). It is the aim of Jodo to have a Sunday school in every one of its temples and to give thorough and systematic religious instruction. As yet it has not succeeded in carrying out its plan in the country temples, but most city temples are provided with schools, and evangelists are sent into the country districts to do something corresponding to Sunday-school work. At the Jodo headquarters temple—Chionin in Kyoto

—they have a large Sunday school which claims to have nearly a thousand members. It is, of course, the Shinshu in its two great branches, the West and East Hongwanji, that does the most work of this sort. Its Sunday schools are by far the most numerous[17] and are probably the most systematically conducted. Taking the Buddhist Sunday school as a whole, one may say that though it is not nearly so widespread as is the Christian Sunday school in America, it has made a fair start. More than half the 1163 Buddhist temples in the city of Tokyo have Sunday schools.[18] In 1920 there were in Japan as a whole 6928 Buddhist Sunday schools, with 18,750 teachers and 788,146 pupils.[19] The numbers have probably increased very considerably since then, though I have recent figures only for the West Hongwanji. In February, 1928, this church (if so I may call it) had two thousand five hundred Sunday schools and announced that each of its temples (nearly ten thousand in number) must establish a Sunday school during the year. A certain amount of system and cooperation is introduced into the many Sunday schools of the various sects by the Bukkyo Shonen Rengo Dan, or Confederation of Young Buddhists Association, a non-denominational Sunday-school union.

It is only the more modern-minded Buddhists that have gone into Sunday-school work, hence most of the Sunday schools are decidedly modern and efficient in their equipment. The Sunday school is never held in the temple proper, but has a hall of its own (which of course may or may not be within the temple enclosure). The assembly room for the school is sometimes supplemented by small classrooms and a library. In the main hall there is an altar and shrine (usually with an image of Amida, Shotoku Taishi, the founder of the sect, or some other member of the Buddhist cycle). For the actual work of the school an ample equipment is provided—an organ or piano, hymn books, blackboards, pictures, charts, children's books and magazines, games for recess time, and a

[17] In 1920 the West Hongwanji carried on, at home and in the mission fields, about 2000 Sunday schools, with 9595 teachers and 385,134 pupils, according to the official pamphlet on *The Buddhist Sunday School* put out in 1920 by the West Hongwanji. In February, 1928, it had twenty-five hundred Sunday schools. (*Young East*, Feb., 1928).

[18] Mrs. Nobaku Shiodome, "Activities of Buddhist Women in Tokyo," *Young East* I, 29.

[19] *The Mahayana Buddhists and Their Work for Children*, 1920.

school flag. Each pupil is given one or two sacred books or leaflets with colored pictures illustrating the story of some Buddhist saint, a hymn-book, a rosary, and a monthly attendance card. This, at least, is the rule in the West Hongwanji Sunday schools, and in the other sects there is no great difference. The pupils are usually divided into classes according to age. The superintendents and head teachers are largely drawn either from the priests or from young men studying for the priesthood. The women of the parish of course assist but the proportion of men teachers in the three Sunday schools I visited was very much larger than it is in American Sunday schools. Some of the sects have a special administrative officer, who has studied religious education in the United States, to supervise all their Sunday-school work.

A Buddhist Sunday school is a very pretty and interesting sight. In the Shingon Sunday school on Mount Koya which we visited there were about one hundred and eighty children present, varying from four to fourteen in age; and with their brilliantly colored kimonos, their black hair, their sparkling eyes, their sunny gladness, they made a very sweet picture. They all sat together in the center of the hall, and (of course) on the floor, with no teachers or other grown-ups among them. The teachers stood around the walls and the children were left to listen and sing, to whisper and play, or to get up and go out as they liked. No effort at discipline was made, but none seemed greatly needed. The Japanese Sunday school depends for order upon the good manners of the children and the interest the speaker can inspire in them.

The service opened with the unveiling of the shrine, before which all bowed, holding their little heads down, down for a few seconds. Then all the little heads bobbed up and all the shrill voices joined in repeating a prayer of veneration. This was followed by the singing of a hymn in unison which all the children knew and which they sang with a will. One of the boys then came forward and offered incense before the shrine and a girl followed him, offering flowers and tea. Then came the serious and difficult part of the morning—an address by the superintendent. The subject of this address was the meaning of the Five Vows which were to be read later on in the service, and while it may have been scholarly and elevated, it was not very interesting to the younger children. Some of them were slightly restless (no one blamed them) and about twenty of the littlest got up and toddled out of the building, at various intervals during the address—returning to their places when it was over. No one objected and it seemed quite the natural thing for them to do. When the address was over and the young wanderers had returned (of their own accord), a student in the seminary told them a story. He was a real story-teller, and though his tale lasted half an hour the children listened with close attention. Story-telling is a part of the Sunday-school work and the first prerequisite of the story is that it shall be interesting. In addition to that it may be instructive and edifying—the story, perhaps, of Kobo Daishi or some other saint; but the one prerequisite is interest. After the story was finished, all the children bowed toward the altar and the assistant superintendent read them the following introduction to the Vows:

> We must be honest and do good. But it is hard to do good things and to be honest. Those who do wrong and tell lies are hated by their emperor, teachers, fathers and mothers. Not only so. Even if we study hard in school, if we tell lies and do wrong we cannot grow up to be great men. Therefore we must ask the Buddha to protect our little hearts and we must try to do right. Kobo Daishi, who lies up there in the Holy of Holies of the temple, is a person of great mercy, and when we worship him with our hands clasped he tells us we are good children and makes us his children. The Bishop of Kongobuji [20] teaches us to become children of Kobo Daishi by making these vows. So let us make these vows to Kobo Daishi.

Hereupon the five following vows were read out in turn by the leader and repeated in unison by all the children:

> We will be diligent in our duties.
> We will worship the Buddha and the Kami.
> We will be loyal to the emperor and dutiful to our parents.
> We will have merciful hearts.
> We will do everything honestly.

After taking these vows to Kobo Daishi the children sang another hymn and a student assistant made a short address.

[20] Kongobuji is the headquarters temple of the principal branch of Shingon and the residence of its Bishop, the Lord Abbot of Koya-san.

Unfortunately it occurred to the superintendent at this point that it would be only courtesy to ask the American visitor to make some remarks, so the poor children had to listen to a fourth talk, which, however, had the interest of being entirely unintelligible until translated to them by my interpreter. I was sorry the children had to stand it, but it was of some interest to me that a Japanese Buddhist Sunday-school superintendent should invite a visiting American Christian to address his children. I have not often heard of a Buddhist being asked to address a Christian Sunday-school.

This school on Koya-san belonged, as I have said, to the Shingon sect. In the Shinshu Sunday schools I visited (both West and East Hongwanji) there was more real instruction and study: as will be shown by the following schedule, which I copy from the official pamphlet published by the Hongwanji:

Opening bell at 8:50 A.M.

1st Period, 9:00 A.M.—9:40 A.M.

1. Opening of the Shrine
2. Worshiping
3. Incense-burning (by a representative of the pupils)
4. Service
5. Hymn
6. Sermon
7. Worshiping
8. Closing of the Shrine

(10 minutes' recess)

2d Period, 9:50 A.M.—10:20 A.M.

1. Moral tales (for each class)
2. Teaching of Hymns (for each class)

(10 minutes' recess)

3d Period, 10:30 A.M.—11:30 A.M.

1. Story-telling (historical, nursery, etc.)
2. Exercise of Chanting
3. Exercise of Hymn-singing

4th Period, 11:30 A.M.

1. Opening of the Shrine
2. Hymn
3. Worshiping
4. Closing of the Shrine

Closing bell

Monthly Topics for Moral Discipline in 1919

April, The Spirit of Progress
May, Piety
June, Prudence
July, Temperance
August, Honoring of Ancestors
September, Order
October, Filial Piety
November, Loyalty
December, Public Service
January, The Grace of Buddha
February, Integrity
March, Gratitude

The order of exercises on the day of my visit was not quite the same as that exhibited above, but followed it fairly well. The children sang with even greater fervor than in the Sunday school on Koya-san. The Sutra which they chanted they knew by heart, and for the hymns each was provided with a hymn book, and their shrill little voices—especially those of the boys—rang out with a peal of irresistible joy. I have never heard such hymn singing by children before nor since. The sermon in this Sunday school seemed to be rather more interesting than the superintendent's address on Koya had been, and consisted in a discussion of the three mottoes of the school namely: "(1) Let us praise the name of the Most Merciful Buddha who is always with us and for us. (2) Let us worship and thank the Most Merciful Buddha who loves us. (3) Let us believe in the Most Merciful Buddha who watches our actions, and be good and kind." In the course of his address upon these mottoes, the preacher emphasized the need of loving one another, and he illustrated one of his points by telling a story about the boyhood of Andrew Carnegie, who was a good boy and worked hard. The whole sermon lasted but seven minutes.

As will be noted from the schedule given above, there are three recesses during the Sunday-school service, and inasmuch as the service lasts from 8:50 to 12 or later, they are needed. They are used for outdoor games. In the second period the children divide into classes, each class going to its own room; while in the third they reassemble in the large hall for moral stories—which are excellently told and illustrated with pictures drawn by the story-teller on the blackboard. Here, as at Koya, no attempt whatever is made at "discipline," and the speaker depends for the order and attention of the children upon the interest he can arouse in them.

Sunday schools are by no means the only educational institutions founded and directed by Buddhists. Like Christian missions, the Buddhist sects are supplementing the government educational system by schools of their own in which the usual subjects are taught but through which they hope to breathe a spirit of religion. These schools are of all grades. Altogether there are nearly a hundred primary schools under Buddhist direction and over a hundred secondary schools, twenty-six "middle schools" (high schools) for boys, and thirteen for girls, forty special schools (including three for the training of nuns),[21] ten colleges and four universities (or colleges of university rank),[22] beside which there are several theological seminaries as we should call them. Of these universities one belongs to the West and one to the East Hongwanji, one to the Soto branch of Zen, one to Nichiren. An additional university is being organized through the amalgamation of three of the lower colleges supported by Tendai, Zen, and Shingon. I should add that the Jodo College in Tokyo is in faculty and curriculum about on a par with the "universities," and that the Reverend Sonyu Otani, abbot of the West Hongwanji, is planning to found a University for Women in Tokyo.[23] Most of the Buddhist colleges are theological seminaries, that is, technical training schools for the priesthood, and every sect [24] has at least one of these. Some of the sects have also summer schools for young priests or for candidates for the priesthood who have had insufficient training. The universities and the better colleges are centers of real scholarship, with generous curricula, good libraries, learned teachers, and fairly adequate equipment. The West Hongwanji University at Kyoto (known as the Ryukoku Daigaku) is typical of the best and

[21] I can vouch for the inexactness of these figures: they are the result of an attempt to harmonize statistics from the pamphlet published by the Federation of Buddhist Organizations for Children, and from *The Young East* for Oct., 1925. I believe, however, that they are *approximately* trustworthy.

[22] These figures are given by *The Young East* for June, 1926.

[23] *The Young East* for April, 1926.

[24] I am not absolutely certain about two or three of the smallest sects.

the content of its curriculum may be of interest. Its regular course is of three years' duration and includes the following subjects: (1) Doctrine of Buddhism, (2) Doctrine of the Shin Sect, (3) History of Buddhism, (4) Outline of the Science of Religion and of the History of Religion, (5) History of European Philosophy, (6) Psychology, (7) Ethics, (8) Pedagogy, (9) Sociology, (10) History of Indian Philosophy and Literature, (11) History of Chinese Philosophy and Literature, (12) History of Japan and of the Japanese Classics, (13) History of European Literature.[26]

The less active sects give less elaborate training in their colleges than that offered in the Ryukoku Daigaku, and education is not necessary for admission to the priesthood. Still all of the larger and more active sects have excellent colleges for those who wish to train in them for the priesthood, and the opportunity is embraced by a steadily increasing number. It seems most probable that when the present generation of students reach middle age, the Buddhist clergy of Japan will be, on the whole, a well-educated and intelligent body of men.

Schools and colleges are not the only institutions made use of by Japanese Buddhism toward the advance of insight and the extension of religious knowledge and of general education. The Jodo sect supports forty-one public libraries, which in 1922 had a circulation of 30,843. Both Jodo and Shin have special courses for study in social service, and Jodo

[26] I take this from Rev. J. T. Addison's valuable paper on "Religious Life in Japan" (in the *Harvard Theolog. Review* for Oct., 1925), who adds the following interesting information concerning the extra-curricular activity of the students: "Despite the lack of college dormitories the social life of the students is active and highly organized. Those 'interests and activities' which in America vie so successfully with the interests of education and the activities of study, are familiar in Kyoto. Most of the numerous clubs (which meet in university buildings, tea-houses, hotels, or the students' own rooms) are organized as departments of a general Student Association. Each club has a Faculty adviser or guide. There are, for instance, four religious clubs which meet for the discussion of religious problems or of current topics. A Sunday-school department conducts Sunday-schools in different parts of Kyoto. Another department publishes two student magazines, one of a scientific, the other of a popular, nature. Several music clubs and an orchestra constitute the music department. And still other interests are represented by the poetry club, the debating club, and the art club. Yet more varied are the athletic activities—jiu-jitsu, wrestling, fencing, archery, riding, rowing, tennis, and baseball. In baseball and tennis especially the university teams compete with other colleges, including the Otani University of the Higashi Hongwanji sect. Sectarian rivalry thus takes a novel form, the spectacle of which would no doubt prove baffling to some of the mediaeval founders."

recently sent three students abroad to study social service methods in the West.[26] In 1925 the West Hongwanji initiated a compaign of political education in view of the coming election (in 1928) in which for the first time the suffrage was exercised by all male citizens over twenty-five years of age (including Buddhist monks, who had never had the franchise till then). With this purpose 300 priests and lecturers were ordered to different parts of the country, and conferences were held with government officials as to programs, etc. Two pamphlets of an educational nature were also prepared for distribution among the new voters, and twenty-eight priests (mostly from the West Hongwanji) ran for Parliament; one was elected.[27] There is a Buddhists' "Temperance Movement League, and various Women's Associations which do propaganda work against the use of intoxicants. The East Hongwanji publishes over a dozen religious periodicals, mostly monthlies; [28] and all the more active sects do much the same. Foremost in the religious periodical literature of Japanese Buddhism should be mentioned the *Eastern Buddhist*, a quarterly for scholarly articles on the philosophy and history of Buddhism, published in Kyoto; and the *Young East*, a monthly, founded in June, 1925, by a group of forward-looking Buddhists, who believe that the world, particularly the Western world, needs the message which Mahayana Buddhism has to give, and who hope to do their share in extending this message by interpreting Japan and especially Japanese Buddhism to Europe and America.

Mention should also be made of the *Mahayana*, the organ of the Koju Society, whose aim is the translation of Sanskrit Buddhist literature into Japanese, *Modern Buddhism*, a monthly magazine in Japanese, of a scholarly nature, and *The Study of Religions*, a monthly of the same sort published by the Interdenominational Association (Kakushu Rengokai) [29] and edited by Professor Anesaki. Buddhism has also two weekly journals and a daily paper. Altogether,

[26] Saneharu Ojima, "Some Aspects of Modern Japanese Buddhism," in the *Christian Movement in Japan* for 1923, p. 294.

[27] *The Young East* for Sept., 1925, Feb. and March, 1928.

[28] *Principal Teachings of the True Sect of Pure Land*, pp. 47-48.

[29] See page 576 above.

according to the *Young East* for April, 1926, "the number of periodicals relating to Buddhism in Japan totals 167." [30]

Perhaps the most important piece of work of a combined scholarly and religious nature which has been undertaken in the Far East for many a year is the new edition of the Chinese Tripitaka or Buddhist Canon.[31] It is to include 2633 books, 717 of which have never been included in any previous edition of the Tripitaka. Professors Takakusu and Watanabe, both of them scholars of the first rank, are the editors, and the work as planned will be complete in fifty-five large volumes. Forty of these have already been published, and the editors expect to complete the work by November, 1928. The editors have collated their material with the three great previous editions, and are adding new material derived from the discoveries of Aurel Stein in the caves of Tun Huang. This immense edition of the Tripitaka is, of course, for scholars only. A work of a more popular nature has been carried out by some of the Buddhists of Nagoya who have written and published a concise exposition of Buddhism in modern Japanese. "Copies of this book have been distributed among the elementary, middle, and girls' higher schools at Nagoya, and in the districts of Aichi Prefecture. Other prefectures will follow suit and shortly present the book to schools of elementary and secondary grades in them." [32]

Some years ago, according to Mr. Reischauer, the leading sects began

> circulating what might be called Sectarian Bibles; namely volumes bound in convenient form which contain the chief scriptures of the sect with standard commentaries on the same. One of these published first in 1911 passed through forty-five reprints in three years. Biographies of Buddhist saints, catechisms, expositions of Buddhist philosophies, essays and sermons on various moral and religious topics are appearing in greater number from year to year.[33]

[30] Classified according to the different sects to which they belong they are as follows:

Shin Sect	71	Soto Sect	10
Shingon Sect	13	Rinzai Sect	10
Jodo Sect	12	Tendai Sect	3
Nichiren Sect	12	Others	36

[31] It is to be known as the Taisho edition.

[32] *The Young East* for Oct., 1925.

[33] *Studies in Japanese Buddhism*, pp. 311-12.

A most elaborate publication of this sort is now being planned, and work on it begun: namely, an edition of all the important Buddhist books and writings that have appeared since the introduction of Buddhism into Japan. The edition will consist of ten large volumes.[34]

Several of the movements and institutions referred to in this chapter, as the reader must have noticed, should be classed not merely under the headings of propaganda or education but also as philanthropic or humanitarian undertakings. One of the principal characteristics of the Buddhist revival in Japan has, in fact, been a renewal of these works of charity and mercy. I say a renewal, for philanthropic activity, in at least spasmodic fashion, characterized Japanese Buddhism from the days of Prince Shotoku until the restoration. In Chapter XXIII reference was made to the charitable institutions which the Prince founded, and we saw that his noble example was followed by many monks and many Buddhist rulers. In the Nara period, the famous monk Gyogi founded orphanages, dispensaries, and homes for the aged, and Ganjin, who introduced the Ritsu or Vinaya sect from China, was distinguished as a physician and is known as the father of medical science in Japan. During these early days the distribution of medicine among the people seems to have been one of the functions of the Buddhist clergy, as well as the distribution of food in time of famine. They seem to have been particularly busy with famine relief during the twelfth and thirteenth centuries, and they also founded homes for beggars and homes for the sick, giving help of various sorts especially to the lepers. As we have seen, many Buddhist activities slowed down during the deadly last years of the Tokugawa régime, and at the restoration a number of the philanthropic undertakings which had been in charge of the Buddhist clergy were taken over by the imperial government. There followed a short period of relative inactivity: but with the arrival of the Christian missionaries and the initiation by them of various charitable movements, the Buddhist leaders were stung into activity once more, and since then the larger sects have sought to emulate the example of the new religion.

[34] *The Young East* for Oct., 1925.

If we compare the number of Japanese Buddhists with the number of Japanese Christians, and on this basis compare the philanthropic work carried on in the land by the two religions, it will be seen that Buddhism is very far in the rear of its rival. Still something of a substantial sort is being done by Buddhism, and when one compares it with conditions of a quarter century ago the contrast is notable, and the promise for the future correspondingly bright. I shall not trouble the reader with a detailed and minute account, but shall simply copy out here a few representative statistics for the year 1919 (I can find no inclusive figures of a later date) given in a government report on the charitable organizations supported and controlled by Buddhism.

Kinds of Institution	No.	No. of the Rescued	Annual Expenses	Property Value
Institutions for the Relief of the Destitute	24	1,354	Yen, 58,232	Yen, 113,518
Homes for the Aged	11	325	56,659	78,403
Institutions for the Relief of Sickness	16	273,485	82,138	183,737
Homes for Children	70	2,843	328,335	876,642
Reformatory Schools	21	528	103,985	....
Free Elementary Schools	12	2,185	27,109	75,228
Schools for Blind or Deaf and Dumb	7	189	18,826	57,110
Infant Day Nurseries	18	865	24,334	93,725
Employment Offices	9	7,385	5,017	42,674
Lodging Houses for Laborers	8	79,963	20,767	....
Institutions for the Care of Ex-convicts	462	Direct 3,218; Indirect 28,529	185,325	323,565
Miscellaneous Charities	33	....	79,256	47,533
Totals	701	Over 400,000	989,983	1,892,135

I might add that of these 701 organizations, eight are supported by Tendai, fifteen by Shingon, forty-five by Jodo, forty-seven by Zen, one hundred and four by Shin, twenty-four by Nichiren, forty by the other sects together, three hundred and sixty-seven by the United Buddhists Organization (three hundred and forty-five of these were organizations for the care of ex-convicts), and fifty-one by non-sectarian Buddhists.[35]

Since the earthquake Buddhist charity has found new

[35] I take these figures concerning the sects from the pamphlet on *The Mahayana Buddhists and Their Work for Children.*

demands upon its care and has, like Christian charity, responded gladly. A large part of the temple land of the Zo-jo-ji—the chief Jodo temple of Tokyo—was for a year and more after the catastrophe covered with temporary huts for the lodging of earthquake sufferers, and several other temples in and near Tokyo and Yokohama were similarly helpful. The West Hongwanji is undertaking the construction of several halls in these two cities for various social welfare works, at an estimated cost of 1,660,000 yen. For the wise administration of their charity funds—not only for earthquake relief but for its philanthropic undertakings in general—several of the sects, including both the Hongwanjis, the Jodo, Soto, and Nichiren, have established social service departments, with trained workers at their heads.

The educational and philanthropic movement within Japanese Buddhism, the activities of which we have been studying in this chapter, owes much of its force to the stimulus and example of Christianity. It is by no means wholly due to Christian influence, for, as we have seen, Buddhism was active in both these directions long before Christianity was heard of in Japan. Japanese Buddhism, indeed, has always been rather notably active, and has been characterized by efforts to mix in politics, spread Chinese culture, and educate children, quite as much as by any tendency to withdraw from the world. The new developments in helpful activity of a modern sort have their roots in the earliest traditions of Japanese Buddhism. Indeed their roots go much deeper than that. They reach back to the teaching and example of the Founder himself. Buddhism has always been a religion of mercy and generosity: and in a sense its modern activities are a natural evolution from the example of the Buddha and from the Bodhisattva ideal of the Mahayana, made efficient in their application through methods borrowed from the West. What we are witnessing in Japan is the spirit of Gotama coming to its own.

But while human helpfulness is natural to Buddhism, it is still true that the activity of Japanese Buddhism and its aim to make this world a better place to live in, rather than to get away from it into some solitary monastery or some unknowable Nirvana, is in considerable contrast to what one finds in China and what one reads about in many works on Pali Buddhism. This is in part the explanation of the rather surprising attitude toward the new movement adopted by many Western critics and not a few missionaries. When in modern Buddhist books or papers they read that the Buddhist aim is in part to make this a better and a happier world, they shake their heads and say with sad disapproval, Not Buddhism! The interest which a certain type of Christian missionary seems to feel in the orthodoxy of his Buddhist neighbors is almost touching. He stamps as non-Buddhistic whatever was not once delivered unto the bonzes by the Arahants, and insists strenuously upon the formula *quod semper, quod ubique, quod ab omnibus.* This, as I have intimated, is not wholly due to the desire to keep all the human merit for his own religion; but also to the notion which so many of us share that Buddhism must necessarily be defined by what we read in the works of Rhys Davids about the original teachings of Gotama. The truth is, of course, that those teachings with the practice that went with them were Buddhism, that the religion of Siam and Burma is Buddhism, that the religion of Japan is Buddhism, and that if we want to know what Buddhism is we must not dogmatize about it but study the religion of Buddhist countries and see. The question how, with their many divergencies, these varied forms of religion can all be Buddhism, how Buddhism or any other religion or any other living thing can change, we shall have occasion to consider in a later chapter.

CHAPTER XXIX

BUDDHIST THOUGHT IN JAPAN—THE EARLIER SECTS

PERHAPS the most fundamental characteristic of Buddhist thought in Japan is its liberality and tolerance. More than once in this book I have had occasion to point out these traits of Buddhism in general. To a greater or less extent they are found in nearly all Japanese Buddhists. Some of the sects, to be sure, are less liberal than others. Members of the Nichiren sect in particular are sometimes relatively intolerant, and assert that salvation in the fullest and highest sense is possible only to followers of Nichiren. The leading abbot of the sect, however, assured me that in his own opinion not only members of other Buddhist sects but also all good and sincerely religious men—Christians as well as Buddhists—would be saved. On this matter we must remember that for Buddhism there is no such absolute division between the sheep and the goats as one finds in Christian teaching. In Buddhist belief you need not necessarily in the next life go *either* to heaven *or* to hell. There are many mansions not only in heaven but in other parts of the universe. Thus some members of Shinshu believe that while only followers of the Pure Land sects, or at most only Buddhists, can go to the Paradise of Amida, good men of other religions will go to some of the other heavens, or will have a desirable rebirth here. The more liberal members of the Shin sect teach that highly earnest and devout Christians will be received by Amida into his Paradise quite as readily as Shinshu believers, because in reality they *are* Shinshu believers without knowing it. One of the most prominent Shinshu abbots of Tokyo—a most kindly and delightful old gentleman—told me that this was his own belief. "But," he added, with just the suggestion of a twinkle in his eye, "I have never yet met such a Christian—not even among my foreign visitors."

The sects that make less of faith and more of philosophy

are naturally rather more liberal than the Nichiren and Pure Land sects. Thus the Lord Abbot and Bishop of Koya-san told me that Shingon teaches the present and actual salvation of all just in the measure in which they apprehend the truth. In this he was expressing not only Shingon doctrine but that also of Tendai, Kegon, and (in a sense) of Zen. "The one truth," he said, "appears in all religions. Whoever reaches the ideal and perfect state in his own religion will reach the same level as the highest in any other religion. Different religions have different methods of attaining the highest state. In the phenomenal world we distinguish between religions. But if each religion developed to the full its highest potentiality, they would all reach an identity. Up to that point our states will be different. But the final fate for all men will be the same." By that fate, he meant, of course, identity with the Real. The thought is not new nor does it owe its source to modern or Western conceptions. In the tenth century a Buddhist poet sang:

> Many the paths that twist and wind
> Through stream-cleft vale or forest maze;
> But those who reach the hill-top find
> (Though they have climbed by different ways)
> On the wide summit, clear and kind,
> Just the same moonlight softly plays,
> Shining on all with equal rays! [1]

This liberal attitude toward other religions, as we have seen, has been made easier for Buddhism by its generous interpretation of symbolism, by its occasional disregard of the niceties of logic, and by its doctrine of the different levels of truth and degrees of reality. It was in this way, as we have seen, that Buddhism was able to adopt, at one time or another, nearly all the Kami of Shinto and thus to become the dominant religion of the land. It is especially by the doctrine of *Hoben,* or the accommodation of truth to the minds of the hearers, that Buddhism was able to absorb so much of Shinto with a good conscience,[2] and that each of the sects is

[1] *The Master Singers of Japan,* Walsh's trans., p. 83.

[2] The Catechism of the Shin sect quotes the great Shin teacher Rennyo as follows: "The so-called gods (Kami) are but transformations of the Buddhas and Bosatsus. But since it is difficult for men of this world to approach the Buddhas and Bosatsus, deity is revealed by accommodation as gods. Thus connection with mankind is made and man is brought finally into Buddhism" (*Tr. A. S. J.*, XXXVIII, 386).

able to recognize that the teachings of all the others—and most of the teachings of Christianity, for that matter—are all true. Three realms are to be recognized and distinguished: the realm of delusion, the realm of accommodated or relative truth, and the realm of absolute truth.[3] Many seemingly contradictory views may be reconciled and accepted by placing them in the second of these realms. "The shield is convex." "The shield is concave." Both these assertions are true—true in the relative sense—spite of their seeming incompatibility. From the higher point of view the shield in one sense is both, in one sense neither.

The nature of both the material world and the self, as viewed by Buddhist thought, must be considered in the light of this distinction if they are to be understood. Neither the self nor the physical world is sheer illusion, but neither is absolute reality. All Buddhist sects in Japan in final theory are idealistic and none explicitly deny the Anatta doctrine, while most of them explicitly affirm it; yet all leave room to speak *as if* the self and the world were real. There is a reality in each, but the reality is not what it seems. What seems to be the self is really (for all but the popular party of the Amida sects) a temporary collection of qualities, themselves as transitory as the collection. Even so non-technical and non-sectarian a periodical as the *Young East* recently printed a paragraph on this subject, ending thus:

> "Anatta signifies unreal, without a substance, without what is generally called soul, I, ego, self, thing-in-itself. Anatta is the fundamental basis of the Buddhist philosophy."[4]

According to Professor Suzuki:

> The refusal of modern psychology to have soul mean anything more than the sum-total of all mental experiences, such as sensations, ideas, feelings, decisions, etc., is precisely a rehearsal of the Buddhist doctrine of non-atman. It does not deny that there is a unity of consciousness, for to deny this is to doubt our everyday experiences, but it refuses to assert that this unity is absolute, unconditioned, and independent. Everything in this phenomenal phase of existence is a combination of certain causes and conditions brought together according to the principle of karma; and

[3] Cf. pp. 241 above. See also Reischauer, *op. cit.*, pp. 184-88; and Knox, *The Development of Religion in Japan* (N. Y., Putnam, 1907), pp. 119-21.

[4] I, 186, for Nov., 1925.

everything that is compound is finite and subject to dissolution and therefore always limited by something else. To maintain the existence of a soul-substance which is supposed to lie hidden behind the phenomena of consciousness is not only misleading, but harmful and productive of some morally dangerous conclusions.[5]

As the last sentence in the passage just quoted indicates, Buddhism rejects the soul theory for both a metaphysical and an ethical reason. The concept is part and parcel of the whole *substance* view of realism, which Buddhist idealism discards; and it involves, moreover, difficulties of both an *a priori* and an empirical nature which in Buddhist opinion are insuperable. No Western student of objective idealism or of psychology needs to be told what these are. But the ethical reasons for the rejection of the soul theory probably appeal to most Buddhist thinkers even more forcibly than do the metaphysical ones. The Founder seems to have taught that it was the thought of self and the belief in it which more than any other one thing has brought sin into the world and all our woe; and it seems to the thinkers of the Mahayana to be incompatible with that unity of all beings which is the basis of every virtue.

Liberality, the belief in degrees of truth and reality, an idealistic interpretation of the external world, and the Anatta doctrine are characteristics of all the Buddhist sects of Japan (with the possible exception of the Amida sects). Nor are these by any means the only things they hold in common. It will, however, save time and probably make for clearness if I take up the more important sects singly and outline briefly their several positions. It is natural to begin with the Hosso sect, both because of its antiquity and also because all the other sects unite in distinguishing it from the rest of Japanese Buddhism as being not "complete" but only "provisional" Mahayana. As I have dealt in previous chapters at some length with the Indian and Chinese forms of this school of thought,[6] it need not here detain us long. I should remind the reader that it was this school that added a seventh and an eighth plane or element to the Indian analysis of mind, the eighth being the Alaya-vijnana, or repository consciousness, a kind of subconscious reservoir, from which the images

[5] *Outlines of Mahayana Buddhism*, p. 41. [6] See pages 242-248, 408-412.

arise that *are* the physical world. The followers of this school in Japan as in China seem to be divided on the question of monism and pluralism. At any rate, Dr. Armstrong informs me that Japanese books expounding the Hosso philosophy teach an ultimate and absolute Reality which they call Nirvana or Shinnyo, and from this they say the Alaya-vijnana (or Alayashiki) is derived. The Hosso monks with whom I have talked, on the other hand, say nothing of an ultimate, monistic Reality, take Nirvana (Shinnyo) to mean merely the state of the individual when enlightened, and insist that each individual has his own Alayashiki (Alaya-vijnana) and that back of this philosophy cannot go. A learned Kegon monk did something to clear up the matter for me by insisting that while Hosso thinkers when pressed have to admit an Ultimate, or (what amounts to the same thing) to recognize the metaphysical reality of Nirvana (Shinnyo) as a trans-individual reality, they suggest no logical relation between it and the Alayashiki and never refer to it nor make use of it in their philosophy.

The two great Hosso temples are Horyuji and Kofuku-ji (at Nara), and I went to both in search of light. The Horyuji abbot was out when I called, but one of his followers listened to my questions and did his best to answer them. The seventh kind of consciousness, the Manashiki, he told me, thinks everything in a bad way and is responsible for the illusion of selfhood, being misled by desire. The Alayashiki, the eighth level or form of mind, though not itself a form of explicit consciousness, is the fountain of all phenomena, the storehouse which contains the seeds of all this phantasmagorial world. Each man has his own Alayashiki which is separate from that of others and which produces for him his own world. Space and time are merely its productions and must be interpreted idealistically. The Buddha is still existent and is now in the highest heaven, though his spirit is everywhere; for heaven is not a place but a state of mind. Good men will go at death to heaven and the bad to hell; and this of course means that their Alayashiki will produce for them the kind of world which, according to the law of Karma, they deserve. For each man's Alayashiki, in creating the external world for him, acts in strict conformity to Karma. Each man thus has his own world; yet this world which every man makes is common to all. But, I asked, how is this to be explained; how do we happen to make our worlds alike? He replied that there was a very learned monk, the Reverend Saikyo, in Kofukuji at Nara, and I had better go and ask him.

As my kind Horyuji monk was evidently getting beyond his depth and was plainly distressed by my persistent questioning, I took his advice, and my interpreter and I mounted our rickshaws, caught the train for Nara, and were rushed with other rickshaws to a modest house within the large enclosure of the ancient and famous monastery of Kofukuji (most of whose buildings have long been destroyed) and inquired for the Reverend Saikyo. The learned monk welcomed us in grave but kindly manner and invited us to sit on the floor in front of him—and partake of the usual cheering cup that certainly could never inebriate. He was a dark little man of perhaps forty-five or fifty years, dressed wholly in black and very simply, with long eyelashes and meditative expression. He had an air of decision and finality about him and spoke with self-confidence and in the long, clear tones of one accustomed to lecturing, repeating his formulas with a relish and at times rolling them under his tongue. After my interpreter had made his usual little introductory speech, filled with Japanese courtesy, and we had bowed to each other several times afresh, I recounted to him, while sipping the honorable tea, the end of our conversation at Horyuji, and put to him the question which the Horyuji monk had been unable to answer: why, though each of us makes his own world, we all make it alike and have a common world to live in. He replied:

Hosso recognizes that the noumenal world cannot be the source of the phenomenal world (this, apparently, in contrast to the teaching of Tendai and Kegon). Phenomena can come only from phenomena. Hosso, therefore, recognizes the relations between things in this world. It does not recognize nor bother with any hypothetical Reality or Substance beyond this world that we know, as the other sects do. I pointed out that all this was interesting and enlightening, but it did not answer just the question I had asked, about our common world. His answer this time was to the point. Each of us, he said, makes his own world; and these worlds which we make *may* in part be the same and they may not. Often they are not the same and never are they completely the same. What we call the same moon may be to one man joyful, to another sad. The world of each depends for its nature on the spirit of each. It will be a good world or a bad world according to the man's character and his past conduct.[7] We are all making our own worlds by ourselves and the world we experience now is the result of our past deeds and our merit or Karma. In each man the ultimate source of the world is the Alayashiki (Alaya-vijnana). Each of us has his own and this is not identical with that of any one else. It does not merge in any cosmic Alayashiki or Butatathata. The Hosso is thus essentially individualistic and pluralistic.[8]

This extreme pluralism and individualism is shared by none of the other Japanese sects. In fact, spite of many superficial contrasts, the other sects are, from the philosophical point of view, closely allied and when put in their ultimate terms they all defend a nearly identical form of spiritual monism. The general trend of the Mahayana would be enough to explain much of this similarity, but some of it must be attributed to the historical fact that the Tendai is, in a sense, the philosophic mother of all these sects,[9] save Kegon and Shingon;[10] and further that Kegon thought is closely related to that of Tendai, and that Shingon has adopted most of its philosophy from Kegon. I shall, therefore, give a rather detailed account of the Kegon-Tendai philosophy and thereby shall be enabled to deal with the theoretical teachings of the other sects much more briefly. For the Kegon-Tendai point of view is the very keel of Japanese Buddhism.

It is the theory of both these schools (which are so nearly

[7] Whatever one may think of this solution for the difficulty which subjectivism makes for itself, surely it is about as good as that which Gentile and his school propose for the same predicament.

[8] Cf. similar statements by my Chinese friends who belonged to this same school, pp. 408, 409, 411, 412.

[9] It will be recalled that the founders of all the more important sects subsequent to Shingon studied Buddhist philosophy on Hiei-san.

[10] I should add that in some respects (as we shall see) Zen is closer to Kegon than to Tendai.

one) that Sakyamuni expounded his doctrine in five stages, or in five grades of teaching: and Tendai pictures these five formulations of his truth as having been given out at five different periods of his life. In the first period, lasting only a few weeks after his enlightenment, he taught the philosophic truth in all its depth, as found in the Avatamsaka Sutra—the great scripture of the Kegon sect. But he soon discovered that only a few could comprehend this great doctrine; and so, following the pedagogical method of all the Buddhas, viz., milk for babes and meat for strong men, he taught in the second period merely the simple truths of the Hinayana. These were all true. The Mahayana never asserts that the Hinayana doctrines are false. They are not false, but they are very incomplete. In the third and fourth periods,[11] therefore, Sakyamuni led his listeners on to larger visions, and finally in the fifth period he gave the full truth of the Saddharma Pundarika.[12] This, in Tendai opinion, differs from the great Kegon Sutra, revealed during the first period, not in philosophical meaning (except for details), but in being inclusive of all the other teachings. Tendai means to deny nothing, but to find a place within itself for the truths of all other Buddhist schools, even the Hinayana.

As the Kegon sect is a little older than the Tendai (both in China and Japan), I shall treat of its philosophy first—and rather briefly, for its importance in Japanese thought is less than that of Tendai. The world, it teaches, may be viewed in four different ways and in fact is so viewed by different schools of Buddhist thought, each of the four having some degree of truth, but only the fourth (which is that of Kegon) being fully true. Some people think of the world as made up of separate things. This first way of viewing reality is, of course, very illusory. A second way is the extreme denial of separate and phenomenal things. This view centers upon the One Being back of phenomena which is Reason itself. "All things returning into Reality are lost."

[11] In these periods Chih K'ai (the Chinese Founder of Tendai) placed a number of the earlier Mahayana Sutras, which had been the chief scripture of the Sunyata, Yogacara, and other early Mahayana schools of thought.

[12] For a more detailed account of these five stages see McGovern's *Introduction to Mahayana Buddhism*, pp. 123-29; Armstrong, *The Doctrine of the Tendai Sect; Eastern Buddhist*, III, 32-34; Reischauer, *op. cit.*, pp. 172-74.

"Individual distinctions are lost and everything disappears, having no place to rest"—thus wrote the philosopher Tojun, expressing this second point of view. This is less untrue than the naïve acceptance of separateness and of the phenomenal, but it needs supplementation. A third and truer view accepts Reason, but not abstract Reason: it teaches Reason in relation to things. The reality of things is no longer denied but everything is looked at from the viewpoint of its source. The water thus is seen to be the wave, and the wave the water, and the one is found in the many. The final truth, which is the fourth world view, the view of Kegon, is a continuation and completion of this third position. Everything is here seen to blend with Absolute Reality. To know one thing truly is to know all—to understand the flower in the crannied wall is to know what God and man is. Things mutually enter into each other like two lights reflected in parallel mirrors. Two things may be different in one sense, yet really the same, as the water and the wave. All things are one, and the one is all. For all things exist in mutual harmony at one and the same time. In the atom all things are at work performing one function, just as one taste of the ocean is revealed in one drop of water. The laws of all things are exhibited in each thing. One sees the Absolute Reality by looking at each detail with understanding eyes.

I am indebted for this exposition of Kegon chiefly to conversations with Dr. Armstrong of Tokyo, and to his book on the sects of Japan, which, though still in manuscript form, he most kindly permitted me to read. Professor Suzuki has presented much the same interpretation in the following brief summary:

> The Kegon conception of the world is not pantheism; for what it teaches is that each object is not only itself but every other object, and that all things are mutually conditioning to such an extent that the withdrawal of one of them means the disturbance of the whole system, which is to say, the world grows imperfect to that extent. When this theory is pushed to its logical conclusion the complete network of interrelationships of all things rests on the point of a single hair. As this pen moves along the lines of this ruled paper, the triple chiliocosm moves with it, and as I think out my thought, in it are reflected all the Buddhas and Bodhisattvas of the past, present, and future, even as the moon and stars and all other heavenly bodies are mirrored in the ocean, eternally serene

and undisturbd. The world of Kegon is thus known as the world of interpenetration, which is regarded as one step further than the idea of the oneness of the phenomenal and the noumenal world—this latter being the doctrine of "imperfect" Mahayana Buddhism.[13]

As I have already said, the chief scripture of Kegon is the Avatamsaka Sutra. The point of view which it expresses is very like that of the Lotus (the chief scripture of Tendai) with, however, more repeated emphasis upon the telescoping of all time into one moment, and upon the interpenetration of all things in each other.

All lands are interpenetrating in the Buddha-land
And they are countless in number,—a phenomenon beyond our understanding;
There is nothing that does not fill up every quarter of the universe,
And things are inexhaustible and unmeasurable and move with perfect spontaneity.
All the Buddha-lands are embraced in one Buddha-land,
And each one of the Buddha-lands embraces all the others in itself;
But the land is neither extended nor compressed:
One land fills up all the ten quarters of the universe,
And in turn the universe with all its contents is embraced in one land,
And yet the world as it is suffers no damage.[14]

It is difficult to get a great deal of insight into the Kegon philosophy from the monks; for Kegon monks are few and (like other monks) not always thorough masters of the doctrine they profess. None the less I mean to set down here some of the things I got from Kegon monks and professors because, as I have more than once stated, my aim in studying Buddhism has been largely to find out what actual living men believe, and not merely what is said in learned books written by men long since dead. The center and headquarters of the Kegon sect is in the ancient Todai-ji monastery in Nara. Unluckily for me, on the day of my visit there, the abbot was ill and could not see me; so I had to content myself with some of the lesser lights. The first monk with whom I conversed was a man of perhaps thirty-five, with a kindly face, large dark eyes, and a direct and friendly way of looking at you. Much of the information he gave me

[13] *The Eastern Buddhist*, I, 235.

[14] From the Avatamsaka Sutra, epitomized and translated by Professors Yamabe, Akanuma, and Suzuki, in the *Eastern Buddhist*, I, 237.

was in substantial agreement with the more exact and learned account I had gleaned from Dr. Armstrong and the Avatamsaka Sutra. He also added that the ultimate aim held out by Kegon is the attainment of Shinnyo, or Nirvana, and that this is a state of mind. It is not to be described but may be achieved and experienced by giving up our desires and denying ourselves. To do this is to become Buddha. We must distinguish, however, between the Shinnyo that may be gained in this life and the complete form of it which the enlightened enter into at death. These were both seen in the case of Shaka. At death Shaka became Shinnyo and is therefore eternal and timeless. One who fully enters Shinnyo becomes also eternal and identical with Shaka and with all the Buddhas. Individuality is thus sloughed off at the death of the enlightened.

Is Shinnyo, then, I asked, to be identified with the Ultimate and Absolute Reality? The honest and kindly monk replied that he could not give me a clear answer to that question, for he was still studying the doctrine; but that there was a very learned monk from Kyoto visiting another temple in Nara that very day, and that he would give me a letter to him. So, armed with the letter, my interpreter and I dashed off in our rickshaws, through the winding lanes of ancient Nara to find out the answer to my tremendous question. But alas, the learned monk, when we reached the temple where he was visiting, was too busy to see us. So back we came, carrying our question with us to Todai-ji once more. This time our friend was reinforced by a colleague who had gone further in Kegon philosophy than he, and was in some ways more alert in mind. He answered my question at once and with confidence: Shinnyo is the Absolute Reality. It is also, already and always (whether we realize it or not) the real being of each of us. The aim of Kegon is thus to make explicit that which is already and eternally implicit.

The statement that Shinnyo is the real being of each of us, I interposed, suggests a relation between it and the Alaya-shiki of the Hosso. What is this relation? The monk replied that there was no relation between them. But at this point a third monk, who had been listening to the discussion, broke in and corrected his colleague. This monk was much more scholarly in appearance than the others. He wore a white kimono with black lace and embroidery over it, had large round spectacles, and looked like a true scholastic. There is no *logical* relation, he said, between Shinnyo and the Alayashiki, but the latter comes from the former—as, in one sense, all things do. Shinnyo is not only the Absolute Reality: it is the phenomenal world as well, for the phenomenal and the Absolute are one. In this Kegon differs from Tendai.

Here, in fact, we have the one difference of any importance between these two great schools of Japanese thought. It is in part a matter of emphasis, Tendai stressing unity and the Absolute, Kegon multiplicity and the phenomenal. My third monk at Todai-ji carried the contrast to what was perhaps an extreme, so as to make Kegon seem at times even realistic. Every particle of matter, he said, partakes of and represents the nature of all things, is at the same time phenomenal and absolute. It would continue to exist if you and I should cease. Trees have the Buddha nature and are therefore just as real as we. Kegon, he said, does not make use of the concept of consciousness and so the question of Berkeleyan idealism does not arise.

Two of the professors in the Koya-san university put the difference between Kegon and Tendai in much the same way. Kegon, I was told, recognizes identity as Tendai does but also recognizes and stresses difference. Tendai thought reaches the Absolute and rests there: Kegon recognizes it but insists upon reverting to this world with its multiplicity and activity. Real activity is something which Tendai fails to find a proper place for. Moreover, Kegon insists that back of both identity and diversity, back of both passivity and activity, there is a third aspect of Reality whose existence we must recognize but about which we can make no predication. This unknowable aspect of the Real is still identical with the world of difference and with the world of identity, and is needed to explain the two. Thus, in brief, Tendai asserts only one thing, namely identity: Kegon asserts three things: identity, difference, and an Unknowable back of both. But the three are one.

It is hardly safe—as a professor of Tendai philosophy once said to me when I read from my notes on this conversation with the professor of Kegon—it is hardly safe to take Western terms such as monism and pluralism and apply them to Tendai and Kegon. In all Buddhist thought, he said, subject and object are unified in one, and no attempt is made to distinguish them sharply. (This would naturally follow from the Anatta doctrine.) Nor is it correct, he insisted, to assert that Tendai fails to recognize multiplicity or to see that each thing is represented in all, and all in each. Still it is true that Tendai stresses unity and identity, while Kegon stresses multiplicity and diversity. The difference (I might suggest) between the two forms of thought seems not unlike that which one finds within English Hegelianism, between the schools of Bradley and of Bosanquet.[15] I think, in fact, that if the Kegon philosophy could be translated into Western terms without warping it too violently, it would prove, in its ultimate assertions, to be rather strikingly like the doctrine taught in Bosanquet's *Principle of Individuality and Value*.[16]

The philosophical views of the Shingon sect are taken over very largely from Kegon. Some details, however, have been added, and at times a different emphasis is given; hence a few words should be said concerning Shingon thought as distinct from Kegon. The relation between the two schools is so close that what is to be said of Shingon should plainly be set down here, before going on to the great Tendai philosophy, in spite of the fact that chronologically Tendai is a little earlier (at least in Japan) than Shingon.

We found the thinkers of the Kegon school putting more emphasis than most Mahayana philosophers upon the phenomenal world and its activities. This tendency is continued in Shingon, with especial emphasis on the body and the

[15] Dr. Kyoson Tsuchida suggests that Japanese Buddhist philosophy in general has close logical relations to Husserl's and Meinong's theory of knowledge. See his *Contemporary Thought of Japan and China* (London, Williams and Norgate, 1927), pp. 65-66.

[16] For a more technical and thoroughly Japanese presentation of the contrast between Tendai and Kegon, see McGovern, *Introduction*, pp. 69-72. He sums up the difference thus: "In this system [Kegon] phenomena are emphasized at the expense of the noumenom; or let us say that instead of trying to understand the nature of the particular by comprehending the universal, as is done in the Tendai school, we must attempt to understand the universal by studying the particular" (pp. 71-72).

elements (material and otherwise) into which all things may be analyzed. These are earth, water, fire, air (or wind), ether (or the Void), and mind.[17] One school of Shingon interprets these elements literally, one symbolically.[18] Both agree that all beings, including even the Buddha, are composed of these elements; which is another way of denying any ultimate difference between beings and a way of insisting that in the last analysis all things possess the Buddha nature. This Buddha nature in the sense of the Absolute, Shingon never wearies of asserting, is not abstract and passive, but concrete and active. It is all things and all things are it. Matter is never separate from mind, nor mind from matter. The expressions of Shingon thinkers often verge upon realism: in fact, the school would, apparently, like to be both realistic and idealistic at once, and as so often happens with semi-mystical forms of thought, logical contradiction gives it very little trouble.

The world is thus truly many. But it is as truly one. In art, ritual, and teaching Shingon lays repeated emphasis upon the doctrine of identity. All things are at last identical with each other and identical with the One. This One is symbolized by the Buddha Dainichi (Vairocana), who, from the religious point of view, is the supreme Buddha for this sect. He is the great Sun, the great source of all being, from which all finite beings stream forth, as from the One of Plotinus. Or, more exactly, Dainichi is the all-inclusive Reality, identical with all finite things.[19] He is matter as well as spirit; in this sense Shingon approaches more nearly to pantheism in the strict sense than any other Buddhist philosophy.

Thus it will hardly do to express the relation of the Absolute to the phenomenal by saying that the phenomenal world is the manifestation of the Absolute.[20] The relation

[17] The first five of these are symbolized by the five geometrical forms of the *sotoba* so often found in Shingon temple enclosures and graveyards. See pp. 505, 506.

[18] Thus earth means eternity or timelessness, etc.

[19] The relation of Dainichi to the world is symbolized particularly in the two great *mandala* representing the Taizo-kai and Kongo-kai (the Womb-store cycle and the Diamond cycle.) For details see Anesaki, *Buddhist Art*, pp. 38-42, with plates.

[20] The relation of the phenomenal and the Absolute is a central problem for Shingon and one on which Shingon thinkers have expended a good deal of thought. Shingon recognizes two worlds—an *a priori* and an empirical. These it calls the Taizo-kai (or Womb-store world) and Kongo-kai (or Diamond world), and these are two aspects of

is one of closer identity than this.[21] The two are one—so a Professor in the Koya-san university told me—in the same way that water is one with its various forms of steam, liquid, and ice. This figure will be helpful to some. To my obstinately realistic mind it suggested further questions. *Is* the phenomenal world (I asked the professor) really the Absolute Reality? For the ice *is* the water, and with no remainder and no difference of quality. Now if the phenomenal world *is* the Absolute in this literal sense, what becomes of the denial of differences? The crux of the matter seems to lie in the problem how to reconcile the reality of the phenomenal world (which Shingon admits) with the identity of all things (which Shingon asserts). The professor could only answer that the One Being takes many shapes: the shapes are different but the essence one.

I am not sure whether this explanation will satisfy the reader. It satisfies the followers of Shingon, and thereby enables them to reach what they regard as a more direct road to Buddhahood than some other sects possess. For on the one hand they adopt almost a realistic recognition of matter, pluralism, activity; yet on the other hand maintain the strictest denial of differences and the most absolute identity between the many and the One. Not only in my mind or spirit do I find the Buddha: I may equally well find Him in my body. His mouth and body as well as his mind are, or may become, mine. The difference between me and the Buddha is one of degree only. Hence salvation—or the complete realization of the Buddha nature—is not difficult. And in fact in this process of salvation the Buddha works with and in me—not indeed expressly for the sake of my salvation, but out of the spontaneous joy of his eternal activity. Buddhahood is the perfect condition of the heart. To know

Reality. The Taizo-kai is the unseen and unexperienced world beyond Time and Space, the Kongo-kai the knowable world. When we look *through* this knowable world it is the Unseen that we see. Thus in a sense the Unknown becomes known; but when it does so it (in a sense) becomes identical with the world which we know. Dainichi, however, or the Absolute, is not to be identified with either one of these worlds, but with both.

[21] Cf. Goethe·

> *Willst du ins Unendliche schreiten,*
> *Geh nur im Endlichen nach allen Seiten.*
> *Willst du dich am Ganzen erquicken,*
> *So musst du das Ganze im Kleinsten erblicken.*

one's own heart truly is to be the Buddha: for the unborn Reality of all things lies in one's heart. This realization *is* Nirvana: and this the central fact of immortality. As to further details the doctors of Shingon are of two opinions. Some hold that the enlightened, having become one with the Universal Mind, loses all distinct personality; while the others maintain that the enlightened becomes Buddha in essence but not in existence, and thus continues distinct while retaining the pure Buddha nature through all eternity.

We come now to the Tendai philosophy, to which more space must be given than I have allotted to Shingon, as it has had such profound influence on the thought of all the Japanese sects except the three thus far considered. Tendai teaches a more thorough-going idealism than does Kegon or Shingon, which, as we have seen, coquet with both pluralism and realism. "One mind, one thought, includes all the 3000 worlds," said a professor of Tendai philosophy to me. And this "one mind" means the mind of each individual—yours and mine. Space itself, in the last analysis, is in the mind. So also is time, past and future, being really parts of an eternal and timeless present. Ideal also are all the relations between particular minds; for only such relations as are recognized by minds are real. Each mind, in one sense, absorbs all of Reality, including all other minds. Each mind is the whole and thus in the last analysis is identical with all the others. Reality is not a collection of minds: it is the One Mind.

Hence this world which seems to be mine in the particularist and separate sense is not mine alone but is the real world in which all minds are one. The aim of Tendai is to realize this oneness of all minds and all being. The world of the many is both real and not real. It is not ultimately real. It is real in the sense of being the expression, the garment of the One. Buddhist thought in dealing with this question seems ever on the verge of hopeless self-contradiction. It is possible that its contradictory assertions about the Many may be explained in the way just suggested (the Many being the *expression* of the One); yet I am not sure a Buddhist philosopher would be very enthusiastic over the help I have sought to bring. For it does not trouble him, as it troubles us, to have his Universe contain contradictory opposites. When their presence is pointed out to him he may perhaps seek to reconcile them, but he may perfectly well smile and ask if we expect Reality to conform to the rules of our logic books. At times the Tendai and its daughter schools seem positively to delight in their defiance of logic. It identifies extreme Buddhistic opposites. Passion *is* enlightenment, it asserts, and birth and death *are* Nirvana.

Buddhism insists that to know the truth we must enter through both the "gate of difference" and the "gate of sameness."

> While we have to acknowledge the world of particulars in which individuality predominates, we must not forget that looking through the gate of sameness all distinctions and contradictions vanish in a higher principle of unity. . . . Sameness without difference is sameness wrongly conceived, while difference without sameness is difference wrongly conceived. . . . From the standpoint of Absolute Truth, there is no such thing as mind or matter or even God or universe. But if we confine ourselves to this view and become blind to the other side which says that the many exist, that the world actually is, we are like the man who has no legs; we are unable to move, we cannot live our daily life.

In one sense contemporary Japanese Buddhism accepts Nagarjuna's doctrine of the Void; but it does not interpret it as absolute Nihilism. Instead it

> teaches the existence of the highest reality that transcends the duality of body and mind as well as the limitations of time and space. Though this highest reality is the source of life, the ultimate reason of existence, and the norm of things multifarious and multitudinous, it has nothing particular in it, it cannot be designated by any determinative terms, it refuses to be expressed in the phraseology we use in our common parlance. . . . It would be madness to deny the reality of the phenomenal world, but in the midst of these realities the enlightened see their non-reality. There towers a huge mountain, here lies a boundless ocean, birds are singing, trees are growing, and I sit here looking over the verdant meadow: yet in spite of all these, nay, indeed by reason of all these, I believe in the nothingness of existence, in the non-reality of realities, and in the absolute oneness of all things; and it is thereby that I gain my peace of mind and realize the sense of perfect freedom in my everyday life.[22]

This identification of all things with each other, of the Absolute with the phenomenal, of the One with the many,

[22] These passages I have taken from the Rev. Soyen Shaku's *Sermons of a Buddhist Abbot*, trans. by Prof. Suzuki, pp. 27, 30, 93, 98, 99.

this emphatic denial and yet assertion of differences, is characteristic of Tendai and of most Mahayana thought. Dr. Armstrong quotes a Tendai philosopher, Dr. Maeda, as saying, in his (Japanese) *Outline of Tendai*, "Reality is nothing but things and things are nothing but Reality." Yet we must remember that things by themselves are unreal, utter vacuity. Dr. Maeda also asserts that there is no more distinction and difference among things than within the Absolute. If there is any distinction at all "there is distinction in both things and reality, and if there is no distinction there is none in either reality or things." "In this way," writes Dr. Armstrong in summing up, "all distinction or separation is destroyed; all things are identical in nature. When the universe is looked at from the standpoint of the absolute it is called phenomena perfected by reality, but when looked at from the standpoint of the relative it is called phenomena produced by things."[23]

Professor Inabe of Kyoto explained the matter to me thus: The world is really One, but there are different degrees of the realization of this truth. Thus we might form a series of what are phenomenally known as minds according to the grade of their realization, and this would extend all the way from the lowest animals through different men with their varying insight, up to the Bodhisattvas and at length up to the Buddha, who alone completely realizes the truth, and with whom all differences fall out. The differences from the Buddha's point of view fall out because in the fullest

[23] "The Doctrine of the Tendai Sect," in the *Eastern Buddhist*, III, 44, 45. Professor Anesaki interprets the Tendai doctrine of the One and the Many as follows: "The synthesis amounts to affirming both vacuity and appearance at the same time. The conception of vacuity has shown us that a particular existence is void, when taken in itself; but it points to the reality of the universal, as an outcome of a thorough-going negation of relativity. On the other hand, the idea of phenomenal appearance has demonstrated that there is a reality in phenomena which is no less essential to our conception of being than the reality attached to the universal. The world of the universal, the unity of all things in the fundamental nature (*dhammata*), is the foundation of every particular existence, pre-existent to all particular manifestations. Yet its manifestations in concrete beings, Dhammas, are as real as the pre-existent universals, being subject to the laws, Dhammas, which rule all. That they are ruled by the same laws shows their unity in the basis. The particular derives its being from the universal nature of things, while the universal could not fully realize its true nature without manifesting itself in a particular. Both are real, but either by itself is imperfectly real. The Middle Path consists in uniting the two aspects of existence, universal and particular, and in seeing therein the true reality" (*Nichiren the Buddhist Prophet*, p. 150).

sense they are not real. Thus the dog and the philosopher are one. They are one to the extent of the dog's nature. All that is in the dog is shared by the philosopher, as a large circle includes a small one. The same qualities, the same nature, except for pure negations and limitations, which are found in the dog are found in the philosopher. (To use a technical term of Western philosophy, they share the same *what,* not the same *that.*) Their existence, as something distinct from their qualities or nature, is not identical, for existence in this realistic sense is an illusion. The real world is a world of *qualities* or *natures,* a logical world.

Two men unenlightened are not identical. Tendai does not deny differences on the lower levels. (In this Professor Inabe would seem to disagree with Dr. Maeda, as quoted on page 613. Tendai admits differences but asserts unity behind the differences. Here the general Buddhist doctrine of the degrees of truth and reality is of assistance. The world of the many is not illusion. It is real, but it is on the lower plane. Its differences are not illusory; but so long as one fails to realize that the differences are conditioned by identity the mind is under illusion. The many things are real because I think them and I think them because the One Mind in me thinks them. This One Mind, which is the One Reality, is the Buddha; and he who realizes this *fully* becomes one with the Buddha. In realizing the full truth he comes to full self-realization; he becomes what he is. The knowing of Reality and the being of It are one.

It is our insistence upon the things of the phenomenal world as merely separate, and especially our insistence upon the separate reality of our finite selves, that keep up the illusion under which all but the Buddha still somehow suffer. From the higher and unclouded view we should see with direct intuition the unity and identity of all things.

In this connection I cannot refrain from quoting the words of an Indian Vedantist (the late Vasudeva Kirtikar) upon what is practically the same assertion, as defended by the Indian Vedanta:

> Many European thinkers consider this last position to be absolutely inconceivable. No doubt, with ordinary humanity, it is so; for, with the egohood such as we ordinarily have, with the distinction of the ego

and the non-ego fully alive and staring us in the face, it is impossible to realize the truth of this position. It belongs to a different plane of thought; and if we cannot reach that plane or will not endeavor to reach it, our attitude should be to let it alone. But it is unphilosophical to comment upon it from the plane which *we* occupy, and pronounce it as absurd and nonsensical. Those who can conceive the possibility of its truth, and those who have realized it to themselves, say that it is impossible to discern the highest spiritual truths with "the eyes of the flesh." [24]

Tendai, like the Vedanta, makes appeal to more than the "eyes of the flesh." It means to be not only a philosophy but a religion as well. It is under no illusion as to the possibility of proving its doctrine of ultimate Unity by any processes of logic; it even disclaims the power of expounding it in perfectly definite terms. It holds its own formulations, like those of other philosophies, ever subject to modification.[25] No verbal statement of the truth, it holds, can be fully true. "The name that can be named is not the Eternal Name." Its truths and all human truths must be taken symbolically. In this sense it admits, or even asserts, an ultimate skepticism. But this skepticism is of the intellectual sort only, and is the reverse side of an absolute spiritual confidence. In turning away from theoretical certitude Tendai appeals to what is, in the last analysis, a kind of mystical experience. This is sometimes known by the Sanskrit word Prajna; which is, after all, only another way of saying religious insight or intuitive faith. Much is made of this form of insight by Soyen Shaku in his sermons; and though he speaks from the point of view of Zen rather than in explicit exposition of Tendai, what he says will hold for nearly all Japanese Buddhism.

In knowledge subject and object coexist and condition each other; in faith they become one, there is identity only and no mutuality. Transcending the reciprocity of the "I" and the "not-I," the Prajna beholds the universe in its ultimate oneness and feels all forms of life in their essential sameness. It knows that the impulse it feels is the quickening spirit of all existence, and that the pulsation of sympathy which beats in response to outside stimuli is the source of universal animation.[26]

[24] *Studies in Vedanta* (Bombay, Taraporevala, 1924), pp. 4-5.

[25] Cf. McGovern, *Introduction*, pp. 34, 39-40.

[26] *Op. cit.*, p. 137. The entire sermon on *Spiritual Enlightenment* (pp. 132-145) should be read.

> The truth [says another recent Japanese writer] is essentially inexpressible, it is beyond antithesis and can be grasped only by experience. To seek to make the inexpressible theoretically comprehensible is naturally an impossible undertaking.[27]

The One Reality, thus known intuitively, is the Buddha. Including all things, He (or It?) includes evil as well as good. The attitude of Mahayana Buddhism toward morality and moral evil is quite different from that of Christianity, Judaism, Zoroastrianism, or even of Hinayana Buddhism. This follows necessarily from its monistic character and its denial of all dualism. The Mahayana feels that morality has its proper place, that in our activities in the phenomenal world we must of course regard it and should make much of it. But the Mahayana insists we should not stop with it. Religion, it teaches, far transcends morality. To the Mahayanist there is in the thought of morality something of *constraint*. Duty usually carries with it a sense of *must* and *must not*. Religion, on the other hand, is free and brings a sense of freedom. Doubtless the religious man should be moral; but he should be much more than that. He should live at least in part in the realm of realization, beyond the sphere of moral activity.

The Buddha is "*jenseits von Gut und Böse*." Like the Bradleyan Absolute, He includes within himself all things, the evil as well as the good, just to the extent that these are real at all. But as in Bradley's or Royce's philosophy once more, so for Buddhism, evil, like other finite things, when taken up into the Absolute, when seen in all its relations, is transcended, is overcome, is evil no longer. Its evil consisted in its separateness, and when taken up into the whole, this separateness disappears. Its evil nature was relatively illusory. The Buddha *includes* evil because He includes all things, but He *is* not evil.

The evil that we find in this world is relatively illusory but not wholly so. Hence, though the Mahayana makes relatively less of morality in its teaching than does Christianity or the Hinayana, it by no means neglects it. As in the teaching of the Christian mystics, morality by itself can never bring one the final insight which alone is of supreme

[27] Schuej Ohasama in *Zen, Der Lebendige Buddhismus in Japan*, p. 48.

value; but one can hardly attain that insight without morality. Monju is not the only Bodhisattva: there is Kwannon as well.

If in one sense the Buddha includes evil, so even the chief of sinners, potentially at least, is in part good. For, whether they know it or not, and whether they display it or not, the Buddha nature is in all men. Tendai claims to carry this doctrine, of the ubiquity of the Buddha nature, further than did the schools that preceded it.

> The Hosso doctrine teaches that all things have the Buddha nature, but that the nature of a Buddha just about to be enlightened is not in everything. In Kegon teaching Reality (Shinnyo) is in all things, but in inanimate things there is not the nature of a Buddha about to enter Buddhahood. The Tendai sect says that in all things there is a Buddha nature. . . . In this way the Tendai doctrine of reality differs from that of other sects, because it includes the nature of Buddha in stones, trees, and men.[28]

When one refers to the Buddha as the Absolute or the inclusive Reality, it is of course the Dharmakaya that one means. Tendai accepts and makes much of the doctrine of the three bodies of the Buddha, discussed in Chapter XIII of this book. It is the Dharmakaya or Body of the Law, which is the ultimate and truly Real. The Avatamsaka Sutra (which the Tendai accepts and uses) says of it:

> The Dharmakaya unfolds itself here, there, and everywhere, responding to the call of Karma. It is not an individual reality, it is not a false existence, but is universal and pure. It comes from nowhere, it goes to nowhere; it does not assert itself, nor is it subject to annihilation. It is forever serene and eternal. It is the one, devoid of all determinations. This Body of Dharma has no boundary, no quarters, but is embodied in all bodies. Its freedom and spontaneity is incomprehensible, its spiritual presence in things corporeal is incomprehensible. All forms of corporeality are involved therein; it is able to create all things. Assuming any concrete material body as required by the nature and condition of karma, it illuminates all creations. Though it is the store-house of intelligence, it is void of particularity. There is no place in the universe where this Dharamakaya does not prevail. The universe becomes, but this forever remains. It is free from all opposites and contraries. Yet it is working in all things to lead them to Nirvana.[29]

[28] Armstrong, *op. cit.*, p. 46.
[29] Quoted by Beatrice Lane Suzuki in the *Eastern Buddhist*, I, 64.

In the Dharmakaya all the Buddhas are one. In that ultimate state (the only one that is fully real in the absolute sense) there is no distinction between Shaka, Amida, Dainichi, or any of the innumerable Buddhas. This absolute identity, in one sense, of course cannot hold of the two more phenomenal Buddha bodies. In these the different Buddhas are distinguishable—in the Sambhogakaya and in the Nirmanakaya, the Body of Bliss which appears to the holy Bodhisattvas and the Body of Transformation which is identical with the historical Buddhas of this phenomenal world. Taken as phenomenal beings, the historical Buddhas and also the great Bodhisattvas may be real and distinct in the way in which other phenomenal beings, you and I, are real and distinct. Within the Tendai fold there is room for various interpretations of the nature and reality of these beings, most of whom we outsiders would call mythical. To the Buddhists they are not merely mythical. To some they are as real as any persons can be. To others they are real only as symbols of great spiritual truths. Thus the abbot Soyen Shaku writes of Kwannon:

> The universal wave of love is vibrating in every sentient being, and when this innermost chord is touched through the deepest spiritual communion one can suffer, it vibrates, and the vibration reaches the very source of life which is the love of Kwannon, and there takes place the phenomenon called communion. The universal love-principle has thus made itself known to the human heart.[80]

For the philosophical Buddhist the important thing about Kwannon and the other great Bodhisattvas is thus the fact that they stand for certain spiritual realities which may be experienced in the human heart. The question whether they have some individual existence, like the gods of the heathen, is relatively unimportant. The Buddhist is able to have faith in them and derive from them spiritual reinforcement without necessarily believing them to be existent. Similarly the historicity of Shaka or Amida (as Hozo) is of much less interest to the Mahayana Buddhist than is the question of the historicity of Jesus to the Christian or the historicity of Gotama to the Hinayanist. If the Christian

[80] *Op. cit.*, p. 169.

and the Hinayanist attack the Mahayanist, saying "Our Jesus and Gotama are historical and your Amida and Dainichi are not," he may answer, "Just for this reason my Amida and Dainichi are superior." Were he acquainted with the writings of Aristotle he would probably quote the Stagirite to the effect that poetry is truer than history. The truth of Amida, he would say, is a universal truth, hence Amida is more real than are either Jesus or Gotama as merely historical beings, bound down to a particular appearance in one place and at one time. As phenomenal beings they could have at best but a low grade of reality. Their true being, in so far as they are real at all, is measured not by dates and external evidence, but by the extent to which they enter into the Eternal, the degree of their identity with the Dharmakaya.

This same principle applies of course to all men, and to the question of man's fate. Tendai accepts the Anatta doctrine. From the ultimate point of view separate selfhood is illusion. Yet in this phenomenal world there is a sense in which we are separate; and this semi-illusory selfhood need not necessarily be ended by the illusory event known as bodily death. It is thus that many thoughtful adherents of Tendai are able to maintain the doctrine of transmigration and of paradise. To other thinkers these terms, paradise and rebirth, are to be taken only symbolically.[31] To only a very few does Nirvana mean annihilation. As Professor Otto has put it (and I think he understands these matters with unusual sympathy):

> It is only conceptually that "Nirvana" is a negation; it is felt in consciousness as in the strongest degree positive; it exercises a "fascination" by which its votaries are as much carried away as are the Hindu or the Christian by the corresponding objects of their worship. I recall vividly a conversation I had with a Buddhist monk. He had been putting before me methodically and pertinaciously the arguments for the Buddhist "theology of negation," the doctrine of anatman and "entire emptiness." When he had made an end, I asked him, what then Nirvana itself is; and after a long pause came at last the single answer, low and restrained: "Bliss—unspeakable." And the hushed restraint of that answer, the solemnity of his voice, demeanor, and gesture, made more clear what was meant than the words themselves.[32]

[31] Cf. Soyen Shaku, *op. cit.*, pp. 57-58, 173-75, 210-13.
[32] *The Idea of the Holy*, trans., p. 39.

This answer is, I think, fairly representative. If the hope of philosophical Buddhism is to be put in one sentence, we may say the eternal life means Nirvana or becoming Buddha: and this means self-realization, the explicit discovery and realization of the Buddha nature which has all along been hidden but actually present within one, the identification of all one's true being with the Dharmakaya.

This picture of merging our personality in the Divine—the dewdrop slipping into the shining sea—has a certain great emotional attraction. Western minds, however, are likely to put the query: Is it anything more than a picture? Has it any real meaning? Is it ultimately thinkable? To say that your personality, your stream of consciousness, your self-awareness, merges in some Absolute Mind, what is this but to say that it absolutely ceases to be? Is it not merely another way of saying that death ends all? Can one put real meaning into any form of immortality other than personal immortality? Does not the figure of the dewdrop and the sea mislead us? We form a visual image of the dewdrop continuing to exist in the ocean. But does not the whole meaning of my continued existence depend upon my continued "power to say I am I"?

It would be difficult to refute this argument. It may be quite unanswerable. But before we can be sure of that we must have a much more definite and certain doctrine of the nature of selfhood than I for one would venture to maintain. The whole problem is illusive: we feel about in the dark. *Omnis individuatio est negatio* is perhaps true; yet is it so sure that if all the limitations of human individuality were broken, there would be nothing left? Could not the small self be continuous with and, to the extent of its reality, identical with a larger and inclusive self, even though after the surrender of the smaller self the realization of what had happened would be felt only by the larger self? What, for example, should we say of those secondary and split-off personalities which are eventually suppressed yet contribute to the resulting total personality? I have in mind cases like those reported by Dr. Morton Prince [38] and by Dr. W. F.

[38] *The Dissociation of a Personality* (London, Longmans, 1906).

Prince.[34] These subordinate personalities faced the prospect of suppression with exactly the same dread that many people have for death: it meant death to them. Yet this death, though it was the end of the sense of just that limited individual, certainly did not mean annihilation. The subordinate personality in one sense lived on in the new, more complete, unified person. And (though this was not true of the cases reported) it is perfectly conceivable that the larger personality in which the smaller was merged might have realized and remembered the whole process and thus might have experienced the fact, from its higher point of view, that the submerged personality really survived as an identical aspect or element of the whole self. I am, therefore, not at all certain that the figure of the dewdrop and the sea, the concept of one's identity with the Dharmakaya, is meaningless.

But let us return to Tendai, and take if we can a rapid, bird's-eye view of its whole position, in large outline. The Tendai universe may be called a divine universe with no "God" in it. The Tendai teaches incarnation, many incarnations, without any deity becoming incarnate. For it, incarnation means not the descent of deity into human flesh, but the ascent of the individual to deity by becoming his true self, which is selfless. "Become what thou art" is its most fundamental command, a command which underlies and transcends all the laws of morality. Many individuals, so Buddhism teaches, have risen from the common level, perhaps an infinite number, to this higher plane of realization and divinization: not in the sense of achieving something essentially new, but by realizing the Buddha nature which was always theirs and which lies, frequently unguessed, in all beings. To know Reality is to be it.

To this realization one attains chiefly through cultivation of the two great Buddhist virtues of insight and compassion. These mean much more than mere morality. They include it, but they include metaphysical comprehension and mystical experience as well. When these qualities of soul are fully attained, when self is completely forgotten in love for others and the illusion of separateness, both in theory and

[34] *The Psychic in the House* (Boston Society for Psychic Research, 1926).

in inner feeling, is overcome, one enters into Buddhahood. This must mean, it would seem, that compassion and insight, in some high sense, constitute the ultimate nature of reality.

So one enters into the Dharmakaya, into the Eternal Peace. For such an one there is no more rebirth, there is no more illusion, no more world of separateness and of particulars. And the Buddhist thinker of a mystical turn, with a feeling for the cosmic realities, looks toward this with a kind of metaphysical longing, sensing the call of the Eternal.

> Here begins the sea that ends not till the world's end. Where we stand,
> Could we know the next high sea-mark set beyond these waves that gleam,
> We should know what never man hath known, nor eye of man hath scanned . . .
> Ah, but here man's heart leaps, yearning toward the gloom with venturous glee,
> From the shore that hath no shore beyond it set in all the sea.

CHAPTER XXX

ZEN

As we saw in the chapter on the history of Japanese Buddhism, Zen was introduced into Japan after the formation of the Yutsu Nembutsu and Jodo sects. It antedated, however, the other Amida sects and also Nichiren; while in the form of its thought it is much older and closer to the original Buddhism than is Amida worship. Hence I shall devote this chapter to Zen and leave the thought of the Amida and Nichiren sects—which together are the most modern divisions of Buddhism—to the following chapter.

It is with much hesitancy that I deal with the mysticism and the philosophy of Zen. There is no other subject connected with Buddhism so difficult for a Westerner to handle intelligently, no other so intangible, so different from everything with which we are acquainted, so hard to make plausible, so unspeakably *queer*. Nor are there many subjects more important to an understanding of the Japanese Buddhism of today—and probably of tomorrow. Fortunately the reader (unless he has skipped a good deal) already knows something about Zen, in fact is already in possession of the central thought of this mystical school.

This central thought, or fundamental insistence, when baldly stated, sounds simple enough: to the effect, namely, that experience and life are primary, while cult, theory, and learning are very secondary. No other school of Buddhism makes so little of its images and of its ritual. One of the great Zen masters of China, getting up one frosty morning and having no fuel, threw into the fire the wooden Buddha that sat upon the altar, and warmed himself ostentatiously before his disciples. Nor is the discursive thought of philosophy of much more value than Buddha images. Zen does not actually inveigh against it but warns its followers that neither logic nor metaphysics is to be relied upon for insight.[1] Theoretical instruction may be positively harmful. A Japanese student of mine on his departure from Japan was directed by his father, an enthusiastic adept in Zen, to beware of studying about the theory of Buddhism. There are a few books, to be sure, which followers of Zen may read with some profit—some of the ancient Sutras and the writings of Zen masters. But even the best of these can do little for one and if wrongly used may be a hindrance rather than a help. The truest of books (to use a favorite Zen figure) can be at best but a "finger pointing at the moon." If we fix our gaze on the finger we miss the heavenly glory. The finger is of use only in pointing away from itself to the light which illumines finger and all.

Where, then, is the "moon" to be found? Where and how shall we discover the Buddha? The answer that Zen gives to this question was formulated long ago by a Chinese Zen master in words that express the conviction of the whole school through the centuries:

> If you wish to seek the Buddha, you ought to see into your own nature: for this nature is the Buddha himself. If you have not seen into your own nature, what is the use of thinking of the Buddha, reciting the Sutras, observing a fast, or keeping the precepts? . . . The Buddha is your own mind: make no mistake to bow to external objects. . . . The mind is the Buddha, the Buddha is the way, and the way is Zen. To see directly into one's original nature, this is Zen. When this original nature is not seen into, there is no Zen. Even if you are well learned in hundreds of the Sutras and Sastras, you still remain an ignoramus in Buddhism when you have not yet seen into your original nature. Buddhism is not there [in mere learning]. The highest truth is unfathomably deep, is not an object of talk or discussion, and even the canonical texts have no way to bring it within our reach. Let us once see into our own original nature and we have the truth even if we are quite illiterate, not

[1] The third patriarch in China wrote as follows concerning thought (I give the German translation found in Ohasama's *Zen*, p. 66):

Dein Denken lass schweigen—
Darauf kommt es an!
Bleibe nicht stehen
Bei gegensätzlichen Gedanken:
Ihnen nachzujagen und sie zu suchen,
Davor hüte dich!
Wer vom Gegensätzlichen
Nur einen Hauch beibehalt
Dessen Geist bleibt verworren.

knowing a word. . . . All the Buddhas in successive ages have spoken only of seeing into one's own nature.[2]

To attain the fruits of Zen one need not read nor think nor pray: but one must do something incomparably more difficult. For, as the reader need hardly be told, this "seeing into one's own nature" is no easy task. For most people, at any rate, a long and intense training, lasting many years, is needed. This training consists partly in reading—for some books may be helpful if one uses them in the proper spirit—and in the study of the experiences and methods of the great Zen masters. But the central part of the training consists in the discipline of self-mastery and concentration given by zazen.

Zen believes that it was through the process of zazen that Sakyamuni gained his illumination. He sat for seven weeks under the Bo Tree at Buddh Gaya rapt in Zen meditation, and as a result the supreme insight suddenly dawned upon him. The novitiate is therefore following the Founder's example as he sits through long hours, cross-legged, regulating his breathing and his thoughts. I have spoken in a previous chapter of the posture and the breathing exercises. These of course are but the externals of zazen and are useful chiefly for beginners. The really important part of the process is concentration of mind. This also is the most difficult part. When one attempts to turn one's thoughts away from every outward thing, one becomes aware of the immense amount of lumber with which one's mind is clogged: so at least say those who have tried zazen. Worries and wishes and longings rise to the surface and must be diligently set aside, and at first the more one tries to forget them the more insistent they become. The man of mystical tendencies, no matter what his religion, is particularly distressed by this inner multiplicity, this cleavage within him, this incipiently divided self. He longs for unity in his life and in his mind. In extreme cases, as Murisier has pointed out,[3] this longing for the unitive state and the destruction of all distractions and all multifariousness, approaches the posi-

[2] Taken from Prof. Suzuki's admirable article on "The Revelation of a New Truth in Zen Buddhism," *Eastern Buddhist*, I, 197-99.

[3] *Les Maladies du Sentiment Religieux* (Paris, Alcan, 1903), Chap. I.

tively morbid. Many Christian mystics are excellent examples of this urge toward the narrowing and unification of consciousness, and they sometimes seek it by means of what Murisier calls "simpliciation."

The process by which the Zen seeker attempts to demolish this state of inward multiplicity and to become one is sometimes through direct attack, sometimes through certain clever devices. By direct attack I mean the explicit effort to empty the mind. As a leading Zen abbot described it to me, one must seek to "think nothing." One knows that the aim is to realize oneself as the Buddha, to find the Buddha nature within one's mind: yet this must not be attempted through any process of auto-suggestion. One does not repeat to oneself, "I am Buddha," or anything else, said the abbot, as the Amida and Nichiren sects repeat their formulas of prayer, or, he might have added, as the followers of Coué repeat his formulas. One simply seeks to empty the mind, to sink oneself into the universe, to give up every attempt at self-guidance, and so to let the subconscious forces act. Yet this emptiness of mind which is sought in zazen is far from unconsciousness or sleep. Those who have practiced zazen long enough to catch some glimpse of the kind of experience sought are unanimous in insisting that the mental condition arrived at and often induced is far from blank emptiness or negation. The mind is empty, but the void which fills it is somehow meaningful and luminous.

This explicit attempt to empty the mind I called, a few lines back, a direct attack upon that multiplicity of our inward life which it is the aim of Zen to destroy. But the Zen spiritual directors long ago devised less obvious and more subtle methods for inducing the unity of enlightenment which they seek. The most systematic of these indirect methods consists in giving the student a problem or *koan* upon which to concentrate his thoughts, not for the sake of the solution but because such concentration has proved to be an excellent means of bringing about the desired inner unity and illumination. It should be clearly understood before any of these problems are read that the aim in presenting them is purely psychological: otherwise they will seem not only meaningless and queer but downright insane. Zen masters through the centuries, in China and Japan, have devised more and more of these koan, so that there are now upward of seventeen hundred of them. They have been likened to the act of knocking on the door; the Buddha who dwells within each of us hears the knock and opens. "Thus," says Ohasama, "every *koan* or problem is to be understood only as a means. Since the Patriarch Engo in China (1063-1135) and Haku-in in Japan (1683-1768), Zen masters have used such problems as the foundation of the training they give their pupils and help them thereby to experience the Truth."[4] They have also arranged some of the more important problems in an order of ascending difficulty and revelation, for pedagogical purposes. The pupil is sometimes instructed to concentrate on his problem during zazen instead of making the effort to empty his mind. But the aim of this is not the revelation of any truth connected with the problem, but the inducement of a state in which the dominance of the many and the worries of the world may be cast out and one may realize immediately the identity of oneself with the Buddha. Concentration upon the problem does this, I was told by a Zen abbot, through keeping the mind taut, on a constant stretch, steadily concentrated, and thus (to that extent) unified.

The problem most commonly presented first of all to the beginner is the famous "Joshu's Mu." Joshu was a distinguished Chinese Zen master who lived (tradition says) from 778 to 897. On one occasion a monk asked him whether the Buddha (who it will be recalled is in all things) is also in the little dog. To this Joshu answered by the syllable "Mu." This word (the equivalent of the modern Mandarin *Pu*) means no. But the significance Joshu gave to the word was that he refused to answer the question. "The question," writes Ohasama in comment, "touches the being of the Absolute, which as above all opposites and all classes, cannot be expressed through any assertion, whether Yes or No, but can only be directly experienced."[5] In other words, yes and no

[4] *Zen: der Lebendige Buddhismus in Japan*, p. 9.

[5] *Op. cit.*, p. 155. Suzuki's comment is: "This *mu* is not at all understood in its literal sense; when it is given as a *koan* it means just '*Mu*' and the masters will not give you any explanation," *Eastern Buddhist*, I, 216, note. See also *Essays in Zen Buddhism*, p. 236 and note.

are both wrong: to assert that the Buddha is or to assert that He is not in the little dog are alike false, for both imply distinctions between the two, and within the Absolute there are no distinctions. A great many Zen pupils have begun by meditating on this problem. Their spiritual director does not give them any explanation such as I have suggested—at least not at first. They are to meditate on the "Mu." They keep in constant touch with their director; and finally if the light has dawned upon them he sees it, not by any words which they speak, but by their faces, by their whole manner, and by that intuitive transmission of thought through which Sakyamuni communicated with Mahakassapa,[6] and which Zen has ever considered the only way of really transmitting truth. For the truth of mysticism can by its nature never be put into words. Words imply distinctions and drag us back into the world of multiplicity and relation. The experience sought has no statable intellectual content.

One of my Japanese students at Williams, whose father was an enthusiastic follower of Zen, had studied for a year in a Zen monastery, and had been given Joshu's Mu as the subject of his meditation. He worked at it throughout the year but got no light (much to his father's disappointment), and was then allowed to leave the monastery and come to America. Here he still meditated at frequent intervals on the Mu, while in his room or while taking lonely walks. He knows now much more about the meaning of the problem than I have expressed above, but this is hardly even the beginning of the solution he seeks. For the answer he is after can never be put into words. It is a unique form of experience and this he has not yet attained. Still, he assures me, the time spent upon Joshu's Mu has been far from wasted. He is conscious that he has gained through his meditation new powers of self-control, and he believes also that he is much happier because of it.

Joshu's Mu is not the only problem for beginners. Another of my Japanese students, who had also studied in a Zen monastery, had been set to work at the following problem. His director clapped his hands and asked, "Do you hear

[6] See page 280.

that?" The boy said, "Yes." Then the monk made the same motion as before with his right hand, the left remaining at his side, so that his right hand beat only the air; and again he asked, "Do you hear that?" The boy replied, "No." "Well," said the monk, "listen until you do." This "listening for the voice of one hand," as the Japanese call it, is not an uncommon problem. My student had never succeeded in hearing the voice of one hand, but others have succeeded where he failed. I once met a Japanese lieutenant, traveling in Arizona, who had been given this same problem and had heard the voice of one hand. It cannot, he said, be described in words. It is not a sound nor a sensation, but a state of mind. A great Zen teacher explained the purpose of the problem to me thus: The sound which is worth hearing is not a sound at all; and the "one hand" that makes it is not one in the numerical sense but in the absolute sense. It is "the One without a second." What the pupil has to do is to realize this One, the Absolute. A sound is made by something which is in relation to something else—as the first sound made by the two hands. In the Absolute there are no relations and no distinctions. The attempt to hear the sound of one hand is merely one of many ways of bringing the pupil to this realization.

There are, as I have said, about seventeen hundred of these problems which have been used on various occasions by Zen masters. A Zen abbot I conversed with near Tokyo makes use of the problem "Why is the summer hot?" It will do the pupil no good in wrestling with this problem to give the scientific answer. He must, rather, contemplate himself as heat, as summer itself, and the whole of Reality as summer. By this means (so the abbot assured me) the pupil reaches such a stage of understanding that he is no longer either hot or cold, and he sees that nothing is hot or cold, or has any real qualities: that all is emptiness. Another problem which has had some importance historically is called the Beardless Barbarian. The question was set by the Zen master Wakuan and is as follows: "Why does the barbarian in the west have no beard?" The point is that the barbarian in the west of course *has* a beard, as every one is supposed to know. The problem thus purposely seems to assert what is obviously false. But just through this obvious falseness it aims to lead the mind beyond the realm of the merely false or true. So, at least, Ohasama interprets it. "The irrelevance of all merely relative partial truths is thus made clear and one is directed onward to the absolute and complete truth."[7]

Closely related to the koan or problems are certain famous replies and statements made by distinguished Zen masters of various times, which seem to have nothing in common but their astounding irrelevancy or paradox, but which by this very characteristic aim to do the same thing for the pupil as the koan. Some of these replies, in fact, are used as koan: the pupil is told of the reply or statement and directed to meditate upon it until the light breaks upon him.

The rehearsal of some of these sayings and doings of the Zen masters makes very queer reading; and I say doings as well as sayings, for hard knocks with fists and clubs were often used instead of words to rouse the dormant insight of the sluggish pupil. Less violent acts also were tried, in the hope that their symbolic significance might strike the mind of the seeker. On one occasion a Chinese master, Yoh Shan by name, was besought by his pupils to preach them a sermon on the Dharma. "Then ring the bell," he replied. "The bell rang and all the monks assembled in the Hall eager to hear the sermon. Yoh Shan went up into the pulpit and descended immediately without saying a word."[8] "A Chinese Zen master, Bokuji, was once asked: 'We have to dress and eat every day, and how can we escape from all that?' The master replied, 'We dress, we eat.' 'I do not understand you,' said the questioner. 'If you don't understand, put your dress on and eat your food.'"[9] "When Kwazan was asked to describe the nature of the Buddha, he said: 'I know how to play the drum, dong-do-ko-dong.'"[10] A monk once said to Joshu, "All things return to the One, but whither does the One return?" To which Joshu replied, "When I was

[7] *Op. cit.*, pp. 95, 157. Ohasama expounds and interprets some thirty-one of the most famous problems.

[8] Nukariya, *The Religion of the Samurai*, p. 55.

[9] Susuki, *Eastern Buddhist*, I, 25.

[10] *Ibid.*, p. 354.

in Seiju I had a monk's robe which weighed seven chin."[11]

It is difficult for us Westerners to consider sayings like these seriously. Instead of digging for some inner meaning, our mind runs off to memories of the Walrus' reply to the oysters when they asked if he were going to eat them: "The night is fine," the walrus said; "do you admire the view?" Or to the remark of Mr. Eff's Aunt (in *Little Dorrit*), to the effect that when she lived at Henly, Miles' gander was stole by tinkers.

Of course for Orientals, trained in the interpretation of subtle suggestions and symbols, and in the use of a language which prides itself on its ability to hide immensities of meaning under the minimum of verbal expression, for men, moreover, who have studied and meditated in Zen monasteries for years, these subtle sayings have an appearance so different from that they present to us as to be utterly transformed. Thus it seems obvious enough to a Japanese trained in Zen that Joshu's remark about the monk's robe, when asked about the One, was intended to suggest to the questioner that the One is to be found in concrete reality and everywhere else; and that the *new* robe was a symbol of the new life of spiritual liberty.[12] Similarly Professor Suzuki interprets Bokuju's answer about dress and food to mean, "Salvation must be found in the finite itself, there is nothing infinite apart from things; if you seek something transcendental, that will cut you off from this world of relativity, which is the same thing as the annihilation of yourself."[13] Of course we Westerners feel like exclaiming, If that was what Joshu and Bokuju meant, why didn't they say so? To which a partial reply would be that if we had been brought up to speak and read Chinese instead of English we should feel very differently on the matter; while a more profound explanation may be sought in the reflection that direct statements would have defeated the whole aim the masters had in view—which was not to communicate verbal conceptions but to put the mind of the pupil on a stretch and

[11] Reported by Ohasama, p. 112 (with comment on 175), and by Suzuki, *Eastern Buddhist*, I, 30.

[12] Ohasama, p. 175.

[13] *Op. cit.*, p. 25.

keep it actively puzzled and concentrated. The pupil must work out his own intuition of the truth, he must *live into* the truth, for himself. A mere verbal solution is but parrot philosophy, and for Zen a mere conceptual solution is little better.

I gather that the slaps and physical violence of ancient Chinese Zen and the irrelevant remarks we have been discussing are less used than they once were. But the irrelevancies, at any rate, have by no means been given up. Thus a Buddhist lady of wealth, who had suddenly lost most of her fortune, a few years ago, went to the abbot of one of the great Hongwanji temples in Kyoto for comfort. He tried to give her the consolation of sympathy, saying, "Dear madam, I can only weep with you." From him she went to one of the Zen abbots and told her story. His only remark was, "What do you think of the wife of Yoritomo?" [14] The question, of course, had no more to do with the poor lady's sorrow than the flowers that bloom in the spring; and that is why the abbot asked it.

The aim of these extraordinary methods, both psychical and physical, is, as I have indicated, to jolt the mind out of its accustomed rut and give the soul such a *bang* that its eyes will be knocked open (as one knocks open the eyes of a Paris doll), and so will suddenly see the light of an utterly new world. The theory seems to be something like James and Starbuck's theory of religious conversion. A process of "incubation" within the subconscious is produced by several months or even years of zazen, meditation, study, training, and "atmosphere." When the time is ripe the new insight will exfoliate suddenly from out the subconscious region if only it receives, so to speak, a last shake or stir.

> It is [writes Professor Suzuki] like picking a hidden lock, the flood of new experiences gushes forth from the opening. It is again like the clock's striking the hours; when the appointed time comes it clicks, and the whole percussion of sounds is released. The mind seems to have something of this mechanism; when a certain moment is reached, a hitherto closed screen is lifted, an entirely new vista opens up, and the tone of one's whole life thereafter changes. This mental clicking or opening

[14] Yoritomo, the reader will recall, was the founder of the Minamoto Shogunate (1192). The incident was told me by one of the monks at the Zen monastery where it happened.

is called "satori" by the Zen masters and is insisted upon as the main object of their discipline.[15]

A large number of "conversion cases," as we should call them, are on record, showing in considerable detail how the strange methods used by the Zen masters have worked in the past, and with what sudden revelation satori comes. There is room here but for one or two instances, but many more like them could be adduced. They will doubtless remind the reader of some of the cases of sudden conversion in James' *Varieties* and in other books dealing with this odd form of experience.

A Japanese Zen master, Bukko by name (1226-1286), one of the most influential teachers of Zen at the time when Japanese Zen was still dependent on China, has recounted the process of his "conversion" in some detail.

When seventeen I made up my mind to study Buddhism and began to unravel the mysteries of "Joshu's Mu." I expected to finish the matter within one year, but I did not come to any understanding of it after all. Another year passed without much avail, and three more years, also finding myself with no progress. In the fifth or sixth year, while no special change came over me, the "Mu" became so inseparably attached to me that I could not get away from it even while asleep. This whole universe seemed to be nothing but the "Mu" itself. In the meantime I was told by an old monk to set it aside for a while and see how things would go with me. According to this advice I dropped the matter altogether and sat quietly. But owing to the fact that the "Mu" had been with me so long, I could in no way shake it off however much I tried. When I was sitting, I forgot that I was sitting; nor was I conscious of my own body. Nothing but a sense of utter blankness prevailed. Half a year passed thus. Like a bird escaped from its cage, my mind, my consciousness moved about (without restraint) sometimes eastward, sometimes westward, sometimes northward, or southward. Sitting through two days in succession, or through one day and night I did not feel any fatigue. . . . [During this period Bukko had an experience of levitation, in which he was thought dead by many of the monks; and after that a continuous vision whenever he closed his eyes. He continues:] One night sitting far into the night I kept my eyes open and was aware of my sitting up in my seat. All suddenly the sound of striking the board in front of the head-monk's room reached my ear, which at once revealed to me the "original man" in full. There was then no more of that vision which appeared at the closing of the eyes. Hastily I came down from the seat and ran out into a moonlit

[15] *The Eastern Buddhist,* I, 201.

night and went up to the garden house called Ganki, where looking up to the sky I laughed loudly, "Oh, how great is the Dharmakaya! Oh, how so great and immense for evermore!" Thence my joy knew no bounds. I could not quietly sit in the Meditation Hall; I went about with no special purpose in the mountains walking this way and that. . . . Thinking thus, I felt all the bonds snapped and broken to pieces that have been tying me for so many ages. How many numberless years have I been sitting in the hole of ants! Today even in the hollow of my hair there lie all the Buddha-lands in the ten quarters! I thought within myself, "Even if I have no greater *satori,* I am now all sufficient unto myself." [16]

Satori need not be the result of direct pondering on one of the problems, though presumably it always requires a certain amount of subconscious incubation. A merely chance occurrence—a sight, a sound—may bring it about. Often it is accompanied by intense emotional phenomena such as trembling, a rush of tears, or a cold sweat.

Hyakujo (724-814) one day went out attending his master Baso. A flock of wild geese was seen flying. Baso asked: "What are they?" "They are wild geese, sir." "Whither are they flying?" "They have flown away, sir." Baso abruptly taking hold of Hyakujo's nose gave it a twist. Overcome with pain, Hyakujo cried aloud, "Oh! Oh!" Said Baso, "You say they have flown away, but all the same they have been here from the very beginning." This made Hyakujo's back wet with cold perspiration. He had *satori.*[17]

Haku-in, who afterwards became a famous Zen master (1683-1768) had, as a student, been set to work on a problem which he could not solve, and after long efforts became so desperate of reaching insight that he left his teacher and wandered away from the monastery, and lived in a neighboring city, begging his meals from house to house. One day while standing before the door of an old woman who had refused to give him anything he fell into so deep meditation over his Zen problem that he did not hear the words of the old lady until she knocked him over the head with a switch. Thereupon he experienced the great insight: the truth he had sought rushed into his mind. Filled with joy he started back to the monastery. His master saw him ap-

[16] From Suzuki, *op. cit.*, pp. 219-21. [17] *Ibid.*, p. 204.

proaching in the distance and knew by his appearance that he had attained satori.[18]

Both for my own sake and for that of my readers I wish I had a perfectly definite and statable notion what these mystical experiences of Zen may really be. But, as all insist, only those who have experienced them can know, and even they can never tell it; for the experience is essentially ineffable, and the very attempt to put it into conceptual terms necessarily defeats itself. This, of course, is only what all the mystics affirm of every sort of mystical experience. One can only say, with the Upanishads, "Neti, Neti," *not this, not this.* The experience is ineffable, unspeakable.

And yet the mystics do speak a good deal. From the things that they say it is plain that there are several sorts of mystical experience, and by careful analysis of the expressions they do give us it is possible even for the non-mystic to form some dim notion of the general nature of the mystical experience and of the larger lines of division and distinction which run within it. We need not, therefore, be too desperate of getting a little light on Zen mysticism for all the insistence of the Zen adepts that the experience is beyond all words and all conceptual distinctions.

The experiences of the Zen masters quoted in these last few pages may have reminded the reader of some of the events recounted in the Book of Acts.[19] Whatever the theological distance between the two, there would seem to be a psychological—or at least superficial—parallel between the coming of satori and the coming of the Holy Ghost. Each is depicted as a perfectly definite and unmistakable experience. It happens suddenly at a specific place and a specific moment. The subject of it realizes at once that something revolutionary has happened: and outside beholders also recognize it without question. Satori has wider relations than this. Otto, the distinguished author of *Das Heilige,* who is much interested in Zen, has pointed out certain similarities between satori and the feeling of the numinous to which his book

[18] Ohasama, *op. cit.,* p. 36.
[19] Cf. Chaps. II, 1-13, X, 44-47, etc.

is devoted.[20] There is no doubt that the experience sought and cultivated by Zen is related more or less closely to all mystical states.

But it is related to some mystical states more closely than to others. It is sometimes classed with those semi-mystical conditions brought about through auto-suggestion or self-hypnosis. Mr. Arthur Waley,[21] for example, seems to class it thus. His knowledge of things Japanese and Chinese is so profound that I should hesitate long before disagreeing with him; moreover, the quotation he gives us[22] from Buddhapriya shows how closely early Zen methods imitated those of the Indian Yoga, in which the narrowing of consciousness was the aim. Yet this process of narrowing and concentrating the attention was probably seldom carried by Zen to the extreme unconscious trance, and so far as I am aware this is never done today. Zazen, to be sure, aims at "emptiness," but the descriptions given us of satori indicate that it is an intense form of consciousness; and even the "emptiness" of zazen (as all the followers of Zen insist) is very far indeed from unconsciousness, trance, or sleep.

On the other hand, the Zen form of experience, whether in zazen or satori, differs noticeably from either Vedantic or Christian mysticism. Otto thinks it "far more naïve than the mysticism of the Vedanta, more blissful, more thoroughly illumined, far richer in potentialities: it is not world-rejecting but world-transfiguring."[23] I cannot agree with this *in toto;* but satori is certainly more naïve than the Vedantic form of mysticism and without any sense of communion or reunion with a Being such as Brahman. The contrast between it and the usual type of Christian mysticism is even greater—chiefly because of the greater emphasis by Christian mystics on the personality of the Divine and on love for Him. Not a few Christian mystics, to be sure, have approximated something like the Zen form of experience; but the more representative mystics have con-

[20] See his article on "Zen Buddhism" in Vol. III of the *Eastern Buddhist* (pp. 117-125); his "Gleitwort" to Ohasama's *Zen, der lebendige Buddhisms in Japan;* and p. 69 of his *The Idea of the Holy.*

[21] See his little monograph on *Zen Buddhism in Its Relation to Art.*

[22] *Op. cit.*, pp. 11-13.

[23] *Eastern Buddhist,* I, 121.

sidered this experience unChristian. Tauler has an instructive passage in which he describes this form of mysticism, of which he disapproves, in terms that distinctly suggest zazen.[24] The follower of Zen does not want communion with God, nor realization of the presence of the Buddha except so far as he and the Buddha are one. "Cleanse your mouth even from the word 'Buddha,'" is a typical Zen saying. It is self-realization, not communion, that Zen seeks and finds.[25]

Zen mysticism, then, differs notably from the usual religious mysticism of either India or Christendom. For a somewhat similar reason it is difficult to class it with Otto's "numinous feeling." Neither in the unitive state produced by zazen nor in satori is the Zen mystic conscious of the presence of any *numen.* The fear, too, the *mysterium tremendum,* of which Otto makes so much, is hardly to be found in Zen mysticism.[26] Yet Zen is beyond all question a form of mysticism. And the great interest which it has for the student of the psychology of religion is largely due just to these contrasts which it sustains to other mystical types. It is, moreover, characteristically Buddhist; and while the Mahayana is the explicit philosophy of its followers, in spirit it is closely related to the Hinayana, and it harks back to the psychical exercises which the Founder is said to have practiced and to have taught his disciples. As Hinayana Buddhism is a religion without a God, Zen is a form of mysticism without communion. But it is without communion because the unity of the individual's nature and the Buddha nature

[24] "What they desire is a type of rest and comfort naturally pleasing to all creatures; and such an experience is possible to any person who only knows the art of emptying himself of imaginations and impulses. Let a man but separate himself from all contingencies and from all works, and there will come over him in this state of emptiness a peace which is very great, lovely, and agreeable, and which is in itself no sin, since it is a part of our human nature. But when it is taken for a veritable possessing of God, or unity with God, then it is a sin; for it is in reality nothing but a state of thorough passivity and apathy untouched by the power from on high, which any man can attain without special grace of God. It is a purely negative state from which (if one in arrogance calls it divine) nothing follows but blindness, failure of understanding, and a disinclination to be governed by the rules of ordinary righteousness." Quoted by Hocking in *Mind,* XXXVII (1912), p. 59.

[25] The best treatment of Satori with which I am acquainted is Suzuki's essay on the subject, namely Essay No. V in his *Essays in Zen Buddhism.*

[26] Otto thinks it is, but seems to depend for evidence chiefly upon the "monstrous" expression given to Bodhidharma by almost all Chinese and Japanese artists, *op. cit.,* p. 118.

is felt to be so complete as to be belied by any term which implies duality.

As I read over the accounts of the various experiences of Zen adepts, and recall what has been told me by Zen monks, it appears to me rather hopeless to attempt to put all these experiences into one category. After all there is absolutely no evidence to show that all Zen experiences are alike, and the antecedent probability is that they differ considerably. Zen writers sometimes recognize this but insist that the various experiences are only different stages or depths of the same thing. How they know they are the same it would be hard to say, and what can be meant by calling them the same when as a fact they are so different can be explained only by leaving the level of psychological description and branching into philosophical theory. If we stick to the lower level of psychology it seems to me we must divide the mystical experiences of Zen into at least two classes (half a dozen or twenty might be better), namely, the state of relative vacuity induced by zazen, and the sudden enlightenment known as satori. That there are innumerable gradations of experience between these two which, taken together, connect them, I doubt not; but the recognition of the two extremes and the difference between them is none the less enlightening.

As I have pointed out in more than one place, the ancient and approved methods of doing zazen are notably like the Yoga methods of India. They fit in admirably with Nagarjuna's denial of differences; and Nagarjuna's philosophy has had deep influence with many of the Zen masters. The answer, moreover, which almost any Zen devotee in Chinese or Japanese monasteries today will give you if you ask him what is the principal aim of zazen will be this: to *empty the mind*. It would seem, therefore, pretty plain that mental concentration and unity, the driving out of details, and the shunning of all relational thought is one type of the Zen experience. In this it is related to the *via negativa* of some of the Neo-Platonic and some of the Christian mystics, and, carried to its extreme, it fulfils fairly well the rather exaggerated description of mysticism given by Royce in *The World and the Individual*.[27]

[27] Vol. I, Lecture IV.

The other type of Zen experience is the illumination found in satori. Satori in Professor Suzuki's opinion is the very heart of Zen, and I shall therefore quote from him again upon this matter.

> *Satori* may be defined as an intuitive looking into the nature of things in contradistinction to the intellectual and logical understanding of it. Practically, it means the unfolding of a new world hitherto unperceived in the confusion of a dualistic mind. Or we may say that with *satori* our entire surroundings are viewed from quite an unexpected angle of perception. Whatever this is, the world for those who have gained a *satori* is no more the old world as it used to be; even with all its flowing streams and burning fires, it is never the same one again. Logically, all its opposites and contradictions are united and harmonized into a consistent organic whole. This is a mystery and a miracle, but according to the Zen masters such is being performed every day. *Satori* therefore, can be had only through our once personally experiencing it. Its semblance or analogy in a more or less feeble way is gained when a difficult mathematical problem is solved, or when a great discovery is made, or when a sudden means of escape is realized in the midst of most desperate complications, in short, when one exclaims, "Eureka! Eureka!" But this refers only to the subjective and emotional aspect of a *satori.* As for its intellectual side, it is concerned with the entirety of one's life. For what Zen proposes to do is a revolution, and a re-valuation as well, of the spiritual aspect of one's existence. The solving of a mathematical problem ends with the solution, it does not affect one's whole life. So with all other particular questions, practical or scientific, they do not necessarily alter the basic life-tone of the individual concerned. But the opening of *satori* is the re-making of life itself. When it is genuine—for there are many simulacra of it—its effects on one's moral and spiritual life are revolutionary, and they are also enhancing, purifying, as well as exacting.[28]

A Chinese Zen master in the tenth century described what satori meant to him in a few verses which Professor Suzuki has translated as follows:

> Something dropped! It is no other thing;
> Right and left, there is nothing earthy:
> Rivers and mountains and the great earth,
> In them all revealed is the Body of the Dharmaraja.[29]

Neither the extreme of the *via negativa* nor the extreme of the intellectual insight of satori is common; and most Zen

[28] *Eastern Buddhist,* I, 195-96.
[29] *Op. cit.,* p. 214.

adepts, I expect, find traces of both in their most precious experiences. A Zen abbot in Kyoto described his own experience to me as follows: "The contemplation of Zen produces *right mind;* and this means a mind not mixed with things. It sometimes approximates an empty mind—a mind without thought. But this does not mean unconsciousness nor sleep. It is difficult to describe. It is not like death. It is life, it is dynamic. It is not a blank emptiness like unconsciousness but is full of life and force."

"In this condition," I asked, "is the mind captivated by some central object, or is it a blank?"

"At first," the abbot responded, "the beginner is given an object for thought in the form of an enigmatic question, in order to keep his mind on a tight stretch. But at last the heavens open and he sees beyond. In this condition one asks oneself, What do I see? What do I hear? What do I feel? What am I? His conclusion is that he sees nothing, hears nothing, feels nothing, is nothing; but that this 'nothing' is no mere blank or negation. It is like waking from a dream. It is not a realization of being in accord with the laws of the universe, for you are then beyond such forms of thought; and to say that you *realize* anything would be to misrepresent the state, for realization comes only after the experience is past. So, after the experience, you may realize that you were in accord with the laws of the universe. The feeling that you are near to God would be too explicit to be good. Every explicit experience must be transcended. Yet when you have transcended every explicit thing, it is not negation that you reach. When you come to the stage where the ice is broken and the tensity of the mind is overcome, you must not be captivated by any object, whether God or Buddha. A sense even of thankfulness to God or the Buddha at such a time would captivate the mind and be an impediment. It would enslave the mind and bind it; and it is unimportant, once the mind is bound, whether the chain be iron or gold."

Satori of this sort is plainly emotional rather than intellectual. It is almost entirely lacking in intellectual content, and yet filled with intense emotion of conviction, and the mystic returns from it with a sense of great illumination. The same phenomenon is common among Christian mystics, who frequently after ecstasy assert that they have had tremendous revelations yet are unable to state explicitly any of them.[30]

Not always are the reports of satori so lacking in definite detail as was the description given me by the Kyoto abbot. Another Kyoto Zen abbot told me that in satori one sees the nature of Buddha in everything, and realizes that we are all identical with each other and with all material things, because we and all things partake of the Buddha nature. This represents fairly well the satori realization described by many Zen writers. It seems perfectly plain that a revelation of this sort is to be set down as interpretation rather than as the immediate experience of satori; or else that the conception of satori must be enlarged so as to include almost any emotional intensification of a philosophical belief otherwise obtained.

That there are all kinds and degrees of satori can, indeed, hardly be questioned. It is a relative term, and many a good Zen scholar is uncertain whether he has had it or not. When the experience comes in its most intense form it is, indeed, unmistakable: but this intense experience is rare in modern Japan, just as ecstasy is rare in Christendom, and *samadhi* in India. It is said that some have experienced satori as many as eighteen times (for it is, of course, a temporary and passing state); but most of those you question will say they are not sure they have ever attained it though they have approximated it two or three times. One abbot told me that after he had studied and done zazen for twelve years his colleagues thought he had attained this insight, but that he himself does not think he has attained it even yet. This poor opinion of himself, however, may have been a matter of deliberate cultivation, for he added that if one thinks one has really attained, that means the beginning of the downward road. One should always be dissatisfied and seek for further enlightenment. The zazen which begins to approximate satori induces, apparently, a kind of relaxation of body and

[30] Cf. Leuba, "Tendances Religieuses chez les Mystiques Chrétiens" (*Revue Philosophique*, LIV, 480); and my book on *The Religious Consciousness*, pp. 405-11.

openness of mind not unrelated to the "beautiful silence" of a Quaker meeting.

I suggested, a few paragraphs back, that the intellectual and statable content of the Zen revelation is really obtained elsewhere. When put into words it turns out to be—as of course we should expect—not something new but a restatement of the leading ideas of Mahayana philosophy. These are learned by reading, lectures, and conversation, are breathed in with the very air of the Zen monastery, become a part of the subconscious or the "apperceiving mass," or whatever else we wish to call that great body of ideas and attitudes which are so fundamental for the individual as to be taken for granted; and when the emotional crisis of satori arrives, or has partially subsided, these ideas are presented to the mind in relatively objective form as a kind of immediate intuition, clad with the joy of a personal discovery. I do not say this is all there is to it: I am by no means persuaded it is all; but it is a large part of it. There can be no doubt that the traditional Mahayana philosophy contributes very much more to the Zen revelation than the Zen revelation contributes to the Mahayana philosophy.

For, spite of Bodhidharma's silence and spite of a thousand and more years of protest against philosophy, there can be no doubt that Zen has a philosophy. A Zen abbot once responded to a question of mine concerning Zen thought by the simple sentence, "Zen has nothing to say." This was orthodox and correct. But I noted that, having made his tribute to Bodhidharma, the abbot had a good deal to say.

What Zen says, however, is far from systematic. Both the Mahayana in general and mysticism in general feel little constraint from the rules of logic: and Zen being a combination of the two is doubly free. Even more than Tendai it fairly revels in contradictions. Since all verbal assertions are bound, in the last analysis, to be false, almost any assertion may be made. The law of contradiction holds only for this world of the many, and one can see how a Tendai philosopher can, with some logic, comfort himself by escaping to the world of the One; but the Zen thinker spurns any such act of discretion. Of course Zen thought is greatly influenced by Tendai; but it is still more influenced by Kegon. Change for Zen is real with nothing illusory about it. The phenomenal world is the real world. "Nirvana is Samsara." [31] The man who has attained the truth, says one of the most famous of Zen hymns, "does not reject error. The true nature of the unintelligible cannot be other than the Buddha nature." Upon which Ohasama comments: "Truth does not need to be sought first, for it is present everywhere, even in error. Hence he who rejects error rejects truth." [32]

The backbone of Zen thought is, as I have said, to be found in the Tendai-Kegon philosophy. But it is plain that Nagarjuna's doctrine of vacuity has also had profound influence upon many Zen thinkers. It is easy to see why the concept of the Void should make a strong appeal to those who believe that they approximate an immediate intuition of the Real in the concentrated and "unified" state produced by zazen. Professor Hocking has pointed out that mystics in general have been led to attribute unity and ineffableness to God because they find their trance ineffable and unitary. "What is a psychological report (and a true one) is taken as a metaphysical statement (and a false one)." [33] Murisier and Ribot have pointed out a similar influence upon mystic theology derived from the "monoideism" of the quietest type.[34] In similar fashion, the process of "emptying the mind" practiced so strenuously by students of Zen most naturally leads to the conclusion that Reality is found in the "complete nothing." Which does not make Zen the less sure that the phenomenal reality of the changing many is thoroughly real and that "Nirvana is Samsara."

In spite of these various contradictions, however, due, I suspect, to the natural and widespread human desire to eat one's cake and keep it too, there is one doctrine or assertion that Zen sticks to with a consistency that would satisfy the nicest lover of logic. I refer to the fundamental conviction that to see the Buddha one must look into one's own

[31] Samsara, it will be recalled, is this world of changing phenomena, which for the Founder and for the Hinayana is at the exact antipodes from Nirvana.

[32] *Op. cit.*, pp. 71, 134.

[33] "Mysticism as Seen through Its Psychology," *Mind*, N. S., XXI (1912), p. 43.

[34] Murisier, *Les Maladies du Sentiment Religieux*, esp. pp. 61-62; Ribot, "L'Ideal Quietiste," *Rev. Philosophique* for 1915, pp. 440-54. Leuba has also treated this influence of mystical psychology upon mystic theology in his *Psychology of Religious Mysticism*, pp. 306f. See also Chap. XVIII of *The Religious Consciousness.*

nature and one's own mind. This I have already dwelt upon in another connection, but it can hardly be repeated too often, for it is the very heart of Zen. The Universal lies within, and only by immediate inner intuition can one know it. Having known it one knows all. Haku-in celebrated this central thought in the first lines of his hymn:

"In their deepest nature men are Buddha, as water is ice. And as there is no ice without water, so without the Buddha there could be no men. Woe to them who seek it in the far distant, and know not that it is very near." [35]

This realization of the identity of oneself with the eternal Buddha gives the point of view from which Zen regards the problem of immortality. On the subordinate aspects of this question there is much disagreement in Zen. Mention is made of reincarnation: yet the self is of course denied, and by some [36] the mind is identified with the body. But the really central doctrine on which nearly all intelligent followers of Zen would unite is to be found, as I have said, in the identity of all things with the Buddha, and in the nature of eternity. An ancient hymn by the third Chinese patriarch of the sect asserts, "A moment is as a thousand years. . . . Past and future, are they not an eternal now?" [37] In spite of the repeated assertion that change is real and that Nirvana is Samsara, it is in a timeless immortality that Zen believes.

The eternal Now and the identity of the Buddha with all things is of course a common belief with Tendai and Kegon and with most of the sects that have grown out of their thought. It is not this belief nor any other doctrine that makes Zen unique. Its uniqueness consists in its persistent attempt (which it maintains is often successful) to find and actually to experience the Buddha nature. It does not stop with faith, it goes on to vision. It *knows* whom it has believed. It has much of the conceptual weakness and much of the empirical strength of all mysticism. Secure within the certainty of its own ineffable experience, it watches with

[35] Quoted by Ohasama, *op. cit.*, p. 62.

[36] E.g., by Kaiten Nukariya, who seems to have fallen under the influence of Haeckel, and whose book on Zen, called *The Religion of the Samurai*, is so largely framed on Western categories as to be misleading.

[37] Quoted by Ohasama, p. 71.

equanimity the fate of the philosophies in which it sometimes dabbles. Your true Zen will discuss philosophy with you as long as you like, he will read books and write them. But he is not troubled by the thought that all the philosophies and all the books may be mistaken. For he knows that the best and truest of these are but "fingers pointing at the moon."

CHAPTER XXXI

PHILOSOPHICAL POSITIONS OF THE NICHIREN AND AMIDA SECTS

NICHIREN, as we have seen, never renounced his allegiance to the Tendai thought in which he had been trained, and so far as he differed from his teachers on Hiei-san it was through a more exclusive and extreme loyalty to the great Tendai gospel, the Saddharma Pundarika Sutra. Tendai seeks to be inclusive of all the truth in all sects: Nichiren is rather bitterly exclusive of all truth but that of the Lotus. In positive philosophical insight Nichiren had little to contribute. He was an intelligent Tendai philosopher; hardly more. His contribution was rather on the religious side, attempting as he did to make the truths of the Lotus gospel live in the hearts of his followers as matters of individual experience, through meditation, active practice, and earnest loyalty to Sakyamuni.[1]

The three leading characteristics of the thought of the Nichiren sect today (so I was told by the abbot of a large Nichiren monastery near Tokyo) are (1) insistence upon history rather than myth, (2) antagonism to the pessimism common in some of the other sects, and (3) emphasis upon the social and national aspect of religion. The first and third of these points are especially stressed by all Nichiren thinkers. Members of this sect, I was told by one of their monks in a Kyoto monastery, refuse to believe in anything imaginary. The other sects talk about mythical Buddhas, Amida, Dainichi, and the rest, and about an imaginary Western Paradise. The Nichiren sect accepts none of these things. It bases itself on actual history and on the facts of life and busies itself about the welfare of individuals here and now and the safety and happiness of society. My monkish informant, I might add, looked like the sort of man who would hold that sort

[1] Cf. Anesaki, *Nichiren*, Chap. VII.

of view, a big, dominating fellow, with a positivist, pragmatist, "cash-value" air. There was certainly little about him suggesting the other-worldly. For him, and for most of his fellows, the welfare of Japan and the spirit of nationalism are a vital part of Buddhism. They come by this view rightly. The three great vows of Nichiren, as popularly known, are the following: "I must be the pillar of Japan; I must be eyes to Japan; I must be a great ship to Japan." [2]

Not all members of the sect would go so far as did the Kyoto monk in denying reality to all members of the Buddhist cycle other than Shaka. My friend the Tokyo abbot assured me the other Buddhas and the Bodhisattvas are as real as you and I. They act and work. They have special natures and exist for special purposes. But they are not ultimately real, as is the One Buddha: and when their work is accomplished they are reabsorbed into the Absolute Source of all things, which is, of course, Sakyamuni. For it is from Him that all beings are rayed out, so to speak, like beams of light from a central sun. Yet though absolute, he is also personal. The Absolute is one with the historical Shaka. And all men are one with both. This, of course, is almost Tendai doctrine and has little new about it except a certain personal aspect which Nichiren stresses in the relation between individual men and the Eternal Buddha. The Buddha is sometimes thought of, not merely as the Dharmakaya, but as our Father. My Kyoto monk found in this a contrast between Nichiren Buddhism and Christianity; and I quote his remark chiefly because of the light it throws on the kind of Christian teaching that seems to have got itself published in many parts of Japan. Christianity, he said, teaches that we are the children of sin, whereas Nichiren taught that we are the children of Buddha.

The Japanese Amida sects, like the Nichiren, in one sense grew out of Tendai and so far as they can be said to have an official philosophy at all the Tendai philosophy is the basis of it. The acceptance of this form of thought, however, is by no means necessary for orthodox members of these sects. Most of their thinkers accept the Tendai view, a few do not; but all agree that no abstruse theory is necessary to salvation.

[2] Coates and Ishizuka, *Honen*, p. 67.

The central character of all these sects is belief in salvation through the grace of Amida given freely to all who have faith in Him.

Amida has as many interpretations as the Christian God, perhaps more. For the rank and file He is hardly different from "Our Heavenly Father," except that in the back of their minds lurks the dim realization that if they were philosophers they would interpret Him in some more profound sense. For the philosophical Amidist (if I may use such a word) Amida is the Absolute, the Tendai Dharmakaya. Even these philosophers, however, still retain the personal view. In philosophy, I was told by a very learned Shinshu abbot, Shin and Jodo thinkers accept pantheism; in faith they insist upon the personal view of God. Like other Orientals (once more) they distinguish between faith and believing to be true. The personal and the impersonal view play back and forth within the mind and speech of the Amidist thinker in interesting fashion. The catechism of the Shin sect deals with the question thus: "Since the Shinshu and Jodo group in general is not argumentative but practical Buddhism, it leads its adherents by teachings which are applicable to our daily life. For this reason Amida is represented as a Buddha who has personal existence."[3]

> As a theistic conception [writes Reischauer] the Amida doctrine breaks down for the reason that no Buddhist philosopher is willing to think of the Ultimate in terms of personality. Amida is spoken of as a personal being, but the term Personal is what Buddhist philosophers of all schools would consider as an accommodation of language when used of the Ultimate. Even in the West it is a common objection to the doctrine of a Personal God to say that personality implies limitation, and that therefore God as the Absolute cannot be personal. The Buddhist philosopher raises the same objection and says that if Amida is spoken of as personal, it is only by way of accommodation to suit the doctrine to the intelligence of the average man who cannot think in the concepts of philosophy.

The combination of the impersonal Absolute with the literally personal is made more striking, for the logically-minded more difficult, and for the religiously-minded per-

[3] Reischauer's trans., *T. A. S. J.*, XXXVII, p. 364. This version of the Shinshu catechism has been republished by the Hongwanji mission in Honolulu in pamphlet form.

haps more fascinating, by the identification of the eternal Amida with the man Hozo. It was as Hozo (Sanskrit Dharmakara), a man who lived at the time when the Buddha Sejizaiobutsu was upon earth, that Amida made his famous forty-eight vows. According to the Shin catechism Hozo "was an historical personage, but he does not belong to the period of authentic history."[4] Just when he lived we cannot tell. Some call it ten kalpas ago, some say he belonged to the eternities of the past.

> But it does not matter whether we say ten Kalpas or eternity, for the essence of the universe is not subject to space and time. Still it is the free and eternal truth which belongs to the timeless and measureless eternity that after all has value for a world which is conditioned by space and time. Therefore the Amida who attained perfection ten Kalpas ago is the same as the one who attained Buddhahood in the eternities of the past. Both are explained in terms suited to meet the degree of intelligence to which they are revealed, and in reality there is no difference between them. Do you regard the moon which has tonight appeared from behind the mountain as just now coming into existence, or is it not the same moon which gave light in the ages past?[5]

The identity of the man Hozo with the Absolute is one of those paradoxes which delights the religious heart in many countries—witness the identification of the child Krishna with the infinite Vishnu, of the infant Jesus with the Eternal Logos by whom all things were made that were made. "Language fails! Language fails! Language fails! One can only exclaim Ah! in wonder and amazement."[6]

Considered in Himself, from the absolute point of view, Amida is the Real Substance which constitutes the essence of the Universe. "It is," says the Shin catechism, "the Acme of Truth." In Spinozistic fashion the catechism continues,

[4] Reischauer's trans., p. 362. We must accept the historicity of Hozo, the catechism continues, on the authority of Shaka, and we must not be too nice in our insistence upon the meticulous rules of evidence. "If we put too much stress on the matter of historical evidence, all events in the mythological age of Japan and in the very ancient periods of Chinese and Western history can be reduced to mere legend. We must doubt therefore not only the historicity of Hozo Bosatsu, but all ancient history will become untrustworthy. Since we live in a world which has neither beginning nor end, we can not deny that at a certain time there appeared such a famous man and that he was of such an ideal character [as Hozo Bosatsu is alleged to have been]. In a world subject to such vicissitudes one must guard against getting too nearsighted and believing only what can be historically established" (*op. cit.*, p. 363).

[5] *Op. cit.*, p. 363-64.

[6] From Mito Giko, quoted in the catechism, p. 365.

There is nothing in this universe which does not come under one or the other of the two realities we call matter and mind. By the Real Substance of the universe then we mean the underlying essence of matter and mind. This Substance, through the law of Cause and Effect, produces things and destroys them; it changes things and maintains them. . . . Real Substance is the Body of Law [the Dharmakaya] which underlies the entire universe. This is the so-called Spiritual Essence which neither is born nor perishes. The apparent differences in the world are but the product of impure thought; outside the mind there are no real differences. Therefore the real essence of the universe is not to be expressed in words, nor can it be reduced to any fixed formula. It is incomprehensible and ultimately it is a Oneness in which there is neither change nor difference. It is indestructible, and because it is a Oneness it is called *Real* Substance.[7]

This, of course, is the Tendai philosophy over again, and from this view it follows that ultimately all the Buddhas are one, and for that matter all deities of all religions are but many names for Amida. It was for this reason that Rennyo, the greatest of the Shinshu teachers after Shinran and the eighth patriarch of the sect, forbade the explicit worship of any members of the Shinto or Buddhist cycles save only Amida, and banished from the domestic shrine of the Shinshu believer the Kami shelf which other Buddhist sects had retained. It is for this reason also that even Shaka is unrepresented in Shinshu temples and Shinshu homes. For "the act of invoking Amida's name includes within it all that would be involved in the invocation of them all."[8] This unification of all that is divine, in fact of all that is real, under the one name Amida of course does not mean that the other Buddhas are in no sense real. They are real in a way, just as you and I are in some sense real. Ultimately we are all one, but practically we are many; just as all the waves are water and therefore one, and yet as waves they are many. Without the waves there would be no water, and without the water no waves. The task of harmonizing the unity of being with the multiplicity of the Buddhas is further advanced by the concept of the Trikaya, the three Bodies of the Buddha. In their Dharmakaya all the Buddhas are one, and this one Dharmakaya is really Amida; in their Sambhogakaya and Nirmanakaya they are many.[9]

[7] *Op. cit.*, pp. 365-66.

[8] Coates and Ishizuka, *Honen*, p. 58.

[9] Amida is of course also one of the Sambhogakaya. Moreover, as the Sambhogakaya is closer to practical reality than the more abstruse Dharmakaya, and hence more repre-

This brings up the question of the relation of Amida to Shaka. The Shinshu catechism says:

> There are two ways in which the relation between Amida and Shaka is conceived. One way regards the two as one and the same being; the other as distinct. When the two are regarded as one and the same being, the teacher Shaka is looked upon as the incarnation of Amida. He is regarded as coming temporarily into this world. When the two are conceived as distinct beings, Shaka is looked upon as the *Teacher* of this world and Amida as the *Saviour* of the world.[10]

In one of his hymns Shinran wrote: "That Buddha that was made flesh in India was in this world manifested that he might preach the Divine Promise of Him who is infinite."[11] One of the professors in the Educational Department of the Nishi Hongwanji temple in Kyoto told me that Shinshu has a Trinity consisting of (1) Shinnyo or the Absolute or the World of Identity (which is really Amida), (2) the personal Amida in the Western Paradise, and (3) Shaka. Shaka is really Amida taking human form. After the death of Shaka he of course became again simply Amida. At present there is no distinct personality Shaka anywhere existent. He added that Shaka has appeared as a saving power many times since his death in India, some say 8000 times. Amida appears in this world in Shaka's form and in thousands of other forms to save people. In fact, as one of these many expressions of Amida, Shaka is always present and active in the world. Naturally at this point I asked how this assertion of Shaka's present activity was consistent with the earlier assertion that Shaka as a distinct personality no longer existed. The professor replied that Shaka as a man died long ago but that Shaka's spirit still continues to live and to act. To make the matter clearer I asked, in Western fashion, Does this mean that it is the same personality, the same self, that continues to live and to act? In reply the professor made the comment that he really did not know what the word *personality* meant. It is a new term, he said, recently introduced from

sentative of wisdom and mercy, it is as a Sambhogakaya rather than as the Dharmakaya that Jodo and Shin love best to envisage Amida. Hence while Tendai and Kegon give their chief emphasis to the Dharmakaya, the Amida sects stress most the Sambhogakaya. Cf. McGovern *Introduction to Mahayana Buddhism*, pp. 95-96.

[10] Pp. 355-56.

[11] Trans. by Yamabe and Beck in *Buddhist Psalms*, p. 29.

the West. (A Shingon monk, two days before, had told me the same thing.) All he could say in answer to my question was that Shaka at his death in Kusinara had been absorbed into Amida. None the less, he frequently comes back as a saving power, and on such occasions he is again Shaka. As such a saving power he is present in the world today. And this, the professor concluded, did not seem to him at all inconsistent with his earlier statement that the Shaka who died in Kusinara in 480 B.C. no longer exists. "But this Shaka who is present in the world today," I insisted, "is he conscious of himself as Shaka?" The professor replied that my question had no definite meaning for him. The Shaka who is active in the world today certainly does not know himself as the son of King Suddhodana, nor is he conscious of his exact identity with a particular Indian prince. Yet he is truly Shaka. In other words, our questions and answers were at cross purposes because of the fundamental contrast between Eastern and Western concepts of individuality—a rather interesting situation. The professor started out on the presupposition of the Anatta doctrine, and his questions and answers implied, what he was too courteous to assert, that it was really the vagueness of our Western concept of personality that made me see a contradiction where to the Eastern mind there was no contradiction at all.

If we may trust Dean Inge, this concept of personality on which the questions I put to the abbot were based, is not only relatively local but relatively new. In his opinion the thought of impervious and separate selves goes back hardly further than Kant; and he insists that at any rate the conception of personality found in the New Testament is "absolutely fluid."

> Jesus Christ was seriously suspected of being Elijah or Jeremiah or even John Baptist who had just been beheaded. And unless we are willing to sacrifice the whole of the deepest and most spiritual teaching of St. Paul and St. John, unless we are prepared to treat all the solemn language of the New Testament about the solidarity of the body and its members, the vine and its branches, as fantastic and misleading metaphor, we must assert roundly that this notion of "impervious" spiritual atoms is flatly contrary to Christianity.[12]

[12] *Personal Idealism and Mysticism*, 3rd ed. (London, Longmans, 1924), pp. 94, 95.

I cite these words of Dean Inge not as being final (for as the reader may have guessed, I am not in full agreement with him), but to remind the reader that the position of Buddhism in general upon the question of personality, and of my friend the abbot in particular, is not peculiar nor merely oriental.

But the central theme of Amidist thought is not the nature of the Godhead but the way of salvation. I have in another connection spoken of the division of Japanese Buddhism into two great sections according as they promise salvation through Shodomen (the Holy Way section) and Jiriki (self-strength) or through Jodomen (the Pure Land section) and Tariki (another's strength). The difference is thus expressed in the Shinshu catechism:

> Shodomen has reference to the holy way in which the saints of this division walk. It is the way for the strong man who relies on his own strength for salvation. The principle of self-culture which the sects belonging to this division teach finds in Shaka Nyorai an example. He revealed in his own life the wisdom attained through meditation and also the way by which such wisdom may be attained; and so he has made it possible for mankind to attain the same through religious observances. Therefore this division of Buddhism is sometimes called the School of Self-Reliance or the Way of Hardships. Jodomon means the Nirvana Entering Division. This division recognizing the insufficiency of one's own strength relies for salvation upon the Great Mercy of Amida Nyorai. It teaches the principle of faith in the strength of Another. Therefore this is sometimes called the School of Reliance on Another or the Easy Way Doctrine.[18]

As will be seen from this quotation, the Amida sects do not deny that salvation is (at least in theory) possible by the Way of Works—morality, meditation, insight. But in the opinion of Honen Shonin and the founders of the other Pure Land sects this road was so difficult that for men of their generation it had become well-nigh impossible as a practical matter. The simplest and surest way was not through one's own merits but through the merits and the grace of the gracious Amida and through the might of his famous eighteenth vow. Honen and Shinran and all their followers have said in substance with St. Paul and Martin Luther, not once but many times, "By grace are ye saved through faith; and that not of yourselves; it is the gift of God." This faith through

[18] Pp. 342-43. Cf. also McGovern, pp. 94-95, 104-08.

which salvation comes is not an easy matter. It does not consist either in the repetition or in the intellectual acceptance of a formula. "Ah," said Shinran, "it is difficult indeed for a man even during a life of many incarnations to meet with the salvation wrought by the Buddha's great vow. Even in eternity it is difficult to rise to pure faith. Let him then who has this faith rejoice: for it was thus predetermined." [14] "Predetermined," however, not by some anthropomorphic Jehovah or Allah, but by one's own merit acquired through striving in many previous lives; and yet the gift of God as well. It is not chiefly nor even largely intellectual but rather a state of the loving heart.

> The union of hearts [wrote Honen Shonin, that real saint of the twelfth century] is the union of our heart with the heart of Amida. The Tendai sect says truly that in the world there is always a lover and a beloved and that love is perfected when lover and beloved meet. Amida is the lover, we are the beloved and when we turn with our whole heart to Amida and surrender ourselves to Him, our hearts become one with His. But a heart that is distracted over many things cannot realize this union. That privilege is reserved for those hearts that are devoted to the thankful remembrance of Amida's mercies.[15]

Faith means complete trust in Amida and therefore utter renunciation of self-help. A devout and mystical member of the Shin sect whose writings are held in much respect,[16] expresses it thus:

> We are to believe deeply in the mercy of Amida, but if you are too concerned with your state of mind, the very mercy of Amida may prove to be a hindrance to the growth of your faith. If you strive to grow in faith thinking this must be accomplished for your salvation, the very effort will smother it. For faith means unconditionally to submit oneself to The Other, and the straining is the outcome of self-power; the heavier you step the deeper you go into the mud of self-power, and the further you stand from the Other-power. . . . There is no need for you to look backward and forward and to carry along such old stuff as Nembutsu [17] or faith or joyful heart. As soon as you realize the destiny

[14] Quoted in the Shinshu catechism, p. 346.

[15] Quoted by Arthur Lloyd in *Shinran and his Work,* p. 98.

[16] Kojun Shichiri, who died in 1900. Professor Suzuki has translated some of his "Sayings" in *The Eastern Buddhist* (Vol. III, No. 2). It is from Suzuki's article that I take the quotation from Shichiri.

[17] As we shall see, Shin in contrast to Jodo teaches that the repetition of the Nembutsu is not necessary to salvation.

of your sinful existence and the infinite, unconditional love of The Other, begone with the last trace of self-assertion in whatever form, and abandon yourself, heart and soul, at the feet of the Saviour.

This matter of salvation by faith is so fundamental to Amidist Buddhism that I am tempted to dwell a little longer upon it. The Shinshu catechism from which I have so often quoted is very explicit upon this point and, as the reader will notice, it has quite the tone of evangelical Christianity. Thus Question 58 reads:

What is faith in Amida Butsu?

[Ans.] When we hear what is the significance of *Namu Amida Butsu*, we recognize that we are deeply involved in sin and evil from which it is impossible to extricate ourselves through whatever efforts we may put forth. We must trust firmly and without a doubt in the might of Amida's Vow to save us and bear in mind his great merciful heart.

To believe the truth is faith (Junshi).

[Q. 59] What is the state of mind of him who believes in Amida?

[Ans.] Before we know Amida we spend our lives in sin as a result of which we are drawn into the evil way and are submerged in suffering. But when we listen to the Voice of Salvation we are saved from our sinful condition, being taken into the eternal light of Buddha; and so we are able to share his merit and receive his favor. We rely upon the great heart of mercy of the Nyorai while we exclaim, "O, thou Nyorai of great mercy, thou Father of true salvation!" Thus we feel as if we had escaped from the jaws of the tiger and entered the rescue boat. Relying upon this Amida Nyorai, we utter the *Nembutsu* with gratitude and reverence, with exultation and devotion. Our heart is filled with a great peace and a great joy. . . .

[Q. 61] When we speak of believing in the Might of Amida's saving Vow, do we not mean that this faith comes from the believer's own power?

[Ans.] Of course it is the believer's heart that does the believing, but that this heart becomes fixed in its belief is due alone to the believer having understood the heart of mercy wherewith Amida saves him. The unwavering faith which submits to the commands of Amida is not the product of the believer's own strength of heart, but it comes through the strength of Another. . . . If a man who has only the faith which relies upon self, prays to Amida for help and salvation, however earnestly he may pray, he cannot attain the great joy which is called the Peace of Heart because he relies on himself. But in the case of the man whose faith comes through the strength of Another, when he prays he relies entirely upon Amida's commandment of great mercy which calls us unto salvation. Therefore the Great Joy which is called either Faith or Peace is the faith which is the gift of Another.[18]

From these quotations it will be seen that evangelical Buddhism has some of the same uncertainties and some of the same difficulties about the relation of faith and works as evangelical Christianity. The way of faith is immensely simpler and easier than the way of works and knowledge, and we should accept through faith the grace of God. Yet this act of acceptance and of faith which we are urged to perform turns out to be not our act at all but the act of God who works within us. The evangelical thus seems with one breath to urge us to do something which in the next breath he tells us only God can do. So eager is he to ascribe all merit to the Divine Giver that he refuses to the creature even the meager credit of accepting the gift, which at the same moment he urges him to take and which he blames him for not taking. It is to man's discredit if he refuses to believe, yet not to his credit if he does believe. Much the same difficulty arises in another connection when the question of the value of works is raised. It is the old controversy between St. James and St. Paul, between the Church of Rome and Martin Luther. The Jodo sect sees the difficulty, perhaps, a little more clearly than the Shinshu and hence hesitates in carrying the doctrine of salvation by faith to its extreme and logical conclusion. We are saved by faith, yet works, too, are helpful, and we must perform them. Shinran and his followers care more for the logic of their presuppositions and less for the paradox of the consequences. According to Shinshu doctrine, works help not at all toward salvation, but are performed as a spontaneous consequence of faith and as a token of our gratitude to Amida.[19]

This matter of faith and works I discussed at some length with a Tokyo Shinshu abbot, a most learned, kindly, and reverend gentleman in whose house I spent a delightful afternoon. It was, as I look back upon it, almost ungracious of me to ply him with unpleasant questions on this difficult matter as I did, in my clumsy, downright, large-footed Western way: particularly after his cordial welcome and in

[18] Pp. 371-73.
[19] Cf. the catechism, pp. 345, 381-83.

the midst of his gentle and abundant hospitality. We had been discussing other topics when the door of his study opened, and his aged mother and his little daughter (of perhaps seven years) entered upon their knees, bowing to me as only Japanese ladies can and bringing with them the implements necessary for making the honorable tea. The old lady —and a lady she was, every inch of her—heated the water over the charcoal brazier, and when it came to a boil poured it first (according to the Japanese fashion) into another receptacle and then, when it had cooled a trifle, upon the tea leaves, so that the bitterest flavor of the tea might not be brought out as it would have been by actually boiling water. And then the little girl with the sweet courtesy of her age and nation brought me the cup, with cakes and other things. The gentleness of Japanese ladies at their best, old and young, the beauty of soul that shines through their bodies and their actions, is surely one of the loveliest flowers of all human culture. Even after I had eaten my cakes and sipped my tea and the little maid and her grandmother had withdrawn, it was hard for me to bring my thoughts back to theology.

But I did. And it was after this idyllic interlude of touching hospitality that I broke out with my almost brutal questions about faith and works. What will happen, said I, after death to a morally bad man who has had faith in Amida? He will, responded the abbot, be born in the Western Paradise. But, I asked, does not this teaching have an evil effect upon morality? Our moral life, replied my patient host (who, I should add, spoke English excellently), our moral life should be the natural and spontaneous consequence of our religious faith. A man with religious faith may occasionally fail to do right, but these failures are due to bad Karma collected in previous lives. Without a religious life a moral life is impossible. Hence if a man has true faith, and to the extent that he has true faith, he will not sin. True faith and a truly moral life are inseparable. What, then, I asked, *is* true faith? It is, said the abbot, the realization of the actuality of Amida's salvation in ourselves. To be more explicit, said I, if a man thoroughly believes that Amida exists in the Western Paradise, that He made the forty-eight vows and will save all who believe in him, has such a man true faith? The abbot answered Yes. I think this was bad tactics on his part and not altogether necessary; but he did say Yes. Whereupon I most discourteously pointed out that a man might believe all these things and be a villain still, and ended up by quoting St. James on the devils who believe and tremble. At this the abbot retracted his Yes of a moment before, and said that as a fact it is not possible for a man who has real faith in Amida to commit great sins. But, he added, one must take into consideration the power of evil Karma, which is so great at times as to suppress temporarily our free wills. That even this was not fully satisfactory he seemed to realize, for he confessed that the point was one of great delicacy and of great difficulty for the Shin sect. Still, in spite of all difficulties of detail, it is true, he insisted, that pure faith is the one thing that matters. How one names the object of one's faith does not matter, whether Amida or Jehovah or Jesus, and those of pure faith in other religions, if such there be, are really Shinshu believers without knowing it. Earnest faith is the one important thing.

The question of works is bound up with the question of the use of the Nembutsu; and this is one of the few points of theory on which Jodo and Shin are divided. The Nembutsu (Namu Amida Butsu), as I have pointed out in a previous chapter, is regarded by all the Pure Land sects as, in a sense, the name of Amida; and Honen Shonin taught that salvation came by the repetition of this divine name with a heart of faith. Thus faith alone was for Honen hardly sufficient. It should be accompanied and expressed by the loving repetition of Amida's name. In other words, the repetition of the Nembutsu had for him and has for his sect, in one sense, an absolute value, and it was for this reason that he made a point of repeating it several thousand times a day.[20] The reason why Honen considered the repetition of this sacred formula so important "was that its efficacy was so explicitly asserted in Amida's Original Vow. In this Vow Amida made the Salvation of all sentient beings by the simple invocation of his name the one condition upon which he would accept Buddhahood, thus transferring to them the full merit of all those religious austerities he had practiced

[20] Ryonin, the founder of the Yutsu Nembutsu sect, did the same.

through many kalpas of time."[21] This view seems, of course, a trifle naïve, and Shinran was quick to see that the logic of the doctrine of salvation by faith made such repetition no longer essential to salvation. He did not, indeed, go the whole distance that his logic implied, for he, too, accepted the authority of the famous eighteenth vow: but he insisted that one invocation of the sacred name, "Namu Amida Butsu" with a heart of faith was quite sufficient to justify the believer in claiming Amida's promise. After that first invocation it is doubtless well to invoke the sacred name frequently, but such repetitions help in no wise toward one's salvation, but are merely expressions—as are all good works—of one's gratitude for the salvation which has already been secured.

Salvation thus begins in this life, and means first of all the union of the human heart with the heart of Amida. It means also, for most members of the sect, something like "going to heaven when you die." The Anatta doctrine, so far as I know, has never been explicitly abandoned by the Amida sects, but for the less philosophical members of these sects it has lapsed into obsolescence. The pious but not profoundly educated follower of Honen or Shinran, or Ryonin or Ippen, believes in a "soul" of much the same indefinite sort as does the pious Christian. The fate of this soul in the future life is left rather vague. Transmigration for those who have not attained to pure faith in Amida is accepted, quite as a matter of course, by all these sects. They also believe in the "Western Paradise," the "Pure Land," where Amida dwells and where he will receive the souls of those who trust in him and claim the merit of his vow by the repetition, with pure faith, of His holy name. Shinran speaks also of a "Temporal Paradise"[22] for those not sufficiently advanced in the life of the spirit for the Pure Land.

For many a pious member of Jodo or of Shin, Amida's glorious heaven is the final term of the imagined future. Yet for the more earnest souls, for those members of Jodo and Shin who have become most saturated with the spirit of

[21] Coates and Ishizuka, p. 45.

[22] "Few are the believers that shall be born into the Land that is promised [i.e., the Pure Land], but many are they that shall be born into the Temporal Paradise," Yamabe and Beck, *Buddhist Psalms*, pp. 75-76.

the founders—and of the great Founder—those, in other words, who are most like Amida himself, even the glories of the Pure Land are but means to further insight and further service rather than the final end of all striving. According to Professor Suzuki, the intelligent Amidist yearns for the Pure Land chiefly as a means for obtaining the same great enlightenment which other sects seek here and now by the more difficult path of self-strength (Jiriki). "The Pure Land School in this respect shows no deviation from the main current of Buddhist thought: indeed if it did it could not at all go under the name of Buddhism. Enlightenment is the one fundamental note that reverberates through all the branches of the teaching of the Buddha."[23] The earnest lover of Amida in fact longs not only for enlightenment but also for endless opportunity to make use of this enlightenment, once gained in the Pure Land, for the salvation of the sad and unenlightened beings who are still held in the clutches of Samsara. Hence Shinran's doctrine of Gensoyeko, which Professor Suzuki translates as "return and transfer," the doctrine that after having attained enlightenment one may, if one will, "come back to this life to dedicate all one's merits toward the enlightenment of one's fellow beings, sentient and non-sentient."[24]

> When [said Shinran] we shall have attained unto the faith and the deeds of the Merciful Promise through our Father that is in all things able to give them unto us, birth and death are henceforward as Nirvana. And this is called the Gift of Departure. And when we shall have attained unto that height which is desire for the ingathering of all beings into Paradise, shall we return again into this world that we may be Saviours of Men. And this is called the Gift of Returning.[25]

The question will very likely present itself to the reader's mind, Who is it that returns to this world after enlightenment in the Pure Land? and how is this notion of "return and transfer" to be squared with the Anatta doctrine? Personally I can of course only join in the reader's wonder. Enlightenment in the Buddhist sense would seem to mean the

[23] "The Development of the Pure Land Doctrine in Buddhism," *Eastern Buddhist*, III (1925), 322.

[24] Suzuki, *op. cit.*, p. 323.

[25] *Buddhist Psalms*, p. 49.

destruction of the illusory limitations of personality, and the merging of the individual into the Supreme. Shinran himself is quoted as saying: "He who is in all things supreme is Himself Nirvana, and Nirvana is that true light that abideth in the land that is to come."[26]

It is plain that the Amidist conception of the future life is quite as lacking in lines of dogmatic precision as is the Christian—a state of things that is probably to be desired. "Eye hath not seen nor ear heard." The indefiniteness, in fact, is carried farther by the Buddhists than I have indicated. For the more philosophically minded, in both Jodo and Shin, have long interpreted the Pure Land of Amida in such philosophic and subjective terms as practically to deny what the orthodox rank and file believe. As long ago as the end of the fourteenth century Ryoyo Shogei, the Seventh Patriarch of the Jodo sect,

> insisted that the ordinary conception of the soul's being transported to Paradise and born there was merely a figure of speech, the fact being that neither Amida nor the sainted beings are to be conceived of as existing over there at all, because the Pure Land is the ultimate and absolute reality, and that is everywhere, so that we may be identified with it right here where we are.[27]

This symbolic interpretation of the Pure Land is plainly a case of the fundamental Tendai philosophy shining through the pictorial garb in which Honen and Shinran had draped it. And while the rank and file of the Amida sects cling to their pleasant and picturesque mythology, a large number of the clergy, including, I suppose, a majority of the professors in their universities, take the more philosophical view. I was told by learned monks in both these sects that for the liberal Amidist, the Western Paradise is really not a place but a state of mind and that the ultimate goal does not consist in being born in a lotus in the Pure Land but in realizing one's essential unity with the Buddha. These more liberal thinkers, moreover, take Hozo and the various Buddhas and Bodhisattvas in purely symbolic fashion, as mere myths to help the childlike mind, while even Amida is, in their interpretation, not a personal God but a name for the Bhutata-

[26] *Ibid.*, p. 37.

[27] Coates and Ishizuka, pp. 56-57.

thata, the Ultimately Real. Such a view differs, of course, in no respect from that of Tendai. There is, however, still a slight difference in emphasis between liberal Shin and Jodo thinkers and those of the older sects and of Zen. Jodo and Shin, as I have said, make little of the Anatta doctrine and on the whole believe in a kind of immortality which is rather more personal than that of the other sects. But the difference is very slight. As one of the Shinshu professors said to me, "In a sense the self is immortal. Still the self that is immortal is the transcendental rather than the empirical ego; and the immortality it is to enjoy is not personal in just the Christian sense."

I should add that the advanced position of the liberals has provoked a good deal of opposition from what might be called the fundamentalist school of Jodo and especially of Shin. Particularly in the Nishi (or Western) Hongwanji has the division between liberals and conservatives been marked and, at times, bitter. A few years ago one of the professors in the Ryukoku university at Kyoto was dismissed for teaching that the personal Amida and the Western Paradise were merely symbols. This is the only case I have come upon in modern Buddhism of anything approximating a prosecution for heresy. Of course it was not really that. One can be a member of Shinshu or Jodo and even a priest in these sects and give any kind of symbolic interpretation one wishes to the formulations of Buddhist thought. But since the distinctive thing within these sects, the justification for their departure from the more philosophic sects and the cause of their great hold upon the common people, is their insistence upon salvation through faith in Amida and his grace, it is but natural that they should object when their official representatives, the professors in their endowed theological seminaries, teach that there is no personal and gracious Amida to have faith in. Thus the problem for Buddhist modernism is almost identical in nature with the problem of Christian modernism. These Buddhist liberals are not only philosophical but deeply religious men. They see the religious and emotional value of their ancient symbols, just as the Christian liberal appreciates the value of the Christian symbols. But if they are to be honest with themselves they cannot give these symbols the old and literal interpretation.

The difficulty goes deeper than at first appears. Ultimately the whole question of God and the Absolute is involved. The position of the philosophic Amidist, whose religious emotions drive him toward Amida and whose philosophical convictions bind him to the Tendai Bhutatathata is very close to that depicted by Bradley in a noted essay: "When you begin to worship the Absolute or the Universe and make it the object of religion, you in fact have transformed it. It has become something forthwith which is less than the Universe." [28] And worship of some sort is of course demanded by the religious consciousness. "The religious consciousness must represent to itself the Good Will in its relation with mine. It must express both our difference and our unity." Yet if you seek to represent this object of worship, this Other than yourself, as something really other—as for example personality—you raise for yourself difficulties no less perplexing.

> A God who has made this strange and glorious Nature outside of which he remains, is an idea at best one-sided. Confined to this idea we lose large realms of what is beautiful and sublime, and even for religion our conception of goodness suffers. Unless the Maker and Sustainer becomes also the indwelling Life and Mind and the inspiring Love, how much of the Universe is impoverished! . . . The so-called "pantheism" which breathes through much of our poetry and art is no less vitally implied in religious practice. Banish all that is meant by the indwelling Spirit of God, in its harmony and discord with the finite soul, and what death and desolation has taken the place of living religion! But how this Spirit can be held consistently with the external individual Person, is a problem which has defied solution. . . . For the reality of God means His own actual presence within individual souls, and apart from this presence both he and they are no more than abstractions.[29]

I cite these passages from the great English thinker because they so well express the position not merely of the Amidist but of the religious Mahayanist in general. And I must remind the reader also of Bradley's rather desperate solution: "From the above it follows that there is a funda-

[28] "On God and the Absolute," in Bradley's *Essays on Truth and Reality* (Oxford, Clarendon Press, 1914), p. 428.

[29] *Op. cit.*, pp. 432-33, 436-37.

mental inconsistency in religion." For on the one hand, it demands that God be perfect and unlimited; yet on the other it insists that he shall stand in relation to my will. The reader may have his own way of getting out of this difficulty, but at any rate it is well for him to realize that the difficulty is a very real one and that it is felt to be insoluble by one of the greatest of our contemporary Western thinkers, and by no means the result of purely local or chance or arbitrary philosophical conceptions or of oriental vagueness. Recognition of this inherent difficulty will explain much of the inconsistency within Mahayana philosophy, and many of its refusals to be forced by the dictum of logical consistency into giving up either its monism or its religious attitude toward the Highest. There is a sense in which, for the religious Mahayanist of every sect, not only Amida but even the Dharmakaya is both God and the Absolute in one.

But while the Mahayana object of reverence or worship is sufficiently distinguishable from the abstract One of philosophy and sufficiently separable from the finite individual to be regarded religiously, Mahayana thought seldom seriously makes for itself the additional difficulty of conceiving it in its ultimate nature as a Person. The latent perplexities of the religious consciousness to which Bradley refers are thus at least reduced to a minimum. And there can be no doubt that, in spite of its great logical difficulties, the attempt to conceive the Divine as at once spiritual and non-personal possesses a certain perennial attraction. Many of the mystics have felt it, and have even felt forced to it by the nature of their mystical experiences.[30] If we could still put full and definite meaning into the term *spiritual* while stripping it of the connotations that cling about the word *personal*, it might well be a refuge for the religious soul who cannot and will not accept naturalism as the last word concerning Reality, and yet who finds it very difficult to interpret the Divine under the limitations which the word personal almost necessarily implies. I do not think that this syn-

[30] E.g., Mlle. Vé, whose experiences have been so thoroughly investigated by Prof. Flournoy. She writes, on one occasion, concerning the Divine as experienced in her progressive trances, "It is more vague and less personal than I had so far regarded the Divine. It soars beyond good and evil." Flournoy, "Une Mystique Moderne," *Archives de Psychologie*, XV. 71.

thesis of the impersonal and the spiritual has yet been found. But I am glad that Mahayana Buddhism is still seeking it.

A partial solution of the problem, and an ancient one, is of course to be had in the intelligent use of symbolism which the Mahayana inherited from India. The many Buddhas and Bodhisattvas and their relation to the fundamental positions of the Tendai-Kegon philosophy are of course illustrative of what I mean. They help to nourish the religious life with its demand for something like a personal deity, while the intellect is quieted with the thought that these beloved figures may, when necessity demands it, be interpreted in terms of a more abstract and monistic conception. The great doctrine of the Trikaya [31] does the same thing even more successfully. Thus the Buddhist is able, on the one hand, to have faith without necessarily believing to be true,[32] and yet, on the other, his religion by no means evaporates into what I have called subjective worship, or the mere attempt to produce a desirable state of mind within oneself. For much that is strictly objective is left, since the symbols are real symbols; [33] they are for the Mahayanist not mere pious names nor conscious appeals to the will to believe. It is his firm conviction that they stand for absolute truths, quite regardless of pleasant or unpleasant effects produced upon him by faith in them.

It is quite in accord with this constant use of a very living symbolism, this interchange of the symbol for the thing symbolized, that Buddhism should be notably lacking in exact definitions for its theological and philosophical terms, and that it should have no one and exclusive name for the Divine. There is nothing in Buddhist terminology to correspond to the words God, Jehovah, Allah. Sometimes the Divine is referred to as Sunyata, sometimes as Bhutatathata; it is called Chen Ru or the Dharmakaya or Shinnyo, or the Buddha Nature that is within all. Buddhist thinkers and mystics would understand very well Goethe's exhortation in *Faust:*

[31] The three Bodies of the Buddha.

[32] This distinction, as the reader will recall, I quote from Keyserling.

[33] Cf. Stanton Coit's excellent treatment of the reality of symbolism in his *National Idealism and a State Church* (London, Williams and Norgate, 1907), pp. 329-30.

Erfühl davon dein Herz, so gross es ist,
Und wenn du ganz in dem Gefühle selig bist
Nenn es dann wie du willst.
Nenn's Glück, Herz, Liebe, Gott.
Ich habe keinen Namen
Dafür! Gefühl ist alles;
Nam' ist Schall und Rauch
Umnebelnd Himmelsgluth.

But while for the Buddhist the Divine is without dogmatic definition and official name, it is (except for the naïve Amidist) emphatically of the monistic rather than of the theistic type. I use the word monistic rather than pantheistic, for pantheism usually has the connotation of interpreting the Divine in terms of the world, and the major drift of Mahayana (as of Hindu) thought is rather to interpret the world in terms of the Divine. Such a view has as a consequence not a belittling of God but an infinite enlarging of the world. Buddhist descriptions of the world of time and space, frankly symbolical of something greater than words can express, are bewildering aggregations of infinite Buddhakshetras and of endless kotis of kalpas. When one turns from these fantastically magnificent attempts to express infinite duration and infinite extent, as symbols of timeless and absolute Reality, to the latest descriptions of the universe given by our Western naturalism,[34] one experiences a sense of al-

[34] Cf. the following from Bertrand Russell: "The physical world is large compared with Man—larger than it was thought to be in Dante's time, but not so large as it seemed a hundred years ago. Both upward and downward, both in the large and in the small, science seems to be reaching limits. It is thought that the universe is of finite extent in space, and that light could travel round it in a few hundred millions of years. It is thought that matter consists of electrons and protons, which are of finite size, and of which there are only a finite number in the world. Probably their changes are not continuous, as used to be thought, but proceed by jerks, which are never smaller than a certain minimum jerk. The laws of these changes can apparently be summed up in a small number of very general principles, which determine the past and the future of the world when any small section of its history is known. Physical science is thus approaching the stage when it will be complete, and therefore uninteresting. Given the laws governing the motions of electrons and protons, the rest is merely geography—a collection of particular facts telling their distribution throughout some portion of the world's history. The total number of facts of geography required to determine the world's history is probably finite; theoretically, they could all be written down in a big book to be kept at Somerset House, with a calculating machine attached, which, by turning a handle, would enable the inquirer to find out the facts at other times than those recorded. It is difficult to imagine anything less interesting, or more different from the passionate delights of incomplete discovery. It is like climbing a high mountain and finding nothing at the top except a restaurant where they sell ginger-beer, surrounded by fog but equipped with wireless." From *What I Believe*, (New York, Dutton, 1925), pp. 1-3.

most unendurable oppression, as though the roof of the world were pressing upon one's head, and the world's walls were squeezing out one's life. Bertrand Russell's universe seems so shrunken one can hardly breathe. After reading about our little up-to-date Western world, the dazzling imagery of a Buddhist Sutra comes like a breath of fresh air or a vision of the sea.

But I should remind the reader that there is a tendency within Buddhism which may well, and at no distant date, develop into a naturalism as narrow and mechanical as that of the West. The contrast between the Tendai and the Kegon is slight but it may prove to be fateful.[35] The discovery of Reality in this world of many changing things, if it stop where Kegon stops, is indeed a healthful counterpoise to the transcendence of Tendai; but the extension of this concept by some Shingon and some Zen thinkers so as practically to deny any other point of view, offers a ready tool, to those who would be thoroughly subservient to "modern science," for stripping Buddhism of most of the spiritual interpretations which the Mahayana has almost always given to Reality. It is possible that our generation stands at the parting of the ways between two forms of Buddhism which will be immensely more antithetic than are any of the sects of the Mahayana.

If this cleavage is to come about, however, it will mean a distinct development within Mahayana philosophy, for, with all its insistence that the water is to be found in the waves and the One in the many, there can be no doubt that Mahayana philosophy, as a whole, and especially so much of it (and that means most of it) as takes its note from Tendai thought, has always insisted that somehow or other there is a spiritual unity back of the phenomenal many, and in the last analysis has agreed with St. Paul that our citizenship is in heaven.[36] Nor is it merely the philosophers of the

[35] A somewhat similar division may be traced within Western idealism. Just as Gentile and his school corresponds to the Hosso philosophy, so Eucken, the Cairds, Royce, and Hocking may be compared with the Tendai, and Bosanquet and Hoernlé with Kegon. Bradley possibly should be classed with Bosanquet and Kegon, but in some ways he is closer to Nagarjuna.

[36] Not only Pauline theology but much of English poetry has a great deal in common with Mahayana thought. Shelley's lines, for example—so often quoted that I hesitate to remind the reader of them—are almost a technical expression of Tendai:

Mahayana that hold this view. It is, I expect, primarily the view of the Buddhist mystics. And when I refer to the mystics of Buddhism I do not mean to refer merely to Zen adepts. For every school of Buddhism has its mystics, and all of them aim at that *Prajna,* that immediate religious insight or intuition which brings one a feeling for the Whole of things.

Western mystics often regard these flashes of insight as special acts of the Divine, interferences, peculiar revelations in which God is present as He is not elsewhere and at other times. The Buddhist mystics seldom thus interpret their experiences. For them the Divine is everywhere, though, of course, more nearly realized, more perfectly *revealed* in some states and some things than in others. Moments of ecstasy and insight, therefore, do not mark any special nearness of God to the soul; they are, in a sense, of psychological interest only. They are not things that God specially does nor things that happen to God. They are things that happen to the individual or acts of apprehension on his part, momentary glimpses of what is always there. And, I suppose, as the Mahayana mystic, or the Christian mystic, progresses in his spiritual career, he trusts less and less to these momentary and peculiar experiences and more and more to finding God always and everywhere. God does not change, but man's realization becomes more constant.

In Buddhism this mystic trend seems to be related to the Anatta doctrine. For, as the Abbot Soyen Shaku tells us, the Prajna or intuition of Buddhist mysticism, feels cabined, cribbed, confined by the limits of the separate self. "Transcending the reciprocity of the 'I' and the 'not-I,' the Prajna beholds the universe in its ultimate oneness and feels all forms

> "The One remains, the many change and pass;
> Heaven's light forever shines, Earth's shadows fly;
> Life, like a dome of many-coloured glass,
> Stains the white radiance of Eternity."

Or take Thomas Moore's familiar strain, which sounds to modern ears perhaps more Buddhist than Christian:

> "This world is all a fleeting show
> For man's delusion given.
> The smiles of joy, the tears of woe,
> Deceitful shine, deceitful flow,
> There's nothing true but Heaven."

of life in essential sameness."[37] And (as the reader will recall) Christian deans as well as Buddhist abbots insist that the separateness of the self must be broken down if the unity of God and man is to be possible.[38] *Intercourse* is conceivable on a basis of pluralism, with God and man presented as separate selves; intercourse but hardly that participation, that mutual interpenetration which many of the mystics, Christian as well as Buddhist, insist upon. The Johannine doctrine that Christ is the vine (not the root or trunk but the whole vine), and we the branches, is essentially one with the Mahayana doctrine that the Buddha nature is in all of us. Surely for the mystics of both religions, the Eternal Buddha and the Eternal Christ have much in common. The words attributed to Christ in the fragment of an unknown gospel recently discovered in Egypt might well have been put into the mouth of the Buddha in some ancient Mahayana Sutra: "Lift the stone and thou shalt find me; cleave the wood, and there am I."

This conception of the Buddha nature in all things is the central thought of the Mahayana. All things share this nature, though not all equally manifest it. Through some it shines directly, in others it is, to our dim eyes, nearly obscured. Yet in reality it penetrates all things, from the little flowers and the graceful bamboo and the great cryptomeria, from haunts even of vice and crime, up through all grades of animals, men, and kami, to the Bodhisattvas and the great Buddhas. This is the Buddhist way of putting it; but very nearly the same thought has been expressed by the greatest of Christendom's religious poets, in the first canto of the *Paradiso:*

> *La gloria di Colui che tutto muove*
> *Per l'universo penetra, e risplende*
> *In una parte più, e meno altrove.*

Each of the Mahayana sects has sought to express and to realize this thought in its own way: Jodo and Shinshu through their loving faith in Amida, by whose grace we shall all some day realize the unity of our souls in the One; Tendai

[37] Soyen Shaku, *Sermons of a Buddhist Abbot,* p. 137.
[38] Cf. Inge, *Personal Idealism and Mysticism,* Chap. IV, p. 144.

and Kegon and their daughter schools in their emphasis upon the identity of all things in the Dharmakaya; Zen with its persistent faith that potentially there is within each of us an

> eye amid the blind
> That dumb and silent readst the Eternal Deep,
> Forever haunted by the Eternal Mind.

The expressions of these various Buddhist sects and others like them are different and crooked ways leading to the one insight which views all beings as broken lights of the Central Fire; they are human symbols of the Unseen, fanciful efforts to express the Unexpressible; in words varying, perhaps contradictory, but one in essential conviction.

Are they mistaken? Is their conviction an illusion? Or is there really some truth hidden here, dimly adumbrated by the thinkers and mystics of the many religions? Ah, if we only knew! Most of us I believe find in our hearts a responsive echo when the great mystic note, telling of cosmic harmony and oneness, is sounded. On the other hand, for many of us, the intellectual formulations of the mystic and the monistic creeds thus far presented seem logically unpersuasive if not actually untenable. Pluralism, also, and personalism have not only much of logic on their sides but make their own great moral appeal. Both the monistic and the pluralistic views have behind them a long and noble tradition of great names. Pity that either should be wholly false! I wonder, sometimes, may both somehow be true? May Aristotle at last be reconciled with Plato, or (what is more difficult and more to the point) may he be reconciled with the Upanishads and with the Mahayana? May we some day open our eyes to an Hegelian synthesis in which all that was true in both the monistic and the pluralistic traditions is preserved?

As yet I, at any rate, know of no such synthesis. All the formulations of the monistic view—including all those which the Mahayana has given us—seem to me, logically considered, quite unsatisfactory. And yet the Mahayana has for me a compelling power over the attention and a growing appeal to my incipient "cosmic sense." I do not see *how* it can be true.

And yet I continue asking myself, May it not be that, in Plato's words, at least, "something like it is true"; that in some deep sense, in some sense that is more than tautology and that is intensely significant, we all do share the Buddha nature?

CHAPTER XXXII

A REVIEW OF THE PRESENT CONDITION OF BUDDHISM

A PICTURE of the Buddhism of our day such as this book has sought to draw would be manifestly incomplete without some attempt to bring together the facts as to the relative strength and weakness of the religion in different lands and to give a general review of its status throughout the Buddhist world. To attempt this in really thorough-going fashion would be a gigantic undertaking for which I am quite unequipped; but even the general and superficial impressions which I have been able to gather may be of some value—the more so, perhaps, because none of those much better equipped than I have had the temerity to present a general bird's-eye view of the entire Hinayana and Mahayana world such as I am going to try to present in this chapter. My only excuse for rushing in as a fool where angels fear to tread is exactly because angels do fear to tread where we should all like to have them lead us. Moreover, the fact that I have studied superficially but with sympathy all the non-Lamaist lands of Buddhism and have specialized minutely in none may give me a certain dispassionate advantage for such a bird's-eye view. Without further apologies, therefore, we shall plunge into the problem, beginning our survey with the Hinayana lands of southern and southeastern Asia.

Southern Buddhism, as a whole—the Buddhism of Ceylon, Burma, Siam, and Cambodia—seems to be in fairly healthy condition. It feels of course, as does every religion of our day, the effects of the two great drifts of contemporary thought, the distrust of authority and the growth of naturalism. I should add at once, however, that Hinayana Buddhism has perhaps less to fear through these two tendencies than any of its rivals; for in its pure form it has never leaned as heavily as most religions do upon authority, and it has always been characterized by a certain hard-headedness—of which its atheism is an effect rather than a cause, and by means of which it has been enabled to look with considerable equanimity upon the advance of naturalism. William James, in a famous passage, once divided all thinkers and all philosophies into two classes which he called the "tender-minded" and the "tough-minded." On such a classification Southern Buddhism, as I have indicated, would fall under the tough-minded class. From its origin on, it has been pretty consistently both hard-headed and soft-hearted. This rather unusual and very useful combination was particularly characteristic of the Founder and constituted perhaps the chief secret of his overwhelming success; and the direction he gave to the movement has never been lost by the Hinayana. No other Founder of a religion ever made so constant and steady an appeal to the cold intellect; no other ever tried to be so thoroughly scientific; and the results of his sowing are being reaped today in this age of scientific and deliberate attack upon authority and upon the will-to-believe. Not that Southern Buddhism can afford to be altogether complacent in the face of an ambitious and militant naturalism. There are positions essential to its life the retention of which is not compatible with the extreme claims of a naturalistic philosophy. As a consequence, even Southern Buddhism is suffering to some extent from the naturalism and agnosticism of the times. But, as it has few weak outlying positions for the enemy to attack, it has as yet suffered less than any of the other great religions from this source; and it is, as I have said, in a fairly healthy condition.

Against the attacks of Christian missionaries it has not been so well intrenched. Especially among the more ignorant portion of the Ceylonese have the gains of Christianity and the losses of Buddhism been considerable. Christian missionaries, both Catholic and Protestant, seeing the great lack of educational facilities in Ceylon, have made excellent use of the opportunity thus offered, and have gained many converts among the children in the mission schools. No such opportunity was offered in Burma, for, as we have seen, most Burmese boys get their education in the monasteries. Yet even here Christian missions have met with considerable success. The new feeling of nationalism that has begun to make itself felt in Burma and Ceylon, the distrust for Europe, its culture and its religion which the Great War inspired, and the general dislike of Western institutions which is so manifest over all the East today, appear to have given a set-back to Christian propaganda and to have lent new life to Buddhism. These wide and deep-going movements have much more to do with the Buddhist revival than have the many little societies with long names and ambitious lists of purposes, the Congresses and resolutions and ephemeral periodicals, which are merely the foam on the crest of the advancing wave.

The most important and business-like organization in the Buddhist revival is the Maha Bodhi Society, to which reference was made in Chapter VII. This has done a good deal for religious education in Ceylon, but it is most interested in propagating Buddhism abroad. In this effort it has joined hands with a group of Germans who in 1912 organized in Halle-am-Saale a "*Bund für Buddhistisches Leben,*" which in 1921 united with a German branch of the Maha Bodhi Society.[1]

The aim of the Maha Bodhi Society is to bring Buddhism into the personal lives of its members and to introduce it to their friends. The *Bund* publishes two periodicals, the *Zeitschrift für Buddhismus* and the *Pfad*, the first learned, the second popular. It also publishes an occasional book and arranges for lectures on Buddhism and kindred topics. There are at least two other Buddhist periodicals in Germany carried on largely for propaganda as well as for scholarly purposes: namely, the *Neu-Buddhistische Zeitschrift*, published by Paul Dahlke, and the *Buddhistisches Weltspiegel*, published by G. Grimm. The Maha Bodhi Society, under the leadership of its founder and head, Mr. Dharmapala, has recently started a branch in London, where it has bought a house as headquarters [2] and is issuing a periodical, the *British Buddhist*.[3] Branches of the society have recently been

[1] See the *Pfad* for Feb., 1926.

[2] In June, 1926. It is also raising funds to build a vihara which is to cost R 100,000, about a quarter of which had been raised in March, 1928.

[3] Another Buddhist periodical has recently been started in London, called *Buddhism in England*, and published by the Buddhist Lodge of the Theosophical Society.

founded in Denmark and in New York City; while a Buddhist academy is to be opened in Leningrad.

Ever since its foundation in 1891 the principal object of the Maha Bodhi Society seems to have been to rescue the great pagoda at Buddh Gaya, where the Buddha attained supreme wisdom, from the hands of the local Hindu Mohunt. Buddhist societies in various parts of Ceylon and Burma have joined with the Maha Bodhi for years in protest, and as the viceroy's government naturally refused to interfere, the matter was at length taken up by the All India Congress. After hearing both sides, the congress ruled that the shrine should hereafter be controlled by a committee of ten, five to be Buddhists and five Hindus. This seemed to many clear-headed Indians a most just and satisfactory solution;[4] but most of the Buddhists of Ceylon, Burma, Nepal and Madras at all interested in the question were[5]—and, I judge, still are —quite unsatisfied. A Buddhist "Mission House" is being erected near the pagoda.

Another aim of the Maha Bodhi is to found a vihara and at length a Buddhist university at Sarnath, where the Buddha delivered his first sermon. The government has donated the necessary land and the plans are drawn. The estimated cost is 130,000 rupees. Mrs. Mary E. Foster of Honolulu gave, several years ago, 30,000 rupees toward this amount, and the Maha Bodhi has been soliciting funds ever since among "the Buddhists of Japan, Burma, Ceylon, Siam, China, Tibet, Chittagong, Arakan, Cambodia, Nepal, Korea, Manchuria and Sikkim"[6] for the remainder. In March, 1928, it had raised 13,989 rupees—totaling, therefore, 43,989. The vihara has already been begun, and it is hoped that the building will at least keep pace with the collection of funds.

There are still a few Buddhists in various parts of India.[7] In Bombay a "Buddha Society" was founded in 1922 (most or all of its members, however, being Buddhists only in the sense of having a scholarly and human interest in the reli-

[4] See the *Indian Social Reformer* for March 13, 1926.

[5] See the protests in the *Maha Bodhi* for April–May, 1926.

[6] I quote from the *Maha Bodhi* appeal, published every month in its magazine.

[7] In addition to the remnants of Indian Buddhism mentioned in this paragraph, there is a degenerate form of Buddhism in some of the villages of Bengal and Orissa. See Dutt's *Early Buddhist Monarchism*, p. 2, with references there given.

gion); it conducts fortnightly lectures and has voted to start a Buddhist Journal,[8] and is raising money to build a vihara. In Kerala, a district of southern India, a considerable number of Buddhists have built a temple and formed a Buddhist Association with headquarters at Calicut.[9] They had been stirred up, it seems, by itinerant Ceylonese monks and have asked the Ceylonese Buddhists to send them more monks to aid in a revival of their religion.[10] They have also initiated a movement to put an end to animal sacrifice by the Hindus.[11] A more effective step toward evangelizing India was the opening of a vihara in Calcutta in November, 1920, the first thoroughly Buddhist vihara on Indian soil for perhaps six or seven hundred years. With this solid possession in the hands of the Buddhists, the invasion of India may be said to have begun.

For nothing less than the winning back of India to Buddhism is the ambition of the more zealous and energetic members of the Maha Bodhi and of the various other missionary societies. It is perhaps unfortunate that so much of their time and energy should have been spent in passing resolutions and protests concerning the possession of the shrine at Buddh Gaya. It would seem that the sending of missionaries to India would be more to the point. But at any rate this vihara in Calcutta, with the editorial office of the

[8] *Buddhist Annual of Ceylon* for 1923, and *Maha Bodhi* for Sept., 1927.

[9] *The Maha Bodhi* for Feb., 1925.

[10] Concerning these Buddhists, the editor of the *Indian Social Reformer* of Bombay has kindly given me the following information. "The association was formed in Kerala, comprising British Malabar and the Native States of Cochin and Travancore, some eight years ago with its headquarters at Calicut. The idea of starting the Association was inspired by lectures on and exposition of Buddhism by itinerant Buddhist monks from Ceylon, who were invited to Malabar by a band of young men interested in the religion. Even at the present day it is not unusual for monks during their frequent sojourn there to convert people to Buddhism. There are said to be about 3,000 converts to Buddhism in Kerala. The President of the Association is Mr. C. Krishnan, High Court Vakil and editor of the *Mitavadi*, a vernacular journal. Mr. Manjeri Rama Iyer, a leading High Court Vakil of Calicut and Secretary of the Theosophical Society in Kerala, renders to the Association much valuable help. The members of the Association are mostly people of the locality belonging to the Thiyya community. This is accounted for by the general belief that the Thiyyas were originally Buddhists who embraced Hinduism on their migration from Ceylon to India. The members also take up social work such as the removal of untouchability, weaning the people from superstitious beliefs and customs by education, improving the position of women, etc., as part of their religious propaganda.

[11] *Indian Social Reformer* for Jan. 15, 1927. This movement in Calicut is in part a protest by non-Brahmins against caste and privilege—so at least thinks a writer in *The Maha Bodhi* for July, 1927.

Maha Bodhi magazine close by, is a real beginning; [12] and the plan to build a vihara at Sarnath where Buddhist monks shall live, and to make it the kernel of a Buddhist university seems wise and promising.

It is the hope of these sanguine Buddhists (whose courage is surely admirable) that through the instructions to be given at their future Sarnath University, and through the Buddhist books which the university staff will translate into the vernacular of India, many of India's millions may be won back to the faith of the great Indian Teacher. It does not seem probable that our generation will see any large effect produced upon India's millions. Yet in the history of religions a few centuries are a very little thing, and what may be the result of a persistent movement by devoted Buddhist missionaries in the course of say five hundred years it is quite impossible to predict. One may argue it either way. One might insist that Buddhism, being native to India, should make a strong appeal to Indians and rapid progress among them if once rightly presented. On the other hand, one might point out that Buddhism once had a large part of India at its feet and then lost it all, thus showing its inability to satisfy permanently the Indian nature. To this the Buddhists will unanimously reply with their oft-repeated explanation of the death of Buddhism in India—namely, that their religion did not die a natural death but was assassinated—murdered by the sword of Islam. Those of us who cannot be satisfied with this simple and easy explanation of the expulsion of Buddhism from India will probably venture no prediction as to the success of the proposed missionary venture, but will merely wish that from the heights of Paranirvana we might be permitted, some five hundred years hence, to observe the issue. But whatever the success of the enterprise in India, there can be no doubt that if it be earnestly pursued its effect upon the Buddhism of Ceylon and Burma will be most salutary. The influence of the Christian missionary enterprise upon the Christianity of the home lands leaves no doubt upon this matter. In this con-

[12] A second Buddhist periodical in India is being projected,—this by the Nepalese Buddhist Mission. It is to be called *Buddhist India* and is to be published in Calcutta. (*The Young East* for Dec., 1926.) A Buddhist quarterly called *Buddhist India* was started in Calcutta in 1927.

nection it is interesting to learn that at a meeting of Ceylonese Buddhists in January, 1928, it was decided to send four monks as missionaries to the Malay States, and (at a meeting in March) to send three to London.

The condition of things in Siam and Cambodia is in some ways quite different from that which one finds in Ceylon and Burma. The form of Buddhism of all four lands is in essentials the same, but the fact that in Siam and Cambodia Buddhism is the state religion makes a considerable difference. The encouragement and support of the governments and the éclat that comes from the favor of kings have made things relatively easy for Buddhism in these lands and enabled it to avoid some of the dangers that it has had to face in Ceylon and Burma. Christian missions have made but slight progress among Siamese Buddhists, their successes having been scored chiefly among the ignorant animistic inhabitants of northern Siam; while among Cambodian Buddhists Christian missions have made practically no progress at all. This being the situation, no need has been felt for special efforts at propaganda such as one finds in Burma and Ceylon, and no organizations such as the Y.M.B.A. or the Maha Bodhi Society have been started or taken over. The Siamese and Cambodians are pretty well content with things as they are. As we have seen, most boys in Siam and practically all the boys in Cambodia go for a time to the wats, or monasteries, and there learn religion and manners and wear the yellow robe. The government schools in Siam have regular religious instruction, which means instruction in Buddhism. This is not true of Cambodia, for there Buddhism is not the state religion in the full sense, as it is in Siam. The government schools of Cambodia are under the French, and no religion of any sort is taught in them. As about one hundred per cent of the boys in Cambodia, however, go also for a time to the wats, to be trained by the monks, there is as yet no noticeable loss to Buddhism from the new educational system. I should add, moreover, that the French Government is rather friendly to Buddhism and in 1915 founded a college at Pnom Penh, *l'École des Hautes Études Pali,* largely for the higher education of Buddhist monks. Promising young monks are here taught Pali and Buddhist philosophy. The

French authorities are also encouraging the publication of a monthly in the Cambodian language devoted to Buddhistic studies.

There is one problem of tendency for Cambodia and Siam which does not exist for Ceylon and Burma. Chinese from Kwangtung and Fukien are landing by thousands every year in Saigon and Bangkok and spreading over all the towns and into the agricultural districts. Two shiploads of Chinese coolies are sent every week to Bangkok from Swatow alone, each load aggregating from three hundred to fifteen hundred. Some of these, of course, return to China, but many of them remain. On the streets of Bangkok it often seems as if all the shops were kept by Chinese, and the situation is somewhat the same in Pnom Penh. These incoming Chinese, of course, so far as they are Buddhists at all, belong to the northern or Mahayana branch, and they bring their religion with them. In both Siam and Cambodia, therefore, one finds Buddhist temples of the Chinese sort, and the Mahayana is beginning to spread in this biological fashion within these two Hinayana lands. Many of the incoming Chinese are not Buddhists in any sense, and what religion they have consists in the cult of their ancestors and of a few of the Chinese gods.

The influx of so large a number of Mahayana and of non-Buddhist immigrants cannot fail to have its great influence on the future religion of both Siam and Cambodia. A hundred years from now these countries will be largely Chinese. In Cambodia, moreover, there is a considerable admixture of Annamese, who, like the Chinese, either are Mahayanists or have no Buddhism at all. The problem is complicated by the mixture of the races. The Chinese and Annamese intermarry readily with both Siamese and Cambodians, and the population of the cities is already becoming very mixed. What will be the religion of this mixed race? In the case of mixed marriages, what is the religion of the children? These are questions of great significance for the future of Southern Buddhism, and I wish I knew how they should be answered. Such meager information as I have been able to obtain is to the following effect: There are relatively few marriages between Southern Buddhists and non-Buddhists, but many between Southern Buddhists and Chinese or Annamese Buddhists. There are many marriages between Chinese men (provided they be Buddhists) and Siamese or Cambodian girls; but relatively few between Chinese girls and men of another race. Thus in the great majority of mixed marriages the husband and father is a Chinese Buddhist, the wife and mother a Southern Buddhist. The daughters of such marriages almost always grow up in their mother's religion. With the sons there is no such regularity. If the father is fervent in his religion the boys will be brought up in the Mahayana faith. The father, however, is seldom fervent. His religious interest is satisfied when the ancestral tablets have been duly revered, and the rest he leaves to the mother. She is much more likely to be religious than her husband, and so will often influence her sons toward the Hinayana form of Buddhism. In Siam the Hinayana has the further advantage that the boys are sure to be taught its principles when they go to school. The tendency varies according to the locality. In the fishing villages along the coast of southern Siam the tendency is strongly Mahayana, while in Bangkok it is as strongly Hinayana. In general one may say that at present the mixed race which is forming in Siam and Cambodia tends to be Hinayanist rather than Mahayanist, but that it would be dangerous to predict what will be the situation in a few years, particularly in Cambodia where education is beginning to pass out of Buddhist hands. But one must remember the fact that both Siamese and Cambodians are very ardent Hinayanists, while the Chinese and Annamese representatives of the Mahayana are not ardent at all on matters religious, a fact that cannot fail to have its influence.

When we pass from Cambodia into Cochin-China, Annam, and Tonquin, we come upon a marked change. For we have here passed the line between the Hinayana and the Mahayana. As I pointed out in a previous chapter, the line is extraordinarily sharp, coinciding as it does with the racial and linguistic boundary between the Khmers and the Annamese. I doubt whether there be another boundary line in the world the two sides of which are so sharply contrasted in matters of religion. Not only in content is the Hinayana of Cambodia strikingly different from the Mahayana of the

Annamese states; the two religions are equally contrasted in fervor. In Cambodia every one is a Buddhist, the land is covered with temples, and the road yellow with bonzes. You cross the border and never a bonze and hardly a temple can you find. In the city of Saigon so far as I could discover—either by my own search or by questioning the inhabitants—there is not a single Buddhist temple, nor a single Buddhist monk. There is indeed a large Chinese temple in the city, which has a tiny image of Kwan-Yin on a subordinate altar; but the deities occupying the central altars, and to whom all the worship is given, are Chinese gods which have no relation to the Buddhist cycle. In the suburbs of the city there is a rude Annamese Buddhist temple closed most of the time and typical in this respect of the Buddhism which extends all the way up the coast from Saigon to Canton. The truth is, Buddhism in French Indo-China outside of the Hinayana belt is in an exceedingly moribund condition. The people are getting on without any religion. The influence of the French has been what the influence of Westerners usually is upon the peoples of the Orient—distinctly anti-religious. Annamese Buddhism had little enough life when the Europeans arrived: their arrival seems to have given it the *coup de grâce*.

And so in our geographical survey of the Buddhist world we come to China! And what shall we say of it? The Buddhism of China is like many other things in this vast land; any statement one makes about it may easily be proved true, and as easily proved false. One may cite chapter and verse, so to speak, and exhibit specific instances to prove almost anything. The first impression a stranger gets of Chinese Buddhism is that there is very little of it. One soon learns that it is almost vain to search for a Buddhist outside of the monasteries; and on visiting the monasteries one finds that it is almost equally vain to search for a Buddhist inside them. In a sense, of course, almost all Chinese are Buddhists—in the sense, namely, that some members of each family occasionally burn incense in a Buddhist temple and that a monk may be called upon to help out at a funeral. All have heard of the Fos and the P'usas and nearly all in some sense "believe" in them. If the word *Buddhist* however be taken to imply any real knowledge of Buddhism, then the number of Buddhists in China would seem to be exceedingly small. To many of those, moreover, who know most about the subject Buddhism is rather an interesting philosophy than a living faith. The situation reminds one somewhat of a famous remark made by Oliver Wendell Holmes in reviewing a book which he had found full of inaccuracies and platitudes: "This book," he said, "contains much that is new and much that is true; but the new isn't true and the true isn't new." So one might say that in China there are many who believe in Buddhism and a few who understand it; but those who believe in it don't understand it and those who understand it don't believe in it.

Such a statement, however, like most general statements, would be far too sweeping to be true. Those to whom Buddhism means most do not reveal themselves to the casual stranger; and first impressions are particularly likely to be misleading in China. The land, moreover, is so enormous that it would be difficult to make any statement which would hold of it all. To approximate the truth, therefore, one must make distinctions.

If we begin with the Tonquin border we shall find Buddhism in much the same moribund condition that we discovered in Tonquin and Annam. In the city of Canton it is difficult to discover any traces of Buddhism. All the temples have been taken over by Dr. Sun and his followers; a few have been left to the monks, while the majority have been sold or given up to the military. The principal temple of the town, the Wa Lum Ssu, is in a state of dirt and decay remarkable even for China. Its central shrine is closed, the place is in the hands of caretakers, no monks are visible, and the former dormitory and main court are now used for barracks. There is hardly a monk left in Canton. This may in part be owing to the continued state of war from which Canton so long suffered. Yet I am not sure that it is, and I have no reason to think that many monks will troop back on the conclusion of a secure peace. But one must not judge Cantonese Buddhism wholly by its temples. Many Cantonese women, I am told, worship Kwan-Yin in their homes. There are, moreover, several large monasteries in the country districts. In its monastic life Kwangtung is not notably behind other provinces; but this is hardly representative of the religious life of the people. In some of the villages, I am told, are still to be found lay Buddhist societies or vegetarian societies, as they are sometimes called. They are rare today but those that exist seem to have retained a rather high and admirable type of Buddhism. The societies are so rare, however, and their membership so limited that they do not greatly influence the general level of Buddhism in the south.

As we travel northward the signs of vitality in Buddhism gradually increase. At Swatow there is a Buddhist temple of no great size, but crowds of Buddhists worship in it and with a fervor that I have never seen surpassed in China. Foochow is a Buddhist center of importance and some of the largest and most flourishing monasteries in China are in its vicinity.

But the center of living Buddhism in China is the lower Yangtse Valley—say from Kiukiang down. At Kiukiang itself, to be sure, the religion seems to be in a far from healthy condition. Its one large temple, possessing a most attractive pagoda visible for miles up and down the river, is ill-kept, some of its buildings, including the pagoda, lapsing into quiet decay. A few monks are left and an occasional worshiper bows before the trio of Buddhas in the main sanctuary, or hires the monks to chant and burn incense for the soul of some departed relative. But there are few signs in the temple of very active faith. On the edges of the town there are two or three small Buddhist shrines, all of them dilapidated in appearance, largely deserted, and speaking chiefly of the past. Farther up the river, in the cluster of cities at the mouth of the Han, the religion appears to be in much healthier condition; for, as we have seen, Hankow and Wuchang form almost the center of the Buddhist revival, while on the outskirts of both Wuchang and Hanyang there are large and flourishing Buddhist monasteries.

As one goes farther up the Yangtse and its tributaries, the force of Buddhism as a living and influential religion gradually declines. In the province of Hunan it retains a certain amount of strength but most of this is confined to isolated monasteries in the country districts. There are two Buddhist temples on the outskirts of the city of Changsha that seem really alive. One of these is particularly worth noting. It is rebuilding some of its shrines at considerable expense, all its buildings and courts are kept up in excellent fashion, the monks appear to be earnest and reverend men, and the whole place has an unmistakably religious atmosphere. Nothing of this sort is to be found within the city. Changsha is undoubtedly a religious place in one sense. Its streets are full of little shrines in which incense and paper money are burned. But these shrines are not Buddhist; the kind of religion which they cater to is of the purely superstitious sort, and the few Buddhist temples one does find are ill-kept and largely deserted.

The number and the condition of Buddhist temples, of course, must not be taken as an absolute criterion of the condition of Buddhism in Changsha, or elsewhere. The most intelligent Buddhist laymen often keep conscientiously—and contemptuously—away from the temples. Yet it is hard to believe that among the uneducated masses Buddhism can be very strong in a city where its temples are almost universally allowed to revert either to dust and solitude, or to purely non-religious uses.

On the upper Yangtse, in Western Hupeh, and in most of Szechuen, one finds but few sparks of real life in Buddhism. There are notable exceptions to this general statement. All the region about Mount Omei is devotedly Buddhist, and on the sacred mountain (as even the professional foes of Buddhism acknowledge) there are many devout, intelligent, and truly religious monks. Nor is Mount Omei the only Buddhist center. Scattered in various parts of this large region there are monasteries and sacred places to which thousands of pilgrims annually troop. In both Chungking and Chengtu, moreover, as we have seen, pronounced efforts at an intelligent revival of Buddhism are being made which are at present meeting with some success. In spite of all this, it is still true that the general impression one gets from most parts of this region is that one is witnessing the last gasps of a dying religion. In the city of Ichang there is not a single Buddhist temple of any size or influence. On the hills about it there are many isolated monasteries, a few in fair condition, most of them in an advanced state of decay, many of them quite deserted. The same story is continued as one follows the river up-stream, through the Gorges, to Chungking. One passes, to be sure, a really impressive series of temples, large and small, perched upon cliffs, hidden away in ravines, or nestling up against small cities. But on investigation it transpires that less than half are or ever were Buddhist, and many more than eighty per cent of these have been deserted by the monks and given up to schools, factories, storehouses, or (most commonly) to the military. In Wusung, for example, there are five large temples, all of them in ruins—not only deserted by the monks but largely demolished; and what is left of them is used by the soldiers. It is a rather sad commentary on the present age in China to find so many temples originally built in honor of the great Indian pacifist, made over into armories and barracks. One large temple that we passed is now the headquarters of a troop of bandits—no longer a house of worshipers but a den of thieves.

In and all about Chungking things continue to be almost as bad. There are indeed two large Buddhist temples in the city with no admixture of Taoist images and with fairly devout and even active monks. Except for these, most Buddhist temples of the region are in a deplorable condition. There is hardly one which has not as many Taoist as Buddhist images; nearly all of them are deserted and filthy; and a very large percentage have been quite handed over to non-religious uses—one, I remember, made into a place for the sorting of pigs' bristles, another (dedicated to Kwan-Yin!) used as a military storehouse for the drying of hams.

In Cheng-tu, I am told, Buddhism is in rather better condition than in Chungking. And even in the latter city there is much more individual worship—especially of Kwan-Yin—than the condition of the temples would indicate. Many shops and homes have little private shrines, in some of which are to be found images of Kwan-Yin and of Yo Wang P'usa, with offerings of red cloth in token of answers to prayer. Still I am assured by a number of men and women who have lived for years in various parts of Szechuen that the influence of Buddhism throughout the province is but slight.

But all this is changed when one goes down the river below Kiu Kiang. Nanking, Soochow, Hangchow, Ningpo, and all the adjacent regions of Kiangsu and Chekiang are filled with very living Buddhism. New temples are being constructed, old ones repaired and pilgrimages carried on, young monks are studying and old monks meditating, throughout all this region.

The repair and cleanliness of the Chekiang temples and the sharp contrast they afford to what one finds in many other parts of China are surely significant. Both monks and people seem to have a pride in the appearance of their temples which is an unmistakable sign of real interest in their faith. Even in this region it is of course chiefly the women who show any great degree of zeal, the men being more interested in rice than in religion. They protect the temples and reverence the Buddhas but do not bother them; in this respect following out the admonitions of Confucius to revere the spirits and avoid them. There are many men, however, especially among the peasants in the agricultural districts, who go on pilgrimages and worship in the temples with a very real fervor. Particularly is the cult of Kwan-Yin a living force, more especially in eastern Chekiang. Almost every day in the year is a day of pilgrimage to her shrines at the upper, middle, and lower "Monasteries of India" in the mountains near Hangchow, and most of all to her chosen home, the little island of P'uto. To the fishermen of the region she occupies much the same place the Madonna holds in the hearts of the Sicilian sailors.

Buddhism, as I have said, has its flood-tide in the lower Yangtse valley. As we travel northward from the river we find the tide once more ebbing. In Shantung the dominant religion is not Buddhism but Taoism. The leading temples of the cities are Taoist, and many of the so-called Buddhist temples which one does find have been invaded by Taoist divinities who seem to receive quite as much of the incense and of the worship as the Fos and the P'usas. There are a few Buddhist monasteries in secluded spots, but many of these are in a condition that is at least somnolent. In the lives of the peasants in the country districts Buddhism is said to play but a small part.

The process is continued in Chihli. How one should characterize the Buddhism of Peking is hard to say. There are many fine temples and monasteries in and around the city, most of them are in a fair state of repair and some of them in excellent condition. They are maintained by a large number of monks. Most of the temples are open at all times and the Fos and P'usas within cannot complain of dearth of incense or lack of praise. On the other hand, the great majority of the monks are almost grotesquely ignorant, and hardly any effort is made for the instruction of the laity. One sees in Peking but little of the fervent worship so common in the lower Yangtse valley. Yet Buddhism here is in a much more healthy condition than in the extreme south. In the eastern part of the province, in fact, it seems to be enjoying a genuine revival. So much is this the case that for a number of years Christian missions in that region have made little or no progress. In the city of Ma Fang, for example, there is said to be not a single Christian convert. And this is due largely to the fervor of Buddhism—a fervor which has shown itself in the recent renovation of a Buddhist temple at the expense of upward of $100,000 gold, collected from among the common people.

As one goes northward from Peking this fervor steadily declines. In Manchuria, I am told, Buddhism is in a more decrepit condition than in Chihli. Toward the edges of the empire the ebbing tide grows even lower, rippling out in a thin stream into Korea, and dying away amid the Lamaism, Shamanism, and Animism of the north. The same story is repeated toward the west. In Shansi one finds Buddhism in much the same condition of decay that characterized Kwangtung. Wutai Shan—one of the four sacred mountains of Buddhism—of course forms a notable exception to this, as does also, to a less extent, Mien Shan farther south. These, however, are isolated spots and spread no great influence through the regions round them. In Taiyuanan Fu, the capital and metropolis of Shansi, there is, so far as I could discover, only one Buddhist temple and this is closed nearly all the time, its influence on the people being almost *nil*. As one travels southward over the great plain of Shansi one finds constant repetition of the same story. Shin Ssu, the largest monastery in the plain, exhibits a strange mixture of Buddhism and Taoism. It has only five resident monks, and most of its shrines are closed the greater part of the time, the only one regularly kept open and the only one that seems at all popular being Taoist. Farther south the large walled city of Wen Shu possesses not a single Buddhist temple. Formerly there was one here but it has recently been torn down and a school built in its place. Fen Chow, a city of 70,000 inhabitants, has, so far as I was able to make out, but one Buddhist temple and but one Buddhist monk. Once in a while a monk from some distant monastery comes through town and burns a little incense, but there are very few monks in the region. P'ing Yao, a city some sixty li south of Fen Chow, likewise possesses one Buddhist temple, but not a single monk. The temple is in charge of a caretaker. A Chinese boy whose home is in P'ing Yao told me that he thought there were a few Buddhists in the city but he himself was not acquainted with any. In the smaller towns and villages one finds Taoist temples but the Buddhist temples have either been made into schools or are falling to pieces. All over central Shansi, in short, Buddhist temples and the Buddhist faith are quietly decaying. The most marked architectural features of the region are the great bottle-shaped tombs of former abbots, mute witnesses to the fervor of the Buddhist faith in this region in a day long past. In some places one can count a score of these great tombs. They mark the graves of dead abbots; do they also mark the grave of a dead religion?

Conditions in Shensi do not differ greatly from those in Shansi. The capital, Si-an Fu, is something of an exception. There are several Buddhist temples in the city and one good-sized monastery with something over fifty monks; and many of the laity make use of Buddhist monks at funerals. The up-keep of the temples, in the city, however, is no sign of popular religious interest, for in Shensi Buddhism gets its financial support largely from one person, the devout and liberal mother of a recent governor. In the country districts, I am told, there is small sign of life in Buddhism, except in the mountain range, where there are several fine monasteries. Across the western border, in the distant province of Kansu, Buddhism is at a very low ebb. Most of the villages are either Mohammedan or "Chinese," i.e., their temples have the usual array of deities who are in part Taoist and in part belong to the ancient superstition of China. Rarely does one come upon a Buddhist temple or a Buddhist monk, and what Buddhism one finds (I am told) is usually of the Lamaist or Mongolian type. Of Chinese (or Mahayana) Buddhism there is very little except perhaps along the southern border of the province, where the influence of Szechuan is slightly felt. The great cave temple at Tun Huang, where Stein found so many Buddhist manuscripts and whose walls are adorned with wonderful Buddhist frescoes from the T'ang dynasty, is now (and apparently has for years or centuries been) in charge of a Taoist priest. Beyond Kansu and Szechuan, to the north and west, Chinese Buddhism of course [13] disappears completely from view.

The gradual decay of Chinese Buddhism is no new thing. It has been going on for years. In 1901 De Groot found much the same situation.

> As to the Buddhist abbeys [he wrote] their days seem numbered. The hundreds of stately edifices with shining curved roofs standing out elegantly against the sky, with lofty pagodas and ancient parks, which, as books so profusely inform us, once studded the empire, picturesquely breaking the monotony of the mountain slopes: buildings where the pious sought salvation by thousands, thronging the broad Mahayana to eternal bliss and perfection, and whither the laity flocked to receive initiation into the commandments—these institutions can now at most be counted by dozens. No crowds of sowers are sent out from there into the world to scatter in all directions faith and piety; no religious councils or synods, formerly attended by thousands, take place there now. Of many of these buildings only the spacious temple halls exist, but the clergy who crowded them to make their hymns resound, have all but a few disappeared. Nuns are a rarity. With the greater part of the convents religious wisdom has vanished. Theological studies belong to history: philosophical works have wellnigh disappeared, and to collect a Tripitaka in China has become an impossibility. Propagation of the doctrines of salvation through preaching, which the Mahayana principles laid upon the sons of Buddha as one of the highest duties, has long since ceased. In short, from whatever point of view one considers the matter—conventual life is at best a shadow of what it was in past centuries.[14]

[13] I feel the more confident that I have not drawn too gloomy a picture of the state of Buddhism in China by finding my own conclusions invariably indorsed by men who are in a better position to judge than I. The larger part of this chapter, for example, was embodied in a paper which I read before the Chinese Social and Political Science Association in Peking, in 1924. In the discussion that followed a number of the members who were intimately acquainted with conditions in various parts of China expressed opinions in substantial agreement with mine.

[14] *Sectarianism and Religious Persecution in China*, I. 132.

When the Chinese traveler Hiuen-Tsiang was in India, toward the middle of the seventh century, he visited most of the places which his predecessor, Fa-Hien, had seen two centuries before. A comparison of the accounts given by the two travelers is instructive. In the central part of Northern India Buddhism had held its own in Hiuen-Tsiang's time, and even increased the number of its monasteries. In several of the outlying regions, however, a notable decline had set in, and in some when Hiuen-Tsiang visited them it was very nearly extinct. One who reads the descriptions given by these two ancient Chinese travelers is inevitably reminded of the present condition of Buddhism in their own land.[15] One recalls how, after Hiuen-Tsiang's time, the Buddhist tide in India, already on the ebb, steadily receded from all the outlying regions toward the center and there at length completely died away. Is history repeating itself in China? Is Buddhism gradually retreating to the Yangtse valley? If so, what will be the next step after that? . . . Matthew Arnold's lines on Dover Beach ring through one's head:

> The Sea of Faith
> Was once too at the full, and round earth's shore
> Lay like the folds of a bright garment furled.
> But now I only hear
> Its melancholy long withdrawing roar,
> Retreating to the breath of the night wind,
> Down the vast edges drear
> And naked shingles of the world.

As to whether Chinese Buddhism is destined to repeat the story of Indian Buddhism I refuse to make any prediction. And lest I leave too gloomy a picture I should remind the reader of the one brighter side of the present situation: one must not forget that there is a new force astir in the heart of Buddhism, the so-called Buddhist revival. An entire chapter has, however, already been devoted to this subject, so I shall say no more of it here. If Chinese

[15] And not only by the decrease in the number of temples and monks but also by the attitude of the clergy. The following description, for example, of the monks of northwestern India in 635 by Hiuen-Tsiang will sound strangely familiar to one acquainted with the monks of China today: "They practice the duty of quiet meditation and have pleasure in reciting texts relating to this subject; but they have no great understanding of them." (Beal, *Buddhist Records of the Western World*, p. 120).

Buddhism could produce many men like Tai Hsu and some of the other leaders of the revival, there would be considerable hope of the success of the movement.

One may well raise the question, however, What can this little band do among nearly 400,000,000? Especially unpromising does the future of Chinese Buddhism appear because of its almost complete lack of anything that could properly be called religious education. China has no monastic schools like those of Burma, Siam, and Cambodia, and almost no religious schools like those of Ceylon. The Chinese boy and girl grow up with only such knowledge of Buddhism as they can get from their parents or their fellows; and this has to do almost exclusively with certain superficial acts, such as kneeling, burning incense, and repeating a few more or less meaningless syllables. The religious education of the monks themselves usually extends only a little beyond this. Under such circumstances, it is not surprising that in many parts of China Christian missionaries, before the present revolution began, made considerable conquests. More serious are the losses Buddhism is suffering before the advancing tide of naturalism. To this great body of students seems to be tending. Not that they have altogether given up Buddhism thereby. They know little or nothing about Buddhist philosophy, but, I am told, many of them have a kind of tacit understanding in the back of their minds that if they had a philosophy it would be a Buddhist philosophy. But this is where their Buddhism begins and ends, and the young men who in former days would have been leaders of Buddhist thought are now almost totally ignorant of Buddhism, and either quite agnostic on ultimate questions or frankly adherents of a naturalistic philosophy which is almost as incompatible with Buddhism as it is with Christianity.

Several of the most enthusiastic and intelligent Buddhists that I met in China expressed themselves as having very little hope for the future of their religion in their native land. One of them questioned whether the present revival of Buddhism was a revival of the true Mahayana, saying that at any rate its influence was narrow and that in his opinion the ruined temples of China would never be rebuilt nor replaced.

Another told me that his only hope for Buddhism was that it might be reintroduced into China by Western scholars. The scientific study of Buddhist history and philosophy that is now being carried on by Europeans and Americans he thought might stimulate a new interest in the religion among the Chinese.[16] Naturally, however, he was not very sanguine over this possibility and contented himself by pointing out that the Buddha himself had predicted the complete disappearance of the Dharma from the earth. After his prophecy is fulfilled Maitreya will come and reestablish the Law, Buddhism will spread throughout the world, and a reign of happiness and universal peace will begin.[17]

If now we turn from China to Korea, the condition of Buddhism grows even worse. In fact Korean Buddhism has been in a very perilous state ever since the year 1472 when the king cleared the capital, Seoul, of Buddhist bonzes and temples. This attack upon the religion, it will be recalled, was followed by a more serious one, a few years later, when the monks were banished from all the cities of the land and had to retire to various secluded monasteries. This had the effect, naturally, of cutting off the monks from the laity, and the people were left to revert to a condition of Animism, with almost no knowledge of Buddhism or care for it. It was only in the early years of the present century that the attitude of the government changed and the monks were allowed back in the cities. By that time, of course, no one wanted them back, and only an energetic missionary campaign could have made any noticeable impression upon the solid heathenism of most of Korea. It need not be said—at least to those acquainted with Korean monks—that no such energetic campaign was made. Yet Buddhism is not quite

[16] That Western encouragement might be of considerable influence in the revival of Buddhism is not so preposterous a suggestion as at first it seems. There is little doubt that Western influence has had a good deal to do with the present revival of self-consciousness in Hinduism. It is interesting to note, for example, that Mahatma Gandhi made his first acquaintance with the Bhagavad Gita through Sir Edwin Arnold's translation and through the influence of an English theosophist in England, and that his first interest in and real knowledge of Hindu philosophical thought came from the same source. See his autobiography, *The Story of My Experiments with Truth* (Eng. trans. Ahmedabad, 1927), Chap. XX.

[17] The total effect of the present revolution upon Buddhism cannot as yet be evaluated. The effects thus far visible are chiefly an increase of superstitious practices on the part of soldiers and peasants. More and more of the temples are being handed over to the military.

dead in Korea, and especially since the advent of the Japanese it is showing a few signs of life. There is one Buddhist temple in Seoul, supported largely by the Japanese. In the monasteries, at least in those among the Diamond mountains and along the east coast, there are some devout and earnest monks, and a few learned ones. As we have seen, some effort is being made at a revival of Buddhism. On the whole, however, the religion is still in a rather moribund condition in Korea. Bishop Trollope told me that in his entire career as a missionary in Korea, extending as it does over a long lifetime, he has only once found Buddhism an impediment to his efforts at conversion. Animism has stood in his way many times but Buddhism only once. The fact that of Korea's 17,000,000 inhabitants only 382,000 are Buddhist speaks for itself.

The contrast between Chinese and Korean Buddhism, on the one hand, and Japanese Buddhism, on the other, is very great. The most rushed and unobservant globe-trotter on his way through Japan on a fast express can hardly fail, if he looks out of the train windows at all, to be impressed with the way in which Buddhism has seized upon every grove and every little hilltop not already preoccupied by Shinto, for the erection of a temple. If the globe-trotter visit the temples he will find not only Buddhist monks chanting verses but large numbers of the laity visiting the shrines and paying their respects to the Butsus. There can be no doubt that Buddhism is a living thing in Japan.

Buddhism is much more evenly spread over Japan than it is over China; there are few of those glaring contrasts between localities that we found in comparing the lower Yangtse valley with Kwangtung or with Shansi. Yet there are local contrasts in Japan which are worth recording, and which, in fact, the hurried visitor to Japan should keep in mind lest he misjudge Japanese Buddhism by what he finds in one province or one city. As to the main island, it may be said that Buddhism is stronger in the southwest than in the northeast. The center of the religion is probably in and about Kyoto, whereas Tokyo and all the region to the northeast of it is relatively weak in Buddhist fervor. The three other large islands differ considerably in the religious interests of their inhabitants. Kyushu, the probable birthplace of the dominant clan, the island on which the heavenly grandson of the Sun Goddess descended to found the race of the Mikados, is naturally a stronghold of Shinto. In one department of this island, in fact—namely, Satsuma—during the latter part of the Tokugawa times, no Buddhist monks were permitted to enter. This veto has, of course, long been revoked, but though Buddhist missionaries have been sent thither, both Satsuma and the rest of Kyushu is distinctly a Shinto rather than a Buddhist region.[18] These conditions are somewhat reversed in Shikoku, which is strongly Buddhist. The fourth large island of Japan, Yezo, which lies to the north, was until fifty years ago inhabited chiefly by the Ainus, the aboriginal race whom the Japanese long since drove out of the southern islands. During the last half century Japanese colonists have been spreading northward and gradually taking possession of this large island, and the process is going on with increased rapidity. I have been told by a Christian missionary who has lived for many years in Yezo and also by a Buddhist professor of my acquaintance, that these incoming Japanese have brought and are bringing their religion with them, and that most of them are Buddhists. The Buddhism they are bringing, moreover, is of a more living and active sort than the average Buddhism of the main island. The monks who go with the immigrants are not always above criticism morally, but they are zealous in their religion and active in their propaganda of it, notably so in getting hold of the children through Sunday schools and in similar ways. Yezo is thus becoming a strong Buddhist center.

If the strength of Japanese Buddhism varies with the locality, it also varies somewhat with the generations. Here as elsewhere religious tradition and belief is stronger with the old than with the young. The adolescent Japanese is agnostic about many things which his father took for granted. "The old women in the country," writes Professor Reisch-

[18] This must not be taken to mean that there is little Buddhist zeal in Kyushu. In some parts of the island there is much of it; as is shown by the fact that the largest seated Buddha image in the world has just been constructed at Beppu (Kyushu). It is "made of reinforced concrete, and is eighty feet in height, twenty feet higher than the famous Daibutsu at Nara." (*The Young East* for March, 1928).

auer, "and some of the old men are still earnest followers of things as they were. The younger generation, though nominally Buddhist, is utterly ignorant of and indifferent to the religion of their fathers."[19] Professor Reischauer knows a great deal more about the Japanese than I do, but I cannot help feeling that such a statement as this is far too sweeping. It is probably true that the contrast between the younger and the older generation, in matters of faith, is greater than it is in most countries; but it is the same sort of contrast that one finds in America, it is due to the same type of causes, and it will probably resolve itself in much the same way that it regularly has done both in Japan and in America, as the younger generation becomes the older generation and feels the increasing need of religious support and consolation.

Another religious contrast among the Japanese is that between the masses and the educated. Over the rank and file of the population Buddhism has a strong hold. It is emphatically the religion of Japan. A large portion of the better educated, especially in and about Tokyo and Yokohama, know little about Buddhism or any other religion, and take little interest in anything religious. So far as they go beyond agnosticism and seek the guidance of any system of thought, it is Confucianism toward which they lean.[20] This position of many of the intellectuals is due, in part, to historical and political causes. Buddhism, as we have seen, was supported by the Tokugawa government and was in a sense the state religion. It therefore shared the unpopularity of the old régime among the intellectual classes who restored the emperor. There are, of course, other reasons. The Japanese have no great interest in metaphysics,[21] and many of them find the ethical, political, and naturalistic position of Neo-Confucianism more interesting than the abstractions of Tendai and Kegon. The simple evangelism of the Pure Land sects makes a great appeal to the masses, but the young men of Jodo and Shin who have studied modern science often find the teachings of these popular sects rather thin, not to say naïve. So it comes about that the Pure Land sects tend

[19] *Studies in Japanese Buddhism*, p. 311.

[20] See Yoshitaro Yamashita in the *Transactions of the Japan Society*, IV. 264.

[21] Cf. J. W. Robertson Scott's *The Foundation of Japan* (Murray).

to lose their hold over many of the intellectual and educated members of the younger generation.

A very prominent Japanese scholar, well known both in his own country and in this—himself a Buddhist and a serious student of Buddhism—expressed to me a very dark view of the situation, so far as institutional Buddhism is concerned. As an organized religion, he said, Buddhism has but poor prospects for the future. Tendai has never recovered from the blow dealt it by Nobunaga when the monasteries on Hiei-san were destroyed, but has been ever since, like Hosso and Kegon, in a rather moribund condition. Shingon retains its hold over the people only by pandering to their superstitions. Zen will doubtless always have a following, but, like other mystical forms of religion, can expect to exert but little influence on an age such as ours. The time was when its mystical appeal, presented largely through the medium of Chinese art and poetry, found a ready response in the aristocratic leaders of the land; but those days of aristocracy and good taste are gone, and the number of mystics in any generation is bound to be limited. The Nichiren sect is weak for another reason. Its priesthood is notably corrupt, intolerant, and ignorant. A minority of them, indeed, are innocent and learned men; but these for the most part lead secluded lives, investigating the minute points in some of the Sutras, and exerting no appreciable influence on the life around them. The great majority are lacking in learning and philosophy, though full of a narrow religious zeal. The laity of the sect are notably intolerant. And as to the great Pure Land sects, their other-worldliness gives them but poor prospects in the age that is ahead of us. They were formed in and for an era of civil war and social turmoil, when despair of this present world was prominent in men's minds and the impress they took on in those times they have never thrown off. Moreover, the largest of these Pure Land sects, Shinshu, has the additional disadvantage of being ever on the edge of something like disruption, because of the ill-concealed dissatisfaction felt by the majority of the members with the two dynasties which rule the great Hongwanjis. Outside of the sects, in the opinion of the scholar whom I quote, the prospects of Buddhism are much brighter. There are many earnest laymen, who, though dissatisfied with all the sects, are filled with the Buddhist spirit and are giving it expression in various ways—in pantheistic philosophy, in scientific thought, in social service, in mystic life. It is in the spread of the Buddhist spirit outside the lines of the sects that the hope for the future of Buddhism is to be found. But within organized Buddhism very little is to be looked for.

My own opinion on this matter is not worth a great deal—except, perhaps, as it reflects the views of many with whom I have talked and whose opinions are worth much. But whether worth much or little I ought, perhaps, to express what conclusions I have come to; and if I am to do so I must venture to disagree with the distinguished Buddhist scholar and thinker whose rather pessimistic views I expressed in the preceding paragraph. I am emboldened to do so, because several Japanese and several foreigners with whom I talked, all of whom were men of much knowledge and sound judgment, had reached in substance the same conclusion as I. It will be noted that the rather dark picture of Buddhism quoted in the preceding paragraph referred in large part to the future rather than to the present. Whatever may come about in the next fifty years, certain it is that today Buddhism has a large, and, in some of the sects, an enthusiastic and devoted following. Now it is doubtless true that there are elements in the present situation which, if they grow and are not counteracted, will promise ill for the future of Buddhism; but before drawing a dismal conclusion on the basis of these factors, we should first ask ourselves whether there are not other factors at work whose influence in the future may well counterbalance those to which we have just referred. If we ask ourselves this question, an affirmative answer seems a very natural one. For it is only within the last few years that Buddhism has awakened to the need of education and reform, and of giving systematic culture to the religious life. The seeds are only now being planted and the probable harvest is surely a factor that cannot be neglected and that puts quite a different face upon the whole situation. Especially would I remind the reader of the fact that in a few years Japan will have, for the first time in her history, a really educated priesthood. These future leaders of Japanese Buddhism are now at school, studying the deeper meaning of their creed, and learning modern and western ways of educating the laity. Reischauer, to be sure, seems to anticipate that the more scholarly study of Buddhist thought and history will tend to weaken rather than strengthen the religion, because it will show how far the Mahayana has diverged from the teachings of the Founder.[22] There may be truth in this, and it may portend the weakening of Buddhism or possibly the gradual substitution of the Hinayana for the Mahayana. It is interesting to recall that this identical change actually took place, centuries ago, in both Burma and Cambodia. An occasional article in some of the Buddhist periodicals of Japan by scholarly Buddhists—especially by European Buddhists—urges a return to something like Pali Buddhism. In spite of all this I should be surprised if such a return ever came about. Your Mahayanist, whether Japanese, Chinese, or (ancient) Indian, cares and ever has cared very little for anything that history could say. The historical Sakyamuni will never be of any great importance in the Mahayana. It could get on without him.

If we look again at the weakness of the various sects to which reference was made a few pages back, it will be seen that most of them may well be remedied or counteracted by the forces that are being set free through the advance of religious education within Buddhism. The Japanese are indeed much interested in the science of the West; but they are also beginning to realize that the philosophy at the basis of all the branches of the Mahayana is of a sort that is quite capable of making room for everything that science has yet discovered or is likely to discover. The more thoroughly educated members of Jodo and Shin, for example, have already gotten back of the symbolism of their sects and are basing their lives and their religion, intellectually, not upon a naïve mythology, but upon a profound philosophy. The same resource is open to the Nichiren and Shingon sects. And both Zen and Tendai consciously and explicitly rest upon a philosophy that has nothing to fear from science.

[22] *Studies in Japanese Buddhism,* p. 310. "Every year's work of Japan's great educational system is bound to help undermine the present basis of Buddhism in Japan."

When these facts are more generally recognized it may well have the effect of increasing the respect of the thinking classes for the Buddhist philosophy and of rousing a new curiosity and interest in it. Surely this is a feature of the situation which must be taken count of in any attempt to forecast the future. In fact, some of the effects of the new intellectual stimulus are already being felt. As Professor Addison of the Episcopal Theological School in Cambridge recently wrote, on his return from a year's study of conditions in Japan:

> Partly as a result, partly as a cause of the Buddhist revival, there is widely observed, especially in the younger generation, an awakened idealism and a growing interest in religion. Far less enthusiasm is now manifested for the older type of materialism and skepticism represented by Herbert Spencer; far more general is the response to the stimulus of idealism in many forms—whether of the latest German philosophy, of Christianity, or of a new Buddhism.[23]

There is an interesting feature in the present religious condition of Japan which has escaped general notice but which is worth considering, if one is to embark on the sea of conjectures as to the future of the land. We have, namely, the anomalous situation of a highly intelligent people who are great readers and much interested in Western science and speculation, a large portion of whom still belong religiously to a faith which, however beautiful, has come, with very little change, straight out of the childhood of the race. The Political Shinto, to which the government is officially devoted, may or may not be a religion,[24] but the Shinto of the great rank and file of the Shintoists certainly is one. It seems exceedingly improbable that the naïve beliefs of this childlike cult will be able to hold for very long a large proportion of the intelligent and increasingly educated Japanese.[25] When they outgrow it, whither will they go? I cannot seriously suppose that new "religions" like the Omo-to-Kyo and Tenri-kyo—more naïve in their way than Shinto itself—will have any lasting appeal for large numbers

[23] *Religious Life in Japan,* p. 344.

[24] See Holton's discussion in "The Political Philosophy of Modern Shinto," *Tr. A. S. J.*, Vol. XLIX, Part II.

[25] If we may accept Dr. Kato's view of Shinto, however, as a developing religion we shall have to revise this verdict. See his *Study of Shinto, the Religion of the Japanese Nation.*

of these bright-minded people. Some of them will doubtless be converted to Christianity. Many will get on with the kind of agnostic indifference which seems to satisfy so many of the intellectual Japanese and so many of the illiterate Chinese at present. But it would be strange, to my thinking, if Buddhism did not come in for its share of the heritage. Buddhism is by this time a Japanese religion and is so regarded by all but a few of the extremely sophisticated. It has therefore certain great advantages of an initial sort over its Western rival.

One further fact should also be noted here: namely, the direction that Buddhism is actually taking today and that it has been following for the past thirty or forty years. When the Shogunate was overthrown the strength of Buddhism, as we have seen, was at low ebb. During the first years of the restoration, after it had been disestablished as the state religion and deprived of many of its temple-lands, it seemed to fall even lower. But from that time to this every year has marked a steady advance both in its influence over the people and in the quality of its teaching and its devotion. The last fifteen years in particular have been marked by a notable advance. It has been stung into new efforts by the advent of a great Western rival and it has deliberately and successfully learned from it many of the Western ways of efficient activity. In education, propaganda, worship, and service it has taken great strides, and we are witnessing today only the first fruits of its new sowings. Doubtless there are many agnostics in Japan. Doubtless many young men and not a few young women belonging to Buddhist families are growing up with much less faith and much less religious interest than their parents and grandparents. But is this a condition peculiar to Japanese Buddhism? Is there, in fact, any religion in the world today except perhaps Mohammedanism in Arabia which is not faced with the same serious problem? I am making no prophecy, be it understood, as to the future of Japanese Buddhism, nor would I for a moment deny that Japanese Buddhism is confronted with serious difficulties: but it does seem to me that, as religions go in our time, the Buddhism of Japan is a religion of great present strength and of pretty fair promise.

If now in closing our survey of the condition of contemporary Buddhism as a whole we cast a rapid glance over the entire Buddhist world (with the exception, as usual, of the Lamaist lands) we shall see that it falls naturally into five sections. The regions at the extreme southwest and at the extreme northeast—namely, the Hinayana lands and Japan—are, on the whole, in a fairly healthy condition. There is also a section in the center, occupying the lower Yangtse valley where Buddhism is still strong. The two other sections—South China with Annam, and North China with Korea—are in a moribund condition religiously, things growing steadily worse as one draws away from the Yangtse, and reaching their lowest just before the boundaries of Cambodia on the one hand, and of Japan on the other, are crossed.

So much for the actual present condition of Buddhism in the world today. As to its prospects in the future, this is of course all a matter of guesswork at best, though there may be a difference between a reasonable guess and a mere shot in the dark. A reasonable guess as to the future of Buddhism, however, if there be really such a thing, must base itself on a study of its inner nature, rather than upon the relatively external facts with which this chapter has been concerned. It is possible, therefore, that further light may be thrown upon the prospects of Buddhism by the considerations to which the next chapter will be devoted.

CHAPTER XXXIII

THE UNITY OF BUDDHISM

AFTER writing on the Buddhist religion pages enough to wear out the patience of the most long-suffering reader, it may seem strange, not to say unkind, of me to raise, at this late hour, the disconcerting question, Is there any such thing as Buddhism at all? Yet the question must be asked; if we do not put it, it will ask itself. Indeed, I fear the attentive reader has long since raised this query in the back of his mind. And this seems as good a place as any to face it.

The visitor to the lands I have tried to describe finds few things so striking as the varied and contrasting forms which Buddhism presents as one passes from the southwest to the northeast. The reader of this volume I hope has been struck with the same peculiarity. Particularly notable, of course, is the difference between the Hinayana and the Mahayana. One familiar with the Buddhism of Burma and Siam when suddenly set down in China feels himself in the midst of an utterly new and unknown religion. In the smoke of incense and paper money, before the Fos and P'usas among the artificial flowers and votive vegetables, he gropes around, at first in vain, for something familiar. And if he has the unusual good luck to find some monk or layman who can explain to him the Mahayana philosophy, he is the more mystified, and is tempted to exclaim: By what right is all this—or any of this—called Buddhism? How, indeed, can the religions of these various lands justly be subsumed under one heading, and be called by one name?

The diversities between Northern and Southern Buddhism are many. The account I have given of the Buddhism of today by no means includes all these diversities, but the reader must have noted a considerable number of them. It may be worth while here to recapitulate a few of the more important contrasts.

Most fundamental, perhaps, among these is the difference in the scriptures used by the two great schools. In theory the Tripitaka (in a Chinese rather than a Pali version, to be sure) is recognized by the Buddhists of China and Japan. But it is practically never read, and the explicit teaching of the Mahayana is to the effect that these Southern scriptures form merely a provisional statement of the truth, and have been entirely transcended by the fuller truth of the Northern school. The Southern school, on its part, refuses to recognize the Northern scriptures as having any authority whatever: in fact, it quite ignores them. Following from this divergence in canonical scripture, an almost equally fundamental contrast is to be found in the attitude of the two schools on metaphysical questions. The Hinayana, in obedience to the warnings of the Founder, refrains almost entirely from metaphysical speculation; the Mahayana is interested in little else. Its emphasis upon morality is relatively slight, whereas the Hinayana teaching might almost be said to begin and end with moral matters. The moral ideals of the two schools have often been contrasted: Southern Buddhism holding up as the supreme norm for admiration and imitation the self-contained and enlightened Arahant, while Northern Buddhism looks upon his attainment as but a little thing, and points the learner instead to the unselfish example of the Boddhisattva. The moral teaching of the Southern school still makes a good deal of the Four Noble Truths and the Noble Eightfold Path. It is rare that one finds a Northern Buddhist who has so much as heard of these things. The Hinayana is emphatically realistic; the Mahayana as emphatically idealistic in its philosophy. In Hinayana lands while there is a recognition of a long series of Buddhas, Sakyamuni alone plays any vital part in either theoretical or practical religion. In China and Korea he is associated with two or more other Buddhas who stand quite on an equality with him, and he is compassed about by a host of P'usas, Taoist deities, and Chinese generals who often seem to form a thoroughly polytheistic pantheon, while some of them frequently take from the Buddhas four-fifths of the offerings and adoration of the worshipers. In Japan the Taoist and Chinese additions to the Buddhist cycle merely give way to the innumerable deities drawn from Shinto; and Sakyamuni, far from coming back to his own, is in three of the most important sects explicitly put on a level greatly inferior to that of some of the other Buddhas. The interest of the Southern school is fixed almost exclusively on the teachings *of* the Buddha; the Northern school is principally interested in the teachings of philosophy *about* the Buddha. On Southern principles (as at present held) there seems logically nothing for the fully enlightened Buddhist at death but annihilation; and the Founder taught that the ultimate fate of the enlightened was one of the questions which ought not to be raised. The Northern school discusses the matter at length and frequently teaches something like a personal immortality for the perfected soul. Southern and Northern teaching are usually alike in their insistence that salvation can be attained only through the individual's own efforts and his intellectual enlightenment; but many Chinese Buddhists and two of the largest and most forward-looking of the Japanese sects deny this, and in Christian fashion offer salvation purely through faith and grace, and by an act of will. Can religions having these enormous divergencies be still called, in any significant sense, one religion? That is our question.

Before attempting to answer this question directly, it may be well to remind ourselves that at any rate Buddhism is not alone in possessing wide varieties of belief. Of the four great religions of the world, Mohammedanism is unique in being capable of formulation within the compass of relatively narrow and exact theological definition; and even here, if one contrasts Sunnis with Shiahs, or better still, orthodox with liberals, one will find very considerable divergencies. Hinduism contains within itself ever greater contrasts than Buddhism. And what shall we say of the use of a single name to designate the religion of the Spanish peasant and the German philosopher, of the South-American half-breed, the Russian ikon-worshiper, the English high-churchman, and the New England Unitarian? In fact, it would not be difficult to point out within Christianity rather interesting parallels to many of the Buddhist variations of belief and practice discussed in the last paragraph.

If Northern and Southern Buddhists do not agree on their authoritative books, Catholic and Protestant Christians agree no better on the question whether the source of authority lies in a book, in a man, in a council, or in the whole body of believers; or in fact whether there is any such thing as authority at all. There is, indeed, within Christianity no such division as to the propriety of metaphysical discussion and the importance of metaphysical doctrines, as we found in contrasting the Hinayana with the Mahayana. All forms of Christianity are more or less interested in problems of this nature. But the answers which different Christian bodies give to these problems vary almost as greatly as those furnished by the various schools of Buddhist thought. Well-nigh innumerable are the philosophical positions carefully expounded by distinguished Christian theologians, varying all the way from a simple realistic anthropomorphic scheme like that of the Old Testament to the most abstruse systems of Absolute Idealism. Particularly noticeable is this divergence when the discussion ranges about the person of the Founder. If Buddhists cannot agree on the nature and position of the Buddha, no more can Christians on the nature and position of the Christ. In Christianity as in Buddhism we find again the perennial disagreement whether the religion consists in the teachings *of* the Founder or in the teachings of the Church *about* the Founder. And as to his nature, there is an almost continuous gradation of beliefs, running all the way from the conception of him as God himself, down to the picture of him as a deluded zealot and even to the denial of his existence altogether. To match the contrast between the Hinayana unitary worship and the popular polytheism of China and Japan, we have the contrast between Unitarianism and the saint worship of various Catholic and "Orthodox" countries. If the Goddess of Mercy has supplanted the Buddha in the shrines and in the worship of many a Buddhist, have we not a striking parallel to this in the way in which the Madonna has taken the place of both God and Christ in the hearts of many a simple Christian? And if the Pure Land sects differ from the rest of Buddhism on the method of salvation, is not this identical disagreement to be found again within the Christian fold?

The truth is that if we try to define any of the great religions (except perhaps Mohammedanism) by means of creeds and doctrines, we shall find it altogether impossible to discover any unity in them. We shall be forced to split each of them into at least four or five quite distinct and even antithetical religions. As a matter of credal agreement there is no such thing as Buddhism, Hinduism, or Christianity.

And yet learned writers and ignorant people, literature, history, and common speech alike, continue to speak of Christianity, Hinduism, and Buddhism, and every one understands in a general way what they mean, and (except in hypercritical moments) every one knows perfectly well that this use of the words is justified. What, then, shall we make of these things, and how shall we come at any defensible definition of the world's great religions? What do we mean when we speak of Christianity, Hinduism, and Buddhism?

As I have already pointed out, one thing is plain: namely, that all credal definitions are hopeless. For the truth is, the great religions of the world are not primarily schools of philosophic thought. They are something very much bigger, very much more living than any creed can be. They are, in fact, living things, organic beings, in a sense, and they can no more be identified with some form of teaching than can you and I. If we take the historical rather than the theological point of view, and consider what as a matter of fact Christianity and Buddhism have been in history and actually are in the world today, we shall see that neither of them is or ever has been a creed, but that each of them is a stream of spiritual life, one of the currents of the spiritual life of the race, taking its source back thousands of years and flowing steadily and continuously down through the ages. Each of these religions is, as I have said, an organic thing, and as such it has the same kind of unity and of self-identity that other organic things possess: not the unity of unchanging creed but the unity of a constantly yet continuously changing life.

If now we ask what constitutes the unity and self identity of living organisms, we shall get the clue to the problem of this chapter. You are the same person that you were twenty years ago, not because your body has remained unchanged, not because your mind has remained unchanged: change, in fact, has been the very condition of your being alive at all. You are the same person that you were for two reasons. In the first place, your life has been a continuous and and unbroken stream from then to now, your self of today has grown out of your self of yesterday, and that grew out of your self of the day before, and so back to the beginning of your conscious existence. And secondly, you are the same with your self of twenty years ago because, in spite of innumerable changes, small and great, there are certain fundamental characteristics which were yours then and which are yours still. These principles hold of every organism and give it what self-identity it possesses. A material thing may be identified by the identity of its constituent atoms; a creed may be identified by its unchanging propositions; but a living, and therefore changing, organic being is identical with its own past self because of the continuity of its life, and because of the persistence of some of its more fundamental characters. A complex organism, moreover, possesses various organs of varied functions, called out and necessitated by the demands of its life and the exigencies of its environment. The eye *is* not the hand; it is very different from the hand; yet the two are one in the sense that they belong to the same organism and serve the same life. Through the unbroken continuity of growth both trace back their origin to the same parent cells, and both are informed with the same spirit and characterized by one dominating purpose, or innate tendency.

We may, I think, properly compare the great religions to living organisms. I do not mean, of course, that they are organisms in the full and biological sense of the word. It would be as appropriate, perhaps, to compare them to rivers. For rivers, too, have the self-identity of continuity and some of them the additional identity of persistent character. But the comparison of the religions to living things seems to me rather better, for religions struggle for existence and adapt themselves to new environments and to changing environments in almost biological fashion.

But whatever figure we use, it is, I trust, now clear that we have a right to speak of "Christianity" and of "Buddhism" and to attribute to each of them a certain unity and self-identity. For each of them is connected with its own past and its own origin by the unbroken transition of a continuous growth, and each of them can be shown to possess certain persistent characters in spite of an enormous amount of constant change. In short, it may be said that each of the great religions has its own controlling genius, which remains fairly constant underneath the almost endless branchings of its variations.

It is, of course, no part of our task here to deal further with the other great religions;[1] but if I am to sustain my thesis that in a real sense there is such a thing as Buddhism I must treat in somewhat greater detail those characteristics on which its unity and self-identity depend. As to the continuity of Buddhism, if it be not unnecessary it is useless for me to deal with it in detail at this point: for the whole of this volume has been an effort to portray it. To me there are few phases of the spiritual life of man more interesting or more impressive than the growth and development and migration of Buddhism. As the title of this book is intended to suggest, Buddhism has been a pilgrim, beginning its career in a little town among the foothills of the Himalayas, wandering down river valleys and over great plains and across mountains; a pilgrim, and after many years an exile, driven from its mother land and making its way through many a hardship and many a danger into strange countries and among strange peoples. Much of its early possessions it has carried with it, much it has left aside, and in the new lands to which it has come it has found many an additional treasure which it has made its own. But throughout its long course there has been no break. Each phase of its career can be traced to the preceding phase, or to the reception by it of some tributary stream. Its course has been like that of a great river which with its tributaries drains an entire continent and, with many a bend, pushes its irresistible, majestic way to the sea. It has had the continuity of an individual

[1] I have made some suggestions toward this in the case of Hinduism in Chapter VI of *India and Its Faiths;* and more specifically on the question of Christianity in a paper entitled "Again What is Christianity?" published in the *Hibbert Journal* and in an address on "The Nature of Christianity" printed by the Peking Union Medical College in 1924.

life, the continuity of an organic species, the continuity (from another point of view) of the Hegelian dialectic.

All this, I trust, is plain enough. Not so obvious, perhaps, are those persistent characteristics which help to make it, in all its ramifications and in all its history, still one religion. I shall not, of course, maintain that all those who burn incense in Buddhist temples or employ Buddhist monks at funerals are Buddhists, any more than I should hold that every ikon-worshiper is necessarily a Christian. What I mean is that there are certain qualities of character and feeling, of point of view, conduct, and belief, which may properly be called Buddhist, and that these are not confined to any one school of Buddhism, whether Hinayana or Mahayana, but are to be found in all those who by common consent would be considered typically Buddhist in all the lands we have studied, from southern Ceylon to northern Japan. These qualities, I hold, transcend not only nations but centuries, and unite the earnest follower of the most up-to-date Japanese sect with the earliest disciples of the Founder. Taken together they constitute what, in a rough and general way, might be called the Spirit of Buddhism.[2]

As fundamental among these qualities I would point out first of all a certain attitude, a certain feeling, a certain way of looking at things, a certain point of view, which is hardly to be described and for which I can think of no better word than the German *Innerlichkeit*. Our English *inwardness* perhaps suggests it, but not so well. Buddhism constantly lays its emphasis upon the subjective as having more importance than the objective. It is interested primarily in psychology and seeks in psychology for the solution to most important questions. Its glance is ever turned inward, and the events that go on within the soul it regards as immensely more significant than anything in the outer or material world can possibly be. Only in the inner life does it feel at grips

[2] Cf. the following from Hiuen-Tsiang's oration to the King of Kan-chang, on taking leave of him:

"In agreement with the mysterious character of this doctrine the world has progressed in its higher destiny: but distant peoples, coming to interpret the doctrine, are not in agreement. The time of the Holy One is remote from us: and so the sense of his doctrine is differently expounded. But as the taste of the fruit of different trees of the same kind is the same, so the principles of the schools as they now exist are not different." (Beal's trans. of the *Life of Hiuen-Tsiang*, p. 31.)

with reality. This has been its point of view from the beginning; and with this fact in mind one sees that the development of the Mahayana idealistic metaphysics is not so out of keeping with the simple teaching of the Founder as at first it seems to be.

With such a view of relative values it is natural that Buddhism in all its forms should regard as of primary importance the cultivation of the inner life. Self-discipline and self-control are the first aims of its earnest adherents in every land. It is for this reason, I suppose, that whatever else of the teachings of the Founder it may have forgotten, Buddhism has never ceased to inculcate the Five Precepts—the five great rules of self-control. These are the primary requisites for reaching the supreme goal, which, whether it be that of the Arahant in this life or of the Buddhas and Buddhisattvas in the spaceless worlds, or of the simple Shinshu believer sitting upon his lotus in the Western Paradise, consists in the attainment of a spiritual freedom and an inner peace that the external world can neither give nor take away. Other religions have taught the value of an independent spiritual calm, but no others have given it such repeated and almost exclusive emphasis. Once this is gained, the Buddhist feels, nothing else counts. He who through strenuous culture of the inner life has attained to this spiritual freedom, who has won the Great Peace, may snap his fingers at whatever comes.

The inner nature of this supreme goal has determined inevitably the characteristic form which the Buddhist moral teaching and moral training have assumed. The destruction of desire, as the chief enemy of inner peace, was the burden of many of the Founder's most significant sermons, and for long years this aim, embodied in the Four Noble Truths, seems to have occupied a very central place in Buddhist teaching. The Four Noble Truths, as I have pointed out, form no real part of Northern Buddhism today, and there is no general attack upon desire as such. But the essence of the matter has been retained in the persistent attack which Buddhism the world over constantly makes upon lust, anger, and worry. In the insatiable nature of sexual desire, the destructive excitement of ill-will, and the steady sapping of our inner strength that comes from anxiety, Buddhism sees the three great dangers to our freedom and our peace, and against these it launches its attacks, in every Buddhist land, with something of the same vehemence and systematic earnestness that the early Brothers and Sisters put into the practice of the Noble Eightfold Path. In all these things the Northern Buddhists and the Southern Buddhists are at one.

As a reenforcement to these three great attacks upon lust, anger, and worry, or rather, as the principal offensive of the entire campaign, Buddhism when in earnest, in every part of the world, brings all its forces to bear against self-centeredness and self-interest, against that common preoccupation with one's own possessions and schemes and wishes and rights which is so notoriously incompatible with the calm life of the spirit. I do not mean that all "Buddhists" do this: but all those in every land who would be singled out as notably and characteristically Buddhist are distinguished for this effort. The attack launched by the Founder upon self-centeredness has never ceased to have its influence upon Buddhism in all the lands to which it has been carried. Sometimes, as I have pointed out in previous chapters, the Buddhist emphasis on the inner life has resulted in a sophisticated sort of spiritual selfishness, quite as ugly as the more brutal and naïve form which it has displaced; but there can be no doubt of the fact that the Buddhist point of view and the Buddhist training have resulted in great efforts, both North and South, to get rid of the more aggressive and obvious forms of selfishness. This has been reflected in the Anatta or non-ego doctrine of both Hinayana and Mahayana, and in the readiness and eagerness of many Buddhists to merge the individual in the Absolute. It is seen more persistently in a trait which I think every one must feel who has much to do with Buddhists who are steeped in the thought and training of their religion, namely, a kind of "negative-self feeling" (to use McDougall's term), a kind of humility, an unwillingness to put themselves forward, a dislike for the aggressive attitude which seeks to emphasize Number One. This lack of aggressiveness is one of the most marked of Buddhist traits. It stands out in strong contrast to the large-footed, self-advertising, red-blooded, self-congratulatory efficiency of the

West. For that matter, it is, of course, a characteristic not only of Buddhism but of the East in general; but in the East itself it belongs peculiarly to Buddhism. It is at the heart of much of Buddhist pacifism. Your typical Buddhist would rather give up his rights than fight for them. Self-display and the instinct of pugnacity have been as nearly eradicated by the Buddhist training as perhaps they ever are or can be in human nature. There is little longing in the Buddhist for a fight as such, or for that positing of the self, that assertion of one's own will, which is at the bottom of so many an altercation. Moreover, nothing that one can fight for is worth so much as that inner peace which a fight is certain to destroy. There is a kind of gentleness in the Buddhist nature which I think every one must feel.

But this is not the gentleness and non-aggressiveness of weakness. It is not fear that prompts it. Behind it there is a spiritual strength of a quiet sort, a power of passive resistance that might well astonish a Western prize-fighter, forever feeling of his biceps. The non-aggressiveness of the typical Buddhist is a kind of strength in reserve; it is the gentleness of the strong man who refuses to push his own way in a crowd, or of the reflective man who is convinced the game is not worth the candle. Partly as an outgrowth of this gentleness of spirit, partly in obedience to the never-forgotten exhortations of the Founder, partly out of contagion from the example and influence of his mesmeric personality, Buddhism in all the lands to which it has gone has never ceased to preach and to practice universal pity and sympathy for all sentient life. *Ahimsa*, harmlessness, is the first law. No other religion, except perhaps Jainism, carries so far this fellow-feeling for all living things, enfolding in its merciful arms even the lowest forms of animal life. As every one knows, it influences even the details of the monks' diet, and is not infrequently seen in what seems to us fantastic forms, as in the refusal of conscientious Buddhists to kill snakes or mosquitoes. Not only so. This feeling of pity sometimes defeats its own end, as in the unwillingness of Buddhists to put a suffering animal out of its misery. For the roots of it are emotional rather than reasoned. The unwillingness of Buddhists to kill animals is often explained in the West as due to the belief in transmigration and the consequent fear of destroying in the animal some deceased friend or relative. There is no doubt that the transmigration theory has something to do with it, setting the whole animal kingdom, as it does, on something like an ultimate equality with man and thus inducing a respect for our brute relations which in the West is difficult to grasp. But I am sure there is more in the attitude of the Buddhist than this. It is by no means purely as a matter of reasoned theory that he feels for the lower forms of life and dislikes to kill them. The *feeling* of pity is quite as fundamental and original as the theory.

Naturally, not all Buddhists obey the law of Ahimsa. Buddhist laymen often encourage or even participate in the killing of animals and fish for food. But this exception to the law is recognized as an exception, and he who practices it knows that in so doing he is not acting wholly as a Buddhist should. The necessities of this present evil world make it very difficult for all save the monks to follow completely the councils of perfection. Nor would I assert that pity for all sentient things and harmlessness toward all human beings are displayed by every Buddhist, any more than efficient love for one's neighbor is seen in every Christian; but I believe it is true that whoever in the lands of the East is conspicuously devoid of these traits is by common consent regarded as a very poor Buddhist, no matter how many candles he may burn to the Fos and the P'usas, to the Butsus and Busatsus. It is not without significance that the only members of the Buddhist cycle who are real rivals in popularity of the Buddhas are the Goddess of Mercy and Jizo. These are loved, I am very sure, not only because they may prove helpful to the worshiper, but because the Buddhist consciousness the world over holds in most reverend esteem and most enthusiastic admiration the qualities of sympathy and helpfulness which they embody. In China they will tell you that the Chinese learned reverence from Confucius and pity from the Buddha. Much the same thing seems to be true of Japan. Whatever be the sins of Buddhist monks, and they are sometimes many, they usually have the reputation, in all lands, for a real feeling of sympathy; and if they teach anything to the layman it is likely to be the law of harmlessness. In the more earnest and consistent Buddhists, lay or cleric, south or north, this sympathy often blossoms into genuine love and a real desire for positive helpfulness.

Another outgrowth of the inwardness, gentleness, and lack of aggressiveness which are so basic in the Buddhist character, is an unusual degree of intellectual tolerance and liberality of thought. This tolerance for the opinions of others has an intellectual or theoretical root as well. It is in part the natural result of the lack of any absolutely authoritative book, church, or pope. Buddhism has never had a theory of literal and plenary inspiration. The Founder seems regularly to have based his teachings upon his own experience or on the common reason of the race. Hence, in Buddhism it is extremely rare to find any trace of that bigotry which has been all too common in religions which like Judaism, Christianity, and Mohammedanism, claim to possess a uniquely inspired and infallible book. In the case of the Mahayana, moreover, this natural tolerance has been reenforced by a theory of different grades or degrees of truth, and the possession of a world-view wide enough to make room for most scientific hypotheses and most non-Buddhist philosophies as approximate pictures of certain aspects of Reality. The universal Buddhist belief, moreover, that there is no absolute division between the sheep and the goats, but that most of us are both goats and sheep at the same time, the conception of many heavens and many hells and many conditions of rebirth in this world, with the refusal to shut the door of effort in the face of any sinner, however vile, or to believe that anywhere in the universe there is a gate bearing the inscription "Who enter here leave hope behind"—all these considerations make it natural for the Buddhist to recognize many ways of salvation besides just his own. In an oft-quoted parable in the Lotus of the Good Law, the Buddha shows not only that in the Eternal Heavens there are many mansions, but that there are many "vehicles" by which one may reach them. Over and over again have I asked monks in both Hinayana and Mahayana lands whether sincere Christians wo lived according to their best light could be saved. In only one case, so far as I remember, have

I received a negative answer; and frequently I have been assured not only that Christianity if followed out conscientiously leads to the same ultimate goal as Buddhism, but that a good Christian *is* really a good Buddhist, without knowing it.

I have dealt thus far with the fruits of what I have called Buddhist *Innerlichkeit* on their positive side. There are also negative results which are quite as characteristic and which must not be passed over. Like other things, Buddhism possesses *les défauts de ses qualities*. The constant preoccupation with the inner and the great emphasis laid upon it naturally works a corresponding neglect of the outer. The typical Buddhist usually pays relatively slight attention to the external world. The consequence of this is seen in the lack of practical efficiency and of serious practical effort so often pointed out in the great majority of consistent Buddhists. A good Buddhist is likely to be "an ineffectual angel." Buddhists are not greatly interested in the regeneration of this evil world, and though they may wish for it in a mild way they are too busy cultivating their own inner lives to do much toward it. The morality which they preach and practice is mostly of a personal sort. It is in danger, in fact, of being largely of a negative sort. It is not insignificant that the Five Precepts—the one set of moral laws taught with emphasis over the entire Buddhist world—are all phrased in negative form. Earnest and efficient effort for social morality, for the reform of society, for cooperation with others in making this a better world, for positive and effectual helpfulness toward one's neighbor, these things are by no means incompatible with Buddhism—in a sense they may even be the natural outflow of Buddhist pity, but there is much in Buddhism that makes them difficult; and, as a fact, outside of Japan they are rare. In all these ways of practical and efficient helpfulness and positive as well as loving service, Buddhism is far behind Christianity.

There are, of course, other causes for this contrast between Buddhism and Christianity besides the fundamental contrast in the genius of the two religions which I have been discussing. Foremost among these are the racial and economic factors. No one will question the obvious fact that the Western races, on the whole, are more practically efficient than the Eastern races. The reason for this may be what you like, but the fact is undeniable. The Western races are also more aggressive, they have a larger share of the sporting, combative spirit than have most Orientals. Now it is quite thinkable—I should say quite probable—that if, by some chance of history, Buddhism had gone west and Christianity east, Buddhism would have been the aggressive, practically efficient religion and Christianity the inactive one. The economic situation has reenforced the contrast of tendency within the two religions so largely brought about by racial characteristics. The charitable institutions and the missionary activities of Christendom have been made possible by the surplus wealth of Christian lands. In the West the population has never caught up with the food supply in the way it did ages ago in the East. It is perhaps more than a coincidence that Protestant missions date exactly from the period at which Protestant countries, as a result of the industrial revolution, began to have an excess of wealth. And it is, of course, perfectly plain that the possession of political and military power, as well as wealth, has done much to make possible the actual development of Christian missions. I do not think these racial and economic factors when combined are enough to explain the contrast in outer activity and efficient helpfulness exhibited by the two religions. I think the original teachings of the two Founders and the ideas developed by their successors must be taken as co-causes in developing the differences we find. All these factors have doubtless had their influence.

Whatever the causes may be, however, there is no doubt that most Buddhist morality and good will are tinged with a certain passivity that is unfortunately almost as characteristic of Buddhism as that morality and that good will themselves. It did not, indeed, characterize the Founder; and innumerable cases of thoroughly consistent Buddhists probably might be cited who did not share it. It is perfectly thinkable, and (as the Shinshu in Japan is demonstrating) it is practically possible, that Buddhism may come to possess the active virtues of positive efficient achievement in the external world. But thus far it has done so only in exceptional cases; and its passivity and disregard of social, political, economic, and material conditions is a natural if not a necessary corollary of its emphasis upon the inner life.

There is another corollary of Buddhist *Innerlichkeit* which is even more unfortunate than its passivity and which must be pointed out. The inner life is necessarily a private life. As William James expressed it: the breaches between "thoughts belonging to different personal minds . . . are the most absolute breaches in nature." It follows that one can do relatively little of a direct sort for the inner life of others. One may, indeed, teach morality and give instructions in zazen. But most of the work of self-cultivation must be done by one's self. *By* one's self and consequently *for* one's self. When the chief business of life is the culture of one's spirit, the constant preoccupation with one's own inner life and one's advance in virtue naturally tends to breed much of the self-centeredness which Buddhism is so deeply concerned to destroy. Only, as I have indicated above, it is a peculiar form of self-centeredness, a kind of sophisticated spiritual priggishness and selfishness which is indeed far removed from the brutal aggressive self-love which Buddhism constantly attacks, but which is hardly more attractive, though it may be much less harmful. The belief in Karma and in the acquisition of merit, with all that these things mean for the future lives of believers, also contributes to this most undesirable result. With the baser sort of Buddhist, the whole thing frequently boils down to a kind of spiritual materialism in which the merit to be acquired by each good deed is nicely calculated, and the cash value of virtue in this or another life is ever present to the mind's eye.

Fortunately, Buddhism possesses still a further characteristic which may in time, and possibly at no distant time, to a considerable extent counteract the unfortunate consequences of its inveterate inwardness. I refer to its remarkable elasticity and its ability to respond to new needs. Of this I shall have something more to say before the close of the chapter. Already, in fact, in both Siam and Japan the needs of the times are bringing out in Buddhism qualities of practical and efficient activity in the external world which show that passivity and selfishness are by no means inevitable and unescapable consequences of its inward nature. And it is possible that these new movements within Buddhism may be only a foretaste of what is yet to develop.

In addition to the qualities I have discussed there are certain fundamental beliefs which all schools of Buddhism hold in common, the more important of which should be mentioned in this connection. Perhaps the most basal of these is the universal confidence of all Buddhists in the complete dominance of the universe by spiritual forces. Southern Buddhism is atheistic in a sense, and neither Southern nor Northern Buddhism has anything to say about creation or a creator. But both schools believe emphatically that the universe itself is supernaturally moral. The fundamental law of Reality, dominating all laws of the material world, is the law of Karma, that whatsoever a sentient being sows, that he shall reap: that virtue and vice have their never-failing recompense. This faith Buddhism of course shares with Hinduism, from which, in fact, it borrowed it. Following naturally from this basal doctrine is the correlative belief in the unimportance of physical death. The laws of matter being so subordinate to the laws of spirit, it is unthinkable on Buddhist presuppositions that the accident of bodily death should put an end to the life of the spirit. It is conceivable, think some members of the Southern school, that absolute enlightenment may bring so full completion that consciousness as we know it will cease, at the expiration of bodily life; but mere bodily death by itself cannot possibly have any such momentous influence upon a member of the spiritual world. What form the future life may take is a matter of detail upon which different schools and different individuals disagree, though all accept transmigration as a partial solution. This common acceptance of the doctrine of transmigration, indeed, deserves more emphasis than I have space here to give it, as one of the great credal bonds that hold the entire Buddhist world together. But more important still is the spiritual and moral conception of the universe which I have been discussing, the basal faith that nothing on the physical plane can destroy the life of the spirit, and that not only the spiritual but the material world is ultimately governed by moral laws. On these great doctrines Buddhists of all schools are firmly agreed.

One other common belief, moreover, should be mentioned, namely, the recognition by all Buddhists that their religion in its present form owes its reintroduction upon this earth to the great Indian Teacher, Sakyamuni. Together with this historical belief and this recognition of indebtedness goes the sense of gratitude and loyalty to him which loses in intensity, to be sure, as one gets farther away from the scenes of his earthly life, yet which has still a certain strength even in distant Japan. Connected with this item of the common Buddhist creed there is the further belief, accepted by all, in a series of supernaturally enlightened beings, the Buddhas, of whom Sakyamuni was one, who out of pity for all sentient things from time to time appear upon the earth to reinstate a knowledge of the truth and of the way to salvation.

Before closing this chapter I must say one further word about a final quality in Buddhism which I have already mentioned and which has been and must of necessity be of great importance in the life of the religion. I refer to its remarkable elasticity and adaptability. Wherever Buddhism has gone it has manifested this characteristic, and manifested it in a superlative and unique degree. I do not think there is another religion that possesses so much of it. Buddhism has been emphatically a missionary religion. Its transplanting to new lands has been accomplished never through conquest or through migration but solely by the spread of ideas. Yet almost everywhere it has gone it has so completely adapted itself to the new people and the new land as to become practically a national religion. This has been partly due to the tolerance and liberality of its thought, to which I have already referred, a tolerance which it has exhibited both within and without. With the most extremely rare exceptions Buddhism has held no heresy trials and has carried on no persecutions. With a daring catholicity that approaches foolhardiness it has recognized every form of rival as a possessor of some degree of truth. Its confidence in the inclusiveness of truth, and of its own truth, has been so great that it has taken up into itself all sorts of foreign cults and superstitions and seemingly incongruous and inconsistent beliefs. The doctrine or policy of *hoben* as the Japanese call it, or "accommodation," has been applied to an extent that astonishes every Western student who reads of it for the first time. The conception that the beliefs and the gods of other religions may be true and real in their way, that they may be symbolic expressions of the truth which we possess in its fullness, hardly dawned upon the Western world prior to our grandfathers' time, and before that was guessed only by an occasional Lessing or *Nathan der Weise*. But from the earliest introduction of Buddhism into Japan and even into China, when our Christian predecessors were anathematizing each other over an iota subscript, the Buddhist missionaries and thinkers were accepting into their religion all sorts of native beliefs as dim and symbolic expressions of the Eternal Dharma.

That Buddhism has carried this tolerance and liberality too far for its own good is beyond question, a fact recognized today by all Buddhist leaders. The adoption of the innumerable deities of the Shinto pantheon as merely Bodhisattvas under new (and extremely long!) names helped indeed to win over the Japanese people, but it brought into Buddhism a mass of primitive and superstitious cult which did much to put the religion into the degenerate condition from which it suffered for so many of the medieval centuries. Fortunately, its rival came to its rescue and through the effort of Shinto scholars who despised Buddhism a reform within Buddhism was initiated which has been carried on with increasing success to our own day. In China the situation has been and is much more serious. The welcoming of Taoist deities into Buddhist temples has been carried on with so liberal a hospitality that not infrequently the guests have deprived their host of all the best rooms and in some cases have turned him out of doors altogether. The deplorable condition of Buddhism in some of the more distant provinces of China is in part due to an excess of tolerance and an extreme extension of the doctrine of symbolic interpretation.

Yet when not carried too far this liberality, this elasticity and adaptability of which I speak, are undoubted elements of strength. Change is a necessity of life, a sign of life; in its readiness to change its outward forms and to adapt itself to all sorts of new conditions Buddhism has shown itself very much alive. When transplanted to a new land it has acted exactly as a virile biological species acts under similar circumstances. It has made the adaptations necessary to the new conditions, it has responded to the new stimuli with an inventiveness and a youthful energy that betoken an almost inexhaustible store of life and strength. Never troubled by an excessive love of consistency, that "vice of little minds," never bound to an absolutely authoritative past, never committed to an unchangeable loyalty to that which has been believed *semper, ubique, et ab omnibus,* it has been able to develop its philosophy and its cult according to the fresh and changing needs of the peoples it has sought to feed. Prejudice and hostility have not stood in its way. Its rivals it has regularly sought to make into friends and allies; and when they refused this relationship and declared open war upon it, it has not been too proud to learn from them and adopt such of their methods as seemed adaptable to its needs. Christian missionaries frequently ridicule the Japanese Buddhists for their adoption of Christian hymn tunes and their imitation of the Y. M. C. A., the Sunday school, the Salvation Army, and other Christian methods and institutions. As a fact this action on the part of Buddhism is a token of its life and its wisdom. If it were the dead thing some missionaries depict, it could not thus adapt itself to the new needs of the new day. This unique ability to adapt itself to new conditions, to develop new organs and functions, is inherent in the fundamental nature of Buddhism. As I have more than once pointed out, the inclusiveness of its philosophy puts it in a better position to make room for new scientific discoveries and new philosophic hypotheses than can either Christianity or Islam. It can also deal with its own outgrown beliefs in a symbolic fashion which must be the envy of religions more explicitly bound to definite and authoritative creeds. The unity that it possesses, the spirit that holds it together, as I have tried to show, are not of the credal sort and not endangered by the new developments which a new age may demand of it.

The results arrived at in this chapter are, therefore, not

without their bearing on the question of the prospects of Buddhism. In particular, the peculiar elasticity of Buddhism puts the whole matter in a different light from that in which we saw it in the preceding chapter when we were considering only the actual conditions from what might be called a quantitative point of view. A religion with the kind of self-identity and unity I have described and with the power of adaptation to changing conditions which Buddhism possesses is far from moribund. Such a religion has still a mission to perform in this world: and provided it has wise and awakened leadership, it may face the future with head erect and with a growing confidence.

CHAPTER XXXIV

BUDDHISM AND CHRISTIANITY

At the close of the preceding chapter we found ourselves faced once more with the problem of the prospects of Buddhism as it looks toward the future. Several of the factors involved in this problem we have already considered; but there is one which we have thus far fought shy of, though its importance must be plain to all. I refer to the state of war that seems to exist between Buddhism and its great competitor, whose militant and aggressive hosts have been invading all the Buddhist lands for a century or more. A candid discussion of this warfare and what it involves leads inevitably into certain topics which I should gladly avoid. But no treatment of the present condition of Buddhism (and that is really what I have wished to present in these pages) would be even approximately complete if it did not give some consideration to the great movement of Christian missions in Buddhist lands, and the present and possible future relations of Buddhism and Christianity to each other.

I shall make no attempt to furnish the reader with statistics of conversions, of schools, hospitals and other achievements of Christian missions. These can be obtained from the various missionary boards and from the many books written on the missionary movement. Some of these statistics are trustworthy and valuable; some of them are misleading. Among misleading statistics should be classed most of those that deal with conversions. They are not misleading if one refuses to be misled, but for the inexperienced and unwary they are likely to be a delusion and a snare. This for two quite different reasons. In the first place, no one can tell, because no one knows, how much a "conversion" may be worth. It may mean that the "heathen" is made over into a new creature, that the old Adam has been replaced by the new, that an inward and heavenly revolution has taken place in the soul. It may also mean that the old conventional restraints and traditional beliefs have been broken and nothing but a new form of words has taken their place; that the old symbols which had the sanction of ages of reverence have been exchanged for new ones which fail to get much hold on the imagination and the character. In most cases of "conversion" I believe a real improvement in life and conduct results. Together with the old beliefs old evil influences are broken, and the individual is brought into a spiritual environment which is morally helpful. The missionaries are fully justified in not making the conditions of admission to the church very high. Their aim in this policy is not (as some critics suppose) to swell the statistics of conversions, but to bring as many as possible of the "interested" into a social relationship where good influences of various sorts may be brought to bear upon them. The policy is wise and laudable, but it has the incidental result of making the statistics of their work rather misleading for those at home who do not know how to interpret them. Thus the work of "evangelizing the world" may seem to the incautious reader to be getting on much faster than it really is. But there is another side to the matter, and this, too, contributes to the unreliability of statistics on this subject. The most important part of the movement toward evangelization is of the kind that can never get into statistics: namely, the indirect and imponderable influence exercised upon the nominally non-Christian masses by the little Christian centers that spring up around every mission. The greatest thing that Christian missions can do is to disseminate the spirit of Christ, and of this work there is and can be no measure. Statistics of the "converted" and of the "heathen" shed little light upon actual results. Not every one that saith "Lord, Lord" has learned the spirit of the Master; and many a Buddhist and Confucianist is a Christian in all but creed and name.

The views that one will hold of the need of Christian missions in general and of the special need of missions in special lands, will depend on all sorts of things. There still are some people—apparently there still are many people—who maintain that the great aim of Christian missions is to save souls from hell, and that all the "heathen" are bound thither and must reside there through all eternity unless they accept the "evangelical" creed. Many of my readers will doubt this statement. They will class the belief in the damnation of the heathen with antediluvian things such as Tutankhamen and the eggs of dinosaurs. But I can assure them that not all ancient things are in museums, and that a considerable minority of the people who support the missionary enterprise still harbor the belief in heathen damnation or something very like it. To one who holds this point of view all "heathen" lands, of course, are equally in need of Christian missions. But the rest of us may properly make distinctions between the various non-Christian lands, and differentiate those which are in great need of the help Christian missionaries can bring from others which are capable of getting on relatively well by themselves.

Among Buddhist lands the contrast here indicated is very striking. In Japan and Siam Buddhism is decidedly alive and is doing real work for the moral and social and religious welfare of the people. Burma, Ceylon and Cambodia are less well off but are still religiously in a fair condition. China, Annam, and Korea, on the other hand, with the exception of a few localities, are drawing but little spiritual and moral nurture from the native religions and are in great need of assistance. The position of those who deny that these lands are in need of the kind of help which wise and truly Christian missionaries can bring, seems to me either based on ignorance, on sentiment, on prejudice, or else to be quite incomprehensible. It is emphatically the position of the sentimentalist rather than that of the realist. I can understand how one who has never been in China may be impressed by an argument against missions which should recite the antiquity of the Chinese civilization, the loftiness of the Confucian code, the law-abiding and moral nature of the Chinese, the beauty of their art and the picturesqueness of their dilapidation. All these things are undeniable. Undeniable also is the fact that we of the West might well learn many things from the Chinese. But despite all this it may still be true that there are a few things which the Chinese might well learn from us. And when one goes to China and looks about, only (as it seems to me) a sentimentally obdurate blindness can prevent one from seeing a considerable number of pitifully crying needs which some one ought to make an effort to satisfy. And no one, so far as I have discerned, is ready to take off his coat and make the sacrifices necessary for this sort of work except the Christian missionary.

There are two classes of writers and talkers about China who are equally misleading. One is made up of those people of mole-like vision and encyclopedic ignorance who assert that the Chinese are barbarians and that there is no civilization except our civilization. The other class is composed of those sentimental enthusiasts who, by magnifying certain things and shutting their eyes to others, manage to believe (or at least to assert) that Chinese art, poetry, religion, morality, politics, and social structure and customs are all superior to those of the West; and that the East is all civilized and the West all barbarian. For my own part, I admire the East; but I also love the East. And loving the East I cannot fail to see that in many ways it is inferior to the West, and that it has great needs which the West is in a position in some degree to satisfy. I cannot shut my eyes to the extreme illiteracy of the Chinese, and the consequent inner poverty of their lives; their lack of individual spiritual development; their almost universally diseased condition; their many bodily ills that come through sheer ignorance, superstition, and evil conventions; the lack of home life and its joys; the sad lot of the majority of the women; the limited nature of their mutual helpfulness, going as it does hardly beyond the family lines; their callousness to the sufferings of others; the low standards of honesty among their officials and among many who are not officials; the cheapness of the lie; the superstitious fears with which they spoil their peace; the unspiritual nature of their outlook; the general materialism of their lives.

Much the same sad state of things exists in Korea and Annam. And in none of these lands are the native religions doing more than a minute percentage of the work required to set things right. It is my thesis that Christian missions are needed, and sorely needed, in all these lands, not to destroy the native religions (so far as these religions are more than demonstrable superstition) but to do the work which the native religions fail to do. And there is work enough of this sort everywhere, and for all. In Siam and Japan, as I have pointed out, Buddhism is stronger and more wide awake than elsewhere; but even in these countries Buddhism needs the help that Christianity can bring.

For the work of the modern missionary is chiefly directed against evils of the very real and undeniable sort recited above. A large percentage of missionaries in our day are school teachers. Many more are physicians and nurses. Some of them are architects and builders, some of them roadmakers. And those who are put down as evangelists give up most of their time to directing native teachers and preachers, settling disputes, giving personal advice, volunteering in famine relief and plague relief, dealing with what wisdom they possess with social questions, attacking evil customs such as footbinding and the opium habit, seeking to arouse and direct a healthy public opinion, in short, teaching people how to live.

It may be said that it is well enough for the missionary to carry on educational, medical, and social work, but that there is no justification for his attempt to change the religion of the natives. Some of the native religions, it is pointed out, are noble, spiritual teachings. Since the Orientals have a good enough religion of their own, why try to substitute ours? Why, as it is sometimes expressed, seek to make Baptists out of Buddhists? I should like those who ask that question to come with me to China, Korea, and Annam and point out to me the Buddhists who are being made into Baptists. I spent upward of eight months in China with the almost exclusive aim of finding Buddhists. Outside of the Yangtse valley and outside of the monasteries I found exceedingly few. Exceedingly few, that is, relatively speaking and in the sense of the anti-missionary argument recited above; exceedingly few in whose lives the noble teachings of Buddhism were a real power; exceedingly few for whom Buddhism was doing anything of striking importance. And those few were in no danger of being converted to Christianity, and, so far as I was aware, the missionaries were not wasting any of their time upon them. The missionaries had too many other, more promising things to do. The converts to Christianity in the three lands I have mentioned are very seldom made from those who have been devout Buddhists or

Confucians. They are made as a rule either from those who had no religion before they met the missionary or from animists and spirit-worshipers whose "religion," if so it can be called, was in many ways much worse than none at all. And I do not see how there can be much argument over the superiority of Christianity to the self-indulgent materialism of the Annamese, the crude and non-moral superstition of the Chinese villager, or the tree-worship and devil-fear of the Korean. In the other Buddhist lands, I confess, the situation is different, and there many efforts are made at the conversion of real Buddhists. This is often a waste of time and it is sometimes positively harmful. Probably it is not wise for missionary boards to spend as much of their money and their energies on these lands as in the others where the need is so much greater. Yet surely the Siamese and Japanese, as well as other peoples, should have an opportunity to learn about Christianity if they care to. With the critics of the Christian missions I agree that the Buddha has a message for many of us in the West—for all of us, perhaps. But I should add that Christ also has a message for the East and for all of it.

In fact, Buddhism itself needs the assistance of Christianity, not only in doing some of the common moral and spiritual work which it is not strong enough to do alone, but also for its own sake. Especially in Ceylon and Japan has Christianity served Buddhism in two distinct and important ways. It has, in the first place, taught it many useful methods of education and propaganda and ceremonial. And more important still, it has been a stimulant to Buddhism, rousing it to renewed life and effort by the very fact of its rivalry. Two earnest Japanese Buddhists of my acquaintance, both of them professors in Buddhist seminaries, assured me—and each quite spontaneously—that Japanese Buddhism owed a large debt of gratitude to the Christian missionaries.

The great majority of the many missionaries I have met in Buddhist lands are liberal, intelligent, open-minded men and women. Most of them are quick to recognize the finer elements in the native religions. Most of them are much more liberal in their point of view than are the rank and file of the churches at home that send them out. Most of them have become decidedly more liberal than they were when they left home. They have done something to educate the "heathen" and the "heathen" have done something to educate them. They have got rid of many of our home-made provincialisms. They have attained, among other things, an international point of view which is seldom found among those who spend all their lives in their native land. Many of them have, in similar fashion, learned to transcend denominational lines and to think in terms of Christianity. A few of them have succeeded in the very difficult task of thinking in terms of religion, of viewing the situation from a point of view that transcends the credal and nominal distinctions between religions, while yet retaining the energy of the partisan in the service of the Good.

In this matter again one should make distinctions between different lands. The missionaries to Japan are as a rule a very liberal group. They have to be. Ignorant and narrow preachers of the gospel stand little chance of making much impression on so intelligent and wide-awake a people as the Japanese. A very large proportion of the missionaries I met in China are also well educated and liberal and wise workers. The level of liberality falls very decidedly when one enters Korea or Annam, though in Korea, at least, I think the majority are still of the liberal sort. In the other countries I visited the average level lies somewhere between these extremes. There is a notable difference also between the missionaries of different churches. I could name names, but I do not wish to hurt feelings or acquire enemies.

As I have implied, by no means all missionaries are of the liberal type. There is a narrow-minded minority, full of the unselfish devotion of the zealot, who mix much harm with the good they do. They are of the stuff the martyrs were made of, and their persecutors. If born in an earlier age they could have gone to the stake, or have tied some one else to it, with equal readiness and fervor. They have come out to destroy the devil and all his works, to smash the idols and convert the heathen, or justify the Almighty in sending them to eternal damnation. As Mr. R. F. Johnston's *Letters to a Missionary* [1] show, there is still a fair minority of both missionaries and mission boards who cling (in name at least) to

[1] London, Watts, 1918.

the dogma that the heathen will be condemned by divine "justice" to everlasting punishment unless they accept some particular form of faith. Missionaries of this narrow type are, so far as I know, invariably earnest, devoted, self-sacrificing souls, ready to give their lives—and in fact actually giving their lives—to the cause they love. In this as in every field, zeal and narrowness commonly go together. Doubtless it is a great impetus to missionary labor if one fervently believes that millions of one's fellows are held suspended, like Jonathan Edward's famous spider, over the fires of hell, and that in a brief time they will all be dropped into the yawning jaws of the fiery abyss unless snatched like a brand from the burning by being made to repeat some sacred formula. There is no doubt that Christian love for their fellows burns very brightly in the hearts of these earnest and often heroic apostles of an ancient creed. It may seem unkind to suggest that a careful psychological analysis of their actual impulse would reveal not only Christian love but also a good deal of the instinct of pugnacity and of the partisanship commonly associated with the Old Adam. Their type of militant missionary zeal not infrequently has much in common with a familiar kind of "one-hundred percent" patriotism which, in the words of Professor Veblin, "belongs under the general caption of sportsmanship rather than of workmanship. . . . It is bent on an invidious success which must involve as its major purpose the defeat and humiliation of some competitor, whatever else may be comprised in its aim."[2] The impelling force within many of these nobly earnest knights of Jehovah is in part the same as that which sent the crusaders on their missions of sanctified conquest. They have come out as soldiers of the Lord to destroy His enemies. His enemies are the rival religions; and hatred for the Lord's enemies often burns quite as brightly as love for the lost sheep. They have been taught that Christianity and Buddhism are antipodal and that there is war to the death between them; and the militant group loyalty they feel for Christianity is unconsciously mingled with, and mistaken for, the spirit of Jesus. They are playing a great game, and their aim is to beat the other fellows. They are striving not only for suc-

[2] *The Nature of Peace* (New York, Macmillan, 1917), p. 33.

cess but for an "invidious success." The thrill of partisanship, which they take for the love of Christ, blinds their eyes. In this they are not alone, nor peculiar. We would all do well to examine our own hearts. If I am not mistaken, a considerable fraction of the motivation of Christian missions among the home churches is more closely related to patriotism, college spirit, party loyalty, and the enthusiasm of the baseball rooter who eagerly "heals his team," than it is to anything in the New Testament. The spirit of partisanship is a sentiment centering around some social group, and having for its chief constituent the instinct of pugnacity. In itself it is neither vicious nor virtuous. Its value depends upon the measure of enlightenment which it possesses.

The partisanship of the narrower type of missionary is not very enlightened. His opponents must be the enemies of Christ and of the Truth, and therefore must be beaten. He is too busy attacking these enemies to examine their real nature. Objective, scientific study of the position of his adversaries would be almost an impossibility for his essentially partisan mind; and such an unprejudiced weighing of values, even if possible, he would consider most reprehensible.

> To doubt would be disloyalty,
> To falter would be sin.

The mission boards and theological schools that send out missionaries of this kind regularly give them no real information as to the nature of the native religions they are to meet. Instead they inspire them, indirectly and unintentionally no doubt, with an almost ineradicable prejudice. Thus equipped, these zealous men and women spend their lives in Buddhist lands, in constant touch with Buddhists, and at the end of their days know little more of the finer elements in Buddhism than did their ignorant teachers at home. They will tell you that they have no time to study Buddhism; that they wish they might have time for such study in order to understand more fully the many falsehoods and evil practices inculcated by that evil religion. The thought that there might be in Buddhism something besides evil practices and falsehoods seems never to enter their heads. If it does, it appears to be strenuously suppressed, lest it weaken the fervor of their blows.

There are, I think, few men who have less of the virtue of magnanimity and fair play than the missionary of this extreme (and fortunately very rare) type. He is frankly unwilling to give the devil his due. The poor heathen in his blindness has no chance at all. Some of the missionaries I have talked with seem to divide all the "heathen" into two groups, both equally bad. There are those, in the first place, who have wickedly forgotten their own religion, never visit any of their own temples, never say any of their own prayers, and are trying to get on without any religion at all. This is dreadful. Then there is another terrible class of heathen, namely those who are "very fanatical" (I quote the words repeatedly used by one of my acquaintances) and who stick to their old religion with wicked obstinacy. The poor heathen, he catches it going and coming! All of which is good orthodoxy after all and has the authority of no less a man than that of the great St. Augustine; who, it will be recalled, taught that no non-Christian could possibly be good, and that the pagan virtues were only "splendid vices" (*splendida peccata*).[8]

The extremely narrow missionary I have been picturing is fortunately a rare being today—though there are possibly more of his kind than some readers of this book may suppose. But there are a good many who more or less nearly or distantly approximate the picture I have drawn. The young missionaries, fresh from America, whom one meets in the North China Language School (where most missionaries to North China get their linguistic training) are in large measure of the conservative type; and I am told the proportion of conservatives among them is on the increase. The mission field, especially in China and Korea, is unfortunately split into two distinct camps which instead of gradually coalescing seem to be steadily drawing farther and farther apart. In this the mission field is, of course, only following the currents of the home churches. In missionary lands, however,

[8] See Nourrisson's discussion of this matter in his *La Philosophie de St. Augustin* (Paris, 1866), I. 467-71, with the references there given, particularly *Contra Julianum Pelagianum*, IV. 3.

one is much more keenly aware of the sharp division of Christian thought than one commonly is at home, because the effectiveness of missionary activity is so seriously curtailed by it. An active campaign is being carried on against liberal teaching and liberal missionaries, in part by a few self-appointed reactionary missionaries who feel it their duty to inquire into the creeds of their fellows, in part by systematically organized "Fundamentalist" forces, subsidized by liberal grants of money from wealthy Fundamentalists at home. The evil that is thus being done to the Christian cause is quite unmeasurable. Cooperation is being prevented, disunion is being sown, mutual suspicion and enmity between missionaries is being disseminated, earnest Christian leaders are being diverted from their work by repeated accusations before the home boards and by threats of removal; and what is, perhaps, worst of all, the Fundamentalist type of missionary is teaching the Chinese and Koreans, the Siamese and Cambodians, and to some extent the Japanese, that Christianity consists in not smoking, not drinking, not dancing, not doing as you like on Sunday; and that it is to be identified with a creed that defies modern science and with a picture of God which, from a moral point of view, would be an insult to an Eastern despot. It is no wonder that many intelligent Orientals regard Christianity as a superstition.

And indeed if Christianity be the sort of thing taught by a considerable number of the Fundamentalist theologians it *is* a superstition and a very ugly one. Christian unity is a desirable thing, but common frankness must force us to recognize the fact, even if we do not talk about it, that liberal Christianity and "Fundamentalism" in its extreme form have very little *of a credal sort* in common. It will not lead to mutual understanding to allow ourselves to be blinded by names. As a fact, most liberal Christians are in their beliefs very much nearer to liberal Buddhism than they are to the creed of Fundamentalist Christianity. Most of the readers of this book, I will venture to suggest, would find it easier to assent to the Dharmakaya doctrine, to the conception of the Buddha Nature that is in us all, to the moral structure of the universe as represented by the law of Karma, according to which each of us reaps, throughout eternity, the due reward of his works, than to accept the picture of the emotional little Jehovah, the eternal damnation of those who do not believe in, or have never heard of, the "evangelical" creed, and the other things with which extreme Fundamentalism would present us.

I have tried to give an outspoken description of the missionary movement in Buddhist lands as I have observed it. If I may judge by those I have met, the majority of the missionaries are liberal-minded and open-minded men and women, who are doing a very splendid work, the value of which is recognized and gratefully recognized by the inhabitants of these lands, whether Christian or non-Christian. Few of these missionaries are as well educated as they should be, nor are they as well informed concerning the nature of the non-Christian religions as we all wish they were. But they are usually well aware of their own shortcomings, and many of them are making earnest, and sometimes scholarly efforts to understand without prejudice and even with sympathy the native forms of the spiritual life. Besides these there is a small but sometimes militant minority, who have come out to destroy Buddhism and are inadvertently doing everything in their power to destroy Christianity. In view of this situation, what shall we say of the possible future relations and of the desirable relations between Christianity and Buddhism?

There are four possible relations that the two religions may hold to each other in the future. They may, namely, continue in the state of mutual warfare which to a considerable extent characterizes them today. Secondly, one of them may succeed in destroying the other. Thirdly, they might conceivably coalesce. Or, finally, they might tacitly agree to settle down and live side by side, as partners, perhaps, in a common business, as friendly rivals, possibly, but not as foes. As the reader may have guessed, this last is in my opinion the consummation most devoutly to be wished.

The present state of warfare may, as a fact, continue into the indefinite future. It is therefore a possible solution, but I think far from a desirable solution of our problem. Particularly undesirable does it seem to me if the warfare between the two religions be universally carried on in the extreme way in which many of the narrowly partisan missionaries now wage it. The mutual recriminations, the constant attacks made and received on both sides would be mutually harmful and would redound to the advantage of no one but the common foe, the enemy of every spiritual view of the cosmos and of every unselfish attitude toward life. When the Ceylonese, Korean, or Chinese is making up his mind how he shall live and how he shall look upon the universe, the unedifying spectacle of the two great leaders of the spiritual life engaged in slinging mud at each other may well be the decisive consideration in favor of materialism and selfishness. Since each ridicules the other, he will end by ridiculing both. And when a large part of the effort of the religious leaders is drafted off into attacks upon each other, much solid educational, charitable, and social work, for which there is crying need, will necessarily go undone.

In this connection it is only just to point out the curious fact that thus far, in most Buddhist lands, the warfare to which I have referred has been, almost wholly, a one-sided affair. It is the Christian missionaries that have done all the attacking and almost all the fighting.[4] Passive resistance or even something that looks like turning the other cheek has been the response of most Buddhists. In Japan and Ceylon, to be sure, Buddhism has made some rather unsystematic efforts at self-defense, but everywhere else it has done almost nothing even to defend itself, and nowhere has it taken the lead and acted aggressively. There are two reasons for this. One is to be found in the passive, non-aggressive and outwardly inefficient nature of Buddhism discussed in the preceding chapter. But there is another reason, namely, the fact that only after great provocation does Buddhism feel any animosity toward Christianity, or toward any other form of religion. The attitude of the great majority of Buddhists toward Christians and toward Christianity is one of genuine friendliness. If there is to be a fierce and long continued war between the two religions it will be all the work of Christianity. For its part, Buddhism would be only too glad

[4] An exception must be made here of the Maha Bodhi Society and its organ, which are very bitter against Christianity.

to ratify a treaty of enduring peace, alliance, and friendship with its great rival.[5]

I think it unlikely that either of the two religions that we are considering will be able to destroy the other. Certainly the conversion of all Buddhist lands to the Christian creed and the Christian form of worship, and the discarding of all native religious beliefs and religious customs, if possible at all, is a goal that can be attained only at a remote time. And I would point out that if one of the two religions is destined to destroy the other, say in Japan or one of the Hinayana lands, it is not at all certain which of the two will be the victim. Christianity, of course, has the advantage of Western energy and Anglo-Saxon money. But one must remember, on the other hand, that it is chiefly the reactionary part of the missionary movement that is set upon the destruction of Buddhism. And when one considers the fantastic teachings of this sect, and their hopeless incompatibility with either science or scholarly criticism, and when in addition one recalls the remarkable elasticity, adaptability, and liberality of Buddhism, whose philosophy is quite capable of welcoming anything that science is likely to establish—when one makes this comparison, it does not appear at all certain that, in a case of dog eat dog, Buddhism would get the worst of it.

Nor does it seem to me even desirable that Buddhism should be destroyed and completely superseded, at any rate by the kind of Christianity which is being preached in the East today by the more militant missionary. By that I mean that if it is to be destroyed, it is highly desirable that the religion which displaces it should contain a good deal of what we now know as Buddhism; and this would be a solution to be described rather by the word *coalescence* than by the word

[5] *The Young East*, the Japanese periodical to which I have several times referred, founded in 1925 explicitly for the propaganda of Buddhism, quoted in a recent number from an American subscriber who both commended the periodical and attacked Christian missions in Japan. The editors commented upon the letter as follows: "We are thankful for these kind words, but it is far from our minds to challenge Christian missionaries in the Far East to any quarrel. We respect them for their enthusiasm and faithful service and know that they are our friends and allies in that part of our aim of ushering in a time of peace and good will into these parts of the world. We publish this little journal with no intention whatever of obstructing or injuring the activities of Christian missionaries, but it is one of our cherished desires to make better known through this medium the real East to the peoples of the West" (I. 98).

destruction. It is of course desirable that a great mass of the superstitions and superstitious evil practices which cluster around Buddhism today should be destroyed—and indeed the same thing may be said concerning Christianity. It is desirable that the narrow inwardness of Buddhism should be supplemented. It is desirable that the Spirit of Christ should be spread abroad everywhere. But I cannot see that this necessarily means the destruction of Buddhism. There are elements of spiritual beauty in Buddhism, sources of spiritual strength, which this old world could ill afford to lose. Many of the nobler aspects of Buddhism are the common property of the two religions. But there are also peculiarly Buddhist qualities, shared possibly but not stressed by Christianity, for which the East has always felt the need—and which possibly the West, too, needs without knowing it. Gentleness of spirit, cultivation of the inner life, the destruction of tyrannous desires, aspiration for spiritual freedom and for the Great Peace, these are things which Buddhism has taught with an emphasis immeasurably greater than official Christianity has dared put upon them since the second century. In its earliest days Christianity seems to have given *Innerlichkeit* almost as great, though not so exclusive, an emphasis as Buddhism. But whatever may have been the teachings of Jesus and his immediate successors, and of the medieval Catholic mystics, certainly the actual Christianity of our day, and particularly Protestant Christianity, even at its best, lays its almost exclusive stress upon a very different, more Western, more external and aggressive set of virtues. These fine manly Christian virtues are certainly needed, but the gentler, inward, Buddhist virtues have a place also and need a champion. Not only so. Many of the methods of moral training of the Hinayana have a psychological insight and a practical efficacy that give them a distinctive value. Many of the conceptions of the Mahayana have a nobility that puts them among the inspiring intellectual treasures of the race. And surely the memory of Gotama and the impress of his magnetic personality is one of the most precious things in the spiritual life of man. It possesses an emotional hold over the imagination of a large part of mankind such as only one other name can boast. It has been and still is an inspiration to noble living in the hearts of an innumerable company of our fellows. That an attempt should be made by earnest lovers of their kind to destroy this memory and end this influence is explicable only through pitiful ignorance or blind prejudice. If these men should succeed in their destructive aim it would be a racial calamity. For the age when that sort of influence and tradition could be originated is forever past. The reverend and loving memory of Moses and Jesus, of Buddha and Confucius, of Zarathustra and Mohammed are among the world's priceless spiritual resources, and once they are destroyed they can no more be replaced than can the planet's coal and oil and iron. In our age the race has awakened to the fact that the earth's riches are not endless and we think and talk much of the conservation of our material resources. It is time that our religious leaders too should see the folly of a policy of reckless and prodigal destruction, and should institute in its stead a cooperative system of conservation for the world's spiritual resources.

Nor am I persuaded that it would be a gain if the more mythical or symbolic names of the Buddhist cycle were all forgotten. When one thinks what Amida, Kwan-Yin, Jizo, mean to the Mahayana Buddhist, the power they have over his imagination in the production of quiet confidence, inner peace, mercy and gentleness toward others, hope for the future, comfort in the hour of bereavement, calmness in the hour of death, one can hardly contemplate their utter destruction with complacency. Doubtless they are unhistorical, but as symbols of spiritual aspects of the Cosmos they are not necessarily unreal. They are symbols only, to be sure, but in religion, as distinct from abstract philosophy, symbols of some sort seem to be a necessity. As Dean Inge has expressed it: "We cannot make our highest intuitions and experiences our own without translating them into symbolical or mythical forms. Myths and cultus seem to be the untransparent middle terms between the spiritual and the temporal."[6] And for a given people the symbols that will exert the most compelling force are those which have behind them the great prestige of an ancient and venerable tradition. You cannot make new symbols and endow them with this power.

[6] *Outspoken Essays*, II. 254 (London, Longmans, 1923).

You cannot transplant the symbols of an alien race and culture and make them glow with the compelling attraction of the native ones.

As I have said, symbols of some sort our Chinese and Japanese fellows must have. So I put the question as a real question, with a real wish that some one would enlighten me: Is it honestly desirable that the venerated names of Amida and the Goddess of Mercy and Jizo who saves little children, around which the faith and love of two nations for centuries have twined and which have blossomed in a kind of inevitable way from the culture and the hearts of these Eastern races, is it, I ask, really desirable that these native, tried and beloved figures should be replaced, in China and Japan, by the worthies of the Old Testament? Is it not possible that we may have overestimated and overemphasized the value of Hebrew culture and ideas? The Jews were a great people certainly—but there have been others. The Yahveh even of pre-prophetic times was a fine conception, and the Yahveh of the Prophets at its best a very noble one. But so at their best were the conceptions of Zeus, Ahura Mazda, Brahman, T'ien; so are the conceptions of Amida, and the Dharmakaya. Surely we are fast getting beyond the time when intelligent Christians can seriously take the Yahveh of the Twelve Tribes as having any *supreme* value for us. A unique value for us, doubtless, he has; it was historically from him that the Christian conception of God developed. But the "gods of the nations" also developed, and some of them developed toward the same larger conception toward which the God of Israel was in process of growing throughout Old Testament times. At best they were all but symbols.

The study of the Old Testament should hold a large place in the education of every American and European, because as an historical fact our culture has been so deeply influenced by Hebrew beliefs and our literature is so shot through with Hebrew thought. But is there any good reason why the details of Hebrew history and Hebrew ideas should be foisted upon peoples to whom they are as foreign as they are to the Japanese, the Chinese, and the Indians? Is it really necessary that the whole world should be brought up upon Abraham, Isaac, and Jacob?

In fine, then, the goal of replacing Buddhism completely by Christianity seems to me as undesirable as it is unlikely of achievement. A certain amount of progress toward this end is, indeed, probable, and is something to be wished. But when I recall various groups of keenly intelligent, lofty-minded Buddhist thinkers I have known in different parts of the world, the thought of converting them to what is commonly known as Christianity seems simply fantastic. I should as lief think of making St. Thomas Aquinas into a Methodist.

Nor am I sure that the actual results of the destruction of Buddhism in so far as already achieved are altogether a gain. In some cases, no doubt, poor Buddhists, or even good Buddhists, have been made into fair Christians. But most of the Christian gain seems to have been made from the non-Buddhist sections of the population, and the real gainer from the weakening of Buddhism has been not Christianity but worldliness and naturalism. I remember climbing a steep and stony hillside in Chihli province, back of the great monastery of Chieh Tai Ssu, to an ancient mountain hermitage called Chi Leh Feng San, which means, I believe, the Peak of Perfect Happiness. It is a cavern, supplemented by side and front walls. The walls are said to have been built and the place consecrated during the Liao dynasty, eleven hundred years ago, by a monk from Chieh Tai Ssu, who wished for more absolute retirement than he could find in the large monastery. The last ten years of his life he spent in this lonely hermitage. His successors continued the worship of the Blessed One at this shrine for nearly a thousand years. It is now deserted. A few decaying images of the Buddha and his attendant P'usas still occupy the central shrine, and a sad little Kwan-Yin still sticks to her post at the entrance. But it is now several years since the cavern and its ruined walls have echoed to the sound of Sutras chanted in honor of the Tathagata. On one of the walls some visitor has traced with chalk in large letters the words, "Ye shall know the Truth, and the Truth shall make you free." The inscription was probably written by some ardent Christian, in exulting triumph over the fall of a false faith. But on reading it I could not repress the query, Are the former worshipers of the Blessed One, who now worship him no longer, free indeed? They who once spent their lives in reverence, meditation, and gentle helpfulness, what are they doing with their new-found liberty? And what was the Truth that has set them free? Was it the truth of a larger spiritual life and of a more efficient love and service, or was it materialism, cold indifference to the cosmic questions and to the life of the spirit, and cynical efforts at self-centered gratification?

Reflections such as the foregoing naturally lead us on to the third of the four possible relations between the two religions that I suggested some pages back. If Buddhism and Christianity are to cease their attacks upon each other, may we not expect them to coalesce, and should we not use our influence to bring about an explicit coalescence? As to the question whether they may in the distant future grow into one, it would be hazardous to make any confident statement; but I feel quite confident in saying that it would be unwise to seek to hasten any such coalescence by an explicit identification of the two. The genius of Buddhism is one, the genius of Christianity is another. The philosophy of Buddhism is one; the philosophy of Christianity is another. Each has its rôle to play, each has arisen in reply to a deep-lying need of the human mind and the human heart. A union of the two, brought about by the deliberate act of the leaders of both, would be ultimately a failure, and so far as it succeeded, it would bring but little gain and would result in real loss. The wiser leaders of both religions realize this fact thoroughly. The attempted union of Buddhism with Taoism in China, and with Shinto in Japan is an object lesson against any such rather artificial mixture. The two religions, to be sure, have a great deal in common. All things considered, their similarities are very much greater in both number and importance than their differences. Yet differences there are, and it will serve no useful purpose to shut our eyes to them. Nor is it desirable that Buddhism and Christianity should become exactly alike. This world has need of both.

My own conclusion is, therefore, as I indicated at the beginning of this discussion, that the desirable solution of our problem will be found only when the two religions settle down to live side by side on terms of amity and cooperation and friendly rivalry. The same principle holds, I believe, of the great religions of the world as that which we have been working out between the various divisions and denominations of Christianity at home. The origin of Protestantism and the origin of many of the Protestant denominations was accompanied with much hostile feeling and militant and destructive activity. At length we have learned that a difference in creed or in ceremonial need not mean war, and we have come to look upon other Christian bodies than our own not as enemies but as cooperating friends. We have even ceased to wish for the reunion of all Christendom into one church with one creed and one form of worship. For we have come to realize that different minds need different religious symbols, and that different temperaments require different ways of worshiping. Some day we shall see that the same principle holds of the wider relations between religions. There are some minds and some temperaments to which the Buddhist conceptions and the Buddhist symbols and the Buddhist worship are more satisfying and helpful than the Christian, while for others the Christian ways of thinking and worshiping are best. This, I know, will be a hard saying for most Christians to accept, but it seems to me pretty plainly true. In the first place Christian theology as it exists today and as it has always been, is notably more conservative and more bound down to the authority and the formulations of the past than is Buddhist theology. In discussing this matter liberal and advanced Christians almost always forget, for the time, what Christianity actually is for the majority of Christians at home and for the great majority of Christian missionaries in foreign lands. The Christianity which the creeds of the churches retain, which the rank and file of good Christians believe in, and which the majority of missionaries preach, though much more liberal than it was twenty-five years ago, still insists upon the actuality of some things which are of very dubious certainty and to which Buddhism has never officially committed itself. It is quite conceivable—many think it almost certain—that in the course of the next century or half century the official Christian position—the position maintained at present by the majority of the churches in their more deliberate utterances and taught by most of the missionaries to their converts—is going to be well-nigh untenable for many reading and thinking men and women who are honest with themselves. The position of the more philosophical sort of Buddhism is much stronger on matters such as these and offers a more helpful form of resistance to the advance of naturalism. At any rate, it can hardly be denied that there are many religous people in both East and West who find and increasingly will find in Christian theology certain grave difficulties from which Buddhism is quite free.

It is of course to be hoped that the liberal party within the Christian church will be able to lead the thought of Christendom in a direction not inconsistent with the scholarship and intelligence of the future. Christianity and Mahayana Buddhism, on many of the points which at present separate them, may come to an ultimate agreement. But in their basal conceptions of the world it would seem that they represent related but distinct philosophies, each of which has its value and neither of which will ever be given up wholly for the other. In the last analysis, I suppose, Christianity stands for monotheism and Buddhism for pantheism. I think that both of these points of view, in some modified form or other, will for a long time be needed by the human race.

There is a certain type of mind to which pantheism must ever seem cold, a type of mind which for its own best spiritual development needs to conceive God under the image of a person. For minds such as these Christianity will have much more to give than Buddhism. Christianity also possesses a certain positive nature which appeals to many minds and which Buddhism has to some extent always lacked. It is not correct, to be sure (and I have pointed this out more than once), to assert that Buddhism is pessimistic. Both Buddhism and Christianity are in some sense pessimistic about the world of sense and sin; both are optimistic about ultimate Reality. But there clings about Buddhism ever a negative note, while Christianity is essentially positive. The Anatta doctrine and the doctrine of impermanence always suggest the negative point of view, with usually a touch of gentle melancholy. In this respect both the Christian and the Hindu views seem more positive and more joyful than the Buddhist. I doubt whether a person converted from Christianity to Buddhism would ever have the joy in religion that so often accompanies a conversion from Buddhism to Christianity. The typical Christian experience at its best is joy; the typical Buddhist experience is peace. Not that Buddhism is without joy. But the joy it produces is usually either a contrast effect—the consequence of the destruction of worry—or it is a kind of philosophic confidence. And as to the matter of morality, there can be no doubt that the Hinayana, even at its best, lacks something of the unreserved self-forgetting devotion of Jesus' teaching and example; that the Mahayana, even with its noble Bodhisattva ideal, lays less emphasis upon the moral life than does Christianity; and that both Mahayana and Hinayana are as yet immeasurably inferior to Christianity in actual and efficient heplfulness. Buddhism has not yet learned to serve in the whole-hearted and effective way of Christ. Even Japanese Buddhism has still a long way to go in the will to help and the energy of full devotion before it can seriously compare with Christianity at its best. And if we abstract from Japan, Buddhism in other parts of the world is still characterized at times by an extreme fear of sorrow, a preoccupation with one's own Karma, a suspicious attitude toward the normally good things of life, in marked contrast to the rational and glad acceptance of the world's true riches which more and more marks the attitude of modern Christianity. For the leaders of Christianity today, as every one knows, say but little of the ascetic aspect of Jesus' teachings and instead dwell upon the words which the Fourth Gospel attributes to Him: "I am come that they might have life and that they might have it more abundantly."

And this inevitably brings up the question of the different effects produced upon the minds of Christians and Buddhists by the figures of the respective Founders. There can be no doubt that the psychological power of the image of Christ is unique. No other figure, human or divine, has ever been able to produce such intense and wide-spreading effects upon the human imagination, and through it upon the whole of human life. This, I think, is one of the great arguments for Christian missions. It is at least conceivable that the inspiring figure of Jesus might be released from much of the mythical jewelry with which he has been so often and so unfortunately bedecked, and from some of the dogmas which hide much of his true glory, and so might be given to all the world, a common possession of mankind, from which intelligent men of all religions might draw endless inspiration. This is being actually done in India by the Brahma Somaj and Mahatma Gandhi, before our eyes. In a very real sense Jesus seems in the process of being taken over into the nobler forms of Hinduism. Gandhi is able to bring this about only because the Christian missionaries have long since made the figure of their Master familiar and glorious in the eyes of most educated Indians. What is being done for India we may well expect will be done for all Buddhist lands and for all lands and all religions. In the end it may well transpire that the great work of Christian missions has not been to convert the "heathen" to "Christianity," but to permeate all the non-Christian religions with the spirit of Christ.

But while the power of the Buddha over the imaginations of men has never worked and probably never will work such miracles of spiritual redemption as has the thought of the living Christ, it must not be forgotten that his power for good has probably been only second to that of Jesus, that his figure is today the actual support of millions of our fellows, and that there is a type of mind to whom the calm, intellectual, loving Sage of India will make an appeal ever greater than that of the Cosmic Logos of the Fourth Gospel or of the eager adolescent reformer of the Synoptics. I was much interested in a remark let fall by the Chinese monk Tai Hsu on this matter. On being asked by a missionary what he thought of Christ, he replied: "Your Christ appears to me to be a great Bodhisattva." A Bodhisattva, notice, worthy of immense admiration and reverence; a being animated by divine love. A Bodhisattva, but not a Buddha; not one fully enlightened. Equal to the Buddha, doubtless, in mercy and self-sacrifice, but still behind him in ultimate insight and supreme wisdom.

And just as there are many minds to whom monotheism is a living force and pantheism could perhaps never be anything but a cold and abstract doctrine, so there are some minds—and are they not an increasing number?—to whom monotheism with its personal deity is a difficult, or even a dead world view, while the Buddhist philosophy with its cosmic largeness and sweep and inclusiveness offers a living vision of the Real and a perennial source of spiritual strength. A Buddhist thinker, accustomed to the immensities and infinities of the Sutras and to the impersonal yet spiritual concept of the Buddha nature which breathes through all things, feels in Christianity a certain sense of confinement, a lack of space and air. The Christian universe he finds too nice and too little.

It may be that as the longings of the human heart and mind are superficially modified in the course of centuries, the conceptions and the hopes of the two great religions will also be modified and that Buddhism and Christianity will more and more approximate each other. Even if this should occur, however, it is unlikely that the forms and symbols under which they present their truths will ever entirely coalesce, nor is it desirable that they should do so. At any rate until that distant and most improbable day when Oriental and Occidental shall feel and be exactly alike, a diversity of spiritual symbols will be needed if all are to find their best satisfaction.

It seems to me, therefore, an unfortunate and misleading question to ask, Which of these two great religions is true and which false? For both possess much truth and neither one is wholly beyond illusion. Nor can we say in any absolute and complete sense that either one is altogether better than the other. There are many souls whose inner life can be best nourished by what Christianity has to give, and there are those who will find their spiritual needs best supplied by Buddhism. Neither of the religions could wholly supplant the other without a real loss to the human race. Each has its peculiar function in the spiritual economy of our human world.

Meanwhile there is much work in common for the two religions to perform, work of a social, educational, philanthropic kind, upon which they may well cooperate.[7] There

[7] I take from recent numbers of the *Young East* two actual examples of the sort of cooperation I have in mind. The January 1927 number announced the formation of a "Purity Union" formed by two Japanese, one an ardent Christian, the other an ardent Buddhist, for the purpose of organizing popular opinion against the licensing of prostitution. The other case (reported in the number for June 1927) is an "example of

is another common task which will be increasingly thrust upon them as the years go by: namely, the united effort to defend a spiritual view of the world, an idealistic view of human life and the way to live it. Materialism both in metaphysics and in morals is the common foe of both, and it will require all the strength both have to muster to drive back the rapid advances of that foe, without wasting any of their forces in civil war. Shoulder to shoulder they may do much.

Nor do social service and the defense of the common truth as they now see it exhaust the field of their desirable cooperation. There is the pursuit of further truth as well, and the mutual assistance in the truth search which each may give the other.[8] Each has something to give from which the other may well learn. As Mr. Dwight Goddard has admirably expressed it:

> We Anglo-Saxon Christians need the Buddhist serenity and aloofness even more than they need our executive ability and energy. We both see humanity entangled in a bewildering maze of causality, dissatisfaction, selfishness, poverty, sickness, old age and death. Gautama saw the way out through an individualistic life of kindness and purity, by the subordination of all physical desire and the will-to-power. Jesus saw the way out through a brotherly life of coöperating good-will and service. The general result of following Gautama's way has been to exaggerate inaction. The general result of following Jesus' way has been to exaggerate nervous activity in social service and institutions. . . . The world needs today—it needs desperately—the mingling of these two: social Christianity with

cooperation between Christians and Buddhists in the village of Tatsuoka in Nagano Prefecture. The village contains more than six hundred families of which about one half are Christians, the remaining half Buddhists. Instead of keeping an attitude of indifference, if not hostility, toward each other, as in other places, the villagers are cooperating for the improvement of the village administration under the direction of the Reverend Kobayasi and his wife, who established a Christian church in the village several years ago and have converted half of the villagers into Christians, and of Dr. Ko Nakada and Mr. Shigeru Kinoshita, who are devoted Buddhists and are doing their best for the propagation of Buddhism among the villagers. No quarrel has ever arisen between them. Half of the members of the village council are Buddhists and the other half Christians, but everything goes on smoothly between them, each party regarding the other with brotherly feeling and trying to render assistance for the promotion of their common welfare."

[8] Cf. the following from Prof. Whitehead: "The decay of Christianity and Buddhism as determinative influences in modern thought, is partly due to the fact that each religion has unduly sheltered itself from the other. The self-sufficient pedantry of learning and the confidence of ignorant zealots have combined to shut up each religion in its own forms of thought. Instead of looking to each other for deeper meanings, they have remained self-satisfied and self-fertilized" (*Religion in the Making*, Macmillan, 1926), p. 146.

its coöperative service and good-will, and Buddhist personal piety, kindness, serenity, and self-control.[9]

Not only in matters such as these may Buddhism and Christianity properly learn from each other; on questions of philosophical theory also each might profitably borrow and each lend. Buddhist thought would do well to take from Christian and from Western ways of thinking, some of that definiteness and logical exactness, the lack of which often makes Buddhist world pictures almost hopelessly self-contradictory. Christian theology, on the other hand, might well borrow from Buddhist thought some of the larger cosmic feeling which so distinguishes it, in contrast to which much of our Protestant and Catholic anthropomorphic systematization often seems as little as it is exact. Nor need their mutual influence stop here. It is neither likely nor desirable that the borrowing and lending of the two religions will cease at any point that we can now definitely name.

[9] From a little pamphlet entitled *A Vision of Christian and Buddhist Fellowship in the Search for Light and Reality,* and printed in Los Gatos, California, in 1924. Mr. Goddard is a former missionary in Southern China. His pamphlet has the merit of making a definite proposal of a method by which better understanding and cooperation might be brought about between Christians and Buddhists—a proposal which has the approval of one of the greatest of Christian missionaries in China, Bishop Roots of the American Episcopal church. The proposal is to the effect that a hospice, after the model of a Buddhist monastery, should be founded in some central locality in China, such as Hangchow or Nanking, which should serve the following functions. It should be, namely:

"1. A place for fellowship and mutual exchange of thought,
2. A place to which missionaries may come for rest and meditation,
3. A place for annual retreat for both Buddhists and Christians,
4. A clearing house for the exchange of speakers at annual conferences,
5. A place for the accumulation and examination of Buddhist books and research material,
6. The publishing of a magazine designed to circulate among both Christians and Buddhists,
7. The publishing of books of mutual interest,
8. A place where British and American scholars may meet Buddhist scholars in a friendly atmosphere,
9. A place for the conservation of the results of research into the early contacts of Buddhism and Christianity,
10. The foregoing are all the immediate objects. The great purpose is more distant, but is all-important: namely, to provide a center from which may radiate that friendly and understanding sympathy which we believe, in the long run, will draw Christianity and Buddhism together into one native church."

Something like Mr. Goddard's dream may be partially realized in Japan in the not-distant future. A convention of representatives of Buddhism, Shinto, and Christianity is being held this year (June 5-9, 1928), for the "promotion of inter-religious co-operation" through the discussion of "questions of common interest bearing on international peace, education, thought, and social welfare" (*The Young East* for May, 1928).

But if this be the case, and if no new important differences in belief arise, it means that the future will witness a gradual and partial approximation of the two religions. Already, when liberal Buddhist and liberal Christian thinkers frankly compare their views, they discover that the principal differences between them consist in the ways in which they express their faith. It is chiefly their symbols that divide them. This gradual approximation of which I speak will be a very different thing from a deliberate and more or less artificial identification or union of the two religions brought about by the specific and conscious acts of the leaders. It will be a natural and almost imperceptible development, a steady growth of mutual respect and friendliness. Both religions will come to place less emphasis on some of the differences that now seem important, and each will come to see that the other's truth may possibly, in some large sense, be true. For in some sense all truth is one. Contradictory opposites, of course, cannot both be true; that much is certain if anything is certain. But we cannot always be sure that opposites which seem to us contradictory are really so. Beliefs that seem mutually incompatible from a lower level may, when grasped by a more inclusive vision, prove to be true and mutually complementary. There is at least this much of justification for the ancient Tendai-Kegon doctrine of the different planes of truth. And, as a Chinese Buddhist philosopher of deep insight recently said, it may be that the Buddhist and the Christian are both viewing the same Supreme Reality from slightly different angles.

For when a last review we take of both Christian and Buddhist philosophical conceptions, we must realize that neither of them is a final and complete picture of the Ultimate and Absolute. At their best, both are but adumbrations of the Real, but fragmentary gleams of the truth which both are seeking—"fingers pointing at the moon." Certainly the Christian insight has taught us much. But for the Christian as well as for the Buddhist there can be but one answer to the question: "Canst thou by searching find out God, or know the Almighty unto perfection? It is high as Heaven; what canst thou do; deeper than hell, what canst thou know?" The Christian conceptions, though containing much that is true, are, like the Buddhist, only symbols after all, symbols of the mystery that no man has solved, the mystery behind the face of things, of which all the religions are acutely conscious, and of which no religion has ever given more than a poetic, a figurative explanation.

It is thoughts such as these that fill my mind these last days of our Buddhist pilgrimage. And now as we board the ship that is to carry us away from Japan, the last of our Buddhist lands, they press with special insistency. What is the truth of it all? What is the significance of the great conceptions of the two religions—the Christian Logos, the eternal Christ, Chen Ru, the Dharmakaya, the Buddha nature that is in us all and rolls through all things? What do the symbols mean? Is it possible that in the end they somehow cover the same Truth? And what may that Truth be? . . .

But now the officer on the bridge is ringing his signal to the engine room, the propeller sluggishly begins its revolutions, the great ship quivers and starts and slowly noses its way between the long protecting arms of the breakwater, on into the outer harbor. The bluff, the green banks and hillsides beyond it, the groves with their hidden temples float past, and before us opens out the sea. Now all Japan lies there astern, stretched along the horizon's edge, and behind it the setting sun. All Japan lies out there, its cities and its paddy fields, its mountains and its valleys, its Buddhist temples, Shinto shrines, and little Christian churches, merging in one thin, green line. Darkness and distance are rapidly shutting them from our view. The horizon is engulfing them—the horizon of space and the horizon of time—as it engulfs all things mortal at the end. Before long nothing will be left our eyes but sky and ocean and night, tremulous night, luminous with its stars. The little lights of man's making are glimmering now on the edge of the world, Buddhist temples, Shinto shrines, Christian churches, all merged in one.

> They are but broken lights of Thee,
> And Thou, O Lord, art more than they.

So the ship sails out into the unknown silent spaces of the sea.

INDEX